Chevrolet Corvette Automotive Repair Manual

by Alan Ahlstrand and John H Haynes

Member of the Guild of Motoring Writers

Models covered:

All Corvette models - 1968 through 1982

(9L10 - 24040)

(274)

ABCDE
F

2

Haynes Publishing Group
Sparkford Nr Yeovil
Somerset BA22 7JJ England

Haynes North America, Inc
861 Lawrence Drive
Newbury Park
California 91320 USA

Acknowledgements

We are grateful for the help and cooperation of Tomco Industries, 1435 Woodson Road, St. Louis, Missouri 63132, for their assistance with technical information and illustrations. Wiring diagrams originated exclusively for Haynes North America, Inc. by George Edward Brodd. Certain illustrations originated by Valley Forge Technical Information Services. Technical writers who contributed to this project include Mike Forsythe and Ed Scott.

A book in the Haynes Automotive Repair Manual Series

Printed in the U.S.A.

ISBN 1 85010 723 8

Library of Congress Catalog Card Number 91-71157

Contents

Haynes photographer, mechanic and author with 1977 Corvette

About this manual

Its purpose

The purpose of this manual is to help you get the best value from your vehicle. It can do so in several ways. It can help you decide what work must be done, even if you choose to have it done by a dealer service department or a repair shop; it provides information and procedures for routine maintenance and servicing; and it offers diagnostic and repair procedures to follow when trouble occurs.

We hope you use the manual to tackle the work yourself. For many simpler jobs, doing it yourself may be quicker than arranging an appointment to get the vehicle into a shop and making the trips to leave it and pick it up. More importantly, a lot of money can be saved by avoiding the expense the shop must pass on to you to cover its labor and overhead costs. An added benefit is the sense of satisfaction and accomplishment that you feel after doing the job yourself.

Using the manual

The manual is divided into Chapters. Each Chapter is divided into numbered Sections, which are headed in bold type between horizontal lines. Each Section consists of consecutively numbered paragraphs.

At the beginning of each numbered Section you will be referred to any illustrations which apply to the procedures in that Section. The reference numbers used in illustration captions pinpoint the pertinent Section and the Step within that Section. That is, illustration 3.2 means the illustration refers to Section 3 and Step (or paragraph) 2 within that Section.

Procedures, once described in the text, are not normally repeated. When it's necessary to refer to another Chapter, the reference will be given as Chapter and Section number. Cross references given without use of the word "Chapter" apply to Sections and/or paragraphs in the same Chapter. For example, "see Section 8" means in the same Chapter.

References to the left or right side of the vehicle assume you are sitting in the driver's seat, facing forward.

Even though we have prepared this manual with extreme care, neither the publisher nor the author can accept responsibility for any errors in, or omissions from, the information given.

NOTE

A **Note** provides information necessary to properly complete a procedure or information which will make the procedure easier to understand.

CAUTION

A **Caution** provides a special procedure or special steps which must be taken while completing the procedure where the Caution is found. Not heeding a Caution can result in damage to the assembly being worked on.

WARNING

A **Warning** provides a special procedure or special steps which must be taken while completing the procedure where the Warning is found. Not heeding a Warning can result in personal injury.

Introduction to the Chevrolet Corvette

The Chevrolet Corvette is the luxury sports car from General Motors first introduced in 1953. Over the years the car has developed from a six-cylinder-with-automatic transmission "personal" car to the high-performance sports car against which all other US sports cars are compared.

The Corvettes in the models covered by this manual come with a variety of small-block and big-block Chevrolet V8 engines as standard and optional equipment, in varying performance configurations.

Three transmissions are available - a three speed or four-speed manual transmission and an automatic transmission.

The suspension is fully independent, with A-arms and coil springs in front, and the Corvette's unique independent rear suspension with transverse leaf spring in back.

Styling has changed over the years, with five distinct "generations" during the years covered by this manual, and convertible models were available up through the 1975 model year.

Vehicle identification numbers

Modifications are a continuing and unpublicized process in vehicle manufacturing. Since spare parts manuals and lists are compiled on a numerical basis, the individual vehicle numbers are essential to correctly identify the component required. The following identification numbers are applicable to the Corvette:

Vehicle Identification Number (VIN)

This very important identification number is stamped on a plate attached to the left side of the dashboard just inside the windshield on the driver's side of the vehicle (see illustration). The VIN also appears on the Vehicle Certificate of Title and Registration. It contains information such as where and when the vehicle was manufactured, the model year and the body style.

Model type numbers

19000 Series - up to 1972
1YZ37 (2-door Sport Coupe) - 1973 on
1YZ67 (2-door Convertible) - 1973 to 1975

Engine number

This ID number is stamped into a pad at the front, right-hand side of the engine block (see illustration).

Manual transmission number

3-speed Warner - located on a boss at the right rear corner of the extension housing
3-speed Muncie - located on a boss above the filler plug
3-speed Saginaw - located on the lower right-hand side of the case, adjacent to the cover
4-speed Warner - located on the rear vertical surface of the extension housing
4-speed Muncie - located on the rear right-hand side of the case flange

4-speed Saginaw - located on the lower right-hand side of the case, adjacent to the cover

Automatic transmission number

Type 350 - located on the right-hand vertical surface of the oil pan
Type 400 - located on a blue tag attached to the right-hand side of the transmission

Rear axle number

This ID number is on the bottom surface of the carrier at the cover mounting flange.

Tune-up decal/Emission Control Information label

This very important label is located in the engine compartment, usually on the under side of the hood or on the radiator cross brace, although it may be on the air cleaner assembly.

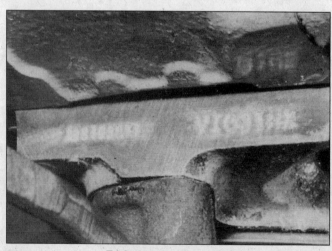

Typical engine ID number

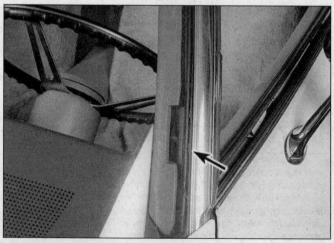

VIN number plate location

Buying parts

Replacement parts are available from many sources, which generally fall into one of two categories - authorized dealer parts departments and independent retail auto parts stores. Our advice concerning these parts is as follows:

Retail auto parts stores: Good auto parts stores will stock frequently needed components which wear out relatively fast, such as clutch components, exhaust systems, brake parts, tune-up parts, etc. These stores often supply new or reconditioned parts on an exchange basis, which can save a considerable amount of money. Discount auto parts stores are often very good places to buy materials and parts needed for general vehicle maintenance such as oil, grease, filters, spark plugs, belts, touch-up paint, bulbs, etc. They also usually sell tools and general accessories, have convenient hours, charge lower prices and can often be found not far from home.

Authorized dealer parts department: This is the best source for parts which are unique to the vehicle and not generally available elsewhere (such as major engine parts, transmission parts, trim pieces, etc.).

Warranty information: If the vehicle is still covered under warranty, be sure that any replacement parts purchased - regardless of the source - do not invalidate the warranty!

To be sure of obtaining the correct parts, have engine and chassis numbers available and, if possible, take the old parts along for positive identification.

Maintenance techniques, tools and working facilities

Maintenance techniques

There are a number of techniques involved in maintenance and repair that will be referred to throughout this manual. Application of these techniques will enable the home mechanic to be more efficient, better organized and capable of performing the various tasks properly, which will ensure that the repair job is thorough and complete.

Fasteners

Fasteners are nuts, bolts, studs and screws used to hold two or more parts together. There are a few things to keep in mind when working with fasteners. Almost all of them use a locking device of some type, either a lockwasher, locknut, locking tab or thread adhesive. All threaded fasteners should be clean and straight, with undamaged threads and undamaged corners on the hex head where the wrench fits. Develop the habit of replacing all damaged nuts and bolts with new ones. Special locknuts with nylon or fiber inserts can only be used once. If they are removed, they lose their locking ability and must be replaced with new ones.

Rusted nuts and bolts should be treated with a penetrating fluid to ease removal and prevent breakage. Some mechanics use turpentine in a spout-type oil can, which works quite well. After applying the rust penetrant, let it work for a few minutes before trying to loosen the nut or bolt. Badly rusted fasteners may have to be chiseled or sawed off or removed with a special nut breaker, available at tool stores.

If a bolt or stud breaks off in an assembly, it can be drilled and removed with a special tool commonly available for this purpose. Most automotive machine shops can perform this task, as well as other repair procedures, such as the repair of threaded holes that have been stripped out.

Flat washers and lockwashers, when removed from an assembly, should always be replaced exactly as removed. Replace any damaged washers with new ones. Never use a lockwasher on any soft metal surface (such as aluminum), thin sheet metal or plastic.

Fastener sizes

For a number of reasons, automobile manufacturers are making wider and wider use of metric fasteners. Therefore, it is important to be able to tell the difference between standard (sometimes called U.S. or SAE) and metric hardware, since they cannot be interchanged.

All bolts, whether standard or metric, are sized according to diameter, thread pitch and length. For example, a standard 1/2 - 13 x 1 bolt is 1/2 inch in diameter, has 13 threads per inch and is 1 inch long. An M12 - 1.75 x 25 metric bolt is 12 mm in diameter, has a thread pitch of 1.75 mm (the distance between threads) and is 25 mm long. The two bolts are nearly identical, and easily confused, but they are not interchangeable.

In addition to the differences in diameter, thread pitch and length, metric and standard bolts can also be distinguished by examining the bolt heads. To begin with, the distance across the flats on a standard bolt head is measured in inches, while the same dimension on a metric bolt is sized in millimeters (the same is true for nuts). As a result, a standard wrench should not be used on a metric bolt and a metric wrench should not be used on a standard bolt. Also, most standard bolts have slashes radiating out from the center of the head to denote the grade or strength of the bolt, which is an indication of the amount of torque that can be applied to it. The greater the number of slashes, the greater the strength of the bolt. Grades 0 through 5 are commonly used on automobiles. Metric bolts have a property class (grade) number, rather than a slash, molded into their heads to indicate bolt strength. In this case, the higher the number, the stronger the bolt. Property class numbers 8.8, 9.8 and 10.9 are commonly used on automobiles.

Strength markings can also be used to distinguish standard hex nuts from metric hex nuts. Many standard nuts have dots stamped into one side, while metric nuts are marked with a number. The greater the number of dots, or the higher the number, the greater the strength of the nut.

Metric studs are also marked on their ends according to property class (grade). Larger studs are numbered (the same as metric bolts), while smaller studs carry a geometric code to denote grade.

It should be noted that many fasteners, especially Grades 0 through 2, have no distinguishing marks on them. When such is the case, the only way to determine whether it is standard or metric is to measure the thread pitch or compare it to a known fastener of the same size.

Standard fasteners are often referred to as SAE, as opposed to metric. However, it should be noted that SAE technically refers to a non-metric fine thread fastener only. Coarse thread non-metric fasteners are referred to as USS sizes.

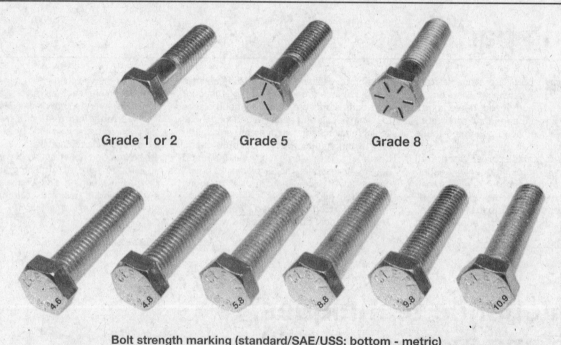

Grade 1 or 2   Grade 5   Grade 8

Bolt strength marking (standard/SAE/USS; bottom - metric)

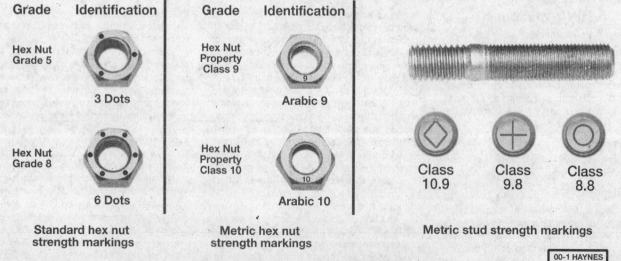

Grade	Identification	Grade	Identification
Hex Nut Grade 5	3 Dots	Hex Nut Property Class 9	Arabic 9
Hex Nut Grade 8	6 Dots	Hex Nut Property Class 10	Arabic 10

Class 10.9   Class 9.8   Class 8.8

Standard hex nut strength markings   **Metric hex nut strength markings**   **Metric stud strength markings**

Since fasteners of the same size (both standard and metric) may have different strength ratings, be sure to reinstall any bolts, studs or nuts removed from your vehicle in their original locations. Also, when replacing a fastener with a new one, make sure that the new one has a strength rating equal to or greater than the original.

Tightening sequences and procedures

Most threaded fasteners should be tightened to a specific torque value (torque is the twisting force applied to a threaded component such as a nut or bolt). Overtightening the fastener can weaken it and cause it to break, while undertightening can cause it to eventually come loose. Bolts, screws and studs, depending on the material they are made of and their thread diameters, have specific torque values, many of which are noted in the Specifications at the beginning of each Chapter. Be sure to follow the torque recommendations closely. For fasteners not assigned a specific torque, a general torque value chart is presented here as a guide. These torque values are for dry (unlubricated) fasteners threaded into steel or cast iron (not aluminum). As was previously mentioned, the size and grade of a fastener determine the amount of torque that can safely be applied to it. The figures listed here are approximate for Grade 2 and Grade 3 fasteners. Higher grades can tolerate higher torque values.

Fasteners laid out in a pattern, such as cylinder head bolts, oil pan bolts, differential cover bolts, etc., must be loosened or tightened in sequence to avoid warping the component. This sequence will normally be shown in the appropriate Chapter. If a specific pattern is not given, the following procedures can be used to prevent warping.

Metric thread sizes	Ft-lbs	Nm
M-6	6 to 9	9 to 12
M-8	14 to 21	19 to 28
M-10	28 to 40	38 to 54
M-12	50 to 71	68 to 96
M-14	80 to 140	109 to 154

Pipe thread sizes		
1/8	5 to 8	7 to 10
1/4	12 to 18	17 to 24
3/8	22 to 33	30 to 44
1/2	25 to 35	34 to 47

U.S. thread sizes		
1/4 - 20	6 to 9	9 to 12
5/16 - 18	12 to 18	17 to 24
5/16 - 24	14 to 20	19 to 27
3/8 - 16	22 to 32	30 to 43
3/8 - 24	27 to 38	37 to 51
7/16 - 14	40 to 55	55 to 74
7/16 - 20	40 to 60	55 to 81
1/2 - 13	55 to 80	75 to 108

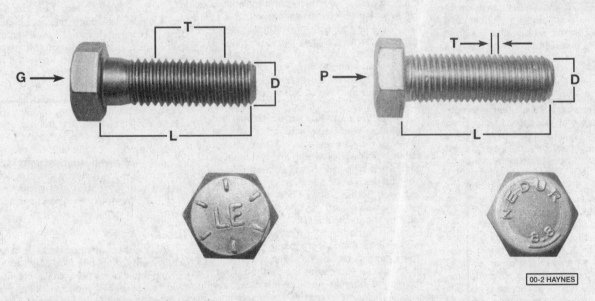

Standard (SAE and USS) bolt dimensions/grade marks

- G Grade marks (bolt strength)
- L Length (in inches)
- T Thread pitch (number of threads per inch)
- D Nominal diameter (in inches)

Metric bolt dimensions/grade marks

- P Property class (bolt strength)
- L Length (in millimeters)
- T Thread pitch (distance between threads in millimeters)
- D Diameter

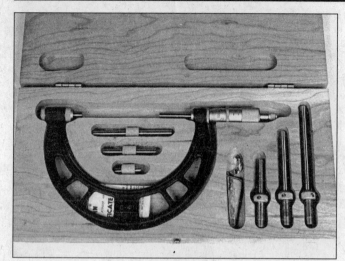

Micrometer set

Dial indicator set

Initially, the bolts or nuts should be assembled finger-tight only. Next, they should be tightened one full turn each, in a criss-cross or diagonal pattern. After each one has been tightened one full turn, return to the first one and tighten them all one-half turn, following the same pattern. Finally, tighten each of them one-quarter turn at a time until each fastener has been tightened to the proper torque. To loosen and remove the fasteners, the procedure would be reversed.

Component disassembly

Component disassembly should be done with care and purpose to help ensure that the parts go back together properly. Always keep track of the sequence in which parts are removed. Make note of special characteristics or marks on parts that can be installed more than one way, such as a grooved thrust washer on a shaft. It is a good idea to lay the disassembled parts out on a clean surface in the order that they were removed. It may also be helpful to make sketches or take instant photos of components before removal.

When removing fasteners from a component, keep track of their locations. Sometimes threading a bolt back in a part, or putting the washers and nut back on a stud, can prevent mix-ups later. If nuts and bolts cannot be returned to their original locations, they should be kept in a compartmented box or a series of small boxes. A cupcake or muffin tin is ideal for this purpose, since each cavity can hold the bolts and nuts from a particular area (i.e. oil pan bolts, valve cover bolts, engine mount bolts, etc.). A pan of this type is especially helpful when working on assemblies with very small parts, such as the carburetor, alternator, valve train or interior dash and trim pieces. The cavities can be marked with paint or tape to identify the contents.

Whenever wiring looms, harnesses or connectors are separated, it is a good idea to identify the two halves with numbered pieces of masking tape so they can be easily reconnected.

Gasket sealing surfaces

Throughout any vehicle, gaskets are used to seal the mating surfaces between two parts and keep lubricants, fluids, vacuum or pressure contained in an assembly.

Many times these gaskets are coated with a liquid or paste-type gasket sealing compound before assembly. Age, heat and pressure can sometimes cause the two parts to stick together so tightly that they are very difficult to separate. Often, the assembly can be loosened by striking it with a soft-face hammer near the mating surfaces. A regular hammer can be used if a block of wood is placed between the hammer and the part. Do not hammer on cast parts or parts that could be easily damaged. With any particularly stubborn part, always recheck to make sure that every fastener has been removed.

Avoid using a screwdriver or bar to pry apart an assembly, as they can easily mar the gasket sealing surfaces of the parts, which must remain smooth. If prying is absolutely necessary, use an old broom handle, but keep in mind that extra clean up will be necessary if the wood splinters.

After the parts are separated, the old gasket must be carefully scraped off and the gasket surfaces cleaned. Stubborn gasket material can be soaked with rust penetrant or treated with a special chemical to soften it so it can be easily scraped off. A scraper can be fashioned from a piece of copper tubing by flattening and sharpening one end. Copper is recommended because it is usually softer than the surfaces to be scraped, which reduces the chance of gouging the part. Some gaskets can be removed with a wire brush, but regardless of the method used, the mating surfaces must be left clean and smooth. If for some reason the gasket surface is gouged, then a gasket sealer thick enough to fill scratches will have to be used during reassembly of the components. For most applications, a non-drying (or semi-drying) gasket sealer should be used.

Hose removal tips

Warning: *If the vehicle is equipped with air conditioning, do not disconnect any of the A/C hoses without first having the system depressurized by a dealer service department or a service station.*

Hose removal precautions closely parallel gasket removal precautions. Avoid scratching or gouging the surface that the hose mates against or the connection may leak. This is especially true for radiator hoses. Because of various chemical reactions, the rubber in hoses can bond itself to the metal spigot that the hose fits over. To remove a hose, first loosen the hose clamps that secure it to the spigot. Then, with slip-joint pliers, grab the hose at the clamp and rotate it around the spigot. Work it back and forth until it is completely free, then pull it off. Silicone or other lubricants will ease removal if they can be applied between the hose and the outside of the spigot. Apply the same lubricant to the inside of the hose and the outside of the spigot to simplify installation.

As a last resort (and if the hose is to be replaced with a new one anyway), the rubber can be slit with a knife and the hose peeled from the spigot. If this must be done, be careful that the metal connection is not damaged.

If a hose clamp is broken or damaged, do not reuse it. Wire-type clamps usually weaken with age, so it is a good idea to replace them with screw-type clamps whenever a hose is removed.

Tools

A selection of good tools is a basic requirement for anyone who plans to maintain and repair his or her own vehicle. For the owner who has few tools, the initial investment might seem high, but when compared to the spiraling costs of professional auto maintenance and repair, it is a wise one.

To help the owner decide which tools are needed to perform the tasks detailed in this manual, the following tool lists are offered: *Maintenance and minor repair,*

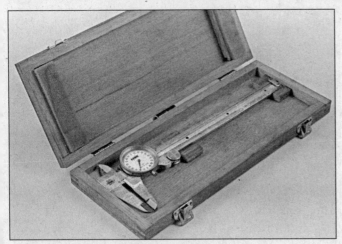

Dial caliper

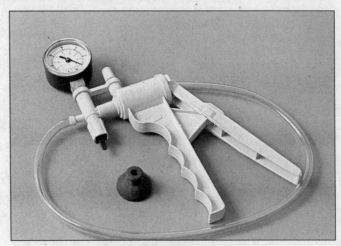

Hand-operated vacuum pump

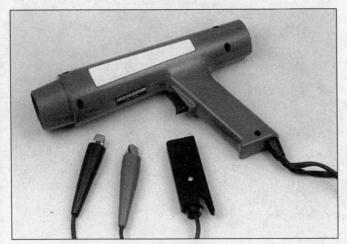

Timing light

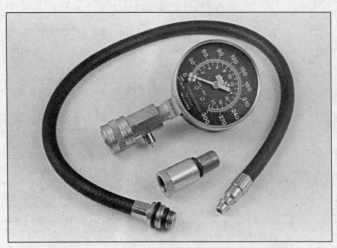

Compression gauge with spark plug hole adapter

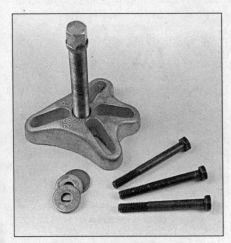

Damper/steering wheel puller

General purpose puller

Hydraulic lifter removal tool

Repair/overhaul and *Special.*

The newcomer to practical mechanics should start off with the *maintenance and minor repair* tool kit, which is adequate for the simpler jobs performed on a vehicle. Then, as confidence and experience grow, the owner can tackle more difficult tasks, buying additional tools as they are needed.

Eventually the basic kit will be expanded into the *repair and overhaul* tool set. Over a period of time, the experienced do-it-yourselfer will assemble a tool set complete enough for most repair and overhaul procedures and will add tools from the special category when it is felt that the expense is justified by the frequency of use.

Maintenance and minor repair tool kit

The tools in this list should be considered the minimum required for performance of routine maintenance, servicing and minor repair work. We recommend the purchase of combination wrenches (box-end and open-

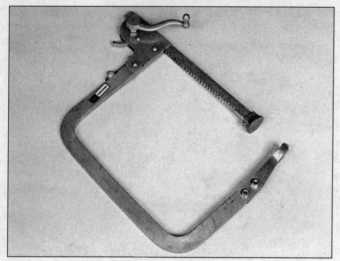

Valve spring compressor

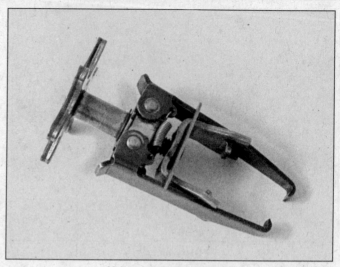

Valve spring compressor

Ridge reamer

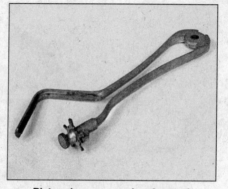

Piston ring groove cleaning tool

Ring removal/installation tool

end combined in one wrench). While more expensive than open end wrenches, they offer the advantages of both types of wrench.

> Combination wrench set (1/4-inch to
>   1 inch or 6 mm to 19 mm)
> Adjustable wrench, 8 inch
> Spark plug wrench with rubber insert
> Spark plug gap adjusting tool
> Feeler gauge set
> Brake bleeder wrench
> Standard screwdriver (5/16-inch x
>   6 inch)
> Phillips screwdriver (No. 2 x 6 inch)
> Combination pliers - 6 inch
> Hacksaw and assortment of blades
> Tire pressure gauge
> Grease gun
> Oil can
> Fine emery cloth
> Wire brush
> Battery post and cable cleaning tool
> Oil filter wrench
> Funnel (medium size)
> Safety goggles
> Jackstands (2)
> Drain pan

Note: *If basic tune-ups are going to be part of routine maintenance, it will be necessary to purchase a good quality stroboscopic timing*

light and combination tachometer/dwell meter. Although they are included in the list of special tools, it is mentioned here because they are absolutely necessary for tuning most vehicles properly.

Repair and overhaul tool set

These tools are essential for anyone who plans to perform major repairs and are in addition to those in the maintenance and minor repair tool kit. Included is a comprehensive set of sockets which, though expensive, are invaluable because of their versatility, especially when various extensions and drives are available. We recommend the 1/2-inch drive over the 3/8-inch drive. Although the larger drive is bulky and more expensive, it has the capacity of accepting a very wide range of large sockets. Ideally, however, the mechanic should have a 3/8-inch drive set and a 1/2-inch drive set.

> Socket set(s)
> Reversible ratchet
> Extension - 10 inch
> Universal joint
> Torque wrench (same size drive as
>   sockets)
> Ball peen hammer - 8 ounce
> Soft-face hammer (plastic/rubber)

Ring compressor

> Standard screwdriver (1/4-inch x 6 inch)
> Standard screwdriver (stubby -
>   5/16-inch)
> Phillips screwdriver (No. 3 x 8 inch)
> Phillips screwdriver (stubby - No. 2)
> Pliers - vise grip
> Pliers - lineman's
> Pliers - needle nose
> Pliers - snap-ring (internal and external)
> Cold chisel - 1/2-inch

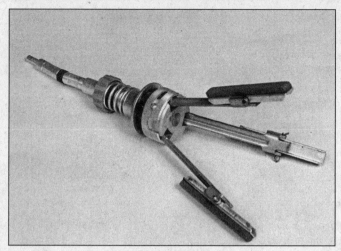

Cylinder hone

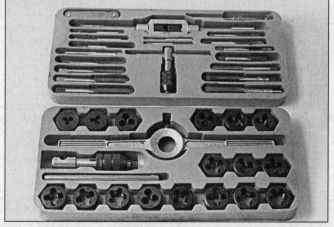

Brake hold-down spring tool

Scribe
Scraper (made from flattened copper
*   tubing)*
Centerpunch
Pin punches (1/16, 1/8, 3/16-inch)
Steel rule/straightedge - 12 inch
Allen wrench set (1/8 to 3/8-inch or
*   4 mm to 10 mm)*
A selection of files

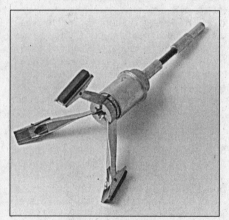

Brake cylinder hone

Wire brush (large)
Jackstands (second set)
Jack (scissor or hydraulic type)
Note: *Another tool which is often useful is an electric drill with a chuck capacity of 3/8-inch and a set of good quality drill bits.*

Special tools

The tools in this list include those which are not used regularly, are expensive to buy, or which need to be used in accordance with their manufacturer's instructions. Unless these tools will be used frequently, it is not very economical to purchase many of them. A consideration would be to split the cost and use between yourself and a friend or friends. In addition, most of these tools can be obtained from a tool rental shop on a temporary basis.

This list primarily contains only those tools and instruments widely available to the public, and not those special tools produced by the vehicle manufacturer for distribution to dealer service departments. Occasionally, references to the manufacturer's special tools are included in the text of this manual. Generally, an alternative method of doing the job without the special tool is offered. How-

ever, sometimes there is no alternative to their use. Where this is the case, and the tool cannot be purchased or borrowed, the work should be turned over to the dealer service department or an automotive repair shop.

Valve spring compressor
Piston ring groove cleaning tool
Piston ring compressor
Piston ring installation tool
Cylinder compression gauge
Cylinder ridge reamer
Cylinder surfacing hone
Cylinder bore gauge
Micrometers and/or dial calipers
Hydraulic lifter removal tool
Balljoint separator
Universal-type puller
Impact screwdriver
Dial indicator set
Stroboscopic timing light (inductive
*   pick-up)*
Hand operated vacuum/pressure pump
Tachometer/dwell meter
Universal electrical multimeter
Cable hoist
Brake spring removal and installation
*   tools*
Floor jack

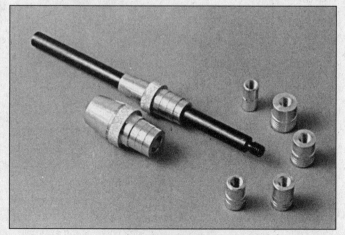

Clutch plate alignment tool

Tap and die set

Buying tools

For the do-it-yourselfer who is just starting to get involved in vehicle maintenance and repair, there are a number of options available when purchasing tools. If maintenance and minor repair is the extent of the work to be done, the purchase of individual tools is satisfactory. If, on the other hand, extensive work is planned, it would be a good idea to purchase a modest tool set from one of the large retail chain stores. A set can usually be bought at a substantial savings over the individual tool prices, and they often come with a tool box. As additional tools are needed, add-on sets, individual tools and a larger tool box can be purchased to expand the tool selection. Building a tool set gradually allows the cost of the tools to be spread over a longer period of time and gives the mechanic the freedom to choose only those tools that will actually be used.

Tool stores will often be the only source of some of the special tools that are needed, but regardless of where tools are bought, try to avoid cheap ones, especially when buying screwdrivers and sockets, because they won't last very long. The expense involved in replacing cheap tools will eventually be greater than the initial cost of quality tools.

Care and maintenance of tools

Good tools are expensive, so it makes sense to treat them with respect. Keep them clean and in usable condition and store them properly when not in use. Always wipe off any dirt, grease or metal chips before putting them away. Never leave tools lying around in the work area. Upon completion of a job, always check closely under the hood for tools that may have been left there so they won't get lost during a test drive.

Some tools, such as screwdrivers, pliers, wrenches and sockets, can be hung on a panel mounted on the garage or workshop wall, while others should be kept in a tool box or tray. Measuring instruments, gauges, meters, etc. must be carefully stored where they cannot be damaged by weather or impact from other tools.

When tools are used with care and stored properly, they will last a very long time. Even with the best of care, though, tools will wear out if used frequently. When a tool is damaged or worn out, replace it. Subsequent jobs will be safer and more enjoyable if you do.

How to repair damaged threads

Sometimes, the internal threads of a nut or bolt hole can become stripped, usually from overtightening. Stripping threads is an all-too-common occurrence, especially when working with aluminum parts, because aluminum is so soft that it easily strips out.

Usually, external or internal threads are only partially stripped. After they've been cleaned up with a tap or die, they'll still work. Sometimes, however, threads are badly damaged. When this happens, you've got three choices:

1) *Drill and tap the hole to the next suitable oversize and install a larger diameter bolt, screw or stud.*

2) *Drill and tap the hole to accept a threaded plug, then drill and tap the plug to the original screw size. You can also buy a plug already threaded to the original size. Then you simply drill a hole to the specified size, then run the threaded plug into the hole with a bolt and jam nut. Once the plug is fully seated, remove the jam nut and bolt.*

3) *The third method uses a patented thread repair kit like Heli-Coil or Slimsert. These easy-to-use kits are designed to repair damaged threads in straight-through holes and blind holes. Both are available as kits which can handle a variety of sizes and thread patterns. Drill the hole, then tap it with the special included tap. Install the Heli-Coil and the hole is back to its original diameter and thread pitch.*

Regardless of which method you use, be sure to proceed calmly and carefully. A little impatience or carelessness during one of these relatively simple procedures can ruin your whole day's work and cost you a bundle if you wreck an expensive part.

Working facilities

Not to be overlooked when discussing tools is the workshop. If anything more than routine maintenance is to be carried out, some sort of suitable work area is essential.

It is understood, and appreciated, that many home mechanics do not have a good workshop or garage available, and end up removing an engine or doing major repairs outside. It is recommended, however, that the overhaul or repair be completed under the cover of a roof.

A clean, flat workbench or table of comfortable working height is an absolute necessity. The workbench should be equipped with a vise that has a jaw opening of at least four inches.

As mentioned previously, some clean, dry storage space is also required for tools, as well as the lubricants, fluids, cleaning solvents, etc. which soon become necessary.

Sometimes waste oil and fluids, drained from the engine or cooling system during normal maintenance or repairs, present a disposal problem. To avoid pouring them on the ground or into a sewage system, pour the used fluids into large containers, seal them with caps and take them to an authorized disposal site or recycling center. Plastic jugs, such as old antifreeze containers, are ideal for this purpose.

Always keep a supply of old newspapers and clean rags available. Old towels are excellent for mopping up spills. Many mechanics use rolls of paper towels for most work because they are readily available and disposable. To help keep the area under the vehicle clean, a large cardboard box can be cut open and flattened to protect the garage or shop floor.

Whenever working over a painted surface, such as when leaning over a fender to service something under the hood, always cover it with an old blanket or bedspread to protect the finish. Vinyl covered pads, made especially for this purpose, are available at auto parts stores.

Booster battery (jump) starting

Observe the following precautions when using a booster battery to start a vehicle:

a) *Before connecting the booster battery, make sure the ignition switch is in the Off position.*

b) *Turn off the lights, heater and other electrical loads.*

c) *Your eyes should be shielded. Safety goggles are a good idea.*

d) *Make sure the booster battery is the same voltage as the dead one in the vehicle.*

e) *The two vehicles MUST NOT TOUCH each other.*

f) *Make sure the transmission is in Neutral (manual transaxle) or Park (automatic transaxle).*

g) *If the booster battery is not a maintenance-free type, remove the vent caps and lay a cloth over the vent holes.*

Connect the red jumper cable to the positive (+) terminals of each battery.

Connect one end of the black cable to the negative (-) terminal of the booster battery. The other end of this cable should be connected to a good ground on the engine block **(see illustration)**. Make sure the cable will not come into contact with the fan, drivebelts or other moving parts of the engine.

Start the engine using the booster battery, then, with the engine running at idle speed, disconnect the jumper cables in the reverse order of connection.

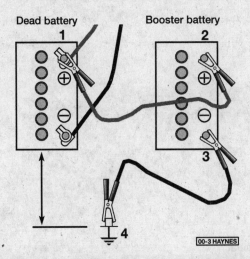

Make the booster battery cable connections in the numerical order shown (note that the negative cable of the booster battery is NOT attached to the negative terminal of the dead battery)

Jacking and towing

Jacking

Warning: *The jack supplied with the vehicle should only be used for raising the vehicle when changing a tire or placing jackstands under the frame. Never work under the vehicle or start the engine while the jack is being used as the only means of support.*

The vehicle must be parked on a level surface with the wheels blocked, the hazard flashers on and the transmission in Park (automatic) or Reverse (manual). Apply the parking brake if the front of the vehicle must be raised. Make sure no one is in the vehicle when using the jack to lift it.

Remove the jack from the storage compartment behind the passenger seat **(see illustration)**. If a flat tire is being changed, you'll also need the lug nut wrench and spare tire. If the spare must be installed, loosen the lug nuts one-half turn, but leave them in place until the tire is off the ground. Some models have wheel covers which must be removed to get at the lug nuts (wheel covers often have sharp edges - be careful not to cut yourself).

Place the jack under the vehicle in the indicated position **(see illustrations)**. Turn the jack handle clockwise until the tire clears the ground. Remove the lug nuts, pull off the wheel and install the spare. Thread the lug nuts back on and tighten them snugly. Don't attempt to tighten them completely until the vehicle is lowered to the ground.

Turn the jack handle counterclockwise to lower the vehicle. Remove the jack and tighten the lug nuts (if loosened or removed) in a criss-cross pattern. If possible, use a torque wrench to tighten them (see Chapter 1 for the torque figures). If you don't have a torque wrench, have the nuts checked by a service station or repair shop as soon as possible.

Stow the tire, jack and wrench and unblock the wheels.

Towing

Vehicles with a manual transmission

The vehicle can be towed with all four wheels on the ground, if the transmission, rear axle and steering system are undamaged. A towing dolly must be used if any of the components are damaged.

Vehicles with an automatic transmission

The vehicle can be towed with all four wheels on the ground if speeds don't exceed 35 mph and the distance is less than fifty miles, otherwise transmission damage can result.

All vehicles

Equipment specifically designed for towing should be used. It should be attached to the main structural members of the vehicle, not the bumpers or brackets. Safety is a major consideration when towing and all applicable state and local laws must be obeyed. A safety chain must be used.

The parking brake must be released and the transmission must be in Neutral. The steering must be unlocked (ignition switch in the Accessory position). Remember that power steering and power brakes won't work with the engine off.

The jack is stowed in a covered compartment behind the passenger seat

Place the jack under the indicated points for the rear . . .

. . . and the front positions

Automotive chemicals and lubricants

A number of automotive chemicals and lubricants are available for use during vehicle maintenance and repair. They include a wide variety of products ranging from cleaning solvents and degreasers to lubricants and protective sprays for rubber, plastic and vinyl.

Cleaners

Carburetor cleaner and choke cleaner is a strong solvent for gum, varnish and carbon. Most carburetor cleaners leave a dry-type lubricant film which will not harden or gum up. Because of this film it is not recommended for use on electrical components.

Brake system cleaner is used to remove grease and brake fluid from the brake system, where clean surfaces are absolutely necessary. It leaves no residue and often eliminates brake squeal caused by contaminants.

Electrical cleaner removes oxidation, corrosion and carbon deposits from electrical contacts, restoring full current flow. It can also be used to clean spark plugs, carburetor jets, voltage regulators and other parts where an oil-free surface is desired.

Demoisturants remove water and moisture from electrical components such as alternators, voltage regulators, electrical connectors and fuse blocks. They are non-conductive, non-corrosive and non-flammable.

Degreasers are heavy-duty solvents used to remove grease from the outside of the engine and from chassis components. They can be sprayed or brushed on and, depending on the type, are rinsed off either with water or solvent.

Lubricants

Motor oil is the lubricant formulated for use in engines. It normally contains a wide variety of additives to prevent corrosion and reduce foaming and wear. Motor oil comes in various weights (viscosity ratings) from 0 to 50. The recommended weight of the oil depends on the season, temperature and the demands on the engine. Light oil is used in cold climates and under light load conditions. Heavy oil is used in hot climates and where high loads are encountered. Multi-viscosity oils are designed to have characteristics of both light and heavy oils and are available in a number of weights from 5W-20 to 20W-50.

Gear oil is designed to be used in differentials, manual transmissions and other areas where high-temperature lubrication is required.

Chassis and wheel bearing grease is a heavy grease used where increased loads and friction are encountered, such as for wheel bearings, balljoints, tie-rod ends and universal joints.

High-temperature wheel bearing grease is designed to withstand the extreme temperatures encountered by wheel bearings in disc brake equipped vehicles. It usually contains molybdenum disulfide (moly), which is a dry-type lubricant.

White grease is a heavy grease for metal-to-metal applications where water is a problem. White grease stays soft under both low and high temperatures (usually from -100 to +190-degrees F), and will not wash off or dilute in the presence of water.

Assembly lube is a special extreme pressure lubricant, usually containing moly, used to lubricate high-load parts (such as main and rod bearings and cam lobes) for initial start-up of a new engine. The assembly lube lubricates the parts without being squeezed out or washed away until the engine oiling system begins to function.

Silicone lubricants are used to protect rubber, plastic, vinyl and nylon parts.

Graphite lubricants are used where oils cannot be used due to contamination problems, such as in locks. The dry graphite will lubricate metal parts while remaining uncontaminated by dirt, water, oil or acids. It is electrically conductive and will not foul electrical contacts in locks such as the ignition switch.

Moly penetrants loosen and lubricate frozen, rusted and corroded fasteners and prevent future rusting or freezing.

Heat-sink grease is a special electrically non-conductive grease that is used for mounting electronic ignition modules where it is essential that heat is transferred away from the module.

Sealants

RTV sealant is one of the most widely used gasket compounds. Made from silicone, RTV is air curing, it seals, bonds, waterproofs, fills surface irregularities, remains flexible, doesn't shrink, is relatively easy to remove, and is used as a supplementary sealer with almost all low and medium temperature gaskets.

Anaerobic sealant is much like RTV in that it can be used either to seal gaskets or to form gaskets by itself. It remains flexible, is solvent resistant and fills surface imperfections. The difference between an anaerobic sealant and an RTV-type sealant is in the curing. RTV cures when exposed to air, while an anaerobic sealant cures only in the absence of air. This means that an anaerobic sealant cures only after the assembly of parts, sealing them together.

Thread and pipe sealant is used for sealing hydraulic and pneumatic fittings and vacuum lines. It is usually made from a Teflon compound, and comes in a spray, a paint-on liquid and as a wrap-around tape.

Chemicals

Anti-seize compound prevents seizing, galling, cold welding, rust and corrosion in fasteners. High-temperature anti-seize, usually made with copper and graphite lubricants, is used for exhaust system and exhaust manifold bolts.

Anaerobic locking compounds are used to keep fasteners from vibrating or working loose and cure only after installation, in the absence of air. Medium strength locking compound is used for small nuts, bolts and screws that may be removed later. High-strength locking compound is for large nuts, bolts and studs which aren't removed on a regular basis.

Oil additives range from viscosity index improvers to chemical treatments that claim to reduce internal engine friction. It should be noted that most oil manufacturers caution against using additives with their oils.

Gas additives perform several functions, depending on their chemical makeup. They usually contain solvents that help dissolve gum and varnish that build up on carburetor, fuel injection and intake parts. They also serve to break down carbon deposits that form on the inside surfaces of the combustion chambers. Some additives contain upper cylinder lubricants for valves and piston rings, and others contain chemicals to remove condensation from the gas tank.

Miscellaneous

Brake fluid is specially formulated hydraulic fluid that can withstand the heat and pressure encountered in brake systems. Care must be taken so this fluid does not come in contact with painted surfaces or plastics. An opened container should always be resealed to prevent contamination by water or dirt.

Weatherstrip adhesive is used to bond weatherstripping around doors, windows and trunk lids. It is sometimes used to attach trim pieces.

Undercoating is a petroleum-based, tar-like substance that is designed to protect metal surfaces on the underside of the vehicle from corrosion. It also acts as a sound-deadening agent by insulating the bottom of the vehicle.

Waxes and polishes are used to help protect painted and plated surfaces from the weather. Different types of paint may require the use of different types of wax and polish. Some polishes utilize a chemical or abrasive cleaner to help remove the top layer of oxidized (dull) paint on older vehicles. In recent years many non-wax polishes that contain a wide variety of chemicals such as polymers and silicones have been introduced. These non-wax polishes are usually easier to apply and last longer than conventional waxes and polishes.

Conversion factors

Length (distance)
Inches (in)	X 25.4	= Millimetres (mm)	X 0.0394	= Inches (in)
Feet (ft)	X 0.305	= Metres (m)	X 3.281	= Feet (ft)
Miles	X 1.609	= Kilometres (km)	X 0.621	= Miles

Volume (capacity)
Cubic inches (cu in; in^3)	X 16.387	= Cubic centimetres (cc; cm^3)	X 0.061	= Cubic inches (cu in; in^3)
Imperial pints (Imp pt)	X 0.568	= Litres (l)	X 1.76	= Imperial pints (Imp pt)
Imperial quarts (Imp qt)	X 1.137	= Litres (l)	X 0.88	= Imperial quarts (Imp qt)
Imperial quarts (Imp qt)	X 1.201	= US quarts (US qt)	X 0.833	= Imperial quarts (Imp qt)
US quarts (US qt)	X 0.946	= Litres (l)	X 1.057	= US quarts (US qt)
Imperial gallons (Imp gal)	X 4.546	= Litres (l)	X 0.22	= Imperial gallons (Imp gal)
Imperial gallons (Imp gal)	X 1.201	= US gallons (US gal)	X 0.833	= Imperial gallons (Imp gal)
US gallons (US gal)	X 3.785	= Litres (l)	X 0.264	= US gallons (US gal)

Mass (weight)
Ounces (oz)	X 28.35	= Grams (g)	X 0.035	= Ounces (oz)
Pounds (lb)	X 0.454	= Kilograms (kg)	X 2.205	= Pounds (lb)

Force
Ounces-force (ozf; oz)	X 0.278	= Newtons (N)	X 3.6	= Ounces-force (ozf; oz)
Pounds-force (lbf; lb)	X 4.448	= Newtons (N)	X 0.225	= Pounds-force (lbf; lb)
Newtons (N)	X 0.1	= Kilograms-force (kgf; kg)	X 9.81	= Newtons (N)

Pressure
Pounds-force per square inch (psi; lbf/in^2; lb/in^2)	X 0.070	= Kilograms-force per square centimetre (kgf/cm^2; kg/cm^2)	X 14.223	= Pounds-force per square inch (psi; lbf/in^2; lb/in^2)
Pounds-force per square inch (psi; lbf/in^2; lb/in^2)	X 0.068	= Atmospheres (atm)	X 14.696	= Pounds-force per square inch (psi; lbf/in^2; lb/in^2)
Pounds-force per square inch (psi; lbf/in^2; lb/in^2)	X 0.069	= Bars	X 14.5	= Pounds-force per square inch (psi; lbf/in^2; lb/in^2)
Pounds-force per square inch (psi; lbf/in^2; lb/in^2)	X 6.895	= Kilopascals (kPa)	X 0.145	= Pounds-force per square inch (psi; lbf/in^2; lb/in^2)
Kilopascals (kPa)	X 0.01	= Kilograms-force per square centimetre (kgf/cm^2; kg/cm^2)	X 98.1	= Kilopascals (kPa)

Torque (moment of force)
Pounds-force inches (lbf in; lb in)	X 1.152	= Kilograms-force centimetre (kgf cm; kg cm)	X 0.868	= Pounds-force inches (lbf in; lb in)
Pounds-force inches (lbf in; lb in)	X 0.113	= Newton metres (Nm)	X 8.85	= Pounds-force inches (lbf in; lb in)
Pounds-force inches (lbf in; lb in)	X 0.083	= Pounds-force feet (lbf ft; lb ft)	X 12	= Pounds-force inches (lbf in; lb in)
Pounds-force feet (lbf ft; lb ft)	X 0.138	= Kilograms-force metres (kgf m; kg m)	X 7.233	= Pounds-force feet (lbf ft; lb ft)
Pounds-force feet (lbf ft; lb ft)	X 1.356	= Newton metres (Nm)	X 0.738	= Pounds-force feet (lbf ft; lb ft)
Newton metres (Nm)	X 0.102	= Kilograms-force metres (kgf m; kg m)	X 9.804	= Newton metres (Nm)

Vacuum
Inches mercury (in. Hg)	X 3.377	= Kilopascals (kPa)	X 0.2961	= Inches mercury
Inches mercury (in. Hg)	X 25.4	= Millimeters mercury (mm Hg)	X 0.0394	= Inches mercury

Power
Horsepower (hp)	X 745.7	= Watts (W)	X 0.0013	= Horsepower (hp)

Velocity (speed)
Miles per hour (miles/hr; mph)	X 1.609	= Kilometres per hour (km/hr; kph)	X 0.621	= Miles per hour (miles/hr; mph)

Fuel consumption*
Miles per gallon, Imperial (mpg)	X 0.354	= Kilometres per litre (km/l)	X 2.825	= Miles per gallon, Imperial (mpg)
Miles per gallon, US (mpg)	X 0.425	= Kilometres per litre (km/l)	X 2.352	= Miles per gallon, US (mpg)

Temperature
Degrees Fahrenheit = (°C x 1.8) + 32

Degrees Celsius (Degrees Centigrade; °C) = (°F - 32) x 0.56

*It is common practice to convert from miles per gallon (mpg) to litres/100 kilometres (l/100km), where mpg (Imperial) x l/100 km = 282 and mpg (US) x l/100 km = 235

Safety first!

Regardless of how enthusiastic you may be about getting on with the job at hand, take the time to ensure that your safety is not jeopardized. A moment's lack of attention can result in an accident, as can failure to observe certain simple safety precautions. The possibility of an accident will always exist, and the following points should not be considered a comprehensive list of all dangers. Rather, they are intended to make you aware of the risks and to encourage a safety conscious approach to all work you carry out on your vehicle.

Essential DOs and DON'Ts

DON'T rely on a jack when working under the vehicle. Always use approved jackstands to support the weight of the vehicle and place them under the recommended lift or support points.

DON'T attempt to loosen extremely tight fasteners (i.e. wheel lug nuts) while the vehicle is on a jack - it may fall.

DON'T start the engine without first making sure that the transmission is in Neutral (or Park where applicable) and the parking brake is set.

DON'T remove the radiator cap from a hot cooling system - let it cool or cover it with a cloth and release the pressure gradually.

DON'T attempt to drain the engine oil until you are sure it has cooled to the point that it will not burn you.

DON'T touch any part of the engine or exhaust system until it has cooled sufficiently to avoid burns.

DON'T siphon toxic liquids such as gasoline, antifreeze and brake fluid by mouth, or allow them to remain on your skin.

DON'T inhale brake lining dust - it is potentially hazardous (see Asbestos below).

DON'T allow spilled oil or grease to remain on the floor - wipe it up before someone slips on it.

DON'T use loose fitting wrenches or other tools which may slip and cause injury.

DON'T push on wrenches when loosening or tightening nuts or bolts. Always try to pull the wrench toward you. If the situation calls for pushing the wrench away, push with an open hand to avoid scraped knuckles if the wrench should slip.

DON'T attempt to lift a heavy component alone - get someone to help you.

DON'T rush or take unsafe shortcuts to finish a job.

DON'T allow children or animals in or around the vehicle while you are working on it.

DO wear eye protection when using power tools such as a drill, sander, bench grinder, etc. and when working under a vehicle.

DO keep loose clothing and long hair well out of the way of moving parts.

DO make sure that any hoist used has a safe working load rating adequate for the job.

DO get someone to check on you periodically when working alone on a vehicle.

DO carry out work in a logical sequence and make sure that everything is correctly assembled and tightened.

DO keep chemicals and fluids tightly capped and out of the reach of children and pets.

DO remember that your vehicle's safety affects that of yourself and others. If in doubt on any point, get professional advice.

Asbestos

Certain friction, insulating, sealing, and other products - such as brake linings, brake bands, clutch linings, torque converters, gaskets, etc. - may contain asbestos. Extreme care must be taken to avoid inhalation of dust from such products, since it is hazardous to health. If in doubt, assume that they do contain asbestos.

Fire

Remember at all times that gasoline is highly flammable. Never smoke or have any kind of open flame around when working on a vehicle. But the risk does not end there. A spark caused by an electrical short circuit, by two metal surfaces contacting each other, or even by static electricity built up in your body under certain conditions, can ignite gasoline vapors, which in a confined space are highly explosive. Do not, under any circumstances, use gasoline for cleaning parts. Use an approved safety solvent.

Always disconnect the battery ground (-) cable at the battery before working on any part of the fuel system or electrical system. Never risk spilling fuel on a hot engine or exhaust component. It is strongly recommended that a fire extinguisher suitable for use on fuel and electrical fires be kept handy in the garage or workshop at all times. Never try to extinguish a fuel or electrical fire with water.

Fumes

Certain fumes are highly toxic and can quickly cause unconsciousness and even death if inhaled to any extent. Gasoline vapor falls into this category, as do the vapors from some cleaning solvents. Any draining or pouring of such volatile fluids should be done in a well ventilated area.

When using cleaning fluids and solvents, read the instructions on the container carefully. Never use materials from unmarked containers.

Never run the engine in an enclosed space, such as a garage. Exhaust fumes contain carbon monoxide, which is extremely poisonous. If you need to run the engine, always do so in the open air, or at least have the rear of the vehicle outside the work area.

If you are fortunate enough to have the use of an inspection pit, never drain or pour gasoline and never run the engine while the vehicle is over the pit. The fumes, being heavier than air, will concentrate in the pit with possibly lethal results.

The battery

Never create a spark or allow a bare light bulb near a battery. They normally give off a certain amount of hydrogen gas, which is highly explosive.

Always disconnect the battery ground (-) cable at the battery before working on the fuel or electrical systems.

If possible, loosen the filler caps or cover when charging the battery from an external source (this does not apply to sealed or maintenance-free batteries). Do not charge at an excessive rate or the battery may burst.

Take care when adding water to a non maintenance-free battery and when carrying a battery. The electrolyte, even when diluted, is very corrosive and should not be allowed to contact clothing or skin.

Always wear eye protection when cleaning the battery to prevent the caustic deposits from entering your eyes.

Household current

When using an electric power tool, inspection light, etc., which operates on household current, always make sure that the tool is correctly connected to its plug and that, where necessary, it is properly grounded. Do not use such items in damp conditions and, again, do not create a spark or apply excessive heat in the vicinity of fuel or fuel vapor.

Secondary ignition system voltage

A severe electric shock can result from touching certain parts of the ignition system (such as the spark plug wires) when the engine is running or being cranked, particularly if components are damp or the insulation is defective. In the case of an electronic ignition system, the secondary system voltage is much higher and could prove fatal.

Troubleshooting

Contents

This section is an easy reference guide to the more common problems which may occur during the operation of your vehicle. The problems and their possible causes are grouped under headings denoting various components or systems, such as Engine, Cooling system, etc. They also refer you to the chapter and/or section which deals with the problem.

Remember, successful troubleshooting isn't a mysterious "black art" practiced only by professional mechanics. It's simply the result of the right knowledge combined with an intelligent, systematic approach to a problem. Always use the process of elimination, starting with the simplest solution and working through to the most complex - and never overlook the obvious. Anyone can run the gas tank dry or leave the lights on overnight, so don't assume it can't happen to you.

Finally, always try to establish a clear idea why a problem has occurred and take steps to ensure it doesn't happen again. For example, if the electrical system fails because of a poor connection, check all other connections in the system to make sure they don't fail as well. If a particular fuse continues to blow, find out why - don't just replace one fuse after another. Remember, failure of a small component often indicates potential failure or malfunction of a more important component or system.

Engine

1 Engine will not rotate when attempting to start

1 Battery terminal connections loose or corroded. Check the cable terminals at the battery. Tighten the cable or remove corrosion as necessary.
2 Battery discharged or faulty. If the cable connections are clean and tight on the battery posts, turn the key to the On position and switch on the headlights and/or windshield wipers. If they fail to function, the battery is discharged.
3 Automatic transmission not completely engaged in Park or clutch not completely depressed.
4 Broken, loose or disconnected wiring in the starting circuit. Inspect all wiring and connectors at the battery, starter solenoid and ignition switch.
5 Starter motor pinion jammed in flywheel ring gear. If equipped with a manual transmission, place the transmission in gear and rock the vehicle to manually turn the engine. Remove the starter and inspect the pinion and flywheel at earliest convenience.
6 Starter solenoid faulty (Chapter 5).
7 Starter motor faulty (Chapter 5).
8 Ignition switch faulty (Chapter 12).

2 Engine rotates but will not start

1 Fuel tank empty.
2 Battery discharged (engine rotates slowly). Check the operation of electrical components as described in previous Section.
3 Battery terminal connections loose or corroded. See previous Section.
4 Carburetor flooded and/or fuel level in carburetor incorrect. This will usually be accompanied by a strong fuel odor from under the hood. Wait a few minutes, depress the accelerator pedal all the way to the floor and attempt to start the engine.
5 Choke control inoperative (Chapter 1).
6 Fuel not reaching carburetor or fuel injectors. With the ignition switch in the Off position, open the hood, remove the top plate of the air cleaner assembly and observe the top of the carburetor (manually move the choke plate back if necessary). Have an assistant depress the accelerator pedal and check that fuel spurts into the carburetor. If not, check the fuel filter (Chapter 1), fuel lines and fuel pump (Chapter 4).
7 Fuel injector or fuel pump faulty (fuel injected vehicles) (Chapter 4).
8 No power to fuel pump (Chapter 4).
9 Worn, faulty or incorrectly gapped spark plugs (Chapter 1).
10 Broken, loose or disconnected wiring in the starting circuit (see previous Section).
11 Distributor loose, causing ignition timing to change. Turn the distributor as necessary to start the engine, then set the ignition timing as soon as possible (Chapter 1).
12 Broken, loose or disconnected wires at the ignition coil or faulty coil (Chapter 5).

3 Starter motor operates without rotating engine

1 Starter pinion sticking. Remove the starter (Chapter 5) and inspect.
2 Starter pinion or flywheel teeth worn or broken. Remove the cover at the rear of the engine and inspect.

4 Engine hard to start when cold

1 Battery discharged or low. Check as described in Section 1.
2 Choke control inoperative or out of adjustment (Chapter 4).
3 Carburetor flooded (see Section 2).
4 Fuel supply not reaching the carburetor (see Section 2).
5 Carburetor/fuel injection system in need of overhaul (Chapter 4).
6 Distributor rotor carbon tracked and/or mechanical advance mechanism rusted (Chapter 5).
7 Fuel injection malfunction (Chapter 4).

5 Engine hard to start when hot

1 Air filter clogged (Chapter 1).
2 Fuel not reaching the injectors (see Section 2).
3 Corroded electrical leads at the battery (Chapter 1).
4 Bad engine ground (Chapter 1).
5 Starter worn (Chapter 5).
6 Corroded electrical leads at the fuel injection (Chapter 4).

6 Starter motor noisy or excessively rough in engagement

1 Pinion or flywheel gear teeth worn or broken. Remove the cover at the rear of the engine (if so equipped) and inspect.
2 Starter motor mounting bolts loose or missing.

7 Engine starts but stops immediately

1 Loose or faulty electrical connections at distributor, coil or alternator.
2 Insufficient fuel reaching the carburetor or fuel injector. Disconnect the fuel line. Place a container under the disconnected fuel line and observe the flow of fuel from the line. If little or none at all, check for blockage in the lines and/or replace the fuel pump (Chapter 4).
3 Vacuum leak at the gasket surfaces of the carburetor or fuel injection unit. Make sure that all mounting bolts/nuts are tightened securely and that all vacuum hoses connected to the carburetor or fuel injection unit and manifold are positioned properly and in good condition.

8 Engine lopes while idling or idles erratically

1 Vacuum leakage. Check mounting bolts/nuts at the carburetor/fuel injection unit and intake manifold for tightness. Make sure that all vacuum hoses are connected and in good condition. Use a stethoscope or a length of fuel hose held against your ear to listen for vacuum leaks while the engine is running. A hissing sound will be heard. Check the carburetor/fuel injector and intake manifold gasket surfaces.
2 Leaking EGR valve or plugged PCV valve (see Chapters 1 and 6).
3 Air filter clogged (Chapter 1).
4 Fuel pump not delivering sufficient fuel to the carburetor/fuel injector (see Section 7).
5 Carburetor out of adjustment (Chapter 4).
6 Leaking head gasket. If this is suspected, take the vehicle to a repair shop or dealer where the engine can be pressure

checked.
7   Timing chain and/or gears worn (Chapter 2).
8   Camshaft lobes worn (Chapter 2).

9   Engine misses at idle speed

1   Spark plugs worn or improperly gapped (Chapter 1).
2   Faulty spark plug wires (Chapter 1).
3   Choke not operating properly (Chapter 1).
4   Sticking or faulty emissions system components (Chapter 6).
5   Clogged fuel filter and/or foreign matter in fuel. Remove the fuel filter (Chapter 1) and inspect.
6   Vacuum leaks at the intake manifold or at hose connections. Check as described in Section 8.
7   Incorrect idle speed or idle mixture (Chapter 1).
8   Incorrect ignition timing (Chapter 1).
9   Uneven or low cylinder compression. Check compression as described in Chapter 1.

10   Engine misses throughout driving speed range

1   Fuel filter clogged and/or impurities in the fuel system (Chapter 1). Also check fuel output at the carburetor/fuel injector (Section 7).
2   Faulty or incorrectly gapped spark plugs (Chapter 1).
3   Incorrect ignition timing (Chapter 1).
4   Check for cracked distributor cap, disconnected distributor wires and damaged distributor components (Chapter 1).
5   Cracked spark plug wires (Chapter 1).
6   Faulty emissions system components (Chapter 6).
7   Low or uneven cylinder compression pressures. Remove the spark plugs and test the compression with gauge (Chapter 1).
8   Weak or faulty ignition system (Chapter 5).
9   Vacuum leaks at the carburetor/fuel injection unit or vacuum hoses (see Section 8).

11   Engine stalls

1   Idle speed incorrect (Chapter 1).
2   Fuel filter clogged and/or water and impurities in the fuel system (Chapter 1).
3   Choke improperly adjusted or sticking (Chapter 1).
4   Distributor components damp or damaged (Chapter 5).
5   Faulty emissions system components (Chapter 6).
6   Faulty or incorrectly gapped spark plugs (Chapter 1). Also check spark plug wires

(Chapter 1).
7   Vacuum leak at the carburetor/fuel injection unit or vacuum hoses. Check as described in Section 8.

12   Engine lacks power

1   Incorrect ignition timing (Chapter 1).
2   Excessive play in distributor shaft. At the same time, check for a worn rotor, faulty distributor cap/wires, etc. (Chapters 1 and 5).
3   Faulty or incorrectly gapped spark plugs (Chapter 1).
4   Fuel injection units not adjusted properly or excessively worn (Chapter 4).
5   Faulty coil (Chapter 5).
6   Brakes binding (Chapter 1).
7   Automatic transmission fluid level incorrect (Chapter 1).
8   Clutch slipping (Chapter 8).
9   Fuel filter clogged and/or impurities in the fuel system (Chapter 1).
10   Emissions control system not functioning properly (Chapter 6).
11   Use of substandard fuel. Fill tank with proper octane fuel.
12   Low or uneven cylinder compression pressures. Test with compression tester, which will detect leaking valves and/or blown head gasket (Chapter 1).

13   Engine backfires

1   Emissions system not functioning properly (Chapter 6).
2   Ignition timing incorrect (Chapter 1).
3   Faulty secondary ignition system (cracked spark plug insulator, faulty plug wires, distributor cap and/or rotor) (Chapters 1 and 5).
4   Carburetor/fuel injection units in need of adjustment or worn excessively (Chapter 4).
5   Vacuum leak at the fuel injection unit(s) or vacuum hoses. Check as described in Section 8.
6   Valve clearances incorrectly set, and/or valves sticking in guides (Chapter 2).
7   Crossed plug wires (Chapter 1).

14   Pinging or knocking engine sounds during acceleration or uphill

1   Incorrect fuel grade. Fill tank with fuel of the proper octane rating.
2   Ignition timing incorrect (Chapter 1).
3   Carburetor/fuel injection units in need of adjustment or overhaul (Chapter 4).
4   Improper spark plugs. Check plug type against Emissions Control Information label located in engine compartment. Also check plugs and wires for damage (Chapter 1).
5   Worn or damaged distributor components (Chapter 5).
6   Faulty emissions system (Chapter 6).

7   Vacuum leak. Check as described in Section 8.
8   Carbon build-up in cylinders (Chapter 2).

15   Engine diesels (continues to run) after switching off

1   Idle speed too high (Chapter 1).
2   Electrical solenoid at side of carburetor not functioning properly (not all models, see Chapter 4).
3   Ignition timing incorrectly adjusted (Chapter 1).
4   Thermo-controlled air cleaner heat valve not operating properly (Chapter 6).
5   Excessive engine operating temperature. Probable causes of this are malfunctioning thermostat, clogged radiator, faulty water pump (Chapter 3).
6   Incorrect fuel grade. Fill tank with fuel of the proper octane rating.

Engine electrical system

16   Battery will not hold a charge

1   Alternator drivebelt defective or not adjusted properly (Chapter 1).
2   Electrolyte level low or battery discharged (Chapter 1).
3   Battery terminals loose or corroded (Chapter 1).
4   Alternator not charging properly (Chapter 5).
5   Loose, broken or faulty wires in the charging circuit (Chapter 5).
6   Short in the vehicle wiring causing a continual drain on the battery.
7   Battery defective internally.

17   Ignition light fails to go out

1   Fault in alternator or charging circuit (Chapter 5).
2   Alternator drivebelt defective or not properly adjusted (Chapter 1).

18   Ignition light fails to come on when key is turned on

1   Warning light bulb defective (Chapter 12).
2   Alternator faulty (Chapter 5).
3   Fault in the printed circuit, dash wiring or bulb holder (Chapter 12).

19   "Check engine" light comes on

See Chapter 6.

Fuel system

20 Excessive fuel consumption

1 Dirty or clogged air filter element (Chapter 1).
2 Incorrectly set ignition timing (Chapter 1).
3 Choke sticking or improperly adjusted (Chapter 1).
4 Emissions system not functioning properly (not all vehicles, see Chapter 6).
5 Carburetor idle speed and/or mixture not adjusted properly (Chapter 1).
6 Carburetor/fuel injection internal parts excessively worn or damaged (Chapter 4).
7 Low tire pressure or incorrect tire size (Chapter 1).

21 Fuel leakage and/or fuel odor

1 Leak in a fuel feed or vent line (Chapter 4).
2 Tank overfilled. Fill only to automatic shut-off.
3 Emissions system filter clogged (Chapter 1).
4 Vapor leaks from system lines (Chapter 4).
5 Carburetor/fuel injection internal parts excessively worn or out of adjustment (Chapter 4).

Cooling system

22 Overheating

1 Insufficient coolant in system (Chapter 1).
2 Water pump drivebelt defective or not adjusted properly (Chapter 1).
3 Radiator core blocked or radiator grille dirty and restricted (Chapter 3).
4 Thermostat faulty (Chapter 3).
5 Fan blades broken or cracked (Chapter 3).
6 Radiator cap not maintaining proper pressure. Have cap pressure tested by gas station or repair shop.
7 Ignition timing incorrect (Chapter 1).

23 Overcooling

1 Thermostat faulty (Chapter 3).
2 Inaccurate temperature gauge or sending unit.

24 External coolant leakage

1 Deteriorated or damaged hoses or loose clamps. Replace hoses and/or tighten clamps at hose connections (Chapter 1).
2 Water pump seals defective. If this is the case, water will drip from the weep hole in the water pump body (Chapter 1).
3 Leakage from radiator core or header tank. This will require the radiator to be professionally repaired (see Chapter 3 for removal procedures).
4 Engine drain plugs or water jacket core plugs leaking (see Chapter 2).

25 Internal coolant leakage

Note: *Internal coolant leaks can usually be detected by examining the oil. Check the dipstick and inside the valve covers for water deposits and an oil consistency like a milkshake.*
1 Leaking cylinder head gasket. Have the cooling system pressure tested.
2 Cracked cylinder bore or cylinder head. Dismantle engine and inspect (Chapter 2).

26 Coolant loss

1 Too much coolant in system (Chapter 1).
2 Coolant boiling away due to overheating (see Section 22).
3 Internal or external leakage (see Sections 24 and 25).
4 Faulty radiator cap. Have the cap pressure tested.

27 Poor coolant circulation

1 Inoperative water pump. A quick test is to pinch the top radiator hose closed with your hand while the engine is idling, then let it loose. You should feel the surge of coolant if the pump is working properly (Chapter 1).
2 Restriction in cooling system. Drain, flush and refill the system (Chapter 1). If necessary, remove the radiator (Chapter 3) and have it reverse flushed.
3 Water pump drivebelt defective or not adjusted properly (Chapter 1).
4 Thermostat sticking (Chapter 3).

Clutch

28 Fails to release (pedal pressed to the floor - shift lever does not move freely in and out of Reverse)

1 Clutch fork off ball stud. Look under the vehicle, on the left side of transmission.
2 Clutch plate warped or damaged (Chapter 8).

29 Clutch slips (engine speed increases with no increase in vehicle speed)

1 Clutch plate oil soaked or lining worn. Remove clutch (Chapter 8) and inspect.
2 Clutch plate not seated. It may take 30 or 40 normal starts for a new one to seat.
3 Pressure plate worn (Chapter 8).

30 Grabbing (chattering) as clutch is engaged

1 Oil on clutch plate lining. Remove (Chapter 8) and inspect. Correct any leakage source.
2 Worn or loose engine or transmission mounts. These units move slightly when clutch is released. Inspect mounts and bolts.
3 Worn splines on clutch plate hub. Remove clutch components (Chapter 8) and inspect.
4 Warped pressure plate or flywheel. Remove clutch components and inspect.

31 Squeal or rumble with clutch fully engaged (pedal released)

1 Improper adjustment; no free play (Chapter 1).
2 Release bearing binding on transmission bearing retainer. Remove clutch components (Chapter 8) and check bearing. Remove any burrs or nicks, clean and relubricate before reinstallation.
3 Weak linkage return spring. Replace the spring.

32 Squeal or rumble with clutch fully disengaged (pedal depressed)

1 Worn, defective or broken release bearing (Chapter 8).
2 Worn or broken pressure plate springs (or diaphragm fingers) (Chapter 8).

33 Clutch pedal stays on floor when disengaged

1 Bind in linkage or release bearing. Inspect linkage or remove clutch components as necessary.
2 Linkage springs being over extended. Adjust linkage for proper free play. Make sure proper pedal stop (bumper) is installed.

Manual transmission

Note: *All the following references are to Chapter 7, unless otherwise noted.*

34 Noisy in Neutral with engine running

1   Input shaft bearing worn.
2   Damaged main drive gear bearing.
3   Worn countershaft bearings.
4   Worn or damaged countershaft end play shims.

35 Noisy in all gears

1   Any of the above causes, and/or:
2   Insufficient lubricant (see checking procedures in Chapter 1).

36 Noisy in one particular gear

1   Worn, damaged or chipped gear teeth for that particular gear.
2   Worn or damaged synchronizer for that particular gear.

37 Slips out of high gear

1   Transmission mounting bolts loose.
2   Shift rods not working freely.
3   Damaged mainshaft pilot bearing.
4   Dirt between transmission case and engine or misalignment of transmission.

38 Difficulty in engaging gears

1   Clutch not releasing completely (see clutch adjustment in Chapter 8).
2   Loose, damaged or out-of-adjustment shift linkage. Make a thorough inspection, replacing parts as necessary.
3   Air in hydraulic system (Chapter 8).

39 Oil leakage

1   Excessive amount of lubricant in transmission (see Chapter 1 for correct checking procedures). Drain lubricant as required.
2   Side cover loose or gasket damaged.
3   Rear oil seal or speedometer oil seal in need of replacement.
4   Clutch hydraulic system leaking (Chapter 8).

Automatic transmission

Note: *Due to the complexity of the automatic transmission, it's very difficult for the home mechanic to properly diagnose and service this component. For problems other than the following, the vehicle should be taken to a dealer or reputable mechanic.*

40 General shift mechanism problems

1   Chapter 7 deals with checking and adjusting the shift linkage on automatic transmissions. Common problems which may be attributed to poorly adjusted linkage are:
    Engine starting in gears other than Park or Neutral.
    Indicator on shifter pointing to a gear other than the one actually being used.
    Vehicle moves when in Park.
2   Refer to Chapter 7 to adjust the linkage.

41 Transmission will not downshift with accelerator pedal pressed to the floor

Chapter 7 deals with adjusting the detent cable to enable the transmission to downshift properly.

42 Transmission slips, shifts rough, is noisy or has no drive in forward or reverse gears

1   There are many probable causes for the above problems, but the home mechanic should be concerned with only one possibility - fluid level.
2   Before taking the vehicle to a repair shop, check the level and condition of the fluid as described in Chapter 1. Correct fluid level as necessary or change the fluid and filter if needed. If the problem persists, have a professional diagnose the probable cause.

43 Fluid leakage

1   Automatic transmission fluid is a deep red color. Fluid leaks should not be confused with engine oil, which can easily be blown by air flow to the transmission.
2   To pinpoint a leak, first remove all built-up dirt and grime from around the transmission. Degreasing agents and/or steam cleaning will achieve this. With the underside clean, drive the vehicle at low speeds so air flow will not blow the leak far from its source. Raise the vehicle and determine where the leak is coming from. Common areas of leakage are:
a) *Pan: Tighten mounting bolts and/or replace pan gasket as necessary (see Chapters 1 and 7).*
b) *Filler pipe: Replace the rubber seal where pipe enters transmission case.*
c) *Transmission oil lines: Tighten connectors where lines enter transmission case and/or replace lines.*
d) *Vent pipe: Transmission overfilled and/or water in fluid (see checking procedures, Chapter 1).*

e) *Speedometer connector: Replace the O-ring where speedometer cable enters transmission case (Chapter 7).*

Driveshaft

44 Oil leak at front of driveshaft

Defective transmission rear oil seal. See Chapter 7 for replacement procedures. While this is done, check the splined yoke for burrs or a rough condition which may be damaging the seal. the can be removed with crocus cloth or a fine whetstone.

45 Knock or clunk when the transmission is under initial load (just after transmission is put into gear)

1   Loose or disconnected rear suspension components. Check all mounting bolts, nuts and bushings (Chapter 10).
2   Loose driveshaft bolts. Inspect all bolts and nuts and tighten them to the specified torque.
3   Splined driveshaft in need of lubrication (Chapter 1).
4   Worn or damaged universal joint bearings. Check for wear (Chapter 8).

46 Metallic grating sound consistent with vehicle speed

Pronounced wear in the universal joint bearings. Check as described in Chapter 8.

47 Vibration

Note: *Before assuming the driveshaft is at fault, make sure the tires are perfectly balanced and perform the following test.*
1   Install a tachometer inside the vehicle to monitor engine speed as the vehicle is driven. Drive the vehicle and note the engine speed at which the vibration (roughness) is most pronounced. Now shift the transmission to a different gear and bring the engine speed to the same point.
2   If the vibration occurs at the same engine speed (rpm) regardless of which gear the transmission is in, the driveshaft is NOT at fault since the driveshaft speed varies.
3   If the vibration decreases or is eliminated when the transmission is in a different gear at the same engine speed, refer to the following probable causes.
4   Bent or dented driveshaft. Inspect and replace as necessary (Chapter 8).
5   Undercoating or built-up dirt, etc. on the driveshaft. Clean the shaft thoroughly and recheck.

6   Worn universal joint bearings. Remove and inspect (Chapter 8).
7   Driveshaft and/or companion flange out of balance. Check for missing weights on the shaft. Remove the driveshaft (Chapter 8) and reinstall 180-degrees from original position, then retest. Have the driveshaft professionally balanced if the problem persists.

Drive axles

48   Noise

1   Road noise. No corrective procedures available.
2   Tire noise. Inspect the tires and check tire pressures (Chapter 1).
3   Rear wheel bearings loose, worn or damaged (Chapter 10).

49   Vibration

See probable causes under Driveshaft. Proceed under the guidelines listed for the driveshaft. If the problem persists, check the rear wheel bearings by raising the rear of the vehicle and spinning the wheels by hand. Listen for evidence of rough (noisy) bearings. Remove and inspect (Chapter 8).

50   Oil leakage

1   Pinion seal damaged (Chapter 8).
2   Axleshaft oil seals damaged (Chapter 8).
3   Differential inspection cover leaking. Tighten the bolts or replace the gasket as required (Chapter 8).

Brakes

Note: *Before assuming that a brake problem exists, make sure the tires are in good condition and inflated properly (see Chapter 1), the front end alignment is correct and the vehicle is not loaded with weight in an unequal manner.*

51   Vehicle pulls to one side during braking

1   Defective, damaged or oil contaminated brake pads on one side. Inspect as described in Chapter 9.
2   Excessive wear of brake pad material or disc on one side. Inspect and correct as necessary.
3   Loose or disconnected front suspension components. Inspect and tighten all bolts to the specified torque (Chapter 10).
4   Defective caliper assembly. Remove the caliper and inspect for a stuck piston or other damage (Chapter 9).

52   Noise (high-pitched squeal with the brakes applied)

Disc brake pads worn out. The noise comes from the wear sensor rubbing against the disc. Replace the pads with new ones immediately (Chapter 9).

53   Excessive brake pedal travel

1   Partial brake system failure. Inspect the entire system (Chapter 9) and correct as required.
2   Insufficient fluid in the master cylinder. Check (Chapter 1), add fluid and bleed the system if necessary (Chapter 9).

54   Brake pedal feels spongy when depressed

1   Air in the hydraulic lines. Bleed the brake system (Chapter 9).
2   Faulty flexible hoses. Inspect all system hoses and lines. Replace parts as necessary.
3   Master cylinder mounting bolts/nuts loose.
4   Master cylinder defective (Chapter 9).

55   Excessive effort required to stop vehicle

1   Power brake booster not operating properly (Chapter 9).
2   Excessively worn brake pads. Inspect and replace if necessary (Chapter 9).
3   One or more caliper pistons seized or sticking. Inspect and rebuild as required (Chapter 9).
4   Brake pads contaminated with oil or grease. Inspect and replace as required (Chapter 9).
5   New pads installed and not yet seated. It will take a while for the new material to seat against the disc.

56   Pedal travels to the floor with little resistance

Little or no fluid in the master cylinder reservoir caused by leaking caliper piston(s), loose, damaged or disconnected brake lines. Inspect the entire system and correct as necessary.

57   Brake pedal pulsates during brake application

1   Wheel bearings not adjusted properly or in need of replacement (Chapter 1).
2   Caliper not sliding properly due to improper installation or obstructions.

Remove and inspect (Chapter 9).
3   Rotor defective. Remove the rotor (Chapter 9) and check for excessive lateral runout and parallelism. Have the rotor resurfaced or replace it with a new one.

Suspension and steering systems

58   Vehicle pulls to one side

1   Tire pressures uneven (Chapter 1).
2   Defective tire (Chapter 1).
3   Excessive wear in suspension or steering components (Chapter 10).
4   Front end in need of alignment.
5   Front brakes dragging. Inspect the brakes as described in Chapter 9.

59   Shimmy, shake or vibration

1   Tire or wheel out-of-balance or out-of-round. Have them balanced by a professional.
2   Loose, worn or out-of-adjustment wheel bearings (Chapters 1 and 8).
3   Shock absorbers and/or suspension components worn or damaged (Chapter 10).

60   Excessive pitching and/or rolling around corners or during braking

1   Defective shock absorbers. Replace as a set (Chapter 10).
2   Broken or weak springs and/or suspension components. Inspect as described in Chapter 10.

61   Excessively stiff steering

1   Lack of fluid in power steering fluid reservoir (Chapter 1).
2   Incorrect tire pressures (Chapter 1).
3   Lack of lubrication at steering joints (Chapter 1).
4   Front end out of alignment.
5   See also section titled Lack of power assistance.

62   Excessive play in steering

1   Loose front wheel bearings (Chapter 1).
2   Excessive wear in suspension or steering components (Chapter 10).

63   Lack of power assistance

1   Steering pump drivebelt defective or not adjusted properly (Chapter 1).
2   Fluid level low (Chapter 1).

3   Hoses or lines restricted. Inspect and replace parts as necessary.
4   Air in power steering system. Bleed the system (Chapter 10).

64   Excessive tire wear (not specific to one area)

1   Incorrect tire pressures (Chapter 1).
2   Tires out-of-balance. Have them balanced by a professional.
3   Wheels damaged. Inspect and replace as necessary.
4   Suspension or steering components excessively worn (Chapter 10).

65   Excessive tire wear on outside edge

1   Inflation pressures incorrect (Chapter 1).
2   Excessive speed in turns.
3   Front end alignment incorrect (excessive toe-in). Have it professionally aligned.
4   Suspension arm bent or twisted (Chapter 10).

66   Excessive tire wear on inside edge

1   Inflation pressures incorrect (Chapter 1).

2   Front end alignment incorrect (toe-out). Have it professionally aligned.
3   Loose or damaged steering components (Chapter 10).

67   Tire tread worn in one place

1   Tires out-of-balance.
2   Damaged or buckled wheel. Inspect and replace if necessary.
3   Defective tire (Chapter 1).

Chapter 1
Tune-up and routine maintenance

Contents

Specifications

Recommended lubricants and fluids

Note: *Listed here are manufacturer recommendations at the time this manual was written. Manufacturers occasionally upgrade their fluid specifications, so check with your auto parts store for current recommendations.*

Engine oil
  Type ..... SF, SF/CC or SF/CD
  Viscosity ..... See accompanying chart

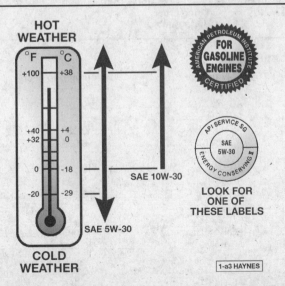

Engine oil viscosity chart

Recommended lubricants and fluids

Engine oil (continued)
    Capacity (approximate)

Small block	5 qts	
Big block	6 qts	

Automatic transmission fluid
    Type .... Dexron II ATF

Capacity	Routine change	Fill from dry
350		
1968 thru 1977	5 pts	20 pts
1978 on	6 pts	20
400	7-1/2 pts	22 pts
700 R-4	10 pts	23 pts

Manual transmission
    USA .... SAE 80 or 90W GL-5 gear lubricant
    Canada .... SAE 80W GL-5 gear lubricant
Differential
    Standard
      USA .... SAE 80 or 90W GL-5 gear lubricant
      Canada .... SAE 80W GL-5 gear lubricant
    Positraction .... Gear lubricant plus special Positraction additive
Chassis grease fittings .... chassis grease
Constant Velocity U-joint .... chassis grease
Engine coolant .... Mixture of water and ethylene glycol base antifreeze
Brake fluid .... DOT-3 fluid
Power steering fluid .... power steering fluid or Dexron II ATF
Manual steering box lubricant .... steering gear grease
Wheel bearing grease .... NLGI no. 2 moly-base wheel bearing grease

Ignition system

Cylinder numbers/locations (front-to-rear)
    Left (driver's) side 1-3-5-7
    Right side 2-4-6-8
    Dwell angle .... 29 to 31 degrees
Firing order 1-8-4-3-6-5-7-2

V8 ENGINE with points-type ignition
Firing order
1-8-4-3-6-5-7-2

V8 ENGINE with electronic (HEI) ignition

Cylinder location and distributor rotation

The blackened terminal shown on the distributor cap indicates the Number One spark plug wire position

Spark plug type/gap and ignition timing

Engine (cu.in.)	Spark plug type	Spark plug gap (inch)	Timing (degrees BTDC)
1968			
327 (all)	AC 44	0.035	4
427 (390 hp)	AC 43N	0.035	4
427 (435 hp)	AC 43N or AC 43XL	0.035	4
427 (430 hp)	AC 43XL	0.035	12
1969			
350	ACR 44	0.035	8
427 (390 hp)	AC 43N	0.035	4
427 (435 hp)	AC 43N or AC 43XL	0.035	4
427 (430 hp)	AC 43XL	0.035	12
1970			
350 (300 hp)	AC R44	0.035	4
350 (350 hp)	AC R44	0.035	8
350 (370 hp)	AC R43	0.035	14
454 (LS6)	AC R43TS	0.035	8
454 (L56)	AC R43TS	0.035	12

Engine (cu.in.)	Spark plug type	Spark plug gap (inch)	Timing (degrees BTDC)
1971			
350 (270 hp)	AC R44TS	0.035	4
350 (330 hp)	AC R44TS	0.035	8*
454 (LS6)	AC R43TS	0.035	8
454 (L56)	AC R43TS	0.035	12

with standard trans, 12 degrees with automatic

Engine (cu.in.)	Spark plug type	Spark plug gap (inch)	Timing (degrees BTDC)
1972			
350 (190 hp)	AC R44T	0.035	8
350 (255 hp)	AC R44T	0.035	4
454 (270 hp)	AC R43T	0.035	8
1973			
350 (200 hp)	AC R44T	0.035	12
350 (250 hp)	AC R44T	0.035	8
454 (275 hp)	AC R43T	0.035	10
1974			
350 (195 hp)	AC R44T	0.035	4*
350 (250 hp)	AC R44T	0.035	8
454 (270 hp)	AC R43T	0.035	10

with standard trans, 8 degrees with automatic

Engine (cu.in.)	Spark plug type	Spark plug gap (inch)	Timing (degrees BTDC)
1975			
All	AC R44TX	0.060	6
1976			
350 (195 hp)	AC R45TS	0.045	6
350 (210 hp)	AC R45TS	0.045	12
350 (270 hp)	AC R45TS	0.045	8
1977			
350 (195 hp)	AC R45TS	0.045	8
350 (270 hp)	AC R45TS	0.045	12
1978 and 1979			
350 (L48)			
California (automatic)	AC R45TS	0.045	8
All others	AC R45TS	0.045	6
350 (L82)	AC R45TS	0.045	12
1980			
305	AC R43TS	0.045	4
350 (L48)	AC R45TS	0.045	6
350 (L82)	AC R45TS	0.045	12

1981 and 1982
Refer to the Vehicle Emissions Control Information label for spark plug specifications

Engine idle speed

1968 .... 750 rpm
1969
    Rochester 4MV only
        350 HP .... 750 rpm
        390 HP .... 800 rpm (M/T), 600 rpm (A/T)
    All others .... 750 rpm
1970 .... 750 rpm
1971
    Holley 4150 .... 700 rpm
    Rochester 4MV .... 600 rpm
1972
    Holley 4150 .... 900 rpm (solenoid de-energized, set to 500 rpm with Allen wrench)
    Rochester 4MV
        350 cu in engine .... 900 rpm (solenoid de-energized, set to 450 rpm with Allen wrench)
        454 cu in engine .... 600 rpm (solenoid de-energized, set to 450 rpm with Allen wrench)
1973
    350 cu in engine (M/T)
        Initial .... 920 rpm
        Final .... 900 rpm
    350 cu in engine (A/T)
        Initial .... 720 rpm
        Final .... 700 rpm
    454 cu in engine
        Initial .... 625 rpm
        Final .... 600 rpm

Engine idle speed (continued)

1974

350 cu in engine
- Solenoid screw (M/T) .... 900 rpm
- Solenoid screw (A/T in Drive) .... 700 rpm
- Lean drop idle mixture (M/T) .... 950 to 900 rpm
- Lean drop idle mixture (A/T in Drive) .... 730 to 700 rpm

454 cu in engine
- Solenoid screw (M/T) .... 800 rpm
- Solenoid screw (A/T in Drive) .... 600 rpm
- Lean drop idle mixture (M/T) .... 850 to 800 rpm
- Lean drop idle mixture (A/T in Drive) .... 630 to 600 rpm

1975

Federal
- M/T .... 800 rpm
- A/T (in Drive) .... 600 rpm

California
- M/T .... 600 rpm
- A/T (in Drive) .... 600 rpm

1976

Initial
- M/T .... 1100 rpm
- A/T .... 750 rpm

Final
- M/T .... 1000 rpm
- A/T (A/C off) .... 700 rpm

1977

	Initial	Final
M/T (low altitude)		
RPO L82 only	900 rpm	800 rpm
All others	800 rpm	700 rpm
A/T (low altitude and California)		
RPO L82 only	750 rpm	700 rpm
All others	550 rpm (in D)	500 rpm (in D)
A/T (high altitude)	650 rpm	600 rpm

Note: *For the remaining model years, the information listed on the Vehicle Emission Control Information label (in the engine compartment) supersedes any information listed here.*

1978

	Base idle	Curb idle	Fast idle
L48 engine			
M/T	800 (N)	700 (N)	1300
A/T (including California)	600 (D)	500 (D)	1600
High altitude (A/T)	650 (D)	600 (D)	1600
L82 engine			
M/T	1000 (N)	900 (N)	1600
A/T	800 (D)	700 (D)	1600

1979

	Curb idle	Enriched rpm	Solenoid speed	Fast idle
L48 engine				
A/T	500 (D)	530 to 570	600 (D)	1600
M/T	700 (N)	800 to 850	-	1300
California (A/T)	500 (D)	520 to 560	600 (D)	1600
High altitude (A/T)	600 (D)	630 to 670	650 (D)	1750
L82 engine				
A/T	700 (D)	730 to 770	800(D)	1600
M/T	900 (N)	975 to 1025	-	1300

1980 (L48 engine, A/T)
- Solenoid screw .... 600 (D)
- Curb idle .... 500 (D)
- Fast idle 1600

1981 and 1982 .... See Vehicle Emission Control Information label in the engine compartment

General

Radiator cap pressure rating .... 15 psi

Drivebelt tension

	7-to-10 inches	13-to-16 inches
Pulley-to-pulley center distance		
Belt deflection	1/4-inch	1/2-inch

Clutch pedal free play
  1968 through 1971
    Standard clutch .... 1-1/4 to 2 in
    Heavy-Duty clutch .... 2 to 2-1/2 in
  1972 .... 1-1/4 to 1-3/4 in
  1973 .... 1-1/4 to 1-1/2 in
  1974 on .... 1 to 1-1/2 in
Front wheel bearing end play .... 0.001 to 0.005 in

Brakes
Brake pad wear limit .... 1/8 in
Parking brake shoe wear limit .... 1/32 in

Torque specifications   **Ft-lbs** (unless otherwise indicated)
Spark plugs 15
Engine oil drain plug 20
Automatic transmission pan bolts
  1968 through 1977 8
  1978 through 1980 .... 130 in-lbs
  1981 and later 13
Wheel lug nuts
  Steel wheels
    1968 through 1977 75
    1978 on 70
  Aluminum wheels
    1968 through 1977 85
    1978 on 80

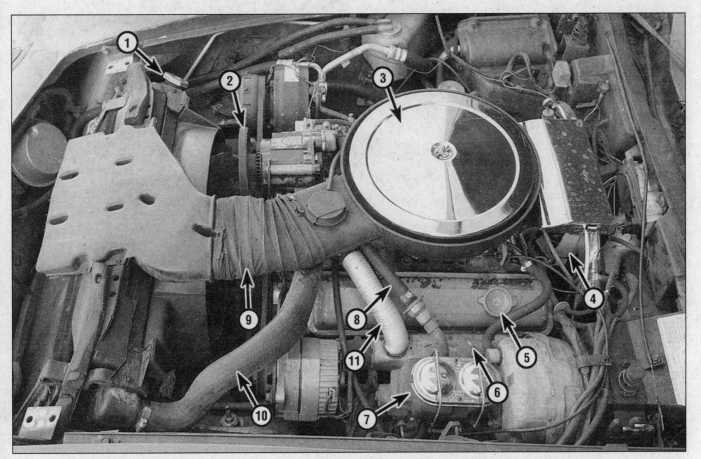

Engine compartment component layout (driver's side)

1	Radiator cap	5	Engine oil filler cap	8	AIR system hose
2	Drivebelt (several used)	6	Engine oil dipstick	9	Intake air duct
3	Air cleaner housing	7	Brake fluid reservoir	10	Upper radiator hose
4	Distributor			11	PCV valve (beneath hose)

Engine compartment component layout (passenger's side)

1	Windshield washer fluid reservoir	3	PCV breather tube
2	EGR valve	4	Automatic transmission fluid dipstick

1   Introduction

This Chapter is designed to help the home mechanic maintain his or her vehicle for peak performance, economy, safety and long life.

On the following pages you will find a maintenance schedule along with Sections which deal specifically with each item on the schedule. Included are visual checks, adjustments and item replacements.

Servicing your vehicle using the time/mileage maintenance schedule and the sequenced Sections will give you a planned program of maintenance. Keep in mind that it is a full plan, and maintaining only a few items at the specified intervals will not give you the same results.

In many cases the manufacturer will recommend additional owner checks such as warning light operation, defroster operation, condition of window glass, etc. We assume these are obvious and have not included such items in the maintenance plan. Consult an owner's manual for additional information.

You'll find as you service your vehicle

Engine compartment underside component layout

1	Brake caliper	4	Brake caliper	7	Steering linkage balljoint grease
2	Radiator drain valve	5	Exhaust pipe		fittings
3	Lower radiator hose	6	Engine oil filter		

that many of the procedures can - and should - be grouped together, due to the nature of the jobs. Examples of this are as follows:

If the vehicle is raised for a chassis lubrication, for example, it's an ideal time for the following checks: Exhaust system, suspension, steering and fuel system.

If the tires and wheels are removed, such as during a routine tire rotation, check the brakes and wheel bearings at the same time.

If you have to borrow or rent a torque wrench, replace the spark plugs and check the carburetor mounting nut torque all in the same day to save time and money.

The first step in the maintenance plan is to prepare yourself before any actual work begins. Read through the appropriate Sections of this Chapter before you begin. Gather up all the necessary parts and tools. If it appears you could have a problem during a particular job, don't hesitate to seek advice from a mechanic or experienced do-it-yourselfer.

2 Corvette Maintenance schedule

The following recommendations are given with the assumption that the vehicle owner will be doing the maintenance or service work, as opposed to having a dealer service department or service station do the work. Most of the intervals are based on factory maintenance recommendations. However, the owner, interested in keeping his or her vehicle in peak condition at all times and with the vehicle's ultimate resale in mind, may want to perform many of these operations more often. Specifically, we would encourage more frequent fluid level checks and oil and filter replacement intervals and have shortened them to reflect this.

Every 250 miles or weekly, whichever comes first

Check the engine oil level (Section 4)
Check the engine coolant level (Section 4)
Check the windshield washer fluid level (Section 4)
Check the battery electrolyte level (Section 4)
Check the brake fluid level (Section 4)
Check the tires and tire pressures (Section 5)
Check the automatic transmission fluid level (Section 6)
Check the power steering fluid level (Section 7)
Check the windshield wiper/washer operation
Check the external light/horn operation
Check the brakes

Every 6000 miles (1968 through 1974 models)/7500 miles (1975 and later models) or 6 months, whichever comes first

All items listed above plus:
Check the seat belts
Check the starter safety switch (Section 8)
Replace the air filter and PCV filter (Section 9)
Replace the fuel filter (Section 10)
Check/adjust the engine drivebelts (Section 11)
Check the carburetor/throttle body mounting nut torque (Section 12)
Check the throttle linkage (Section 13)
Check the emission control system hoses and wires (Section 14)
Check the carburetor choke operation (Section 15)
Check the thermostatically-controlled air cleaner (Section 16)
Check and adjust, if necessary, the engine idle speed (Section 17)
Change the engine oil and oil filter (Section 18)
Lubricate the chassis components (Section 19)
Inspect the suspension and steering components (Section 20)
Inspect the exhaust system (Section 21)

Check the EFE (heat riser) system (Section 22)
Check and adjust, if necessary, the clutch pedal free play (Section 23)
Check the manual transmission oil level (Section 24)
Check the differential (rear axle) oil level (Section 25)
Rotate the tires (Section 26)
Check the brakes (Section 27)
Inspect the fuel system (Section 28)

Every 12,000 miles (1968 through 1974 models)/15,000 miles (1975 and later models) or 12 months, whichever comes first

All items listed above plus:
Inspect and replace, if necessary, the windshield wiper blades (Section 29)
Check and service the battery (Section 30)
Check the cooling system (Section 31)
Inspect and replace, if necessary, all underhood hoses (Section 14)
Check the EGR valve (Section 32)
Check the AIR system (Section 33)
Replace the PCV valve and clean the flame arrestor (Section 34)
Replace the spark plugs (vehicles with ignition points only) (Section 35)
Inspect the spark plug wires, distributor cap and rotor (Sections 36 and 37)
Check/adjust the valve clearances (solid lifters only) (Section 38)
Have the headlight alignment checked
Have the front wheel alignment checked

Every 18,000 miles (1968 through 1974 models)/22,500 miles (1975 and later models) or 18 months, whichever comes first

Replace the ignition points (Section 39)
Check/adjust the ignition timing (Section 40)

Every 24,000 miles (1968 through 1974 models)/30,000 miles (1975 and later models) or 24 months, whichever comes first

Replace the ECS canister filter (Section 41)
Check the steering gear grease seals for leaks (Section 20)
Check and repack the front wheel bearings (Section 42)
Service the cooling system (drain, flush and refill) (Section 43)
Change the automatic transmission fluid and filter (Section 44)
Have the brake fluid replaced

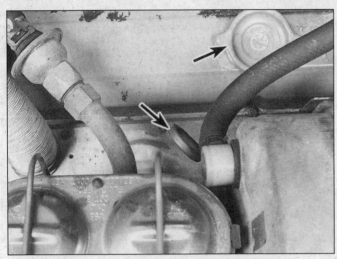

4.2 Typical engine oil dipstick (lower arrow) and oil filler cap (upper arrow) locations

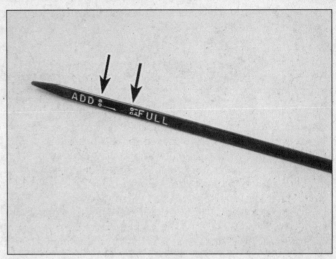

4.4 The engine oil level must be maintained between the marks at all times - it takes one quart to raise the level from the ADD mark to the FULL mark

3 Tune-up general information

The term tune-up is used in this manual to represent a combination of individual operations rather than one specific procedure.

If, from the time the vehicle is new, the routine maintenance schedule is followed closely and frequent checks are made of fluid levels and high wear items, as suggested throughout this manual, the engine will be kept in relatively good running condition and the need for additional work will be minimized.

More likely than not, however, there will be times when the engine is running poorly due to lack of regular maintenance. This is even more likely if a used vehicle, which has not received regular and frequent maintenance checks, is purchased. In such cases an engine tune-up will be needed outside of the regular routine maintenance intervals.

The first step in any tune-up or engine diagnosis to help correct a poor running engine would be a cylinder compression check. A check of the engine compression will give valuable information regarding the overall condition of many internal components and should be used as a basis for tune-up and repair procedures. If, for instance, a compression check indicates serious internal engine wear, a conventional tune-up will not improve engine performance and would be a waste of time and money. Due to its importance, compression checking should be performed by someone who has the proper compression testing gauge and who is knowledgeable with its use. Further information on compression testing can be found in Chapter 2 of this manual.

The following series of operations are those most often needed to bring a generally poor running engine back into a proper state of tune.

Minor tune-up

Clean, inspect and test the battery
Check all engine related fluids
Check and adjust the drivebelts
Replace the spark plugs
Inspect the distributor cap and rotor
Inspect the spark plug and coil wires
Check/clean/adjust the ignition points
Check and adjust the ignition timing
Check the PCV valve
Check and adjust the idle speed
Check the air and PCV filters
Check the cooling system
Check all underhood hoses

Major tune-up

All operations listed under Minor tune-up plus . . .
Check the EGR system
Check the ignition system
Check the charging system
Check the fuel system
Replace the air and PCV filters
Replace the distributor cap and rotor
Replace the ignition points and adjust the dwell (if applicable)
Replace the spark plug wires

4 Fluid level checks

Note: *The following are fluid level checks to be done on a 250 mile or weekly basis. Additional fluid level checks can be found in specific maintenance intervals which follow. Regardless of intervals, be alert to fluid leaks under the vehicle which would indicate a fault to be corrected immediately.*

1   There are a number of components on a vehicle which rely on the use of fluids to operate properly. During normal operation of the vehicle, these fluids are used up and must be replenished before damage occurs. See *Recommended lubricants and fluids* at the beginning of this Chapter for the specific lubricant or fluid to be used when more is required. When checking fluid levels, make sure the vehicle is on a level surface.

Engine oil

Refer to illustrations 4.2 and 4.4

2   The engine oil level is checked with a dipstick that travels through a tube and into the oil pan at the bottom of the engine **(see illustration)**.

3   The oil level should be checked before the vehicle has been driven, or about 15 minutes after the engine has been shut off. If the oil is checked immediately after driving the vehicle, some of the oil will remain in the upper engine components, producing an inaccurate reading on the dipstick.

4   Pull the dipstick from the tube and wipe all the oil off the end with a clean rag or paper towel. Insert the clean dipstick all the way back into the tube until it seats, then pull it out again. Note the oil level at the end of the dipstick. Add oil as necessary to keep the level between the ADD mark and the FULL mark on the dipstick **(see illustration)**.

5   Do not overfill the engine by adding too much oil since this may result in oil fouled spark plugs, oil leaks or oil seal failures.

6   Oil is added to the engine after removing a twist off cap located on the rocker arm cover **(see illustration 4.2)**. A funnel may help to reduce spills.

7   Checking the oil can be an important preventive maintenance step. If you find the oil level dropping abnormally, it's an indication of oil leakage or internal engine wear which should be corrected. If there are water droplets in the oil, or if it's milky looking, component failure is indicated and the engine should be checked immediately.

Engine coolant

Refer to illustration 4.8

8   Later vehicles covered by this manual

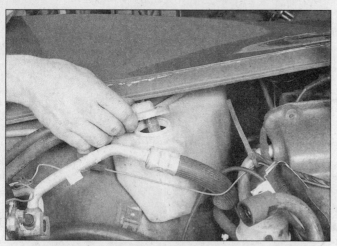

4.8 The coolant level should be checked at the reservoir, not the radiator

4.14 The windshield washer fluid reservoir is located next to the brake master cylinder on most models

are equipped with a pressurized coolant recovery system. A white coolant reservoir at the front of the engine compartment is connected by a hose to the base of the radiator cap **(see illustration)**. As the engine heats up during operation, coolant is forced from the radiator, through the connecting tube and into the reservoir. As the engine cools, the coolant is automatically drawn back into the radiator to keep the level correct.

9   On reservoir equipped models, coolant level checks are very easy; merely locate the coolant reservoir and note the level of fluid in the reservoir. With the engine cold, this should be at or slightly above the FULL COLD mark on the reservoir. Some reservoirs also have a FULL HOT mark to check the level when the engine is hot. On a periodic basis, or if the coolant in the reservoir runs completely dry, check the coolant level in the radiator as well (see Step 10).

10   If your particular vehicle isn't equipped with a coolant recovery system, the level should be checked by removing the radiator cap. **Warning:** *Never remove the radiator cap when the engine is hot - escaping steam and coolant could cause serious injury. Wait until the engine has completely cooled, then wrap a thick cloth around the cap and turn it to the first stop. If any steam escapes from the cap, allow the engine to cool further, then remove the cap and check the level in the radiator. It should be just below the bottom of the filler neck.*

11   If only a small amount of coolant is required to bring the system up to the proper level, plain water can be used. However, to maintain the proper antifreeze/water mixture in the system, both should be mixed together to replenish a low level. High quality antifreeze should be mixed with water in the proportion specified on the container. **Warning:** *Do not allow antifreeze to come in contact with your skin or painted surfaces of the vehicle. Flush contacted areas immediately with plenty of water.*

12   As the level is checked, note the condition of the coolant. It should be relatively

4.17 Remove the cell caps to check the water level in the battery - if the level is low, add distilled water only

transparent. If it's brown or a rust color, the system should be drained, flushed and refilled (Section 43).

13   If the cooling system requires repeated additions to maintain the proper level, have the radiator cap checked for proper sealing ability and check for leaks in the system from cracked hoses, loose hose connections, leaking gaskets, etc.

Windshield washer fluid

Refer to illustration 4.14

14   On later models, fluid for the windshield washer system is located in a plastic reservoir in the engine compartment **(see illustration)**. Don't confuse the windshield washer fluid reservoir and the coolant overflow reservoir.

15   The reservoir should be kept no more than 2/3 full to allow for expansion if it freezes. Additives such as windshield washer concentrate, available at auto parts stores, will help lower the freezing point of the fluid and result in better cleaning of the windshield surface. **Caution:** *Do not use cooling system antifreeze - it will cause damage to the vehicle's paint.*

16   To help prevent icing in cold weather, warm the windshield with the defroster before using the washer.

Battery electrolyte

Refer to illustration 4.17

Warning: *There are certain precautions to be taken when working on or near a battery. Never expose a battery to open flames or sparks, which could ignite the hydrogen gas given off by it. Wear protective clothing and eye protection to reduce the possibility of the corrosive sulfuric acid solution inside the battery harming you. If the fluid is splashed or spilled, flush the contacted area immediately with plenty of water. Remove all metal jewelry which could contact the positive terminal and another grounded metal source and cause a short circuit. Always keep batteries and battery acid out of the reach of children.*

Note: *The battery is located in a covered compartment behind the driver's seat.*

17   Later model vehicles are equipped with maintenance-free batteries which are permanently sealed (except for vent holes) and have no filler caps. Water does not have to be added to these batteries. If a maintenance-type battery is installed, the caps on the top of the battery should be removed periodically to check for a low electrolyte level **(see illustration)**. This check is most critical during warm summer months.

4.20 The brake fluid level should be within 1/4-inch of the top of the reservoir

Brake fluid

Refer to illustration 4.20

18   The brake master cylinder is mounted on the front of the power booster unit in the engine compartment.

19   You have to remove the cover to check the brake fluid level. Clean the area around the sealing lip and use a long screwdriver to pry the heavy wire retainers off the cover.

20   Carefully lift off the cover and check the fluid inside. It should be approximately 1/4-inch below the top edge of the reservoir **(see illustration)**.

21   If additional fluid is necessary to bring the level up to the proper height, carefully pour the specified brake fluid into the master cylinder. Be careful not to spill any.

22   When adding fluid, pour it carefully into the reservoir and don't spill any on surrounding painted surfaces. Be sure the specified fluid is used, since mixing different types of brake fluid can cause damage to the system. See *Recommended lubricants and fluids* at the front of this Chapter or your owner's manual.

23   At this time the fluid and master cylinder can be inspected for contamination. The system should be drained and refilled if rust deposits, dirt particles or water droplets are seen in the fluid.

24   After filling the reservoir to the proper level, make sure the cover is on tight to pre-vent fluid leakage and contamination.

25   The brake fluid level in the master cylinder will drop slightly as the pads at each wheel wear down during normal operation. If the master cylinder requires repeated replenishing to keep it at the proper level, it's an indication of leakage in the system, which should be corrected immediately. Check all brake lines, hoses and fittings (see Section 27).

26   If you discover one or both reservoirs empty or nearly empty when checking the master cylinder fluid level, the brake system should be bled (Chapter 9).

5   Tire and tire pressure checks

Refer to illustration 5.3

1   Periodically inspecting the tires may not only prevent you from being stranded with a flat tire, but can also give you clues as to possible problems with the steering and suspension systems before major damage occurs.

2   Proper tire inflation adds miles to the lifespan of the tires, allows the vehicle to achieve maximum miles per gallon of gas and contributes to the overall quality of the ride.

3   When inspecting the tires, first check the tread. Irregularities in the tread pattern (cupping, flat spots, more wear on one side than the other) are indications of front end

UNDERINFLATION

CUPPING

Cupping may be caused by:
- Underinflation and/or mechanical irregularities such as out-of-balance condition of wheel and/or tire, and bent or damaged wheel.
- Loose or worn steering tie-rod or steering idler arm.
- Loose, damaged or worn front suspension parts.

OVERINFLATION

INCORRECT TOE-IN OR EXTREME CAMBER

FEATHERING DUE TO MISALIGNMENT

5.3 This chart will help you determine the condition of the tires, the probable cause(s) of abnormal wear and the corrective action necessary

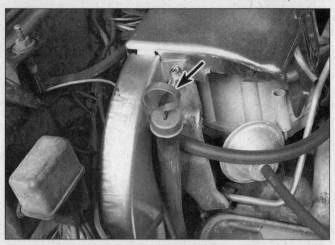

6.3 Automatic transmission fluid dipstick (arrow)

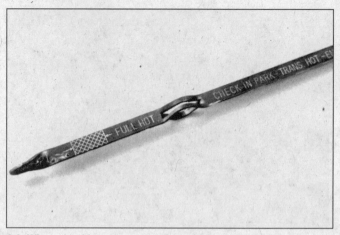

6.6 When checking the automatic transmission fluid level, be sure to note the fluid temperature

alignment and/or balance problems **(see illustration)**. If any of these conditions are noted, take the vehicle to a repair shop to correct the problem.

4   Check the tread area for cuts and punctures. Many times a nail or other object will embed itself in the tire tread and the tire will hold air pressure for a period of time. In most cases, a repair shop or gas station can repair the punctured tire.

5   It's important to check the sidewalls of the tires, both inside and out. Check for deteriorated rubber, cuts, and punctures. Inspect the inner side of the tire for signs of brake fluid leakage, indicating that a brake inspection is needed immediately.

6   Incorrect tire pressure can't be determined merely by looking at the tire. This is especially true for radial tires. A tire pressure gauge must be used. If you don't already have a reliable gauge, purchase one and keep it in the glovebox. Built-in pressure gauges at gas stations are often inaccurate.

7   Always check tire inflation when the tires are cold. Cold, in this case, means the vehicle hasn't been driven more than one mile after sitting for three hours or more. It's normal for the pressure to increase four to eight pounds when the tires are hot.

8   Unscrew the valve cap protruding from the wheel or hubcap and press the gauge firmly onto the valve. Note the reading on the gauge and compare the figure to the recommended tire pressure listed on the tire placard. The tire placard is usually attached to the driver's door jamb. The recommended maximum pressure for the tires is usually also stamped on the tire sidewall. However, the information on the tire placard should always be top priority since it applies to tires used on your particular vehicle.

9   Check all tires and add air as necessary to bring them up to the recommended pressure levels. Don't forget the spare tire. Be sure to reinstall the valve caps, which will keep dirt and moisture out of the valve stem mechanism.

6   Automatic transmission fluid level check

Refer to illustrations 6.3 and 6.6

1   The automatic transmission fluid level should be carefully maintained. Low fluid level can lead to slipping or loss of drive, while overfilling can cause foaming and loss of fluid.

2   With the parking brake set, start the engine, then move the shift lever through all the gear ranges, ending in Park. The fluid level must be checked with the vehicle level and the engine running at idle. **Note:** *Incorrect fluid level readings will result if the vehicle has just been driven at high speeds for an extended period, in hot weather in city traffic, or if it has been pulling a trailer. If any of these conditions apply, wait until the fluid has cooled (about 30 minutes).*

3   With the transmission at normal operating temperature, remove the dipstick from the filler tube. The dipstick is located at the rear of the engine compartment on the passenger's side **(see illustration)**.

4   Carefully touch the fluid at the end of the dipstick to determine if the fluid is cool, warm or hot. Wipe the fluid off the dipstick with a clean rag and push it back into the filler tube until the cap seats.

5   Pull the dipstick out again and note the

fluid level.

6   If the fluid felt cool, the level should be about 1/8 to 3/8-inch above the ADD mark **(see illustration)**. If it felt warm, the level should be between the ADD and FULL HOT marks. If the fluid was hot, the level should be at the FULL HOT mark. If additional fluid is required, add the recommended type directly into the tube using a funnel. It takes about one pint to raise the level from the ADD mark to the FULL HOT mark with a hot transmission, so add the fluid a little at a time and keep checking the level until it's correct.

7   The condition of the fluid should also be checked along with the level. If the fluid at the end of the dipstick is a dark reddish-brown color, or if it has a burned smell, the fluid should be changed. If you're in doubt about the condition of the fluid, purchase some new fluid and compare the two for color and smell.

7   Power steering fluid level check

Refer to illustrations 7.2 and 7.6

1   The power steering system relies on fluid which may, over a period of time, require replenishing.

2   The fluid reservoir for the power steering pump is located on the pump body at the front of the engine **(see illustration)**.

3   For this check, the front wheels should

7.2 Power steering fluid dipstick (arrow)

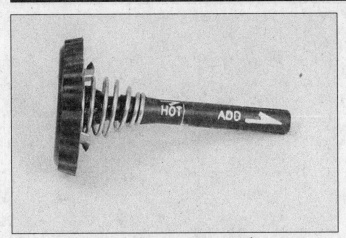

7.6 The marks on the power steering fluid dipstick indicate the safe range with the fluid either HOT or COLD

9.8 The PCV filter fits into a small holder in the air cleaner housing

be pointed straight ahead and the engine should be off.

4   Use a clean rag to wipe off the reservoir cap and the area around it. This will help prevent any foreign matter from entering the reservoir during the check.

5   Twist off the cap and check the temperature of the fluid at the end of the dipstick with your finger.

6   Wipe off the fluid with a clean rag, reinsert the dipstick, then withdraw it and read the fluid level. The level should be at the HOT mark if the fluid was hot to the touch **(see illustration)**. It should be at the COLD mark if the fluid was cool to the touch. Never allow the fluid level to drop below the ADD mark.

7   If additional fluid is required, pour the specified type directly into the reservoir, using a funnel to prevent spills.

8   If the reservoir requires frequent fluid additions, all power steering hoses, hose connections and the power steering pump should be carefully checked for leaks.

8   Starter safety switch check

Warning: *During the following checks there is a chance the vehicle could lunge forward, possibly causing damage or injuries. Allow plenty of room around the vehicle, apply the parking brake and hold down the regular brake pedal during the checks.*

1   Most vehicles are equipped with a starter safety switch which prevents the engine from starting unless the clutch pedal is depressed (manual) or the shift lever is in Neutral or Park (automatic).

2   On automatic transmission vehicles, try to start the vehicle in each gear. The engine should crank only in Park or Neutral.

3   If equipped with a manual transmission, place the shift lever in Neutral. The engine should crank only with the clutch pedal depressed.

4   Make sure the steering column lock allows the key to go into the Lock position only when the shift lever is in Park (automatic transmission) or Reverse (manual transmission).

5   The ignition key should come out only in the Lock position.

9   Air filter/PCV filter replacement

Refer to illustration 9.8

1   At the specified intervals, the air filter and PCV filter should be replaced with new ones. A thorough program of preventive maintenance would call for the two filters to be inspected between changes. The engine air cleaner also supplies filtered air to the PCV system.

2   The filter is located on top of the carburetor or Throttle Body Injection (TBI) units and is replaced by unscrewing the wing nut(s) from the top of the filter housing and lifting off the cover.

3   While the top plate is off, be careful not to drop anything down into the carburetor, TBI or air cleaner assembly.

4   Lift the filter element out and wipe out the inside of the air cleaner housing with a clean rag.

5   If so equipped, remove the polywrap band from the paper element and discard the element. If the band is in good condition, rinse it in kerosene or solvent and squeeze it dry. Dip the band in clean engine oil and gently squeeze out the excess. Install the band

on a new paper element and reassemble.

6   Place the new filter in the air cleaner housing. Make sure it seats properly in the bottom of the housing.

7   The PCV filter is also located inside the air cleaner housing. Remove the top plate and air filter as previously described, then locate the PCV filter on the inside of the housing.

8   Remove the old filter **(see illustration)**.

9   Install the new PCV filter and the new air filter.

10   Install the top plate and any hoses that were disconnected. Don't overtighten the wing nut(s).

10   Fuel filter replacement

Warning: *Gasoline vapors are extremely flammable! Do not smoke or allow open flames or sparks in or near the work area when servicing the fuel system. Also, do not perform this procedure in a garage where a natural gas appliance such as a water heater or clothes dryer is present.*

Carburetor equipped models

Refer to illustrations 10.1, 10.6 and 10.8

1   On these models, the fuel filter is located inside the fuel inlet nut at the carburetor **(see illustration)**. It's made of either

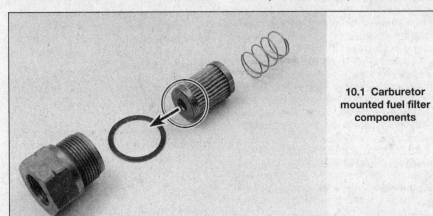

10.1 Carburetor mounted fuel filter components

10.6   Use a flare-nut wrench on the fuel line fitting to avoid rounding off the hex

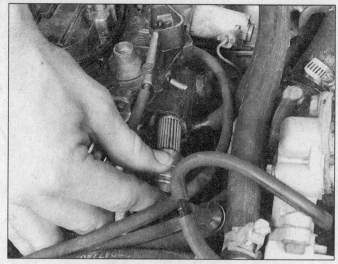

10.8   The filter fits into the recess in the carburetor

pleated paper or porous bronze and can't be cleaned or reused.

2   The job should be done with the engine cold (after sitting at least three hours). The necessary tools include open-end wrenches to fit the fuel line nuts. Flare-nut wrenches (which wrap around the nut) should be used if available. In addition, you have to obtain the replacement filter (make sure it's for your specific vehicle and engine) and some clean rags.

3   Remove the air cleaner assembly. If vacuum hoses must be disconnected, be sure to note their positions and/or tag them to ensure they're reinstalled correctly.

4   Follow the fuel line from the fuel pump to the point where it enters the carburetor. In most cases the fuel line will be metal all the way from the fuel pump to the carburetor.

5   Place some rags under the fuel inlet fittings to catch spilled fuel as the fittings are disconnected.

6   Using a large, thin wrench, hold the fuel inlet nut immediately next to the carburetor body. Now loosen the fitting at the end of the metal fuel line. Make sure the fuel inlet nut next to the carburetor is held securely while the fuel line is disconnected **(see illustration)**.

7   After the fuel line is disconnected, move it aside for better access to the inlet nut. Do not crimp the fuel line.

8   Unscrew the fuel inlet nut, which was previously held steady. As this fitting is drawn away from the carburetor body, be careful not to lose the thin washer-type gasket on the nut or the spring, located behind the fuel filter. Also pay close attention to how the filter is installed **(see illustration)**.

9   Compare the old filter with the new one to make sure they're the same length and design.

10   Reinstall the spring in the carburetor body.

11   Place the filter in position (a gasket is

usually supplied with the new filter) and tighten the nut. Make sure it isn't cross-threaded. Tighten it securely, but be careful not to overtighten it (the threads can strip easily, causing fuel leaks). Reconnect the fuel line to the fuel inlet nut, again using caution to avoid cross-threading the nut. Use a back-up wrench on the fuel inlet nut while tightening the fuel line fitting.

12   Start the engine and check carefully for leaks. If the fuel line fitting leaks, disconnect it and check for stripped or damaged threads. If the fuel line fitting has stripped threads, remove the entire line and have a repair shop install a new fitting. If the threads look all right, purchase some thread sealing tape and wrap the threads with it. Inlet nut repair kits are available at most auto parts stores to overcome leaking at the fuel inlet nut.

Fuel injected models

13   Fuel injected engines employ an in-line fuel filter. The filter is located on the right side frame rail and is accessible from underneath the vehicle.

14   Raise the front of the vehicle and support it securely on jackstands. Apply the parking brake and block the rear wheels.

15   Place a container, newspapers or rags under the fuel filter.

16   Disconnect the fuel lines and detach the filter from the frame.

17   Install the new filter by reversing the removal procedure. Tighten the fittings securely, but don't cross-thread them.

---

11   Drivebelt check, adjustment and replacement

Check and adjustment

Refer to illustrations 11.3, 11.4 and 11.6

1   The drivebelts, or V-belts as they're

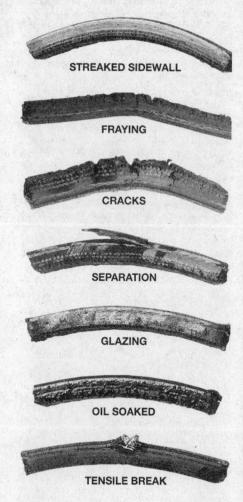

STREAKED SIDEWALL

FRAYING

CRACKS

SEPARATION

GLAZING

OIL SOAKED

TENSILE BREAK

11.3   Here are some of the more common problems associated with drivebelts (check the belts very carefully to prevent an untimely breakdown)

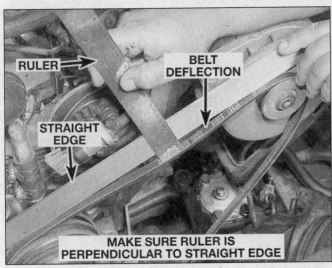

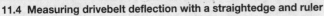

11.4 Measuring drivebelt deflection with a straightedge and ruler

11.6 Alternator drivebelt adjustment bolt (arrow)

often called, are located at the front of the engine and play an important role in the overall operation of the engine and other components. Due to their function and material make-up, the belts are prone to failure after a period of time and should be inspected and adjusted periodically to prevent major engine damage.

2   The number of belts used on a particular vehicle depends on the accessories installed. Drivebelts are used to turn the alternator, power steering pump, water pump, air pump and air-conditioning compressor. Depending on the pulley arrangement, more than one of these components may be driven by a single belt.

3   With the engine off, open the hood and locate the various belts at the front of the engine. Using your fingers (and a flashlight, if necessary), move along the belts checking for cracks and separation of the belt plies. Also check for fraying and glazing, which gives the belt a shiny appearance (see illustration). Both sides of each belt should be inspected, which means you will have to twist the belt to check the underside.

4   The tension of each belt is checked by pushing on the belt at a distance halfway between the pulleys. Push firmly with your thumb and see how much the belt moves (deflects) (see illustration). A rule of thumb is if the distance from pulley center-to-pulley center is between 7 and 10 inches, the belt should deflect 1/4-inch. If the belt travels between pulleys spaced 13 to 16 inches apart, the belt should deflect 1/2-inch.

5   If you have to adjust the belt tension, either to make the belt tighter or looser, it's done by moving the belt-driven accessory on the bracket.

6   For each component there will be an adjusting bolt and a pivot bolt (see illustration). Both bolts must be loosened slightly to move the component.

7   After the two bolts have been loosened, move the component away from the engine

to tighten the belt or toward the engine to loosen the belt. Hold the accessory in position and check the belt tension. If it's correct, tighten the two bolts until just snug, then recheck the tension. If the tension is all right, tighten the bolts.

8   Some sort of pry bar is often needed to move the accessory while the belt is adjusted. If this must be done to gain the proper leverage, be very careful not to damage the component being moved or the part being pried against.

Replacement

9   To replace a belt, follow the above procedures for drivebelt adjustment, but slip the belt off the pulleys and remove it after loosening the adjustment and pivot bolts. Since belts tend to wear more or less at the same rate, it's a good idea to replace all of them at the same time. Mark each belt and the corresponding pulley grooves so the new belts can be installed properly.

10   Take the old belts with you when purchasing new ones (so you can compare them for length, width and design).

11   After the new belts have been installed, adjust them as described above.

12   Carburetor/throttle body mounting nut torque check

1   The carburetor (or TBI units) is attached to the top of the intake manifold by bolts or nuts. These fasteners can sometimes work loose from vibration and temperature changes during normal engine operation and cause a vacuum leak.

2   If you suspect a vacuum leak exists at the bottom of the carburetor or throttle body, obtain a length of fuel hose. Start the engine and place one end of the hose next to your ear as you probe around the base with the other end. You'll hear a hissing sound if a

leak exists (be careful of hot or moving engine components).

3   Remove the air cleaner assembly, tagging each hose to be disconnected with a piece of numbered tape to make reassembly easier.

4   Locate the mounting nuts or bolts at the base of the carburetor or throttle body. Decide what special tools or adapters will be necessary, if any, to tighten the fasteners.

5   Tighten the nuts or bolts securely and evenly. Do not overtighten them, as the threads could strip or the carburetor/TBI unit could distort.

6   If, after the nuts or bolts are properly tightened, a vacuum leak still exists, the carburetor or throttle body must be removed and a new gasket installed. See Chapter 4 for more information.

7   After tightening the fasteners, reinstall the air cleaner and return all hoses to their original positions.

13   Throttle linkage check

1   Check the throttle linkage for damaged or missing parts and for binding and interference when the accelerator pedal is operated.

2   Lubricate the various linkage pivot points with light-weight oil.

14   Underhood hose check and replacement

Refer to illustration 14.1

Warning: Replacement of air conditioning hoses must be left to a dealer service department or service station with the proper equipment to depressurize the system safely. Never remove air conditioning components or hoses until the system has been depressurized.

14.1 Check the rubber hoses and clamps (arrows) for deterioration and secure attachment

15.3 Choke plate location

General

1   High temperatures under the hood can cause deterioration of the rubber and plastic hoses used for engine, accessory and emission systems operation. Periodic inspection should be made for cracks, loose clamps, material hardening and leaks **(see illustration)**.

2   Information specific to the cooling system hoses can be found in Section 31.

3   Some, but not all, hoses are secured to the fittings with clamps. Where clamps are used, check to be sure they haven't lost their tension, allowing the hose to leak. Where clamps aren't used, make sure the hose hasn't expanded and/or hardened where it slips over the fitting, allowing it to leak.

Vacuum hoses

4   It's quite common for vacuum hoses, especially those in the emissions systems, to be color coded or identified by colored stripes molded into the hose. Various systems require hoses with different wall thicknesses, collapse resistance and temperature resistance. When replacing hoses, be sure the new ones are the same material as the originals.

5   Often the only effective way to check a hose is to remove it completely from the vehicle. If more than one hose is removed, be sure to label the hoses and fittings to ensure proper reattachment.

6   When checking vacuum hoses, be sure to include any plastic T-fittings in the check. Check the fittings for cracks and the hose where it fits over the fitting for distortion, which could cause leakage.

7   A small piece of vacuum hose (1/4-inch inside diameter) can be used as a stethoscope to detect vacuum leaks. Hold one end of the hose to your ear and probe around vacuum hoses and fittings, listening for the "hissing" sound characteristic of a vacuum leak. **Warning:** *When probing with the vacuum hose stethoscope, be careful not to allow your body or the hose to come into contact with moving engine components such as the drivebelt, cooling fan, etc.*

Fuel hose

Warning: There are certain precautions which must be taken when inspecting or servicing fuel system components. Work in a well ventilated area and do not allow open flames (cigarettes, appliance pilot lights, etc.) or bare light bulbs near the work area. Mop up any spills immediately and do not store fuel soaked rags where they could ignite. On vehicles equipped with fuel injection, the fuel system is under pressure, so if any fuel lines must be disconnected, the pressure in the system must be relieved (see Chapter 4 for more information).

8   Check all rubber fuel lines for deterioration and chafing. Check especially for cracks where the hose bends and just before clamping points, such as where a hose attaches to the fuel filter.

9   High quality fuel line, usually identified by the word Fluroelastomer printed on the hose, should be used for fuel line replacement. Never use unreinforced vacuum line, clear plastic tubing or water hose for fuel line replacement.

10   Spring-type clamps are commonly used on fuel lines. These clamps often lose their tension over a period of time, and can be "sprung" during the removal process. Therefore it is recommended that all spring type clamps be replaced with screw clamps whenever a hose is replaced.

Metal lines

11   Sections of metal line are often used for fuel line between the fuel pump and carburetor or fuel injection units. Check carefully to be sure the line isn't bent, crimped or cracked.

12   If a section of metal fuel line must be replaced, only seamless steel tubing should be used, since copper and aluminum tubing do not have the strength necessary to withstand normal engine operating vibration.

13   Check the metal brake lines where they enter the master cylinder and brake proportioning unit (if used) for cracks in the lines and loose fittings. Any sign of brake fluid leakage calls for an immediate thorough inspection of the brake system.

---

15   Carburetor choke check

Refer to illustration 15.3

1   The choke operates when the engine is cold, so this check can only be performed before the engine has been started for the day.

2   Open the hood and remove the top plate of the air cleaner assembly. It's usually held in place by a wing nut at the center. If any vacuum hoses must be disconnected, make sure you tag the hoses for reinstallation in their original positions. Place the top plate and wing nut aside, out of the way of moving engine components.

3   Look at the center of the air cleaner housing. You'll notice a flat plate at the carburetor opening **(see illustration)**.

4   Have an assistant press the accelerator pedal to the floor. The plate should close completely. Start the engine while you watch the plate at the carburetor. Do not position your face directly over the carburetor, as the engine could backfire, causing serious burns. When the engine starts, the choke plate should open slightly.

5   Allow the engine to continue running at an idle speed. As the engine warms up to operating temperature, the plate should slowly open, allowing more air to enter through the top of the carburetor.

6   After a few minutes, the choke plate should be fully open to the vertical position. Blip the throttle to make sure the fast idle cam disengages.

7   You'll notice that engine speed corresponds with the plate opening. With the plate fully closed, the engine should run at a fast idle speed. As the plate opens and the throttle is moved to disengage the fast idle cam, the engine speed will decrease.

8   Refer to Chapter 4 for specific information on adjusting and servicing the choke components.

16.3 The thermostatic air cleaner door is located in the snorkel and is visible after removing the duct

16   Thermostatic air cleaner check

Refer to illustration 16.3

1   These vehicles are equipped with a thermostatically-controlled air cleaner which draws air to the carburetor from different locations, depending on engine temperature.

2   This is a visual check. If access is limited, a small mirror may have to be used.

3   Open the hood and locate the damper door inside the air cleaner assembly. It's inside the snorkel on the metal air cleaner housing **(see illustration)**.

4   If there is a flexible air duct attached to the end of the snorkel, leading to an area behind the grille, disconnect it at the snorkel. This will enable you to look through the end of the snorkel and see the damper inside.

5   The check should be done when the engine is cold. Start the engine and look through the snorkel at the damper, which should move to a closed position. With the damper closed, air cannot enter through the end of the snorkel, but instead enters the air cleaner through the flexible duct attached to the exhaust manifold and the heat stove passage.

6   As the engine warms up to operating temperature, the damper should open to allow air through the snorkel end. Depending on outside temperature, this may take 10 to 15 minutes. To speed up this check you can reconnect the snorkel air duct, drive the vehicle, then check to see if the damper is completely open.

7   If the thermo-controlled air cleaner isn't operating properly see Chapter 6 for more information.

17   Idle speed check and adjustment

General information

1   Engine idle speed is the speed at which the engine operates when no accelerator pedal pressure is applied. On fuel injected models this speed is governed by the ECM, while on carbureted models the idle speed can be adjusted. The idle speed is critical to the performance of the engine itself, as well as many engine sub-systems.

2   A hand-held tachometer must be used when adjusting idle speed to get an accurate reading. The exact hook-up for these meters varies with the manufacturer, so follow the particular directions included with the instrument.

3   Since the manufacturer used many different carburetors over the time period covered by this manual, and each one requires a specific approach for setting idle speed, the following procedures are quite detailed. Keep in mind that 1974 and later models have a label located in the engine compartment with instructions for setting idle speed.

4   For most applications, the idle speed is set by turning an adjustment screw located on the side of the carburetor. This screw changes the amount the throttle plate is held open by the throttle linkage. The screw may be on the linkage itself or may be part of a device such as an idle stop solenoid. **Note:** *Refer to Chapter 4 for illustrations of the carburetors to locate the idle speed screw and mixture screw mentioned in the following procedures.*

5   Once you've found the idle speed screw/idle mixture screw, experiment with different length screwdrivers until the adjustment can be easily made without coming into contact with hot or moving engine components.

6   Make sure the parking brake is firmly set and the wheels blocked to prevent the vehicle from rolling. This is especially true if the transmission must be in Drive. An assistant inside the vehicle pressing on the brake pedal is the safest method.

7   For all applications, the engine must be completely warmed up to operating temperature, which will automatically render the choke fast idle inoperative.

Holley 2300/4150 carburetors

8   The manual transmission must be in Neutral/automatic transmission in Drive.

9   Turn the idle speed screw until the engine is running at the specified idle speed.

10   If the vehicle is equipped with air conditioning, switch the system off during adjustment.

11   Slowly turn the idle mixture screw until the idle speed reaches its maximum.

12   Adjust the idle speed screw until the engine is running at the specified idle speed, then turn the mixture screw to obtain a drop (lean roll) in the idle speed of 20 rpms.

13   Finally, turn the mixture screw out 1/4-turn.

Rochester 4MV carburetor

14   The procedure is the same as the one described for the Holley 2300, but also refer to the vehicle Emission Control Information label or tune-up decal.

15   After 1973, the carburetor mixture screws are equipped with plastic limiter caps. Normally, adjustment should be restricted to turning the screws within the limits of the cap stops. If major disassembly has been done, and the limiter caps have been broken to remove the screws, set the idle as described above, then install new caps on the screws so they're positioned at the mid-point of adjustment.

Rochester M4MC carburetor

16   Make sure the engine is at normal operating temperature, with the ignition timing correctly set.

17   Remove the air cleaner but keep the vacuum hoses connected.

18   Refer to the Emission Control Information label, then disconnect and plug the other hoses.

19   Make sure the air conditioner is off.

20   Connect an accurate tachometer to the engine.

21   Carefully pry the limiter caps off the idle mixture screws. Lightly seat the screws, then back them out equally (about two turns) until the engine will run. The idle mixture screw is located just below the fuel inlet on the side of the carburetor.

22   Place the shift lever in Neutral (manual) or Drive (automatic).

23   Unscrew each mixture screw 1/8-turn (to richen the mixture) at a time, until maximum idle speed is obtained on the tachometer.

24   Now set the specified initial idle speed and then turn the mixture screws again to make sure maximum idle speed has been obtained.

25   Turn each idle mixture screw in 1/8-turn at a time until the specified lean drop idle speed is obtained.

26   Reset the idle speed to the specification by turning the throttle speed screw.

27   Remove the tachometer and install the air cleaner.

Rochester M4ME carburetor

28   Refer to the Emission control Information label in the engine compartment when adjusting the idle speed on this carburetor (used on 1980 and 1981 models).

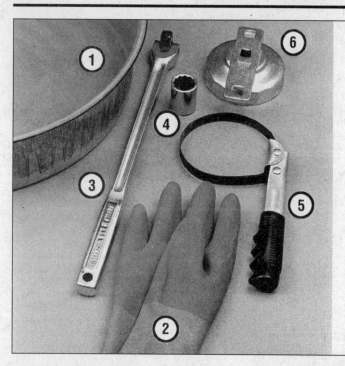

18.3 **These tools are required when changing the engine oil and filter**

1 **Drain pan** - It should be fairly shallow in depth, but wide to prevent spills
2 **Rubber gloves** - When removing the drain plug and filter, you will get oil on your hands (the gloves will prevent burns)
3 **Breaker bar** - Sometimes the oil drain plug is tight, and a long breaker bar is needed to loosen it
4 **Socket** - To be used with the breaker bar or a ratchet (must be the correct size to fit the drain plug - six-point preferred)
5 **Filter wrench** - This is a metal band-type wrench, which requires clearance around the filter to be effective
6 **Filter wrench** - This type fits on the bottom of the filter and can be turned with a ratchet or breaker bar (different-size wrenches are available for different types of filters)

All carburetors

29 On cars equipped with air conditioning, a solenoid is installed on the carburetor to increase idle speed slightly when the air conditioning is switched on. The idle speed adjustment operations are slightly different.

18 Engine oil and filter change

Refer to illustrations 18.3, 18.9, 18.14 and 18.18

1 Frequent oil changes may be the best form of preventive maintenance available to the home mechanic. When engine oil ages, it becomes diluted and contaminated, which leads to premature engine wear.
2 Although some sources recommend oil filter changes every other oil change, we feel the minimal cost of an oil filter and the relative ease with which it is installed dictate that a new filter be used whenever the oil is changed.
3 Gather together all necessary tools and materials before beginning the procedure **(see illustration)**.
4 You should have plenty of clean rags and newspapers handy to mop up any spills. Access to the underside of the vehicle is greatly improved if the vehicle can be lifted on a hoist, driven onto ramps or supported by jackstands. **Warning:** *Do not work under a vehicle which is supported only by a bumper, hydraulic or scissors-type jack.*
5 If this is your first oil change, get under the vehicle and familiarize yourself with the locations of the oil drain plug and the oil filter. The engine and exhaust components will be warm during the actual work, so figure out any potential problems before the engine and accessories are hot.

6 Warm the engine to normal operating temperature. If new oil or any tools are needed, use this warm-up time to gather everything necessary for the job. The correct type of oil for your application can be found in *Recommended lubricants and fluids* at the beginning of this Chapter.
7 With the engine oil warm (warm engine oil will drain better and more built-up sludge will be removed with the oil), raise and support the vehicle. Make sure it's safely supported!
8 Move all necessary tools, rags and newspapers under the vehicle. Position the drain pan under the drain plug. Keep in mind that the oil will initially flow from the pan with some force, so locate the pan accordingly.
9 Being careful not to touch any of the hot exhaust components, use the wrench to remove the drain plug near the bottom of the oil pan **(see illustration)**. Depending on how hot the oil is, you may want to wear gloves while unscrewing the plug the final few turns.

10 Allow the old oil to drain into the pan. It may be necessary to move the pan farther under the engine as the oil flow slows to a trickle.
11 After all the oil has drained, wipe off the drain plug with a clean rag. Small metal particles may cling to the plug and would immediately contaminate the new oil.
12 Clean the area around the drain plug opening and reinstall the plug. Tighten the plug securely with the wrench. If a torque wrench is available, use it to tighten the plug.
13 Move the drain pan into position under the oil filter.
14 Use the filter wrench to loosen the oil filter **(see illustration)**. Chain or metal band filter wrenches may distort the filter canister, but this is of no concern as the filter will be discarded anyway.
15 Completely unscrew the old filter. Be careful - it's full of oil. Empty the oil inside the filter into the drain pan.
16 Compare the old filter with the new one

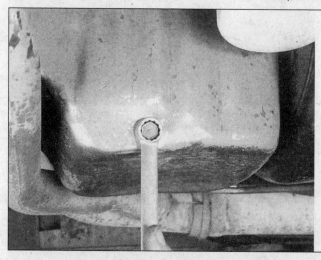

18.9 **The oil drain plug is located at the bottom of the pan and should be removed using either a socket or a box-end wrench - DO NOT use an open-end-wrench, as the corners on the bolt can easily be rounded off**

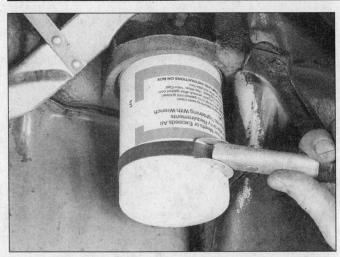

18.14 A strap-type oil filter wrench is used to loosen the oil filter (if access makes removal difficult, other types of filter wrenches are available)

18.18 Lubricate the oil filter gasket with clean engine oil before installing the filter on the engine

to make sure they're the same type.

17   Use a clean rag to remove all oil, dirt and sludge from the area where the oil filter mounts to the engine. Check the old filter to make sure the rubber gasket isn't stuck to the engine mounting surface. If the gasket is stuck to the engine (use a flashlight if necessary), remove it.

18   Apply a light coat of oil around the full circumference of the rubber gasket of the new oil filter **(see illustration)**.

19   Attach the new filter to the engine, following the tightening directions printed on the filter canister or packing box. Most filter manufacturers recommend against using a filter wrench due to the possibility of over-tightening and damage to the seal.

20   Remove all tools, rags, etc. from under the vehicle, being careful not to spill the oil in the drain pan, then lower the vehicle.

21   Move to the engine compartment and locate the oil filler cap.

22   Pour the fresh oil into the filler opening. A funnel may be used.

23   Pour four quarts of fresh oil into the engine. Wait a few minutes to allow the oil to drain into the pan, then check the level on the oil dipstick (see Section 4 if necessary). If the oil level is above the ADD mark, start the engine and allow the new oil to circulate.

24   Run the engine for only about a minute and then shut it off. Immediately look under the vehicle and check for leaks at the oil pan drain plug and around the oil filter. If either is leaking, tighten with a bit more force.

25   With the new oil circulated and the filter now completely full, recheck the level on the dipstick and add more oil as necessary.

26   During the first few trips after an oil change, make it a point to check frequently for leaks and proper oil level.

27   The old oil drained from the engine can-

not be reused in its present state and should be disposed of. Oil reclamation centers, auto repair shops and gas stations will normally accept the oil, which can be refined and used again. After the oil has cooled it can be drained into a suitable container (capped plastic jugs, topped bottles, milk cartons, etc.) for transport to one of these disposal sites.

19 Chassis lubrication

Refer to illustrations 19.1, 19.6 and 19.7

1   Refer to *Recommended lubricants and fluids* at the front of this Chapter to obtain the necessary grease, etc. You'll also need a grease gun **(see illustration)**. Occasionally plugs will be installed rather than grease fittings. If so, grease fittings will have to be pur-

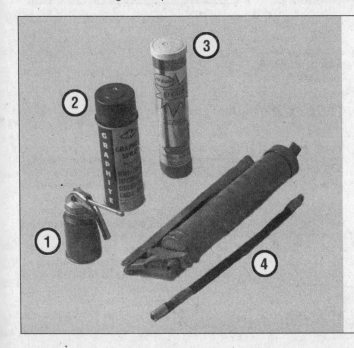

19.1 Materials required for chassis and body lubrication

1   *Engine oil - Light engine oil in a can like this can be used for door and hood hinges*
2   *Graphite spray - Used to lubricate lock cylinders*
3   *Grease - Grease, in a variety of types and weights, is available for use in a grease gun. Check the Specifications for your requirements*
4   *Grease gun - A common grease gun, shown here with a detachable hose and nozzle, is needed for chassis lubrication. After use, clean it thoroughly*

19.6 Be sure to lubricate the steering linkage balljoints . . .

19.7 . . . and the steering control valve adapter

chased and installed.

2   Look under the vehicle and see if grease fittings or plugs are installed. If there are plugs, remove them and buy grease fittings, which will thread into the component. A dealer or auto parts store will be able to supply the correct fittings. Straight, as well as angled, fittings are available.

3   For easier access under the vehicle, raise it with a jack and place jackstands under the frame. Make sure it's safely supported by the stands. If the wheels are removed at this interval for tire rotation or brake inspection, loosen the lug nuts slightly while the vehicle is still on the ground.

4   Before beginning, force a little grease out of the nozzle to remove any dirt from the end of the gun. Wipe the nozzle clean with a rag.

5   With the grease gun and plenty of clean rags, crawl under the vehicle and begin lubricating the component.

6   Wipe the balljoint grease fitting nipple clean and push the nozzle firmly over it **(see illustration)**. Squeeze the trigger on the grease gun to force grease into the component. Each balljoint should be lubricated until the rubber seal is firm to the touch. Do not pump too much grease into the fittings as it could rupture the seal.

7   For all other suspension and steering components, continue pumping grease into the fitting until it oozes out of the joint between the two components **(see illustration)**. If it escapes around the grease gun nozzle, the nipple is clogged or the nozzle isn't completely seated on the fitting. Resecure the gun nozzle to the fitting and try again. If necessary, replace the fitting with a new one.

8   Wipe the excess grease from the components and the grease fitting. Repeat the procedure for the remaining fittings.

9   If equipped with a manual transmission, lubricate the shift linkage and clutch linkage pivot points with clean engine oil. Lubricate the pushrod-to-fork contact points with chas-

sis grease. Some models also have a grease fitting on the clutch cross-shaft (frame-to-block) and at the clutch ball pivot on the bellhousing.

10   While you're under the vehicle, clean and lubricate the parking brake cable along with the cable guides and levers. This can be done by smearing some of the chassis grease onto the cable and its related parts with your fingers.

11   Open the hood and smear a little chassis grease on the hood latch mechanism. Have an assistant pull the hood release lever from inside the vehicle as you lubricate the cable at the latch.

12   Lubricate all the hinges (door, hood, etc.) with engine oil to keep them in proper working order.

13   The key lock cylinders can be lubricated with spray-on graphite or silicone lubricant, which is available at auto parts stores.

14   Lubricate the door weatherstripping with silicone spray. This will reduce chafing and retard wear.

20 Suspension and steering check

1   Raise the front of the vehicle periodically and visually check the suspension and steering components for wear.

2   Indications of a fault in these systems are excessive play in the steering wheel before the front wheels react, excessive sway around corners, body movement over rough roads or binding at some point as the steering wheel is turned.

3   Raise the front end of the vehicle and support it securely on jackstands placed under the frame rails. Because of the work to be done, make sure the vehicle cannot fall from the stands.

4   Check the wheel bearings. Do this by spinning the front wheels. Listen for any abnormal noises and watch to make sure the wheel spins true (doesn't wobble). Grabbing the top and bottom of the tire, pull in and out,

noticing any movement which would indicate a loose wheel bearing assembly. If the bearings are suspect, refer to Section 42 and Chapter 10 for more information or see a dealer for a more thorough inspection.

5   Working under the vehicle, check for loose bolts, broken or disconnected parts and deteriorated rubber bushings on all suspension and steering components. Look for grease or fluid leaking from the steering assembly. Check the power steering hoses and connections for leaks.

6   Have an assistant turn the steering wheel from side-to-side and check the steering components for free movement, chafing and binding. If the wheels don't respond to movement of the steering wheel, try to determine where the slack is located.

21 Exhaust system check

Refer to illustrations 21.2a, 21.2b, 21.3a and 21.3b

1   With the engine cold (at least three hours after the vehicle has been driven), check the complete exhaust system from the manifolds to the ends of the tailpipes. Be careful around the catalytic converter, which may be hot even after three hours. The inspection should be done on a hoist where unrestricted access is available.

2   Check the pipes and connections for signs of leakage and/or corrosion indicating a potential failure **(see illustrations)**.

3   Make sure all brackets and hangers are in good condition and tight **(see illustrations)**.

4   Inspect the underside of the body for holes, corrosion, open seams, etc. which may allow exhaust gases to enter the passenger compartment. Seal all body openings with silicone or body putty.

5   Rattles and other noises can often be traced to the exhaust system, especially the hangers, mounts and heat shields. Try to move the pipes, mufflers and catalytic con-

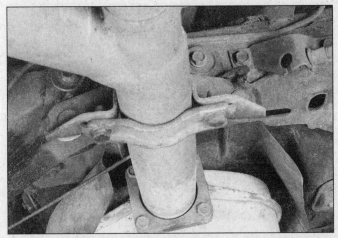

21.2a Check the catalytic converter mounting bolts

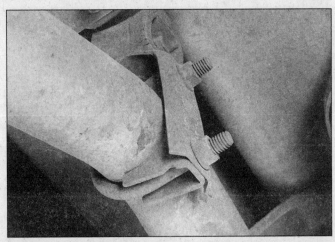

21.2b Look for holes in the exhaust pipes like the one shown here

21.3a Check the clamp nuts to make sure they're tight

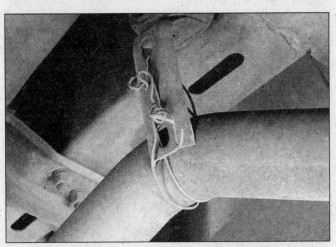

21.3b Check the hangers and brackets for missing parts

verter. If the components can come in contact with the body or suspension parts, secure the exhaust system with new brackets and hangers.

6   This is an ideal time to check the running condition of the engine by inspecting the very ends of the tailpipes. The exhaust deposits here are an indication of engine state-of-tune. If the pipe is black and sooty or bright white deposits are found here, the engine is in need of a tune-up, including a thorough carburetor inspection and adjustment.

22   EFE (heat riser) system check

Refer to illustrations 22.5a and 22.5b

1   The heat riser and the Early Fuel Evaporation (EFE) system both perform the same job, but each functions in a slightly different manner.

2   The heat riser is a valve inside the exhaust pipe, near the junction between the exhaust manifold and pipe. It can be identified by an external weight and spring.

3   With the engine and exhaust pipe cold, try moving the weight by hand. It should

move freely.

4   Start the engine (cold) and watch the heat riser. When the engine starts, the weight should move to the closed position. As the engine warms to normal operating temperature, the weight should move the valve to the open position, allowing a free flow of exhaust through the tailpipe. Since it could take sev-

eral minutes for the system to heat up, you could mark the cold weight position, drive the vehicle, then check the weight.

5   The EFE system also blocks off exhaust flow when the engine is cold. However, this system uses more precise temperature sensors and vacuum to open and close the exhaust pipe valve **(see illustrations)**.

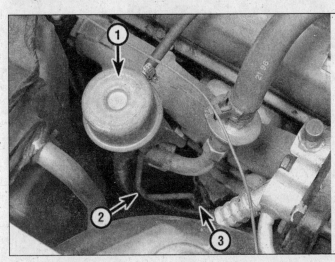

22.5a EFE system upper components

1 Power actuator
2 Actuator rod
3 Exhaust heat valve

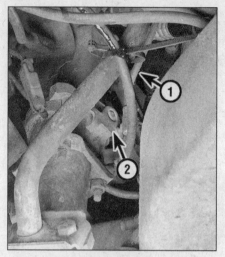

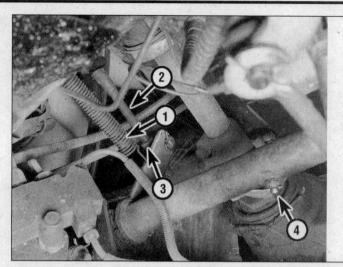

23.5 Clutch adjustment details

1   *Spring*
2   *Clutch adjustment rod*
3   *Front adjusting nut*
4   *Lubrication point for clutch cross-shaft*

22.5b From below, the actuator rod (1) connects to the heat valve (2)

6   Locate the EFE actuator, which is bolted to a bracket on the right side of the engine. It will have an actuating rod attached to it which will lead down to the valve inside the pipe.

7   With the engine cold, have an assistant start it as you watch the actuating rod. It should immediately move to close off the valve as the engine warms. This process may take some time, so you might want to mark the position of the rod when the valve is closed, drive the vehicle to reach normal operating temperature, then open the hood and see if the rod has moved the valve to the open position.

8   More information on the EFE system can be found in Chapter 6.

23 Clutch pedal free play check and adjustment

Refer to illustration 23.5

Check

1   On manual transmission models, it's important to have the proper clutch free play. Free play is the distance between the clutch pedal when it's all the way up and the point at which the clutch starts to disengage.

2   Slowly depress the clutch pedal until you can feel resistance. Do this a number of times until you can pinpoint exactly where the resistance is felt.

3   Now measure the distance the pedal travels before the resistance is felt.

4   If the distance is not as indicated in this Chapter's Specifications, the clutch pedal free play should be adjusted.

Adjustment

5   If the free play is not as specified, disconnect the spring **(see illustration)** and pull the clutch pedal all the way back against the stop.

6   Loosen the nuts, then move the adjustment rod until you can just feel the release bearing make contact with the pressure plate fingers (all linkage free play will be eliminated).

7   Adjust the front nut against the swivel, then back it off 4-1/2 turns. Hold the front nut and tighten the rear nut against the swivel.

8   Reinstall the spring, then recheck the free play.

24 Manual transmission oil level check

Refer to illustration 24.1

1   Manual transmissions do not have a dipstick. The lubricant level is checked by removing the plug from the side of the transmission case **(see illustration)**.

2   If the oil level is not at the bottom of the plug opening, use a syringe to squeeze the appropriate lubricant into the opening until it just starts to run out of the hole.

3   Install the plug and tighten it securely. Drive the vehicle a short distance, then check for leaks.

25 Differential oil level check

Refer to illustration 25.1

1   Remove the oil check/fill plug from the side of the differential **(see illustration)**.

2   The oil level should be at the bottom of the plug opening. If not, use a syringe to add the proper lubricant until it just starts to run out of the opening.

24.1 Typical manual transmission check/filler plug

25.1 Typical differential check/filler plug

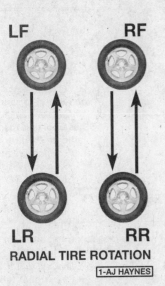

RADIAL TIRE ROTATION

1-AJ HAYNES

26.2 Tire rotation diagram

26 Tire rotation

Refer to illustration 26.2

1   The tires should be rotated at the specified intervals and whenever uneven wear is noticed.

2   Refer to the accompanying illustration for the preferred tire rotation pattern.

3   Refer to the information in *Jacking and towing* at the front of this manual for the proper procedures to follow when raising the vehicle and changing a tire. If you're going to check the brakes, don't apply the parking brake as stated. Make sure the tires are blocked to prevent the vehicle from rolling as it's raised.

4   If possible, the entire vehicle should be raised at the same time. This can be done on a hoist or by jacking up each corner and then lowering the vehicle onto jackstands placed under the frame rails. Always use four jackstands and make sure the vehicle is safely supported.

5   After rotation, check and adjust the tire pressures as necessary and be sure to check the lug nut tightness.

6   For more information on the wheels and tires, refer to Chapter 10.

27 Brake check

Refer to illustrations 27.6a and 27.6b

Note: *For detailed illustrations of the brakes, refer to Chapter 9.*

1   In addition to the specified intervals, the brakes should be inspected every time the wheels are removed or whenever a problem arises.

2   To check the brakes, raise the vehicle and place it securely on jackstands. Remove the wheels (see *Jacking and towing* at the front of the manual, if necessary).

Disc brakes

3   Disc brakes are used on all four wheels of these models. Extensive rotor damage can occur if the pads are not replaced when needed.

4   Most vehicles are equipped with a wear sensor attached to the inner pad. This is a small, bent piece of metal visible from the inner side of the brake caliper. When the pad wears to the specified limit, the metal sensor rubs against the rotor and makes a screeching sound.

5   The disc brake calipers, which contain the pads, are visible with the wheels removed. There is an outer pad and an inner pad in each caliper. All pads should be inspected.

6   The caliper has a "window" to inspect the pads. Check the thickness of the pad linings by looking into the caliper opening **(see illustrations).** If the wear sensor is very close to the rotor or the pad material has worn to about 1/8-inch or less, the pads require replacement.

7   If you're unsure about the exact thickness of the remaining lining material, remove the pads for further inspection or replacement (refer to Chapter 9).

8   Before installing the wheels, check for leakage and/or damage (cracks, splitting, etc.) around the brake hose connections. Replace the hose or fittings as necessary (Chapter 9).

9   Check the condition of the rotors. Look for score marks and burned spots. If these conditions exist, the hub/rotor assembly should be removed for servicing (Chapter 9).

Parking brake

10   The parking brake operates from a hand lever and locks the rear brake system. The easiest, and perhaps most obvious method of periodically checking the operation of the parking brake assembly is to park the vehicle on a steep hill with the parking brake set and the transmission in Neutral. If the parking brake cannot prevent the vehicle from rolling, it should be adjusted (see Chapter 9).

Brake pedal travel

11   The brakes should be periodically checked for pedal travel, which is the distance the brake pedal moves toward the floor from a fully released position. The brakes must be cold while performing this test.

12   Using a ruler, measure the distance from the floor to the brake pedal.

13   Pump the brakes at least three times. On power brake models do this without starting the engine. Press firmly on the brake pedal and measure the distance between the floor and the pedal.

14   The distance the pedal travels should not exceed 3-1/2 inches (manual brakes) or 4-1/2 inches (power brakes).

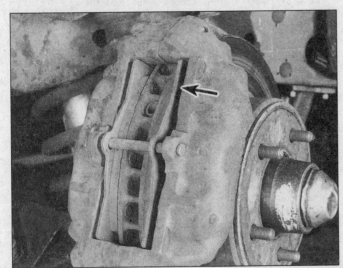

27.6a Check the front brake pad lining thickness by looking into the caliper through the large opening (arrow)

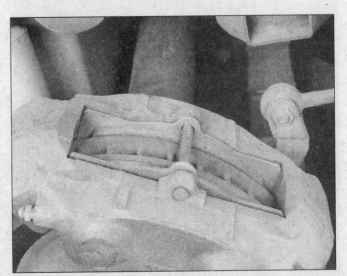

27.6b The rear brake pads can be checked in the same fashion

28   Fuel system check

Warning: *There are certain precautions to take when inspecting or servicing the fuel system components. Work in a well-ventilated area and do not allow open flames (cigarettes, appliance pilot lights, etc.) in the work area. Mop up spills immediately and do not store fuel soaked rags where they could ignite. On fuel injection equipped models, the fuel system is under pressure - no components should be disconnected until after the pressure has been relieved (Chapter 4).*

1   The fuel system is most easily checked with the vehicle raised on a hoist so the components underneath the vehicle are readily visible and accessible.

2   If the smell of gasoline is noticed while driving or after the vehicle has been in the sun, the system should be thoroughly inspected immediately.

3   Remove the gas filler cap and check for damage, corrosion and an unbroken sealing imprint on the gasket. Replace the cap with a new one if necessary.

4   With the vehicle raised, inspect the gas tank for punctures, cracks and other damage. **Warning:** *Do not, under any circumstances, try to repair a fuel tank yourself (except rubber components) unless you have considerable experience. A welding torch or any open flame can easily cause the fuel vapors to explode if the proper precautions are not taken.*

5   Carefully check all rubber hoses and metal lines leading away from the fuel tank. Check for loose connections, deteriorated hoses, crimped lines and other damage. Follow the lines to the front of the vehicle, carefully inspecting them all the way. Repair or replace damaged sections as necessary.

6   If a fuel odor is still evident after the inspection, refer to Section 43.

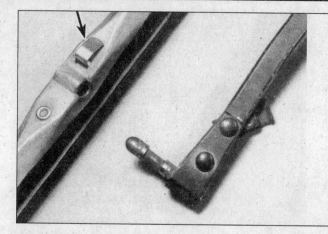

29.6 Depress the tab (arrow) to slide the wiper blade assembly off the stud on the arm

29   Wiper blade check and replacement

Refer to illustration 29.6

1   The windshield wiper and blade assembly should be inspected periodically for damage, loose components and cracked or worn blade elements.

2   Road film can build up on the wiper blades and affect their efficiency, so they should be washed regularly with a mild detergent solution.

3   The action of the wiping mechanism can loosen the bolts, nuts and fasteners, so they should be checked and tightened, as necessary, at the same time the wiper blades are checked.

4   If the wiper blade elements (sometimes called "inserts") are cracked, worn or warped, they should be replaced with new ones.

5   Pull the wiper blade/arm assembly away from the glass.

6   Depress the blade-to-arm connector **(see illustration)** and slide the blade assembly off the wiper arm and over the retaining stud.

7   Pinch the tabs at the end and then slide the element out of the blade assembly.

8   Compare the new element with the old for length, design, etc.

9   Slide the new element into place. It will automatically lock at the correct location.

10   Reinstall the blade assembly on the arm, wet the windshield and test for proper operation.

30   Battery check and maintenance

Refer to illustrations 30.1a, 30.1b, 30.8a, 30.8b, 30.8c and 30.8d

Warning: *Certain precautions must be followed when checking and servicing the battery. Hydrogen gas, which is highly flammable, is always present in the battery cells, so keep lighted tobacco and all other open flames and sparks away from the battery. The electrolyte inside the battery is actually dilute sulfuric acid, which will cause injury if splashed onto your skin or into your eyes. It will also ruin clothes and painted surfaces. When removing the battery cables, always detach the negative cable*

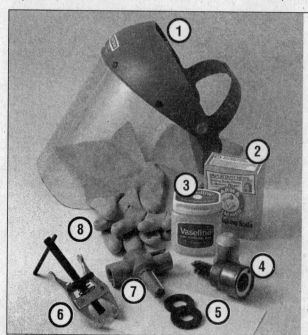

30.1a Tools and materials required for top-terminal battery maintenance

1   **Face shield/safety goggles** - *When removing corrosion with a brush, the acidic particles can easily fly up into your eyes*

2   **Baking soda** - *A solution of baking soda and water can be used to neutralize corrosion*

3   **Petroleum jelly** - *A layer of this on the battery posts will help prevent corrosion*

4   **Battery post/cable cleaner** - *This wire brush cleaning tool will remove all traces of corrosion from the battery posts and cable clamps*

5   **Treated felt washers** - *Placing one of these on each post, directly under the cable clamps, will help prevent corrosion*

6   **Puller** - *Sometimes the cable clamps are very difficult to pull off the posts, even after the nut/bolt has been completely loosened. This tool pulls the clamp straight up and off the post without damage*

7   **Battery post/cable cleaner** - *Here is another cleaning tool which is a slightly different version of Number 4 above, but it does the same thing*

8   **Rubber gloves** - *Another safety item to consider when servicing the battery; remember that's acid inside the battery!*

30.1b Tools and materials required for side-terminal battery maintenance

1 *Face shield/safety goggles* - *When removing corrosion with a brush, the acidic particles can easily fly up into your eyes*
2 *Rubber gloves* - *Another safety item to consider when servicing the battery - remember that's acid inside the battery!*
3 *Battery terminal/cable cleaner* - *This wire brush cleaning tool will remove all traces of corrosion from the battery and cable*
4 *Treated felt washers* - *Placing one of these on each terminal, directly under the cable end, will help prevent corrosion (be sure to get the correct type for side-terminal batteries)*
5 *Baking soda* - *A solution of baking soda and water can be used to neutralize corrosion*
6 *Petroleum jelly* - *A layer of this on the battery terminal bolts will help prevent corrosion*

first and hook it up last!

1   Battery maintenance is an important procedure that will help ensure you aren't stranded because of a dead battery. Several tools are required for this procedure **(see illustrations)**.
2   When checking/servicing the battery, always turn the engine and all accessories off.
3   A sealed (sometimes called maintenance-free), side-terminal battery is standard equipment on all later model vehicles. The cell caps cannot be removed, no electrolyte checks are required and water cannot be added to the cells. However, if you have a vehicle with a standard top terminal battery, or if a standard aftermarket battery has been installed, the following maintenance procedure can be used.

4   Remove the caps and check the electrolyte level in each of the battery cells (Section 4). It must be above the plates. There's usually a split-ring indicator in each cell to indicate the correct level. If the level is low, add distilled water only, then reinstall the cell caps. **Caution:** *Overfilling the cells may cause electrolyte to spill over during periods of heavy charging, causing corrosion and damage to nearby components.*
5   If the positive terminal and cable clamp on your vehicle's battery is equipped with a rubber protector, make sure it's not torn or damaged. It should completely cover the terminal.
6   The external condition of the battery should be checked periodically. Look for damage such as a cracked case.

7   Check the tightness of the battery cable clamps to ensure good electrical connections and inspect the entire length of each cable, looking for cracked or abraded insulation and frayed conductors.
8   If corrosion (visible as white, fluffy deposits) is evident, remove the cables from the terminals, clean them with a battery brush and reinstall them **(see illustrations)**. Corrosion can be kept to a minimum by installing specially treated washers available at auto parts stores or by applying a layer of petroleum jelly or grease to the terminals and cable clamps after they are assembled.
9   Make sure the battery carrier is in good condition and the hold-down clamp is tight. If the battery is removed (see Chapter 5 for the

30.8a Battery terminal corrosion usually appears as light, fluffy powder

30.8b Removing the cable from a battery post with a wrench - sometimes a special battery pliers is required for this procedure if corrosion has caused deterioration of the nut hex (always remove the ground cable first and hook it up last!)

30.8c Regardless of the type of tool used on the battery posts, a clean, shiny surface should be the result

30.8d When cleaning the cable clamps, all corrosion must be removed (the inside of the clamp is tapered to match the taper on the post, so don't remove too much material)

Check for a chafed area that could fail prematurely.

Check for a soft area indicating the hose has deteriorated inside.

Overtightening the clamp on a hardened hose will damage the hose and cause a leak.

Check each hose for swelling and oil-soaked ends. Cracks and breaks can be located by squeezing the hose.

31.4 Hoses, like drivebelts, have a habit of failing at the worst possible time - to prevent the inconvenience of a blown radiator or heater hose, inspect them carefully as shown here

removal and installation procedure), make sure no parts remain in the bottom of the carrier when it's reinstalled. When reinstalling the hold-down clamp, don't overtighten the bolt.

10   Corrosion on the carrier, battery case and surrounding areas can be removed with a solution of water and baking soda. Apply the mixture with a small brush, let it work, then rinse it off with plenty of clean water.

11   Any metal parts of the vehicle damaged by corrosion should be coated with a zinc-based primer, then painted.

12   Additional information on the battery, charging and jump starting can be found in the front of this manual and in Chapter 5.

31   Cooling system check

Refer to illustration 31.4

1   Many major engine failures can be attributed to a faulty cooling system. If the vehicle is equipped with an automatic transmission, the cooling system also cools the transmission fluid and plays an important role in prolonging transmission life.

2   The cooling system should be checked with the engine cold. Do this before the vehicle is driven for the day or after it has been shut off for at least three hours.

3   Remove the radiator cap by turning it to the left until it reaches a stop. If you hear a hissing sound (indicating there is still pressure in the system), wait until it stops. Now press down on the cap with the palm of your hand and continue turning to the left until the cap can be removed. Thoroughly clean the cap, inside and out, with clean water. Also clean the filler neck on the radiator. All traces of corrosion should be removed. The coolant inside the radiator should be relatively transparent. If it's rust colored, the system should be drained and refilled (Section 43). If the coolant level isn't correct, add additional antifreeze/coolant mixture (see Section 4).

4   Carefully check the large upper and lower radiator hoses along with the smaller diameter heater hoses which run from the engine to the firewall. Inspect each hose along its entire length, replacing any hose which is cracked, swollen or shows signs of deterioration. Cracks may become more apparent if the hose is squeezed **(see illustration)**.

5   Make sure all hose connections are tight. A leak in the cooling system will usually show up as white or rust colored deposits on the areas adjoining the leak. If wire-type clamps are used at the ends of the hoses, it may be wise to replace them with more secure screw type clamps.

6   Use compressed air or a soft brush to remove bugs, leaves, etc. from the front of the radiator or air conditioning condenser. Be careful not to damage the delicate cooling fins or cut yourself on them.

7   Every other inspection, or at the first indication of cooling system problems, have the cap and system pressure tested. If you don't have a pressure tester, most gas stations and repair shops will do this for a minimal charge.

32   EGR valve check

Refer to illustration 32.2

1   The EGR valve is usually located on the intake manifold, adjacent to the carburetor. Most of the time when a problem develops in this emissions system, it's due to a stuck or dirty EGR valve.

2   With the engine cold to prevent burns, reach under the EGR valve and push on the diaphragm. Using moderate pressure, you should be able to press the diaphragm up-and-down within the housing **(see illustration)**.

3   If the diaphragm doesn't move or moves only with much effort, remove the EGR valve and clean it or replace it with a new one. If in doubt about the condition of the valve, compare the free movement of your EGR valve with a new valve.

4   Refer to Chapter 6 for more information on the EGR system.

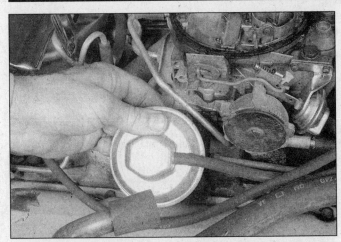

32.2 The EGR valve should be checked with the engine cold!

34.2 The PCV valve is attached to the valve cover - you may have to remove the air cleaner assembly to get at the valve

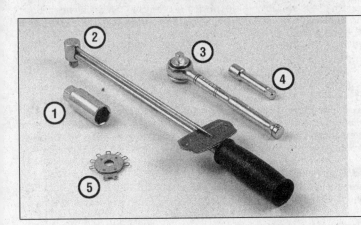

35.1 Tools required for changing spark plugs

1 *Spark plug socket* - This will have special padding inside to protect the spark plug's porcelain insulator
2 *Torque wrench* - Although not mandatory, using this tool is the best way to ensure the plugs are tightened properly
3 *Ratchet* - Standard hand tool to fit the spark plug socket
4 *Extension* - Depending on model and accessories, you may need special extensions and universal joints to reach one or more of the plugs
5 *Spark plug gap gauge* - This gauge for checking the gap comes in a variety of styles. Make sure the gap for your engine is included

33 AIR system check

Refer to Chapter 6 for this procedure.

34 PCV valve check and replacement

Refer to illustration 34.2
1   The PCV valve is located in the valve cover.
2   With the engine idling at normal operating temperature, pull the valve (with hose attached) out of the rubber grommet in the valve cover **(see illustration)**.
3   Place your finger over the end of the valve. If there's no vacuum at the valve, check for a plugged hose, manifold port or valve. Replace any plugged or deteriorated hoses.
4   Turn off the engine and shake the PCV valve, listening for a rattle. If the valve doesn't rattle, replace it with a new one.
5   To replace the valve, pull it out of the end of the hose, noting its installed position and direction.
6   When purchasing a replacement PCV valve, make sure it's for your particular vehicle and engine size. Compare the old valve with the new one to make sure they're the same.

7   Push the valve into the end of the hose until it's seated.
8   Check the rubber grommet for damage and replace it with a new one if necessary.
9   Push the PCV valve and hose securely into position.

35 Spark plug replacement

Refer to illustrations 35.1, 35.4a, 35.4b, 35.5 and 35.9
1   Before beginning, obtain the necessary tools, which will include a special spark plug wrench or socket and a gap measuring tool **(see illustration)**.
2   The best procedure to follow when replacing the spark plugs is to purchase the new spark plugs beforehand, adjust them to the proper gap, and then replace each plug one at a time. When buying the new spark plugs it's important to obtain the correct plugs for your specific engine. This information can be found on the tune-up or Vehicle Emissions Control Information label located under the hood or in the owner's manual. If differences exist between these sources, purchase the spark plug type specified on the label, because the information was printed for your specific engine.
3   Allow the engine to cool completely

35.4a Spark plug manufacturers recommend using a wire-type gauge when checking the gap - if the wire does not slide between the electrodes with a slight drag, adjustment is required

before attempting plug removal. During this time, each of the new spark plugs can be inspected for defects and the gaps can be checked.
4   The gap is checked by inserting the proper thickness gauge between the electrodes at the tip of the plug **(see illustration)**.

35.4b To change the gap, bend the side electrode only, as indicated by the arrows, and be very careful not to crack or chip the porcelain insulator surrounding the center electrode

The gap between the electrodes should be the same as that given in the Specifications or on the Emissions Control label. The wire should just touch each of the electrodes. If the gap is incorrect, use the notched adjuster on the feeler gauge body to bend the curved side electrode slightly until the proper gap is obtained **(see illustration)**. If the side electrode is not exactly over the center electrode, use the notched adjuster to align the two. Check for cracks in the porcelain insulator, indicating the spark plug should not be used.

5   With the engine cool, remove the spark plug wire from one spark plug. Do this by grabbing the boot at the end of the wire, not the wire itself **(see illustration)**. Sometimes you have to use a twisting motion to free the boot from the plug.

6   If compressed air is available, use it to blow any dirt or foreign material away from the spark plug area. A common bicycle pump will also work. The idea here is to eliminate the possibility of debris falling into the cylin-der as the spark plug is removed.

7   Place the spark plug socket over the plug and remove it from the engine by turning in a counterclockwise direction.

8   Compare the spark plug with the chart on the inside back cover of this manual to get an indication of the overall running condition of the engine.

9   Thread the new plug into the engine until you can no longer turn it with your fingers, then tighten it with the socket. Where there might be difficulty in inserting the spark plugs into the spark plug holes, or the possibility of cross-threading them into the head, a short piece of 3/16-inch rubber tubing can be attached to the end of the spark plug **(see illustration)**. The flexible tubing will act as a universal joint to help align the plug with the plug hole, and if the plug begins to cross-thread, the hose will slip on the spark plug, preventing thread damage. If one is available, use a torque wrench to tighten the plug to ensure that it's seated correctly. The correct torque figure is included in the Specifications at the front of this Chapter.

10   Before pushing the spark plug wire onto the end of the plug, inspect the wire following the procedures outlined in Section 36.

11   Attach the plug wire to the new spark plug, again using a twisting motion on the boot until it's firmly seated on the spark plug. Make sure the wire is routed away from the exhaust manifold.

12   Follow the above procedure for the remaining spark plugs, replacing them one at a time to prevent mixing up the spark plug wires.

36   Spark plug wire check and replacement

1   The spark plug wires should be checked at the recommended intervals and whenever new spark plugs are installed in the engine.

2   The wires should be inspected one at a time to prevent mixing up the order, which is essential for proper engine operation.

3   Disconnect the plug wire from the spark plug. To do this, grab the rubber boot, twist slightly and pull the wire free. Do not pull on the wire itself, only on the rubber boot.

4   Check inside the boot for corrosion, which will look like a white crusty powder. Push the wire and boot back onto the end of the spark plug. It should be a tight fit on the plug. If it isn't, remove the wire and use pliers to carefully crimp the metal connector inside the boot until it fits securely on the end of the spark plug.

5   Using a clean rag, wipe the entire length of the wire to remove any built-up dirt and grease. Once the wire is clean, check for burns, cracks and other damage. Do not bend the wire excessively or pull on it since the conductor inside might break.

6   Disconnect the wire from the distributor cap. A retaining ring at the top of the distributor may have to be removed to free the wires. Again, pull only on the rubber boot. Check for corrosion and a tight fit in the same manner as the spark plug end. Replace the wire in the distributor cap.

7   Check the remaining spark plug wires one at a time, making sure they're securely fastened at the distributor and spark plugs when the check is complete.

8   If new spark plug wires are required, purchase a set for your specific engine model. Wire sets are available pre-cut, with the rubber boots already installed. Remove and replace the wires one at a time to avoid mix-ups in the firing order.

37   Distributor cap and rotor check and replacement

1   It's common practice to install a new distributor cap and rotor whenever new spark plug wires are installed. Although the point-less electronic distributor used on later models requires much less maintenance than a conventional distributor, periodic inspections should be performed when the plug wires are checked. **Note:** *On later models with electronic ignition, if the distributor cap must be replaced, the ignition coil will have to be removed from the cap and installed in the new one.*

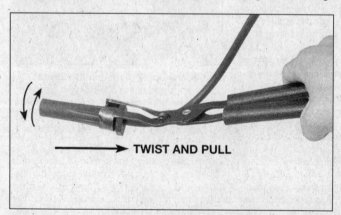

35.5 When removing the spark plug wires, pull only on the boot and twist it back-and-forth

35.9 A length of 3/8-inch ID rubber hose will save time and prevent damaged threads when installing the spark plugs

Check

Refer to illustrations 37.2, 37.3a, 37.3b, 37.4, 37.5 and 37.7

2   To gain access to the distributor cap it may be necessary to remove the shroud **(see illustration)**.

3   The cap is held in place with latches that look like screws - to release them, push down with a screwdriver and turn them about 1/2-turn **(see illustration)**. Pull up on the cap, with the wires attached, to separate it from the distributor, then position it to one side **(see illustration)**.

4   The rotor is now visible on the end of the distributor shaft. Check it carefully for cracks and carbon tracks. Make sure the center terminal spring tension is adequate and look for corrosion and wear on the rotor tip **(see illustration)**. If in doubt about its condition, replace it with a new one.

5   If replacement is required, detach the rotor and install a new one. The rotor is attached to the distributor shaft with two

37.2 Remove the bolts and detach the shroud from the distributor to get at the cap and wires

screws **(see illustration)**.

6   The rotor is indexed to the shaft so it can only be installed one way. It has one square and one round peg on the underside

that must fit into holes with the same shape.

7   Check the distributor cap for carbon tracks, cracks and other damage. Closely examine the terminals on the inside of the

37.3a Depress and turn the screws to release the distributor cap

37.3b Lift up on the cap with the wires attached to remove it from the distributor

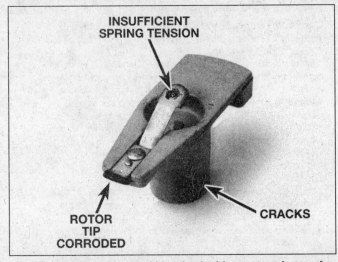

37.4 The ignition rotor should be checked for wear and corrosion as indicated here (if in doubt about its condition, buy a new one)

37.5 The rotor is attached to the distributor shaft with two screws

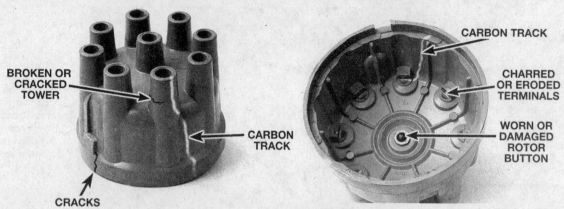

37.7 Shown here are some of the common defects to look for when inspecting the distributor cap (if in doubt about its condition, install a new one)

cap for excessive corrosion and damage **(see illustration)**. Slight deposits are normal. Again, if in doubt about the condition of the cap, replace it with a new one.

Replacement

Conventional distributor

8   On models with a separately mounted ignition coil, simply separate the cap from the distributor and transfer the spark plug wires, one at a time, to the new cap. Be very careful not to mix up the wires!

9   Reattach the cap to the distributor, then reposition the latches to hold it in place.

Coil-in-cap distributor

10   Use your thumbs to push the spark plug wire retainer latches away from the coil cover.

11   Lift the retainer ring away from the distributor cap with the spark plug wires attached to the ring. It may be necessary to work the wires off the distributor cap towers

so they remain with the ring.

12   Disconnect the battery/tachometer/coil electrical connector from the distributor cap.

13   Remove the two coil cover screws and lift off the coil cover.

14   There are three small spade connectors on wires extending from the coil into the electrical connector hood at the side of the distributor cap. Note which terminals the wires are attached to, then use a small screwdriver to push them free.

15   Remove the four coil mounting screws and lift the coil out of the cap.

16   When installing the coil in the new cap, be sure to install the rubber arc seal in the cap.

17   Install the coil screws, the wires in the connector hood, and the coil cover.

18   Install the cap on the distributor.

19   Plug in the coil electrical connector to the distributor cap.

20   Install the spark plug wire retaining ring on the distributor cap.

38   Valve lash check and adjustment

This procedure is required only on engines with solid lifters. Refer to Chapter 2, Part A, for the steps to follow.

39   Ignition point replacement and dwell adjustment

Refer to illustrations 39.1, 39.2, 39.7, 39.9, 39.16, 39.17 and 39.29

Ignition point replacement

1   The ignition points must be replaced at regular intervals on vehicles not equipped with electronic ignition. Occasionally the rubbing block will wear enough to require adjustment of the points. It's also possible to clean and dress them with a fine file, but replacement is recommended since they are relatively inaccessible and very inexpensive. Sev-

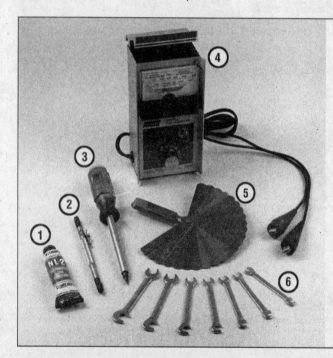

39.1 Tools and materials needed for contact point replacement and dwell angle adjustment

1   *Distributor cam lube - Sometimes this special lubricant comes with the new points; however, it's a good idea to buy a tube and have it on hand*

2   *Screw starter - This tool has special claws which hold the screw securely as it's started, which helps prevent accidental dropping of the screw*

3   *Magnetic screwdriver - Serves the same purpose as 2 above. If you don't have one of these special screwdrivers, you risk dropping the point mounting screws down into the distributor body*

4   *Dwell meter - A dwell meter is the only accurate way to determine the point setting (gap). Connect the meter according to the instructions supplied with it.*

5   *Blade-type feeler gauges - These are required to set the initial point gap (space between the points when they are open)*

6   *Ignition wrenches - These special wrenches are made to work within the tight confines of the distributor. Specifically, they are needed to loosen the nut/bolt which secures the leads to the points*

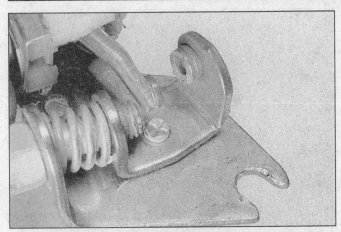

39.2 Although it is possible to restore ignition points that are pitted, burned and corroded (as shown here), they should be replaced instead

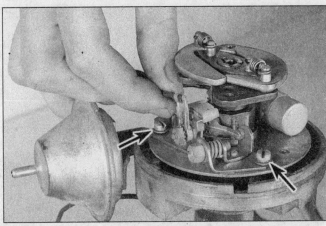

39.7 Loosen the nut and disconnect the primary and condenser wires from the points - note the ignition point mounting screws (arrows)

eral special tools are required for this procedure **(see illustration)**.

2   After removing the distributor cap and rotor (Section 37), the ignition points are visible. They can be examined by gently prying them open to reveal the condition of the contact surfaces **(see illustration)**. If they're rough, pitted, covered with oil or burned, they should be replaced, along with the condenser. **Caution:** *This procedure requires the removal of small screws which can easily fall down into the distributor. To retrieve them, the distributor would have to be removed and disassembled. Use a magnetic or spring-loaded screwdriver and be extra careful.*

3   If not already done, remove the distributor cap by positioning a screwdriver in the slotted head of each latch. Press down on the latch and rotate it 1/2-turn to release the cap from the distributor body (see Section 37).

4   Position the cap (with the spark plug wires still attached) out of the way. Use a length of wire to hold it out of the way if necessary.

5   Remove the rotor, which is held in place with two screws.

6   If equipped with a radio frequency interference shield (RFI), remove the mounting

screws and the two-piece shield to gain access to the ignition points.

7   Note how they are routed, then disconnect the primary and condenser wire leads from the points **(see illustration)**. The wires may be attached with a small nut (which should be loosened, but not removed) a small screw or by a spring loaded terminal. **Note:** *Some models are equipped with ignition points which include the condenser as an integral part of the point assembly. If your vehicle has this type, the condenser removal procedure below will not apply and there will be only one wire to detach from the points, rather than the two used with a separate condenser assembly.*

8   Loosen the two screws which secure the ignition points to the breaker plate, but don't completely remove the screws (most ignition point sets have slots at these locations). Slide the points out of the distributor.

9   The condenser can now be removed from the breaker plate. Loosen the mounting strap screw and slide the condenser out or completely remove the condenser and strap **(see illustration)**. If you remove both the condenser and strap, be careful not to drop the mounting screw down into the distributor

body.

10   Before installing the new points and condenser, clean the breaker plate and the cam on the distributor shaft to remove all dirt, dust and oil.

11   Apply a small amount of distributor cam lube (usually supplied with the new points, but also available separately) to the cam lobes.

12   Position the new condenser and tighten the mounting strap screw securely.

13   Slide the new point set under the mounting screw heads and make sure the protrusions on the breaker plate fit into the holes in the point base (to properly position the point set), then tighten the screws securely.

14   Attach the primary and condenser wires to the new points. Make sure the wires are routed so they don't interfere with breaker plate or advance weight movement.

15   Although the gap between the contact points (dwell angle) will be adjusted later, make the initial adjustment now, which will allow the engine to be started.

16   Make sure the point rubbing block is resting on one of the high points of the cam **(see illustration)**. If it isn't, turn the ignition

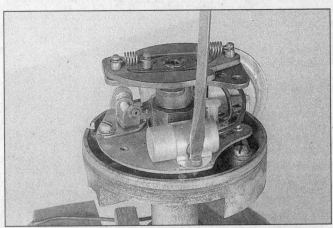

39.9 The condenser is attached to the breaker plate by a single screw

39.16 Before adjusting the point gap, the rubbing block must be resting on one of the cam lobes (which will open the points)

39.17 With the points open, insert a 0.019-inch thick feeler gauge and turn the adjustment screw with a 1/8-inch Allen wrench

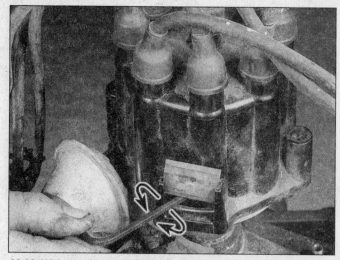

39.29 With the distributor cap door open, a 1/8-inch Allen wrench can be inserted into the adjustment screw socket and turned to adjust the point dwell

switch to Start in short bursts to reposition the cam. You can also turn the crankshaft with a breaker bar and socket attached to the large bolt that holds the vibration damper in place.

17   With the rubbing block on a cam high point (points open), insert a 0.019-inch thick feeler gauge between the contact surfaces and use an Allen wrench to turn the adjustment screw until the point gap is equal to the thickness of the feeler gauge **(see illustration)**. The gap is correct when a slight amount of drag is felt as the feeler gauge is withdrawn.

18   If equipped, install the RFI shield.

19   Before installing the rotor, check it as described in Section 37.

20   Install the rotor. The rotor is indexed with a square peg underneath on one side and a round peg on the other side, so it will fit on the advance mechanism only one way. Tighten the rotor mounting screws securely.

21   Before installing the distributor cap, inspect it (Section 37).

22   Install the distributor cap and lock the latches under the distributor body by depressing and turning them with a screwdriver.

23   Start the engine and check the dwell angle and ignition timing.

Dwell angle adjustment

24   Whenever new ignition points are installed or the original points are cleaned, the dwell angle must be checked and adjusted.

25   Precise adjustment of the dwell angle requires an instrument called a dwell meter. Combination tach/dwell meters are commonly available at reasonable cost from auto parts stores. An approximate setting can be obtained if a meter isn't available.

26   If a dwell meter is available, hook it up following the manufacturer's instructions.

27   Start the engine and allow it to run at idle until normal operating temperature is reached (the engine must be warm to obtain an accurate reading). Turn off the engine.

28   Raise the metal door in the distributor cap. Hold it in the open position with tape if necessary.

29   Just inside the opening is the ignition point adjustment screw. Insert a 1/8-inch Allen wrench into the adjustment screw socket **(see illustration)**.

30   Start the engine and turn the adjustment screw as required to obtain the specified dwell reading on the meter. Dwell angle specifications can be found at the beginning of this Chapter and on the tune-up decal in the engine compartment. If there's a discrepancy between the two, assume the tune-up decal is correct. **Note:** *When adjusting the dwell, aim for the lower end of the dwell specification range. Then, as the points wear, the dwell will remain within the specified range over a longer period of time.*

31   Remove the Allen wrench and close the door on the distributor. Turn off the engine and disconnect the dwell meter, then check the ignition timing (see Section 40).

32   If a dwell meter isn't available, use the following procedure to obtain an approximate dwell setting.

33   Start the engine and allow it to idle until normal operating temperature is reached.

34   Raise the metal door in the distributor cap. Hold it in the open position with tape if necessary.

35   Just inside the opening is the ignition point adjustment screw. Insert a 1/8-inch Allen wrench into the adjustment screw socket **(see illustration 39.29)**.

36   Turn the Allen wrench clockwise until the engine begins to misfire, then turn the screw 1/2-turn counterclockwise.

37   Remove the Allen wrench and close the door. As soon as possible have the dwell angle checked and/or adjusted with a dwell meter to ensure optimum performance.

40   Ignition timing check and adjustment

Refer to illustrations 40.2, 40.6 and 40.11

Note: The procedures included on the Tune-up or Vehicle Emissions Control Information (VECI) label must be followed when adjusting the ignition timing. The label will include all information concerning preliminary steps to be performed before adjusting the timing, as well as the timing specifications.

1   At the specified intervals, whenever the ignition points have been replaced, the distributor removed or a change made in the fuel type, the ignition timing should be checked and adjusted.

2   Locate the Tune-up or VECI label under the hood and read through and perform all preliminary instructions concerning ignition timing. Some special tools will be needed for this procedure **(see illustration)**.

3   Before attempting to check the timing, make sure the ignition point dwell angle is correct (Section 39) and the idle speed is as specified (Section 17).

4   If specified on the tune-up label, disconnect the vacuum hose from the distributor and plug the open end of the hose with a rubber plug, rod or bolt of the proper size.

5   Connect a timing light in accordance with the manufacturer's instructions. Generally, the light will be connected to the battery terminals and the number one spark plug wire. The number one spark plug is the first one on the right hand (driver's side) as you're facing the engine from the front.

6   Locate the timing scale on the front cover of the engine **(see illustration)**. It's located just behind the crankshaft pulley/vibration damper. Clean it off with solvent if necessary to see the numbers and lines.

7   Use chalk or paint to mark the groove in the vibration damper.

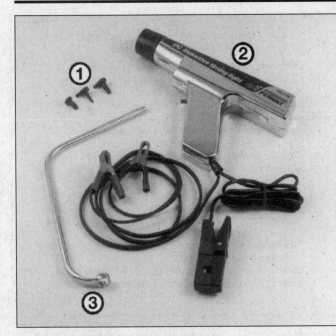

40.2 Tools needed to check and adjust the ignition timing

1 **Vacuum plugs** - *Vacuum hoses will, in most cases, have to be disconnected and plugged. Molded plugs in various shapes and sizes are available for this*
2 **Inductive pick-up timing light** - *Flashes a bright, concentrated beam of light when the number one spark plug fires. Connect the leads according to the instructions supplied with the light*
3 **Distributor wrench** - *On some models, the hold-down bolt for the distributor is difficult to reach and turn with conventional wrenches or sockets. A special wrench like this must be used*

8   Put a mark on the timing scale in accordance with the number of degrees called for on the VECI label or the tune-up label in the engine compartment. Each peak or notch on the scale represents 2-degrees. The word Before or the letter A indicates advance and the letter 0 indicates Top Dead Center (TDC). For example, if your vehicle specifications call for 8-degrees BTDC (Before Top Dead Center), you should make a mark on the timing scale 4 notches before the 0.

9   Make sure the wiring for the timing light is clear of all moving engine components, then start the engine and warm it up to normal operating temperature.

10   Aim the flashing timing light at the timing scale. The marks should appear to be stationary. If they are aligned, the timing is correct.

11   If the groove in the vibration damper is not lining up with the correct mark, loosen the distributor hold-down bolt **(see illustra-**tion**)** and rotate the distributor until the groove is lined up with the correct timing mark.

12   Retighten the hold-down bolt and recheck the timing.

13   As the engine speed is increased, the mark on the vibration damper should move away from the mark on the timing scale. If it does, the mechanical advance is working properly. If it doesn't, check the advance weights and distributor cam for binding.

14   Run the engine at about 1000 rpm and watch the timing marks as the distributor vacuum advance hose is disconnected. When the hose is disconnected, the timing mark on the vibration damper should appear to move closer to the zero on the timing scale. When the hose is reconnected, the mark should move away again. If reconnecting the hose produces an abrupt increase in advance, or none at all, the vacuum advance unit is probably defective (see Chapter 5).

15   Turn off the engine and disconnect the timing light. Reconnect the vacuum advance hose if removed, and any other components which were disconnected.

41   ECS system canister filter replacement

This procedure is covered in Chapter 6 under ECS system.

42   Front wheel bearing check, repack and adjustment

Refer to illustrations 42.1, 42.6, 42.7, 42.8, 42.9, 42.11 and 42.15

1   In most cases the front wheel bearings won't need servicing until the brake pads are changed. However, the bearings should be

40.6 The ignition timing marks are located low on the front of the engine, near the crankshaft pulley, and can be seen from the driver's side of the vehicle

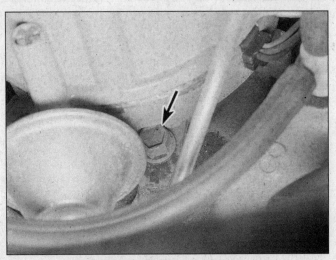

40.11 Distributor hold-down bolt (arrow)

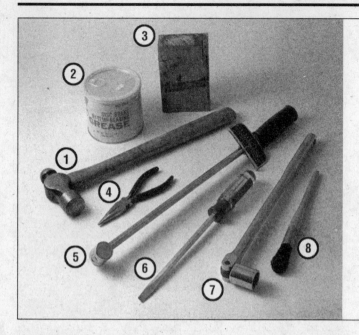

42.1 Tools and materials needed for front wheel bearing maintenance

1 *Hammer* - A common hammer will do just fine
2 *Grease* - High-temperature grease that is formulated specially for front wheel bearings should be used
3 *Wood block* - If you have a scrap piece of 2x4, it can be used to drive the new seal into the hub
4 *Needle-nose pliers* - Used to straighten and remove the cotter pin in the spindle
5 *Torque wrench* - This is very important in this procedure; if the bearing is too tight, the wheel won't turn freely - if it's too loose, the wheel will "wobble" on the spindle. Either way, it could mean extensive damage
6 *Screwdriver* - Used to remove the seal from the hub (a long screwdriver is preferred)
7 *Socket/breaker bar* - Needed to loosen the nut on the spindle if it's extremely tight
8 *Brush* - Together with some clean solvent, this will be used to remove old grease from the hub and spindle

checked whenever the front wheels are raised for any reason. Several items, including a torque wrench and special grease, are required for this procedure **(see illustration)**.

2 With the vehicle securely supported on jackstands, spin each wheel and check for noise, rolling resistance and free play.
3 Grasp the top of each tire with one hand and the bottom with the other. Move the wheel in-and-out on the spindle. If there's any noticeable movement the bearings should be checked and then repacked with grease or replaced if necessary.
4 Remove the wheel.
5 Fabricate a wood block which can be slid between the brake pads to keep them separated. Remove the brake caliper (Chapter 9) and hang it out of the way on a piece of wire.
6 Pry the dust cap out of the hub using a screwdriver or hammer and chisel **(see illustration)**.
7 Straighten the bent ends of the cotter pin, then pull it out of the spindle **(see illustration)**. Discard the cotter pin and use a new one during reassembly.
8 Remove the spindle nut and washer from the end of the spindle **(see illustration)**.
9 Pull the hub assembly out slightly and then push it back into its original position. This should force the outer bearing off the

42.6 The wheel bearing dust cap can be pried out of the hub with a chisel

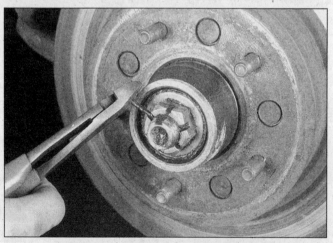

42.7 Pull out the cotter pin and discard it . . .

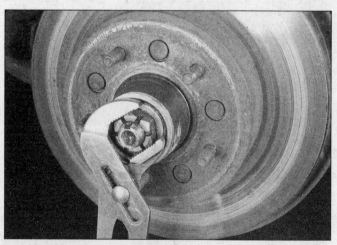

42.8 . . . then remove the spindle nut

42.9 Pull the hut out slightly to dislodge the outer wheel bearing

42.11 The seal (arrow) must be pried out of the rear of the hub

spindle enough so it can be removed **(see illustration)**.

10 Pull the hub assembly off the spindle.

11 Use a screwdriver to pry the seal out of the rear of the hub **(see illustration)**. As this is done, note how the seal is installed.

12 Again noting how it's installed, remove the inner bearing from the hub.

13 Use solvent to remove all traces of the old grease from the bearings, hub and spindle. A small brush may prove helpful; however make sure no bristles from the brush embed themselves inside the bearing rollers. Allow the parts to air dry.

14 Carefully inspect the bearings for cracks, heat discoloration, worn rollers, etc. Check the bearing races inside the hub for cracks, scoring and uneven surfaces. If the bearing races are defective, the hubs should be taken to a machine shop to have new races installed. Note that bearings and races come as matched sets, and old bearings should never be installed on new races.

15 Use high-temperature front wheel bearing grease to pack the bearings. Work the grease completely into the bearings, forcing it between the rollers, cone and cage from the back side **(see illustration)**.

16 Apply a thin coat of grease to the spindle at the outer bearing seat, inner bearing seat, shoulder and seal seat.

17 Put a small quantity of grease inboard of each bearing race inside the hub. Using your finger, form a dam at these points to provide extra grease availability and to keep thinned grease from flowing out of the bearing.

18 Place the grease-packed inner bearing into the rear of the hub and put a little more grease outboard of the bearing.

19 Place a new seal over the inner bearing and tap the seal evenly into place with a hammer and block of wood until it's flush with the hub.

20 Carefully place the hub assembly onto the spindle and push the grease-packed outer bearing into position.

21 Install the washer and spindle nut. Tighten the nut only slightly (no more than 12 ft-lbs of torque).

22 Spin the hub in a forward direction to seat the bearings and remove any grease or burrs which could cause excessive bearing play later.

23 Check to see that the tightness of the spindle nut is still approximately 12 ft-lbs.

24 Loosen the spindle nut until it is just loose, no more.

25 Using your hand (not a wrench of any kind), tighten the nut until it's snug (hub end play should be 0.001 to 0.005-inch). Install a

new cotter pin through the hole in the spindle and spindle nut. If the nut slots don't line up, loosen the nut slightly until they do. From the hand-tight position, the nut should not be loosened more than one-half flat to install the cotter pin.

26 Bend the ends of the cotter pin until they are flat against the nut. Cut off any extra length which could interfere with the dust cap.

27 Install the dust cap, tapping it into place with a hammer.

28 Place the brake caliper near the rotor and carefully remove the wood spacer. Install the caliper (Chapter 9).

29 Install the tire/wheel assembly on the hub and tighten the lug nuts.

30 Grasp the top and bottom of the tire and check the bearings in the manner described earlier in this Section.

31 Lower the vehicle.

43 Cooling system servicing (draining, flushing and refilling)

1 Periodically, the cooling system should be drained, flushed and refilled to replenish the antifreeze mixture and prevent formation of rust and corrosion, which can impair the performance of the cooling system and cause engine damage.

2 At the same time the cooling system is serviced, all hoses and the radiator cap should be inspected and replaced if defective (see Section 31).

3 Since antifreeze is a corrosive and poisonous solution, be careful not to spill any of the coolant mixture on the vehicle's paint or your skin. If this happens, rinse immediately with plenty of clean water. Consult your local authorities about the dumping of antifreeze before draining the cooling system. In many areas, reclamation centers have been set up to collect automobile oil and drained antifreeze/water mixtures, rather than allowing them to be added to the sewage system.

4 With the engine cold, remove the radia-

42.15 Work grease into the bearing rollers by pressing it against the palm of your hand

44.5 Loosen all the bolts - remove the bolts from the sides and one end of the transmission pan, but leave two at the other end in place to keep the pan from falling as it's pried loose

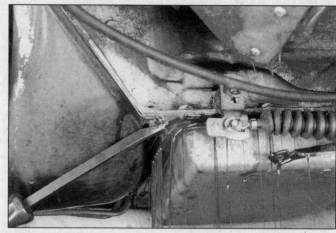

44.7 Carefully pry the pan loose and allow the fluid to drain out, then remove it completely

tor cap.

5   Move a large container under the radiator to catch the coolant as it's drained.

6   Drain the radiator by opening the fitting at the bottom. If the drain has excessive corrosion and cannot be turned easily, or if the radiator isn't equipped with a drain, disconnect the lower radiator hose to allow the coolant to drain. Be careful that none of the solution is splashed on your skin or into your eyes - wear safety glasses!

7   Disconnect the hose from the coolant reservoir and remove the reservoir. Flush it out with clean water.

8   Place a garden hose in the radiator filler neck and flush the system until the water runs clear at all drain points.

9   In severe cases of contamination or clogging of the radiator, remove it (see Chapter 3) and reverse flush it. This involves inserting the hose in the bottom radiator outlet to allow the water to run against the normal flow, draining through the top. A radiator repair shop should be consulted if further cleaning or repair is necessary.

10   When the coolant is regularly drained and the system refilled with the correct antifreeze/water mixture, there should be no need to use chemical cleaners or descalers.

11   To refill the system, reconnect the radiator hoses and install the reservoir and the overflow hose.

12   Fill the radiator with the proper mixture of antifreeze and water (see Section 4) to the base of the filler neck, then add more coolant to the reservoir until it reaches the lower mark.

13   With the radiator cap still removed, start the engine and run it until normal operating temperature is reached. With the engine idling, add additional coolant to the radiator to bring up to the proper level. Install the radiator and reservoir caps.

14   Keep a close watch on the coolant level and the cooling system hoses during the first few miles of driving. Tighten the hose clamps and/or add more coolant as necessary.

44 Automatic transmission fluid and filter change

Refer to illustrations 44.5, 44.7 and 44.10

1   At the specified time intervals, the transmission fluid should be drained and replaced. Since the fluid will remain hot long after driving, perform this procedure only after sufficient cooling.

2   Before beginning work, purchase the specified transmission fluid (see *Recommended lubricants and fluids* at the front of this Chapter) and filter.

3   Other tools necessary for this job include jackstands to support the vehicle in a raised position, a drain pan, newspapers and clean rags.

4   Raise the vehicle and support it securely on jackstands. **Note:** *Later models may be equipped with a transmission fluid drain plug. The transmission fluid can be drained before the pan is removed on these models (like changing the engine oil). Those models without a transmission drain plug must use the following procedure.*

5   With a drain pan in place, remove the front and side pan bolts **(see illustration)**.

6   Loosen the rear pan bolts approximately four turns.

7   Carefully pry the transmission pan loose with a screwdriver, allowing the fluid to drain **(see illustration)**.

8   Remove the remaining bolts, pan and gasket. Carefully clean the gasket surface of the transmission to remove all traces of the old gasket and sealant.

9   Drain the fluid from the transmission pan, clean it with solvent and dry it with compressed air.

10   Remove the filter from the mount inside the transmission **(see illustration)**.

11   Install a new filter screen and gasket or O-ring.

12   Make sure the gasket surface on the transmission pan is clean, then install a new gasket. Put the pan in place against the transmission and, working around the pan, tighten each bolt a little at a time until the final torque figure is reached.

13   Lower the vehicle and add the specified amount of automatic transmission fluid through the filler tube (Section 6).

14   With the selector in Park and the parking brake set, run the engine at a fast idle, but do not race the engine.

15   Move the gear selector through each range and back to Park. Check the fluid level.

16   Check under the vehicle for leaks during the first few trips.

44.10 The filter is attached to the transmission with bolts or screws

Chapter 2 Part A
Engines

Contents

Specifications

General

Cylinder numbers (front-to-rear)	
Left (driver's) side	1-3-5-7
Right side	2-4-6-8
Firing order	1-8-4-3-6-5-7-2
Bore and stroke	
305	3.74 x 3.48 in
327	4.0 x 3.25 in
350	4.0 x 3.48 in
427	4.25 x 3.76 in
454	4.25 x 4.00 in

V8 ENGINE with points-type ignition
Firing order
1-8-4-3-6-5-7-2

0786H

V8 ENGINE with electronic (HEI) ignition

0787H

Cylinder location and distributor rotation

The blackened terminal shown on the distributor cap indicates the Number One spark plug wire position

Camshaft

Bearing journal diameter	
Small block	1.8682 to 1.8692 in
Big block	1.9482 to 1.9492 in
End play	0.0015 in maximum
Lobe lift, allowable variation	0.005 in

Torque specifications

	Ft-lbs (unless otherwise indicated)
Rocker arm cover	
Small block	45 in-lbs
Big block	50 in-lbs
Intake manifold bolts	30
Exhaust manifold bolts	
1968 through 1977	20
1978 on	
Outer bolts	20
Inner bolts	30
Cylinder head bolts	
Small block	
Step 1	30
Step 2	50
Step 3	65
Big block	
Step 1	40
Step 2	60
Step 3	80*

* On engines with aluminum heads, tighten the short bolts to 65 ft-lbs and the long bolts to 75 ft-lbs.

Timing cover bolts	80 in-lbs
Camshaft sprocket bolts	20
Torsional (vibration) damper bolt	
Small block	60
Big block	85
Oil pan	
Small block	
1/4-20	80 in-lbs
5/16-18	165 in-lbs
Big block	
Oil pan-to-front cover bolts	55 in-lbs
Oil pan-to-block bolts	145 in-lbs
Oil pump bolt	65
Rear main bearing cap bolts	
Small block	
1968 through 1976	75
1977 on	80
Big block	110
Flywheel mounting bolts	
327, 350	60
427, 454	65

1   General information

This Part of Chapter 2 is devoted to in-vehicle repair procedures for the engine. All information concerning engine removal and installation and engine block and cylinder head overhaul can be found in Part B of this Chapter.

Since the repair procedures included in this Part are based on the assumption the engine is still installed in the vehicle, if they're being used during a complete engine over-haul (with the engine already out of the vehi-cle and on a stand) many of the steps included here won't apply.

The Specifications included in this Part of Chapter 2 apply only to the procedures found here. The specifications necessary for rebuilding the block and cylinder heads are included in Part B.

The V8 engines used in the Corvette during the years covered by this manual vary in size from 305 cubic inches to 454 cubic inches. The 305, 307 and 350 cubic inch engines are collectively known as Small Block engines. The 427 and 454 cubic inch engines are known as Big Block engines.

2   Repair operations possible with the engine in the vehicle

Many major repair operations can be accomplished without removing the engine from the vehicle.

Clean the engine compartment and the exterior of the engine with some type of pres-sure washer before any work is done. A clean engine will make the job easier and help keep dirt out of the internal areas of the engine.

Depending on the components involved, it may be a good idea to remove the hood to improve access to the engine as repairs are performed (refer to Chapter 11 if necessary).

If oil or coolant leaks develop, indicating a need for gasket or seal replacement, the repairs can generally be made with the engine in the vehicle. The oil pan gasket, cylinder head gaskets, intake and exhaust manifold gaskets, timing cover gaskets and crankshaft oil seals are accessible with the engine in place.

Exterior engine components, such as the water pump, starter motor, alternator, distributor and the carburetor or fuel injection units, as well as the intake and exhaust manifolds, can be removed for repair with the engine in place.

Since the cylinder heads can be removed without pulling the engine, valve component servicing can also be accomplished with the engine in the vehicle.

Replacement of, repairs to or inspection of the timing chain and sprockets and the oil pump are all possible with the engine in place.

---

3 Rocker arm covers - removal and installation

---

1   Disconnect the negative cable from the battery, then remove the air cleaner assembly and the heat stove duct.

Removal

2   Remove or reposition all hoses, brackets, wires and lines that could interfere with rocker arm removal. If air conditioning lines must be moved, do not loosen or disconnect the compressor lines.
3   Remove the rocker arm cover mounting nuts or bolts. If equipped, slip the spark plug wire clip brackets and washers off the lower rocker arm cover studs and position the brackets/wires out of the way.
4   Detach the spark plug wires from the plugs, then lay the spark plug wire harness up over the distributor and remove the rocker arm cover(s). **Note:** *If the cover sticks to the cylinder head, use a block of wood and a hammer to dislodge it. If it still won't come loose, try to slip a flexible putty knife between the head and cover to break the seal. Do not pry at the cover-to-head joint or damage to the sealing surface and cover flange will result and oil leaks could develop.*

Installation

5   The mating surfaces of each cylinder head and rocker arm cover must be perfectly clean when the covers are installed. Use a gasket scraper to remove all traces of sealant or old gasket, then clean the mating surfaces with lacquer thinner or acetone (if there's old sealant or oil on the mating surfaces when the cover is installed, oil leaks may develop). If the covers are made of aluminum, be extra careful not to nick or gouge the mating surfaces with the scraper.
6   If studs are used to mount the rocker

arm covers, clean the threads with a die to remove any corrosion and restore damaged threads. On models that utilize bolts, make sure the threaded holes in the head are clean. Run a tap into them to remove corrosion and restore damaged threads.
7   Mate the new gaskets to the covers before the covers are installed. Apply a thin coat of RTV sealant to the cover flange, then position the gasket inside the cover lip and allow the sealant to set up so the gasket adheres to the cover (if the sealant isn't allowed to set, the gasket may fall out of the cover as it's installed on the engine).
8   Carefully position the cover on the head and install the nuts or bolts. Don't forget to slip the spark plug wire clip brackets and washers over the studs before the nuts are threaded on.
9   Tighten the nuts or bolts in three or four steps to the specified torque.
10   The remaining installation steps are the reverse of removal.
11   Start the engine and check carefully for oil leaks as the engine warms up.

---

4 Rocker arms and pushrods - removal, inspection and installation

---

Removal

Refer to illustration 4.4
1   Refer to Section 3 and detach the rocker arm covers from the cylinder heads.
2   Beginning at the front of one cylinder head, loosen and remove the rocker arm stud nuts. Store them separately in marked containers to ensure they'll be reinstalled in their original locations. **Note:** *If the pushrods are the only items being removed, loosen each nut just enough to allow the rocker arms to be rotated to the side so the pushrods can be lifted out.*
3   Lift off the rocker arms and pivot balls and store them in the marked containers with the nuts (they should be reinstalled in their original locations).
4   Remove the pushrods and store them in order to make sure they will not get mixed up during installation **(see illustration)**.

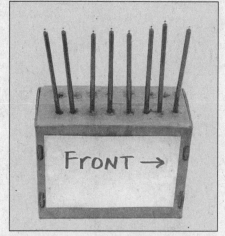

4.4 A perforated cardboard box can be used to store the pushrods to ensure they are reinstalled in their original locations

Inspection

5   Check each rocker arm for wear, cracks and other damage, especially where the pushrods and valve stems contact the rocker arm faces.
6   Make sure the hole at the pushrod end of each rocker arm is open.
7   Check each rocker arm pivot area for wear, cracks and galling. If the rocker arms are worn or damaged, replace them with new ones and use new pivot balls as well.
8   Inspect the pushrods for cracks and excessive wear at the ends. Roll each pushrod across a piece of plate glass to see if it's bent (if it wobbles, it's bent).

Installation

Refer to illustrations 4.10 and 4.11
9   Lubricate the lower end of each pushrod with clean engine oil or moly-base grease and install them in their original locations. Make sure each pushrod seats completely in the lifter socket.
10   Apply moly-base grease to the ends of the valve stems and the upper ends of the pushrods before positioning the rocker arms over the studs **(see illustration)**.

4.10 The ends of the pushrods and the valve stems should be lubricated with moly-base grease prior to installation of the rocker arms

4.11 Moly-base grease applied to the pivot balls will ensure adequate lubrication as oil pressure builds up when the engine is started

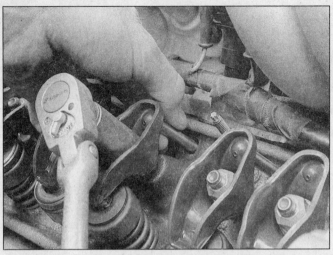

4.13 Rotate each pushrod as the rocker arm nut is tightened to determine the point at which all play is removed, then tighten each nut an additional one full turn

11   Set the rocker arms in place, then install the pivot balls and nuts. Apply moly-base grease to the pivot balls to prevent damage to the mating surfaces before engine oil pressure builds up **(see illustration)**. Be sure to install each nut with the flat side against the pivot ball.

Valve adjustment

Engines with hydraulic lifters

Refer to illustration 4.13

12   Refer to Section 9 and bring the number one piston to top dead center on the compression stroke.

13   Tighten the rocker arm nuts (number one cylinder only) until all play is removed at the pushrods. This can be determined by rotating each pushrod between your thumb and index finger as the nut is tightened **(see illustration)**. At the point where a slight drag is just felt as you spin the pushrod, all lash has been removed.

14   Tighten each nut an additional 3/4 turn to center the lifters. Valve adjustment for cylinder number one is now complete.

15   Turn the crankshaft 90-degrees in the normal direction of rotation until the next piston in the firing order is at TDC on the compression stroke. The distributor rotor should be pointing in the direction of terminal number eight on the cap (see Section 9 for additional information).

16   Repeat the procedure described in Steps 13 and 14 for the cylinder number eight valves.

17   Turn the crankshaft another 90-degrees and adjust the number four cylinder valves. Continue turning the crankshaft 90-degrees at a time and adjust both valves for each cylinder before proceeding. Follow the firing order sequence. A cylinder number illustration and the firing order is included in the Specifications.

18   Refer to Section 3 and install the rocker arm covers. Start the engine, listen for unusual valve train noises and check for oil leaks at the rocker arm cover joints.

Engines with solid lifters

Note: *On engines with solid (mechanical) lifters, adjustment must be done with the engine at normal operating temperature. After major repairs or an overhaul, initially set the lash as described below, run the engine until normal operating temperature is reached, then repeat the procedure with the engine hot.*

19   Refer to Section 9 and bring the number one piston to top dead center on the compression stroke.

20   Turn the rocker arm adjusting nuts for the exhaust valves of cylinders four and eight, and the intake valves of cylinders two and seven, until a feeler gauge of the specified thickness can be inserted between the rocker arm and the end of the valve stem with a slight amount of drag.

21   Rotate the crankshaft 180-degrees clockwise and repeat the procedure for the exhaust valves of cylinders three and six, and the intake valves of cylinders one and eight.

22   Rotate the crankshaft another 180-degrees clockwise (the timing marks should be aligned) and repeat the procedure for the exhaust valves of cylinders five and seven, and intake valves of cylinders three and four.

23   Rotate the crankshaft an additional 180-degrees clockwise and repeat the procedure for the exhaust valves of cylinders one and two, and intake valves of cylinders five and six.

---

5   Valve springs, retainers and seals - replacement

Refer to illustrations 5.4, 5.8, 5.9, 5.17 and 5.18

Note: *Broken valve springs and defective valve stem seals can be replaced without removing the affected cylinder head. Two special tools and a compressed air source are normally required to perform this operation, so read through this Section carefully and rent or buy the tools before beginning the job. If compressed air isn't available, a length of nylon rope can be used to keep the valves from falling into the cylinder during this procedure.*

1   Refer to Section 3 and remove the rocker arm cover from the affected cylinder head. If all of the valve stem seals are being replaced, remove both rocker arm covers.

2   Remove the spark plug from the cylinder which has the defective component. If all of the valve stem seals are being replaced, all of the spark plugs should be removed.

3   Turn the crankshaft until the piston in the affected cylinder is at top dead center on the compression stroke (refer to Section 9 for instructions). If you're replacing all of the valve stem seals, begin with cylinder number one and work on the valves for one cylinder at a time. Move from cylinder-to-cylinder following the firing order sequence (see the Specifications at the beginning of this Chapter).

4   Thread an adapter into the spark plug hole and connect an air hose from a compressed air source to it **(see illustration)**. Most auto parts stores can supply the air hose adapter. **Note:** *Many cylinder compression gauges utilize a screw-in fitting that may work with your air hose quick-disconnect fitting.*

5   Remove the nut, pivot ball and rocker arm for the valve with the defective part and pull out the pushrod. If all of the valve stem seals are being replaced, all of the rocker arms and pushrods should be removed (refer to Section 4).

6   Apply compressed air to the cylinder. **Warning:** *The piston may be forced down by compressed air, causing the crankshaft to turn suddenly. If the wrench used when positioning the number one piston at TDC is still*

5.4 This is what the air hose adapter that threads into the spark plug hole looks like - they're commonly available from auto parts stores

5.8 Once the spring is depressed, the keepers can be removed with a small magnet or a pair of needle-nose pliers

attached to the bolt in the crankshaft nose, it could cause damage or injury when the crankshaft moves.

7   The valves should be held in place by the air pressure. If the valve faces or seats are in poor condition, leaks may prevent the air pressure from retaining the valves (refer to the following procedure). If you don't have access to compressed air, an alternative method can be used. Position the piston at a point just before TDC on the compression stroke, then feed a long piece of nylon rope through the spark plug hole until it fills the combustion chamber. Be sure to leave the end of the rope hanging out of the engine so it can be removed easily. Use a large breaker bar and socket to rotate the crankshaft in the normal direction of rotation until slight resistance is felt as the piston comes up against the rope in the combustion chamber.

8   Stuff shop rags into the cylinder head holes above and below the valves to prevent parts and tools from falling into the engine, then use a valve spring compressor to compress the spring/damper assembly. Remove the keepers with a pair of small needle-nose pliers or a magnet **(see illustration).** Note: *A couple of different types of tools are available for compressing the valve springs with the head in place. One type grips the lower spring coils and presses on the retainer as the knob is turned, while the other type utilizes the rocker arm stud and nut for leverage. Both types work very well, although the lever type is usually less expensive.*

9   Remove the spring retainer or rotator, oil shield and valve spring assembly, then remove the valve stem O-ring seal (if used). Three different types of valve stem oil seals are used on these engines, depending on year, engine size and horsepower rating. The most common is a small O-ring which simply fits around the valve stem just above the guide boss. A second type is a flat O-ring which fits into a groove in the valve stem just below the valve stem keeper groove **(see illustration).** On most high-horsepower

5.9 The flat O-ring valve stem seal fits into a groove just below the keeper groove on the valve stem

applications, an umbrella type seal which extends down over the valve guide boss is used over the valve stem. In some cases the umbrella type seal is used in conjunction with the flat O-ring type seal. The O-ring type seals will most likely be hardened and will probably break when removed, so plan on installing a new one each time the original is removed. **Note:** *If air pressure fails to hold the valve in the closed position during this operation, the valve face or seat is probably damaged. If so, the cylinder head will have to be removed for additional repair operations.*

10   Wrap a rubber band or tape around the top of the valve stem so the valve won't fall into the combustion chamber, then release the air pressure. **Note:** *If a rope was used instead of air pressure, turn the crankshaft slightly in the direction opposite normal rotation.*

11   Inspect the valve stem for damage. Rotate the valve in the guide and check the end for eccentric movement, which would indicate the valve is bent.

12   Move the valve up-and-down in the guide and make sure it doesn't bind. If the valve stem binds, either the valve is bent or

the guide is damaged. In either case, the head will have to be removed for repair.

13   Inspect the rocker arm studs for wear. Worn studs on most small block engines can only be replaced by an automotive machine shop, since they must be pressed in to a precise depth. On some big block engines, however, and some high performance versions of the small block, the studs are threaded into the head and can be replaced if worn. In addition, in some applications of screw-in studs, a guide plate is installed between the stud and head to locate the pushrod in relation to the rocker arm. Be sure to replace the guide plate if the studs are removed and reinstalled and use gasket sealant on the studs when threading them into the head.

14   Reapply air pressure to the cylinder to retain the valve in the closed position, then remove the tape or rubber band from the valve stem. If a rope was used instead of air pressure, rotate the crankshaft in the normal direction of rotation until slight resistance is felt.

15   Lubricate the valve stem with engine oil and install a new umbrella-type oil seal (if used - see Step 9).

16   Install the spring/damper assembly and shield in position over the valve.

17   Install the valve spring retainer or rotator and compress the valve spring assembly. Carefully install the new O-ring seal in the lower groove in the valve stem. Make sure the seal isn't twisted; it must lie perfectly flat in the groove **(see illustration)**.

18   Position the keepers in the upper groove. Apply a small dab of grease to the inside of each keeper to hold it in place if necessary **(see illustration)**. Remove the pressure from the spring tool and make sure the keepers are seated.

19   Disconnect the air hose and remove the adapter from the spark plug hole. If a rope was used in place of air pressure, pull it out of the cylinder.

20   Refer to Section 4 and install the rocker arms and pushrods.

21   Install the spark plugs and hook up the wires.

22   Refer to Section 3 and install the rocker arm covers.

23   Start and run the engine, then check for oil leaks and unusual sounds coming from the rocker arm cover area.

6   Intake manifold - removal and installation

Refer to illustrations 6.9, 6.10a, 6.10b, 6.11, 6.12, 6.13a, 6.13b, 6.15a, 6.15b and 6.15c

Removal

1   Disconnect the negative cable from the battery, then refer to Chapter 1 and drain the cooling system.

2   Refer to Chapter 4 and remove the air cleaner assembly.

3   While in Chapter 4, refer to the appropriate Sections and remove the carburetor or the fuel injection units as necessary to expose the intake manifold mounting bolts.

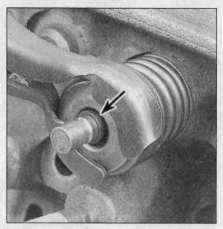

5.17 Make sure the O-ring seal under the retainer is seated in the groove and not twisted before installing the keepers

4   Refer to Chapter 3 and detach the upper radiator hose from the thermostat housing cover. Remove the alternator brace (if not already done). The thermostat housing cover may have to be detached to provide room for removal of the left-front manifold bolt.

5   Remove the rocker arm covers (Section 3).

6   Refer to Chapter 5 and remove the distributor.

7   If there is a heater hose fitting in the intake manifold, remove the hose.

8   Loosen the manifold mounting bolts in 1/4-turn increments until they can be removed by hand. The manifold will probably be stuck to the cylinder heads and force may be required to break the gasket seal. A large pry bar can be positioned under the cast-in lug near the thermostat housing to pry up the front of the manifold. **Caution:** *Do not pry between the block and manifold or the heads and manifold or damage to the gasket sealing surfaces may result and vacuum leaks could develop.*

5.18 Apply a small dab of grease to each keeper as shown here before installation - it'll hold them in place on the valve stem as the spring is released

Installation

Note: The mating surfaces of the cylinder heads, block and manifold must be perfectly clean when the manifold is installed. Gasket removal solvents in aerosol cans are available at most auto parts stores and may be helpful when removing old gasket material that's stuck to the heads and manifold. Be sure to follow the directions printed on the container.

9   Use a gasket scraper to remove all traces of sealant and old gasket material, then clean the mating surfaces with lacquer thinner or acetone (if there's old sealant or oil on the mating surfaces when the manifold is installed, oil or vacuum leaks may develop). When working on the heads and block, cover the lifter valley with shop rags to keep debris out of the engine **(see illustration)**. Use a vacuum cleaner to remove any gasket material that falls into the intake ports in the heads.

10   Use a tap of the correct size to chase the threads in the bolt holes, then use compressed air (if available) to remove the debris

6.9 After covering the lifter valley, use a gasket scraper to remove all traces of sealant and old gasket material from the head and manifold mating surfaces

6.10a The bolt hole threads must be clean and dry to ensure accurate torque readings when the manifold mounting bolts are installed

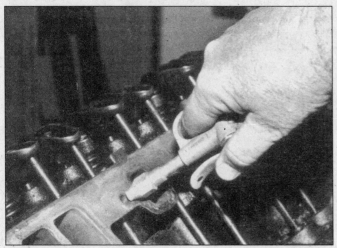

6.10b Clean the bolt holes with compressed air, but be careful - wear safety goggles!

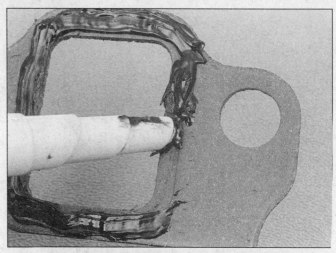

6.11 RTV sealant should be used around the coolant passage holes in the new intake manifold gaskets

6.12 Make sure the intake manifold gaskets are installed right side up or all the passages and bolt holes may not line up properly!

6.13a The rubber end seals . . .

from the holes **(see illustrations)**. **Warning:** *Wear safety glasses or a face shield to protect your eyes when using compressed air!*

11   Apply a thin coat of RTV sealant around the coolant passage holes on the cylinder head side of the new intake manifold gaskets **(see illustration)** (there's normally one hole at each end).

12   Position the gaskets on the cylinder heads. Make sure all intake port openings, coolant passage holes and bolt holes are aligned correctly and the THIS SIDE UP mark is visible **(see illustration)**.

13   Install the front and rear end seals on the block **(see illustrations)**. Note that most seals have either rubber spikes which fit into matching holes in the block, or rubber tabs which fit over the edge of the block to locate the seals. On some early models there's a tab on the rear seal which may have to be cut off for proper fit. Refer to the instructions with the gasket set for further information. Apply a dab of RTV sealant to the seal-to-gasket

6.13b . . . and the intake manifold gaskets must be positioned properly - use RTV at the four seal-to-gasket joints

joints. **Note:** *Later models do not have rubber seals; a bead of RTV sealant is used instead. Make sure it extends up onto the gaskets at each end.*

14   Carefully set the manifold in place. Do not disturb the gaskets and do not move the manifold fore-and-aft after it contacts the front and rear seals.

15   Apply a non-hardening sealant (such as Permatex Number 2) to the manifold bolt threads, then install the bolts. While the sealant is still wet, tighten the bolts to the

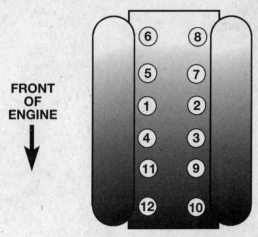

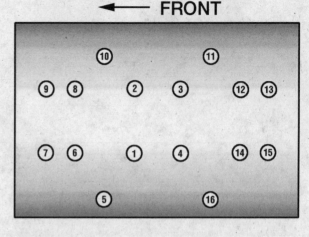

6.15a Small block intake manifold (through 1981)
TIGHTENING sequence

6.15b Big block intake manifold TIGHTENING sequence

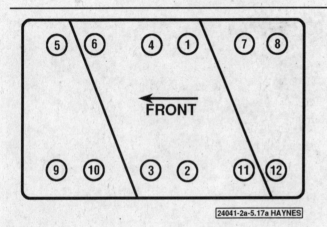

24041-2a-5.17a HAYNES

6.15c 1982 small block intake manifold TIGHTENING sequence

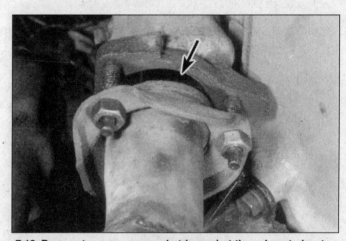

7.13 Be sure to use a new gasket (arrow) at the exhaust pipe-to-manifold joint

specified torque following the recommended sequence **(see illustrations)**. Work up to the final torque in three steps.

16   The remaining installation steps are the reverse of removal. Start the engine and check carefully for oil, vacuum and coolant leaks at the intake manifold joints.

7   Exhaust manifolds - removal and installation

Refer to illustration 7.13

Removal

1   Disconnect the negative cable from the battery.
2   Remove the carburetor heat stove pipe between the exhaust manifold and air cleaner snorkel (if equipped).
3   Disconnect the electrical connector to the oxygen sensor (if equipped).
4   Remove the AIR hose at the check valve and the AIR pipe bracket from the manifold stud (if equipped).
5   Disconnect the spark plug wires from

the spark plugs (refer to Chapter 1 if necessary). If there's any danger of mixing the plug wires up, we recommend labeling them with small pieces of tape.
6   Remove the spark plugs (Chapter 1).
7   Remove the spark plug heat shields.
8   Disconnect the exhaust pipe from the manifold outlet. Often an application of penetrating oil is necessary to remove frozen exhaust pipe nuts. Don't apply excessive force to frozen nuts, which could shear off the exhaust manifold studs.
9   Remove any accessories such as the alternator or air conditioning compressor bolted to the exhaust manifold, along with any mounting brackets.
10   Remove the two front and two rear manifold mounting bolts first, then the two center bolts to separate the manifold from the head. Some models have tabbed washers to keep the bolts from vibrating loose. On these models, the tabs will have to be flattened before the bolts can be removed.

Installation

11   Installation is basically the reverse of the removal procedure. Clean the manifold and

head gasket surfaces to remove old gasket material, then install new gaskets. Do not use gasket cement or sealant on exhaust system gaskets. Be sure to transfer the heat stove assembly if a new manifold is being installed.
12   Install all the manifold bolts and tighten them to the specified torque. Work from the center out toward the ends and approach the final torque in three steps.
13   Apply anti-seize compound to the exhaust manifold-to-exhaust pipe studs and use a new exhaust "doughnut" gasket **(see illustration)**.

8   Cylinder heads - removal and installation

Refer to illustrations 8.5, 8.12, 8.13, 8.15, 8.16a and 8.16b

Removal

1   Refer to Section 3 and remove the rocker arm covers.
2   Refer to Section 6 and remove the intake manifold. Note that the cooling system

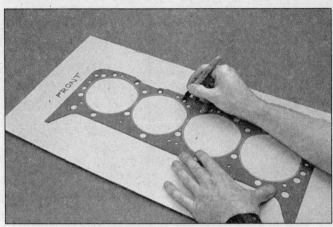

8.5 To avoid mixing up the head bolts, use a new gasket to transfer the bolt hole pattern to a piece of cardboard, then punch holes to accept the bolts

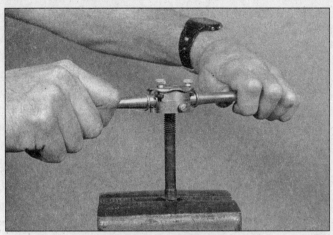

8.12 A die should be used to remove sealant and corrosion from the head bolt threads prior to installation

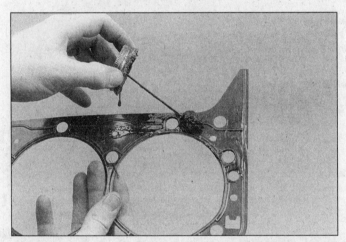

8.13 Steel gaskets - used with cast iron heads - should be coated with a sealant such as K&W Copper Coat before installation

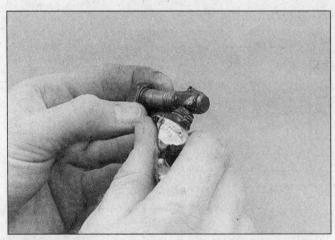

8.15 The head bolts MUST be cooled with a non-hardening sealant (such as Permatex no. 2) before they are installed - coolant will leak past the bolts if this isn't done

must be drained to prevent coolant from getting into internal areas of the engine when the manifold and heads are removed. The alternator, power steering pump, air pump and air conditioner compressor brackets (if equipped) must be removed as well.

3   Refer to Section 7 and detach both exhaust manifolds.

4   Refer to Section 4 and remove the pushrods.

5   Using a new head gasket, outline the cylinders and bolt pattern on a piece of cardboard **(see illustration)**. Be sure to indicate the front of the engine for reference. Punch holes at the bolt locations.

6   Loosen the head bolts in 1/4-turn increments until they can be removed by hand. Work from bolt-to-bolt in a pattern that's the reverse of the tightening sequence. **Note:** *Don't overlook the row of bolts on the lower edge of each head, near the spark plug holes. Store the bolts in the cardboard holder as they're removed. This will ensure the bolts are reinstalled in their original holes.*

7   Lift the heads off the engine. If resistance is felt, do not pry between the head

and block as damage to the mating surfaces will result. To dislodge the head, place a block of wood against the end of it and strike the wood block with a hammer. Store the heads on blocks of wood to prevent damage to the gasket sealing surfaces.

8   Cylinder head disassembly and inspection procedures are covered in detail in Chapter 2, Part B.

Installation

9   The mating surfaces of the cylinder heads and block must be perfectly clean when the heads are installed.

10   Use a gasket scraper to remove all traces of carbon and old gasket material, then clean the mating surfaces with lacquer thinner or acetone (if there's oil on the mating surfaces when the heads are installed, the gaskets may not seal correctly and leaks may develop). When working on the block, cover the lifter valley with shop rags to keep debris out of the engine. Use a vacuum cleaner to remove any debris that falls into the cylinders.

11   Check the block and head mating sur-

faces for nicks, deep scratches and other damage. If damage is slight, it can be removed with a file. If it's excessive, machining may be the only alternative.

12   Use a tap of the correct size to chase the threads in the head bolt holes in the block. Mount each bolt in a vise and run a die down the threads to remove corrosion and restore the threads **(see illustration)**. Dirt, corrosion, sealant and damaged threads will affect torque readings.

13   Position the new gaskets over the dowel pins in the block. **Note:** *If a steel gasket is used (shim-type gasket), apply a thin, even coat of sealant such as K&W Copper Coat to both sides prior to installation* **(see illustration)**. *Steel gaskets must be installed with the raised bead UP. Composition gaskets must be installed dry; do not use sealant.*

14   Carefully position the heads on the block without disturbing the gaskets.

15   Before installing the head bolts, coat the threads with a non-hardening sealant such as Permatex Number 2 **(see illustration)**.

16   Install the bolts in their original locations and tighten them finger-tight. Following the

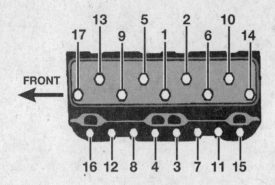

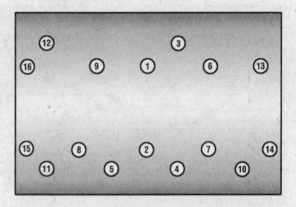

8.16a Cylinder head bolt tightening sequence - small-block V8

8.16b Cylinder head bolt tightening sequence - big-block V8

recommended sequence, tighten the bolts in several steps to the specified torque **(see illustrations)**.

17   The remaining installation steps are the reverse of removal.

9   Top Dead Center (TDC) for number one piston - locating

Refer to illustration 9.6
Note: *The following procedure is based on the assumption the spark plug wires and distributor are correctly installed. If you're trying to locate TDC to install the distributor correctly, piston position must be determined by feeling for compression at the number one spark plug hole, then aligning the ignition timing marks as described in Step 8.*

1   Top Dead Center (TDC) is the highest point in the cylinder each piston reaches as it travels up-and-down when the crankshaft turns. Each piston reaches TDC on the compression stroke and again on the exhaust stroke, but TDC generally refers to piston position on the compression stroke. The timing marks on the vibration damper installed on the front of the crankshaft are referenced to the number one piston at TDC on the compression stroke.

2   Positioning the pistons at TDC is an essential part of many procedures such as rocker arm removal, valve adjustment, timing chain and sprocket replacement and distributor removal.

3   To bring any piston to TDC, the crankshaft must be turned using one of the methods outlined below. When looking at the front of the engine, normal crankshaft rotation is clockwise. **Warning:** *Before beginning this procedure, be sure to place the transmission in Neutral and disable the ignition system by removing the coil wire from the distributor cap and grounding it (remote coil systems) or disconnecting the BAT wire to the coil-in-cap type distributor.*

a) *The preferred method is to turn the crankshaft with a large socket and ratchet attached to the vibration damper*

bolt threaded into the front of the crankshaft.
b) *A remote starter switch, which may save some time, can also be used. Attach the switch leads to the S (switch) and B (battery) terminals on the starter solenoid. Once the piston is close to TDC, use a socket and ratchet as described in the previous paragraph.*
c) *If an assistant is available to turn the ignition switch to the Start position in short bursts, you can get the piston close to TDC without a remote starter switch. Make sure your assistant is out of the vehicle, away from the ignition switch, then use a socket and ratchet as described in Paragraph a) to complete the procedure.*

4   Use a felt-tip pen or chalk to make a mark on the distributor body directly below the number one spark plug wire terminal in the distributor cap (or make a mark on the intake manifold directly across from the number one spark plug wire terminal in the distributor cap).

5   Remove the distributor cap as described in Chapter 1.

6   Turn the crankshaft (see Step 3 above) until the line on the vibration damper is aligned with the zero mark on the timing plate **(see illustration)**. The timing plate and vibration damper are located low on the front of the engine, behind the pulley that turns the drivebelts.

7   The rotor should now be pointing directly at the mark on the distributor base or intake manifold. If it isn't, the piston is at TDC on the exhaust stroke.

8   To get the piston to TDC on the compression stroke, turn the crankshaft one complete turn (360-degrees) clockwise. The rotor should now be pointing at the mark. When the rotor is pointing at the number one spark plug wire terminal in the distributor cap (which is indicated by the mark on the distributor body or intake manifold) and the timing marks are aligned, the number one piston is at TDC on the compression stroke.

9   After the number one piston has been

9.6 Turn the crankshaft until the line on the vibration damper is directly opposite the zero mark on the timing plate as shown here

positioned at TDC on the compression stroke, TDC for any of the remaining cylinders can be located by turning the crankshaft 90-degrees at a time and following the firing order (refer to the Specifications).

10   Timing cover, chain and sprockets - removal and installation

Refer to illustrations 10.6, 10.12 and 10.14

Removal

1   Refer to Chapter 3 and remove the water pump.

2   Remove the bolts and separate the crankshaft drivebelt pulley from the vibration damper.

3   Refer to Section 9 and position the number one piston at TDC on the compression stroke. **Caution:** *Once this has been done, do not turn the crankshaft until the timing chain and sprockets have been reinstalled.*

4   Most, but not all V8 engines, have a large bolt threaded into the nose of the crankshaft to secure the vibration damper in

10.6 A putty knife can be used to break the timing chain cover-to-block seal, but don't pry it off or the cover may be distorted

10.12 Align the timing marks (arrows) before bolting the camshaft sprocket in place. With the sprockets in this position the number 1 cylinder will be at TDC on the exhaust stroke (TDC on the compression stroke for number 6 cylinder)

position. If your engine has a bolt, remove it from the front of the crankshaft, then use a puller to detach the vibration damper. **Caution:** *Do not use a puller with jaws that grip the outer edge of the damper. The puller must be the type that utilizes bolts to apply force to the damper hub only.*

5   On most small block V8 engines, the timing cover cannot be removed with the oil pan in place. The pan bolts will have to be loosened and the pan lowered approximately 1/4-inch for the timing cover to be removed. If the pan has been in place for an extended period of time it's very likely the gasket will break when the pan is lowered. In this case, the pan should be removed and a new gasket installed.

6   Remove the bolts and separate the timing chain cover from the block. It may be stuck. If so, use a putty knife to break the gasket seal **(see illustration)**. The cover is easily distorted, so don't attempt to pry it off.

7   On big block engines, pull the cover forward far enough to insert a knife between the cover and the block, cut the forward portion of the oil pan gasket on each side, then remove the cover.

8   Remove the three bolts from the end of the camshaft, then detach the camshaft sprocket and chain as an assembly. The sprocket on the crankshaft can be removed with a two or three jaw puller, but be careful not to damage the threads in the end of the crankshaft. **Note:** *If the timing chain cover oil seal has been leaking, refer to Section 15 and install a new one.*

Installation

9   Use a gasket scraper to remove all traces of old gasket material and sealant from the cover and engine block. Stuff a shop rag into the opening at the front of the oil pan to keep debris out of the engine. Clean the cover and block sealing surfaces with lacquer thinner or acetone.

10   Check the cover flange for distortion, particularly around the bolt holes. If necessary, place the cover on a block of wood and use a hammer to flatten and restore the gasket surface.

11   If new parts are being installed, be sure to align the keyway in the crankshaft sprocket with the Woodruff key in the end of the crankshaft. **Note:** *The timing chain and sprockets must be replaced as a set - never put a new chain on old sprockets.* Align the sprocket with the Woodruff key and press the sprocket onto the crankshaft with the vibration damper bolt, a large socket and some washers (or tap it gently into place) until it's completely seated. **Caution:** *If resistance is encountered, do not hammer the sprocket onto the crankshaft. It may eventually move onto the shaft, but it may be cracked in the process and fail later, causing extensive engine damage.*

12   Loop the new chain over the camshaft sprocket, then turn the sprocket until the timing mark is in the 12 o'clock position **(see illustration)**. Mesh the chain with the crankshaft sprocket and position the camshaft sprocket on the end of the cam. If necessary, turn the camshaft so the dowel pin fits into the sprocket hole with the timing mark in the 12 o'clock position. **Note:** *The number one piston must be at TDC on the compression stroke as the chain and sprockets are installed (see Step 3 above).*

13   Apply Loctite to the camshaft sprocket bolt threads, then install and tighten them to the specified torque. Lubricate the chain with clean engine oil.

14   On small block V8 engines, apply a small amount of RTV sealant to the U-shaped channel on the bottom of the cover, then position a new rubber oil pan seal in the channel **(see illustration)**. The sealant should hold it in place as the cover is installed.

15   On big block V8 engines, cut the tabs off a new front oil pan seal and use gasket

sealant to hold the seal in the bottom of the cover. Apply a 1/8-inch bead of RTV-type gasket sealant to the junction of the oil pan and front face of the block on each side.

16   Apply a thin layer of RTV sealant to both sides of the new gasket, then position it on the engine block. The dowel pins and sealant will hold it in place.

17   Install the timing chain cover on the block, tightening the bolts finger-tight.

18   If the oil pan was removed on a small block V8 engine, reinstall it (Section 12). If it was only loosened, tighten the oil pan bolts, bringing the oil pan up against the lower seal in the timing chain cover.

19   Tighten the timing chain cover bolts to the specified torque.

20   Lubricate the oil seal contact surface of the vibration damper hub with moly-base grease or clean engine oil, then install the damper on the end of the crankshaft. The keyway in the damper must be aligned with the Woodruff key in the crankshaft nose. If

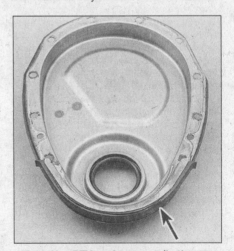

10.14 Use RTV sealant to retain the new rubber oil pan seal (arrow) in the timing chain cover

11.3 When checking the camshaft lobe lift, the dial indicator plunger must be positioned directly above the pushrod

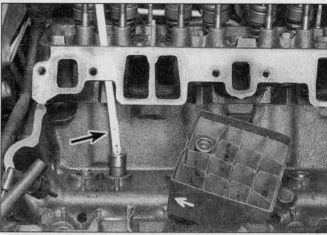

11.11 The lifters on an engine that has accumulated many miles may have to be removed with a special tool (arrow) - store the lifters in an organized manner to make sure they're reinstalled in their original locations

the damper can't be seated by hand, slip a large washer over the bolt, install the bolt and tighten it to push the damper into place. Remove the large washer and tighten the bolt to the specified torque.

21 The remaining installation steps are the reverse of removal.

11 Camshaft, bearings and lifters - removal, inspection and installation

Refer to illustrations 11.3, 11.11, 11.15, 11.18a, 11.18b, 11.18c, 11.18d, 11.20 and 11.22

Camshaft lobe lift check

1 To determine the extent of cam lobe wear, the lobe lift should be checked prior to camshaft removal. Refer to Section 3 and remove the rocker arm covers.

2 Position the number one piston at TDC on the compression stroke (see Section 9).

3 Beginning with the number one cylinder, mount a dial indicator on the engine and position the plunger against the top surface of the first rocker arm. The plunger should be directly above and in line with the pushrod **(see illustration)**.

4 Zero the dial indicator, then very slowly turn the crankshaft in the normal direction of rotation until the indicator needle stops and begins to move in the opposite direction. The point at which it stops indicates maximum cam lobe lift.

5 Record this figure for future reference, then reposition the piston at TDC on the compression stroke.

6 Move the dial indicator to the other number one cylinder rocker arm and repeat the check. Be sure to record the results for each valve.

7 Repeat the check for the remaining valves. Since each piston must be at TDC on

the compression stroke for this procedure, work from cylinder-to-cylinder following the firing order sequence.

8 After the check is complete, compare the results between lobes. The variation between lobes should not exceed Specifications. The results can be more accurately checked when the camshaft is withdrawn from the engine and the lobes measured with a precision micrometer.

Removal

9 Refer to the appropriate Sections and remove the intake manifold, the rocker arms, the pushrods, timing chain, camshaft sprocket, fuel pump and rod. The radiator should be removed as well (Chapter 3). **Note:** *If the vehicle is equipped with air conditioning it may be necessary to remove the air conditioning condenser to remove the camshaft. If the condenser must be removed, the system must first be depressurized by a dealer service department or a service station. Do not disconnect any air conditioning lines until the system has been depressurized.*

10 There are several ways to extract the lifters from the bores. A special tool designed to grip and remove lifters is manufactured by many tool companies and is widely available, but it may not be required in every case. On newer engines without a lot of varnish buildup, the lifters can often be removed with a small magnet or even with your fingers. A machinist's scribe with a bent end can be used to pull the lifters out by positioning the point under the retainer ring inside the top of each lifter. **Caution:** *Do not use pliers to remove the lifters unless you intend to replace them with new ones (along with the camshaft). The pliers will damage the precision machined and hardened lifters, rendering them useless.*

11 Before removing the lifters, arrange to store them in a clearly labeled box to ensure they are reinstalled in their original locations. Remove the lifters and store them where they

will not get dirty **(see illustration)**. Do not attempt to withdraw the camshaft with the lifters in place.

12 Thread a 6-inch long 5/16 - 18 bolt into one of the camshaft sprocket bolt holes to use as a handle when removing the camshaft from the block.

13 Carefully pull the camshaft out. Support the cam near the block so the lobes don't nick or gouge the bearings as it's withdrawn.

Inspection

Camshaft and bearings

14 After the camshaft has been removed from the engine, cleaned with solvent and dried, inspect the bearing journals for uneven wear, pitting and evidence of seizure. If the journals are damaged, the bearing inserts in the block are probably damaged as well. Both the camshaft and bearings will have to be replaced. Replacement of the camshaft bearings requires special tools and techniques which place it beyond the scope of the home mechanic. The block will have to be removed from the vehicle and taken to an automotive machine shop for this procedure.

15 Measure the bearing journals with a micrometer to determine if they're excessively worn or out-of-round **(see illustration)**.

16 Check the camshaft lobes for heat discoloration, score marks, chipped areas, pitting and uneven wear. If the lobes are in good condition and if the lobe lift measurements are as specified, the camshaft can be reused.

Lifters

17 Clean the lifters with solvent and dry them thoroughly without mixing them up.

18 Check each lifter wall, pushrod seat and foot for scuffing, score marks and uneven wear. Each lifter foot (the surface that rides on the cam lobe) must be slightly convex, although this can be difficult to determine by eye. If the base of the lifter is concave **(see illustrations)**, the lifters and camshaft must be replaced. If the lifter walls are damaged or

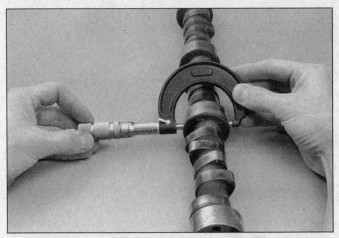

11.15 Check the diameter of each camshaft bearing journal to pinpoint excessive wear and out-of-round conditions

11.18a If the lifters are pitted or rough, they shouldn't be reused

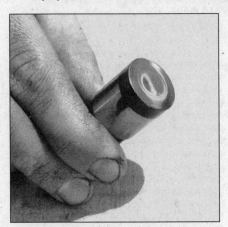

11.18b If the bottom of any lifter is worn concave, scratched or galled, replace the entire set with new lifters

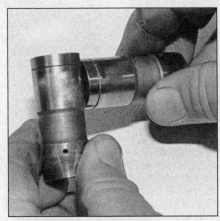

11.18c The foot of each lifter should be slightly convex - the side of another lifter can be used as a straightedge to check it; if it appears flat, it is worn and must not be reused

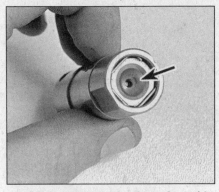

11.18d Check the pushrod seat (arrow) in the top of each lifter for wear

worn (which is not very likely), inspect the lifter bores in the engine block as well. If the pushrod seats (see illustration) are worn, check the pushrod ends.

19   If new lifters are being installed, a new camshaft must also be installed. If a new camshaft is installed, then use new lifters as well. Never install used lifters unless the original camshaft is used and the lifters can be installed in their original locations.

Installation

20   Lubricate the camshaft bearing journals and cam lobes with moly-base grease or engine assembly lube (see illustration).

21   Slide the camshaft into the engine. Support the cam near the block and be careful not to scrape or nick the bearings.

22   Turn the camshaft until the dowel pin is in the 9 o'clock position (see illustration).

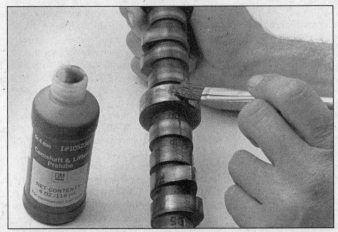

11.20 Be sure to apply moly-base grease or camshaft and lifter prelube to the cam lobes and bearing journals before installing the camshaft

11.22 After the camshaft is in place, turn it until the dowel pin (arrow) is in the 9 o'clock position as shown here

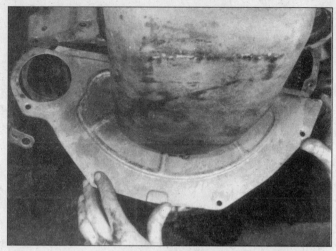

12.7 Remove the flywheel cover

13.3 Make sure the nylon sleeve is in place between the oil pump and oil pump driveshaft

23   Refer to Section 10 and install the timing chain and sprockets.

24   Lubricate the lifters with clean engine oil and install them in the block. If the original lifters are being reinstalled, be sure to return them to their original locations. If a new camshaft was installed, be sure to install new lifters as well.

25   The remaining installation steps are the reverse of removal.

26   Before starting and running the engine, change the oil and install a new oil filter (see Chapter 1).

12   Oil pan - removal and installation

Refer to illustration 12.7

Removal

1   Disconnect the negative cable from the battery.

2   Raise the vehicle and support it securely on jackstands.

3   Drain the engine oil (Chapter 1).

4   Disconnect the idler arm and lower steering linkage (Chapter 10).

5   Disconnect the exhaust pipe from the manifold and converter and lower it out of the way.

6   If equipped with an automatic transmission, remove the converter inspection cover.

7   If equipped with a manual transmission, remove the starter (Chapter 5) and flywheel inspection cover **(see illustration)**.

8   On models with a big block engine, remove the oil filter and disconnect the oil pressure gauge line from the side of the block.

9   Turn the crankshaft until the timing mark on the on the vibration damper is pointed straight down.

10   Remove the oil pan mounting bolts.

11   Separate the pan from the block. If it sticks, tap it with a soft-face hammer to break the gasket seal.

Installation

12   Use a scraper on the mounting surfaces of the oil pan and engine block to remove all old gasket material and sealant. Clean them with lacquer thinner or acetone. Make sure the bolt holes in the block are clean.

13   Check the oil pan flange for distortion, particularly around the bolt holes. If necessary, place the pan on a block of wood and use a hammer to flatten and restore the gasket sealing surface.

14   Remove the old rubber seals from the rear main bearing cap and the timing chain cover, then clean the grooves and install new seals. Use RTV or "Gaskacinch" contact cement to hold the new seals in place.

15   Apply a thin layer of RTV-type sealant to the oil pan flanges and attach new oil pan gaskets. Apply a bead of RTV to the rubber seal-to-block joints as well.

16   Carefully position the pan against the block and install the bolts/nuts finger-tight.

17   Make sure the seals/gaskets haven't shifted, then tighten the bolts/nuts in three steps to the specified torque. Start at the center of the pan and work out toward the ends in a spiral pattern.

18   The remainder of the installation procedure is the reverse of removal.

19   Fill the engine with new oil, start it and check for leaks before placing the vehicle back in service.

13   Oil pump - removal and installation

Refer to illustration 13.3

1   Remove the oil pan as described in Section 12.

2   While supporting the oil pump, remove the pump-to-rear main bearing cap bolt.

3   Lower the pump and remove it, along with the pump driveshaft. Note that on most models a hard nylon sleeve is used to align the oil pump driveshaft and the oil pump

shaft. Make sure the sleeve is in place on the oil pump driveshaft **(see illustration)**. If it isn't there, check the oil pan for the pieces of the sleeve, clean them out of the pan, then get a new sleeve for the oil pump driveshaft.

4   If a new oil pump is installed, make sure the pump driveshaft is mated with the shaft inside the pump.

5   Position the pump on the engine and make sure the slot in the upper end of the driveshaft is aligned with the tang on the lower end of the distributor shaft. The distributor drives the oil pump, so it's absolutely essential that the components mate properly.

6   Install the mounting bolt and tighten it to the specified torque.

7   Install the oil pan.

14   Flywheel/driveplate - removal and installation

Refer to illustration 14.4

1   Raise the vehicle and support it securely on jackstands, then refer to Chapter 7 and remove the transmission. If it's leaking, now would be a very good time to replace the front pump seal/O-ring (automatic transmission only).

2   Remove the pressure plate and clutch disc (see Chapter 8) (manual transmission equipped vehicles). Now is a good time to check/replace the clutch components and pilot bearing.

3   Use a center punch to make alignment marks on the flywheel/driveplate and crankshaft to ensure correct alignment during reinstallation.

4   Remove the bolts that secure the flywheel/driveplate to the crankshaft **(see illustration)**. If the crankshaft turns, wedge a screwdriver through the starter opening to jam the flywheel.

5   Remove the flywheel/driveplate from the crankshaft. Since the flywheel is fairly heavy, be sure to support it while removing the last bolt.

14.4 The flywheel bolts are very tight and will require a large sprocket and 1/2-inch drive breaker bar for removal

15.2 While supporting the cover near the seal bore, drive the old seal out from the inside with a hammer and punch or screwdriver

6   Clean the flywheel to remove grease and oil. Inspect the surface for cracks, rivet grooves, burned areas and score marks. Light scoring can be removed with emery cloth. Check for cracked and broken ring gear teeth. Lay the flywheel on a flat surface and use a straightedge to check for warpage.

7   Clean and inspect the mating surfaces of the flywheel/driveplate and the crankshaft. If the crankshaft rear seal is leaking, replace it before reinstalling the flywheel/driveplate.

8   Position the flywheel/driveplate against the crankshaft. Be sure to align the marks made during removal. Note that some engines have an alignment dowel or staggered bolt holes to ensure correct installation. Before installing the bolts, apply thread locking compound to the threads.

9   Wedge a screwdriver through the starter motor opening to keep the flywheel/driveplate from turning as you tighten the bolts to the torque listed in this Chapter's Specifications.

10   The remainder of installation is the reverse of the removal procedure.

15 Crankshaft oil seals - replacement

Refer to illustrations 15.2, 15.4, 15.11, 15.12a, 15.12b, 15.13 and 15.14

Front seal

Note: *The front seal can be replaced without removing the timing chain cover if you work carefully. The vibration damper must be removed first (Section 10). Next, a seal removal tool should be used to pry the old seal out and the new one should be driven into place with a large socket or piece of pipe and a hammer (the socket or pipe should have an outside diameter that matches the seal). Be sure to apply moly-base grease to the new seal lips and the outer edge to facilitate installation.*

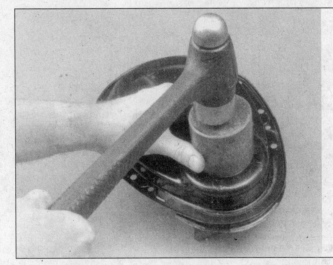

15.4 Clean the bore, then apply a small amount of oil to the outer edge of the seal and drive it squarely into the opening with a large socket or a piece of pipe and a hammer - do not damage the seal in the process!

1   Remove the timing chain cover as described in Section 10.

2   Use a punch or screwdriver and hammer to drive the seal out of the cover from the back side. Support the cover as close to the seal bore as possible **(see illustration)**. Be careful not to distort the cover or scratch the wall of the seal bore. If the engine has accumulated a lot of miles, apply penetrating oil to the seal-to-cover joint on each side and allow it to soak in before attempting to drive the seal out.

3   Clean the bore to remove any old seal material and corrosion. Support the cover on blocks of wood and position the new seal in the bore with the open end of the seal facing in. A small amount of oil applied to the outer edge of the new seal will make installation easier.

4   Drive the seal into the bore with a large socket and hammer until it's completely seated **(see illustration)**. Select a socket that's the same outside diameter as the seal (a section of pipe can be used if a socket isn't available).

5   Reinstall the timing chain cover.

Rear seal

6   The rear main seal can be replaced with the engine in the vehicle. Refer to the appropriate Sections and remove the oil pan and oil pump.

7   Remove the bolts and detach the rear main bearing cap from the engine.

8   The seal section in the bearing cap can be pried out with a screwdriver.

9   To remove the seal section in the block, tap on one end with a hammer and brass punch or wood dowel until the other end protrudes far enough to grip it with a pair of pliers and pull it out. Be very careful not to nick or scratch the crankshaft journal or seal surface as this is done.

10   Inspect the bearing cap and engine block mating surfaces, as well as the cap seal grooves, for nicks, burrs and scratches. Remove any defects with a fine file or deburring tool.

11   A small seal installation tool is usually included when a new seal is purchased. If you didn't receive one, they can also be purchased separately at most auto parts stores

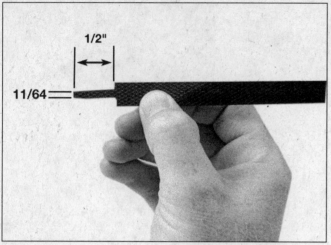

15.11 If the new seal didn't include an installation tool, make one from a piece of brass shim stock 0.004-inch thick

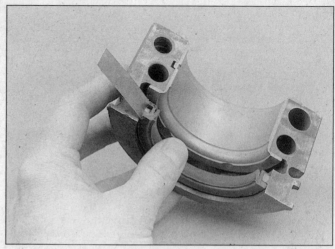

15.12a Using the tool like a "shoehorn", attach the seal section to the bearing cap . . .

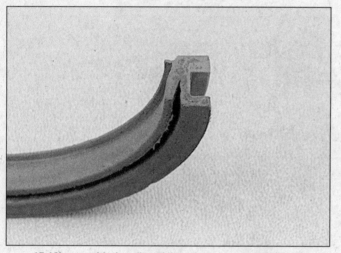

15.12b . . . with the oil seal lip pointing toward the front of the engine

15.13 Position the tool to protect the back side of the seal as it passes over the sharp edge of the ridge - note that the seal straddles the ridge

or you can make one from an old feeler gauge or a piece of brass shim stock **(see illustration).**

12   Using the tool, install one seal section in the cap with the lip facing the front of the engine (if the seal has two lips, the one with the helix must face the front) **(see illustrations).** The ends should be flush with the mating surface of the cap. Make sure it's completely seated.

13   Position the narrow end of the tool so it will protect the back side of the seal as it passes over the sharp edge of the ridge in the block **(see illustration).**

14   Lubricate the seal lips and the groove in the back side with moly-base grease or clean engine oil - do not get any lubricant on the seal ends. Insert the seal into the block, over the tool **(see illustration). Caution:** *Make sure the lip points toward the front of the engine when the seal is installed.*

15   Push the seal into place, using the tool like a "shoehorn". Turning the crankshaft may help to draw the seal into place. When both

15.14 Make sure the seal lip faces the front of the engine and hold the tool in place to protect the seal as it's installed

ends of the seal are flush with the block surface, remove the tool.

16   Apply a thin, even coat of anaerobic sealer to the ends of the seal and also to the block surface adjoining the seal where the

bearing cap touches it. Don't get any sealant on the bearing face, crankshaft journal, seal ends or seal lips. Lubricate the cap seal lips with moly-base grease or clean engine oil.

17   Carefully position the bearing cap on the

block, install the bolts and tighten them to 10-to-12 ft-lbs only. Tap the crankshaft forward and backward with a lead or brass hammer to line up the main bearing and crankshaft thrust surfaces, then tighten the rear bearing cap bolts to the specified torque.
18   Install the oil pump and oil pan.

16   Engine mounts - check and replacement

Refer to illustration 16.1

1   Engine mounts seldom require attention, but broken or deteriorated mounts should be replaced immediately or the added strain placed on the driveline components may cause damage **(see illustration)**.

Check

2   During the check, the engine must be raised slightly to remove the weight from the mounts. Refer to Chapter 1 and remove the distributor cap before raising the engine.
3   Raise the vehicle and support it securely on jackstands, then position the jack under the engine oil pan. Place a large block of wood between the jack head and the oil pan, then carefully raise the engine just enough to take the weight off the mounts.
4   Check the mounts to see if the rubber is cracked, hardened or separated from the metal plates. Sometimes the rubber will split

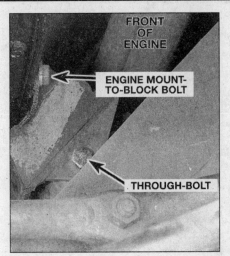 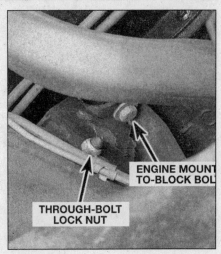

16.1 Typical engine mounting

right down the center. Rubber preservative should be applied to the mounts to slow deterioration.
5   Check for relative movement between the mount plates and the engine or frame (use a large screwdriver or pry bar to attempt to move the mounts). If movement is noted, lower the engine and tighten the mount fasteners.

Replacement

6   Disconnect the negative cable from the

battery, then raise the vehicle and support it securely on jackstands.
7   Remove the nut and withdraw the mount through-bolt from the frame bracket.
8   Raise the engine slightly, then remove the mount-to-block bolts and detach the mount.
9   Installation is the reverse of removal. Use thread locking compound on the mount bolts and be sure to tighten them securely.

Notes

Chapter 2 Part B
General engine overhaul procedures

Contents

Specifications

General

Compression pressure	
Standard	150 psi
Maximum variation between cylinders	20 psi
Oil pressure	40 to 45 psi at 2000 rpm

Block

Cylinder bore diameter	
305	3.7350 to 3.7385 in
327 and 350	3.9995 to 4.0025 in
427 and 454	4.2495 to 4.2525 in
Taper limit	0.001 in
Out-of-round limit	0.002 in

Heads and valve train

Warpage limit	0.003 in per 6 in
Valve seat angle	46-degrees
Valve seat width	
Intake	1/32 to 1/16 in
Exhaust	1/16 to 3/32 in
Valve face angle	45-degrees
Minimum valve margin width	1/32 in

Heads and valve train (continued)

Valve stem-to-valve guide clearance
    Intake valves .... 0.0010 to 0.0027 in
    Exhaust valves
        327 (1968 only) .... 0.0017 to 0.0027 in
        305 and 350 .... 0.0010 to 0.0027 in
        427 (1968 only).. 0.0015 to 0.0032 in
        427 and 454 (1969 to 1974).. 0.0012 to 0.0027 in
Valve spring free length
    Small block .... 2.03 in
    Big block .... 2.12 in
Valve spring installed height
    Small block .... 1-45/64 in
    Big block .... 1-56/64 in

Crankshaft

Main journal diameter
    327
        1 .... 2.4502 in
        2,3, 4 .... 2.4505 in
        5 .... 2.4507 in
    305, and 350
        1 .... 2.4484 to 2.4493 in
        2, 3 and 4 .... 2.4481 to 2.4490 in
        5 .... 2.4479 to 2.4488 in
    427 and 454
        1, 2, 3 and 4 .... 2.7481 to 2.7490 in
        5 .... 2.7476 to 2.7486 in
Main journal taper limit .... 0.001 in
Main journal out-of-round limit .... 0.001 in
Main bearing oil clearance
    1968 and 1969, all engines .... 0.0018 in
    305 and 350
        1 .... 0.0008 to 0.0020 in
        2, 3 and 4 .... 0.0011 to 0.0023 in
        5 .... 0.0017 to 0.0032 in
    427 and 454
        1, 2, 3 and 4 .... 0.0013 to 0.0025 in
        5 .... 0.0024 to 0.0040 in
Rod journal diameter
    305 and 350 .... 2.0988 to 2.0998 in
    427 and 454 .... 2.1990 to 2.2000 in
Rod journal taper limit .... 0.001 in
Rod journal out-of-round limit .... 0.001 in
Rod bearing oil clearance
    327 .... 0.0018 in
    305 and 350 .... 0.0013 to 0.0035 in
    427 and 454 .... 0.0009 to 0.0025 in
Rod end play
    Small block .... 0.008 to 0.014 in
    Big block .... 0.015 to 0.025 in
Crankshaft end play
    327 .... 0.008 in
    305, and 350 .... 0.002 to 0.006 in
    427 and 454 .... 0.006 to 0.010 in

Pistons and rings

Piston-to-bore clearance
    Small block
        Standard .... 0.0007 to 0.0013 in
        Service limit .... 0.0027 in
    Big-block
        Standard .... 0.0024 to 0.0034 in
        Service limit .... 0.0045 in
Piston ring side clearance
    305, 327 and 350
        Both compression rings.. 0.0012 to 0.0032 in
        Oil control .... 0.0010 to 0.0030 in

427 and 454
    Compression (both) .... 0.0017 to 0.0032 in
    Oil control .... 0.000 to 0.005 in
Piston ring end gap
    Top compression (all) .... 0.010 to 0.020 in
    2nd compression (all) .... 0.010 to 0.025 in
    Oil control
        Small block .... 0.015 to 0.055 in
        427 .... 0.010 to 0.030 in
        454 .... 0.015 to 0.055 in

Torque specifications*

Ft-lbs (unless otherwise indicated)

Connecting rod cap nuts
    305, 327 and 350 45
    427 and 454 50
Main bearing cap bolts
    Small block
        2-bolt main caps 80
        4-bolt main caps (to 1976)
            Inner 70
            Outer 65
        4-bolt main caps (1977 on)
            Inner 80
            Outer 70
    Big block (all) 110
Rocker arm studs (screw-in type).. 50

* **Note**: *Refer to Part A for additional torque specifications.*

1 General information

Included in this portion of Chapter 2 are the general overhaul procedures for cylinder head and internal engine components. The information ranges from advice concerning preparation for an overhaul and the purchase of replacement parts to detailed, step-by-step procedures covering removal and installation of internal engine components and the inspection of parts.

The following Sections have been written based on the assumption the engine has been removed from the vehicle. For information concerning in-vehicle engine repair, as well as removal and installation of the external components necessary for the overhaul, see Part A of this Chapter and Section 7 of this Part.

The Specifications included here in Part B are only those necessary for the inspection and overhaul procedures which follow. Refer to Part A for additional Specifications.

2 Engine removal - methods and precautions

If you've decided an engine must be removed for overhaul or major repair work, several preliminary steps should be taken.

Locating a work area is extremely important. A shop is, of course, the most desirable place to work. Adequate work space, along with storage space for the vehicle, will be needed. If a shop or garage isn't available, at the very least a flat, level, clean work surface made of concrete or asphalt is required.

Cleaning the engine compartment and engine before beginning the removal procedure will help keep tools clean and organized.

An engine hoist or A-frame will be needed. Make sure the equipment is rated in excess of the combined weight of the engine and accessories. Safety is of primary importance, considering the potential hazards involved in lifting the engine out of the vehicle.

If the engine is being removed by a novice, a helper should be available. Advice and aid from someone more experienced would also be helpful. There are many instances when one person cannot simultaneously perform all of the operations required when lifting the engine out of the vehicle.

Plan the operation ahead of time. Arrange for or obtain all of the tools and equipment you'll need prior to beginning the job. Some of the equipment necessary to perform engine removal and installation safely and with relative ease are (in addition to an engine hoist) a heavy duty floor jack, complete sets of wrenches and sockets as described at the front of this manual, wooden blocks and plenty of rags and cleaning solvent for mopping up spilled oil, coolant and gasoline. If the hoist must be rented, make sure you arrange for it in advance and perform beforehand all of the operations possible without it. This will save you money and time.

Plan for the vehicle to be out of use for a considerable amount of time. A machine shop will be required to perform some of the work the do-it-yourselfer can't accomplish due to a lack of special equipment. These shops often have a busy schedule, so it would be wise to consult them before removing the engine to accurately estimate the amount of time required to rebuild or repair components that may need work.

Always use extreme caution when removing and installing the engine. Serious injury can result from careless actions. Plan ahead, take your time and a job of this nature, although major, can be accomplished successfully.

3 Engine overhaul - general information

It's not always easy to determine when, or if, an engine should be completely overhauled, as a number of factors must be considered.

High mileage is not necessarily an indication that an overhaul is needed, while low mileage doesn't preclude the need for an overhaul. Frequency of servicing is probably the most important consideration. An engine that has had regular and frequent oil and filter changes, as well as other required maintenance, will most likely give many thousands of miles of reliable service. Conversely, a neglected engine may require an overhaul very early in its life.

Excessive oil consumption is an indication that piston rings and/or valve seals or guides are in need of attention. Make sure oil leaks aren't responsible before deciding the rings and/or guides are bad. Have a cylinder compression or leakdown test performed by an experienced tune-up mechanic to determine the extent of the work required.

If the engine is making obvious knocking or rumbling noises, the connecting rod and/or main bearings are probably at fault. If your vehicle is equipped with an oil pressure warning light instead of an oil pressure gauge, check the pressure with a gauge temporarily installed in place of the oil pressure sending unit and compare it to the Specifications. If the pressure is extremely low, the bearings and/or oil pump are probably worn out.

Loss of power, rough running, excessive valve train noise and high fuel consumption rates may also point to the need for an overhaul, especially if they are all present at the same time. If a complete tune-up doesn't remedy the situation, major mechanical work is the only solution.

An engine overhaul involves restoring the internal parts to the specifications of a new engine. During an overhaul, the piston rings are replaced and the cylinder walls are reconditioned (rebored and/or honed). If a rebore is done, new pistons are required. The main bearings, connecting rod bearings and camshaft bearings are generally replaced with new ones and, if necessary, the crankshaft may be reground to restore the journals.

Generally, the valves are serviced as well, since they're usually in less-than-perfect condition at this point. While the engine is being overhauled, other components, such as the carburetor, distributor, starter and alternator, can be rebuilt as well. The end result should be a like new engine that will give many trouble free miles. **Note:** *Critical cooling system components such as the hoses, the drivebelts, the thermostat and the water pump MUST be replaced with new parts when an engine is overhauled. The radiator should be checked carefully to ensure it isn't clogged or leaking. If in doubt, replace it with a new one. Also, we do not recommend overhauling the oil pump - always install a new one when an engine is rebuilt.*

Before beginning the engine overhaul, read through the entire procedure to familiarize yourself with the scope and requirements of the job. Overhauling an engine isn't difficult, but it is time consuming. Plan on the vehicle being tied up for a minimum of two weeks, especially if parts must be taken to an automotive machine shop for repair or reconditioning. Check on availability of parts and make sure any necessary special tools and equipment are obtained in advance. Most work can be done with typical hand tools, although a number of precision measuring tools are required for inspecting parts to determine if they must be replaced. Often an automotive machine shop will handle the inspection of parts and offer advice concerning reconditioning and replacement. **Note:** *Always wait until the engine has been completely disassembled and all components, especially the engine block, have been inspected before deciding what service and*

repair operations must be performed by an automotive machine shop. Since the block's condition will be the major factor to consider when determining whether to overhaul the original engine or buy a rebuilt one, never purchase parts or have machine work done on other components until the block has been thoroughly inspected. As a general rule, time is the primary cost of an overhaul, so it doesn't pay to install worn or substandard parts.

As a final note, to ensure maximum life and minimum trouble from a rebuilt engine, everything must be assembled with care in a spotlessly clean environment.

4 Cylinder compression check

1   A compression check will tell you what mechanical condition the upper end (pistons, rings, valves, head gaskets) of your engine is in. Specifically, it can tell you if the compression is down due to leakage caused by worn piston rings, defective valves and seats or a blown head gasket. **Note:** *The engine must be at normal operating temperature for this check and the battery must be fully charged.*

2   Begin by cleaning the area around the spark plugs before you remove them (compressed air works best for this). This will prevent dirt from getting into the cylinders as the compression check is being done. Remove all of the spark plugs from the engine.

3   Block the throttle wide open and disconnect the wire from the BAT terminal on the distributor cap (coil-in-cap models). On remote coil models, remove the coil wire from the distributor cap and ground the wire on the engine block.

4   With the compression gauge in the number one spark plug hole, crank the engine over at least four compression strokes and watch the gauge. The compression should build up quickly in a healthy engine. Low compression on the first stroke, followed by gradually increasing pressure on successive strokes, indicates worn piston rings. A low compression reading on the first stroke, which does not build up during successive strokes, indicates leaking valves or a blown head gasket (a cracked head could also be the cause). Deposits on the undersides of the valve heads can also cause low compression. Record the highest gauge reading obtained.

5   Repeat the procedure for the remaining cylinders and compare the results to this Chapter's Specifications.

6   Add some engine oil (about three squirts from a plunger-type oil can) to each cylinder, through the spark plug hole, and repeat the test.

7   If the compression increases after the oil is added, the piston rings are definitely worn. If the compression does not increase significantly, the leakage is occurring at the valves or head gasket. Leakage past the valves may be caused by burned valve seats and/or faces or warped, cracked or bent valves.

8   If two adjacent cylinders have equally

low compression, there is a strong possibility the head gasket between them is blown. The appearance of coolant in the combustion chambers or the crankcase would verify this condition.

9   If the compression is unusually high, the combustion chambers are probably coated with carbon deposits. If that's the case, the cylinder head(s) should be removed and decarbonized.

10   If compression is way down or varies greatly between cylinders, it would be a good idea to have a leak-down test performed by an automotive repair shop. This test will pinpoint exactly where the leakage is occurring and how severe it is.

5 Engine rebuilding alternatives

The do-it-yourselfer is faced with a number of options when performing an engine overhaul. The decision to replace the engine block, piston/connecting rod assemblies and crankshaft depends on a number of factors, with the number one consideration being the condition of the block. Other considerations are cost, access to machine shop facilities, parts availability, time required to complete the project and the extent of prior mechanical experience on the part of the do-it-yourselfer.

Some of the rebuilding alternatives include:

Individual parts - If the inspection procedures reveal the engine block and most engine components are in reusable condition, purchasing individual parts may be the most economical alternative. The block, crankshaft and piston/connecting rod assemblies should all be inspected carefully. Even if the block shows little wear, the cylinder bores should be surface honed.

Crankshaft kit - This rebuild package consists of a reground crankshaft and a matched set of pistons and connecting rods. The pistons will already be installed on the connecting rods. Piston rings and the necessary bearings will be included in the kit. These kits are commonly available for standard cylinder bores, as well as for engine blocks which have been bored to a regular oversize.

Short block - A short block consists of an engine block with a crankshaft and piston/connecting rod assemblies already installed. All new bearings are incorporated and all clearances will be correct. The existing camshaft, valve train components, cylinder heads and external parts can be bolted to the short block with little or no machine shop work necessary.

Long block - A long block consists of a short block plus an oil pump, oil pan, cylinder heads, rocker arm covers, camshaft and valve train components, timing sprockets and chain and timing cover. All components are installed with new bearings, seals and gaskets incorporated throughout. The installation of manifolds and external parts is all that's necessary.

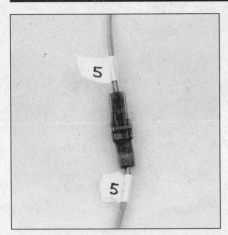

6.5 Label each wire before unplugging the connector

Give careful thought to which alternative is best for you and discuss the situation with local automotive machine shops, auto parts dealers or parts store countermen before ordering or purchasing replacement parts.

6 Engine - removal and installation

Refer to illustrations 6.5, 6.19 and 6.24
Warning: *The air conditioning system is under high pressure! Have a dealer service department or service station discharge the system before disconnecting any air conditioning system hoses or fittings.*

Removal

1 Refer to Chapter 4 and relieve the fuel system pressure (TBI equipped vehicles only), then disconnect the negative cable from the battery.
2 Cover the fenders and cowl and remove the hood (see Chapter 11). Special pads are available to protect the fenders, but an old

bedspread or blanket will also work.
3 Remove the air cleaner assembly.
4 Drain the cooling system (see Chapter 1).
5 Label the vacuum lines, emissions system hoses, wiring connectors, ground straps and fuel lines, to ensure correct reinstallation, then detach them. Pieces of masking tape with numbers or letters written on them work well **(see illustration)**. If there's any possibility of confusion, make a sketch of the engine compartment and clearly label the lines, hoses and wires.
6 Label and detach all coolant hoses from the engine.
7 Remove the cooling fan, shroud and radiator (see Chapter 3).
8 Remove the drivebelts (see Chapter 1).
9 **Warning:** *Gasoline is extremely flammable, so extra precautions must be taken when working on any part of the fuel system. DO NOT smoke or allow open flames or bare light bulbs near the vehicle. Also, don't work in a garage if a natural gas appliance with a pilot light is present.* Disconnect the fuel lines running from the engine to the chassis (see Chapter 4). Plug or cap all open fittings/lines.
10 Disconnect the throttle linkage (and TV linkage/speed control cable, if equipped) from the engine (see Chapter 4).
11 On power steering equipped vehicles, unbolt the power steering pump (see Chapter 10). Leave the lines/hoses attached and make sure the pump is kept in an upright position in the engine compartment (use wire or rope to restrain it out of the way).
12 On air conditioned models, unbolt the compressor (see Chapter 3) and set it aside. Do not disconnect the hoses.
13 Drain the engine oil (Chapter 1) and remove the filter.
14 Remove the starter motor (see Chapter 5).
15 Remove the alternator (see Chapter 5).
16 Unbolt the exhaust system from the engine (see Chapter 4).

17 If you're working on a vehicle with an automatic transmission, refer to Chapter 7 and remove the torque converter-to-driveplate fasteners.
18 Support the transmission with a jack. Position a block of wood between them to prevent damage to the transmission. Special transmission jacks with safety chains are available - use one if possible.
19 Attach an engine sling or a length of chain to the lifting brackets on the engine **(see illustration)**.
20 Roll the hoist into position and connect the sling to it. Take up the slack in the sling or chain, but don't lift the engine. **Warning:** *DO NOT place any part of your body under the engine when it's supported only by a hoist or other lifting device.*
21 Remove the transmission-to-engine block bolts.
22 Remove the engine mount-to-frame bolts.
23 Recheck to be sure nothing is still connecting the engine to the transmission or vehicle. Disconnect anything still remaining.
24 Raise the engine slightly. Carefully work it forward to separate it from the transmission. If you're working on a vehicle with an automatic transmission, be sure the torque converter stays in the transmission (clamp a pair of vise-grips to the housing to keep the converter from sliding out). If you're working on a vehicle with a manual transmission, the input shaft must be completely disengaged from the clutch. Slowly raise the engine out of the engine compartment **(see illustration)**. Check carefully to make sure nothing is hanging up.
25 Remove the flywheel/driveplate and mount the engine on an engine stand.

Installation

26 Check the engine and transmission mounts. If they're worn or damaged, replace them.
27 If you're working on a manual transmis-

6.19 Make sure the chain is bolted securely to the engine at two points diagonally across from each other, then connect the hoist and take up the slack in the chains

6.24 Have an assistant steady the engine as it's raised out of the vehicle

sion equipped vehicle, install the clutch and pressure plate (see Chapter 7). Now is a good time to install a new clutch.

28   Carefully lower the engine into the engine compartment - make sure the engine mounts line up.

29   If you're working on an automatic transmission equipped vehicle, guide the torque converter into the crankshaft following the procedure outlined in Chapter 7.

30   If you're working on a manual transmission equipped vehicle, apply a dab of high-temperature grease to the input shaft and guide it into the crankshaft pilot bearing until the bellhousing is flush with the engine block.

31   Install the transmission-to-engine bolts and tighten them securely. **Caution:** *DO NOT use the bolts to force the transmission and engine together!*

32   Reinstall the remaining components in the reverse order of removal.

33   Add coolant, oil, power steering and transmission fluid as needed.

34   Run the engine and check for leaks and proper operation of all accessories, then install the hood and test drive the vehicle.

35   Have the air conditioning system recharged and leak tested.

7   Engine overhaul - disassembly sequence

1   It's much easier to disassemble and work on the engine if it's mounted on a portable engine stand. These stands can often be rented quite cheaply from an equipment rental yard. Before the engine is mounted on a stand, the flywheel/driveplate should be removed from the engine.

2   If a stand isn't available, it's possible to disassemble the engine with it blocked up on a sturdy workbench or on the floor. Be extra careful not to tip or drop the engine when working without a stand.

3   If you're going to obtain a rebuilt engine, all external components must come off first, to be transferred to the replacement engine, just as they will if you are doing a complete engine overhaul yourself. These include:

Alternator and brackets
Emissions control components
Distributor, spark plug wires and spark plugs
Thermostat and housing cover
Water pump
Carburetor or TBI components
Intake/exhaust manifolds
Oil filter
Engine mounts
Clutch and flywheel/driveplate

Note: *When removing the external components from the engine, pay close attention to details that may be helpful or important during installation. Note the installed position of gaskets, seals, spacers, pins, washers, bolts and other small items.*

4   If you're obtaining a short block, which consists of the engine block, crankshaft, pis-

8.2 A small plastic bag, with an appropriate label, can be used to store the valve train components so they can be kept together and reinstalled in the original position

tons and connecting rods all assembled, then the cylinder heads, oil pan and oil pump will have to be removed as well. See *Engine rebuilding alternatives* for additional information regarding the different possibilities to be considered.

5   If you're planning a complete overhaul, the engine must be disassembled and the internal components removed in the following general order:

Rocker arm covers
Rocker arms and pushrods
Intake and exhaust manifolds
Valve lifters
Cylinder heads
Oil pan
Timing chain cover
Timing chain and sprockets
Camshaft
Oil pump
Piston/connecting rod assemblies
Crankshaft and main bearings

6   Critical cooling system components such as the hoses, the drivebelts, the thermostat and the water pump MUST be replaced with new parts when an engine is overhauled. Also, we do not recommend overhauling the oil pump - always install a new one when an engine is rebuilt.

7   Before beginning the disassembly and overhaul procedures, make sure the following items are available:

Common hand tools
Small cardboard boxes or plastic bags for storing parts
Gasket scraper
Ridge reamer
Vibration damper puller
Micrometers
Telescoping gauges
Dial indicator set
Valve spring compressor
Cylinder surfacing hone
Piston ring groove cleaning tool
Electric drill
Tap and die set
Wire brushes
Oil gallery brushes
Cleaning solvent

8   Cylinder head - disassembly

Refer to illustrations 8.2, 8.3a and 8.3b

Note: New and rebuilt cylinder heads are commonly available for most engines at dealerships and auto parts stores. Due to the fact that some specialized tools are necessary for the disassembly and inspection procedures, and replacement parts may not be readily available, it may be more practical and economical for the home mechanic to purchase replacement heads rather than taking the time to disassemble, inspect and recondition the originals.

Caution: *On Big Block engines, two head designs are generally available - "open chamber" and "closed chamber." While these heads will interchange as far as bolt patterns, accessory mounting, etc. is concerned, the different combustion chamber designs require different piston dome shapes. If you're purchasing a set of reconditioned cylinder heads, make sure the new heads match the combustion chamber design of the originals.*

1   Cylinder head disassembly involves removal of the intake and exhaust valves and related components. If they're still in place, remove the rocker arm nuts, pivot balls and rocker arms from the cylinder head studs. Label the parts or store them separately so they can be reinstalled in their original locations.

2   Before the valves are removed, arrange to label and store them, along with their related components, so they can be kept separate and reinstalled in the same valve guides they are removed from **(see illustration)**.

3   Compress the springs on the first valve with a spring compressor and remove the keepers **(see illustration)**. Carefully release the valve spring compressor and remove the retainer and (if used) rotator, shield, springs and spring seat or shims (if used). Remove the oil seal(s) from the valve stem and the umbrella-type seal from over the guide boss (if used), then pull the valve out of the head. If the valve binds in the guide (won't pull

8.3a Use a valve spring compressor to compress the spring, then remove the keepers from the valve stem

8.3b If the valve won't pull through the guide, deburr the edge of the stem end and the area around the top of the keeper groove with a file or whetstone

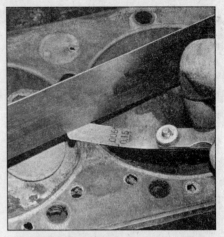

9.12a Check the cylinder head gasket surface for warpage by trying to slip a feeler gauge under the straightedge (see this Chapter's Specifications for the maximum warpage allowed and use a feeler gauge of that thickness)

through), push it back into the head and deburr the area around the keeper groove with a fine file or whetstone **(see illustration)**.

4   Repeat the procedure for the remaining valves. Remember to keep all the parts for each valve together so they can be reinstalled in the same locations.

5   Once the valves and related components have been removed and stored in an organized manner, the head should be thoroughly cleaned and inspected. If a complete engine overhaul is being done, finish the engine disassembly procedures before beginning the cylinder head cleaning and inspection process.

9   Cylinder head - cleaning and inspection

Refer to illustrations 9.12a, 9.12b, 9.14, 9.15, 9.16, 9.17, 9.18 and 9.19

1   Thorough cleaning of the cylinder heads and related valve train components, followed by a detailed inspection, will enable you to decide how much valve service work must be done during the engine overhaul. **Note:** *If the engine was severely overheated, the cylinder heads may be warped.*

Cleaning

2   Scrape away all traces of old gasket material and sealing compound from the head gasket, intake manifold and exhaust manifold sealing surfaces. Be very careful not to gouge the cylinder head. Special gasket removal solvents, which soften gaskets and make removal much easier, are available at auto parts stores.

3   Remove any built up scale from the coolant passages.

4   Run a stiff wire brush through the various holes to remove any deposits that may have formed in them.

5   Run an appropriate size tap into each of the threaded holes to remove any corrosion and thread sealant that may be present. If

compressed air is available, use it to clear the holes of debris produced by this operation.

6   Clean the rocker arm pivot stud threads with a wire brush.

7   Clean the cylinder head with solvent and dry it thoroughly. Compressed air will speed the drying process and ensure that all holes and recessed areas are clean. **Note:** *Decarbonizing chemicals are available and may prove very useful when cleaning cylinder heads and valve train components. They are very caustic and should be used with caution. Be sure to follow the instructions on the container.*

8   Clean the rocker arms, pivot balls, nuts and pushrods with solvent and dry them thoroughly (don't mix them up during the cleaning process). Compressed air will speed the drying process and can be used to clean out the oil passages.

9   Clean all the valve springs, shields, keepers and retainers (or rotators) with solvent and dry them thoroughly. Do the components from one valve at a time to avoid mixing up the parts.

10   Scrape off any heavy deposits that may have formed on the valves, then use a motorized wire brush to remove deposits from the

valve heads and stems. Again, make sure the valves don't get mixed up.

Inspection

Note: *Be sure to perform all of the following inspection procedures before concluding machine shop work is required. Make a list of the items that need attention.*

Cylinder head

11   Inspect the head very carefully for cracks, evidence of coolant leakage and other damage. If cracks are found, a new cylinder head should be obtained.

12   Using a straightedge and feeler gauge, check the head gasket mating surface for warpage **(see illustrations)**. If the warpage exceeds the specified limit, it can be resurfaced at an automotive machine shop. **Note:** *If the heads are resurfaced, the intake manifold flanges will also require machining.*

13   Examine the valve seats in each of the combustion chambers. If they're pitted, cracked or burned, the head will require valve service that's beyond the scope of the home mechanic.

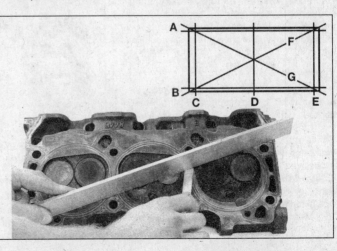

9.12b Make the check with the straightedge positioned lengthwise (on each side), across the head (at three places) and diagonally (corner-to-corner)

9.14 A dial indicator can be used to determine the valve stem-to-guide clearance (move the valve stem as indicated by the arrows)

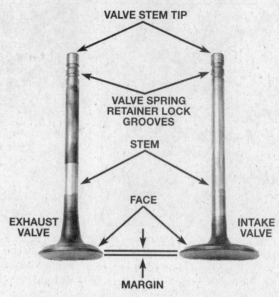

9.15 Check for valve wear at the points shown here

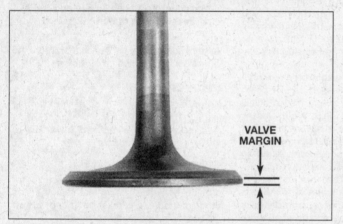

9.16 The margin width on each valve must be as specified (if no margin exists, the valve cannot be reused)

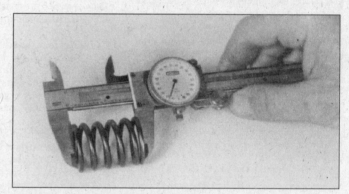

9.17 Measure the free length of each valve spring with a dial or vernier caliper

14   Check the valve stem-to-guide clearance by measuring the lateral movement of the valve stem with a dial indicator attached securely to the head **(see illustration)**. The valve must be in the guide and approximately 1/16-inch off the seat. The total valve stem movement indicated by the gauge needle must be divided by two to obtain the actual clearance. After this is done, if there is still some doubt regarding the condition of the valve guides, they should be checked by an automotive machine shop (the cost should be minimal).

Valves

15   Carefully inspect each valve face for uneven wear, deformation, cracks, pits and burned spots. Check the valve stem for scuffing and galling and the neck for cracks. Rotate the valve and check for any obvious indication that it's bent. Look for pits and excessive wear on the end of the stem **(see illustration)**. The presence of any of these conditions indicates the need for valve service by an automotive machine shop.

16   Measure the margin width on each valve. Any valve with a margin narrower than

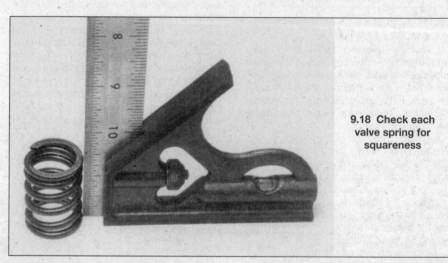

9.18 Check each valve spring for squareness

1/32-inch will have to be replaced with a new one **(see illustration)**.

Valve components

17   Check each valve spring for wear (on the ends) and pits. Measure the free length and compare it to the Specifications **(see illustration)**. Any springs that are shorter

than specified have sagged and shouldn't be reused. The tension of all springs should be checked with a special fixture before deciding they are suitable for use in a rebuilt engine (take the springs to an automotive machine shop for this check).

18   Stand each spring on a flat surface and check it for squareness **(see illustration)**. If

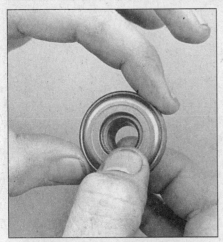

9.19 The exhaust valve rotators can be checked by turning the inner and outer sections in opposite directions - feel for smooth movement and excessive play

any of the springs are distorted or sagged, replace all of them with new parts.

19 Check the spring retainers (or rotators) and keepers for obvious wear and cracks **(see illustration)**. Any questionable parts should be replaced with new ones, as extensive damage will occur if they fail during engine operation.

Rocker arm components

20 Check the rocker arm faces (the areas that contact the pushrod ends and valve stems) for pits, wear, galling, score marks and rough spots. Check the rocker arm pivot contact areas and pivot balls as well. Look for cracks in each rocker arm and nut.

21 Inspect the pushrod ends for scuffing and excessive wear. Roll each pushrod on a flat surface, such as a piece of plate glass, to determine if it's bent.

22 Check the rocker arm studs in the cylinder heads for damaged threads and secure installation. The press-in rocker arm studs used in most small block applications cannot be replaced by the home mechanic due to the need for precision reaming equipment and a press suitable for the job. If any studs are damaged, the head should be taken to an automotive machine shop for stud replacement.

23 Some small block engines and most big block engines use screwed in rather than pressed in rocker arm studs. Also, most engines with screw-in studs use a guide plate, attached to the head by the studs, to maintain pushrod-to-rocker arm alignment. If an engine equipped with screw-in studs is found to have worn, bent or otherwise damaged studs, the studs can be removed individually and replaced. Be sure to replace the guide plates under the studs and apply RTV sealant to the stud threads.

All components

24 Any damaged or excessively worn parts must be replaced with new ones.

25 If the inspection process indicates the valve components are in generally poor condition and worn beyond the limits specified, which is usually the case in an engine that's being overhauled, reassemble the valves in the cylinder head and refer to Section 10 for valve servicing recommendations.

26 If the inspection turns up no excessively worn parts, and if the valve faces and seats are in good condition, the valve train components can be reinstalled in the cylinder head without major servicing. Refer to the appropriate Section for the cylinder head reassembly procedure.

10 Valves - servicing

1 Because of the complex nature of the job and the special tools and equipment needed, servicing of the valves, the valve seats and the valve guides, commonly known as a valve job, is best left to a professional.

2 The home mechanic can remove and disassemble the heads, do the initial cleaning and inspection, then reassemble and deliver the heads to a dealer service department or an automotive machine shop for the actual valve servicing.

3 The dealer service department, or automotive machine shop, will remove the valves and springs, recondition or replace the valves and valve seats, recondition the valve guides, check and replace the valve springs, spring retainers or rotators and keepers (as necessary), replace the valve seals with new ones, reassemble the valve components and make sure the installed spring height is correct. The cylinder head gasket surface will also be resurfaced if it's warped.

4 After the valve job has been performed by a professional, the head will be in like-new condition. When the head is returned, be sure to clean it again before installation on the engine to remove any metal particles and abrasive grit that may still be present from the valve service or head resurfacing operations. Use compressed air, if available, to blow out all the oil holes and passages.

11 Cylinder head - reassembly

Refer to illustration 11.8

1 Regardless of whether or not the heads were sent to an automotive machine shop for valve servicing, make sure they are clean before beginning reassembly.

2 If the heads were sent out for valve servicing, the valves and related components will already be in place. Begin the reassembly procedure with Step 8.

3 Beginning at one end of the head, lubricate and install the first valve. Apply moly-base grease or clean engine oil to the valve stem.

4 Three different types of valve stem oil seals are used on these engines, depending on year, engine size and horsepower rating. The most common is a small O-ring which simply fits around the valve stem just above the guide boss. A second type is a flat O-ring which fits into a groove in the valve stem just below the valve stem keeper groove. On most high horsepower applications, an umbrella-type seal which extends down over the valve guide boss is used over the valve stem. In most cases the umbrella type seal is used in conjunction with the flat O-ring type seal.

5 Drop the spring seat or shim(s) over the valve guide and set the valve springs, shield and retainer (or rotator) in place.

6 Compress the springs with a valve spring compressor and install the O-ring oil seal in the lower groove of the valve stem. Make sure the seal is not twisted - it must lie perfectly flat in the groove **(see illustration 5.9 in Chapter 2, Part A)**. Position the keepers in the upper groove, then slowly release the compressor and make sure the keepers seat properly. Apply a small dab of grease to each keeper to hold it in place if necessary.

7 Repeat the procedure for the remaining valves. Be sure to return the components to their original locations - do not mix them up!

8 Once all the valves are in place in both heads, the valve stem O-ring seals must be checked to make sure they don't leak. This procedure requires a vacuum pump and spe-

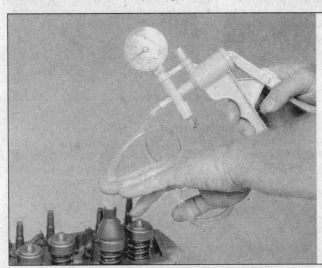

11.8 A special adapter and a vacuum pump are required to check the O-ring valve stem seals for leaks

12.1 A ridge reamer is required to remove the ridge from the top of each cylinder - do this before removing the pistons!

12.3 Check the connecting rod side clearance with a feeler gauge as shown

12.4 Mark the rods and caps (arrow) with a center punch so they can be reassembled as matched sets

12.5 To prevent damage to the crankshaft journals and cylinder walls, slip sections of rubber or plastic hose over the rod bolts before removing the pistons

cial adapter, so it may be a good idea to have it done by a dealer service department, repair shop or automotive machine shop. The adapter is positioned on each valve retainer or rotator and vacuum is applied with the hand pump (see illustration). If the vacuum cannot be maintained, the seal is leaking and must be checked/replaced before the head is installed on the engine.

9   Check the installed valve spring height with a ruler graduated in 1/32-inch increments or a dial caliper. If the heads were sent out for service work, the installed height should be correct (but don't automatically assume that it is). The measurement is taken from the top of each spring seat or shim(s) to the top of the oil shield (or the bottom of the retainer/rotator, the two points are the same). If the height is greater than specified, shims can be added under the springs to correct it. **Caution:** *Do not, under any circumstances, shim the springs to the point where the installed height is less than specified.*

10   Apply moly-base grease to the rocker arm faces and the pivot balls, then install the rocker arms and pivots on the cylinder head studs. Thread the nuts on three or four turns only.

12   Piston/connecting rod assembly - removal

Refer to illustrations 12.1, 12.3, 12.4 and 12.5
Note: *Prior to removing the piston/connecting rod assemblies, remove the cylinder heads, the oil pan and the oil pump by referring to the appropriate Sections in Chapter 2, Part A.*

1   Completely remove the ridge at the top of each cylinder with a ridge reaming tool (see illustration). Follow the manufacturer's instructions provided with the tool. Failure to remove the ridge before attempting to remove the piston/connecting rod assem-

blies will result in piston breakage.
2   After the cylinder ridges have been removed, turn the engine upside-down so the crankshaft is facing up.
3   Before the connecting rods are removed, check the end play with feeler gauges. Slide them between the first connecting rod and the crankshaft throw until the play is removed (see illustration). The end play is equal to the thickness of the feeler gauge(s). If the end play exceeds the service limit, new connecting rods will be required. If new rods (or a new crankshaft) are installed, the end play may fall under the specified minimum. If it does, the rods will have to be machined to restore it - consult an automotive machine shop for advice if necessary. Repeat the procedure for the remaining connecting rods.
4   Check the connecting rods and caps for identification marks. If they aren't plainly marked, use a small center punch to make the appropriate number of indentations on

13.2 Checking crankshaft end play with a dial indicator

13.3 Checking crankshaft endplay with a feeler gauge

13.4a Use a center-punch or number stamping dies to mark the main bearing caps to ensure installation in their original locations on the block (make the punch marks near one of the bolt heads)

13.4b The arrow on the main bearing cap indicates the front of the engine

each rod and cap (see illustration).

5   Loosen each of the connecting rod cap nuts 1/2-turn at a time until they can be removed by hand. Remove the number one connecting rod cap and bearing insert. Don't drop the bearing insert out of the cap. Slip a short length of plastic or rubber hose over each connecting rod cap bolt to protect the crankshaft journal and cylinder wall when the piston is removed (see illustration). Push the connecting rod/piston assembly out through the top of the engine. Use a wooden hammer handle to push on the upper bearing insert in the connecting rod. If resistance is felt, double-check to make sure all of the ridge was removed from the cylinder.

6   Repeat the procedure for the remaining cylinders. After removal, reassemble the connecting rod caps and bearing inserts in their respective connecting rods and install the cap nuts finger-tight. Leaving the old bearing inserts in place until reassembly will help pre-

vent the connecting rod bearing surfaces from being accidentally nicked or gouged.

13   Crankshaft - removal

Refer to illustrations 13.2, 13.3, 13.4a and 13.4b
Note: *The crankshaft can be removed only after the engine has been removed from the vehicle. It's assumed the flywheel or driveplate, vibration damper, timing chain, oil pan, oil pump and piston/connecting rod assemblies have already been removed.*

1   Before the crankshaft is removed, check the end play. Mount a dial indicator with the stem aligned with the crankshaft and just touching one of the crank throws.

2   Push the crankshaft all the way to the rear and zero the dial indicator. Next, pry the crankshaft to the front as far as possible and

check the reading on the dial indicator (see illustration). The distance it moves is the end play. If it's greater than specified, check the crankshaft thrust surfaces for wear. If no wear is evident, new main bearings should correct the end play.

3   If a dial indicator isn't available, feeler gauges can be used. Gently pry or push the crankshaft all the way to the front of the engine. Slip feeler gauges between the crankshaft and the front face of the thrust main bearing to determine the clearance (see illustration).

4   Check the main bearing caps to see if they're marked to indicate their locations. They should be numbered consecutively from the front of the engine to the rear. If they aren't, mark them with number stamping dies or a center punch (see illustration). Main bearing caps generally have a cast-in arrow (see illustration), which points to the front of the engine. Loosen the main bearing cap

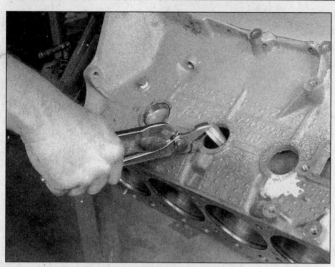

14.1 The core plugs should be removed with a puller - if they're driven into the block, they may be impossible to retrieve

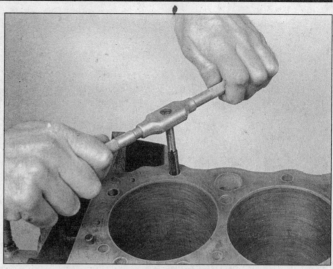

14.8 All bolt holes in the block - particularly the main bearing cap and head bolt holes - should be cleaned and restored with a tap (be sure to remove debris from the holes after this is done)

bolts 1/4-turn at a time each, until they can be removed by hand.

5   Gently tap the caps with a soft-face hammer, then separate them from the engine block. If necessary, use the bolts as levers to remove the caps. Try not to drop the bearing inserts if they come out with the caps.

6   Carefully lift the crankshaft out of the engine. It's a good idea to have an assistant available, since the crankshaft is quite heavy. With the bearing inserts in place in the engine block and main bearing caps, return the caps to their respective locations on the engine block and tighten the bolts finger-tight.

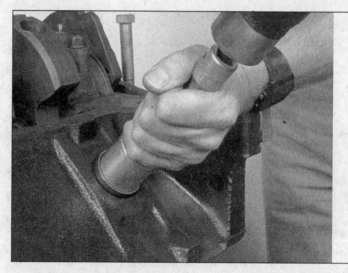

14.10 A large socket on an extension can be used to drive the new core plugs into the bores

14 Engine block - cleaning

Refer to illustrations 14.1, 14.8 and 14.10
Caution: *The core plugs (often known as freeze or soft plugs) may be difficult or impossible to retrieve if they're driven into the block coolant passages.*

1   Drill a small hole in the center of each core plug and pull them out with an auto body type dent puller **(see illustration)**.

2   Using a gasket scraper, remove all traces of gasket material from the engine block. Be very careful not to nick or gouge the gasket sealing surfaces.

3   Remove the main bearing caps and separate the bearing inserts from the caps and the engine block. Tag the bearings, indicating which cylinder they were removed from and whether they were in the cap or the block, then set them aside.

4   Using a 1/4-inch drive breaker bar or ratchet, remove all of the threaded oil gallery plugs from the rear of the block. Discard the plugs and use new ones when the engine is reassembled.

5   If the engine is extremely dirty, it should be taken to an automotive machine shop to be steam cleaned or hot tanked.

6   After the block is returned, clean all oil holes and oil galleries one more time. Brushes specifically designed for this purpose are available at most auto parts stores. Flush the passages with warm water until the water runs clear, dry the block thoroughly and wipe all machined surfaces with a light, rust preventive oil. If you have access to compressed air, use it to speed the drying process and to blow out all the oil holes and galleries.

7   If the block isn't extremely dirty or sludged up, you can do an adequate cleaning job with warm soapy water and a stiff brush. Take plenty of time and do a thorough job. Regardless of the cleaning method used, be sure to clean all oil holes and galleries very thoroughly, dry the block completely and coat all machined surfaces with light oil.

8   The threaded holes in the block must be clean to ensure accurate torque readings during reassembly. Run the proper size tap into each of the holes to remove any rust, corrosion, thread sealant or sludge and to restore any damaged threads **(see illustra-**

tion). If possible, use compressed air to clear the holes of debris produced by this operation. Now is a good time to clean the threads on the head bolts and the main bearing cap bolts as well.

9   Reinstall the main bearing caps and tighten the bolts finger-tight.

10   After coating the sealing surfaces of the new soft plugs with RTV sealant, install them in the engine block. Make sure they are driven in straight and seated properly or leakage could result. Special tools are available for this purpose, but equally good results can be obtained using a large socket, with an outside diameter that will just slip into the soft plug, and a hammer **(see illustration)**.

11   Apply non-hardening sealant (such as Permatex number 2 or Teflon tape) to the new oil gallery plugs and thread them into the holes at the rear of the block. Make sure they're tightened securely.

12   If the engine isn't going to be reassembled right away, cover it with a large plastic trash bag to keep it clean.

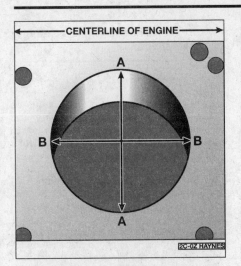

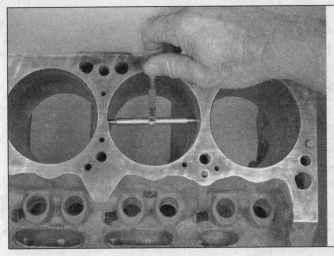

15.4b Use a telescoping gauge to measure the bore - the ability to "feel" when it is at the correct point will be developed over time, so work slowly and repeat the check until you're satisfied the bore measurement is accurate

15.4a Measure the diameter of each cylinder at a right angle to the engine centerline (A), and parallel to engine centerline (B) - out-of-round is the distance between A and B; taper is the difference between A and B at the top of the cylinder and A and B at the bottom of the cylinder

15 Engine block - inspection

Refer to illustrations 15.4a, 15.4b and 15.4c

1   Before the block is inspected, it should be cleaned as described in Section 14. Double-check to make sure the ridge at the top of each cylinder has been completely removed.
2   Visually check the block for cracks, rust and corrosion. Look for stripped threads in the threaded holes. It's also a good idea to have the block checked for hidden cracks by an automotive machine shop with the special equipment to do this type of work. If defects are found, have the block repaired, if possible, or replaced.
3   Check the cylinder bores for scuffing and scoring.
4   Measure the diameter of each cylinder at the top (just under the ridge area), center

and bottom of the cylinder bore, parallel to the crankshaft axis (see illustrations). Note: *These measurements should not be made with the bare block mounted on an engine stand - the cylinders will be distorted and the measurements will be inaccurate.*
5   Next, measure each cylinder's diameter at the same three locations across the crankshaft axis. Compare the results to the Specifications. If the cylinder walls are badly scuffed or scored, or if they're out-of-round or tapered beyond the limits given in the Specifications, have the engine block rebored and honed at an automotive machine shop. If a rebore is done, oversize pistons and rings will be required.
6   If the cylinders are in reasonably good condition and not worn to the outside of the limits, and if the piston-to-cylinder clearances can be maintained properly, then they don't have to be rebored. Honing is all that is necessary (Section 16).

16 Cylinder honing

Refer to illustrations 16.3a and 16.3b

1   Prior to engine reassembly, the cylinder

bores must be honed so the new piston rings will seat correctly and provide the best possible combustion chamber seal. Note: *If you don't have the tools or don't want to tackle the honing operation, most automotive machine shops will do it for a reasonable fee.*
2   Before honing the cylinders, install the main bearing caps and tighten the bolts to the specified torque.
3   Two types of cylinder hones are commonly available - the flex hone or "bottle brush" type and the more traditional surfacing hone with spring-loaded stones. Both will do the job, but for the less experienced mechanic the "bottle brush" hone will probably be easier to use. You'll also need plenty of light oil or honing oil, some rags and an electric drill. Proceed as follows:

a) *Mount the hone in the drill, compress the stones and slip it into the first cylinder* (see illustration).
b) *Lubricate the cylinder with plenty of oil, turn on the drill and move the hone up-and-down in the cylinder at a pace which will produce a fine crosshatch pattern on the cylinder walls. Ideally, the crosshatch lines should intersect at approximately a 60-degree angle* (see

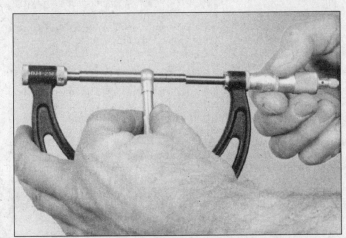

15.4c The gauge is then measured with a micrometer to determine the bore size

16.3a A "bottle brush" hone will produce better results if you've never honed cylinders before

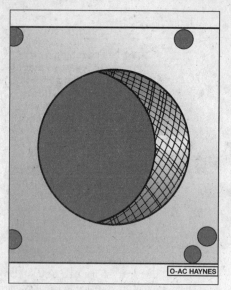

16.3b The cylinder hone should leave a smooth, crosshatch pattern with the lines intersecting at approximately a 60-degree angle

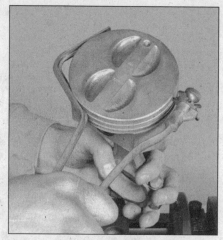

17.4a The piston ring grooves can be cleaned with a special tool, as shown here, . . .

illustration). *Be sure to use plenty of lubricant and don't take off any more material than absolutely necessary to produce the desired finish.* **Note:** *Piston ring manufacturers may specify a smaller crosshatch angle than the traditional 60-degrees - read and follow any instructions printed on the piston ring packages.*

c) *Do not withdraw the hone from the cylinder while it's running. Instead, shut off the drill and continue moving the hone up-and-down in the cylinder until it comes to a complete stop, then compress the stones and withdraw the hone. If you're using a "bottle brush" type hone, stop the drill, then turn the chuck in the normal direction of rotation while withdrawing the hone from the cylinder.*

d) *Wipe the oil out of the cylinder and repeat the procedure for the remaining cylinders.*

4   After the honing job is complete, chamfer the top edges of the cylinder bores with a small file so the rings won't catch when the pistons are installed. Be very careful not to nick the cylinder walls with the end of the file.

5   The entire engine block must be washed again very thoroughly with warm, soapy water to remove all traces of the abrasive grit produced during the honing operation. **Note:** *The bores can be considered clean when a white cloth - dampened with clean engine oil - used to wipe down the bores doesn't pick up any more honing residue, which will show up as gray areas on the cloth. Be sure to run a brush through all oil holes and galleries and flush them with running water.*

6   After rinsing, dry the block and apply a coat of light rust preventive oil to all machined surfaces. Wrap the block in a plastic trash bag to keep it clean and set it aside until reassembly.

17 Piston/connecting rod assembly - inspection

Refer to illustrations 17.4a, 17.4b, 17.10 and 17.11

1   Before the inspection process can be carried out, the piston/connecting rod assemblies must be cleaned and the original piston rings removed from the pistons. **Note:** *Always use new piston rings when the engine is reassembled.*

2   Using a piston ring installation tool, carefully remove the rings from the pistons. Be careful not to nick or gouge the pistons in the process.

3   Scrape all traces of carbon from the top (known as the crown) of the piston. A hand-held wire brush or a piece of fine emery cloth can be used once the majority of the deposits have been scraped away. Do not, under any circumstances, use a wire brush mounted in an electric drill to remove deposits from the pistons. The piston material is soft and will be eroded away by the wire brush.

4   Use a piston ring groove cleaning tool to remove carbon deposits from the ring grooves **(see illustration)**. If a tool isn't available, a piece broken off the old ring will do the job **(see illustration)**. Be very careful to remove only the carbon deposits - don't remove any metal and do not nick or scratch the sides of the ring grooves.

5   Once the deposits have been removed, clean the piston/rod assemblies with solvent and dry them with compressed air (if available). Make sure the oil return holes in the back sides of the ring grooves are clear.

6   If the pistons aren't damaged or worn excessively, and if the engine block isn't rebored, new pistons will not be necessary. Normal piston wear appears as even vertical wear on the piston thrust surfaces and slight looseness of the top ring in its groove. New piston rings, on the other hand, should always be used when an engine is rebuilt.

7   Carefully inspect each piston for cracks

17.4b . . . or a section of a broken ring

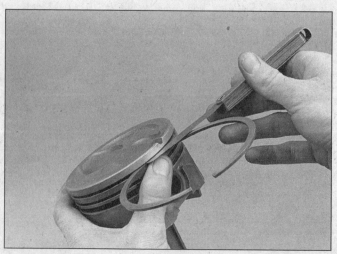

17.10 Check the ring side clearance with a feeler gauge at several points around the groove

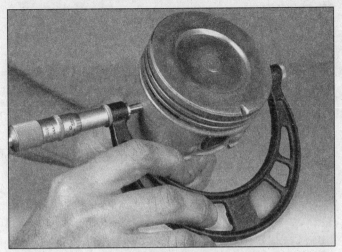

17.11 Measure the piston diameter at a 90-degree angle to the piston pin and in line with it

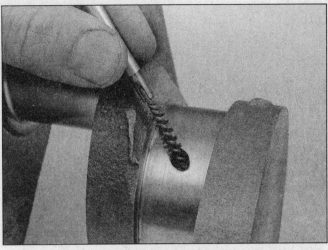

18.1 Use a wire or stiff plastic bristle brush to clean the oil passages in the crankshaft

around the skirt, at the pin bosses and at the ring lands.

8   Look for scoring and scuffing on the thrust faces of the skirt, holes in the piston crown and burned areas at the edge of the crown. If the skirt is scored or scuffed, the engine may have been suffering from over-heating and/or abnormal combustion, which caused excessively high operating temperatures. The cooling and lubrication systems should be checked thoroughly. A hole in the piston crown is an indication that abnormal combustion (preignition) was occurring. Burned areas at the edge of the piston crown are usually evidence of spark knock (detonation). If any of the above problems exist, the causes must be corrected or the damage will occur again. The causes may include intake air leaks, incorrect fuel/air mixture, incorrect ignition timing and EGR system malfunctions.

9   Corrosion of the piston, in the form of small pits, indicates coolant is leaking into the combustion chamber and/or the crankcase. Again, the cause must be corrected or the problem may persist in the rebuilt engine.

10   Measure the piston ring side clearance by laying a new piston ring in each ring groove and slipping a feeler gauge in beside it **(see illustration)**. Check the clearance at three or four locations around each groove. Be sure to use the correct ring for each groove; they are different. If the side clearance is greater than specified, new pistons will have to be used.

11   Check the piston-to-bore clearance by measuring the bore (see Section 15) and the piston diameter. Make sure the pistons and bores are correctly matched. Measure the piston across the skirt, at a 90-degree angle to and in line with the piston pin **(see illustration)**. Subtract the piston diameter from the bore diameter to obtain the clearance. If it's greater than specified, the block will have to be rebored and new pistons and rings installed.

12   Check the piston-to-rod clearance by

18.3 Rubbing a penny lengthwise on each journal will reveal its condition - if copper rubs off and is embedded in the crankshaft, the journals should be reground

twisting the piston and rod in opposite directions. Any noticeable play indicates excessive wear, which must be corrected. The piston/connecting rod assemblies should be taken to an automotive machine shop to have the pistons and rods rebored and new pins installed.

13   If the pistons must be removed from the connecting rods for any reason, they should be taken to an automotive machine shop. While they are there, have the connecting rods checked for bend and twist, since automotive machine shops have special equipment for this purpose. **Note:** *Unless new pistons and/or connecting rods must be installed, do not disassemble the pistons and connecting rods.*

14   Check the connecting rods for cracks and other damage. Temporarily remove the rod caps, lift out the old bearing inserts, wipe the rod and cap bearing surfaces clean and inspect them for nicks, gouges and scratches. After checking the rods, replace

18.4 The oil holes should be chamfered so sharp edges don't gouge or scratch the new bearings

the old bearings, slip the caps into place and tighten the nuts finger-tight.

18   Crankshaft - inspection

Refer to illustrations 18.1, 18.3, 18.4, 18.6 and 18.8

1   Clean the crankshaft with solvent and dry it with compressed air (if available). **Warning:** *Wear eye protection when using compressed air!* Be sure to clean the oil holes with a stiff brush and flush them with solvent **(see illustration)**.

2   Check the main and connecting rod bearing journals for uneven wear, scoring, pits and cracks.

3   Rub a penny across each journal several times **(see illustration)**. If a journal picks up copper from a penny, it's too rough and must be reground.

4   Remove all burrs from the crankshaft oil holes with a stone, file or scraper **(see illustration)**.

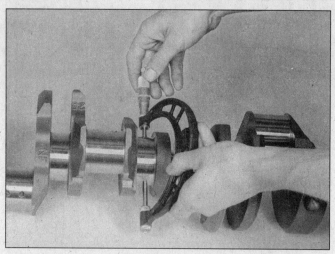

18.6 Measure the diameter of each crankshaft journal at several points to detect taper and out-of-round conditions

18.8 If the seals have worn grooves in the crankshaft journals, or if the seal contact surfaces are nicked or scratched, the new seals will leak

5   Check the rest of the crankshaft for cracks and other damage. It should be magnafluxed to reveal hidden cracks - an automotive machine shop will handle the procedure.

6   Using a micrometer, measure the diameter of the main and connecting rod journals and compare the results to the Specifications (see illustration). By measuring the diameter at a number of points around each journal's circumference, you'll be able to determine whether or not the journal is out-of-round. Take the measurement at each end of the journal, near the crank throws, to determine if the journal is tapered.

7   If the crankshaft journals are damaged, tapered, out-of-round or worn beyond the limits given in the Specifications, have the crankshaft reground by an automotive machine shop. Be sure to use the correct size bearing inserts if the crankshaft is reconditioned.

8   Check the oil seal journals at each end of the crankshaft for wear and damage. If the seal has worn a groove in the journal, or it it's nicked or scratched (see illustration), the new seal may leak when the engine is reassembled. In some cases, an automotive machine shop may be able to repair the journal by pressing on a thin sleeve. If repair isn't feasible, a new or different crankshaft should be installed.

9   Refer to Section 19 and examine the main and rod bearing inserts.

19   Main and connecting rod bearings - inspection

Refer to illustration 19.1

1   Even though the main and connecting rod bearings should be replaced with new ones during the engine overhaul, the old bearings should be retained for close examination, as they may reveal valuable information about the condition of the engine (see illustration).

2   Bearing failure occurs because of lack of lubrication, the presence of dirt or other foreign particles, overloading the engine and corrosion. Regardless of the cause of bearing failure, it must be corrected before the engine is reassembled to prevent it from happening again.

3   When examining the bearings, remove them from the engine block, the main bearing caps, the connecting rods and the rod caps and lay them out on a clean surface in the same general position as their location in the

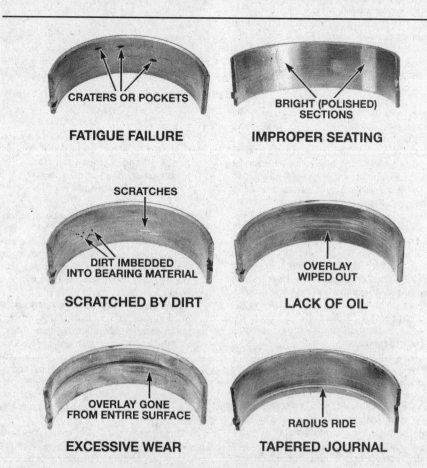

CRATERS OR POCKETS

FATIGUE FAILURE

BRIGHT (POLISHED) SECTIONS

IMPROPER SEATING

SCRATCHES

DIRT IMBEDDED INTO BEARING MATERIAL

SCRATCHED BY DIRT

OVERLAY WIPED OUT

LACK OF OIL

OVERLAY GONE FROM ENTIRE SURFACE

EXCESSIVE WEAR

RADIUS RIDE

TAPERED JOURNAL

19.1 Typical bearing failures

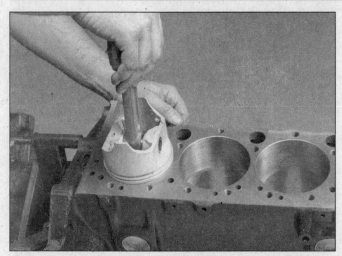

21.3 When checking piston ring end gap, the ring must be square in the cylinder bore (this is done by pushing the ring down with the top of a piston as shown)

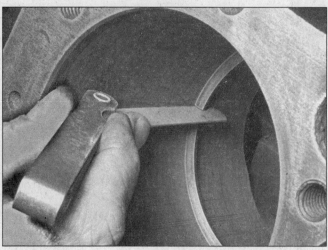

21.4 With the ring square in the cylinder, measure the end gap with a feeler gauge

engine. This will enable you to match any bearing problems with the corresponding crankshaft journal.

4   Dirt and other foreign particles get into the engine in a variety of ways. If may be left in the engine during assembly, or it may pass through filters or the PCV system. It may get into the oil, and from there into the bearings. Metal chips from machining operations and normal engine wear are often present. Abrasives are sometimes left in engine components after reconditioning, especially when parts are not thoroughly cleaned using the proper cleaning methods. Whatever the source, these foreign objects often end up embedded in the soft bearing material and are easily recognized. Large particles will not embed in the bearing and will score or gouge the bearing and journal. The best prevention for this cause of bearing failure is to clean all parts thoroughly and keep everything spotlessly clean during engine assembly. Frequent and regular engine oil and filter changes are also recommended.

5   Lack of lubrication (or lubrication breakdown) has a number of interrelated causes. Excessive heat (which thins the oil), overloading (which squeezes the oil from the bearing face) and oil leakage or throw off (from excessive bearing clearances, worn oil pump or high engine speeds) all contribute to lubrication breakdown. Blocked oil passages, which usually are the result of misaligned oil holes in a bearing shell, will also oil starve a bearing and destroy it. When lack of lubrication is the cause of bearing failure, the bearing material is wiped or extruded from the steel backing of the bearing. Temperatures may increase to the point where the steel backing turns blue from overheating.

6   Driving habits can have a definite effect on bearing life. Full throttle, low speed operation in too high a gear (lugging the engine) puts very high loads on bearings, which tends to squeeze out the oil film. These loads cause the bearings to flex, which produces

fine cracks in the bearing face (fatigue failure). Eventually the bearing material will loosen in pieces and tear away from the steel backing. Short trip driving leads to corrosion of bearings because insufficient engine heat is produced to drive off the condensed water and corrosive gases. These products collect in the engine oil, forming acid and sludge. As the oil is carried to the engine bearings, the acid attacks and corrodes the bearing material.

7   Incorrect bearing installation during engine assembly will lead to bearing failure as well. Tight fitting bearings leave insufficient bearing oil clearance and will result in oil starvation. Dirt or foreign particles trapped behind a bearing insert result in high spots on the bearing which lead to failure.

20 Engine overhaul - reassembly sequence

1   Before beginning engine reassembly, make sure you have all the necessary new parts, gaskets and seals as well as the following items on hand:

Common hand tools
1/2-inch drive torque wrench
Piston ring installation tool
Piston ring compressor
Short lengths of rubber or plastic hose to fit over connecting rod bolts
Plastigage
Feeler gauges
A fine-tooth file
New engine oil
Engine assembly lube or moly-base grease
RTV-type gasket sealant
Anaerobic-type gasket sealant
Thread locking compound

2   To save time and avoid problems, engine reassembly must be done in the following general order:

New camshaft bearings (must be done by an automotive machine shop)
Piston rings
Crankshaft and main bearings
Piston/connecting rod assemblies
Oil pump and oil strainer
Camshaft and lifters
Cylinder heads, pushrods and rocker arms
Timing chain and sprockets
Timing chain cover
Oil pan
Intake and exhaust manifolds
Rocker arm covers
Flywheel/driveplate

21 Piston rings - installation

Refer to illustrations 21.3, 21.4, 21.5, 21.9a, 21.9b and 21.12

1   Before installing the new piston rings, the ring end gaps must be checked. It's assumed the piston ring side clearance has been checked and verified correct (Section 17).

2   Lay out the piston/connecting rod assemblies and the new ring sets so the ring sets will be matched with the same piston and cylinder during the end gap measurement and engine assembly.

3   Insert the top (number one) ring into the first cylinder and square it up with the cylinder walls by pushing it in with the top of the piston **(see illustration)**. The ring should be near the bottom of the cylinder, at the lower limit of ring travel.

4   To measure the end gap, slip feeler gauges between the ends of the ring until a gauge equal to the gap width is found **(see illustration)**. The feeler gauge should slide between the ring ends with a slight amount of drag. Compare the measurement to the Specifications. If the gap is larger or smaller than specified, double-check to make sure you have the correct rings before proceeding.

21.5 If the end gap is too small, clamp a file in a vise and file the ring ends (from the outside in only) to enlarge the gap slightly

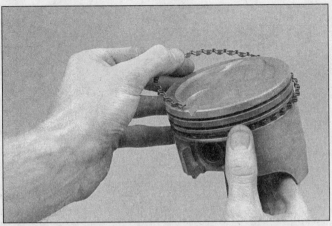

21.9a Installing the spacer/expander in the oil control ring groove

21.9b DO NOT use a piston ring installation tool when installing the oil ring side rails

21.12 Installing the compression rings with a ring expander - the mark (arrow) must face up

5   If the gap is too small, it must be enlarged or the ring ends may come in contact with each other during engine operation, which can cause serious damage to the engine. The end gap can be increased by filing the ring ends very carefully with a fine file. Mount the file in a vise equipped with soft jaws, slip the ring over the file with the ends contacting the file face and slowly move the ring to remove material from the ends **(see illustration)**. When performing this operation, file only from the outside in.

6   Excess end gap isn't critical unless it's greater than 0.040-inch. Again, double-check to make sure you have the correct rings for the engine.

7   Repeat the procedure for each ring that will be installed in the first cylinder and for each ring in the remaining cylinders. Remember to keep rings, pistons and cylinders matched up.

8   Once the ring end gaps have been checked/corrected, the rings can be installed on the pistons.

9   The oil control ring (lowest one on the piston) is installed first. It's composed of three separate components. Slip the spacer/expander into the groove **(see illus-**

tration). If an anti-rotation tang is used, make sure it's inserted into the drilled hole in the ring groove. Install the lower side rail. Do not use a piston ring installation tool on the oil ring side rails, as they may be damaged. Instead, place one end of the side rail into the groove between the spacer/expander and the ring land, hold it firmly in place and slide a finger around the piston while pushing the rail into the groove **(see illustration)**. Next, install the upper side rail in the same manner.

10   After the three oil ring components have been installed, check to make sure both the upper and lower side rails can be turned smoothly in the ring groove.

11   The number two (middle) ring is installed next. It's stamped with a mark which must face up, toward the top of the piston. **Note:** *Always follow the instructions printed on the ring package or box - different manufacturers may require different approaches. Do not mix up the top and middle rings, as they have different cross sections.*

12   Use a piston ring installation tool and make sure the identification mark is facing the top of the piston, then slip the ring into the middle groove on the piston **(see illustration)**. Do not expand the ring any more than

is necessary to slide it over the piston.

13   Install the number one (top) ring in the same manner. Make sure the mark is facing up. Be careful not to confuse the number one and number two rings.

14   Repeat the procedure for the remaining pistons and rings.

22   Rear main oil seal installation

1   Inspect the rear main bearing cap and engine block mating surfaces, as well as the seal grooves, for nicks, burrs and scratches. Remove any defects with a fine file or deburring tool.

2   Install one seal section in the block with the lip facing the front of the engine (if the seal has two lips, the one with the helix must face the front) **(see illustration 15.12b in Part A)**. Leave one end protruding from the block approximately 1/4 to 3/8-inch and make sure it's completely seated.

3   Repeat the procedure to install the remaining seal half in the rear main bearing cap. In this case, leave the opposite end of the seal protruding from the cap the same distance the block seal is protruding from the block.

23.10 Lay the Plastigage strips (arrow) on the main bearing journals, parallel to the crankshaft centerline

4   During final installation of the crankshaft (after the main bearing oil clearances have been checked with Plastigage) as described in Section 23, apply a thin, even coat of anaerobic-type gasket sealant to the areas of the cap or block, described in Section 15, Step 16 of Part A. Don't get any sealant on the bearing face, crankshaft journal, seal ends or seal lips. Also, lubricate the seal lips with moly-base grease or clean engine oil.

23 Crankshaft - installation and main bearing oil clearance check

Refer to illustrations 23.10, 23.14, 23.18 and 23.20

1   Crankshaft installation is the first step in engine reassembly. It's assumed at this point that the engine block and crankshaft have been cleaned, inspected and repaired or reconditioned.
2   Position the engine with the bottom facing up.
3   Remove the main bearing cap bolts and lift out the caps. Lay them out in the proper order to ensure they're installed correctly.
4   If they're still in place, remove the old bearing inserts from the block and the main bearing caps. Wipe the main bearing surfaces of the block and caps with a clean, lint free cloth. They must be kept spotlessly clean.

Main bearing oil clearance check

Note: *Don't touch the faces of the new bearing inserts with your fingers. Oil and acids from your skin can etch the bearings.*

5   Clean the back sides of the new main bearing inserts and lay one bearing half in each main bearing saddle in the block. Lay the other bearing half from each bearing set in the corresponding main bearing cap. Make sure the tab on the bearing insert fits into the recess in the block or cap **(see illustration 24.3). Caution:** *The oil holes in the block*

23.14 Compare the width of the crushed Plastigage to the scale on the envelope to determine the main bearing oil clearance (always take the measurement at the widest point of the Plastigage); be sure to use the correct scale - standard and metric ones are included

must line up with the oil holes in the bearing insert. Do not hammer the bearing into place and do not nick or gouge the bearing faces. No lubrication should be used at this time.
6   The flanged thrust bearing must be installed in the rear cap and saddle.
7   Clean the faces of the bearings in the block and the crankshaft main bearing journals with a clean, lint-free cloth. Check or clean the oil holes in the crankshaft, as any dirt here can go only one way - straight through the new bearings.
8   Once you're certain the crankshaft is clean, carefully lay it in position (an assistant would be very helpful here) in the main bearings.
9   Before the crankshaft can be permanently installed, the main bearing oil clearance must be checked.
10   Cut several pieces of the appropriate size Plastigage (they should be slightly shorter than the width of the main bearings) and place one piece on each crankshaft main bearing journal, parallel with the journal axis **(see illustration)**.
11   Clean the faces of the bearings in the

caps and install the caps in their respective positions (do not mix them up) with the arrows pointing toward the front of the engine. Do not disturb the Plastigage.
12   Starting with the center main and working out toward the ends, tighten the main bearing cap bolts, in three steps, to the specified torque. Do not rotate the crankshaft at any time during this operation.
13   Remove the bolts and carefully lift off the main bearing caps. Keep them in order. Do not disturb the Plastigage or rotate the crankshaft. If any of the main bearing caps are difficult to remove, tap them gently from side-to-side with a soft-face hammer to loosen them.
14   Compare the width of the crushed Plastigage on each journal to the scale printed on the Plastigage envelope to obtain the main bearing oil clearance **(see illustration)**. Check the Specifications to make sure it's correct.
15   If the clearance is not as specified, the bearing inserts may be the wrong size (which means different ones will be required). Before deciding different inserts are needed, make sure no dirt or oil was between the bearing inserts and the caps or block when the clearance was measured. If the Plastigage was wider at one end than the other, the journal may be tapered (refer to Section 18).
16   Carefully scrape all traces of the Plastigage material off the main bearing journals and/or the bearing faces. Use your fingernail or the edge of a credit card - don't nick or scratch the bearing faces.

Final crankshaft installation

17   Carefully lift the crankshaft out of the engine.
18   Clean the bearing faces in the block, then apply a thin, uniform layer of clean moly-base grease or engine oil to each of the bearing surfaces **(see illustration)**. Be sure to coat the thrust faces as well as the journal face of the rear bearing.
19   If not already done, refer to Section 22 and install the rear main oil seal sections in the block and bearing cap. Lubricate the seal faces with moly-base grease or clean engine oil.
20   Make sure the crankshaft journals are

23.18 Apply moly-base grease or clean engine oil to the main bearings . . .

23.20 . . . before installing the crankshaft for the final time

24.3 Make sure the tab on the bearing fits into the recess in the rod or cap

clean, then lay the crankshaft back in place in the block **(see illustration)**.

21   Clean the faces of the bearings in the caps, then apply lubricant to them.

22   Install the caps in their original locations with the arrows pointing toward the front of the engine.

23   Install the bolts.

24   Tighten all except the rear cap bolts (the one with the thrust bearing) to the specified torque. Work from the center out and approach the final torque in three steps.

25   Tighten the rear cap bolts to 10-to-12 ft-lbs.

26   Tap the ends of the crankshaft forward and backward with a lead or brass hammer to line up the main bearing and crankshaft thrust surfaces.

27   Retighten all main bearing cap bolts to the specified torque, starting with the center main and working out toward the ends. On models with four bolt main bearing caps, tighten the inner bolts first, then the outer bolts, and be sure to note that different torque figures are supplied for the inner and outer bolts.

28   On manual transmission equipped models, install a new pilot bearing in the end of the crankshaft (see Chapter 8).

29   Rotate the crankshaft a number of times by hand to check for any obvious binding.

30   The final step is to check the crankshaft end play with a feeler gauge or dial indicator as described in Section 13. The end play should be correct if the crankshaft thrust faces aren't worn or damaged and new bearings have been installed.

24 Piston/connecting rod assembly - installation and rod bearing oil clearance check

Refer to illustrations 24.3, 24.9, 24.11, 24.13 and 24.17

1   Before installing the piston/connecting rod assemblies, the cylinder walls must be perfectly clean, the top edge of each cylinder must be chamfered and the crankshaft must be in place.

2   Remove the connecting rod cap from the end of the number one connecting rod. Remove the old bearing inserts and wipe the bearing surfaces of the connecting rod and cap with a clean, lint-free cloth. They must be kept spotlessly clean.

Connecting rod bearing oil clearance check

Note: *Don't touch the faces of the new bearing inserts with your fingers. Oil and acids from your skin can etch the bearings.*

3   Clean the back side of the new upper bearing half, then lay it in place in the connecting rod. Make sure the tab on the bearing fits into the recess in the rod **(see illustration)**. Don't hammer the bearing insert into place and be very careful not to nick or gouge the bearing face. Don't lubricate the bearing at this time.

4   Clean the back side of the other bearing insert and install it in the rod cap. Again, make sure the tab on the bearing fits into the recess in the cap, and don't apply any lubricant. It's critically important that the mating surfaces of the bearing and connecting rod are perfectly clean and oil free when they're assembled.

5   Position the piston ring gaps at 120-degree intervals around the piston.

6   Slip a section of plastic or rubber hose over each connecting rod cap bolt.

7   Lubricate the piston and rings with clean engine oil and attach a piston ring compressor to the piston. Leave the skirt protruding about 1/4-inch to guide the piston into the cylinder. The rings must be compressed until they're flush with the piston.

8   Rotate the crankshaft until the number one connecting rod journal is at BDC (bottom dead center) and apply a light coat of engine oil to the cylinder walls.

9   With the notch on top of the piston facing the front of the engine **(see illustration)**, carefully insert the piston/connecting rod assembly into the number one cylinder bore

24.9 The notch in the piston must face the front of the engine when the piston/connecting rod assembly is installed

and rest the bottom edge of the ring compressor on the engine block.

10   Tap the top edge of the ring compressor to make sure it's contacting the block around its entire circumference.

11   Gently tap on the top of the piston with the end of a wooden hammer handle while guiding the end of the connecting rod into place on the crankshaft journal **(see illustration)**. The piston rings may try to pop out of the ring compressor just before entering the cylinder bore, so keep some downward pressure on the ring compressor. Work slowly, and if any resistance is felt as the piston enters the cylinder, stop immediately. Find out what's hanging up and fix it before proceeding. Do not, for any reason, force the piston into the cylinder - you might break a ring and/or the piston.

12   Once the piston/connecting rod assembly is installed, the connecting rod bearing oil clearance must be checked before the rod cap is permanently bolted in place.

13   Cut a piece of the appropriate size Plastigage slightly shorter than the width of the

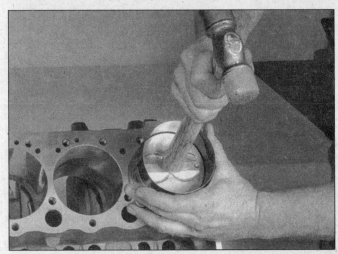

24.11 Drive the piston gently into the cylinder bore with the end of a wooden or plastic hammer handle

24.13 Lay the Plastigage strips on each rod bearing journal, parallel to the crankshaft centerline

connecting rod bearing and lay it in place on the number one connecting rod journal, parallel with the journal axis **(see illustration)**.

14   Clean the connecting rod cap bearing face, remove the protective hoses from the connecting rod bolts and install the rod cap. Make sure the mating mark on the cap is on the same side as the mark on the connecting rod.

15   Install the nuts and tighten them to the specified torque, working up to it in three steps. **Note:** *Use a thin-wall socket to avoid erroneous torque readings that can result if the socket becomes wedged between the rod cap and nut. If the socket tends to wedge itself between the nut and cap, lift up on it slightly until it no longer contacts the cap. Do not rotate the crankshaft at any time during this operation.*

16   Remove the nuts and detach the rod cap, being very careful not to disturb the Plastigage.

17   Compare the width of the crushed Plastigage to the scale printed on the Plastigage envelope to obtain the oil clearance **(see illustration)**. Compare it to the Specifications to make sure the clearance is correct.

18   If the clearance is not as specified, the bearing inserts may be the wrong size (which means different ones will be required). Before deciding different inserts are needed, make sure no dirt or oil was between the bearing inserts and the connecting rod or cap when the clearance was measured. Also, recheck the journal diameter. If the Plastigage was wider at one end than the other, the journal may be tapered (refer to Section 18).

Final connecting rod installation

19   Carefully scrape all traces of the Plastigage material off the rod journal and/or bearing face. Be very careful not to scratch the bearing - use your fingernail or the edge of a credit card.

20   Make sure the bearing faces are perfectly clean, then apply a uniform layer of

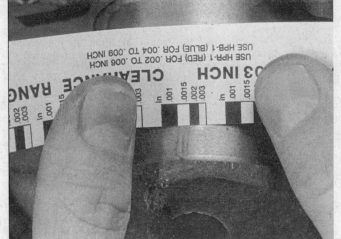

24.17 Measuring the width of the crushed Plastigage to determine the rod bearing oil clearance (be sure to use the correct scale - standard and metric ones are included)

clean moly-base grease or engine oil to both of them. You'll have to push the piston into the cylinder to expose the face of the bearing insert in the connecting rod - be sure to slip the protective hoses over the rod bolts first.

21   Slide the connecting rod back into place on the journal, remove the protective hoses from the rod cap bolts, install the rod cap and tighten the nuts to the specified torque. Again, work up to the torque in three steps.

22   Repeat the entire procedure for the remaining piston/connecting rod assemblies.

23   The important points to remember are . . .

a) *Keep the back sides of the bearing inserts and the insides of the connecting rods and caps perfectly clean when assembling them.*

b) *Make sure you have the correct piston/rod assembly for each cylinder.*

c) *The notch on the piston faces to the front of the engine when the piston is installed.*

d) *Lubricate the cylinder walls with clean oil.*

e) *Lubricate the bearing faces adequately when the rod caps are installed after the oil clearance has been checked.*

24   After all the piston/connecting rod assemblies have been properly installed, rotate the crankshaft a number of times by hand to check for any obvious binding.

25   As a final step, the connecting rod end play must be checked. Refer to Section 12 for this procedure.

26   Compare the measured end play to the Specifications to make sure it's correct. If it was correct before disassembly and the original crankshaft and rods were reinstalled, it should still be right. If new rods or a new crankshaft were installed, the end play may be too small. If so, the rods will have to be removed and taken to an automotive machine shop for resizing.

25   Pre-oiling the engine after overhaul

Refer to illustrations 25.3, 25.5 and 25.6

1   After an overhaul, it's a good idea to pre-oil the engine before it's installed in the vehicle and started for the first time. Pre-oiling will reveal any problems with the lubrication system at a time when corrections can

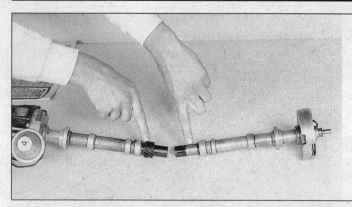

25.3 The pre-oil distributor (right) has the gear ground off and the advance weights removed

be made easily and will prevent major engine damage. It'll also allow the internal engine parts to be lubricated thoroughly in the normal fashion without the heavy loads associated with combustion placed on them.

2   The engine should be completely assembled with the exception of the distributor and rocker arm covers. The oil filter and oil pressure sending unit must be in place and the specified amount of oil must be in the crankcase (see Chapter 1).

3   A modified Chevrolet distributor will be needed for this procedure - a junkyard should be able to supply one for a reasonable price. In order to function as a pre-oil tool, the distributor must have the gear on the lower end of the shaft ground off **(see illustration)** and, if equipped, the advance weights on the upper end of the shaft removed.

4   Install the pre-oil distributor in place of the original distributor and make sure the lower end of the shaft mates with the upper end of the oil pump driveshaft. Turn the distributor shaft until they're aligned and the distributor body seats on the block. Install the distributor hold-down clamp and bolt.

5   Mount the upper end of the shaft in the chuck of an electric drill and use the drill to turn the pre-oil distributor shaft, which will drive the oil pump and circulate the oil throughout the engine **(see illustration)**. **Note:** *The drill must turn in a clockwise direction.*

6   It may take two or three minutes, but oil should soon start to flow out of all the rocker arm holes, indicating the oil pump is working properly **(see illustration)**. Let the oil circulate for several seconds, then shut off the drill.

7   Remove the pre-oil distributor, then install the rocker arm covers. The distributor should be installed after the engine is installed in the vehicle, so plug the hole with a clean cloth.

26 Initial start-up and break-in after overhaul

1   Once the engine has been installed in the vehicle, double-check the engine oil and

coolant levels.

2   With the spark plugs out of the engine and the distributor disabled by disconnecting the BAT connector (coil-in-cap models) or grounding the coil wire (separate coil models), crank the engine until oil pressure registers on the gauge.

3   Install the spark plugs, hook up the plug wires and reconnect the distributor.

4   Start the engine. It may take a few moments for the gasoline to reach the carburetor or TBI units, but the engine should start without a great deal of effort.

5   After the engine starts, it should be allowed to warm up to normal operating temperature. While the engine is warming up, make a thorough check for oil and coolant leaks.

6   Shut the engine off and recheck the engine oil and coolant levels.

7   Drive the vehicle to an area with minimum traffic, accelerate at full throttle from 30 to 50 mph, then allow the vehicle to slow to 30 mph with the throttle closed. Repeat the procedure 10 or 12 times. This will load the piston rings and cause them to seat properly against the cylinder walls. Check again for oil and coolant leaks.

8   Drive the vehicle gently for the first 500 miles (no sustained high speeds) and keep a constant check on the oil level. It's not unusual for an engine to use oil during the break-in period.

9   At approximately 500 to 600 miles, change the oil and filter.

10   For the next few hundred miles, drive the vehicle normally. Don't pamper it or abuse it.

11   After 2000 miles, change the oil and filter again and consider the engine fully broken in.

25.5 An electric drill connected to the modified distributor shaft drives the oil pump - make sure it turns clockwise as viewed from the top

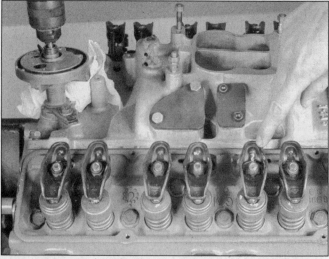

25.6 Oil or grease, depending on what was used during engine assembly, will begin to flow from all of the rocker arm holes if the oil pump and lubrication system are functioning properly

Chapter 3
Cooling, heating and air conditioning systems

Contents

Specifications

General

Radiator cap pressure rating	See Chapter 1
Coolant type	See Chapter 1
Thermostat rating	
1968 through 1974	
Engines with AIR system	195-degrees F
All others	180-degrees F
1975 on	
Optional 350 engine	180-degrees F
All others	195-degrees F

Torque specifications

	Ft-lbs
Water pump mounting bolts	30
Thermostat housing cover (water outlet) bolts	
1968 through 1977	20
1978 on	30
Coolant temperature sending unit	20
Fan clutch hub bolts	25

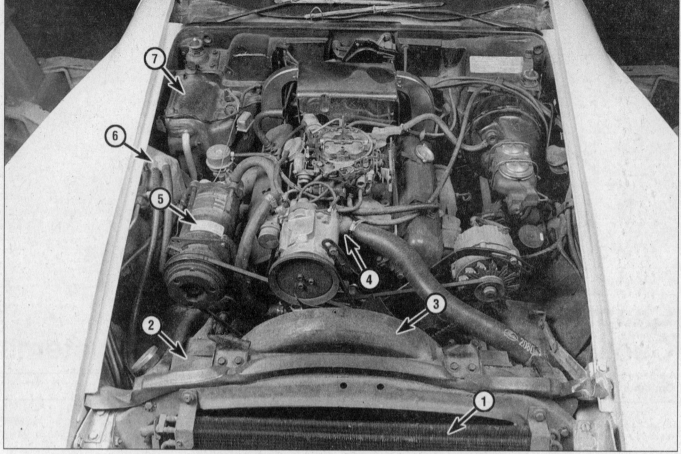

1.1 Cooling, heating and air-conditioning components underhood

1	.Condenser	4	Thermostat housing
2	Radiator	5	Compressor
3	Engine cooling fan and shroud	6	Coolant recovery tank
		7	Evaporator and blower housing

1   General information

Refer to illustration 1.1

Engine cooling system

All vehicles covered by this manual employ a pressurized engine cooling system with thermostatically-controlled coolant circulation **(see illustration)**. An impeller-type water pump mounted on the front of the block pumps coolant through the engine. The coolant flows around each cylinder and toward the rear of the engine. Cast-in coolant passages direct coolant around the intake and exhaust ports, near the spark plug areas and in close proximity to the exhaust valve guides.

A wax pellet-type thermostat is located in the thermostat housing near the front of the engine. During warm up, the closed thermostat prevents coolant from circulating through the radiator. When the engine reaches normal operating temperature, the thermostat opens and allows hot coolant to travel through the radiator, where it's cooled before returning to the engine.

The cooling system is sealed by a pressure type radiator cap. This raises the boiling point of the coolant, and the higher boiling point of the coolant increases the cooling efficiency of the radiator. If the system pressure exceeds the cap pressure relief value, the excess pressure in the system forces the spring-loaded valve inside the cap off its seat and allows the coolant to escape through the overflow tube into a coolant reservoir. When the system cools, the excess coolant is automatically drawn from the reservoir back into the radiator.

The coolant reservoir does double duty as both the point at which fresh coolant is added to the cooling system to maintain the proper fluid level and as a holding tank for overheated coolant.

This type of cooling system is known as a closed design because coolant that escapes past the pressure cap is saved and reused.

Heating system

The heating system consists of a blower fan and heater core located within the heater box, the inlet and outlet hoses connecting the heater core to the engine cooling system and the heater/air conditioning control head on the dashboard. Hot engine coolant is circulated through the heater core. When the heater mode is activated, a flap door opens to expose the heater box to the passenger compartment. A fan switch on the control head activates the blower motor, which forces air through the core, heating the air.

Air conditioning system

The air conditioning system consists of a condenser mounted in front of the radiator, an evaporator mounted adjacent to the heater core, a compressor mounted on the engine, a receiver-drier (accumulator) which contains a high pressure relief valve and the plumbing connecting all of the above.

A blower fan forces the warmer air of the passenger compartment through the evaporator core (sort of a radiator-in-reverse), transferring the heat from the air to the refrigerant. The liquid refrigerant boils off into low pressure vapor, taking the heat with it when it leaves the evaporator.

3.7 Testing a thermostat

3.13 The thermostat housing cover is held in place with two bolts (arrows) - if the cover is stuck, use a soft-face hammer to dislodge it

2 Antifreeze - general information

Warning: *Do not allow antifreeze to come in contact with your skin or painted surfaces of the vehicle. Rinse off spills immediately with plenty of water. Antifreeze is highly toxic if ingested. Never leave antifreeze lying around in an open container or in puddles on the floor; children and pets are attracted by it's sweet smell and may drink it. Check with local authorities about disposing of used antifreeze. Many communities have collection centers which will see that antifreeze is disposed of safely. Never dump used anti-freeze on the ground or into drains.*
Note: *Non-Toxic coolant is available at local auto parts stores. Although the coolant is non-toxic when fresh, proper disposal is still required.*

The cooling system should be filled with a water/ethylene glycol-based antifreeze solution, which will prevent freezing down to at least -20-degrees F, or lower if local climate requires it. It also provides protection against corrosion and increases the coolant boiling point.

The cooling system should be drained, flushed and refilled at the specified intervals (see Chapter 1). Old or contaminated antifreeze solutions are likely to cause damage and encourage the formation of rust and scale in the system. Use distilled water with the antifreeze.

Before adding antifreeze, check all hose connections, because antifreeze tends to search out and leak through very minute openings. Engines don't normally consume coolant, so if the level goes down, find the cause and correct it.

The exact mixture of antifreeze-to-water which you should use depends on the relative weather conditions. The mixture should contain at least 50 percent antifreeze, but should never contain more than 70 percent antifreeze. Consult the mixture ratio chart on the antifreeze container before adding coolant. Hydrometers are available at most auto parts stores to test the coolant. Use antifreeze which meets the vehicle manufacturer's specifications.

3 Thermostat - check and replacement

Refer to illustrations 3.7 and 3.13
Warning: *Do not attempt to remove the radiator cap, coolant or thermostat until the engine has cooled completely.*
Caution: *Do not drive the vehicle without a thermostat. The computer (when equipped) may stay in open loop and emissions and fuel economy will suffer.*

Check

1 Before assuming the thermostat is to blame for a cooling system problem, check the coolant level (Chapter 1), drivebelt tension (Chapter 1) and temperature gauge (or light) operation.
2 If the engine takes a long time to warm up, the thermostat is probably stuck open. Replace the thermostat.
3 If the engine runs hot, use your hand to check the temperature of the upper radiator hose. If the hose isn't hot, but the engine is, the thermostat is probably stuck in the closed position, preventing the coolant inside the engine from escaping to the radiator. Replace the thermostat.
4 If the upper radiator hose is hot, it means the coolant is flowing and the thermostat is open. Consult the Troubleshooting Section at the front of this manual for further diagnosis.
5 A more thorough test of the thermostat can only be made when it is removed from the vehicle (see below). If the thermostat remains in the open position at room temperature, it is faulty and must be replaced.
6 To test it fully, suspend the (closed) thermostat on a length of string or wire in a container of cold water, with a thermometer (cooking type that reads beyond 212 de-grees F). A clear Pyrex cooking container is easiest to use.
7 Heat the water on a stove while observing the temperature and the thermostat. Neither should contact the sides of the container **(see illustration)**.
8 Note the temperature when the thermostat begins to open and when it is fully open. Compare the temperatures to the Specifications in this Chapter. The number stamped into the thermostat is generally the fully-open temperature. Some manufacturers provide Specifications for the beginning-to-open temperature, the fully-open temperature, and sometimes the amount the valve should open.
9 If the thermostat doesn't open and close as specified, or sticks in any position, replace it.

Replacement

Note: *You may have to remove the air cleaner assembly to provide room to work on the thermostat.*
10 Disconnect the negative battery cable.
11 Drain the cooling system (Chapter 1). If the coolant is relatively new or in good condition, save it and reuse it.
12 Follow the upper radiator hose to the engine to locate the thermostat housing. Loosen the clamp and remove the upper radiator hose from the thermostat housing cover fitting. If the hose is stuck, grasp it near the end with a pair of Channelock pliers and twist it to break the seal, then pull it off. If the hose is old or deteriorated, cut it off and install a new one.
13 Remove the bolts and detach the housing cover **(see illustration)**. Be prepared for some coolant to spill as the gasket seal is broken.
14 Note how it's installed (which end is up), then remove the thermostat.
15 Use a scraper or putty knife to remove all traces of gasket material and sealant from the mating surfaces. Make sure nothing falls into the coolant passage; it's a good idea to stuff a rag into the opening. Clean the mating

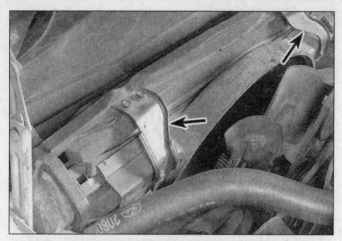

4.4a The shroud on this 1975 Corvette is retained at the top by these brackets (arrows)

4.4b The lower corners are secured by nuts (arrow, seen from below)

surfaces with lacquer thinner or acetone.

16   Apply a thin layer of RTV sealant to the mating surfaces of the housing and cover, then install the new thermostat in the engine, followed by the gasket. Make sure the correct end faces up - the spring is normally directed into the housing.

17   Install the cover and bolts. Tighten the bolts to the specified torque, but don't over-tighten them or the cover may distort.

18   Reattach the radiator hose to the fitting and tighten the clamp (now would be a good time to install new hoses and clamps).

19   Refill the cooling system (Chapter 1), then run the engine until it reaches normal operating temperature and check for leaks.

4   Radiator - removal and installation

Refer to illustrations 4.4a and 4.4b
Warning: *The engine must be completely cool before beginning this procedure!*

1   Disconnect the negative battery cable. **Note:** *On later models, the air cleaner snorkel should be removed to provide more room.*

2   Drain the radiator (refer to Chapter 1).

3   Detach the radiator hoses, overflow hose and automatic transmission cooling lines (if applicable).

4   Detach the radiator shroud and hang it over the fan assembly. The shroud is attached with screws and nuts **(see illustrations)**. On later models with an auxiliary elec-tric fan, the electric fan may be in the way and may have to be removed.

5   Remove the upper mounting panel at the top of the radiator.

6   Remove the brackets and lift the radia-tor out of the engine compartment. Be careful not to scratch the paint on the body. If coolant drips on any body paint, immediately wash it off with clear water as the antifreeze solution can damage the finish.

7   With the radiator removed, it can be inspected for leaks and damage. If it needs repairs, have a professional radiator shop or

dealer service department perform the work, as special equipment and techniques are required.

8   Bugs and dirt can be cleaned from the radiator with compressed air and a soft brush. Do not bend the cooling fins as this is done.

9   Inspect the rubber mounting pads which the radiator sits on and replace as necessary.

10   Set the radiator in position (make sure it's seated in the mounting pads).

11   Install the upper panel, shroud and hoses in the reverse order of removal.

12   Connect the negative battery cable and fill the radiator as described in Chapter 1.

13   Start the engine and check for leaks. Allow the engine to reach normal operating temperature (upper radiator hose hot) and add coolant until the level reaches the bot-tom of the filler neck.

5   Cooling fan and clutch - check and replacement

1   The vehicles covered by this manual are equipped with a thermostatically-controlled mechanical fan clutch. Later models (1981 on) also have an auxiliary electric cooling fan.

Fan clutch check

2   Begin the clutch check with a lukewarm engine (start it when cold and let it run for two minutes only).

3   Remove the key from the ignition switch for safety purposes.

4   Turn the fan blades and note the resis-tance. There should be moderate resistance, depending on temperature.

5   Drive the vehicle until the engine is warmed up. Shut it off and remove the key.

6   Turn the fan blades and again note the resistance. There should be a noticeable increase in resistance.

7   If the fan clutch fails this check or is locked up, replacement is required. If exces-sive fluid is leaking from the hub or lateral play over 1/4-inch is noted, replace the fan clutch.

8   If any fan blades are bent, don't straighten them! The metal will be weakened and blades could fly off during engine opera-tion. Replace the fan with a new one.

Auxiliary electric fan check

9   If the fan doesn't run when it should, check the fuse first.

10   If the fuse is okay, detach the wire from the temperature switch and ground it on the engine block. If the fan runs, the temperature switch is defective.

11   Use jumper wires to attach battery volt-age directly to the fan motor. If it runs, the problem is in the circuit, not the motor.

Fan clutch replacement

12   Disconnect the negative battery cable from the battery, then remove the air cleaner intake duct (if necessary).

13   Remove the upper radiator support or fan shroud (as necessary).

14   Remove the drivebelts (Chapter 1).

15   Remove the fan clutch hub-to-water pump bolts (or nuts) and pull the fan clutch away from the pump.

16   Check the hub mating surfaces for burrs and other damage (use a file to smooth them if necessary).

17   Align the balance marks on the hubs, then attach the new fan clutch to the water pump and tighten the bolts in a criss-cross pattern.

18   Install and adjust the drivebelts (Chap-ter 1). The remaining steps are the reverse of removal.

6   Coolant temperature sending unit - check and replacement

Warning: *Wait until the engine is completely cool before beginning this procedure.*
Refer to illustration 6.1

1   The coolant temperature indicator sys-tem is composed of a light or temperature gauge mounted in the instrument panel and a

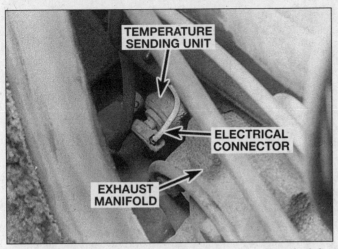

6.1 The coolant temperature sending unit is located on the left cylinder head, between the number 1 and number 3 spark plugs

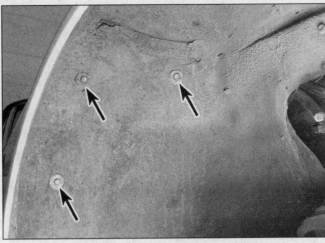

7.5 These screws (arrows) fasten the coolant reservoir to the inner fender

coolant temperature sending unit mounted on the engine **(see illustration)**. Some vehicles have more than one sending unit, but only one is used for the indicator system. **Warning:** *If the vehicle is equipped with an electric cooling fan, stay clear of the fan blades, which can come on at any time.*

2 If an overheating indication occurs, check the coolant level in the system and then make sure the wiring between the light or gauge and the sending unit is secure and all fuses are intact.

3 When the ignition switch is turned on and the starter motor is turning, the indicator light should be on (overheated engine indication).

4 If the light is not on, the bulb may be burned out, the ignition switch may be faulty or the circuit may be open. Test the circuit by grounding the wire to the sending unit while the ignition is on (engine not running for safety). If the gauge deflects full scale or the light comes on, replace the sending unit.

5 As soon as the engine starts, the light should go out and remain out unless the engine overheats. Failure of the light to go out may be due to a grounded wire between the light and the sending unit, a defective sending unit or a faulty ignition switch. Check

the coolant to make sure it's the proper type. Plain water may have too low a boiling point to activate the sending unit.

6 If the sending unit must be replaced, simply unscrew it from the engine and install the new one. Use sealant on the threads. Make sure the engine is cool before removing the defective sending unit. There will be some coolant loss as the unit is removed, so be prepared to catch it. Check the level after the replacement has been installed.

7 Coolant reservoir - removal and installation

Refer to illustration 7.5

1 Remove the air cleaner assembly.

2 Remove the air conditioning compressor (if equipped) and position it out of the way. Do not disconnect the hoses from the compressor!

3 Remove the air cleaner duct from over the radiator (vehicles with air conditioning only).

4 Remove the air cleaner duct along the fender.

5 Loosen the clamp and detach the hose from the coolant reservoir fitting **(see illus-**

tration).

6 Remove the screws and detach the reservoir.

7 Before reinstalling it, make sure the reservoir is clean - if necessary, wash it out with hot, soapy water and rinse it thoroughly.

8 Installation is the reverse of removal.

8 Water pump - check

Refer to illustration 8.4

1 A failure in the water pump can cause serious engine damage due to overheating.

2 There are three ways to check the operation of the water pump while it's installed on the engine. If the pump is defective, it should be replaced with a new or rebuilt unit.

3 With the engine running at normal operating temperature, squeeze the upper radiator hose. If the water pump is working properly, a pressure surge should be felt as the hose is released. **Warning:** *Keep your hands away from the fan blades!*

4 Water pumps are equipped with weep or vent holes. If a failure occurs in the pump seal, coolant will leak from the hole. In most cases you'll need a flashlight to find the hole on the water pump from underneath to check for leaks **(see illustration).**

5 If the water pump shaft bearings fail, there may be a howling sound at the front of the engine while it's running. Shaft wear can be felt if the water pump pulley is rocked up and down. Don't mistake drivebelt slippage, which causes a squealing sound, for water pump bearing failure.

9 Water pump - replacement

Warning: *Wait until the engine is completely cool before beginning this procedure.*

Refer to illustrations 9.7, 9.10 and 9.11

1 Disconnect the negative battery cable from the battery.

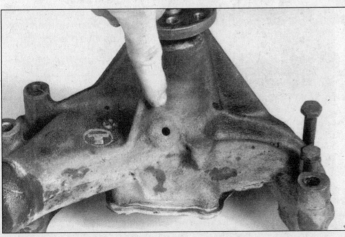

8.4 If coolant leaks out of the weep hole in large quantities, the seal in the water pump is defective and the pump should be replaced (the weep hole is at the bottom of the pump - an inspection mirror will be needed to see it)

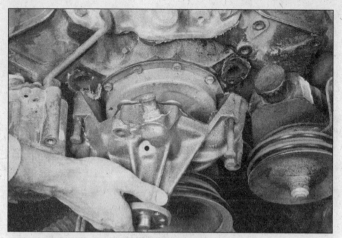

9.7 Remove all the bolts, set the accessories aside and rock the water pump to break the gaskets seal or tap it with a wooden hammer

9.10 Be sure to remove the old gaskets and clean the mating surfaces of the block before installing the new pump

2   Drain the cooling system (see Chapter 1). If the coolant is relatively new or in good condition, save it and reuse it.

3   Remove the cooling fan and shroud.

4   Remove the drivebelts (see Chapter 1) and the fan/fan clutch.

5   Loosen the clamps and detach the hoses from the water pump. If they're stuck, grasp each hose near the end with a pair of Channelock pliers and twist it to break the seal, then pull it off. If the hoses are deteriorated, cut them off and install new ones.

6   Remove all accessory brackets from the water pump. When removing the power steering pump and air conditioning compressor, don't disconnect the hoses. Tie the units aside with the hoses attached.

7   Remove the bolts and detach the water pump from the engine. Note the locations of the various lengths and different types of bolts as they're removed to ensure correct installation **(see illustration)**.

8   clean the bolt threads and the threaded holes in the engine to remove corrosion and sealant.

9   Compare the new pump to the old one to make sure they're identical.

10   Remove all traces of old gasket material from the engine with a gasket scraper **(see illustration)**.

11   If a new pump is being installed, transfer ant hose fittings from the old pump to the new one **(see illustration)**. Clean the thread on the old hose fitting and install in the new pump with pipe sealant.

12   Clean the engine and new water pump mating surfaces with lacquer thinner or acetone.

13   Apply a thin coat of RTV sealant to the engine side of the new gaskets.

14   Apply a thin layer of RTV sealant to the gasket mating surfaces of the new pump, then carefully mate the gaskets and the pump. Slip the bolts through the pump mounting holes to hold the gaskets in place.

15   Carefully attach the pump and gaskets to the engine and thread the bolts into the holes finger-tight.

16   Install any remaining bolts (if they also hold an accessory bracket in place, be sure to reposition the bracket at this time). Tighten them to the torque listed in this Chapter's Specifications in 1/4-turn increments. Don't overtighten them or the pump may be distorted.

17   Reinstall all parts removed for access to the pump.

18   Refill the cooling system and check the drivebelt tension (see Chapter 1). Run the engine and check for leaks.

10   Heater core - replacement

1   Disconnect the negative battery cable from the battery.

2   Drain the radiator (Chapter 1).

3   Loosen the clamps and detach the heater hoses from the core fittings. If they're stuck, slit them with a sharp knife and install new ones.

4   Plug the core fittings to prevent coolant spills.

5   Remove the nuts from the heater distrib-

9.11 Use a wrench to carefully unscrew the heater hose pipe, so it can be transferred to the new pump

utor studs on the engine side of the firewall.

6   Remove the right side instrument pad and the right-hand dash braces.

7   Remove the center dash console duct and the floor outlet duct (see Chapter 11).

8   Remove the radio and center dash console.

9   Pull the heater distributor out of the dash panel mount. Be careful not to bend or kink the control cables.

10   When it's clear, disconnect the cables and the resistor wire from the heater assembly.

11   Pull out the heater core.

12   Installation is the reverse of removal.

11   Blower unit - removal and installation

Refer to illustration 11.4

1   Disconnect the negative battery cable.

2   Where applicable, remove the screws and lay the coolant reservoir tank on one side.

3   Disconnect the blower motor wires.

4   Remove the mounting screws and detach the blower motor from the case **(see illustration)**.

5   Remove the nut and detach the blower wheel from the motor shaft, if necessary.

6   Installation is the reverse of removal. **Note:** *Make sure the open end of the blower wheel is facing away from the motor.*

12   Air conditioning system - check and maintenance

Warning: *The air conditioning system is under high pressure. Do not loosen any hose fittings or remove any components until after the system has been discharged and the refrigerant recovered by an air conditioning shop. Always wear eye protection when disconnecting air conditioning system fittings.*

1   The following maintenance checks

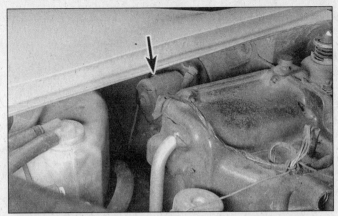

11.4 The blower motor is located under the fender lip (arrow)

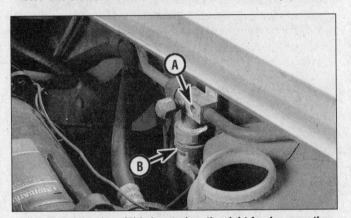

12.7 The sight glass (A) is located on the right fender, near the compressor - B indicate location of the refrigerant pressure switch

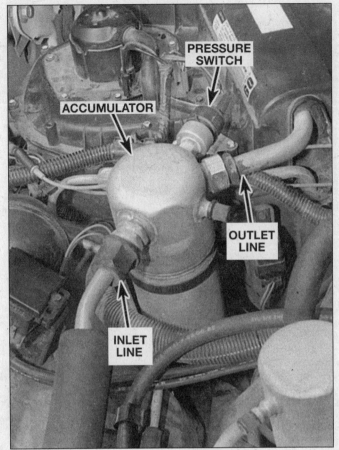

13.4 A typical GM accumulator

should be performed on a regular basis to ensure the air conditioner continues to operate at peak efficiency.

a) *Check the compressor drivebelt. If it's worn or deteriorated, replace it (see Chapter 1).*

b) *Check the drivebelt tension and, if necessary, adjust it (see Chapter 1).*

c) *Check the system hoses. Look for cracks, bubbles, hard spots and deterioration. Inspect the hoses and all fittings for oil bubbles and seepage. If there's any evidence of wear, damage or leaks, replace the hose(s).*

d) *Check the condenser fins for leaves, bugs and other debris. Use a "fin comb" or compressed air to clean the condenser.*

e) *Make sure the system has the correct refrigerant charge.*

2   It's a good idea to operate the system for about 10 minutes at least once a month, particularly during the winter. Long term non-use can cause hardening, and subsequent failure, of the seals.

3   Because of the complexity of the air conditioning system and the special equipment necessary to service it, in-depth troubleshooting and repairs are not included in this manual. However, simple checks and component replacement procedures are pro-vided in this Chapter.

4   The most common cause of poor cooling is simply a low system refrigerant charge. If a noticeable drop in cool air output occurs, one of the following quick checks will help determine if the refrigerant level is low.

Check

Refer to illustration 12.7

5   Warm the engine up to normal operating temperature.

6   Place the air conditioning temperature selector at the coldest setting and put the blower at the highest setting. Open the doors (to make sure the air conditioning system doesn't cycle off as soon as it cools the passenger compartment).

7   With the compressor engaged - the clutch will make an audible click and the center of the clutch will rotate - inspect the sight glass **(see illustration)**. If the refrigerant looks foamy, it's low. Charge the system as described later in this Section.

8   If there's no sight glass, feel the inlet and outlet pipes at the compressor. One side should be cold and one hot. If there's no perceptible difference between the two pipes, there's something wrong with the compressor or the system. It might be a low charge - it might be something else. Take the vehicle to a dealer service department or service station.

Adding refrigerant

Note: *Because of Federal regulations by the Environmental Protection Agency, 14-ounce cans of R-12 refrigerant are not available to the home mechanic. Take your vehicle to a licensed air conditioning mechanic for charging.*

13   Air conditioning system accumulator - removal and installation

Refer to illustration 13.4

Warning: *The air conditioning system is under high pressure. Do not loosen any hose fittings or remove any components until after the system has been discharged and the refrigerant recovered by an air conditioning shop. Always wear eye protection when disconnecting air conditioning system fittings.*

1   Have the air conditioning system discharged (see Warning above).

2   Disconnect the negative battery cable from the battery.

3   Unplug the electrical connector from the pressure switch near the top of the accumulator.

4   Disconnect the refrigerant lines from the accumulator **(see illustration)**. Use a back-

14.5 Typical compressor installation - disconnect the electrical connector at the clutch (1), unbolt the refrigerant lines (2) at the rear, then remove the mounting bolts (3 indicates upper bolt)

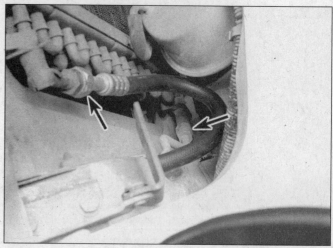

15.5 Disconnect the refrigerant lines (arrows) at the right front of the condenser

up wrench to prevent twisting the tubing.

5   Plug the open fittings to prevent entry of dirt and moisture.

6   Loosen the mounting bracket bolt(s) and lift the accumulator out.

7   If a new accumulator is being installed, remove the Schrader valve and pour the oil out into a measuring cup, noting the amount. Add fresh refrigerant oil to the new accumulator equal to the amount removed from the old unit, plus one ounce.

8   Installation is the reverse of removal.

9   Take the vehicle back to the shop that discharged it. Have the air conditioning system evacuated, charged and leak tested.

15.6 Remove the condenser mounting bolts (arrow indicates one of two)

14   Air conditioning system compressor - removal and installation

Warning: *The air conditioning system is under high pressure. Do not loosen any hose fittings or remove any components until after the system has been discharged and the refrigerant recovered by an air conditioning shop. Always wear eye protection when disconnecting air conditioning system fittings.*

Note: *The accumulator (see Section 13) should be replaced whenever the compressor is replaced.*

Refer to illustration 14.5

1   Have the air conditioning system discharged (see Warning above).

2   Disconnect the negative battery cable from the battery.

3   Disconnect the compressor clutch wiring harness.

4   Remove the drivebelt (see Chapter 1).

5   Disconnect the refrigerant lines from the rear of the compressor. Plug the open fittings to prevent entry of dirt and moisture **(see illustration)**.

6   Unbolt the compressor from the mounting brackets and lift it out of the vehicle.

7   If a new compressor is being installed, follow the directions with the compressor regarding the draining of excess oil prior to installation.

8   The clutch may have to be transferred from the original to the new compressor.

9   Installation is the reverse of removal. Replace all O-rings with new ones specifically made for air conditioning system use and lubricate them with refrigerant oil.

10   Have the system evacuated, recharged and leak tested by the shop that discharged it.

15   Air conditioning system condenser - removal and installation

Warning: *The air conditioning system is under high pressure. Do not loosen any hose fittings or remove any components until after the system has been discharged and the refrigerant recovered by an air conditioning shop. Always wear eye protection when disconnecting air conditioning system fittings.*

Note: *The accumulator (see Section 13)*

should be replaced whenever the condenser is replaced.

Refer to illustrations 15.5 and 15.6

1   Have the air conditioning system discharged (see Warning above).

2   Disconnect the negative battery cable.

3   Drain the cooling system (see Chapter 1).

4   Remove the radiator.

5   Disconnect the refrigerant lines from the condenser **(see illustration)**.

6   Remove the mounting bolts from the condenser brackets **(see illustration)**.

7   Lift the condenser out of the vehicle and plug the lines to keep dirt and moisture out.

8   If the original condenser will be reinstalled, store it with the line fittings on top to prevent oil from draining out.

9   If a new condenser is being installed, pour one ounce of refrigerant oil into it prior to installation.

10   Reinstall the components in the reverse order of removal. Be sure the rubber pads are in place under the condenser.

11   Have the system evacuated, recharged and leak tested by the shop that discharged it.

16.2 Remove the four corner screws (arrows) and lift out the floor console cover

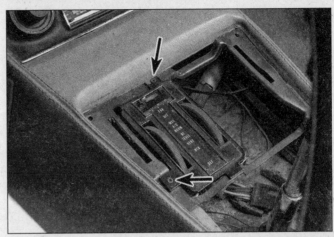

16.3 Remove these two screws (arrows) and lift out the heater/air conditioner control panel far enough to disconnect the electrical connectors at the back of the panel

16   Air conditioner and heater control assembly - removal and installation

Refer to illustrations 16.2 and 16.3

1   Disconnect the negative battery cable from the battery.

2   Remove the screws and take off the floor console trim plate **(see illustration)**.

3   Remove the screws and pull the control assembly up and to the rear **(see illustration)**.

4   Label and disconnect the control cables, vacuum hoses and wire harnesses, then remove the control assembly.

5   Installation is the reverse of removal.

Notes

Chapter 4
Fuel and exhaust systems

Contents

Specifications

Note: *All dimensions in inches unless otherwise stated*

Fuel tank capacity

1968 through 1970	20 gals
1971 and later models	18 gals

Carburetors - application

Engine (cu in)	HP	Carburetor
1968		
327	300	Rochester 4MV
327	350	Rochester 4MV
427	390	Rochester 4MV
427	400	Holley 3x2300 or 4150
427	430	Holley 3x2300 or 4150
427	435	Holley 3x2300 or 4150
1969		
350	350	Rochester 4MV
427	390	Rochester 4MV
427	400	Holley 3x2300
427	435	Holley 3x2300
427	430	Holley 4150
1970		
350	300	Rochester 4MV
350	350	Rochester 4MV
350	370	Holley 4150
427	390	Holley 4150
427	400	Holley 4150
427	430	Holley 4150
427	435	Holley 2300
1971		
350	270	Rochester 4MV
350	330	Holley 4150
454	365	Rochester 4MV
454	425	Holley 4150
1972		
350	200	Rochester 4MV
350	255	Holley 4150
454	270	Rochester 4MV
1973		
350	190	Rochester 4MV
350	250	Rochester 4MV
454	275	Rochester 4MV
1974		
350	195	Rochester 4MV
350	250	Rochester 4MV
454	270	Rochester 4MV
1975 through 1977	350	All models Rochester M4MC
1978 and later models	all	Check number on carburetor

Carburetor data

1968 Holley 2300

Float level	
Primary	0.350 in
Secondary	0.50 in
Accelerator pump stroke	0.015 in
Choke vacuum break	0.250 in
Choke unloader	0.275 in
Main metering jet	
Primary	No 64
Secondary	No 62
Throttle bore	
Primary	1-1/2 in
Secondary	1-3/4 in

1968 Holley 4150

As Holley 2300 except:

Choke vacuum break	0.300 in
Choke unloader	0.350 in

Main metering jet
    Primary .... No 69
    Secondary .... No 76
Throttle bore
    Primary .... 1-11/16 in
    Secondary .... 1-11/16 in

1968 Rochester 4MV

Float level
    300/350 hp .... 9/32 in
    390 hp .... 1/16 in
Accelerator pump stroke .... 9/32 in
Idle vent .... 3/8 in
Fast idle .... 2 complete turns to give 2400 rpm
Carburetor choke rod .... 0.100 in
Choke vacuum break
    300/350 hp .... 0.245 in
    390 hp .... 0.160 in
Choke unloader .... 0.300 in
Air valve spring .... 7/8 in
Secondary closing .... 0.020 in
Secondary opening.. 0.070 in
Secondary lockout... 0.010 in
Main metering jet .... 0.071 in
Throttle lever
    Primary .... 1-3/8 in
    Secondary .... 2-1/4 in
Air valve dashpot .... 0.015 in
Secondary metering rod .... 27/32 in

1969 Holley 2300

As 1968 except for:
Main metering jet
    Primary .... No 63
    Secondary .... No 76

1969 Holley 4150

Float level.. 0.50 in
Accelerator pump .... 0.015 in
Choke vacuum break .... 0.300 in
Choke unloader .... 0.350 in
Secondary stop .... 1/2 turn open
Main metering jet
    Primary .... No 68
    Secondary .... No 76
Throttle bore
    Primary .... 1 9/16 in
    Secondary .... 1 9/16 in

1969 Rochester 4MV

Float level
    350 hp .... 3/16 in
    390 hp .... 1/4 in
Accelerator pump .... 5/16 in
Idle vent .... 3/8 in
Fast idle .... 2 complete turns giving 2400 rpm
Carburetor choke rod .... 0.100 in
Choke vacuum break.. 0.245 in
Choke unloader .... 0.450 in
Air valve spring .... 13/16 in
Secondary closing .... 0.020 in

1969 Rochester 4MV

Secondary opening.. 0.070 in
Secondary lockout... 0.015 in
Main metering jet
    350 hp .... 0.066 in
    390 hp .... 0.071 in
Throttle bore
    Primary .... 1-3/8 in
    Secondary .... 2-1/4 in
Air valve dashpot .... 0.015 in

1970 Holley 4150

As 1969 Holley 4150 except for:

Choke vacuum break	0.350 in
Main metering jet	
Primary	
Throttle side	No 82
Choke side	No 78
Secondary	
Throttle side	No 80
Choke side	No 82
Throttle bore	
Primary	1-3/4 in
Secondary	1-3/4 in

1970 Rochester 4MV

Float level	1/4 in
Accelerator pump	5/16 in
Fast idle	2 full turns to give 2400 rpm
Carburetor choke rod	0.100 in
Choke vacuum break	0.275 in
Choke unloader	0.450 in
Air valve spring	7/16 in
Main metering jet	0.076 in
Throttle bore	
Primary	1-3/8 in
Secondary	2-1/4 in
Air valve dashpot	0.015

1971 Holley 4150

Float level	
Carburetor installed	Fuel level with bottom of sight plug
Bowl inverted	Float centered in bowl
Accelerator pump	0.015 in
Fast idle	0.025 in (2200 rpm)
Choke rod adjustment	1.32±0.015 in
Choke vacuum break	0.350 in
Choke unloader	0.350 in
Secondary stop	1/2 turn open
Main metering jet	
Primary	No 70
Secondary	No 76
Throttle bore	
Primary	1-11/16 in
Secondary	1-11/16 in

1971 Rochester 4MV

Float level	1/4 in
Choke rod	0.100 in
Air valve dashpot	0.020 in
Vacuum break	
Manual	0.275 in
Automatic	0.260 in

1972 Holley 4150

As 1971 Holley 4150 except for:

Main metering jet	
Primary	No 68
Secondary	No 73

1972 Rochester 4MV

Float level	1/4 in
Pump rod	3/8 in
Choke rod (fast idle cam)	0.100 in
Air valve dashpot	0.020 in
Vacuum break	0.215 in
Unloader	0.450 in

1973 Rochester 4MV

Float level	
350 cu in	7/32 in
454 cu in	1/4 in
Pump rod	1-13/32 in (inner location)
Choke rod (fast idle cam)	0.430 in
Air valve wind up	
350 cu in	1/2 turn
454 cu in	11/16 turn
Vacuum brake	0.250 in
Unloader	0.450 in

1974 Rochester 4MV

Float level	
350 cu in engine	1/4 in
454 cu in engine	3/8 in
Pump rod	13/32 (inner location)
Choke rod (fast idle cam)	0.430
Air valve wind up	
350 cu in	
Federal	1 turn
California	7/8 turn
454 cu in	7/16 turn
Vacuum break	0.250 in
Unloader	0.450 in

1975 Rochester M4MC

Float level	15/32
Pump rod	0.275 in (inner location)
Choke coil lever	0.120 in
Choke rod (fast idle cam)	0.300 in
Air valve dashpot	0.015 in
Front vacuum break	0.180 in
Rear vacuum break	0.170 in
Air valve spring wind up	7/8 turn
Choke unloader	0.325 in

1976 and 1977 Rochester M4MC

Float level	13/32 in
Pump rod	9/32 in (inner location)
Choke coil lever	0.120 in
Choke rod (fast idle cam)	0.325 in
Air valve dashpot	0.015 in
Front vacuum break	
All carburetors except No 17056211	0.185 in
Carburetor No 17056211	0.170 in

1978 Rochester M4MC

Float level	15/32 in
Pump rod adjustment	9/32 in
Choke coil lever adjustment	0.120 in
Choke rod (fast idle cam) adjustment	46-degrees (0.314 in)
Air valve dashpot adjustment	0.015 in
Front vacuum break adjustment	
17058202	27-degrees (0.157 in) below 22500 miles
17058203	30-degrees (0.179 in) above 22500 miles
17058204	
17058502	28-degrees (0.164 in) below 30000 miles
17058504	31-degrees (0.187 in) above 30000 miles
17058210	30-degrees (0.179 in) below 22500 miles
17058211	33-degrees (0.203 in) above 22500 miles
17058228	
17058582	
17058584	
Automatic choke coil	2 notches lean
Unloader adjustment	42-degrees (0.277 in)
Secondary lockout adjustment	0.015 in
Secondary closing adjustment	0.020 in
Secondary opening adjustment	link must be in center of slot

1978 Rochester M4MC (continued)

Air valve spring adjustment
17058202	7/8 turn
17058203	
17058204	
17058228	
17058502	
17058504	
17058582	
17058584	
17058210	1 turn
17058211	

1979 Rochester M4MC

Note: *Items not specifically listed here are unchanged from 1978 M4MC.*

Pump rod adjustment
17059203	1/4 in (inner hole)
17059216	
17059217	
17059502	
17059504	
17059582	11/32 in (outer hole)
17059584	
17059210	9/32 in (inner hole)
17059211	
17059228	

Choke rod (fast idle cam)
adjustment	38-degrees (0.243 in)

Front vacuum break adjustment
17059203	27-degrees (0.157 in)
17059210	
17059211	
17059216	
17059217	
17059228	
17059502	28-degrees (0.164 in)
17059504	
17059582	33-degrees (0.203 in)
17059584	

Unloader adjustment
17059203	38-degrees(0.243 in)
17059210	
17059211	
17059216	
17059217	
17059228	
17059502	
17059504	
17059582	46-degrees (0.314 in)
17059584	

Automatic choke coil
17059202	1 notch lean
17059204	
17059210	
17059228	
17059582	
17059584	
17059216	
17059217	
17059203	2 notches lean
17059211	
17059502	
17059504	

Air valve spring adjustment
17049203	7/8 turn
17059216	
17059217	
17059502	
17059504	
17049582	

```
17059584
17059210 .................................................................  1 turn
17059211
17059228
```
Air valve spring wind up
    All carburetors Nos 17056210, 17056211, 17056226 .... 7/8 turn
    Carburetors Nos 17056210, 17056211, 17056226 .... 1 turn
Choke unloader .... 0.325 in

1980 49-state Rochester M4ME

Note: *Items not specifically listed here are unchanged from 1978/1979 M4MC.*

Float level
    17080274 .... 15/32 in
    17080243 .... 3/16 in
    All others .... 7/16 in
Pump rod adjustment
    17080202 .... 1/4 in (inner hole)
    17080204
    17080207
    17080282 .... 11/32 in (outer hole)
    17080284
    17080228 .... 9/32 in (inner hole)
    17080243
    17080274 .... 5/16 in (outer hole)
Choke rod (fast idle cam) adjustment
    17080274 .... 16-degrees (0.083 in)
    17080243 .... 14.5-degrees (0.074 in)
    All others .... 20-degrees (0.110 in)
Air valve dashpot adjustment .... 0.025 in
Front vacuum break adjustment
    17080202 .... 27-degrees (0.157 in)
    17080204
    17080207
    17080282 .... 25-degrees (0.142 in)
    17080284
    17080228 .... 30-degrees (0.179 in)
    17080243 .... 16-degrees (0.083 in)
    17080274 .... 20-degrees (0.110 in)
Rear vacuum break adjustment
    17080274 .... 28-degrees (0.164 in)
    17080243 .... 16-degrees (0.083 in)
Unloader adjustment
    17080243 .... 30-degrees (0.179 in)
    17080274 .... 33-degrees (0.203 in)
    All others .... 38-degrees (0.243 in)
Air valve spring adjustment
    17080243 .... 9/16 turn
    17080274 .... 5/8 turn
    All others .... 7/8 turn

1980 California Rochester E4ME

Note: *Items not specifically listed here are unchanged from 1978/1979 M4MC.*

Float level
    17080542 .... 3/8 in
    17080543
    17080502 .... 1/2 in
    17080504
Pump rod adjustment .... Not required
Choke rod (fast idle cam) adjustment
    17080542 .... 14.5-degrees (0.074 in)
    17080543
    17080502 .... 20-degrees (0.110 in)
    17080504
Front vacuum break adjustment
    17080542 .... 19-degrees (0.103 in)
    17080543
    17080502 .... 24-degrees (0.136 in)
    17080504

1980 California Rochester E4ME (continued)
Rear vacuum break adjustment
17080542	13-degrees (0.066 in)
17080543	23-degrees (0.129 in)
17080502	30-degrees (0.179 in)
17080504	
Unloader adjustment	38-degrees (0.243 in)
Air valve spring adjustment	7/8 turn

1981 Rochester E4ME
Note: *Items not specifically listed here are unchanged from 1978/1979 M4MC.*
Float level	11/32 in
Pump rod adjustment	Not required
Choke rod (fast idle cam) adjustment	20-degrees (0.110 in)
Air valve dashpot adjustment	0.025 in
Front vacuum break adjustment	26-degrees (0.149 in)
Unloader adjustment	38-degrees (0.243 in)
Air valve spring adjustment	7/8 turn
Idle mixture needle adjustment	3 1/3 turns out from seated position

1982 (Cross-Fire injection system)
Note: *Adjustment must be performed only by an authorized dealer service department or properly equipped repair shop.*

1 General information

Warning: *Gasoline is extremely flammable, so take extra precautions when you work on any part of the fuel system. Don't smoke or allow open flames or bare light bulbs near the work area, and don't work in a garage where a natural gas-type appliance (such as a water heater or a clothes dryer) with a pilot light is present. Since gasoline is carcinogenic, wear latex gloves when there's a possibility of being exposed to fuel, and, if you spill any fuel on your skin, rinse it off immediately with soap and water. Mop up any spills immediately and do not store fuel-soaked rags where they could ignite. The fuel system is under constant pressure on 1982 fuel-injected models, so, if any fuel lines are to be disconnected, the fuel pressure in the system must be relieved first. When you perform any kind of work on the fuel system, wear safety glasses and have a Class B type fire extinguisher on hand.*

The fuel system consists of a rear-mounted fuel tank, a fuel pump, an air cleaner and either a carburetor(s) or two throttle body fuel injection units (cross-fire injection - 1982 only).

The carburetor on most models is a four-barrel unit manufactured by either Holley or Rochester. Some earlier performance big-block models are equipped with a "tri-power" system, which incorporates three two-barrel carburetors.

A ducted hood is installed to allow a greater flow of cold air to the air cleaner during acceleration.

The exhaust system consists of a pair of exhaust manifolds, head pipes, mufflers and tailpipes. Later models are equipped with catalytic converters.

2 Air filter - servicing

Most models are equipped with a dry paper element air filter; however, some earlier models have oiled paper, oiled paper with a polyurethane band or wire mesh with a polyurethane band. Information on servicing the air filter is in Chapter 1.

3 Ducted hood air door - description and testing

1   An air control door is installed to the hood which opens when the accelerator pedal is fully depressed.
2   Actuation is by means of a solenoid that is energized by a pedal-operated kickdown assembly.
3   If it is thought that the door is inoperative, first check the connecting wiring and the fuse. Where a radio or map reading lamp is used, the air door shares the fuse and circuit with either of these accessories. If these accessories are working, the electrical supply side of the air door mechanism must be in order.
4   To check the solenoid, connect a jumper wire from the horn relay to the air door solenoid. If the solenoid is not heard to "click", replace it.
5   Check all linkage pivots for rust or binding.

4 Fuel pump - check and replacement

Warning: *Gasoline is extremely flammable, so take extra precautions when you work on any part of the fuel system. Don't smoke or allow open flames or bare light bulbs near the work area, and don't work in a garage where a natural gas-type appliance (such as a water heater or a clothes dryer) with a pilot light is present. Since gasoline is carcinogenic, wear latex gloves when there's a possibility of being exposed to fuel, and, if you spill any fuel on your skin, rinse it off immediately with soap and water. Mop up any spills immediately and do not store fuel-soaked rags where they could ignite. The fuel system is under constant pressure on 1982 fuel-injected models, so, if any fuel lines are to be disconnected, the fuel pressure in the system must be relieved first. When you perform any kind of work on the fuel system, wear safety glasses and have a Class B type fire extinguisher on hand.*

1   The fuel pump is a sealed unit and cannot be serviced in the event of malfunction. Models through 1981 have an engine-mounted fuel pump. 1982 models have an electric fuel pump mounted in the fuel tank.

1968 through 1981
Refer to illustrations 4.3, 4.4, 4.5a and 4.5b
2   If a faulty pump is suspected, remove the ignition coil primary lead, remove the fuel pipe at the carburetor, position an approved gasoline container to catch any fuel, then arrange for an assistant to crank the engine at the starter. If little or no fuel flows out, the pump is defective or the lines are clogged or leaking. Fuel should gush out in well-defined spurts.
3   To remove the pump, remove the fuel inlet and outlet lines **(see illustration)**. Use two wrenches to prevent damage to the pump and connections. **Warning:** *Wear eye protection when working under the fuel pump.*
4   Remove the fuel pump mounting bolts, the pump, and the gasket **(see illustration)**.

4.3 Use backup wrenches when removing the fuel pump lines
(arrow indicates line to carburetor)

4.4 After removing the mounting bolts, pull the fuel pump away
from the engine block

5   If the pushrod is to be removed, first remove the pump adapter plate and gasket **(see illustrations)**.

6   When installing, first install the pushrod using gasket sealant on the gasket (where applicable). Retain the pushrod in position using heavy grease.

7   Install the pump using a new gasket. Use gasket sealant on the screw threads.

8   Connect the fuel lines, start the engine and check for leaks.

1982

9   The fuel pump is part of the fuel tank metering unit and is located in the fuel tank. Access is through the fuel filler door in the body.

10   Disconnect the battery ground cable from the battery, then remove the fuel filler door assembly. It is held in place by screws located on the inside surface.

11   Remove the filler neck seal and the drain hose, then disconnect the fuel lines, the vapor line and the electrical connector.

12   Remove the screws around the circumference of the fuel metering unit, then lift the assembly out of the tank. The fuel pump can be removed from the fuel metering unit once the assembly is out of the tank.

13   Installation is the reverse of removal. Be sure to use a new gasket between the tank and the fuel metering unit. Check for leaks around the fuel line connections before installing the fuel filler door assembly.

5   Steel fuel tank without evaporation control system - removal and installation

Refer to illustrations 5.1, 5.2 and 5.5

Warning: *Gasoline is extremely flammable, so take extra precautions when you work on any part of the fuel system. Don't smoke or allow open flames or bare light bulbs near the work area, and don't work in a garage where a natural gas-type appliance (such as a water heater or a clothes dryer) with a pilot light is present. Since gasoline is carcinogenic, wear latex gloves when there's a possibility of being exposed to fuel, and, if you spill any fuel on your skin, rinse it off immediately with soap and water. Mop up any spills immediately and do not store fuel-soaked rags where they could ignite. The fuel system is under constant pressure on 1982 fuel-injected models, so if any fuel lines are to be disconnected,*

4.5a If necessary, remove the lower two screws and pull off the fuel pump adapter plate and gasket . . .

the fuel pressure in the system must be relieved first. When you perform any kind of work on the fuel system, wear safety glasses and have a Class B type fire extinguisher on hand.

1   The tank is located between the frame rails to the rear of the rear axle **(see illustration)**.

4.5b . . . then pull out the fuel pump pushrod

5.1 The fuel tank support is mounted using bolts (arrows)
at each end

5.5 Filler neck details

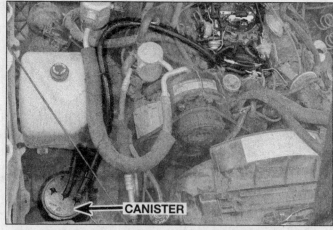

6.2 Typical fuel evaporative control system lines and carbon (charcoal) canister

2   The fuel level metering and fuel pick-up pipe assembly is located on the bottom surface of the tank.
3   Before removing the tank, the fuel must be siphoned out by disconnecting the fuel outlet pipe from the tank and connecting a temporary piece of hose to it. Drain the fuel into an approved gasoline container.
4   Disconnect the battery.
5   Remove the gas cap and the boot from the filler neck **(see illustration)**.
6   Disconnect the drain line.
7   Raise the rear of the vehicle and support it securely.
8   Remove the spare tire from its carrier, then remove the carrier.
9   Disconnect the exhaust system from the transmission support bracket.
10   Disconnect the exhaust rear mountings and move the system to one side.
11   Remove the fuel tank retaining strap bolts.
12   Disconnect the wires from the tank unit.
13   Remove the tank support-to-frame bolts and withdraw the support.
14   Lower the tank carefully, turning it to remove it. Installation is the reverse of removal.

6   Steel fuel tank with Evaporation Control System (EVAP or ECS) - maintenance, removal and installation

Refer to illustration 6.2
1   This system incorporates a separator and carbon canister to control the emission of vapor fumes from the fuel tank to atmosphere.
2   At the special intervals, the carbon canister filter should be replaced. To do this, first mark the hoses in respect of their positions on the canister, which is mounted within the engine compartment **(see illustration)**.
3   Disconnect the hoses and remove the canister. Pry out the filter from the base of the canister and install a new one.

4   If the gas cap must be replaced at any time because of its failure to seal or any other fault, ensure that it is replaced with one that is exactly the same as the one which was removed.
5   Removal and installation of the fuel tank is similar to the operations described in Section 5, except that the additional hoses must be disconnected before the tank can be withdrawn.

7   Steel fuel tank with internal flexible liner - removal and installation

1   This type of fuel tank is installed to very late models as a safety device against tank rupture in the event of a collision.
2   The tank consists of three parts, the steel outer tank, the internal liner or bladder, the top plate assembly which incorporates the metering unit, filler opening, fuel feed and return and vapor pipes.
3   Removal of this type of tank is similar to that described in Section 5.
4   Once removed, the plate assembly can be unbolted, the bladder withdrawn and the metering unit inspected. A fuel tank cover is installed to these models which may be detached after the tank has been removed.
5   Cars with this type of tank liner should not remain empty. If the car is to be stored for any length of time, the tank cover plate should be removed and non-detergent 10W oil sprayed on the inner surface of the bladder.
6   Installation is as described in Section 5.

8   Fuel tank cleaning and repair - general information

1   All repairs to the fuel tank or filler neck should be carried out by a professional who has experience in this critical and potentially dangerous work. Even after cleaning and flushing of the fuel system, explosive fumes

can remain and ignite during repair of the tank.
2   If the fuel tank is removed from the vehicle, it should not be placed in an area where sparks or open flames could ignite the fumes coming out of the tank. Be especially careful inside garages where a natural gas-type appliance is located, because the pilot light could cause an explosion.

9   Accelerator controls (early models)

1   On cars built up until 1973, the following throttle linkage adjustments can be carried out.
2   Disconnect the throttle rod swivel at the throttle lever on the carburetor.
3   Depress the accelerator pedal fully to its stop on the floor and then have an assistant open the throttle lever on the carburetor fully. Without moving either component, tighten the cable clamp bolt.
4   If the car is equipped with automatic transmission, disconnect the kickdown rod at the throttle lever.
5   Hold the throttle lever at the carburetor wide open, push the throttle rod to the rear so that the accelerator pedal touches the floor mat. Adjust the position of the swivel so that it just enters the hole in the throttled lever.
6   Attach the swivel to the throttle lever and install the accelerator return spring.
7   On cars equipped with automatic transmission, hold the throttle lever in the fully open position, pull the kickdown rod to its full detent position and adjust the effective length of the rod so that it just enters the hole in the throttle lever. Reconnect the rod.

10   Accelerator controls (later models)

Refer to illustration 10.2
1   On vehicles built after 1974, no adjustment is provided for.

10.2 Throttle connections on a typical later four-barrel carburetor

11.1a Typical model 2300 Holley carburetor - the list number is on the front of the choke housing (arrow)

11.1b A typical Rochester 4MV carburetor

11.1c A typical Holley 4150/4160 carburetor (arrow points to list number)

2   If full throttle conditions cannot be obtained when the pedal is depressed fully to the floor, the operating cable is binding or the pedal arm has been bent **(see illustration)**.

11 Carburetors - description

Refer to illustrations 11.1a, 11.1b and 11.1c

1   The carburetor(s) used depends upon the year of production of the vehicle and the engine and rated horsepower **(see illustrations)**.

2   The make of carburetor will either be a Rochester or Holley, and reference should be made to the specifications given in this Chapter and Chapter 1 for application of the units to particular vehicles.

12 Holley 2300 carburetor - adjustments without removal from engine

Refer to illustrations 12.4, 12.7 and 12.13
Warning: *Gasoline is extremely flammable,*

so take extra precautions when you work on any part of the fuel system. Don't smoke or allow open flames or bare light bulbs near the work area, and don't work in a garage where a natural gas-type appliance (such as a water heater or a clothes dryer) with a pilot light is present. Since gasoline is carcinogenic, wear

12.4 Fuel level sight plug location (typical Holley 2-barrel or 4-barrel)

latex gloves when there's a possibility of being exposed to fuel, and, if you spill any fuel on your skin, rinse it off immediately with soap and water. Mop up any spills immediately and do not store fuel-soaked rags where they could ignite. The fuel system is under constant pressure on 1982 fuel-injected models, so, if any fuel lines are to be disconnected, the fuel pressure in the system must be relieved first. When you perform any kind of work on the fuel system, wear safety glasses and have a Class B type fire extinguisher on hand.

1   The following adjustments may be carried out with the carburetors installed on the vehicle. **Note:** *For clarity, the photographs show the carburetor removed from the vehicle.*

Float adjustment

2   Remove the air cleaner and unscrew and unscrew the fuel level sight plugs.

3   Start the engine and let it idle.

4   With the vehicle standing on a level surface, the fuel level should be up to the threads at the bottom of the sight plug hole **(see illustration)**.

12.7 Measure the clearance between the lever and the end of the push rod (arrow) when adjusting the accelerator pump

12.13 When setting the fast idle speed there should be 0.250-inch clearance between the throttle blade and the carburetor housing (arrow 1) - bend the lever (arrow 2) to adjust it

5   If adjustment is required, release the inlet needle lock screw and turn the adjusting nut clockwise to lower the level or counter-clockwise to raise it 1/6 of a turn of the adjusting nut will alter the fuel level by 1/16 inch). Tighten the needle lock screw.

6   To ensure the correct secondary float level setting, open the primary throttles slightly and open the secondary throttle by hand. This will give a stabilized secondary fuel level.

Accelerator pump adjustment (primary carburetor)

7   Retain the throttle lever in the fully open position with a rubber band. Hold the accelerator pump lever fully down and measure the distance between the spring adjusting nut and the arm of the pump lever (see illustration). This should be 0.15 in. Adjust if necessary by turning the nut or screw. Hold the pump lever securely as it is not threaded.

Choke vacuum break (primary carburetor) adjustment

8   Hold the choke valve plate fully closed with a rubber band.

9   Hold the vacuum break against its stop and then measure the gap between the lower edge of the choke valve plate and the carburetor body. This should be 0.250 inch. If necessary, bend the vacuum break rod to adjust.

Choke unloader (primary carburetor) - adjustment

10   Hold the throttle lever in the fully open position using a rubber band.

11   Hold the choke valve plate towards the closed position against the unloader tang of the throttle shaft, then measure the gap between the lower edge of the choke valve and the carburetor body. This should be 0.275 inch. If necessary, bend the choke rod at its cranked part to alter the gap.

Fast idle speed (primary carburetor) adjustment

12   Open the throttle slightly then close the choke valve plate, so positioning the fast idle lever against the top step of the fast idle cam.

13   Actuate the fast idle cam. There should be a gap between the throttle plate and the carburetor (idle transfer slot side) of 0.25 inch. Bend the fast idle lever if necessary to adjust (see illustration).

14   When correctly set, the fast idle speed at cold start should be 2200 rpm.

13 Holley 2300 carburetor - removal, overhaul and installation

Refer to illustrations 13.2, 13.4a, 13.4b, 13.4c, 13.6a, 13.6b and 13.9

Warning: *Gasoline is extremely flammable, so take extra precautions when you work on any part of the fuel system. Don't smoke or allow open flames or bare light bulbs near the work area, and don't work in a garage where a natural gas-type appliance (such as a water heater or a clothes dryer) with a pilot light is present. Since gasoline is carcinogenic, wear latex gloves when there's a possibility of being exposed to fuel, and, if you spill any fuel on your skin, rinse it off immediately with soap and water. Mop up any spills immediately and do not store fuel-soaked rags where they could ignite. The fuel system is under*

13.2 Use a back-up wrench when disconnecting the fuel line at the carburetor (Rochester carburetor shown)

13.4a Disconnecting the throttle cable from the carburetor

13.4b Disconnect this . . .

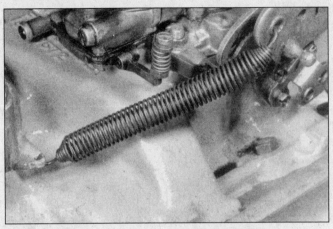

13.4c . . . and this carburetor control spring

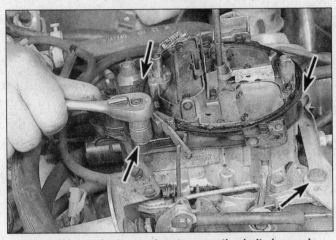

13.6a Remove the four carburetor mounting bolts (arrows) -
Rochester carburetor shown

13.6b Carburetor mounting flange shim

constant pressure on 1982 fuel-injected models, so, if any fuel lines are to be disconnected, the fuel pressure in the system must be relieved first. When you perform any kind of work on the fuel system, wear safety glasses and have a Class B type fire extinguisher on hand.

1 Remove the air cleaner.
2 Disconnect the fuel line from the carburetor **(see illustration)**.
3 Disconnect the vacuum lines from the carburetor.
4 Disconnect the accelerator linkage and return springs **(see illustrations)**.
5 Disconnect the choke mechanism.
6 Unscrew and remove the carburetor flange nuts, then remove the carburetor, gasket and the shim - if equipped - **(see illustrations)**.
7 Clean away all external dirt.
8 Loosen the fuel inlet union, the fuel bowl sight plugs, the needle valve and seat lock screws.
9 Extract the primary fuel bowl screws and detach the fuel bowl **(see illustration on next page)**. Remove the metering block from the primary carburetor, the splash shield and the gasket.
10 On secondary carburetors, remove the

metering block screws, detach the metering block and gasket.
11 Disconnect the vacuum break hose at the primary carburetor vacuum break.
12 On the secondary carburetor, disconnect the secondary diaphragm housing at the throttle lever, and remove it together with gasket.
13 Remove the throttle body and gasket.
14 Remove the sight plug and gasket.
15 Remove the fuel inlet fitting, the fuel filter, spring and gasket.
16 Remove the pump diaphragm cover, the diaphragm and spring from the primary carburetor.
17 The main metering jets can be removed from the primary carburetor using a wide blade screwdriver. The power valve can also be extracted, if necessary, using a one inch, 12 point socket.
18 From the primary carburetor, remove the vacuum fitting and the idle mixture needles and seals.
19 From secondary carburetors, remove the plate and gasket from the metering block dowel pins.
20 The secondary throttle operating assembly can be disassembled by removing the diaphragm cover, followed by the spring

and diaphragm.
21 The secondary carburetor main body cannot be dismantled, but to disassemble the primary main body, remove the choke vacuum break retaining screws. Disconnect the link at the choke lever and remove the choke vacuum break.
22 Remove the choke lever retaining clip, the choke lever and fast idle cam.
23 Remove the pump discharge nozzle screw, the nozzle and gasket then turn the body upside down and extract the pump discharge check valve.
24 Do not disassemble the throttle valve plates unless essential, in which case the staked ends of the retaining screws will have to be filed off.
25 Clean all components in fuel or other suitable solvent and examine for wear or damage. Obtain a repair kit, which will contain all the necessary gaskets and other renewable components.
26 Reassembly is a reversal of dismantling. As an initial setting, turn the idle speed screw in until it contacts the throttle lever, then turn the screw in a further 1 1/2 turns. Turn the idle mixture screw in lightly, until it seats, and then unscrew it one complete turn.
27 When reassembly is complete, carry out

CENTER TRIPLE INST. UNIT

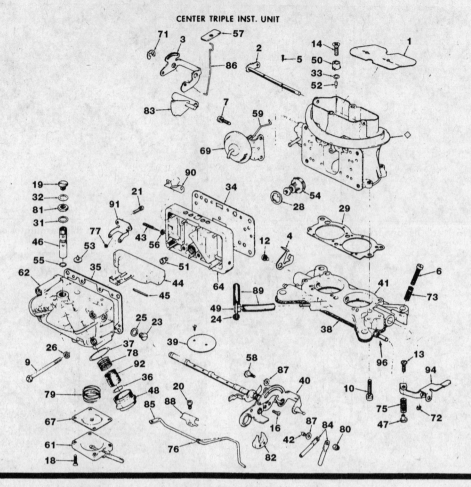

FRONT AND REAR TRIPLE INST. UNIT

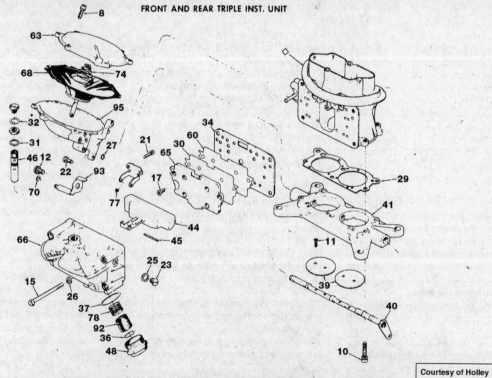

Courtesy of Holley

13.9 Components of Holley 2300-C primary and secondary carburetors

Index Number	Part Name	Index Number	Part Name
1	Choke Plate	46	Fuel Inlet Valve & Seat Assy.
2	Choke Shaft & Lever Assembly	47	Pump Operating Lever Adj. Screw Fitting
3	Choke Control Lever	48	Fuel Inlet Fitting
4	Fast Idle Cam Lever	49	Tee Connector
5	Choke Plate Screw	50	Pump Discharge Nozzle
6	Throttle Stop Screw	51	Main Metering Jet
7	Choke Diaphragm Assy. Bracket Screw & Lock Washer	52	Pump Discharge Needle Valve
8	Diaph. Cover Assy. Scr. & L.W.	53	Air Vent Valve
		54	Power Valve Assy.
9	Fuel Bowl to Main Body Screw	55	Fuel Valve Seat "O" Ring
10	Throttle Body Screw & L.W.	56	Idle Adjusting Needle Seal
11	Throttle Plate Screw	57	Choke Rod Seal
12	Fast Idle Cam Lever Screw & L.W.	58	Throttle Connector Pin
13	Pump Operating Lever Adj. Screw	59	Choke Diaphragm Assy. Link
		60	Metering Body Plate
14	Pump Discharge Nozzle Screw	61	Fuel Pump Diaphragm Cover Assy.
15	Fuel Bowl To Main Body Scr. Sec.	62	Fuel Bowl & Plugs Assy.
16	Pump Cam Lock Screw	63	Diaphragm Housing Cover Sec.
17	Metering Body Screw Sec.	64	Metering Body & Plugs Assy.
18	Fuel Pump Cover Screw	65	Sec. Metering Body
19	Fuel Valve Seat Lock Screw	66	Sec. Fuel Bowl
20	Air Vent Rod Clamp Screw	67	Pump Diaphragm Assy.
21	Float Shaft Bracket Scr. & L.W.	68	Sec. Diaphragm Assy.
		69	Choke Diaphragm Assy. Complete
22	Diaphragm Mounting Scr. & L.W.	70	Sec. Diaphragm Link Retainer
23	Fuel Level Check Plug	71	Choke Control Lever Retainer
24	Tee Connector Plug	72	Pump Operating Lever Retainer
25	Fuel Level Check Plug Gasket	73	Throttle Stop Screw Spring
26	Fuel Bowl Screw Gasket	74	Diaphragm Spring Sec.
27	Diaphragm Housing Gasket Sec.	75	Pump Operating Lever Adj. Spring
28	Power Valve Body Gasket	76	Air Vent Rod Spring
29	Throttle Body Gasket	77	Float Spring
30	Metering Body Plate Gasket Sec.	78	Fuel Inlet Filter Spring
31	Fuel Inlet Adjusting Nut Gasket	79	Diaphragm Return Spring
		80	Throttle Connector Pin Nut
32	Fuel Valve Seat Screw Gasket	81	Fuel Valve Seat Adj. Lock Nut
33	Pump Discharge Nozzle Gasket	82	Pump Cam
34	Metering Body Gasket	83	Fast Idle Cam
35	Fuel Bowl Gasket	84	Throttle Connector Bar
36	Fuel Inlet Filter Gasket	85	Air Vent Rod
37	Fuel Inlet Fitting Gasket	86	Choke Rod
38	Flange Gasket	87	Throttle Connector Pin Spacer
39	Throttle Plate	88	Air Vent Rod Clamp
40	Throttle Lever & Shaft Assy.	89	Choke Vacuum Hose
41	Throttle Body & Shaft Assy.	90	Metering Body Vent Baffle
42	Throttle Connector Pin Bushing	91	Float Shaft Retaining Bracket
		92	Fuel Inlet Filter
43	Idle Adjusting Needle	93	Diaphragm Lever & Pin Assy.
44	Float & Hinge Assy.	94	Pump Operating Lever
45	Float Lever Shaft	95	Sec. Diaphragm Housing
		96	Pump Oper. Lever Stud

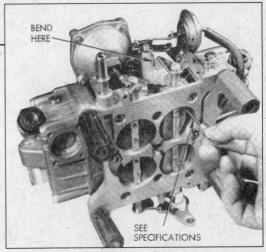

14.5 Adjusting fast idle speed (Holley 4150)

14.6 Adjusting secondary throttle valve stop screw (Holley 4150)

all the adjustments described in Section 12.

28   Install the carburetor to the engine by reversing the removal operations and then adjust the idle speed (see Chapter 1).

14   Holley 4150 carburetor - adjustments without removal from the engine

Refer to illustrations 14.5 and 14.6

Float adjustment

1   The adjustment is as described in Section 12.

Accelerator pump adjustment

2   The adjustment is as described in Section 12.

Choke vacuum break adjustment

3   The adjustment is as described in Section 12 but the gap between the valve plate and carburetor body should be as given in the Specifications according to year of production.

Choke unloader adjustment

4   The adjustment is as described in Section 12, but the gap between the valve plate

and the carburetor body should be as given in Specifications according to year of production.

Fast idle speed adjustment

5   The adjustment is as described in Section 12 (see illustration).

Secondary throttle valve stop screw adjustment

6   Back off the adjustment screw until the throttle plates are fully closed (see illustration).

7   Rotate the adjustment screw until it just touches the throttle lever then rotate it an additional half-turn.

15   Holley 4150 carburetor - removal, overhaul and installation

Refer to illustrations 15.2 and 15.8

1   Removal of the carburetor is as described for the Holley 2300 in Section 13.

2   Initially loosen the fuel inlet fitting, fuel

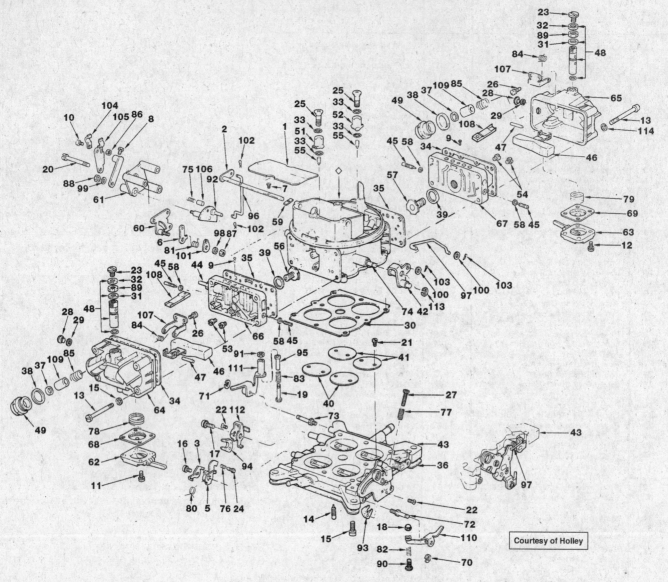

15.2 Exploded view of Holley 4150 carburetor

Courtesy of Holley

**15.8 The upper screw serves only as a
lock-nut - loosen it and then use a wrench
on the nut to remove the float
adjustment assembly**

bowl sight plugs; and the needle and seat lockscrews **(see illustration)**.

3   Remove the primary fuel bowl (four screws), the metering block, splash shield and gasket.

4   Remove the secondary fuel bowl (four screws), the metering block and gasket.

5   Disconnect the secondary throttle operating rod at the throttle lever, followed by the throttle operating assembly and gasket.

6   Disconnect the hose at the vacuum break.

7   Remove the throttle body-to-main body screws, the throttle body and the gasket.

8   Loosen the inlet needle and seat lockscrew, then turn the adjusting nut counterclockwise to remove the needle and seat assembly **(see illustration)**.

9   Remove the hinge pin retainer and slide

out the float. Remove the spring if necessary.

10   Remove the sight plug and gasket, and the inlet fitting, fuel filter, spring and gaskets.

11   From the primary bowl remove the air vent valve assembly (where applicable) and the pump diaphragm screws, pump housing, diaphragm and spring. Check the pump inlet ball for damage and correct operation; if unserviceable, a new bowl assembly will be required.

12   Using a wide bladed screwdriver, remove the main metering jets. Remove the power valves using a one-inch 12-point socket. From the primary side only, remove the idle mixture screws and seals.

13   To disassemble the secondary throttle operating assembly, remove the diaphragm cover, spring and diaphragm.

14   From the main body, remove the vac-

Index Number	Part Name	Index Number	Part Name
1	Choke Plate	56	Power Valve Assy. Pri.
2	Choke Shaft & Lever Assy.	57	Power Valve Assy. or Plug Sec.
3	Fast Idle Pick-up Lever	58	Idle Needle Seal Pri. & Sec.
4	Choke Lever & Swivel Assy.	59	Choke Rod Seal
5	Fast Idle Cam Lever	60	Back-up Plate & Stud Assy.
6	Choke Rod Lever & Bushing Assy.	61	Fast Idle Cam Plate
7	Choke Plate Screw	62	Pump Cover Assy. Pri.
8	Choke Swivel Screw	63	Pump Cover Assy. Sec.
9	Drive Screw	64	Fuel Bowl & Plugs Assy. Pri.
10	Clamp Screw	65	Fuel Bowl & Plugs Assy. Sec.
11	Fuel Pump Cover Screw Pri.	66	Metering Body & Plugs Assy. Pri.
12	Fuel Pump Cover Screw Sec.	67	Metering Body & Plugs Assy. Sec.
13	Fuel Bowl Screw	68	Pump Diaphragm Assy. Pri.
14	Secondary Idle Adjusting Screw	69	Pump Diaphragm Assy. Sec.
15	Throttle Body Screw & L.W.	70	Pump Operating Lever Retainer Pri.
16	Fast Idle Cam Lever Screw & L.W.	71	Pump Operating Lever Retainer Sec.
17	Secondary Pump Cam Lever Screw & L.W.	72	Pump Lever Stud Pri.
18	Pump Lever Adjusting Screw Pri.	73	Pump Lever Stud Sec.
19	Pump Lever Adjusting Screw Sec.	74	Cam Follower Lever Stud
20	Fast Idle Cam Plate Screw & L.W.	75	Plunger Spring
21	Throttle Plate Screw Pri. & Sec.	76	Fast Idle Cam Lever Screw Spring
22	Pump Cam Lock Screw Pri. & Sec.	77	Throttle Stop Screw Spring
23	Fuel Valve Seat Lock Screw	78	Diaphragm Return Spring Pri.
24	Fast Idle Cam Lever Adj. Screw	79	Diaphragm Return Spring Sec.
25	Pump Discharge Nozzle Screw Pri. & Sec.	80	Fast Idle Cam Lever Spring
26	Float Shaft Bracket Screw & L.W. Pri. & Sec.	81	Choke Spring
		82	Pump Lever Adj. Screw Spring Pri.
27	Throttle Stop Screw	83	Pump Lever Adj. Screw Spring Sec.
28	Fuel Level Check Plug Pri. & Sec.	84	Float Spring Pri. & Sec.
29	Fuel Level Check Plug Gasket Pri. & Sec.	85	Fuel Inlet Filter Spring
30	Throttle Body Gasket	86	Bracket Clamp Screw Nut
31	Fuel Valve Seat Adjusting Nut Gasket	87	Choke Spring Nut
		88	Choke Lever Nut
32	Fuel Valve Seat Lock Screw Gasket	89	Fuel Valve Seat Adjusting Nut Pri. & Sec.
33	Pump Discharge Nozzle Gasket	90	Pump Lever Adjusting Screw Nut Pri.
34	Fuel Bowl Gasket Pri. & Sec.		
35	Metering Body Gasket Pri. & Sec.	91	Pump Lever Adjusting Screw Nut Sec.
36	Flange Gasket	92	Fast Idle Cam & Shaft Assy.
37	Fuel Inlet Filter Gasket	93	Pump Cam Pri.
38	Fuel Inlet Fitting Gasket	94	Pump Cam Sec.
39	Power Valve Gasket	95	Pump Operating Lever Screw Sleeve
40	Throttle Plate Primary	96	Choke Rod
41	Throttle Plate Secondary	97	Secondary Connecting Rod
42	Cam Follower Lever Assy.	98	Choke Spring Nut L.W.
43	Throttle Body & Shaft Assy.	99	Choke Control Lever L.W.
44	Spark Tube	100	Connecting Rod Washer
45	Idle Adjusting Needle Pri. & Sec.	101	Choke Spring Washer
46	Float & Hinge Assy. Pri. & Sec.	102	Choke Rod Retainer
47	Float Shaft Pri. & Sec.	103	Cotter Pin
48	Fuel Inlet Needle & Seat Assy. Primary & Sec.	104	Choke Control Wire Bracket Clamp
49	Fuel Inlet Fitting Primary	105	Choke Control Wire Bracket
50	Fuel Inlet Fitting Secondary	106	Fast Idle Cam Plunger
51	Pump Discharge Nozzle Pri.	107	Float Shaft Retaining Bracket Pri. & Sec.
52	Pump Discharge Nozzle Sec.		
53	Main Jet Pri.	108	Fuel Bowl Vent Baffle Pri. & Sec.
54	Main Jet Sec.	109	Fuel Inlet Filter Pri. & Sec.
55	Pump Discharge Needle Valve Pri. & Sec.	110	Pump Operating Lever Pri.
		111	Pump Operating Lever Sec.
		112	Pump Cam Lever Sec.
		113	E. Ring Retainer
		114	Fuel Bowl Screw Gasket

20 Remove the secondary throttle shaft diaphragm lever and the primary throttle shaft fast idle cam lever.

21 Remove the key and disconnect the secondary lockout throttle connecting link from the shaft levers.

22 File off the staked ends of the throttle plate attaching screws, then remove the screws and plates. Remove any burrs from the shafts and withdraw them out of the flange.

23 Remove the throttle lever accelerator pump can and the vacuum break hose.

24 Clean all metal parts in a suitable cold solvent (this includes the choke rod seal - see Step 17). Do not immerse rubber parts, plastic parts (e.g.: secondary throttle shaft bushings and accelerator pump cam), vacuum break unit and other non-metallic parts. Do not probe the jets, but blow through them with clean, dry, compressed air. Examine all fixed and moving parts for cracks, distortion, wear and other damage; replace as necessary. Discard all gaskets. Check the secondary throttle operating diaphragm by moving the diaphragm rod to the up position, plugging the vacuum passage opening and checking that the diaphragm holds upwards until the passage is unplugged.

25 Assembly is essentially the reverse of the removal procedure, but the following points should be noted;

a) Throttle shaft plastic bushings should be rolled between the finger and thumb to help shape them.

b) When installing the throttle valves, the identification numbers should be downwards (to the manifold side).

c) Install the idle speed screw to just contact the throttle lever, then turn the 1 1/2 turns further.

d) Ensure that the choke valve can fall freely under its own weight.

e) When installing the idle mixture screws, use new seals. Preliminary adjustment is made by screwing them in lightly to just seat, then screwing them out one turn.

f) Adjust the floats initially by inverting the fuel bowls and turning the adjustable needle seat until the top of the float is the specified distance from the top of the fuel bowl. (0.350 in primary 0.50 in secondary).

g) On completion of assembly, install the carburetor and adjust the float, the secondary throttle stop valve, fast idle cam, accelerator, pump, choke unloader and vacuum break, as described in Section 14.

16 Automatic choke - description and adjustment (Holley 2300 and 4150 carburetors)

Refer to illustrations 16.1 and 16.3

1 The choke mechanism is controlled by a temperature sensing choke coil mounted on the intake manifold over the exhaust

uum break retaining screws. Remove the assembly, disconnecting the link at the choke lever.

15 Remove the choke lever retaining clip followed by the lever itself and the fast idle cam.

16 Remove the pump discharge nozzle screw, nozzle and gasket, then invert the body to remove the discharge check valve.

17 If further disassembling is required, file off the staked ends of the shaft screws and remove them. Remove the choke rod (upward, through the seal), followed by the seal. Remove the valve from the shaft slot and slide the shaft from the main body.

18 To disassemble the throttle body, remove the pump operating lever assembly and disassemble the spring, bolt and nut.

19 Remove the idle speed screw and spring.

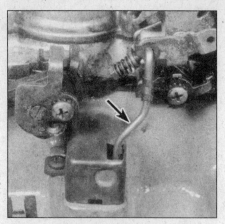

16.1 Automatic choke rod (arrow)

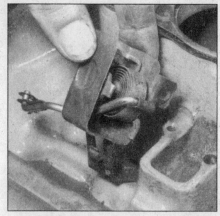

16.3 Removing the automatic choke assembly from the intake manifold

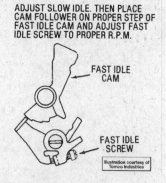

17.1 Fast idle adjustment diagram (Rochester 4MV)

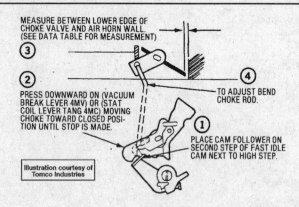

17.3 Choke rod (fast idle cam) adjustment diagram (Rochester 4MV)

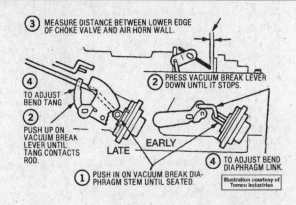

17.6 Choke vacuum break adjustment diagram (Rochester 4MV)

crossover passage **(see illustration)**.

2   The choke can be removed by prying the choke coil shield with a screwdriver.

3   Remove the choke rod, bracket screw and choke coil assembly **(see illustration)**.

4   When installing a new choke coil assembly, make sure that the locating tab is in the forward hole of the intake manifold.

5   Install the choke rod and adjust by bending (without coil shield installed) so that the choke valve plate moves freely from fully open, to fully closed.

6   Start and warm up engine, observing the operation of the choke.

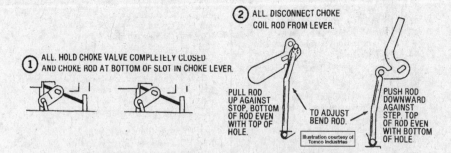

17.9 Choke coil rod adjustment diagram (Rochester 4MV)

17 Rochester 4MV carburetor - adjustments without removal from the engine

Refer to illustrations 17.1, 17.3, 17.6, 17.9 and 17.15

Fast idle adjustment

1   With the transmission in neutral, position the fast idle lever on the high step of the fast idle cam **(see illustration)**.

2   With the engine warm and the choke wide open, adjust the fast idle screw to obtain the specified engine speed.

Choke rod adjustment

3   Place the cam follower on the second step of the fast idle cam and against the high step **(see illustration)**.

4   Rotate the choke valve towards the closed position by turning the external lever counterclockwise.

5   Check that the dimension between the lower edge of the choke valve and the air

horn wall (at the lever end) is as specified. Bend the choke rod if adjustment is required.

Choke vacuum break adjustment

6   Using an external source of suction, seat the choke vacuum break diaphragm **(see illustration)**.

7   Open the throttle slightly so that the cam follower clears the fast idle cam steps, then rotate the vacuum break lever towards the direction of closed choke. Ensure that the

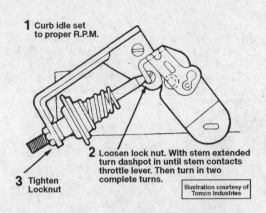

17.15 Rochester 4MV carburetor air valve dashpot adjustment (typical)

18.1 An identification number will be stamped on the side of the carburetor body - copy the numbers when purchasing a rebuild kit or new/rebuilt carburetor

vacuum break rod is in the outer end of the slot in the diaphragm plunger. A rubber band can be used to hold the vacuum break lever in position.

8   Measure the distance from the lower edge of the choke valve to the air horn wall. Bend the vacuum break link if adjustment is required.

Choke coil rod adjustment

9   Rotate the choke coil lever counter-clockwise to fully close the choke (see illustration).
10   With the coil rod disconnected and the cover removed, push down on the rod until it contacts the bracket surface.
11   The coil rod must fit in the choke lever notch, bend the rod to adjust if necessary.
12   Install the choke coil cover.
13   Install the coil rod in the choke coil lever slot and install the retaining clip.
14   Check that the choke operates freely over its full range of travel.

Air valve dashpot adjustment

15   Seat the choke vacuum break diaphragm using an outside source of suction, then measure the dimension between the end of the slot in the vacuum break plunger lever and the air valve when the air valve is fully closed (see illustration).
16   If adjustment is necessary, bend the rod at the air valve end.

18   Rochester 4MV carburetor - removal, overhaul and installation

Refer to illustrations 18.1, 18.2 and 18.32
Warning: *Gasoline is extremely flammable, so take extra precautions when you work on any part of the fuel system. Don't smoke or allow open flames or bare light bulbs near the work area, and don't work in a garage where a natural gas-type appliance (such as a water heater or a clothes dryer) with a pilot light is present. Since gasoline is carcinogenic, wear latex gloves when there's a possibility of being exposed to fuel, and, if you spill any fuel on your skin, rinse it off immediately with soap and water. Mop up any spills immediately and do not store fuel-soaked rags where they could ignite. The fuel system is under constant pressure on 1982 fuel-injected models, so, if any fuel lines are to be disconnected, the fuel pressure in the system must be relieved first. When you perform any kind of work on the fuel system, wear safety glasses and have a Class B type fire extinguisher on hand.*

1   When a carburetor develops faults after a considerable mileage, it is usually more economical to replace the complete unit rather than to completely disassemble it and replace individual components. However, if it is decided to strip and rebuild the unit, first obtain a repair kit, which will contain all the necessary gaskets and other renewable items, and proceed in the following sequence (see illustration).
2   To remove the carburetor, withdraw the air cleaner, disconnect the fuel and vacuum lines, disconnect the choke coil rod and accelerator linkage (see illustration on next page).
3   If the vehicle is equipped with automatic transmission disconnect the kickdown rod. Disconnect the idle stop wiring.
4   Bend back the lockwasher tabs, then remove the idle stop solenoid.
5   Remove the larger idle stop solenoid bracket screw from the float bowl.
6   Remove the clip from the upper end of the choke rod; disconnect the rod. Disconnect the rod from the upper choke shaft lever and remove the rod from the lower lever in the bowl.
7   Drive the pump lever pivot inward to remove the roll pin then remove the pump lever from the air horn and pump rod.
8   Remove the vacuum break hose, and the diaphragm unit from the bracket.
9   Disconnect the choke assist spring.
10   Remove the metering rod hanger and secondary rods after removing the small screw at the top of the hanger.
11   Lift off the air horn, but leave the gasket in position. Do not attempt to remove the air bleed tubes or accelerating well tubes.
12   If the choke valve is to be replaced, remove the valve attaching screws, then measure the valve and shaft.
13   The air valves and air valve shaft are calibrated and should not be removed. A shaft spring repair kit is available and contains all the necessary instructions, if these parts require renewal.
14   Remove the pump plunger from the well. Carefully remove the air horn gasket and remove the pump return spring from the pump well.
15   Remove the plastic filter over the float valve.
16   Press the power piston down and release it to remove it. Remove the spring from the well. Note the power piston plastic retainer that is used for ease of assembly.
17   Remove the metering rods from the power piston by disconnecting the spring from the top of each rod, then rotating the rod to remove it from the hanger.
18   Remove the float assembly by pulling up on the retaining pin until it can be removed, then sliding the float towards the front of the bowl to carefully disengage the needle pull clip.
19   Remove the pull clip and the fuel inlet needle, then unscrew the needle seat and remove the gasket.
20   Unscrew the primary metering jets; do not attempt to remove the secondary metering jets.
21   Remove the discharge ball retainer and the check ball.
22   Remove the baffle from the secondary side of the bowl.
23   Remove the choke assembly after removing the retaining screw on the side of the bowl. Remove the secondary lockout lever from the cast boss on the bowl.
24   Remove the fast idle cam and the choke assembly.

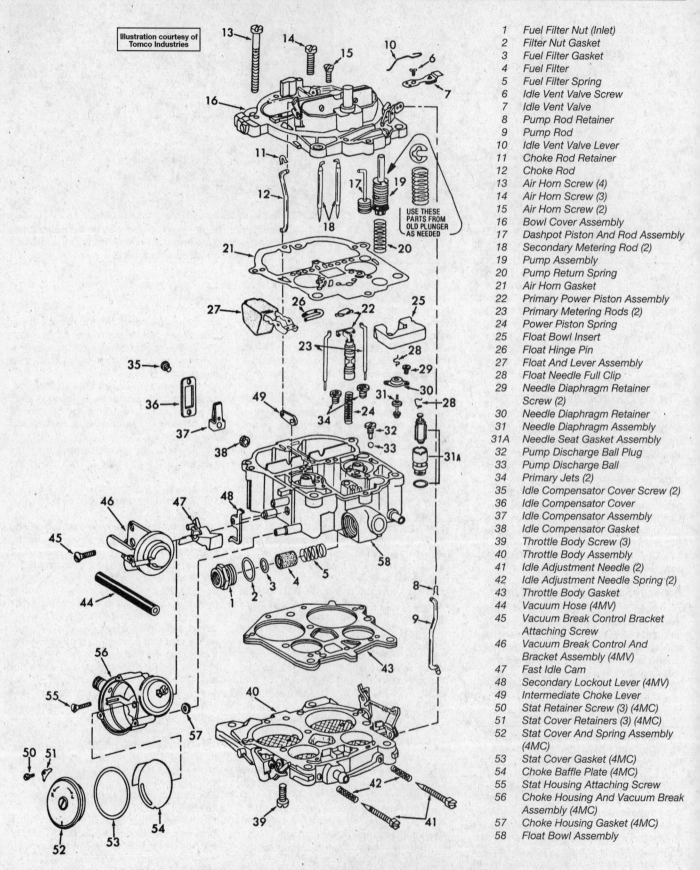

Illustration courtesy of Tomco Industries

USE THESE PARTS FROM OLD PLUNGER AS NEEDED

1   Fuel Filter Nut (Inlet)
2   Filter Nut Gasket
3   Fuel Filter Gasket
4   Fuel Filter
5   Fuel Filter Spring
6   Idle Vent Valve Screw
7   Idle Vent Valve
8   Pump Rod Retainer
9   Pump Rod
10 Idle Vent Valve Lever
11 Choke Rod Retainer
12 Choke Rod
13 Air Horn Screw (4)
14 Air Horn Screw (3)
15 Air Horn Screw (2)
16 Bowl Cover Assembly
17 Dashpot Piston And Rod Assembly
18 Secondary Metering Rod (2)
19 Pump Assembly
20 Pump Return Spring
21 Air Horn Gasket
22 Primary Power Piston Assembly
23 Primary Metering Rods (2)
24 Power Piston Spring
25 Float Bowl Insert
26 Float Hinge Pin
27 Float And Lever Assembly
28 Float Needle Full Clip
29 Needle Diaphragm Retainer
    Screw (2)
30 Needle Diaphragm Retainer
31 Needle Diaphragm Assembly
31A Needle Seat Gasket Assembly
32 Pump Discharge Ball Plug
33 Pump Discharge Ball
34 Primary Jets (2)
35 Idle Compensator Cover Screw (2)
36 Idle Compensator Cover
37 Idle Compensator Assembly
38 Idle Compensator Gasket
39 Throttle Body Screw (3)
40 Throttle Body Assembly
41 Idle Adjustment Needle (2)
42 Idle Adjustment Needle Spring (2)
43 Throttle Body Gasket
44 Vacuum Hose (4MV)
45 Vacuum Break Control Bracket
    Attaching Screw
46 Vacuum Break Control And
    Bracket Assembly (4MV)
47 Fast Idle Cam
48 Secondary Lockout Lever (4MV)
49 Intermediate Choke Lever
50 Stat Retainer Screw (3) (4MC)
51 Stat Cover Retainers (3) (4MC)
52 Stat Cover And Spring Assembly
    (4MC)
53 Stat Cover Gasket (4MC)
54 Choke Baffle Plate (4MC)
55 Stat Housing Attaching Screw
56 Choke Housing And Vacuum Break
    Assembly (4MC)
57 Choke Housing Gasket (4MC)
58 Float Bowl Assembly

18.2 Exploded view of typical Rochester 4MV series carburetor

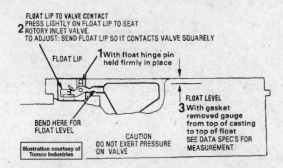

18.32 Float level adjustment diagram (Rochester 4MV)

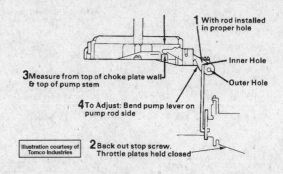

19.1 Pump adjustment diagram (Rochester M4MC)

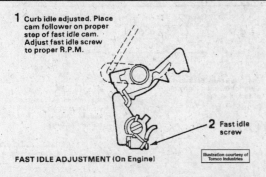

19.6 Fast idle adjustment diagram (Rochester M4MC)

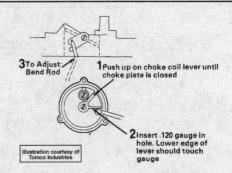

19.10 Choke coil lever adjustment diagram (Rochester M4MC)

25   Remove the intermediate choke rod and actuating lever from the float bowl.

26   Remove the fuel inlet filter nut, gasket, filter and spring.

27   Remove the throttle body-to-bowl screws. Remove the throttle body.

28   Remove the throttle body-to-bowl insulator gaskets.

29   Remove the pump rod from the throttle lever by rotating the rod out of the primary lever.

30   Further disassembling is not recommended. If it is essential to remove the idle mixture needles, pry out the plastic limiter caps then count the number of turns to bottom the needles and install replacements in exactly the same position. New limiter caps should be installed after running adjustments have been made.

31   Clean all metal parts in a suitable cold solvent. Do not immerse rubber parts, plastic parts, the vacuum break assembly or the idle stop solenoid, or permanent damage will result. Do not probe the jets, but blow them through with clean dry compressed air. Examine all fixed and moving parts for cracks, distortion, wear and other damage; replace as necessary. Discard all gaskets and the fuel inlet filter.

32   Assembly is essentially the reverse of the removal procedure, but the following points should be noted:

a) *If new idle mixture screws are used, and the original setting was not noted, install the screws finger-tight to seat them, then back off four full turns.*

b) *Having installed the float, measure from the top of the float bowl gasket surface (gasket not installed) to the top of the float at a point 3/16 inch from the toe. Bend the float up, or down, to obtain the specified dimension* (see illustration).

c) *Tighten the air horn retaining screws, starting with the center screws and working out.*

d) *When connecting the pump lever to the upper pump rod, install the rod in the inner hole.*

e) *After reassembly, carry out all the settings and adjustments listed previously in this Chapter, Section 17.*

33   Installing the carburetor is a reversal of removal, but use a new flange gasket. When the engine has reached normal operating temperature, adjust the idle speed (see Chapter 1).

19 Rochester M4MC carburetor - adjustments without removal from the engine

Refer to illustrations 19.1, 19.6, 19.10, 19.17, 19.22, 19.26, 19.33, 19.36, 19.39, 19.41, 19.45 and 19.51

Pump adjustment

1   With the fast idle cam follower off the steps of the fast idle cam, back out the idle speed screw until the throttle valves are completely closed in the bore (see illustration).

Make sure that the secondary actuating rod is not restricting movement; bend the secondary closing tang if necessary to readjust it after pump adjustment.

2   Place the pump rod in the specified hole in the lever.

3   Measure from the top of the choke valve wall (next to the vent stack) to the top of the pump stem.

4   If necessary, adjust to obtain the specified dimension (given in Specifications) by bending the lever while supporting it with a screwdriver.

5   Adjust the idle speed (see Chapter 1).

Fast idle adjustment

6   Place the cam follower lever on the highest step of the fast idle cam (see illustration).

7   Turn the fast idle screw out until the primary throttle valves are closed.

8   Turn in the fast idle screw to contact the lever then screw in a further three full turns.

9   Refer to the tune-up decal or Vehicle Emissions Control Information label and readjust if necessary to obtain the correct idle speed.

Choke coil lever adjustment

10   Loosen the three retaining screws and remove the cover and coil assembly from the choke housing (see illustration).

11   Push up on the thermostatic coil tang (counterclockwise) until the choke valve is closed.

12   Check that the choke rod is at the bot-

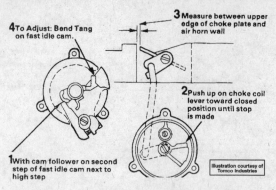

19.17   Choke rod (fast idle cam) adjustment diagram (Rochester M4MC)

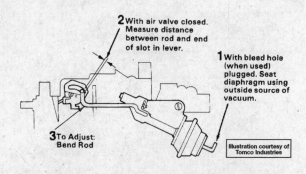

19.22   Air valve dashpot adjustment diagram (Rochester M4MC)

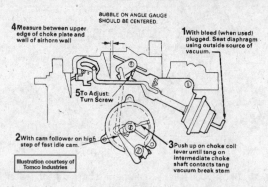

19.26   Vacuum break adjustment diagram (Rochester M4MC)

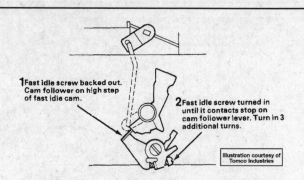

19.33   Automatic choke coil adjustment diagram (Rochester M4MC)

tom of the slot in the choke lever.

13   Insert a plug gauge (an unmarked drill shank is suitable) of the specified size (0.120 in) in the hole in the choke housing.

14   The lower edge of the choke coil lever should just contact the side of the plug gauge.

15   If necessary, bend the choke rod at the point shown to adjust.

Fast idle cam (choke rod) adjustment

16   Turn the fast idle screw in until it contacts the fast idle cam follower lever, then turn in three full turns more.

17   Place a lever on the second step of the fast idle cam against the rise of the high step (see illustration).

18   Push upward on the choke coil lever inside the housing to close the choke valve.

19   Measure between the upper edge of the choke valve and the air horn wall. The gap should be as given in the Specifications.

20   If necessary, bend the tang on the fast idle cam to adjust, but ensure that the tang lies against the cam after bending.

21   Re-check the fast idle adjustment.

Air valve dashpot adjustment

22   Using an external source of suction, seat the front vacuum break diaphragm (see illustration).

23   Ensure that the air valves are completely closed, then measure between the air valve dashpot and the end of the slot in the air

valve lever. The gap should be as given in Specifications.

24   Bend the air valve dashpot rod at the point shown, if adjustment is necessary.

Vacuum break adjustment

25   Loosen the three retaining screws and remove the choke coil cover and coil assembly from the choke housing.

26   Place the cam follower lever on the highest step of the fast idle cam (see illustration).

27   Using an outside source of suction, seat the diaphragm unit.

28   Push up on the inside choke coil lever until the tang on the vacuum break lever contacts the tang on the plunger.

29   Measure between the upper edge of the choke valve and the inside of the air horn wall.

30   Turn the adjustment screw on the vacuum break plunger to obtain the specified dimension.

31   Install the vacuum hose on completion.

Automatic choke coil adjustment

32   Install the choke coil and cover assembly with a gasket between the cover and housing. The tang in the coil must be installed in the slot inside the choke coil lever pick-up arm.

33   Place the fast idle cam follower on the highest step of the fast idle cam, then rotate the cover counterclockwise until the choke

just closes (see illustration).

34   Align the index mark on the cover with the specified point on the choke housing then tighten the retaining screws. The index marks should be set two notches lean on carburetors 17057202/4/10 and 17057502/4/10/28/82/228 and three notches lean on 17057203/211.

Unloader adjustment

35   Adjust the choke coil, as described in the previous Section.

36   Hold the throttle valves wide open and the chokes fully closed (see illustration). A rubber band can be used on the tang of the intermediate choke lever if the engine is warm.

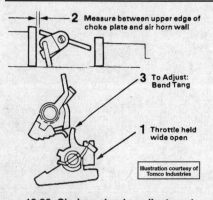

19.36   Choke unloader adjustment diagram (Rochester M4MC)

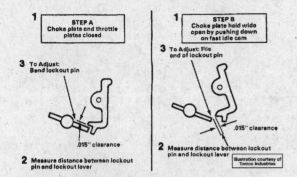

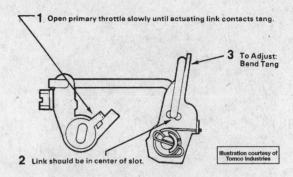

19.39 Secondary lockout adjustment diagram (Rochester M4MC)

19.41 Secondary opening adjustment diagram (Rochester M4MC)

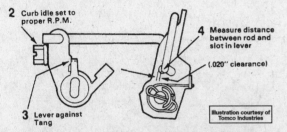

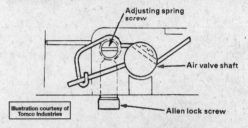

19.45 Secondary closing adjustment diagram (Rochester M4MC)

19.51 Air valve spring wind-up adjustment diagram (Rochester M4MC)

37   Measure between the upper edge of the choke valve and the air horn wall. The gap should be given in Specifications.

38   If adjustment is necessary, bend the tang on the fast idle lever to obtain the specified dimension. Ensure that the tang on the fast idle cam lever contacts the center point of the fast idle cam after adjustment.

Secondary throttle valve lockout adjustment

Lockout lever clearance

39   Hold the choke valves and secondary lockout valves closed, then measure the clearance between the lockout pin and lockout lever **(see illustration)**.

40   If adjustment is necessary, bend the lockout pin to obtain the specified clearance.

Opening clearance

41   Push down on the tail of the fast idle cam to hold the choke wide open **(see illustration)**.

42   Hold the secondary throttle valves partly open then measure between the end of the lockout pin and the toe of the lockout lever. The gap should be as specified.

43   If adjustment is necessary, file the end of the lockout pin but ensure that no burrs remain afterwards.

Secondary closing adjustment

44   Adjust the engine idle speed (see Chapter 1).

45   Hold the choke valve wide open with the cam follower lever off the steps of the fast idle cam **(see illustration)**.

46   Measure the clearance between the slot in the secondary throttle valve pick-up lever and the secondary actuating rod. The gap should be as specified in Specifications.

47   If adjustment is necessary, bend the secondary closing tang on the primary throttle lever to obtain the specified clearance.

Secondary opening adjustment

48   Lightly open the primary throttle lever until the link just contacts the tang on the secondary lever.

49   Bend the tang on the secondary lever, if necessary, to position the link in the center of the secondary lever slot.

Air valve spring wind-up adjustment

50   Remove the front vacuum break diaphragm unit and the air valve dashpot rod.

51   Using a suitable hexagonal wrench, loosen the lock screw, then turn the tension adjusting screw counterclockwise until the air valve is partly open **(see illustration)**.

52   Hold the air valve closed, then turn the tension adjusting screw clockwise the specified number of turns after the spring contacts the pin (one turn for carburetors 17057228/10/11 and 7/8 turn for carburetors 17057204/502/504/582/584/203).

53   Tighten the lockscrew and install the air valve dashpot rod, and the front break diaphragm unit and bracket.

20 Rochester M4MC carburetor - removal, overhaul and installation

Warning: *Gasoline is extremely flammable, so take extra precautions when you work on any part of the fuel system. Don't smoke or allow open flames or bare light bulbs near the work area, and don't work in a garage where a natural gas-type appliance (such as a water heater or a clothes dryer) with a pilot light is present. Since gasoline is carcinogenic, wear latex gloves when there's a possibility of being exposed to fuel, and, if you spill any fuel on your skin, rinse it off immediately with soap and water. Mop up any spills immediately and do not store fuel-soaked rags where they could ignite. The fuel system is under constant pressure on 1982 fuel-injected models, so, if any fuel lines are to be disconnected, the fuel pressure in the system must be relieved first. When you perform any kind of work on the fuel system, wear safety glasses and have a Class B type fire extinguisher on hand.*

1   Removal operations are similar to those described in Section 18. When a carburetor fault develops after considerable mileage, it is usually more economical to replace the

20.1a After removing the carburetor, make notes or diagrams of levers, slots or holes that linkage connects to or anything that could be difficult to remember during reassembly

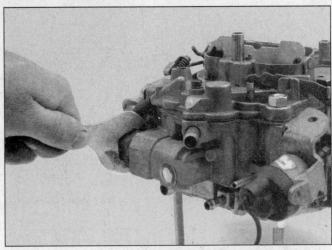

20.1b Using a 1-inch wrench, remove the fuel inlet from the main body of the carburetor

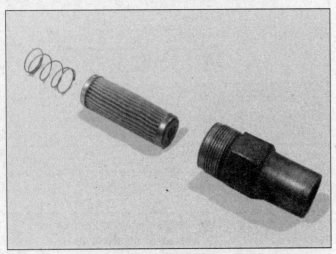

20.1c Remove the filter and spring from the carburetor - always replace the filter during an overhaul

20.1d Remove the choke lever screw and lever - leave the linkage rod that the lever is connected to in place for now

20.1e Remove the two screws and the front vacuum break diaphragm

20.1f If your choke housing has screws, remove the three screws (arrows) and the choke cover retainers beneath the screws - be careful not to lose the retainers

20.1g On some later model carburetors, the choke cover is riveted - drill off the rivet heads - new self-tapping screws usually come with the carburetor kit

20.1h With the cover off, remove the gasket and check the condition of the coil (arrow) - replace the coil if it's broken, bent or corroded

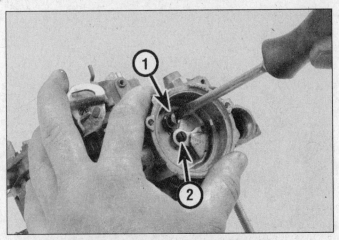

20.1i Remove the choke housing screw (1) and the screw attaching the lever to the shaft (2) . . .

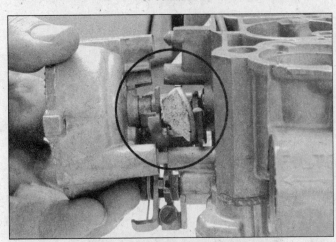

20.1j . . . then remove the choke housing, being careful to note how the linkage (circled area) is assembled

complete unit rather than to completely disassemble it and replace individual components. However, if it is decided to strip and rebuild the unit, first obtain a repair kit, which will contain all the necessary gaskets and other renewable items, and proceed in the following manner. Read the text, then refer to the photo sequence **(see illustrations 20.1a through 20.1cc)** for rebuilding information.

2   If the carburetor has an idle stop solenoid, remove the bracket retaining screws and lift away the solenoid and bracket assembly.

3   Remove the upper choke lever from the end of the choke shaft (one screw) then

20.1k Reassemble the choke parts to avoid confusion in reassembly - the lever (arrow) is located inside the main body, attached to a linkage rod

20.1l Use a small punch and hammer to drive out the roll pin and remove the accelerator pump lever

20.1m If your carburetor has a idle-stop solenoid (shown) or Idle Speed Control (ISC) motor, remove the two screws and lift it off

20.1n Remove the screw on the secondary metering rod holder and lift out the holder with the rods attached

20.1o Remove the nine screws (arrows) that secure the air horn to the main body

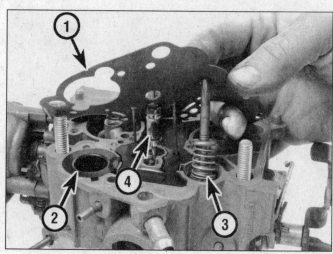

20.1p Carefully remove the gasket (1), the plastic cup (2) if equipped, and the accelerator pump assembly (3) - the power piston (4) and metering rods can be pulled out with the gasket - the power piston doesn't pull out easily, so push it down and release it

20.1q Carefully lift out the float bowl insert

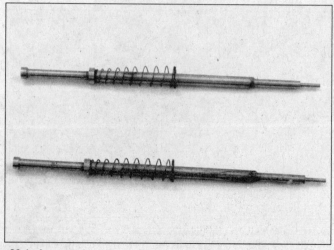

20.1r Inspect the primary metering rods with a magnifying glass to check for scoring or wear

20.1s The baffle on the secondary side just lifts out

20.1t Remove the float assembly with the needle, then use a large screwdriver to unscrew the seat (arrow) from the body

20.1u Unscrew and remove the two main metering jets (arrow)

20.1v Remove the accelerator pump discharge screw (plug) and remove the check ball, either use a magnet or turn the carburetor over to catch the ball as it falls out

20.1w On some late-model carburetors, there are plugs over the idle-mixture screws - cut as shown with a hacksaw, then chisel the piece out as shown at the right, giving access to the screws, which require a special D-shaped screwdriver to remove

20.1x Select the new throttle body-to-main body gasket based on your old one - screw the throttle body back on evenly and don't overtighten

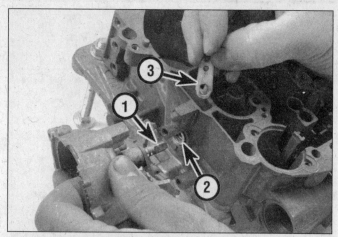

20.1y Assemble the automatic choke linkage on the carburetor - the shaft (1) goes through the seal (2, use a new one) - hook the linkage rod to the lever (3) and lower it into the carburetor body until the shaft goes through it

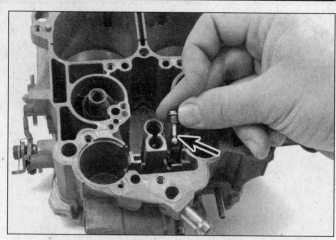

20.1z Be sure to reinstall the check ball and screw (arrow) for the accelerator pump circuit

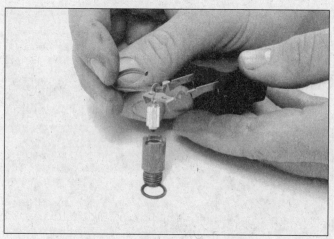

20.1aa Install the new seat with a new gasket, then attach the new needle to the float with the spring and lower the float and needle into the carburetor

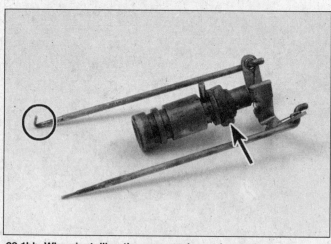

20.1bb When installing the power valve and metering rods, press the retainer (arrow) into the body, then check that the assembly is firmly in place by pushing down on the power valve and releasing it to make sure it stays

rotate the lever to remove it, to disengage it from the choke rod.

4   Remove the choke rod from the lower lever inside the float bowl by holding the lever outward with a small screwdriver and twisting the rod counterclockwise.

5   Remove the vacuum hose from the front vacuum break unit.

6   Remove the small screw at the top of the metering rod hanger and remove the secondary metering rods and hanger.

7   Using a suitable drift, drive the small pump lever pivot roll pin inward to permit removal of the lever.

8   Remove two long screws, five short screws, and two countersunk head screws to detach the air horn. Remove the secondary air baffle deflector (where applicable) from beneath the two center air horn screws.

9   Remove the air horn, but leave the gasket in position at this stage. Do not attempt to remove the small tubes protruding from the air horn.

10   Remove the front vacuum break bracket screws and lift off the unit. detach the air valve dashpot rod from the diaphragm assembly and detach the air valve lever.

11   If considered necessary, remove the staked choke valve attaching screws then remove the choke valve and shaft from the air horn. Do not remove the air valve and the air valve shaft. The air valve closing spring or center plastic cam can be replaced by following the instructions in the appropriate repair kit.

12   Remove the air horn gasket from the float bowl, taking care not to distort the springs that hold the main metering rods.

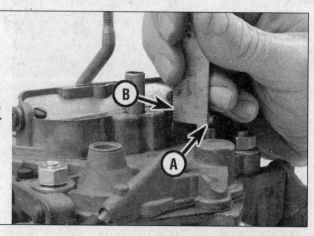

20.1cc After assembly, and having made the adjustments shown in Section 19, measure the height of the accelerator pump rod (point A to point B) and compare it to the Specifications

13   Remove the pump plunger and pump return spring from the pump well.

14   Depress the power piston stem and allow it to snap free, withdrawing the metering rods with it. Remove the power piston spring from the well.

15   Taking care to prevent distortion, remove the metering rods from the power piston by disconnecting the retaining springs, then rotating the rods.

16   Remove the plastic filler block over the float valve, then remove the float assembly and needle by pulling up on the pin. Remove the needle seat and gasket.

17   Remove the metering rod and aneroid from the float bowl.

18   Remove the primary main metering jets. Do not attempt to remove the secondary metering orifice plates.

19   Remove the pump discharge check ball retainer and the ball.

20   Press down on the fast idle cam and remove the vacuum break rod.

21   Move the end of the rod away from the float bowl, then disengage the rod from the hole in the intermediate choke lever.

22   Remove the choke cover attaching screws and retainers. Pull off the cover and remove the gasket. Do not remove the baffle plate from below the thermostatic coil.

23   Remove the choke housing assembly from the float bowl by removing the retaining screw and washer.

24   Remove the secondary throttle valve lockout lever from the float bowl.

25   Remove the lower choke lever by inverting the float bowl.

26   Remove the plastic tube seal from the choke housing.

27   If it is necessary to remove the intermediate choke shaft from the choke housing, remove the coil lever retaining screw and withdraw the lever. Slide out the shaft and (if necessary), remove the fast idle cam.

28   Remove the fuel inlet filter nut, gasket and filter from the float bowl.

29   If necessary, remove the pump well fill slot baffle and the secondary air baffle.

30   Remove the throttle body attaching screws and lift off the float bowl. Remove the insulator gasket.

31   If it is essential to remove the idle mixture needles, pry out the plastic limiter caps then count the number of turns to seat the needles and install replacements in exactly the same position.

32   New limiter caps should be installed after running adjustments have been made when the carburetor has been reinstalled.

33   Clean all metal parts in a suitable cold solvent. Do not immerse rubber parts, plastic parts, pump plunger, filler spools or aneroids, or vacuum breaks. If the choke housing is to be immersed, remove the cup seal from inside the choke housing shaft hole. If the bowl is to be immersed remove the cup seal from the plastic insert; do not attempt to remove the plastic insert. Do not probe the jets, but blow through with clean, dry compressed air. Examine all fixed and moving parts for cracks, distortion, wear and other damage; replace as necessary. Discard all gaskets and the fuel inlet filter.

34   Assembly is essentially the reverse of the disassembly procedure, but the following points should be noted:

a) If new idle mixture screws were used, and the original setting was not noted, install the screws finger-tight to seat them, ten back off four full turns.

b) The lip on the plastic inset cup seal (on the side of the float bowl) faces outwards.

c) The lip on the inside choke housing shaft hole cup seal faces in, towards the housing.

d) When installing the assembled choke body, install the choke rod lever into the cavity in the float bowl. Install the plastic tube seal into the housing cavity before installing the housing. Ensure that the intermediate choke shaft engages into the lower choke lever. The choke coil is installed at the last stage of assembly.

e) Where applicable, the notches on the secondary float bowl air baffle are towards the top, and the top edge of the baffle must be flush with the bowl casting.

f) To adjust the float, hold the retainer firmly in place and push down lightly against the needle. Measure from the top of the float bowl casting (air horn gasket removed) to a point on the top of the float 3/16-inch back from the toe. Bend the float arm to obtain the specified dimension (15/32 inch) by pushing on the pontoon.

g) Tighten the air horn screws, starting with the center screws and working to the outside.

21   Rochester M4ME carburetor (1980) - overhaul

1   The overhaul procedure for the Rochester M4ME carburetor is identical to the procedure for the Rochester M4MC carburetor, with the following exceptions:

2   To disassemble the automatic choke on the M4ME carburetor:

a) Remove the choke cover by drilling out the three cover rivets with a No. 21 (0.159 in) drill bit mounted in a drill motor. Remove only enough metal to separate the rivet head from the rivet (see illustration 20.1g).

b) Once the rivet heads are removed, drive the rivet shanks out of the cover retainers and choke housing with a small pin punch and a hammer.

c) Remove the three retainers, the choke cover assembly and the cover gasket from the housing.

d) Detach the choke housing assembly from the float bowl by removing the retaining screw and washer inside the choke housing. The complete choke assembly can be removed from the float bowl by sliding it outward.

3   After the vacuum break, the fast idle cam (choke rod) and the inside thermostatic coil lever have been adjusted, the choke coil and cover assembly should be installed as follows:

a) Start the three self-tapping screws (supplied with the carburetor service kit) into the choke housing, checking to be sure they are aligned properly. Thread the screws into the housing until they bottom on the screw heads, then remove them.

b) Place the cam follower on the highest step of the fast idle cam.

c) Install the thermostatic cover and coil assembly in the choke housing. Make sure the coil tang engages the inside coil pickup lever.

d) Install the retainer with the tab at location A and align the notch in the cover with the tab on the retainer. Install one of the self-tapping screws.

e) Install the two remaining retainers and screws, then tighten all three screws evenly and securely.

22   Rochester E4ME carburetor (1980 and 1981) - overhaul

Because of the complexity of this particular carburetor and the special tools required to overhaul and adjust it, it is recommended that major service work be left to a dealer service department or a carburetor specialist.

23   Carburetor adjustment (E4ME)

Because of the special tools and equipment required to properly adjust the E4ME carburetor, it is recommended that carburetor diagnosis and adjustment be performed by a dealer service department or a properly equipped tune-up and repair facility.

24   Cross-Fire Injection system (1982 only)

Description

1   The Cross-Fire Injection system (also known as Throttle Body Injection or TBI) is used in place of a carburetor to control the fuel/air mixture fed into the engine's cylinders.

2   It consists of two throttle body injection units (one feeding the right bank and one feeding the left bank of cylinders), an Electronic Control Module (ECM) and a number of sensors.

3   The ECM (which is a miniature computer) and the sensors control the amount of fuel sprayed into the intake manifold through the injectors by monitoring such things as

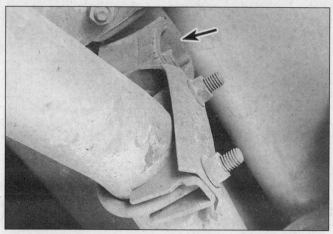

25.1 The exhaust system is hung with rubber hangers like this (arrow)

25.2 The most common cause of exhaust leaks is the gasket at the manifold-to-exhaust pipe - soak the nuts (arrows indicate two of the three), then remove them and lower the pipe to install a new gasket

throttle position, vehicle speed and load, coolant temperature and altitude. During operation of the vehicle, the oxygen sensor in the exhaust and the other sensors continually send electrical "feedback" information to the ECM, which refers to stored program memory and makes high-speed calculations of fuel requirements. The ECM signals each fuel injector, which then cycles open or closed to adjust the fuel/air mixture. This all happens in a fraction of a second and the cycle is repeated thousands of times per minute. The result is to achieve as near as possible an ideal fuel/air mixture regardless of conditions, improved driveability compared to a carbureted vehicle and low levels of emissions.

4   Due to the complexity of the electronic controls and the special tools required to check and service this system, diagnosis and repair must be left to a dealer service department or a reputable repair shop.

TBI/intake manifold cover assembly - removal and installation

Note: *The following procedure is intended to be used only when intake manifold removal or engine disassembly require removal of the fuel injection system components. If the throttle body injectors require repair or servicing, the vehicle should be taken to a dealer service department or a properly-equipped repair facility.*

5   Disconnect the negative cable from the battery.

6   Remove the air cleaner, then disconnect the fuel inlet and return lines from the injectors.

7   Remove the EGR solenoid (located just to the rear of the front injector).

8   Disconnect the wiring leads at the idle air motors, the fuel injectors and the throttle position sensor.

9   Remove the power brake vacuum booster line, then disconnect the accelerator cable and Cruise Control (if so equipped).

10   Disconnect the PCV hose and all vacuum hoses (label them to prevent confusion during reassembly).

11   Remove the bolts attaching the manifold cover to the intake manifold (the fuel transfer tube may have to be removed from the injector units to gain access to the front bolts). **Note:** *The two outermost bolts that fasten the injector units to the manifold cover also thread into the intake manifold and must be removed before the cover can be separated from the manifold. Do not remove the remaining injector mounting bolts or separate the injectors from the manifold cover. If this is done, the curb idle speed must be checked and adjusted (a procedure requiring special tools and expertise beyond the scope of the average home mechanic).*

12   Carefully lift the manifold cover/injector assembly away from the intake manifold.

13   To install the cover assembly, reverse the above procedure. Be sure to thoroughly clean the mating surfaces of the cover and intake manifold and use a new gasket during reassembly. Tighten the mounting bolts in several steps, following a criss-cross pattern, to 20 to 34 ft-lbs.

25   Exhaust system servicing - general information

Refer to illustrations 25.1 and 25.2
Warning: *Inspection and repair of exhaust system components should be done only after enough time has elapsed after driving the vehicle to allow the system components to cool completely. Also, when working under the vehicle, make sure it is securely supported on jackstands.*

1   The exhaust system consists of the exhaust manifold(s), the head pipes, the mufflers, the tailpipes and all brackets, hangers and clamps. The exhaust system is attached to the body with mounting brackets and rubber hangers **(see illustration)**. If any of the

parts are improperly installed, excessive noise and vibration will be transmitted to the body.

2   Conduct regular inspections of the exhaust system to keep it safe and quiet. Look for any damaged or bent parts, open seams, holes, loose connections, excessive corrosion or other defects which could allow exhaust fumes to enter the vehicle **(see illustration)**. Deteriorated exhaust system components should not be repaired; they should be replaced with new parts.

3   If the exhaust system components are extremely corroded or rusted together, welding equipment will probably be required to remove them. The convenient way to accomplish this is to have a muffler repair shop remove the corroded sections with a cutting torch. If, however, you want to save money by doing it yourself (and you don't have a welding outfit with a cutting torch), simply cut off the old components with a hacksaw. If you have compressed air, special pneumatic cutting chisels can also be used. If you do decide to tackle the job at home, be sure to wear safety goggles to protect your eyes from metal chips and work gloves to protect your hands.

4   Here are some simple guidelines to follow when repairing the exhaust system:

a) *Work from the back to the front when removing exhaust system components.*

b) *Apply penetrating oil to the exhaust system component fasteners to make them easier to remove.*

c) *Use new gaskets, hangers and clamps when installing exhaust systems components.*

d) *Apply anti-seize compound to the threads of all exhaust system fasteners during reassembly.*

e) *Be sure to allow sufficient clearance between newly installed parts and all points on the underbody to avoid overheating the floor pan and possibly damaging the interior carpet and insulation. Pay particularly close attention to the catalytic converter and heat shield.*

Chapter 5
Engine electrical systems

Contents

1 General information

The engine electrical systems include all ignition, charging and starting components. Because of their engine-related functions, these components are discussed separately from chassis electrical devices such as the lights, the instruments, etc. (which are included in Chapter 12).

Always observe the following precautions when working on the electrical systems:

a) Be extremely careful when servicing engine electrical components. They are easily damaged if checked, connected or handled improperly.
b) Never leave the ignition switch on for long periods of time with the engine off.
c) Don't disconnect the battery cables while the engine is running.
d) Maintain correct polarity when connecting a battery cable from another vehicle during jump starting.
e) Always disconnect the negative cable first and hook it up last or the battery may be shorted by the tool being used to loosen the cable clamps.

It's also a good idea to review the safety-related information regarding the engine electrical systems located in the Safety first section near the front of this manual before beginning any operation included in this Chapter.

2 Battery - emergency jump starting

Refer to the *Booster battery (jump) starting* procedure at the front of this manual.

3 Battery - removal and installation

Caution: *Always disconnect the negative cable first and hook it up last or the tool being used to loosen the cable clamps may short the battery.*
Note: *On 1968 and 1969 models, the battery is located in the engine compartment. On later models, the battery is located in the storage compartment behind the seats.*

1 Disconnect both cables from the battery terminals.

2 Remove the battery hold-down clamp or strap.
3 Lift out the battery. Be careful - it's heavy.
4 While the battery is out, inspect the carrier (tray) for corrosion (see Chapter 1).
5 If you are replacing the battery, make sure that you get one that's identical, with the same dimensions, amperage rating, cold cranking rating, etc.
6 Installation is the reverse of removal.

4 Battery cables - check and replacement

1 Periodically inspect the entire length of each battery cable for damage, cracked or burned insulation and corrosion. Poor battery cable connections can cause starting problems and decreased engine performance.
2 Check the cable-to-terminal connections at the ends of the cables for cracks, loose wire strands and corrosion. The presence of white, fluffy deposits under the insulation at the cable terminal connection is a sign that the cable is corroded and should be

replaced. Check the terminals for distortion, missing mounting bolts and corrosion.

3   When removing the cables, always disconnect the negative cable first and hook it up last or the tool used to loosen the cable clamps may short the battery. Even if only the positive cable is being replaced, be sure to disconnect the negative cable from the battery first (see Chapter 1 for further information regarding battery cable removal).

4   Disconnect the old cables from the battery, then trace each of them to their opposite ends and detach them from the starter solenoid and ground terminals. Note the routing of each cable to ensure correct installation.

5   If you are replacing either or both of the old cables, take them with you when buying new cables. It is vitally important that you replace the cables with identical parts. Cables have characteristics that make them easy to identify: positive cables are usually red, larger in cross-section and have a larger diameter battery post clamp; ground cables are usually black, smaller in cross-section and have a slightly smaller diameter clamp for the negative post.

6   Clean the threads of the solenoid or ground connection with a wire brush to remove rust and corrosion. Apply a light coat of battery terminal corrosion inhibitor, or petroleum jelly, to the threads to prevent future corrosion.

7   Attach the cable to the solenoid or ground connection and tighten the mounting nut/bolt securely.

8   Before connecting a new cable to the battery, make sure that it reaches the battery post without having to be stretched.

9   Connect the positive cable first, followed by the negative cable.

5   Charging system - general information and precautions

The charging system includes the alternator, an internal or external voltage regulator, a gauge or charge indicator, the battery, a fusible link and the wiring between all the components. The charging system supplies electrical power for the ignition system, the lights, the radio, etc. The alternator is driven by a drivebelt at the front of the engine.

The purpose of the voltage regulator is to limit the alternator's voltage to a preset value. This prevents power surges, circuit overloads, etc., during peak voltage output. On early models, the voltage regulator is a mechanical unit located inside a small metal box; on later models it's a solid-state electronic unit inside the alternator.

The fusible link is a short length of insulated wire integral with the engine compartment wiring harness. The link is four wire gauges smaller in diameter than the circuit it protects. Production fusible links and their identification flags are identified by the flag color. See Chapter 12 for additional information regarding fusible links.

The charging system doesn't ordinarily require periodic maintenance. However, the drivebelt, battery and wires and connections should be inspected at the intervals outlined in Chapter 1.

The dashboard warning light should come on when the ignition key is turned to Start, then go off immediately. If it remains on, there is a malfunction in the charging system (see Section 6). Some vehicles are also equipped with a voltmeter. If the voltmeter indicates abnormally high or low voltage, check the charging system (see Section 6).

Be very careful when making electrical circuit connections to a vehicle equipped with an alternator and note the following:

a) *When reconnecting wires to the alternator from the battery, be sure to note the polarity.*
b) *Before using arc welding equipment to repair any part of the vehicle, disconnect the wires from the alternator and the battery terminals.*
c) *Never start the engine with a battery charger connected.*
d) *Always disconnect both battery leads before using a battery charger.*
e) *The alternator is turned by an engine drivebelt, which could cause serious injury if your hands, hair or clothes become entangled in it with the engine running.*
f) *Because the alternator is connected directly to the battery, it could arc or cause a fire if overloaded or shorted out.*
g) *Wrap a plastic bag over the alternator and secure it with rubberbands before steam cleaning the engine.*

6   Charging system - check

Refer to illustration 6.6

1   If a malfunction occurs in the charging circuit, don't automatically assume that the alternator or regulator is causing the problem. First check the following items:

a) *Check the drivebelt tension and condition (see Chapter 1). Replace it if it's worn or deteriorated.*
b) *Make sure the alternator mounting and adjustment bolts are tight.*
c) *Inspect the alternator wiring harness and the electrical connectors at the alternator and voltage regulator. They must be in good condition and tight.*
d) *Check the fusible link (if equipped) located between the starter solenoid and the alternator. If it's burned, determine the cause, repair the circuit and replace the link (the vehicle won't start and/or the accessories won't work if the fusible link blows). Sometimes a fusible link may look good, but still be bad. If in doubt, remove it and check for continuity.*
e) *Start the engine and check the alternator for abnormal noises (a shrieking or squealing sound indicates a bad bearing).*

f) *Check the specific gravity of the battery electrolyte. If it's low, charge the battery - doesn't apply to maintenance free batteries - (see Chapter 1).*
g) *Make sure the battery is fully charged (one bad cell in a battery can cause overcharging by the alternator).*
h) *Disconnect the battery cables (negative first, then positive). Inspect the battery posts and the cable clamps for corrosion. Clean them thoroughly if necessary (see Chapter 1). Reconnect the cable to the positive terminal.*
i) *With the key off, connect a test light between the negative battery post and the disconnected negative cable clamp.*

   1) *If the test light does not come on, reattach the clamp and proceed to the next Step.*
   2) *If the test light comes on, there is a short (drain) in the electrical system of the vehicle. The short must be repaired before the charging system can be checked.*
   3) *Disconnect the alternator wiring harness.*
      (a) *If the light goes out, the alternator is bad.*
      (b) *If the light stays on, pull each fuse until the light goes out (this will tell you which component is shorted).*

2   Using a voltmeter, check the battery voltage with the engine off. If should be approximately 12-volts.

3   Start the engine and check the battery voltage again. It should now be approximately 14-to-15 volts.

4   Turn on the headlights. The voltage should drop, and then come back up, if the charging system is working properly.

5   If the voltage reading is more than the specified charging voltage, replace the voltage regulator (see Section 7 or 9). If the voltage is less, the alternator diode(s), stator or rectifier may be bad or the voltage regulator may be malfunctioning.

6   You can determine whether an undercharging condition is caused by the alternator or regulator with a full-field test. **Caution:** *The full-field test sends high voltage through the vehicle's electrical system, which can damage components, particularly electronic components. Carefully monitor the charging system voltage to be sure it doesn't exceed 16 volts. Also, do not operate a full-fielded alternator for an extended period of time. Operate it only long enough to take the voltage reading.*

a) *On early models with an external voltage regulator, disconnect the battery negative terminal. Disconnect the F-R electrical connector from the alternator and connect a jumper wire between the F and BATT terminals on the alternator. Re-connect the battery negative terminal, start the engine, turn on the headlights and run the engine at about 1500 to 2000 rpm.*

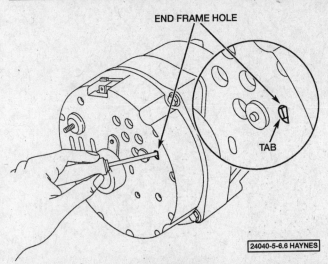

END FRAME HOLE

TAB

24040-5-6.6 HAYNES

6.6 To full-field a later model (SI) alternator, use a screwdriver to ground the tab to the end frame

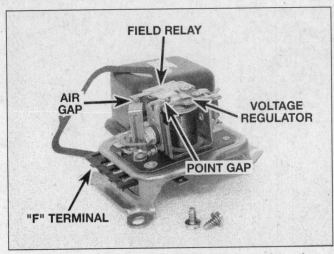

FIELD RELAY

AIR GAP

VOLTAGE REGULATOR

POINT GAP

"F" TERMINAL

7.4 On early models with a separate voltage regulator, the regulator point and air gap adjustments can be checked with a feeler gauge

b) On later models where the voltage regulator is integral with the alternator, start the engine, turn on the headlights, run the engine at about 1500 to 2000 rpm and reach the tip of a screwdriver through the end frame hole (see illustration). Touch the tip of the screwdriver to the tab and ground the side of the screwdriver against the end frame. Caution: Be careful not to touch the alternator fan or other rotating engine components. Do not wear loose clothing.

Measure the battery voltage again. The voltage reading should now be high (about 15 to 16 volts). If it's high, the voltage regulator is probably bad (see Section 7 or 9). If it's still low, the alternator is probably bad.

7   Voltage regulator (early models) - check and replacement

Refer to illustration 7.4

1   A discharged or overcharged battery is often due to a fault in the voltage regulator, but before testing the unit, do the following:

a) Check the alternator drivebelt tension
b) Test the condition of the battery (see Chapter 1).
c) Check the charging circuit for loose connections and broken wires.
d) Make sure that lights or other electrical accessories have not been switched on inadvertently.
e) Check the alternator indicator light or gauge for normal illumination with the ignition switched on and off, and with the engine idling and vehicle stationary.

2   Disconnect the battery negative cable. Disconnect the electrical connector from the regulator.

3   Under no circumstances should the voltage regulator or field relay contacts be cleaned, since any abrasive materials will

destroy the contact material.

4   Voltage regulator point (0.014-inch) and air gap (0.067-inch) adjustments can be checked with a feeler gauge of the specified thickness. Check the voltage regulator point opening of the upper contacts with the lower contacts just touching. Adjustments are made by carefully bending the upper contact arm. Check the voltage regulator air gap with the lower contacts touching and adjust it, if necessary, by turning the nylon nut (see illustration).

5   The field relay point opening (0.030-inch) may be adjusted by bending the armature stop. The air gap (0.015-inch) is checked with the points just touching and is adjusted by bending the flat contact support spring. Note: The field relay will normally operate satisfactorily even if the air gap is outside the specified limits, and should not be adjusted when the system is functioning satisfactorily.

3   If the regulator must be replaced, simply remove the mounting screws.

4   Installation is the reverse of removal. Ensure the rubber gasket is in place on the regulator base.

8   Alternator - removal and installation

Refer to illustration 8.3

Note: If the vehicle is an early model with an external voltage regulator, we recommend replacing the regulator whenever the alternator is replaced (see Section 7).

1   Detach the cable from the negative terminal of the battery.

2   Detach the electrical connectors from the alternator.

3   Loosen the alternator adjustment and pivot bolts, push the alternator toward the engine and detach the drivebelt - see Chapter 1, if necessary - (see illustration).

4   Remove the adjustment and pivot bolts and separate the alternator from the engine.

5   If you are replacing the alternator, take the old one with you when purchasing a replacement unit. Make sure the new/rebuilt unit looks identical to the old alternator. Look at the terminals - they should be the same in number, size and location as the terminals on the old alternator. Finally, look at the identifi-

8.3 Loosen the adjuster bolt (upper arrow) and the pivot bolt (lower arrow)

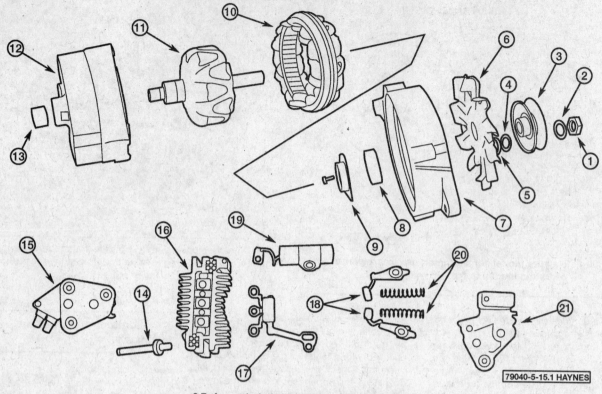

9.7 An exploded view of the 10SI alternator

1	Nut	7	Drive end frame	12	Slip-ring end frame	17	Diode trio
2	Washer	8	Bearing	13	Bearing	18	Brushes
3	Pulley	9	Plate	14	Terminal component stud	19	Capacitor
4	Washer	10	Stator	15	Voltage regulator	20	Brush springs
5	Collar	11	Rotor	16	Rectifier bridge	21	Brush holder
6	Fan						

cation numbers - they will be stamped into the housing or printed on a tag attached to the housing. Make sure the numbers are the same on both alternators.

6   Many new/rebuilt alternators DO NOT have a pulley installed, so you may have to switch the pulley from the old unit to the new/rebuilt one. When buying an alternator, find out the shop's policy regarding pulleys - some shops will perform this service free of charge.

7   Installation is the reverse of removal.

8   After the alternator is installed, adjust the drivebelt tension (see Chapter 1).

9   Check the charging voltage to verify proper operation of the alternator (see Section 6).

9   Alternator - brush replacement and overhaul

Refer to Illustration 9.7

Note: *Since many internal alternator components are delicate, and static testing may not always reveal the source of an alternator problem, it may be advisable for the home*

mechanic to simply replace a faulty unit with a new or factory rebuilt model. If you decide to perform the overhaul procedure yourself, make sure that replacement parts are available before proceeding.

1   Remove the alternator and pulley (see Section 8).

2   Secure the alternator in the jaws of a vice, applying the pressure to the mounting flange. **Caution:** *Do not apply too much pressure and break the delicate cast-aluminum case.*

3   Remove the four through-bolts, and separate the slip-ring end frame and stator assembly from the drive end and rotor assembly. Use a screwdriver to lever them apart and mark the relative position of the end frames to facilitate reassembly.

4   Remove the stator lead securing nuts and separate the stator from the end frame.

1D, 10DN and 100B series (early models)

5   Extract the screws and remove the brush holder assembly.

6   Remove the heat sink from the end frame after extracting the BAT and GRD terminals and single securing screws.

10 S1 series (later models)

7   Continue disassembling by removing the rectifier bridge, securing screw and the BAT terminal screw. Disconnect the condenser lead and remove the rectifier bridge from the end frame **(see illustration).**

8   Unscrew the two securing screws and remove the brush holder and regulator. Carefully retain the insulating sleeves and washers. Note how they're installed for reassembly.

9   Remove the condenser (one screw) from the end frame.

All models

10   If the slip-ring end frame bearing is dry or noisy when rotated, it must be replaced (not greased). Greasing will not extend its service life. Press out the old bearing and discard the oil seal. Press in the new bearing, squarely, until the bearing is flush with the outside of the end frame. Install a new oil seal. During these operations, support the end frame adequately to prevent cracking or distorting the frame.

11   If not already done, insert a 5/16-inch Allen wrench into the socket in the center of the shaft at the drive pulley end. Using this to prevent the shaft from rotating, unscrew the

pulley retaining nut and remove the washer, pulley, fan and the spacer.

12   Remove the rotor and spacers from the drive end frame.

13   If the bearing in the drive end frame is dry or noisy it must be replaced. Do not grease it in the hope that this will extend its life. Access to the bearing is obtained after removing the retainer plate screws and separating the plate/seal assembly. Press the bearing out by using a piece of tube applied to the inner race and press the new one in by applying the tube to the outer race. Make sure that the slinger is correctly located and the recommended grease is applied to the bearing before installation.

14   With the alternator completely dismantled, wipe all components clean (do not use solvent on the stator or rotor windings - use electrical contact cleaner), and examine for wear or damage. Purchase new components as necessary.

15   If the slip rings are dirty they should be cleaned by spinning the rotor and holding a piece of 400-grain abrasive paper against them. This method will avoid the creation of flat spots on the rings. If the rings are badly scored, out-of-round or otherwise damaged, the complete rotor assembly must be replaced.

16   Check the brushes for wear. If they are worn halfway or more in length, do not re-use them. Purchase new springs only if they appear weak or are distorted.

17 Reassembly is the reverse of disassembly. Observe the following points:

a) *Tighten the pulley nut securely. Take great care to position the insulating washers and sleeves correctly on the brush clip screws.*

b) *Clean the brush contact surfaces before installing the slip-ring end frame and hold the brushes up in their holders by passing a thin rod through the opening in the slip-ring end frame to permit the brushes to pass over the slip rings.*

c) *Finally, make sure that the marks on the slip-ring and drive end frame (which were made before disassembly) are in alignment.*

10   Ignition system - general information

1   In order for the engine to run correctly, it is necessary for an electrical spark to ignite the fuel/air mixture in the combustion chamber at exactly the right moment in relation to engine speed and load. The ignition coil converts low-tension (LT) voltage from the battery into high-tension (HT) voltage, powerful enough to jump the spark plug gap in the cylinder, providing that the system is in good condition and that all adjustments are correct.

2   The ignition system installed on pre-1975 models as standard equipment is a conventional distributor with mechanical contact (breaker) points; breakerless (transistor-ized) ignition was an option. On 1975 and later models, a breakerless High Energy Ignition (HEI) system is used.

Mechanical breaker point type (most pre-1975 models)

3   The ignition system is divided into the primary (low-tension) circuit and the secondary (high-tension) circuit.

4   The primary circuit consists of the battery cable to the starter motor, the wire to the ignition switch, the calibrated resistance wire from the ignition switch to the primary coil winding and the wire from the low-tension coil windings to the contact (breaker) points and condenser in the distributor.

5   The secondary circuit consists of the secondary coil winding, the high-tension wire from the coil to the distributor cap, the rotor and the spark plug wires and spark plugs.

6   The system functions in the following manner: Low-tension voltage in the coil is converted into high-tension voltage by the opening and closing of the contact (breaker) points in the distributor. This high-tension voltage is carried through the coil high-tension wire to the brush in the center of the distributor cap, which contacts the arm of the rotor in the distributor. Every time the rotating rotor contacts one of the spark plug terminals in the cap, high-tension voltage jumps the gap from the rotor arm to the terminal and is carried by the spark plug wire to the spark plug, where it jumps the spark plug gap to ground.

7   Ignition advance is controlled by both mechanical and vacuum-operated systems. The mechanical advance mechanism increases spark advance when engine speed is increased. It consists of two weights that, due to centrifugal force, move out from the distributor shaft as the engine speed rises. As they move out, they rotate the cam relative to the distributor shaft, advancing spark timing. The weights are held in position by two light springs. It is the tension of these springs that determines correct spark advance.

8   The vacuum control system consists of a diaphragm, one side of which is connected via a vacuum line to the carburetor, the other side to the contact breaker plate. Vacuum in the intake manifold and carburetor varies with engine speed and throttle opening. As the vacuum changes, it moves the diaphragm, which rotates the contact breaker plate slightly in relation to the rotor, thus advancing or retarding the spark. Control is fine-tuned by a spring in the vacuum assembly. This vacuum system provides optimum spark advance while the vehicle is cruising, maximizing fuel economy.

9   On some models, a Transmission Controlled Spark (TCS) system eliminates vacuum advance (see Chapter 6).

Breakerless and HEI ignition systems (through 1980)

10   These are pulse-triggered, transistor-controlled, inductive discharge systems. Pre-1975 models were commonly referred to as "breakerless". 1975 and later models are called High Energy Ignition (HEI) systems because of their high voltage - approximately 50,000 volts.

11   A magnetic pick-up inside the distributor contains a permanent magnet, pole-piece and pick-up coil. A timer core, rotating inside the pole piece, induces a voltage in the pick-up coil. When the teeth on the timer and pole piece line up, a signal passes to the electronic module to open the coil primary circuit. The primary circuit current collapses and a high voltage is induced in the coil secondary winding. This high voltage is directed to the spark plugs by the distributor rotor in a manner similar to the breaker point type system described above. A condenser suppresses radio interference.

12   These systems feature a longer spark duration than a conventional breaker point ignition system, and the dwell period increases automatically with engine speed. These characteristics are desirable for lean firing and EGR-diluted mixtures (see Chapter 6).

13   On 1975 and later HEI systems, the ignition coil and the electronic module are both housed in the distributor cap. On earlier models, the coil and module are separate from the distributor. The distributor does not require routine servicing.

14   Spark timing is advanced by mechanical and vacuum devices similar to those used on conventional breaker point distributors (described above). The TCS system is eliminated.

HEI systems (1980 California models and all 1981 and 1982 models)

15   These HEI systems are equipped with Electronic Spark Timing (EST). All spark timing changes are carried out by the Electronic Control Module (ECM), which monitors data from various engine sensors, computes the desired spark timing and signals the distributor to alter spark timing accordingly. Vacuum and mechanical advance is eliminated.

16   An Electronic Spark Control (ESC) system utilizes a knock sensor and the ECM to allow maximum spark advance without spark knock. The ESC system improves driveability and fuel economy.

11   Ignition system - check

Refer to illustration 11.2

Warning: Because of the very high voltage generated by the ignition system, extreme care should be taken whenever an operation is performed involving ignition components. This not only includes the distributor, coil, control module and spark plug wires, but related items such as the plug connections, tachometer and any test equipment.

Calibrated ignition tester method

1   If the engine turns over but will not start, disconnect the spark plug wire from any spark plug and attach it to a calibrated ignition tester (available at most auto parts stores).

2   Connect the clip on the tester to a ground such as a metal bracket **(see illustration)**, crank the engine and observe the tip of the tester to see if a spark occurs.

3   If a spark occurs, sufficient voltage is reaching the plugs to fire the engine.

4   If there is no spark, check another wire in the same manner. A few sparks followed by no spark is the same condition as no spark at all. If there's spark at some wires but not others, the spark plug wires are bad or the distributor cap is wet, cracked or carbon tracked (see Chapter 1).

5   If there's still no spark on models with a point-type system or 1968 through 1974 breakerless ignition system, disconnect the coil high-tension wire from the center of the distributor cap and repeat the test, using the disconnected end of the wire. If there's now strong sparking, the distributor cap or rotor is probably faulty, or the engine timing chain is broken or slipping (check to see if the rotor turns when the engine is cranked).

6   On models with a point-type ignition system, if there's still no spark, check and/or replace the breaker points and condenser, check the dwell angle and check to make sure the primary ignition wires are in good shape and securely connected (see Chapter 1). Check carefully where the primary wire connects to the points, as this is a common place to find a grounded or pinched wire.

7   If there's still no spark, the ignition coil, pick-up coil or module is probably faulty.

8   If there is a good spark, check the spark plugs (see Chapter 1) and/or the fuel system (see Chapter 4).

9   Further checks of the breakerless and HEI ignition systems must be done by a dealer service department or repair shop.

Alternative method

Note: *If you are unable to obtain a calibrated tester, the following method will enable you to determine whether the ignition system has*

spark, but it will not tell you if there is enough voltage present to actually initiate combustion.

10   Remove the spark plug wire from a spark plug. Using an insulated tool, hold the wire about 1/4-inch from a good ground and have an assistant crank the engine. Thick, bright-blue sparks should be visible between the wire and ground. Proceed to Steps 3 through 9 above.

---

12   Ignition coil - check and replacement

Check

1   If the engine is hard to start (particularly when it's already hot), misses at high speed or cuts out during acceleration, the coil may be faulty. First, make sure that the battery and the distributor and cap are in good condition, the points (pre-1975 vehicles) are properly adjusted and the spark plugs and plug wires are in good shape. If the problem persists, perform the following test:

Separately mounted coils (pre-1975 models)

2   Before performing any of the following coil electrical checks, make sure that the coil is clean, free of any carbon tracks and that all connections are tight and free of corrosion. Also make sure that both battery terminals are clean and that the cables are securely attached (especially the ground strap at the negative terminal).

3   Perform the ignition system check described in the preceding Section.

a) If the spark is weak, yellowish or red, spark voltage is insufficient. If the points, condenser and battery are in good condition, the coil is probably weak. Take it to a dealer and have the output checked. If it tests weak when compared to a new coil of the same specifications, replace it.

b) If there is no spark at all, try to locate the trouble before replacing the coil. Remove the distributor cap. Turn the engine until the points are open, or separate the points with a small piece of

cardboard. Turn on the ignition switch. Using a 12-volt bulb with two test wires, attach one wire to ground somewhere on the engine and the other wire to first one of the coil's primary terminals and then the other.

1) If the bulb lights when touched to the primary terminal that leads to the distributor, the coil is getting current and the primary windings are okay.

2) If the bulb lights when touched to the other primary terminal but not when attached to the one leading to the distributor, the primary windings are faulty. Replace the coil.

3) If the light does not go on when connected to either primary connection, the coil is not the problem. Check the ignition switch, primary wire connections and starter solenoid.

4) If the bulb lights when touched to both primary terminals (the coil is receiving current at both primary terminals), remove the high-tension cable from the center distributor cap tower and try shorting across the open distributor points with the tip of a clean (no oil) screwdriver.

  a) If a spark jumps from the coil's high-tension secondary wire to a grounded point on the engine as the screwdriver is removed, the points are either contaminated by oil, dirt or water, or they're burned.

  b) If the screwdriver fails to produce a spark at the high-tension wire, disconnect the primary wire that passes between the coil and the distributor and attach a test wire to the coil in its place. Ground the other end of the wire against the engine block, then pull it away (the test wire is simulating the points: grounding the wire is just like closing the points; pulling it away creates the same effect - producing a spark from the coil's high-tension wire - as opening the points).

    1) If a spark jumps from the high-tension cable when the test wire is removed from the ground, the coil is okay. Either the points are grounded or the condenser is shorted.

    2) If a spark does not jump during this test, the secondary windings of the coil are faulty. Replace the coil.

4   Sometimes, a coil checks out perfectly but the engine is still hard to start and misses at higher speeds. The problem may be inadequate spark voltage caused by reversed coil polarity. If you have recently tuned up the engine or performed any service work involving the coil, it's possible that the primary wires to the coil were accidentally reversed. To check for reversed polarity, remove one of the spark plug wires and hold it about 1/4-inch from the spark plug terminal or any

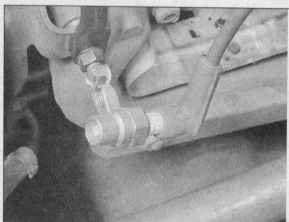

11.2 To use a calibrated ignition tester, disconnect a spark plug wire, hook the wire to the tester, clip the tester to a convenient ground and operate the starter - if there's enough power to fire the plug, sparks will be visible between the electrode tip and the tester body

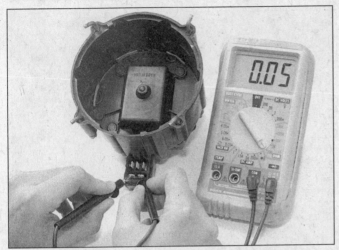

12.6a To test the HEI-type coil-in-cap, attach the leads of an ohmmeter to the primary terminals and verify the indicated resistance is zero or very near zero (1),

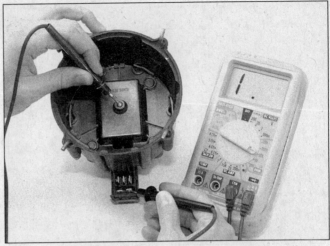

12.6b Using the high scale on the ohmmeter, attach one lead to the high tension terminal and the other to each of the primary terminals and verify both readings are not infinite

12.10 To remove a separate coil, detach the high-tension cable and the two primary wires, then remove the mounting bracket screws

12.14a To get to the coil, remove the coil cover screws and the cover

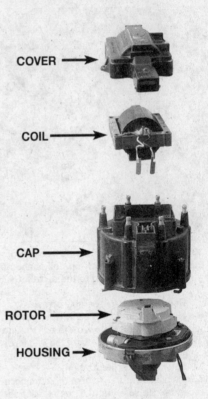

COVER →
COIL →
CAP →
ROTOR →
HOUSING →

12.14b An exploded view of an HEI-type distributor

ground point. Then insert the point of a pencil between the ignition wire and the spark plug while the engine is running (if the plug connector terminals are deeply recessed in a boot or insulating shield, straighten all but one bend in a paper clip and insert the looped end into the plug connector).

a) If the spark flares on the ground or spark plug side of the pencil, the polarity is correct.

b) If the spark flares between the ignition wire and the pencil, however, the polarity is wrong and the primary wires should be switched at the coil.

HEI-type coil-in-cap (1975 and later models)

Refer to illustrations 12.6a and 12.6b

5   Remove the distributor cap (see Chapter 1).

6   Attach the two wires of an ohmmeter to the two primary terminals as shown **(see illustrations)**. The indicated resistance

should be zero or very near zero. If it isn't, replace the coil.

7   Using the high scale, attach one lead of the ohmmeter to the high-tension terminal in the middle of the distributor and the other lead to each of the primary terminals. If both of the readings indicate infinite resistance, replace the coil.

Replacement

Separately mounted coils (pre-1975 models)

Refer to Illustration 12.10

8   Detach the cable from the negative terminal of the battery.

9   Disconnect the high-tension cable from the coil.

10   Detach the electrical connections from the coil primary and secondary terminals. Be sure to mark the connections before removal to ensure that they are re-installed correctly. Remove the coil **(see illustration)**.

11   Installation is the reverse of removal

HEI-type coil-in-cap (1975 and later models)

Refer to Illustrations 12.14a, 12.14b, 12.16 and 12.17

12   Detach the cable from the negative terminal of the battery.

13   Disconnect the battery wire and harness connector from the distributor cap.

14   Remove the coil cover screws and the cover **(see illustrations)**.

12.16 To separate the coil from the distributor cap, clearly mark the wires, detach the coil ground wire and push the wires from the underside of the connectors

12.17 Before installing a new coil, make sure the center electrode is in good condition - the carbon button often burns either on the top or bottom (inside the distributor cap)

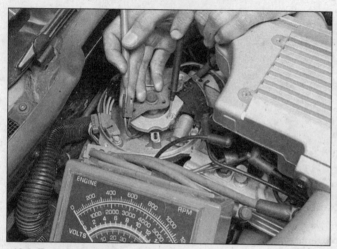

13.3 To test the pick-up coil, hook an ohmmeter lead to each of the terminals of the pick-up coil connector and ground the other lead to the distributor base

13.4 Place the leads in both terminals of the pick-up coil connector and flex the wires by hand to check for intermittent opens

15   Remove the coil assembly screws.
16   Note the position of each wire, marking them if necessary. Remove the coil ground wire, then push the leads from the underside of the connectors. Remove the coil from the distributor cap **(see illustration)**.
17   Installation is the reverse of the removal procedure. Be sure that the center electrode is in good shape **(see illustration)** and that the leads are connected to their original positions.

13   Ignition pick-up coil (breakerless and HEI models) - check and replacement

Refer to illustrations 13.3, 13.4, 13.7, 13.9 and 13.10

1   Remove the distributor cap (see Chapter 1).
2   Remove the rotor and disconnect the pick-up coil wires from the module.

13.7 Place the distributor in a bench vise and drive out the roll pin that locks the drive gear to the bottom of the shaft

Check

3   Connect an ohmmeter to each terminal of the pick-up coil wire and ground it to the distributor base **(see illustration)**. The ohmmeter reading should indicate infinite resis-

tance. If it doesn't, the pick-up coil is defective.
4   Connect the ohmmeter between both terminals of the pick-up coil connector **(see illustration)**. Flex the wires by hand to check for intermittent opens. The ohmmeter reading

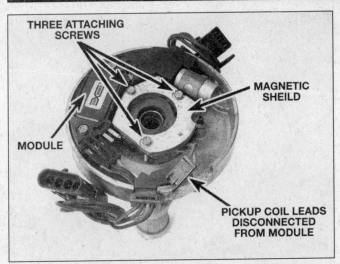

13.9 Remove the three screws attaching the magnetic shield to the distributor base and remove the shield

13.10 Remove the C-clip retaining the pick-up coil/magnet pole piece assembly and remove the assembly from the distributor

should indicate one steady value within the 500 to 1500 ohm range as the wires are flexed. If it doesn't, the pick-up coil is defective.

5   If the pick-up coil fails either test, replace it.

Replacement

6   Remove the distributor (see Section 15). Mark the distributor shaft and gear so that they can be reassembled in the same position.

7   Secure the distributor shaft housing in a bench vise and drive out the roll pin with a hammer and punch (see illustration).

8   Remove the gear and tanged washer, then pull the shaft from the distributor.

9   Remove the three attaching screws and detach the magnetic shield, if equipped (see illustration).

10   If equipped, remove the C-clip (see illustration) and detach the pick-up coil, magnet and pole piece.

11   Install the new pick-up coil, magnet and pole piece assembly.

12   Install the shaft. Make sure that it's clean and lubricated.

13   Install the tanged washer (with the tangs facing up), the drive gear and the roll pin.

14   Spin the shaft to ensure that the teeth on the distributor shaft do not touch the teeth on the pick-up coil pole piece.

15   If the teeth touch, loosen, adjust and retighten the pole piece to eliminate contact.

16   Install the distributor in the engine (see Section 15).

17   Install the rotor and cap (see Chapter 1).

14   Ignition module (HEI models) - replacement

Refer to illustration 14.4

Note: Since special equipment is required, the module must be checked by a dealer ser-

14.4 To remove the module, remove the two mounting screws (1) and unplug the two electrical connectors (2) - if you are installing a new module, apply silicone grease (included with the module) to the module and the spot on which the module is mounted

vice department or other qualified repair shop. It is not necessary to remove the distributor from the engine to replace the ignition module.

1   Disconnect the cable from the negative terminal of the battery.

2   Remove the distributor cap (see Chapter 1).

3   Mark the position of the rotor in relation to the distributor housing. Remove the rotor retaining screws and the rotor.

4   Remove both module mounting screws and detach the module from the distributor (see illustration).

5   Disconnect the electrical connectors from the module. Note that they cannot be interchanged.

6   Do not wipe the grease from the module or the distributor base if the same module is to be reinstalled. If a new module is to be installed, a package of silicone grease will be included with it. Wipe the distributor base and the new module clean, then apply the silicone grease to the face of the module and the distributor base where the module seats. This grease is necessary for heat dissipation.

7   Installation is the reverse of removal.

15   Distributor - removal and installation

Refer to illustrations 15.6, 15.7a and 15.7b

Removal

1   On models with breaker points, disconnect the primary lead from the coil.

2   On breakerless and HEI models, unplug the electrical connector for the module. Follow the wires as they exit the distributor to find the connector.

3   Look for a raised "1" on the distributor cap. This marks the location for the number one cylinder spark plug wire terminal. If the cap does not have a mark for the number one terminal, locate the number one spark plug and trace the wire back to the terminal on the cap.

4   Remove the distributor cap (see Chapter 1) and turn the engine over until the rotor is pointing toward the number one spark plug terminal (see locating TDC procedure in Chapter 2). Note: To move the cap enough provide clearance so you can remove the distributor, it's often necessary to release the

15.6 On some early models, you'll have to unscrew the tachometer drive cable at the base of the distributor (arrow)

15.7a Some distributor hold-down bolts can be removed with a combination wrench . . .

spark plug wire routing clips on the engine or disconnect the wires from the cap. If the wires must be disconnected, be sure to mark them carefully so they can be returned to their original positions.

5   Make a mark on the edge of the distributor base directly below the rotor tip and in line with it. Also, mark the distributor base and the engine block to ensure that the distributor is installed correctly.

6   Disconnect the tachometer drive cable - if equipped - **(see illustration)**, then disconnect the hose from the vacuum advance unit on the distributor (if equipped).

7   Remove the distributor hold-down bolt and clamp **(see illustrations)**, then pull the distributor straight up to remove it. **Caution:** *DO NOT turn the crankshaft while the distributor is out of the engine, or the alignment marks will be useless.*

Installation

Note: *If the crankshaft has been moved while the distributor is out, the number one piston must be repositioned at TDC. This can be done by feeling for compression pressure at the number one plug hole as the crankshaft is turned. Once compression is felt, align the ignition timing zero mark with the pointer.*

8   Insert the distributor into the engine in exactly the same relationship to the block that it was in when removed. Be sure to use a new gasket.

9   To mesh the helical gears on the camshaft and the distributor, it may be necessary to turn the rotor slightly. Recheck the alignment marks between the distributor base and the block to verify that the distributor is in the same position it was in before removal. Also check the rotor to see if it's aligned with the mark you made on the edge of the distributor base.

10   Place the hold-down clamp in position and loosely install the bolt.

11   Install the distributor cap.

12   Re-connect the coil and/or module.

13   Re-attach the spark plug wires (if

removed).

14   Re-connect the vacuum hose and tachometer drive cable.

15   Connect the cable to the negative terminal of the battery.

16   Check the ignition timing (see Chapter 1) and tighten the distributor hold-down bolt securely.

16   Distributor - overhaul

Breaker point type (1968 through 1974)

Refer to illustration 16.2

1   Remove the distributor (See Section 15), then pull out the tachometer drive gear (if equipped).

2   Remove the rotor (two screws), the advance weight springs and the weights **(see illustration)**. Where applicable, also remove the radio frequency interference (RFI) shield.

3   Drive out the roll pin retaining the gear to the shaft then pull off the gear and spacers.

4   Ensure the shaft is not burred, then slide it from the housing. If the shaft is burred in

the area where the gear was, remove the burring with #400 emery cloth.

5   Remove the cam weight base assembly.

6   Remove the screws retaining the vacuum advance unit and lift off the unit itself.

7   Remove the spring retainer (snap-ring), then remove the breaker plate assembly.

8   Remove the contact points and condenser, followed by the felt washer and plastic seal located beneath the breaker plate.

9   Wipe all components clean with a solvent-moistened cloth and examine them for wear, distortion and scoring. Replace parts as necessary. Pay particular attention to the rotor and distributor cap to ensure that they are not cracked.

10   Fill the lubricating cavity in the housing with general purpose grease, then fit a new plastic seal and felt washer.

11   Install the vacuum advance unit and the breaker plate in the housing, and the spring retainer on the upper bushing.

12   Lubricate the cam weight base and slide it on the mainshaft; install the weights and springs.

13   Insert the mainshaft in the housing then fit the shims and drivegear. Install a new roll pin.

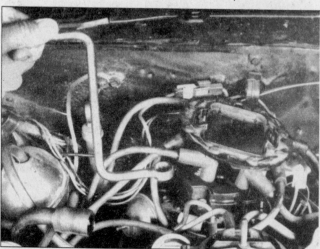

15.7b . . . others may require a special distributor wrench

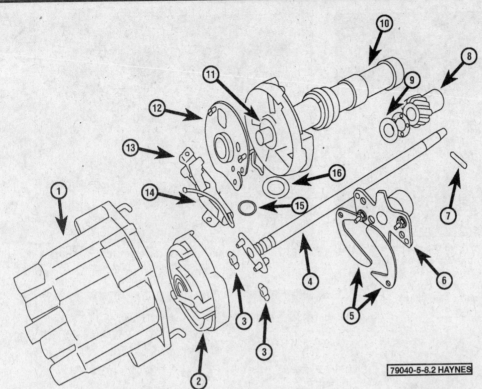

16.2 An exploded view of a typical breaker point type distributor

1 Distributor cap
2 Rotor
3 Advance weight springs
4 Mainshaft
5 Advance weights
6 Cam and advance weight base
7 Drive gear roll pin
8 Distributor drive gear
9 Washer and shim
10 Distributor housing
11 Plastic washer
12 Breaker plate
13 Contact point assembly
14 Condenser
15 retaining ring
16 Felt washer

79040-5-8.2 HAYNES

14 Install the contact point set (see Chapter 1).

15 Install the rotor, aligning the round and square pilot holes.

16 Install the distributor (see Section 15).

Breakerless type (1968 through 1972)

17 Remove the distributor (see Section 15).

18 Remove the rotor (see Chapter 1, if necessary).

19 Remove the centrifugal advance weights and springs.

20 Remove the tachometer drive gear from the distributor.

21 Drive out the roll-pin, then pull the drive gear and washer from the shaft.

22 Remove the distributor shaft.

23 Pull the centrifugal weight support and rotating pole piece from the shaft.

24 Remove the connector from the magnetic pick-up assembly.

25 Remove the retaining ring that holds the magnetic pick-up assembly to the distributor shaft bushing.

26 Lift the complete magnetic pick-up assembly from the distributor housing. Extract the brass washer and felt pad.

27 Detach the vacuum advance unit.

28 Reassembly is the reverse of disassembly.

HEI type (1975 through 1980 - except 1980 California)

Refer to illustrations 16.30, 16.31, 16.33, 16.37a and 16.37b

29 Remove the distributor (see Section 15).

30 Remove the rotor (two screws) **(see illustration)**.

31 Remove the two screws retaining the module. Move the module aside and remove the connector from the 'B' and 'C' terminals **(see illustration)**.

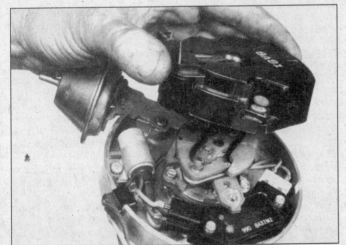

16.30 To detach the rotor from the HEI distributor, remove the two screws on top that attach it to the centrifugal advance mechanism

16.31 To detach the ignition module from the HEI distributor, remove the two mounting screws and unplug the connector from the B and C terminals

16.33 To remove the distributor shaft, drive the roll pin out of the shaft with a hammer and punch, remove the gear, shim and tanged washer from the shaft, inspect the shaft for any burrs that might prevent its removal, then pull it out (be careful not to lose the washer at the upper end of the shaft)

16.37a Remove the three screws (arrows) and detach the pole piece, magnet and pick-up coil

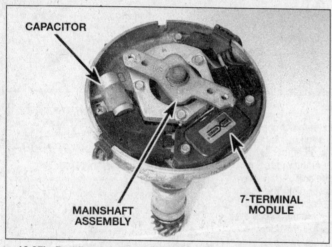

CAPACITOR

MAINSHAFT ASSEMBLY

7-TERMINAL MODULE

16.37b Details of a typical HEI distributor (1975 through 1980)

16.60 To remove the distributor shaft, mark the relative positions of the gear and shaft, drive out the pin retaining the distributor gear to the shaft, remove the gear and pull out the shaft

32 Remove the connections from the 'W' and 'G' terminals.

33 Carefully drive out the roll pin from the drive gear **(see illustration)**.

34 Remove the gear, shim and tanged washer from the distributor shaft.

35 Ensure that the shaft is not burred, then remove it from the housing. If the shaft is burred in the area where the gear was, remove the burring with #400 emery cloth.

36 Remove the washer from the upper end of the distributor housing.

37 Remove the three screws and take out the pole-piece, magnet and pick-up coil **(see illustrations)**.

38 Remove the lock ring, then take out the pick-up coil retainer, shim and felt washer.

39 Remove the vacuum advance unit (two screws).

40 Disconnect the condenser lead and remove the condenser (one screw).

41 Disconnect the wiring harness from the distributor housing.

42 Wipe all components clean with a sol-vent-moistened cloth and examine them for wear, distortion and other damage. Replace parts as necessary.

43 To assemble, position the vacuum advance unit to the housing and secure with the two screws.

44 Position the felt washer over the lubricant reservoir at the top of the housing, then position the shim on top of the felt washer.

45 Position the pick-up coil retainer on the housing. The vacuum advance arm goes over the actuating pin of the advance mechanism. Secure it with the lock-ring.

46 Install the pick-up coil magnet and pole-piece. Loosely install the three screws to retain the pole-piece.

47 Install the washer to the top of the housing. Install the distributor shaft, then rotate it and check for equal clearance all round between the shaft projections and pole-piece. Secure the pole-piece when correctly positioned.

48 Install the tanged washer, shim and drive-gear. Align the gear and install a new roll pin.

49 Loosely install the condenser with one screw.

50 Install the connector to the 'B' and 'C' terminals on the module, with the tab at the top.

51 Apply silicone grease to the base of the module and secure it with two screws. The grease is essential to ensure good heat conduction.

52 Position the wiring harness, with the grommet in the housing notch, then connect the pink wire to the condenser stud and the black wire to the condenser mounting screw. Tighten the screw.

53 Connect the white wire from the pick-up coil to the module "W" terminal and the green to the 'G' terminal.

54 Install the advance weights, weight retainer (dimple down), and springs.

55 Install the rotor and secure with the two screws. Ensure that the notch on the side of the rotor engages with the tab on the cam weight base.

56 Install the distributor (see Section 15).

HEI type (1980 California and all later models)

Refer to illustration 16.60

57   Later model HEI distributors vary somewhat from those described above. Most later distributors are not equipped with vacuum advance units, as an Electronic Control module (ECM) controls advance.
58   Remove the distributor (see Section 15).
59   Place the distributor in a vice, using blocks of wood to protect it.
60   Mark the relative positions of the gear and shaft. Drive the roll pin out **(see illustration)**. Remove the gear and pull the shaft from the distributor housing.
61   Remove the aluminum shield for access to the pick-up coil and module. The pick-up coil can be lifted out after removal of the C-washer. Remove the two screws and lift the module, capacitor and harness assembly from the distributor base.
62   Wipe the distributor base and module with a clean cloth and inspect it for cracks and damage.
63   Reassembly is the reverse of the disassembly procedure. Be sure to apply a coat of silicone lubricant to the distributor base under the module. After reassembly, spin the distributor shaft to make sure there is no contact with the pick-up coil. Loosen and retighten to eliminate the contact.

17   Starting system - general information and precautions

The sole function of the starting system is to turn over the engine quickly enough to allow it to start.

The starting system consists of the battery, the starter motor, the starter solenoid and the wires connecting them. The solenoid is mounted directly on the starter motor. Models with automatic transmissions are equipped with a neutral start switch, mounted next to the base of the shifter, that allows the starter to operate only when the shifter is in Park or Neutral (see Chapter 7B for more information on this switch). Many models with manual transmissions are equipped with a switch that allows the starter to operate only when the clutch is depressed (see Chapter 8 for more information on this switch).

The solenoid/starter motor assembly is installed on the lower part of the engine, next to the transmission bellhousing.

When the ignition key is turned to the Start position, the starter solenoid is actuated through the starter control circuit. The starter solenoid then connects the battery to the starter. The battery supplies the electrical energy to the starter motor, which does the actual work of cranking the engine.

Always observe the following precautions when working on the starting system:

a) *Excessive cranking of the starter motor can overheat it and cause serious damage. Never operate the starter motor for* more than 15 seconds at a time without pausing to allow it to cool for at least two minutes.
b) *The starter is connected directly to the battery and could arc or cause a fire if mishandled, overloaded or shorted out.*
c) *Always detach the cable from the negative terminal of the battery before working on the starting system.*

18   Starter motor - in-vehicle check

Note: *Before diagnosing starter problems, make sure the battery is fully charged.*

1   If the starter motor does not turn at all when the switch is operated, make sure that the shift lever is in Neutral or Park (automatic transmission) or that the clutch pedal is depressed (manual transmission).
2   Make sure that the battery is charged and that all cables, both at the battery and starter solenoid terminals, are clean and secure.
3   If the starter motor spins but the engine is not cranking, the overrunning clutch in the starter motor is slipping and the starter motor must be replaced. Also check that the ring gear on the flywheel or driveplate is not damaged.
4   If, when the switch is actuated, the starter motor does not operate at all but the solenoid clicks, the problem lies with either the battery, the main solenoid contacts or the starter motor itself (or the engine is seized).
5   If the solenoid plunger cannot be heard when the switch is actuated, the battery is bad, the fusible link is burned (the circuit is open) or the solenoid itself is defective.
6   To check the solenoid, connect a jumper lead between the battery positive terminal and the ignition switch wire terminal (the small terminal) on the solenoid. If the starter motor now operates, the solenoid is OK and the problem is in the ignition switch, neutral start switch, clutch switch or the wiring.
7   If the starter motor still does not operate, remove the starter/solenoid assembly for disassembly, testing and repair.
8   If the starter motor cranks the engine at an abnormally slow speed, first make sure the battery is fully charged and that all terminal connections are tight. If the engine is partially seized or has the wrong viscosity oil in it (in cold weather), it will crank slowly. Also, verify the battery's Cold Cranking Amp (CCA) rating is sufficient for the engine (an auto parts store can usually tell you what the minimum should be).
9   Run the engine until normal operating temperature is reached, then disconnect the coil wire from the distributor cap and ground it on the engine.
10   Connect a voltmeter positive lead to the positive battery post and connect the negative lead to the negative post. A fully charged battery should read about 12.6 volts. If the reading is lower, charge the battery before proceeding.
11   Crank the engine and take the voltmeter readings as soon as a steady figure is indicated. Do not allow the starter motor to turn for more than 15 seconds at a time. A reading of 9 volts or more, with the starter motor turning at normal cranking speed, is normal. If the reading is 9 volts or more but the cranking speed is slow, the solenoid contacts are burned, there is a bad connection or the starter motor is faulty. If the reading is less than 9 volts and the cranking speed is slow, the starter motor is bad or the battery is discharged.

19   Starter motor - removal and installation

Refer to illustration 19.4

Note: *On some vehicles, it may be necessary to remove the exhaust pipe(s) or frame cross-member to gain access to the starter motor. In extreme cases it may even be necessary to unbolt the mounts and raise the engine slightly to get the starter out.*

1   Detach the cable from the negative terminal of the battery.
2   Raise the vehicle and support it securely on jackstands.
3   Clearly label, then disconnect the wires from the terminals on the starter motor and solenoid.
4   Remove the mounting bolts and detach

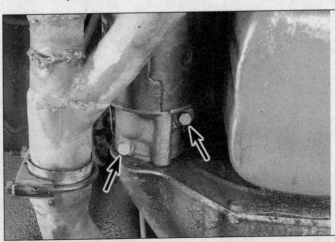

19.4 Two special bolts (arrows) secure the starter - a bracket is also sometimes used at the front

the starter **(see illustration)**. **Note:** *Some models are equipped with a mounting bracket at the rear of the starter that must also be unbolted.*

5   Installation is the reverse of removal. Be sure to replace the exact number of shims that were originally installed between the starter and engine block.

20   Starter solenoid - removal and installation

Refer to illustration 20.5

1   Disconnect the cable from the negative terminal of the battery.
2   Remove the starter motor (see Section 19).
3   Disconnect the strap from the solenoid to the starter motor terminal.
4   Remove the two screws that secure the solenoid to the starter motor.

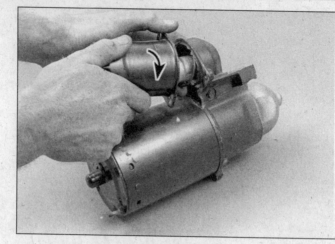

20.5 To remove the solenoid from the starter motor, remove the screws and twist it clockwise

5   Twist the solenoid in a clockwise direction to disengage the flange from the starter body **(see illustration)**. **Note:** *There's a spring between the starter motor and the starter. Keep pressure against the solenoid, then, as the flange is disengaged, slowly release the spring pressure.*
6   Installation is the reverse of removal.

Chapter 6
Emissions control systems

Contents

1 General information

To prevent pollution of the atmosphere from incompletely burned or evaporating gases, and to maintain good driveability and fuel economy, a number of emission control systems are used on these vehicles. Your vehicle is equipped with some (but not all) of the following systems, depending on year and model.

Air Injection Reactor (AIR) system
Exhaust Gas Recirculation (EGR) system
Evaporation Control System (ECS)
Positive Crankcase Ventilation (PCV) system
Inlet air temperature control systems
Catalytic converter
Electronic Spark Timing (EST)
Transmission Controlled Spark (TCS) system
Computer Controlled Catalytic Converter (C4) or Computer Command Control (C3) system

The Sections in this Chapter include general descriptions, checking procedures within the scope of the home mechanic and component replacement procedures (when possible) for each of the systems listed above.

Before assuming that an emissions control system is malfunctioning, check the fuel and ignition systems carefully. The diagnosis of some emission control devices requires specialized tools, equipment and training. If checking and servicing become too difficult or if a procedure is beyond your ability, consult a dealer service department.

This doesn't mean, however, that emission control systems are particularly difficult to maintain and repair. You can quickly and easily perform many checks and do most of the regular maintenance at home with common tune-up and hand tools.

Pay close attention to any special precautions outlined in this Chapter. It should be noted that the illustrations of the various systems may not exactly match the system installed on your vehicle because of changes made by the manufacturer during production or from year to year. Remember - the most frequent cause of emissions problems is simply a loose or broken vacuum hose or wire, so always check the hose and wiring connections first.

On most models, a Vehicle Emissions Control Information (VECI) label is located in the engine compartment. This label contains important emissions specifications and adjustment information, and a vacuum hose routing and emission component location schematic. When servicing the engine or emissions systems, the VECI label in your particular vehicle should always be checked for up-to-date information.

2   Positive Crankcase Ventilation (PCV) system

General description

Refer to illustrations 2.1 and 2.2

1   The Positive Crankcase Ventilation system (or PCV as it is more commonly called), reduces hydrocarbon emissions by circulating fresh air through the crankcase to pick up blow-by gases, which are then re-routed through the carburetor or intake manifold to be reburned by the engine **(see illustration)**.
2   The main components of this simple system are vacuum hoses and a PCV valve which regulates the flow of gases according to engine speed and manifold vacuum **(see illustration)**.

Checking

Refer to illustrations 2.6 and 2.9

3   The PCV system can be checked for proper operation quickly and easily. This system should be checked regularly, as carbon and gunk deposited by the blow-by gases will eventually clog the PCV valve and/or sys-

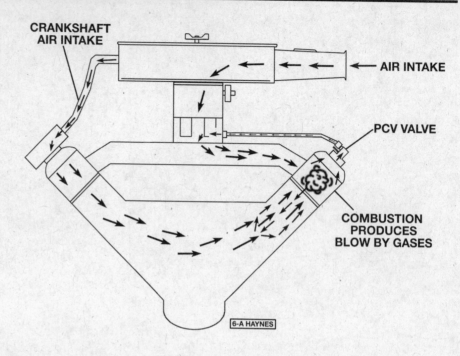

2.1 Operation of a typical Positive Crankcase Ventilation (PCV) system

tem hoses. When the flow of the PCV system is reduced or stopped, common symptoms are rough idling or a reduced engine speed at idle.
4   To check for proper vacuum in the system, remove the top plate of the air cleaner and locate the small PCV filter on the inside of the air cleaner housing.
5   Disconnect the hose leading to this filter. Be careful not to break the molded fitting on the filter.
6   With the engine idling, place your thumb lightly over the end of the hose **(see illustration)**. Leave it there for about 30 seconds.

You should feel a slight pull, or vacuum. The suction may be heard as your thumb is released. This will indicate that air is being drawn all the way through the system. If a vacuum is felt, the system is functioning properly. Check that the filter inside the air cleaner housing is not clogged or dirty. If in doubt, replace the filter with a new one, which is an inexpensive safeguard.
7   If there is very little vacuum, or none at all, at the end of the hose, the system is clogged and must be inspected further.
8   Shut off the engine and locate the PCV valve. Carefully pull it from its rubber grom-

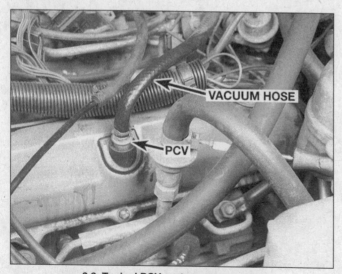

2.2 Typical PCV system components

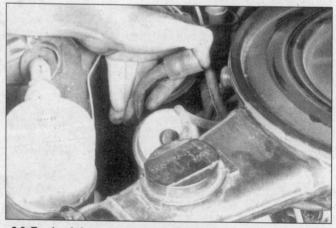

2.6 To check for proper vacuum, remove the top plate of the air cleaner housing, locate the small PCV filter on the inside of the air cleaner housing, detach the hose leading to this filter and, with the engine idling, place your thumb lightly over the end of the hose and leave it there for about 30 seconds - you should feel a slight suction

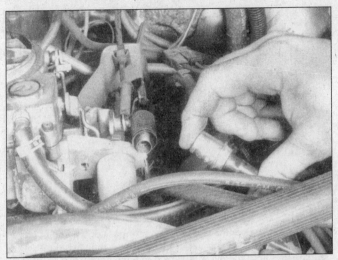

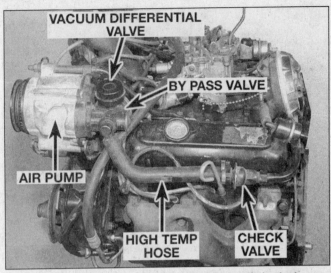

2.9 To check for a clogged PCV valve, remove the valve from the valve cover and, with the engine running, place your finger over the end of the valve and feel for suction - it should be fairly strong

3.1 Typical AIR system (V6 engine shown, V8 similar) - the bypass valve is also called the diverter valve

met. Shake it and listen for a clicking sound. If the valve does not click freely, replace the valve with a new one.

9   Now start the engine and run it at idle speed with the PCV valve removed. Place your thumb over the end of the valve and feel for suction (see illustration). This should be relatively strong vacuum which will be felt immediately.

10   If little or no vacuum is felt at the PCV valve, turn off the engine and disconnect the vacuum hose from the other end of the valve. Run the engine at idle speed and check for vacuum at the end of the hose just disconnected. No vacuum at this point indicates that the vacuum hose or inlet fitting at the engine is plugged or leaking. If it is the hose, replace it with a new one. A clogged passage at the carburetor or manifold requires that the component be removed and thoroughly cleaned of carbon build-up. A strong vacuum felt going into the PCV valve, but little or no vacuum coming out of the valve, indicates a failure of the PCV valve, requiring replacement with a new one.

11   When purchasing a new PCV valve make sure it is the proper one. Each PCV valve is metered for specific engine sizes and model years. An incorrect PCV valve may pull too much or too little vacuum, possibly causing damage to the engine.

12   Information on removing and installing the PCV valve can be found in Chapter 1.

3   Air Injection Reactor (AIR) system

General description

Refer to illustration 3.1

1   The Air Injection Reactor (AIR) system reduces hydrocarbons in the exhaust by pumping additional oxygen into the exhaust port of the cylinder head, exhaust manifold

(see illustration), or the catalytic converter. The oxygen-rich air helps combust the unburned hydrocarbons before they are expelled as exhaust.

2   The AIR system operates at all engine speeds, but it bypasses air for a short time during deceleration and at high speeds, because air added to the over-rich fuel/air mixture present in the exhaust during these conditions can cause backfiring or popping through the exhaust.

3   The AIR system consists of an engine-driven injection pump at the front of the engine, air diverter valve attached to the pump housing, the manifold and injection tubes running into each port at the exhaust manifolds, and a check valve for each hose between the pump and the injection tubes on either side of the engine.

4   Later versions of the AIR system are controlled by the computer (ECM):

a) When the engine is cold, the ECM energizes an AIR control solenoid. This allows air to flow to an AIR switching valve. The AIR switching valve is energized to direct air to the exhaust ports.

b) On a warm engine, or in "closed loop" mode, the ECM de-energizes the AIR switching valve, directing air between the beds of the catalytic converter. This provides extra oxygen for the oxidizing catalyst to decrease HC and CO levels, while keeping oxygen levels low in the first bed of the converter. This enables the reducing catalyst to effectively decrease the levels nitrogen oxides (NOX).

c) If the AIR control valve detects a rapid increase in manifold vacuum (deceleration) certain operating modes (wide open throttle, for example), or the ECM self-diagnostic system detects a problem in the CCC system, air is diverted (divert mode) to the air cleaner or directly to the atmosphere.

d) The divert mode prevents backfiring through the exhaust system. Throttle closure at deceleration creates a fuel-air mixture which is temporarily too rich to burn completely. This mixture, when it reaches the exhaust, becomes burnable when combined with injected air. The next spark would ignite this mixture, causing an exhaust backfire, but momentary diverting of injected air prevents it.

e) The air flow and control hoses transmit pressurized air to the catalytic converter or to the exhaust ports via internal passages in the intake manifold, or through external firing.

f) The check valve prevents backflow of exhaust gas into the AIR distribution system. The valve prevents backflow when the air pump bypasses at high speeds and loads, or when the air pump malfunctions.

Checking

Refer to illustrations 3.6, 3.7 and 3.8

Note: *The following checks generally apply to all AIR systems. However, where ECM-controlled systems differ in design from older types, diagnosis is beyond the scope of the home mechanic.*

5   Properly installed and adjusted air injection systems are fairly reliable and seldom cause problems. However, a malfunctioning system can cause engine surge, backfiring and over-heated spark plugs. The air pump is the most critical component of this system and the belt at the front of the engine which drives the pump should be your first check. If the belt is cracked or frayed, replace it with a new one. Check the tension of the drivebelt by pressing it with your finger. There should be about 1/2-inch of play in the belt when pushed halfway between the pulleys. If the belt is too loose, adjust it (see Chapter 1).

6   To check for proper air delivery from the

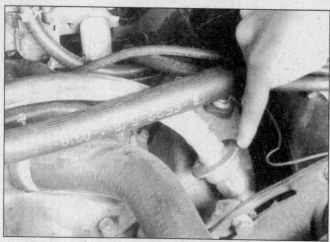

3.6 To check for proper air delivery from the pump, follow the hoses from the pump to where they meet the injection tube/manifold assembly on each side of the engine, loosen the clamps, disconnect the hoses . . .

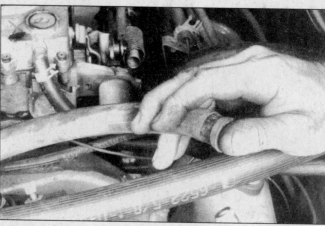

3.7 . . . start the engine and, with your fingers or a piece of paper, verify that air is flowing out of these hoses, then accelerate the engine and note the air flow, which should increase in relation to engine speed - if it does, the pump is working satisfactorily; if it doesn't, check for crimps in the hoses, a loose drivebelt or a leaky diverter valve

pump, follow the hoses from the pump to where they meet the injection tube/manifold assembly on each side of the engine **(see illustration)**. Loosen the clamps and disconnect the hoses.

7   Start the engine and, with your fingers or a piece of paper, verify that air is flowing out of these hoses **(see illustration)**. Accelerate the engine and observe the air flow, which should increase in relation to engine speed. If this is the case, the pump is working satisfactorily. If air flow was not present, or did not increase, check for crimps in the hoses, proper drivebelt tension and for a leaking diverter valve, which can be heard with the pump operating.

8   To check the diverter valve, sometimes called the "gulp" valve or anti-backfire valve, make sure all hoses are connected and start the engine. Locate the muffler on the valve, which is a canister unit with holes in it **(see illustration)**.

9   Being careful not to touch any of the moving engine components, place your hand near the muffler outlet holes and check that no air is escaping with the engine at idle speed. Now have an assistant depress the accelerator pedal to accelerate the engine and then quickly let off the pedal. A momentary blast of air should be felt discharging through the diverter valve muffler. **Warning:** *Stay away from rotating engine components during this test!*

10   If no air discharge was felt, disconnect the smaller vacuum hose at the diverter valve. Place your finger over the end of the hose and again have your assistant depress the accelerator and let it off. As the engine is decelerating, a vacuum should be felt. If vacuum was felt, replace the diverter valve with a new one. If no vacuum was felt, the vacuum hose or engine vacuum source is plugged, requiring a thorough cleaning to eliminate the problem.

11   Two check valves are located on the air manifold assembly. Their function is to pre-

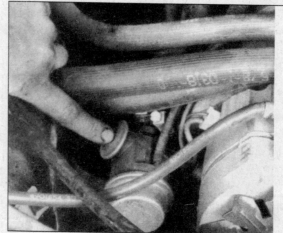

3.8 To check the diverter valve, make sure all hoses are connected, start the engine, locate the muffler (the small perforated canister) on the valve, place your hand near the muffler outlet holes and verify that no air is escaping while the engine is idling, then accelerate the engine and quickly let off the pedal - a momentary blast of air should be felt discharging through the diverter valve muffler

vent exhaust gases from flowing back into the air pump. To find out if they are functioning properly, disconnect the two air supply hoses where they attach to the check valves. Start the engine and, being careful not to touch any moving engine components, place a piece of paper over the outlet of the check valve. No exhaust should flow out of the check valve. The valve can be further checked by turning off the engine, allowing it to cool, and blowing through the check valve (toward the air manifold). Then attempt to suck back through it. If the valve is allowing you to suck back towards the air pump, it is faulty and should be replaced.

12   Another check for this system is for leaks in the hose connection and/or hoses themselves. Leaks can often be detected by sound or feel with the pump in operation. If a leak is suspected, use a soapy water solution to verify this. Pour or sponge the solution of detergent and water on the hoses and connections. With the pump running, bubbles will form if a leak exists. The air delivery hoses are of a special design to withstand engine temperatures, so if they are replaced make sure the new hoses are of the proper standards.

Component replacement
Air pump

13   As mentioned earlier, some air pumps share a common drivebelt with the alternator while others use their own belt. The particular layout on the vehicle being serviced will affect the removal and installation procedure somewhat.

14   With the engine off, disconnect the air delivery hoses at the air pump. Note the position of each hose for assembly.

15   Disconnect the vacuum source hose at the diverter valve.

16   Compress the drivebelt to keep the air pump pulley from turning, and remove the bolts and washers securing the pulley to the pump.

17   To get some slack in the belt, loosen the air pump or alternator adjusting bolt and the pivot bolt (see the drivebelt replacement procedure in Chapter 1, if necessary). Push the component toward the engine until the belt and air pump pulley can be removed from the pump.

18   Remove the bolts which secure the air pump to its brackets and then lift the pump

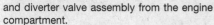
3.36 Use a flare-nut wrench to loosen the injector tube nuts

3.38 External extension tubes must be pressed out after the exhaust manifold is removed from the engine

3.44 To remove the check valve from the air manifold assembly, use two wrenches (one as a backup) on the threaded fittings - be sure that you don't bend or twist the delicate manifold or injection tubes while loosening the check valve

and diverter valve assembly from the engine compartment.

19   If the diverter valve is to be installed on the new air pump, remove the bolts securing it to the pump and separate the two components.

20   Check the pump for evidence that exhaust gas has entered it, indicating a failure of one or both check valves.

21   Install the diverter valve to the new air pump using a new gasket. Tighten the attaching bolts securely.

22   Install the air pump to its engine mounting brackets with the attaching bolts loose. The exception to this is on models where the mounting bolts are inaccessible with the pulley installed. In this case, the pump mounting bolts should be tightened securely at this point.

23   Install the pump pulley with the bolts, only hand tight at this time.

24   Place the drivebelt into position on the air pump pulley and adjust the belt as described in Chapter 1.

25   Keep the pump pulley from turning by compressing the drive belt and tighten the pulley bolts securely.

26   Connect the hoses to the air pump and diverter valve. Make sure the connections are tight.

27   Tighten the mounting bolts for the pump securely.

28   Check the operation of the air pump as outlined previously.

Diverter valve

29   Disconnect the vacuum signal line and air delivery hoses at the diverter valve. Note the position of each for assembly.

30   Remove the bolts which secure the valve to the air pump and remove the diverter valve from the engine compartment.

31   When purchasing a new diverter or bypass valve, keep in mind that, although many of the valves are similar in appearance, each is designed to meet particular requirements of various engines. Therefore, be sure to install the correct valve.

32   Install the new diverter valve to the air pump or pump extension with a new gasket. Tighten the securing bolts.

33   Connect the air delivery and vacuum source hoses and check the operation of the valve as outlined previously.

Air manifold and injection tubes

Refer to illustrations 3.36 and 3.38

34   Due to the high temperatures at this area, the connections at the exhaust manifold may be difficult to loosen. Penetrating oil applied to the thread of the injection tubes may help in the removal procedure.

35   With the engine off and completely cold, disconnect the air delivery hoses at the mani-

fold check valves.

36   Loosen the threaded connectors on the exhaust manifold at each exhaust port **(see illustration)**. Slide the connectors up on the injection tubes so the threads are out of the exhaust manifold.

37   Pull the injection tube/air manifold assembly from the engine exhaust manifold and out of the engine compartment. Depending on the model year, injection tube extensions leading inside the engine may come out with the assembly.

38   On models where the extension tubes remain inside the exhaust manifold, they must be pressed out after the exhaust manifold is removed from the engine **(see illustration)**.

39   If the exhaust manifold was removed from the engine to clean or replace the extensions, reinstall the manifold with extensions to the engine, using a new gasket. Torque to the proper specifications (see Chapter 2).

40   Thread each of the injection tube connectors loosely into the exhaust manifold, using an anti-seize compound on the threads. After each of the connectors is sufficiently started, tighten each securely.

41   Connect the air supply hoses to the check valves.

42   Start the engine and check for leaks as previously described.

Check valve

Refer to illustration 3.44

43   Disconnect the air supply hose at the check valve.

44   Using two wrenches on the flats provided, remove the check valve from the air manifold assembly **(see illustration)**. Be careful not to bend or twist the delicate manifold or injection tubes as this is done.

45   Installation is a reverse of the removal procedure.

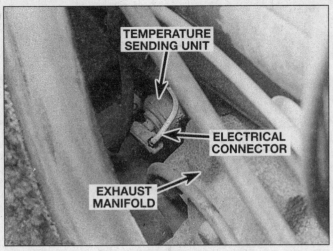

4.7 TCS system - typical coolant temperature switch location in the left cylinder head

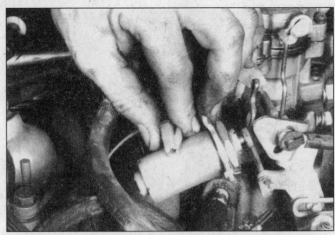

4.17 The idle stop solenoid, which is attached to the right side of the carburetor, can be identified by this wiring connector at one end and the bolt-head plunger at the other

4   Transmission Controlled Spark (TCS) system

General description

1   This system is designed to eliminate the vacuum advance at the distributor under certain driving conditions. The system is incorporated on many models built during the 1970's. The Transmission Controlled Spark (TCS) system used for 1971 models is also known as the Combination Emission Control (CEC) system.

2   Vacuum for the advancing mechanism in the distributor is shut off until the transmission is in High gear or 3rd and 4th gears with the 4-speed transmission. Vacuum is allowed in Reverse for automatic transmissions.

3   This system is made up of: a transmission switch; engine coolant temperature switch; time delay relay; vacuum advance solenoid; and an idle stop solenoid. Although this system is somewhat more difficult to service, check and maintain than the other emissions systems, when each component is examined individually, the operation of the TCS system can be easily understood.

Transmission switch

4   On manual transmissions, the electrical switch is actuated by the internal shifter shaft. The switch is located on the left side of the transmission case, just below the 3rd/4th shifting arm.

5   Automatic transmissions use a pressure-sensitive switch which is actuated by the fluid pressure as the transmission reaches High gear and Reverse. This switch is located on the outside of the transmission on Turbo Hydra-Matic 350 transmissions. Turbo Hydra-Matic 400 transmissions have the switch mounted internally in the transmission.

6   When activated in the proper transmission gears, the switch sends an electrical input to the vacuum advance solenoid. This TCS component remained basically unchanged through the time it was used.

Temperature switch

Refer to illustration 4.7

7   The function of this switch is to sense the engine temperature and send a signal to the vacuum advance solenoid. It is the same switch which operates the dashboard-mounted warning light or water temperature gauge. The switch **(see illustration)** is located in the left cylinder head, between the number one and number three exhaust ports on small-block V8 engines.

8   The temperature switch monitors engine coolant temperatures and sends electrical current to the vacuum advance solenoid. On 1969 through 1972 models, the temperature switch reacts with the vacuum advance solenoid to allow full vacuum advance whenever the engine temperature is below 82-degrees. For 1973 and 1974, this temperature was raised to 93-degrees. This means that, regardless of the transmission gear or any other engine condition, the TCS system is not functional and should have no effect on engine operation until the engine has warmed up to these operating temperatures.

Time delay relay

9   This electrically-operated relay has undergone some changes in the various TCS systems. In each model year, however, its main function is to delay the operation of the vacuum advance solenoid.

10   In all years except 1972, the time delay relay will allow full distributor vacuum advance during the first 20 seconds of engine operation. This means that every time the ignition switch is turned on, no matter if the engine is warm or cold, the delay relay will render the TCS system inoperative for the first 20 seconds.

11   On 1972 models the delay relay performs a different function. The relay does not come into play until the transmission reaches High gear as signaled by the transmission switch. When this happens, the time relay delays the operation of the vacuum advance solenoid for about 20 seconds. In other

words, the engine distributor does not receive full vacuum until about 20 seconds after the transmission reaches High gear.

12   It should also be noted that the 1972 delay relay automatically recycles whenever the transmission is taken out of High gear, as in a downshift or when put into passing gear. Once the transmission is back into High, it will again take about 20 seconds to achieve full vacuum advance at the distributor.

13   The 1972 relay is located under the dashboard. For the other years, the relay is mounted inside the engine compartment.

Vacuum advance solenoid

14   This is the heart of the TCS system, with its function being to supply or deny vacuum to the distributor.

15   This canister-shaped unit is located on the right side of the engine, attached to the intake manifold. It can be readily located by simply following the vacuum hose out of the distributor vacuum advance unit.

16   In the energized position, the plunger inside the solenoid opens the vacuum port from the carburetor/throttle body to the vacuum advance unit, and at the same time blocks off the clean air port at the other end. In the de-energized mode, the clean air port is uncovered, which allows the distributor to vent to the atmosphere and shuts off vacuum to the distributor.

Idle stop solenoid

Refer to illustrations 4.17 and 4.18

17   This solenoid is attached to the right side of the carburetor with brackets. It can be identified by a wiring connector at one end and a bolt-head plunger on the other **(see illustration)**.

18   The idle stop solenoid is an electrically operated, two-position control. It is used to provide a predetermined throttle setting **(see illustration)**.

19   In the energized position, the plunger extends from the solenoid body and contacts the carburetor throttle lever. This prevents the carburetor throttle plates from closing

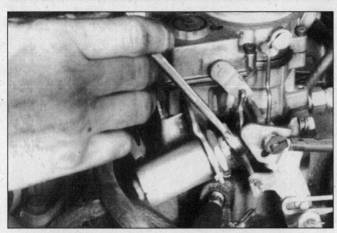

4.18 The idle stop solenoid is an electrically operated two-position control device that can be used to provide a predetermined throttle setting

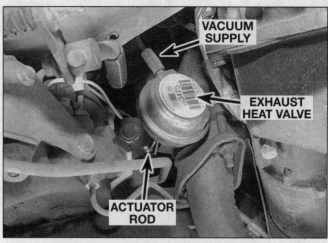

5.2a Typical lower EFE system components

fully. When de-energized (key off), the solenoid plunger retracts into the solenoid body to allow the throttle plates to fully close, which 'starves' the engine and prevents run-on, or "dieseling".

20 The 1971 system also incorporates a solid state timing device which allows the air conditioning compressor (if equipped) to come on when the ignition is turned off. The added load of the air conditioning compressor helps to shut off the engine to further prevent dieseling.

Checking

21 This system is difficult to check due to the fact that the vehicle must be in full operation. This means that the checks must be made with the car traveling at speed.

22 If a problem in this system is suspected, first check that all electrical wires and connections are in good condition and intact. Also inspect the vacuum hoses at the vacuum advance solenoid and the distributor vacuum advance unit. A blown fuse in the fuse box can also cause problems in this system.

23 To ascertain if the TCS system is in fact malfunctioning, connect a vacuum gauge in the hose between the solenoid and the distributor. A length of vacuum hose must be used to enable you to route the gauge inside the passenger's compartment. Make sure the hose is not crimped and will not be damaged by moving or hot engine parts.

24 Drive the car and have an assistant watch the vacuum gauge. Make a log of vacuum gauge readings and transmission gears. If the system is functioning properly, the following conditions will be met:

a) *When the engine is cold, vacuum will show on the gauge until the engine has warmed to operating temperature.*

b) *Vacuum should be present on the gauge during the first 20 seconds after the engine is started, regardless of temperature.*

c) *At normal operating temperature there should be vacuum showing on the gauge in High gear only.*

25 The system should be tested with the engine cold, and also after it has reached normal operating temperature. Don't forget about the time delay function and how it relates to your particular vehicle.

26 The above test will tell you if the system as a whole is functioning properly. The following are test procedures for the individual TCS components if a fault is detected in the driving test.

Idle stop solenoid

27 Have an assistant turn the ignition switch on as you watch the idle stop solenoid plunger. With the key on, the plunger should extend against the throttle linkage. With the key off, the plunger should retract into the solenoid.

Transmission switch

28 With the engine warm and running, have an assistant put the transmission in a low forward gear (make sure the front wheels are blocked, parking brake is on and the assistant has the brake pedal depressed). There should be no vacuum going to the distributor. If there is vacuum going to the distributor, remove the transmission switch connection. Replace the transmission switch if the vacuum stops when the transmission switch connection was removed.

Temperature switch

29 When the engine is cold, there should be vacuum going to the distributor. If this is not the case, ground the wire from the cold terminal of the temperature switch. If the vacuum advance solenoid energizes, replace the temperature switch with a new one.

30 A failure of the temperature switch may also show up on the driving test with the engine at different operating temperatures, and/or as a malfunction of the temperature gauge or dash warning light.

Vacuum advance solenoid

31 Check the vacuum running into the solenoid from the intake manifold or carburetor. You should be able to feel this vacuum

with the engine running.

32 Now reconnect the vacuum inlet hose and disconnect the vacuum hose leading to the distributor. Disconnect the electrical connectors at the solenoid and run a 12-volt jumper wire to the solenoid. The solenoid should be energized, allowing vacuum to reach the distributor.

Time delay relay (1972)

33 With the ignition on, check for 12 volts at the tan colored lead to the relay. Use a test light for this.

34 Install a 12-volt jumper wire to the terminal with the tan lead, and ground the terminal with the black lead. If, after 26 seconds, the advance solenoid does not energize (meaning vacuum to the distributor), replace the delay relay.

Time delay relay (except 1972)

35 Remove the temperature switch connector at the time delay relay.

36 Check to make sure the relay is cool, then turn the ignition to the On position.

37 The vacuum advance solenoid should energize for about 20 seconds and then de-energize. If it does not de-energize, remove the blue lead from the time relay. If this causes the solenoid to de-energize, the relay is faulty and should be replaced.

5 Inlet air temperature control systems

General description

Refer to illustrations 5.2a, 5.2b, and 5.5

1 Various versions of this system go by different names, but their purpose is always the same - to improve engine efficiency and reduce hydrocarbon emissions during the initial warm-up period of the vehicle.

2 Two basic systems are used to achieve this goal:

a) *Forced air pre-heat or EFE system: Some form of exhaust heat valve is*

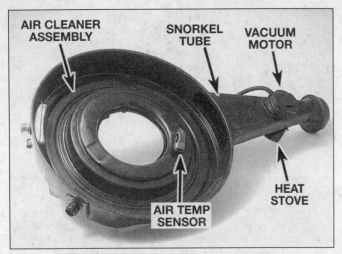

5.2b A typical Thermostatic Air Cleaner (THERMAC) system - this design draws warm air from the exhaust manifold directly into the carburetor

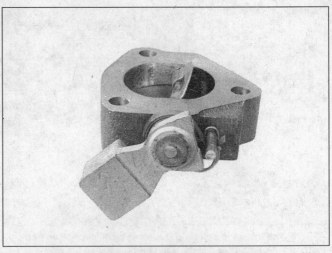

5.5 A typical manifold heat control valve (or heat riser, as it's known on 1970 through 1974 models)

incorporated inside the exhaust pipe **(see illustration)** *to recirculate warm exhaust gases which are then used to pre-heat the carburetor and choke.*

b) *Thermostatic Air Cleaner (THERMAC or TAC): Warm air from the exhaust manifold is routed into the air cleaner, then through the carburetor* **(see illustration)**.

3   This system has its greatest effect on engine performance and emissions output during the first few miles of driving (depending on the outside temperature). Once the engine reaches its normal operating temperature, the flapper valves in the exhaust pipe and air cleaner open, allowing for normal engine operation.

4   Because of this cold-engine-only function, it is important to periodically check this system to prevent poor cold engine performance and overheating of the fuel mixture once the engine has reached operating temperatures. If either the exhaust heat valve or air cleaner valve sticks in the 'no heat' position, the engine will run poorly, stall and waste gas until it has warmed up on its own. A valve sticking in the 'heat' position causes the engine to run as if it is out of tune, because of the constant flow of hot air to the carburetor.

5   The main component of the forced air pre-heat or EFE system is a heat valve **(see illustration)** inside the exhaust pipe on the right side of the engine (called a heat riser on 1969 through 1974 models). In 1975, General Motors introduced a new inlet air temperature control system known as the Early Fuel Evaporation (EFE) system. It also has a valve in the exhaust pipe, but uses manifold vacuum to actuate the valve. Instead of a spring and weight, an actuator and Thermal Vacuum Switch (TVS) control the heat valve. A Thermostatic Air Cleaner (TAC or THERMAC) consisting of a temperature sensor, vacuum diaphragm and heat stove comprise the second system. Initial checking procedures for this system can be found in Chapter 1.

5.10 This vacuum servo (arrow) controls EFE system operation

Checking

Forced air pre-heat system

6   The conventional heat riser, installed on cars built through 1974, should be checked often for free operation. Because of the high exhaust temperatures and its location, which is open to the elements, corrosion frequently keeps the valve from operating freely, or even freezes it in position.

7   To check the heat riser operation, locate it on the exhaust manifold (it can be identified by an external weight and spring), and, with the engine cold, try moving the counterweight. The valve should move freely with no binding. Now have an assistant start the engine (still cold) while the counterweight is observed. The valve should move to the closed position and then slowly open as the engine warms.

8   A stuck or binding heat riser valve can usually be loosened by soaking the valve shaft with solvent as the counterweight is moved back and forth. Light taps with a hammer may be necessary to free a tightly stuck valve. If this proves unsuccessful, the heat riser must be replaced with a new one after disconnecting it from the exhaust pipe.

Early Fuel Evaporation (EFE) system

Refer to illustrations 5.10 and 5.11

9   In 1975, General Motors introduced a replacement for the heat riser known as the Early Fuel Evaporation (EFE) system. The EFE system performs the same function as the heat riser but uses manifold vacuum to open and close the heat valve. Some models may be equipped with an electrical type EFE, which uses a ceramic heater grid located underneath the primary base of the carburetor.

10   To check the EFE system, locate the actuator and rod assembly **(see illustration)** which is located on a bracket attached to the right exhaust manifold. Have an assistant start the engine (it must be cold). Observe the movement of the actuator rod which leads to the heat valve inside the exhaust pipe. It should immediately operate the valve to the closed position. If it does, the system is operating correctly.

11   If the actuator rod doesn't move, disconnect the vacuum hose at the actuator and place your thumb over the open end **(see illustration)**. With the engine cold and at idle,

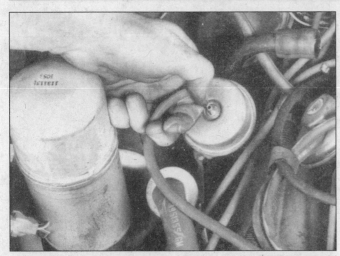

5.11 If the actuator rod is not working properly, you can check the EFE system by disconnecting the vacuum hose at the actuator and placing your thumb over the open end - with the engine cold and at idle, you should feel a suction indicating proper vacuum - if you do, replace the actuator

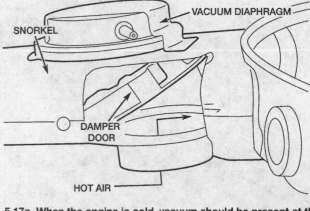

5.17a When the engine is cold, vacuum should be present at the diaphragm, closing the damper door to block all but heater air to the carburetor

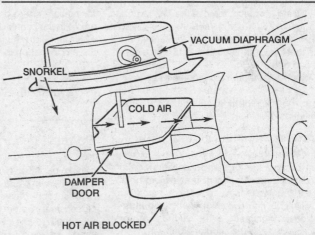

5.17b Once the engine has warmed up, vacuum should be shut off to the diaphragm, allowing only cold air to the carburetor

you should feel a suction, indicating proper vacuum. If there is vacuum at this point, replace the actuator with a new one.

12   If there is no vacuum in the line, this is an indication that either the hose is crimped, plugged or damaged; or the thermal vacuum switch threaded into the water outlet is not functioning properly. Replace the hose or switch as necessary.

13   To make sure the Early Fuel Evaporation system is disengaging once the engine has warmed, continue to observe the actuating rod as the engine reaches normal operating temperature (approximately 180-degrees, depending on engine size). The rod should again move, indicating the valve is in the open position.

14   If, after the engine has warmed, the valve does not open, disconnect the vacuum hose at the actuator and check for vacuum with your thumb. If there is no vacuum, replace the actuator. If there is vacuum, replace the TVS switch on the water outlet housing.

Thermostatic Air Cleaner (TAC/THERMAC)

Refer to illustrations 5.17a and 5.17b

15   THERMAC components can be quickly and easily checked for proper operation, (see Chapter 1 for routine checking procedures and illustrations).

16   With the engine off, observe the damper door inside the air cleaner snorkel (some models with two snorkels may have two damper doors, one in each snorkel). If this is difficult because of the direction in which the snorkel is pointing, use a small mirror. The valve should be open (all air flows through the snorkel and none through the exhaust manifold hot-air duct at the underside of the air cleaner housing).

17   Have an assistant start the engine while you observe the flapper door inside the

snorkel. With the engine cold and at idle, the damper door should close off all air from the snorkel, allowing heated air from the exhaust manifold to enter the air cleaner intake. As the engine warms to operating temperature, the damper door should move, allowing outside air through the snorkel to be included in the mixture **(see illustrations)**. Eventually, the door should recede to the point where most of the incoming air is through the snorkel and not the exhaust manifold passage.

18   If the damper door does not close off the snorkel to outside air when the cold engine is first started, disconnect the vacuum hose at the snorkel vacuum motor, place your thumb over the hose end and check for vacuum. If there is vacuum to the motor, verify that the damper door and link are not frozen or binding within the air cleaner snorkel. Hook up a hand vacuum pump to the fitting on the vacuum motor, in place of the hose, and apply vacuum. If the motor does not hold vacuum, replace the motor.

19   If there is no vacuum to the motor in the above test, check the hoses for cracks, crimps or disconnections and verify there is vacuum to the temperature sensor inside the

air cleaner housing. If the hoses are clear and in good condition, replace the temperature sensor.

Component replacement

Actuator and rod assembly

20   Disconnect the vacuum hose from the actuator.

21   Remove the two nuts which attach the actuator to the bracket.

22   Disconnect the rod from the heat valve and remove the actuator and rod from the engine compartment.

23   Installation is the reverse of removal.

Exhaust heat valve

24   Disconnect the exhaust pipe from the manifold.

25   Disconnect the actuating rod from the heat valve (if equipped).

26   Remove the valve from the exhaust manifold.

27   Installation is the reverse of removal.

Thermal vacuum switch (TVS)

28   Drain the engine coolant until the fluid level is below the engine water outlet (thermostat) housing.

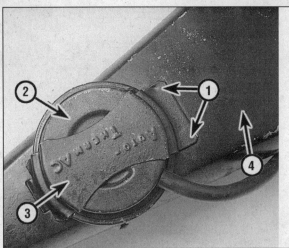

5.35 To replace the air cleaner vacuum motor, drill out the two spot welds which secure the motor retaining strap, remove the attaching strap, lift up the motor, then cock it to one side to unhook the linkage at the control damper assembly

1 *Spot welds*
2 *Vacuum diaphragm motor*
3 *Retaining strap*
4 *Snorkel*

5.44 The sensor retainer must be pried off with a screwdriver

29 Disconnect the hoses from the TVS switch. Note their positions for reassembly.
30 Using a wrench, remove the TVS switch.
31 Apply a soft-setting sealant uniformly to the threads of the new TVS switch. Make sure that none of the sealant gets on the sensor end of the switch.
32 Install the switch and tighten it securely.
33 Connect the vacuum hoses to the switch in their original positions and add coolant as necessary.

Air cleaner vacuum motor

Refer to illustration 5.35

34 Remove the air cleaner assembly from the engine and disconnect the vacuum hose from the motor.
35 Drill out the two spot welds **(see illustration)** which secure the vacuum motor retaining strap to the snorkel tube.
36 Remove the motor attaching strap.
37 Lift up the motor, cocking it to one side to unhook the motor linkage at the control damper assembly.
38 To install, drill a 7/64-inch hole in the snorkel tube at the center of the retaining strap.
39 Insert the vacuum motor linkage into the control damper assembly.
40 Using the sheet metal screw supplied with the motor service kit, attach the motor and retaining strap to the snorkel. Make sure the sheet metal screw does not interfere with the operation of the damper door.
41 Connect the vacuum hose to the motor and install the air cleaner assembly.

Air cleaner temperature sensor

Refer to illustration 5.44

42 Remove the air cleaner from the engine and disconnect the vacuum hoses at the sensor.
43 Carefully note the position of the sensor. The new sensor must be installed in exactly the same position.
44 Pry up the tabs on the sensor retaining clip and remove the sensor and clip from the air cleaner **(see illustration)**.
45 Install the new sensor with a new gasket in the same position as the old one.
46 Press the retaining clip on the sensor, taking care not to damage the control mechanism in the center of the sensor.
47 Connect the vacuum hoses and install the air cleaner on the engine.

6 Evaporative Control System (ECS)

General description

1 The Evaporative Control System is one of the most trouble-free systems in the emissions network. Its function is to reduce hydrocarbon emissions. Basically, this is a closed fuel system which reroutes wasted fuel back to the gas tank and stores fuel vapors instead of venting them to the atmosphere.
2 Because it has few moving parts, the ECS system requires no periodic maintenance other than replacement of the filter in the bottom the charcoal canister at the recommended intervals.
3 The strong smell of fuel vapors is a tip-off that the system is not operating properly.
4 A pressure/vacuum gasoline filler cap must be used on vehicles equipped with ECS. A standard cap can render the system ineffective and possibly even collapse the fuel tank. The ECS system consists of a special gas tank with fill limiters and vent connections, a charcoal canister with an integral purge valve and a filter which stores vapor from the fuel tank to be burned by the carburetor/throttle body, a carburetor bowl vent valve and the system of hoses connecting these components.
5 Earlier versions of the purge valve are regulated by coolant temperature: at coolant temperatures below the switching point, canister purge is controlled by an internal orifice in the switch. At coolant temperatures above the switching point, the switch opens, allowing canister purge to be controlled by manifold vacuum from the carburetor port.
6 With the engine cold and at room tem-

perature, disconnect the fuel tank line at the charcoal canister (on all models, the canister is located inside the engine compartment). Each of the hose connections should be labeled. Make sure you label them yourself if they're not already marked, to prevent improper assembly.
7 As this hose is disconnected, check for the presence of liquid fuel in the line. Fuel in this vapor hose is an indication that the vent controls or pressure-vacuum relief valve in the gas cap are not functioning properly.
8 Hook up a pressure suction device on the end of the fuel vapor line. Apply 15 psi pressure to the line and check for excessive loss of pressure.
9 Check for a fuel vapor smell in the engine compartment and around the gas tank.
10 Remove the fuel filler cap and check for pressure in the gas tank.
11 If there is a large loss of pressure or a fuel odor, inspect all lines for leaks or deterioration.
12 With the fuel filler cap removed, apply pressure again and check for obstructions in the vent line.
13 To check the purge valve built into the canister, start the engine, allow it to reach normal operating temperature and disconnect the vacuum signal line running from the engine to the canister. With your thumb over the end of the hose, raise the engine speed to about 1500 rpm and check for vacuum. If there is no vacuum signal, check the EGR operation as described in this Chapter. The vacuum signal for the canister and the EGR valve originate from the same source.
14 The purge line to the charcoal canister functions with the PCV vacuum source, so if there is no vacuum when this hose is disconnected from the canister, check the PCV valve vacuum.

Servicing

15 Chapter 1 contains all information concerning the servicing of the Evaporative Control System.

7.2 You can't see much of the EGR exhaust passages because they are cast into the intake manifold (arrows). Carbon deposits in the passages should be cleaned out when possible

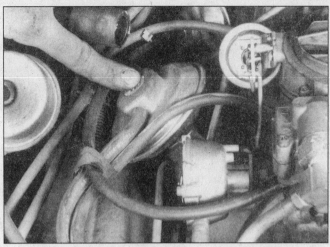

7.6 On most models, the EGR valve is located on the intake manifold, adjacent to the carburetor

7 Exhaust Gas Recirculation (EGR) system

General description

Refer to illustration 7.2

1   The EGR system is used to reduce nitrogen oxides (NOx) from the exhaust. Formation of these pollutants takes place at very high temperatures; consequently, it occurs during the peak temperature period of the combustion process. To reduce peak temperatures, and thus the formation of NOx, a small amount of exhaust gas is taken from the exhaust system and recirculated in the combustion cycle.

2   To tap this exhaust supply without an extensive array of pipes and connections in the exhaust system, additional exhaust passages are cast into the intricate runner system of the intake manifold **(see illustration)**. Because of this arrangement, most of the EGR routing components are hidden from view under the manifold.

3   Two basic types of EGR valves are used - Vacuum Modulated EGR and Exhaust Back Pressure EGR. When Vacuum Modulated EGR is used, the amount of exhaust gas admitted to the intake manifold depends on a vacuum signal (ported vacuum) which is controlled by throttle position. When the throttle is closed (idle or deceleration), there is no vacuum signal to the EGR valve because the vacuum port is above the closed throttle valve. As the throttle valve is opened, a ported vacuum signal is supplied to the EGR valve, admitting exhaust gas to the intake manifold. The Exhaust Backpressure Modulated EGR uses a transducer located inside the EGR valve to control the operating vacuum signal. The vacuum signal is generated in the same manner as for the Vacuum Modulated EGR system. The integral transducer uses exhaust gas pressure to control an air bleed within the valve to modify the vacuum signal from the carburetor or fuel injection

system. The EGR valve is known as a positive transducer type. The latest versions of the EGR valve are ECM-controlled. EGR flow is regulated by an ECM-controlled solenoid in the vacuum line. The ECM uses data from various combinations of sensors - such as the coolant temperature sensor, throttle position sensor, MAP sensor and distributor signal - to regulate the solenoid.

4   The EGR system does not recirculate gases when the engine is idling or decelerating. The system is also regulated by the thermal vacuum switch, which does not allow the system to operate until the engine has reached normal operating temperature.

5   Common engine problems associated with the EGR system are rough idling or stalling when at idle or low speeds. This is usually a result of the EGR valve being stuck in the open position.

Checking

Refer to illustrations 7.6 and 7.13

6   Locate the EGR valve. The location varies from year to year, but on most models it is located on the intake manifold, adjacent to the right side of the carburetor/throttle body **(see illustration)**. Initial checking, with illustrations, can be found in Chapter 1.

7   Place your finger under the EGR valve and push up on the diaphragm plate. The diaphragm should move freely from the open to the closed position. If it doesn't, replace the EGR valve.

8   Now start the engine and run it at idle speed. With your finger, manually depress the EGR diaphragm. If the valve or adjacent accessories are hot, wear gloves to prevent burning your fingers. When the diaphragm is pressed (valve closed to recirculate exhaust), the engine should lose speed, stumble or even stall. If the engine does not change speed, the EGR passages should be checked for blockage. This will require that the intake manifold be removed (see Chapter 2). Any further checking of the positive backpressure type EGR valve will require special tools, so a ques-

tionable valve is best replaced with a new one at this point. Negative backpressure type EGR valves can be further tested as follows:

9   Allow the engine to reach its normal operating temperature. Have an assistant depress the accelerator slightly and hold the engine at a constant speed above idle.

10   Detach the vacuum signal line at the EGR valve and verify that the diaphragm plate moves downward and engine speed increases.

11   Reattach the vacuum line to the valve. The diaphragm plate should move upward with a decrease in engine speed.

12   If the diaphragm doesn't move, make sure the engine is at its normal operating temperature. Repeat the test if in doubt.

13   To verify that vacuum is reaching the EGR valve, detach the vacuum hose at the

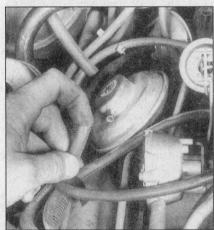

7.13 If a check of the EGR valve reveals that it's not working, verify that vacuum is reaching the EGR valve: detach the vacuum hose from the valve and, with the engine running slightly above idle, place your thumb over the end of the hose - if there is vacuum, replace the EGR valve; if there isn't, trace the vacuum hose to its source and look for cracks, breaks or blockage

valve and, with the engine running and the accelerator slightly pressed, verify that there's vacuum at the end of the hose with your thumb (see illustration). If there is vacuum, replace the EGR valve with a new one. If there is no vacuum signal, follow the vacuum hose to its source, inspecting for disconnections, cracks, breaks or blockage in the lines.

14 On all model years except 1973, the EGR system uses some kind of vacuum valve to regulate the amount of exhaust gas admitted to the intake air/fuel mixture. Some of the more common valves are the Vacuum Controlled Valve (VCV), which regulates the EGR in accordance with engine intake vacuum; the Thermal Vacuum Switch (TVS) which regulates EGR valve operation in relation to engine temperature; and the electronically operated, ECM-controlled solenoid, which also acts in accordance with engine coolant temperature. 1973 models have the vacuum source routed directly to the carburetor.

15 The TVS opens as the coolant temperature increases, allowing vacuum to reach the EGR valve. The exact temperature varies from year to year, but is indicative of the normal operating temperature of the particular engine.

16 To test a vacuum-actuated switch, check the vacuum signal with a vacuum gauge (if the switch on your vehicle is a solenoid under ECM control, diagnosis should be left to a dealer).

17 Disconnect the vacuum hose at the EGR valve, connect the vacuum gauge to the disconnected end of the hose and start the engine, then have an assistant depress the accelerator slightly and note this reading. As the accelerator is depressed, the vacuum reading should increase.

18 If the gauge does not respond to the throttle opening, disconnect the hose that leads from the carburetor/throttle body to the vacuum switch. Repeat the test with the vacuum gauge attached to the vacuum hose end of the switch. If the vacuum gauge responds to accelerator opening, the vacuum switch is defective and should be replaced with a new one.

19 If the gauge still does not respond to an increase in throttle opening, check for a plugged hose or a problem with the carburetor or fuel injection system.

Component replacement

EGR valve

20 Disconnect the vacuum hose at the EGR valve.

21 Remove the nuts or bolts which secure the valve to the intake manifold.

22 Lift the EGR valve from the engine.

23 Clean the mounting surfaces of the EGR valve. Remove all traces of gasket material.

24 Place the new EGR valve, with a new gasket, on the intake manifold. Install the spacer, if used. Tighten the attaching bolts or nuts.

25 Connect the vacuum signal hose.

Thermal vacuum switch

26 Drain the engine coolant until the coolant level is beneath the switch.

27 Disconnect the vacuum hose at the EGR valve, noting their positions for reassembly.

28 Using a wrench, remove the switch.

29 When installing the switch, apply thread sealer to the threads, being careful not to allow the sealant to touch the bottom of the sensor.

30 Install the switch and tighten it securely.

8   Catalytic converter

General description

1 The catalytic converter is an emission control device added to the exhaust system to reduce pollutants from the exhaust gas stream. There are two types of converters. The conventional oxidation catalyst (used on earlier models) reduces the levels of hydrocarbon (HC) and carbon monoxide (CO). The three-way catalyst lowers the levels of oxides of nitrogen (NOx) as well as hydrocarbons (HC) and carbon monoxide (CO).

Checking

2 The test equipment for a catalytic converter is expensive and highly sophisticated. If you suspect that the converter on your vehicle is malfunctioning, take it to a dealer service department or authorized emissions inspection facility for diagnosis and repair.

3 Whenever the vehicle is raised for servicing of underbody components, check the converter for leaks, corrosion, dents and other damage. Check the welds/flange bolts that attach the front and rear ends of the converter to the exhaust system. If damage is discovered, the converter should be replaced.

4 Although catalytic converters don't malfunction too often, they do become plugged. The easiest way to check for a restricted converter is to use a vacuum gauge to diagnose the effect of a blocked exhaust on intake vacuum.

a) Open the throttle until the engine speed is about 2000 RPM.
b) Release the throttle quickly.
c) If there is no restriction, the gauge will quickly drop to not more than 2 in Hg or more above its normal reading.
d) If the gauge does not show 5 in Hg or more above its normal reading, or seems to momentarily hover around its highest reading for a moment before it returns, the exhaust system, or the converter, is plugged (or an exhaust pipe is bent or dented, or the core inside the muffler has shifted).

Component replacement

5 Because the converter is bolted to the exhaust system, refer to the exhaust system removal and installation Section in Chapter 4.

9   Computer Controlled Catalytic Converter (C4) or Computer Command Control (CCC or C3) system and information sensors

General description

Refer to illustrations 9.1a and 9.1b

1 The C4 system first became available on 1980 California models. In 1981, the C4 system was replaced by the Computer Command Control (CCC or C3) System. Both systems control exhaust emissions while retaining driveability by maintaining a continuous interaction between all of the emissions systems on your vehicle (see illustrations). A malfunction in the system is signaled by a Check Engine or Service Engine Soon light on the dash. On the C4 system, the Check Engine light will remain on as long as the engine is running. With the CCC diagnostic system activated, this same light will flash the trouble code related to the cause of the malfunction. On the C3 system, the Check Engine or Service Engine Soon light will remain on until the problem is identified and repaired and the code is erased from memory. In other words, the C3 system stores trouble codes in its memory, but the C4 system doesn't.

2 The C4/C3 System requires special tools for maintenance and repair, so most service work on it should be left to your dealer or a qualified technician. Although it seems complex, the system is easily understood in terms of its various components and their functions.

Electronic control module (ECM)

3 The electronic control module (ECM) is essentially a small on-board computer (located under the dash on most models) which monitors numerous engine functions and controls as many as nine engine-related systems. The ECM contains a Programmable Read Only Memory (PROM) calibration unit which tailors each ECM's performance to conform to the vehicle. The PROM is programmed with the vehicle's particular design, weight, axle ratio, etc., and cannot be used in another ECM in a car which differs in any way.

4 The ECM receives continuous data from the various information sensors, processes it in accordance with PROM instructions, then sends electronic signals to system components, modifying their performance (see the next Section).

Oxygen sensor

5 The oxygen sensor is mounted in the exhaust pipe or manifold, upstream of the catalytic converter. It monitors the exhaust stream and sends information to the ECM on how much oxygen is present. The oxygen level is determined by how rich or lean the fuel mixture is.

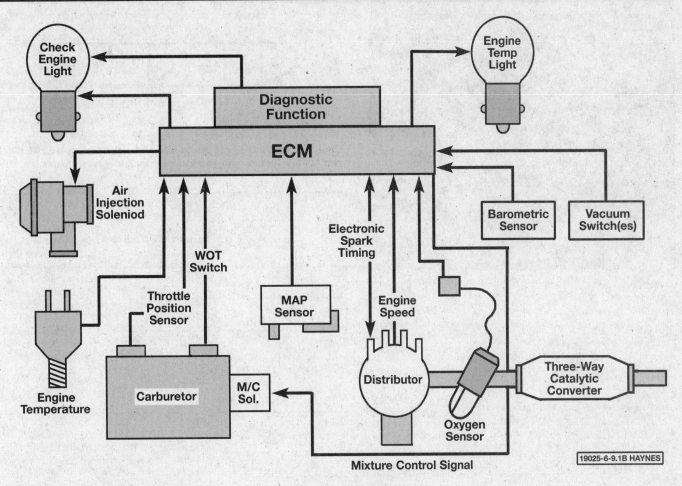

9.1a C4 system component diagram

Mixture Control (M/C) solenoid

6   The M/C solenoid controls the fuel flow through the carburetor idle and main metering circuits. The solenoid cycles ten times per second, constantly adjusting the fuel/air mixture. The ECM energizes the solenoid to keep emissions within limits based on information it receives from the oxygen sensor. Fuel-injected models have no M/C solenoid. The fuel injector pulse width (the amount of time the injectors are open) is altered to control mixture.

Coolant temperature sensor

7   This sensor monitors coolant temperature and sends this information to the ECM. The ECM alters the air/fuel ratio accordingly for conditions such as cold starting. The ECM also performs various switching functions on the EGR, EFE and AIR management systems, depending on engine temperature. This feedback from the coolant sensor can also activate the hot temperature light.

Pressure sensors

Refer to illustration 9.9

8   The ECM uses information from the Barometric Pressure Sensor (BARO) and

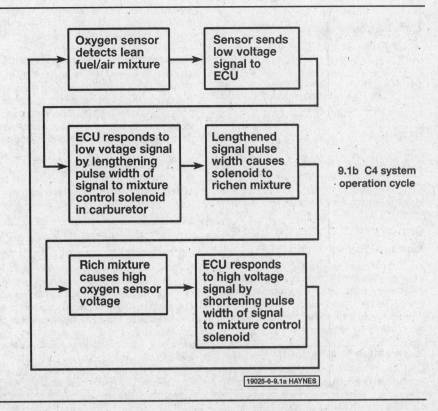

9.1b C4 system operation cycle

9.9 Typical MAP sensor location on the firewall

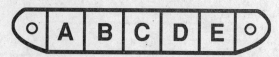

10.4a On 1981 models, the ALDL connector is located in the center console, below the ashtray - to retrieve trouble codes, remove the ashtray and jumper with a spade terminal between terminals D and E

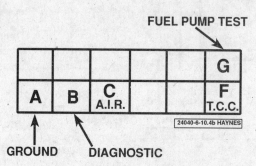

10.4b On 1982 models, the ALCL connector is also located in the center console - to retrieve trouble codes, remove the ashtray and connect a jumper wire between terminals A and B

Manifold Absolute Pressure (MAP) sensor to adjust engine performance. The BARO sensor senses ambient pressure changes that occur as a result of changes in the weather and the altitude of the vehicle. It then sends an electronic signal to the ECM that is used to adjust the air/fuel ratio and spark timing.

9   The MAP sensor **(see illustration)** measures changes in manifold pressure and provides this information to the ECM. The pressure changes reflect the need for adjustments in air/fuel mixture, spark timing (EST), etc., that are needed to maintain good vehicle performance under various driving conditions.

Throttle position sensor (TPS)

10   Mounted on the carburetor or throttle body, the TPS is actuated by the throttle plate and sends a variable voltage signal to the ECM: when the throttle plate is closed, the voltage signal is low, but as the throttle plate is opened, the voltage increases. The ECM uses this voltage signal to recognize throttle position.

Idle speed control (ISC)

11   The idle speed control maintains a low idle speed without stalling under changing conditions. The ECM controls the idle speed control motor on the carburetor or throttle body to adjust the idle.

Electronic spark timing (EST)

12   The High Energy Ignition (HEI) distributor used with the C4 or C3 system does not use centrifugal or vacuum advance. Spark timing is controlled electronically by the ECM, except under certain conditions, such as cranking the engine.

Air injection reactor (AIR)

13   When the engine is cold, the ECM energizes an air switching valve which allows air to flow to the exhaust ports to lower carbon

monoxide (CO) and hydrocarbon (HC) levels in the exhaust.

Exhaust gas recirculation (EGR)

14   The ECM controls ported vacuum to the EGR with a solenoid valve. When the engine is cold, the solenoid is energized to block vacuum to the EGR valve until the engine is warm.

Evaporative emission system (ECS)

15   When the engine is cold or idling, the ECM solenoid blocks vacuum to the valve at the top of the charcoal canister. When the engine is warm and at a specified rpm, the ECM de-energizes the valve, releasing the collected vapors into the intake manifold.

Early fuel evaporation (EFE)

16   The ECM controls a valve which shuts off the system until the engine is warm.

10 C4/C3 system and trouble codes

Refer to illustrations 10.4a and 10.4b

The C4 or C3 system is analogous to the central nervous system in the human body. The sensors (nerve endings) constantly relay information to the ECM (brain), which processes the data and, if necessary, sends out a command to change the operating parameters of the engine (body).

Here's a specific example of how one portion of this system operates: An oxygen sensor, located in the exhaust manifold, con-

stantly monitors the oxygen content of the exhaust gas. If the percentage of oxygen in the exhaust gas is incorrect, an electrical signal is sent to the ECM. The ECM takes this information, processes it and then sends a command to the carburetor or fuel injection system, telling it to change the air/fuel mixture. This happens in a fraction of a second and it goes on continuously when the engine is running. The end result is an air/fuel mixture ratio that is constantly maintained at a predetermined ratio, regardless of driving conditions.

One might think that a system which uses an on-board computer and electrical sensors would be difficult to diagnose. This is not necessarily the case. The C4 or C3 system has a built-in diagnostic feature which indicates a problem by flashing a Check Engine or Service Engine Soon light on the instrument panel. When this light comes on during normal vehicle operation, a fault in one of the information sensor circuits or the ECM itself has been detected. More importantly, on the C3 system, the source of the malfunction is stored in the ECM's memory.

To retrieve this information from the ECM memory, you must ground a diagnostic terminal. On most models, this terminal is part of a wiring connector known as the Assembly Line Data Link (ALDL) or Assembly Line Communication Link (ALCL). The ALDL, ALCL or test lead is located underneath the dashboard or in the center console **(see illustrations)**.

When the diagnostic terminal is grounded with the ignition On and the engine stopped, the system will enter the Diagnostic Mode. In this mode the ECM will display a Code 12 by flashing the light, indicating that the system is operating. A Code 12 is simply one flash, followed by a brief pause, then two flashes in quick succession. This code will be flashed three times.

If no other codes are stored, Code 12 will continue to flash until the diagnostic terminal ground is removed.

After flashing Code 12 three times, the ECM will display any stored trouble codes. Each code will be flashed three times, then Code 12 will be flashed again, indicating that

the display of any stored trouble codes has been completed.

When the ECM sets a trouble code, the light will come on and a trouble code will be stored in memory. If the problem is intermittent, the light will go out after ten seconds, when the fault goes away. However, the trouble code will stay in the ECM memory until the battery voltage to the ECM is interrupted. Removing battery voltage for ten seconds will clear all stored trouble codes. Trouble codes should always cleared after repairs have been completed. **Caution:** *To prevent damage to the ECM, the ignition switch must be*

Off when disconnecting power to the ECM.

Following is a list of the typical trouble codes which may be encountered while diagnosing the C4 or C3 system. The trouble codes do not necessarily indicate a problem with a particular component, but rather a failure of a particular sub-system in the C4 or C3 system. Dealer service departments (and many other shops) have special "scan" tools that can identify the particular problem. These tools are very expensive, and the procedures for using them are very complex. If you wish a more detailed diagnosis, have the system checked with a scan tool.

Trouble codes	Circuit or system	Probable cause
Code 12 . . . (1 flash, pause, 2 flashes)	Distributor-to-ECM . . .	This is the normal code when the engine isn't running. It is not stored in memory. It will flash only when a fault is present, the diagnostic terminal is grounded with the ignition turned on and the engine is not running. If additional codes are stored in the ECM, they will appear after this code has flashed 3 times. If the code appears while the engine is running, no reference pulses from the distributor are reaching the ECM.
Code 13 . . . (1 flash, pause, 3 flashes)	Oxygen sensor . . .	The engine must run up to 5 minutes at part throttle under road load before this code will set. Check for a sticking or misadjusted throttle position sensor. Check the oxygen sensor wires and connectors. Replace the oxygen sensor if necessary.
Code 14 . . . (1 flash, pause, 4 flashes)	Coolant sensor . . .	This code indicates a shorted coolant sensor circuit. The engine must run up to 2 minutes before this code will set. If the engine is experiencing overheating problems, the problem must be rectified before continuing. Check all wiring and connectors associated with the coolant temperature sensor. Replace the sensor if necessary.
Code 13 and 14 . . . at same time	Coolant sensor	See Code 43.
Code 13 and 43 . . . at same time	Coolant sensor	See Code 43.
Code 15 . . . (1 flash, pause, 5 flashes)	Coolant sensor . . .	The temperature sensor circuit is open. The engine must run for 5 minutes under 800 rpm to set this code. See Code 14 probable cause, then check the wiring connections at the ECM.
Code 21 . . . (2 flashes, pause, 1 flash)	TPS switch . . .	The throttle position sensor signal voltage is high. Check for a sticking or misadjusted Throttle Position Sensor (TPS) plunger. The engine must run for at least 10 seconds at 800 rpm, or at the specified curb idle, to set the code. Check all wiring and connectors between the TPS and the ECM. Adjust or replace the TPS if necessary.
Code 22 (1982 only) . . . (2 flashes, pause, 2 flashes)	TPS switch . . .	The TPS signal voltage is low.
Code 23 . . . (2 flashes, pause, 3 flashes)	M/C solenoid . . .	The Mixture Control (M/C) solenoid is open or grounded.
Code 24 . . . (2 flashes, pause, 4 flashes)	VSS	A fault in the Vehicle Speed Sensor (VSS) circuit should appear only when the vehicle is in motion and the engine has run at least 5 minutes. Disregard this code if it is set when the drive wheels are not turning. Check the connectors at the ECM. Check the TPS adjustment.

Trouble codes	Circuit or system	Probable cause
Code 33 (1982 only) . . . (3 flashes, pause, 3 flashes)	MAP sensor . . .	Check for a plugged or leaking MAP sensor vacuum line
Code 34 . . . (3 flashes, pause, 4 flashes)	Vacuum sensor or MAP sensor . . .	This code will set when the signal voltage from the Manifold Absolute Pressure (MAP) sensor circuit signal is too high. The engine must idle for up to 5 minutes to set this code. The ECM will substitute a fixed MAP value and use the TPS to control fuel delivery. Replace the MAP sensor.
Code 35 . . . (3 flashes, pause, 5 flashes)	TPS . . .	Check for a sticking TPS plunger.
Code 41 . . . (4 flashes, pause, 1 flash)	EST circuit . . .	No distributor reference pulses to the ECM at specified engine vacuum (about 8 inches Hg). This code will store in memory. Also, see below.
Code 41 . . . (4 flashes, pause, 1 flash)	EST circuit . . .	The Electronic Spark Timing (EST) bypass circuit or the EST circuit is grounded or open. A malfunctioning HEI module can set this code.
Code 42 . . . (4 flashes, pause, 2 flashes)	EST circuit . . .	Electronic Spark Timing bypass circuit or EST circuit is grounded or open. A malfunctioning HEI module can cause this code.
Code 43 . . . (4 flashes, pause, 3 flashes)	TPS switch . . .	Throttle Position Sensor (TPS) out of adjustment. Engine must run for at least 10 seconds to set this code. Also, see below.
Code 43 (1982 only) . . . (4 flashes, pause, 3 flashes)	ESC unit . . .	The Electronic Spark Control (ESC) retard signal has been on for too long or the voltage is too low.
Code 44 . . . (4 flashes, pause, 4 flashes)	Oxygen sensor . . .	The exhaust is lean. Indicated by the oxygen sensor after the engine has run in closed loop, part throttle at road load up to 5 minutes. Check the ECM wiring connectors. Check for vacuum leakage at the base gasket, vacuum hoses or the intake manifold gasket. Replace the oxygen sensor.
Code 45 . . . (4 flashes, pause, 5 flashes)	Oxygen sensor . . .	The exhaust is rich. Indicated by the oxygen sensor after the vehicle has run in closed loop, part throttle at road load up to 5 minutes. Check the evaporative charcoal canister and its components for the presence of fuel. Replace the oxygen sensor.
Code 44 and 45 . . . at same time	Oxygen sensor . . .	Indicates a faulty oxygen sensor circuit.
Code 51 (1979 only) . . . (5 flashes, pause, 1 flash)	ECM unit . . .	Faulty Electronic Control Module (ECM).
Code 51 . . . (5 flashes, pause, 1 flash)	PROM unit . . .	Faulty Programmed Read Only Memory (PROM) or improper PROM installation. Make sure that the PROM or MEM-CAL is properly in the ECM. Replace the PROM or MEM-CAL.
Code 52 . . . (5 flashes, pause, 2 flashes)	ECM unit . . .	Faulty ECM. Replace the ECM.
Code 53 . . . (5 flashes, pause, 3 flashes)	ECM unit . . .	Faulty ECM. Replace the ECM.
Code 54 . . . (5 flashes, pause, 4 flashes)	M/C solenoid . . .	The Mixture Control (M/C) solenoid voltage is high at the ECM because of a shorted M/C solenoid circuit and/or faulty ECM.

Trouble codes	Circuit or system	Probable cause
Code 55 (1980 only) . . . (5 flashes, pause, 5 flashes)	TPS or ECM . . .	Faulty Throttle Position Sensor (TPS) or Electronic Control Module.
Code 55 . . . (5 flashes, pause, 5 flashes)	ECM or oxygen sensor . . .	Make sure that the ECM ground connectors are tight. If they are, either the ECM or the oxygen sensor is faulty. Replace the ECM and/or the oxygen sensor.

Note: *A Code 33 or 34 may also cause a Code 44 - so check them first.*

Note: *A Code 34 may also cause a Code 45 - so check it first.*

Note: *Where replacement of one of the above systems, units or devices is recommended, it should be recognized that simply replacing some of the above components will not always solve the problem. For this reason, you may want to seek professional advice before purchasing any replacement parts.*

Notes

Chapter 7 Part A
Manual transmission

Contents

Specifications

Transmission type ... 3 or 4 forward speeds (all synchromesh) with one reverse. Floor shift

Torque specifications — Ft-lbs

Three-speed Muncie
Clutch gear retainer bolts	18
Side cover bolts	18
Extension housing bolts	45
Shift shaft to lever bolts	20
Filler plug	15
Drain plug	30
Case to clutch housing bolts	55

Three-speed Saginaw
Clutch gear retainer bolts	22
Side cover bolts	22
Extension to case bolts	45
Shifter shaft to lever bolts	20
Filler plug	15
Case to clutch housing bolts	55

Four-speed Muncie
Clutch gear retainer bolts	25
Side cover bolts	20
Extension housing/bearing retainer bolts	
Upper	20
Lower	30
Filler plug	30
Shifter shaft to lever nuts	20

Torque specifications

	Ft-lbs
Four-speed Saginaw	
Clutch gear retainer bolts	
1968 through 1977	22
1978 through 1982	15
Side cover bolts	
1968 through 1977	22
1978 through 1982	15
Extension housing bolts	45
Shifter shaft to lever bolts	
1968 through 1977	20
1978 through 1982	25
Filler plug	
1968 through 1977	15
1978 through 1982	13
Case to clutch housing bolts	
1968 through 1977	55
1978 through 1982	75
Four-speed Warner	
Clutch gear retainer bolts	20
Side cover bolts	20
Extension housing bolts	50
Shifter shaft to lever nuts	25
Filler and drain plugs	20
Case to clutch housing bolts	55
Four-speed Warner	
Clutch gear retainer bolts	18
Side cover bolts	18
Extension housing bolts	40
Shifter shaft to lever bolts	20
Filler plug	15
Case to clutch housing bolts	52
Rear bearing retainer bolts	25
Retainer to case bolts	35
Drain plug	20

1 General information

All vehicles covered in this manual come equipped with either a three-speed or four-speed manual transmission or an automatic transmission. All information on the manual transmission is included in this Part of Chapter 7. Information on the automatic transmission can be found in Part B of this Chapter.

Due to the complexity, unavailability of replacement parts and the special tools necessary, internal repair by the home mechanic is not recommended. The information in this Chapter is presented if you choose to overhaul the transmission yourself.

Depending on the expense involved in having a faulty transmission overhauled, it may be a good idea to replace the unit with either a new or rebuilt one. Your local dealer or transmission shop should be able to supply you with information concerning cost, availability and exchange policy. Regardless of how you decide to remedy a transmission problem, you can still save a lot of money by removing and installing the unit yourself.

2 Shift linkage (1968 and 1969 three-speed models) - adjustment

1   Loosen the locknuts on both shift rods.
2   Set the shift control lever within the car in Neutral then insert a suitable gauge (0.640 in thick) in the notch of the lever and bracket assembly.
3   Move the shift lever on the side of the transmission to Neutral (center detent) position.
4   Hold the first/reverse rod and lever against the gauge and then tighten the locknut against the swivel.
5   Press second/third rod and lever against the gauge then run the front nut up against the swivel, finally tightening the rear locknut.
6   Remove the gauge and check the shift lever positions. Move the shift lever to neutral and re-insert the gauge into the notch. If the gauge does not freely enter the bracket assembly, re-adjust the linkage.

3 Shift linkage (1970 three-speed models) - adjustment

1   Turn the ignition switch to Lock. Raise the vehicle and support it securely on jackstands.
2   Loosen the locknuts on both shift rods.
3   Disconnect the back drive cable from the column lock tube lever.
4   Set the shift control lever in the car to Neutral.
5   Make up a locking gauge (0.640 in thick) and insert it in the notch in the lever/bracket assembly.
6   Move the lever on the side of the transmission to Neutral.
7   Press first/reverse rod and lever against the gauge, then tighten the locknut against the swivel.
8   Press second/third rod and lever against the gauge and tighten the forward nut against the swivel. Finally tighten the rear locknut against the swivel and then remove the gauge.
9   Check the operation in all the shift lever

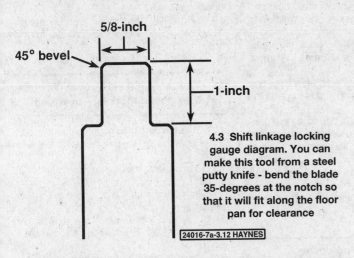

5/8-inch

45° bevel

1-inch

4.3 Shift linkage locking gauge diagram. You can make this tool from a steel putty knife - bend the blade 35-degrees at the notch so that it will fit along the floor pan for clearance

24016-7a-3.12 HAYNES

7.8 Use a seal removal tool or a long screwdriver to carefully pry the seal out of the end of the transmission

positions. If the shift lever has any tendency to contact the console, shim the support bracket as necessary, but make sure that sufficient clearance is maintained between the support and the transmission extension.

10   Working inside the car, loosen the two nuts on the steering column to dash panel bracket.

11   Place the shift lever in Reverse.

12   Rotate the lock tube lever counterclockwise (viewed from the front of the column) to remove any freeplay. Reposition the cable bracket until the cable eye passes over the retaining pin on the bracket.

13   Hold the bracket in position while an assistant tightens the steering column-to-dash panel nuts.

14   Install the cotter pin and washer to retain the back drive cable to the lever pin.

4   Shift linkage (1968 and 1969 four-speed models) - adjustment

Refer to illustration 4.3

1   Loosen the locknuts on the shift rods.

2   Set the three shift levers on the side of the transmission in the neutral detent.

3   Inside the car, move the shift control lever to Neutral and insert a locking gauge into the control lever bracket assembly. Use the accompanying template to fabricate the gauge **(see illustration)**.

4   Tighten the jam nuts on the reverse lever swivel.

5   Tighten the jam nuts on first/second lever swivel and the third/fourth lever swivel.

6   Remove the gauge.

5   Shift linkage (1970 through 1982 four-speed models) - adjustment

1   Carry out the operations described in the preceding Section.

2   If the back drive interlock linkage

requires adjustment, refer to Section 3, Steps 10 through 14.

6   Shift lever assembly - removal and installation

Three-speed models

1   Working inside the car, remove the control lever knob.

2   Remove the console trim plate and seat assembly.

3   Disconnect the control rods from the levers at the base of the shift control lever.

4   Unscrew and remove the bolts that hold the shift control to the support bracket.

5   Unbolt the support bracket from the crossmember and remove the support assembly from the car.

6   Pull down on the shift control assembly to withdraw it from the console boot.

7   The shift control can be dismantled to replace worn components by removing the circlips and pivot pins as necessary.

Four-speed models

8   The operations for removal and dismantling are similar to those just described for three-speed assemblies, but once the shift control knob has been removed, remove the spring and T handle.

7   Transmission oil seals - replacement

1   The following oil seals can be replaced without removing the transmission from the car.

Speedometer gear seal

2   Raise the vehicle to gain access to the transmission.

3   Disconnect the speedometer cable, remove the lockplate to extension bolt and

lockwasher, then remove the lockplate.

4   Insert a screwdriver in the lockplate fitting, and pry the fitting gear and shaft from the extension.

5   Pry out the O-ring.

6   Installation is the reverse of removal, but lubricate the new seal with transmission lubricant and hold the assembly so that the slot in the fitting is towards the lockplate boss on the extension.

Extension housing oil seal

Refer to illustration 7.8

7   Remove the driveshaft (see Chapter 8). Remove any adjacent items necessary to provide additional clearance.

8   Carefully pry out the old seal **(see illustration)**.

9   Carefully clean the counterbore and examine for any damage.

10   Pre-lubricate between the lips of the new seal with transmission lubricant and coat the outer diameter with sealant.

11   Carefully install the seal, lips inward, until the flange seats. Use a tubular spacer for this job.

12   Reinstall the driveshaft (refer to Chapter 8) and any other adjacent items removed.

8   Transmission side cover (Saginaw and Muncie three-speed models) - overhaul

1   Shift transmission into Neutral and rise the vehicle to gain access to the transmission.

2   Disconnect the control rods from the levers on the side of the transmission.

3   Remove the cover assembly from the transmission case and allow the oil to drain.

4   Remove both shift forks from the shifter shaft assemblies and both shifter shaft assemblies from the cover.

5   Pry out the shaft O-ring seals if replacement is required.

6   Remove the detent cam spring and

pivot retainer C-ring. Remove both detent cams.

7   Inspect all parts for damage and wear, and replace as necessary.

8   With the detent spring tang projecting up over the 2nd/3rd shifter shaft cover opening, install the 1st/reverse detent cam onto the detent cam pivot pin. With the detent spring tang projecting up over the 1st and reverse shifter shaft cover hole, install the 2nd/3rd detent cam.

9   Install the C-ring to the pivot shaft and hook the spring into the detent cam notches.

10   Install the shifter shaft assemblies carefully into the cover and the shift forks to the shifter shaft assemblies. Lift up on the detent cam to allow the forks to seat properly.

11   Set the shifter levers into the neutral detent (center position) and position the gasket on the case.

12   Carefully position the side cover, ensuring that the shift forks are aligned with their appropriate mainshaft clutch sliding sleeves.

13   Install and tighten the cover bolts to the torque listed in this Chapter's Specifications.

14   Add the specified lubricant to the transmission (refer to Chapter 1) and lower the vehicle to the ground.

9   Transmission side cover (Warner three-speed models) - overhaul

1   Drain the transmission, then disconnect the control rod and cross shaft from the levers on the side of the transmission.

2   Unscrew the bolts and remove the side cover and gasket.

3   Remove the shift forks from the shift lever assemblies.

4   Remove the nut and lockwasher from each shifter lever shaft.

5   Remove the outer shifter levers and then lightly tap the shifter lever shafts out of the cover.

6   Remove the two steel balls, poppet spring, interlock pins and interlock sleeve from the cover.

7   Remove the O-ring seals from the shifter lever shafts.

8   Replace any worn components. Reassemble by fitting new O-rings to the shifter lever shafts.

9   Install low/reverse shifter shaft and plate to the cover.

10   Set the shifter shaft and plate assembly in neutral (middle detent) and install the interlock sleeve.

11   Fit the ball, poppet spring and interlock pin.

12   Fit the remaining ball followed by the 2nd/3rd shifter shaft and plate. Installation will be made easier if the shaft/plate assembly passes over the ball while it is in its neutral position.

13   Check the clearance between the end of the interlock sleeve, and shifter shaft and plate cams when one plate is in Neutral and the other is in "gear engaged" position. The

clearance should be between 0.002 and 0.008 in. Interlock sleeves are available in four sizes to provide the correct clearance.

14   Install the outer shift levers to the shafts using lockwashers and nuts. Tighten securely.

15   Install shift forks to shift levers making sure that the 1st/reverse hump is towards the bottom of the fork.

16   Install the side cover using a new gasket. Note that the two closest side cover bolts have special oil seals and must be used only in these positions.

17   Connect the control rod and cross shaft to the transmission levers.

18   Refill the transmission (refer to Chapter 1).

10   Transmission side cover (Saginaw and Muncie four-speed models) - overhaul

1   Shift Saginaw models into Neutral and Muncie models into second gear.

2   Raise the vehicle to gain access to the transmission. Place it securely on jackstands.

3   Remove the shift levers from the shifter shafts.

4   Remove the cover assembly and allow the oil to drain.

5   Remove the outer shifter levers.

6   Remove the shift forks from the shifter shaft assemblies, and the three shifter shaft assemblies from the cover.

7   If necessary, pry out the O-ring on the first, 1-2 and reverse shafts.

8   On Saginaw models remove the reverse shifter shaft detent ball and spring.

9   Remove the detent cam spring and the pivot pin C-ring. Mark the cams for identification on reassembly, then remove them.

10   Inspect all the parts for damage and wear and replace as necessary.

11   With the detent spring tang projecting up over the 3rd/4th shifter shaft cover opening, install the 1st/2nd detent cam onto the detent cam pivot pin. With the detent spring tang projecting up over the 1st/2nd shifter shaft cover hole, install the 3rd/4th detent cam.

12   Install the detent cam C-ring to the pivot shaft and hook the spring into the cam notches.

13   Install the 1st/2nd and 3rd/4th shifter shaft assemblies carefully into the cover.

14   Install the shift forks to the shifter shaft assemblies, lifting up on the detent cam to permit the forks to seat.

15   Install the reverse detent ball and spring, then install the reverse shifter shaft assembly to the cover.

16   Move the shifter levers into Neutral (Saginaw) or second gear (Muncie).

17   Position the cover gasket on the case and carefully position the side cover, ensuring that the shift forks are aligned with their appropriate mainshaft clutch sliding sleeves.

18   Screw in the side cover bolts and tighten to the torque listed in this Chapter's

Specifications.

19   Add oil to the transmission (refer to Chapter 1) and lower the vehicle to the ground.

11   Transmission side cover (Warner four-speed models) - overhaul

1   Shift the transmission into second gear.

2   Raise the car to gain access to the side cover.

3   Disconnect the wiring from the TCS switch.

4   Remove the shift levers from the shifter shafts.

5   Unscrew and remove the nine cover screws, remove the cover and allow the oil to drain.

6   Remove the TCS switch from the cover.

7   Remove the outer shifter lever nuts and pull the levers from the shafts.

8   Push the shifter shafts into the cover allowing the detent balls to fall free. Extract the shifter shafts.

9   Remove the interlock sleeve, the interlock pin and poppet spring.

10   Inspect and replace components as necessary.

11   Reassemble by reversing the overhaul procedure.

12   Before installing the side cover, move the shifter levers to second gear position.

13   Install a new gasket on the transmission.

14   Place the side cover into position making sure that the shift forks are aligned with their respective synchronizer sliding sleeve grooves.

15   Insert the cover bolts and tighten to the torque listed in this Chapter's Specifications.

16   Connect the shift levers and the TCS switch wiring.

17   Add lubricant to level of the filler plug hole.

18   Lower the car to the ground.

12   Transmission - removal and installation

1   Disconnect the battery ground cable.

2   Working inside the car, remove the shift lever (see Section 6).

3   Remove the console trim plate.

4   Raise the vehicle and support it securely on jackstands to provide adequate under-vehicle clearance for transmission removal.

5   Remove the dual exhaust system. On cars with a 427 cubic inch engine, the front stud on each manifold will have to be removed.

6   Disconnect the driveshaft at the transmission slip yoke (refer to Chapter 8). Lower the front end of the transmission and then remove the slip yoke from the transmission.

7   Remove the bolts that attach the transmission rear mounting to the bracket. Raise the engine slightly, using a jack and wooden block under the oil pan, until the transmission

is lifted off the mounting bracket.

8 Disconnect the shift linkage bracket from the frame.

9 Remove the shift mechanism complete with rods.

10 Disconnect the shifter levers at the transmission.

11 Disconnect the speedometer cable from the transmission and the wiring from the TCS switch, where fitted.

12 With the engine still well supported, remove the rear mounting crossmember mount bracket, the rear mount cushion and the exhaust pipe yoke.

13 Unscrew and remove the bolts that hold the transmission to the clutch bellhousing, also the extension bottom bolt.

14 Pull the transmission to the rear, at the same time turning it clockwise until it is clear of the clutch housing. An assistant will now have to gently lower the engine until the tachometer drive cable, at the distributor, just clears the ledge on the firewall. The transmission can now be moved further to the rear, until it can be tipped downwards at its front end and removed completely from the car.

15 Installation is the reversal of removal.

13 Transmission overhaul - general information

Overhauling a manual transmission is a difficult job for the do-it-yourselfer. It involves the disassembly and reassembly of many small parts. Numerous clearances must be precisely measured and, if necessary, changed with select fit spacers and snap-rings. As a result, if transmission problems arise, it can be removed and installed by a competent do-it-yourselfer, but overhaul should be left to a transmission repair shop. Rebuilt transmissions may be available - check with your dealer parts department and auto parts stores. At any rate, the time and money involved in an overhaul is almost sure to exceed the cost of a rebuilt unit.

Nevertheless, it's not impossible for an inexperienced mechanic to rebuild a transmission if the special tools are available and the job is done in a deliberate step-by-step manner so nothing is overlooked.

The tools necessary for an overhaul include internal and external snap-ring pliers, a bearing puller, a slide hammer, a set of pin punches, a dial indicator and possibly a hydraulic press. In addition, a large, sturdy workbench and a vise or transmission stand will be required.

During disassembly of the transmission, make careful notes of how each piece comes off, where it fits in relation to other pieces and what holds it in place. Making careful notes and sketches as you disassemble the transmission will make reassembly much easier. Lay each component out in order on a clean table as you proceed.

Before taking the transmission apart for repair, it will help if you have some idea what

area of the transmission is malfunctioning. Certain problems can be closely tied to specific areas in the transmission, which can make component examination and replacement easier. Refer to the *Troubleshooting* section at the front of this manual for information regarding possible sources of trouble.

14 Saginaw three-speed transmission - overhaul

1 Remove the transmission, drain the oil and remove the side cover assembly (refer to Section 8).

2 Remove the drivegear bearing retainer and gasket.

3 Remove the drivegear bearing snap-ring, then pull out the gear until a large screwdriver can be used to lever the drivegear bearing from its location.

4 Remove the speedometer driven gear from the rear extension, then remove the extension retaining bolts.

5 Remove the reverse idler shaft E-ring.

6 Withdraw the drivegear, mainshaft and extension assembly together through the rear casing.

7 From the mainshaft, detach the drivegear, needle bearings and synchronizer ring.

8 Expand the snap-ring in the rear extension, which retains the rear bearing and then withdraw the rear extension.

9 Using a dummy shaft or special tool drive the countershaft (complete with Woodruff key) out of the rear of the transmission case. Carefully remove the dummy shaft and extract the countergear, bearings and thrust washers from the interior of the transmission case using a long drift.

10 Drive the reverse idler shaft out of the rear of the transmission case using a long driver.

11 The mainshaft should only be dismantled if a press or bearing puller is available; otherwise take the assembly to a transmission shop.

12 Remove the 2nd/3rd synchro hub snap-ring from the mainshaft. Do not mix up the synchro unit components; although identical, the components of each unit are matched in production.

13 Remove the synchro unit, second speed blocker ring and second speed gear from the front end of the mainshaft.

14 Depress the speedometer drivegear retaining clip and remove the gear from the mainshaft.

15 Remove the rear bearing snap-ring from its mainshaft groove.

16 Support the reverse gear and press the mainshaft out of the rear bearing, and snap-ring from the rear end of the mainshaft.

17 Remove 1st/reverse synchro hub snap-ring from the mainshaft and remove the synchro unit.

18 Remove the 1st speed blocker ring and 1st speed gear from the rear end of the mainshaft.

19 Clean all components in kerosene and dry thoroughly. Check for wear or chipped teeth. If there has been a history of hard or noisy shifts, then replace the appropriate synchro unit.

20 Withdraw the oil seal from the rear end of the rear extension and drive in a new one with a tubular drift.

21 Clean the transmission case inside and out and check for cracks, particularly around the bolt holes.

22 Withdraw the drivegear bearing retainer seal and drive in a new one.

23 Rebuild the transmission by first reassembling the mainshaft. Install 2nd speed gear so that the rear face of the gear butts against the flange on the mainshaft.

24 Fit the blocker ring, followed by the 2nd/3rd synchro assembly (shift fork groove near rear end of the mainshaft). Make sure that the notches of the blocker ring align with the keys of the synchro assembly.

25 Fit the snap-ring that retains the synchro hub to the mainshaft.

26 To the rear end of the mainshaft, install the 1st speed gear followed by the blocker ring.

27 Install the 1st/reverse synchro unit (shift fork groove nearer the front end of the mainshaft), again making sure that the notches of the blocker ring align with the keys of the synchro unit.

28 Install the snap-ring, reverse gear, reverse gear thrust washer and spring washer.

29 Install the mainshaft rear ball bearing with the outer snap-ring groove nearer the front of the shaft.

30 Install the rear bearing shaft snap-ring.

31 Fit the speedometer drive gear and retaining clip.

32 Insert a dummy shaft through the countergear, and stick the roller bearings (27 at each end), needle retainer washers and the transmission case thrust washers, in position using thick grease. Note that the tangs on the thrust washers are away from the gear faces. **Note:** *If no dummy shaft is available, carefully stick the roller bearings in place, but when installing the shaft (step 34), take care that they are not dislodged.*

33 Install reverse idler gear and shaft with Woodruff key from the rear of the transmission case. Do not install the idler shaft E-ring at this time.

34 Install the countergear assembly from the rear of the transmission case and then insert the countershaft so that it picks up the roller bearings and the thrust washers, at the same time displacing the dummy shaft or tool (if used). The countershaft should be inserted so that its slot is at its rear end when installed.

35 Expand the snap-ring in the rear extension and locate the extension over the rear end of the mainshaft and onto the rear bearing. Make sure that the snap-ring seats in the rear bearing groove.

36 Insert the mainshaft pilot bearings (14 of them) into the clutch gear cavity and then

assemble the 3rd speed blocker ring onto the clutch drive gear.

37 Locate the clutch drive gear, pilot bearings and 3rd speed blocker ring over the front of the mainshaft. Do not fit the drive gear bearing at this time; also make sure that the notches in the blocker ring align with the keys in the 2nd/3rd synchro unit.

38 Stick a new gasket (using grease) to the rear face of the transmission case and then from the rear, insert the combined clutch drive gear/mainshaft and rear extension. Make sure that the 2nd/3rd synchro sleeve is pushed fully forward so that the clutch drive gear engages with the countergear anti-lash plate.

39 Install the rear extension to transmission case bolts.

40 Fit the outer snap-ring to the clutch drive gear bearing and install the bearing over the drive gear and into the front of the transmission case.

41 Fit the clutch drive gear bearing shaft snap-ring.

42 Install the clutch drive gear bearing retainer and its gasket making sure that the oil return hole is at the bottom.

43 Now install the reverse idler gear E-ring to the shaft.

44 With the synchronizer sleeves in the neutral position, install the side cover, gasket and fork assembly (see Section 8). Tighten all the bolts to the torque listed in this Chapter's Specifications.

45 Install the speedometer driven gear in the rear extension.

15 Muncie three-speed transmission - overhaul

1 The operations are very similar to those described in the preceding section for the three-speed Saginaw, but note the following differences and the detail variations in some of the components.

2 Once the extension is unbolted, turn it until the groove in the extension housing flange lines up with the reverse idler shaft. The reverse idler shaft can then be driven out of the gear and transmission case.

3 Keep the synchro components together as originally assembled. If the keys and springs are worn they should be replaced. Before dismantling mark the relative position of hub and sleeve for exact reassembly, Where a groove is visible around the outside of the synchronizer hub, then this must always be positioned opposite the fork slot in the sleeve.

4 When reassembling the breather vent to the extension housing, make sure that it is tightly fitted, and that the internal spout faces the left-hand side of the transmission.

16 Warner three-speed transmission - overhaul

1 Remove the transmission and drain the oil, then remove the transmission side cover (refer to Section 9).

2 Unbolt the extension housing and rotate it clockwise to expose the end of the reverse idler shaft.

3 Drive the reverse idler shaft out of the rear of the case.

4 Again, rotate the extension housing to expose the end of the countershaft. Drive the shaft out of the rear of the transmission case and lower the countergear carefully to the bottom of the case.

5 Remove the complete mainshaft and rear extension housing from the transmission case.

6 Extract the snap-ring in the extension housing to release the mainshaft rear bearing. Withdraw the extension housing from the mainshaft.

7 Remove the clutch gear bearing retainer from the front face of the transmission.

8 Extract the clutch gear bearing snap-ring and washer.

9 Using a soft-face mallet, drive the clutch gear into the transmission case through its bearing.

10 Now remove the bearing by tapping it out of the foot of the transmission case.

11 Extract the countergear and roller bearings, the two countergear thrust washers, reverse idler gear and thrust washers, all from inside the transmission case.

12 Unless a suitable press or bearing puller is available, dismantling the mainshaft should be left to your dealer. Where such equipment is available, carry out the following operations.

13 Remove the 2nd/3rd speed synchro hub snap-ring from the mainshaft.

14 Extract the rear bearing snap-ring from the mainshaft.

15 Support the reverse gear and apply pressure to the rear end of the mainshaft to withdraw the reverse gear, the rear bearing, special washer, snap-ring and the speedo drive gear from the rear end of the mainshaft. When carrying out this work, make sure that the special washer does not get trapped in the snap-ring groove.

16 Extract the first/reverse synchro hub snap-ring from the mainshaft. Remove the synchro unit, 1st speed blocker ring and 1st speed gear from the rear of the mainshaft.

17 Clean, inspect and replace all components as necessary. The synchro units should be dismantled and reassembled if necessary as described in Sections 14 and 15. Replace all oil seals as a matter of routine.

18 Begin reassembly of the mainshaft by installing 1st speed gear to its rear end so that its synchro teeth are to the rear.

19 Fit the 1st gear blocker ring.

20 Fit the 1st/reverse synchro unit over the rear end of the mainshaft, making sure that the three keys engage in the blocker ring notches.

21 Use the thickest snap-ring (selected from the three thicknesses available) which will fit into the groove with the components pressed tightly together.

22 Install reverse gear over the end of the mainshaft so the synchro teeth are towards the front.

23 Press the mainshaft rear bearing into position so the snap-ring groove, on its outer race, is nearest to the reverse gear.

24 Fit the rear bearing special washer and snap-ring to the mainshaft. Select the thickest snap-ring that will fit from the six thicknesses available.

25 Press the speedo drive gear onto the mainshaft and center it on its boss.

26 To the front end of the mainshaft fit the 2nd speed gear so that its synchro teeth are towards the front of the shaft.

27 Install the 2nd speed gear blocker ring and then the 2nd/3rd synchro unit, making sure that the synchro key engages with the blocker ring notches.

28 Install the synchro snap-ring. Use the thickest snap-ring that will fit from the four thicknesses available. The mainshaft is now assembled.

29 Assemble the countergear as described in Section 14, Step 32. At each end of the countergear, assemble 20 rollers, a spacer, then a further 20 rollers, and the final spacer.

30 Using a dummy countershaft as described in Section 14, Step 34, install the countergear and shaft. Note the larger thrust washer is towards the front of the transmission.

31 Fit the Woodruff key to the rear end of the countershaft.

32 The countergear end-play should now be checked. If it exceeds 0.025-in. new thrust washers must be installed.

33 Use thick grease to hold the 25 reverse idler needle rollers in position. Stick a thrust washer on each end of the gear and locate the reverse idler assembly inside the transmission case. Make sure that the beveled side of the gear teeth face towards the front of the transmission.

34 Install the pilot bearing rollers into the clutch gear using heavy grease to retain them.

35 Hold the clutch gear shaft inside the transmission case with the 3rd speed blocker ring over the clutch gear. Now pass the mainshaft assembly into the case from the rear end picking up the spacer, the pilot bearings and the 3rd speed blocker ring. Make sure that the clutch gear engages with the teeth of the countergear anti-lash plate.

36 Install the reverse idler shaft and the Woodruff key.

37 Stick a new extension housing gasket to the rear of the transmission case.

38 Expand the extension housing to bearing snap-ring, and push the housing over the mainshaft and rear bearing. Make sure the snap-ring has partially passed over the rear bearing then fit and tighten to the torque listed in this Chapter's Specifications. The two lower extension housing bolts should have their threads smeared with sealant.

39 Tap the front end of the clutch gear shaft to force the mainshaft rear bearing snap-ring to seat in its groove.

40   Using a piece of tubing applied to the clutch gear bearing inner race, drive the bearing onto the shaft and into the case. Install the washer and snap-ring to the clutch shaft. Use the thickest snap-ring that will fit from the five thicknesses available.
41   Install the snap-ring to the outer race of the clutch gear bearing. If the groove is partly obscured by the transmission casing, tap on the inner face of the bearing outer race using a rod inserted through the side cover opening.
42   Install the gaskets, clutch gear bearing retainer and oil seal, making sure that the oil drain passage is at the bottom. Apply sealant to the retainer bolt threads and tighten to the torque listed in this Chapter's Specifications. It is normal to install two gaskets between the bearing retainer and the front face of the transmission case (one 0.010-in. thick, one 0.015-in. thick) to replace the single 0.025-in. thick gasket fitted in production.
43   Install the side cover as described in Section 9.
44   Fill the transmission with the recommended lubricant (see Chapter 1) after it has been installed in the vehicle.

17 Saginaw four-speed transmission - overhaul

1   Carry out the operations of Steps 1 through 9 of Section 14 but note that an E-ring is not fitted to the reverse idler shaft.
2   Remove the reverse idler gear stop-ring (where applicable), then use a long drift to drive the reverse idler shaft out of the rear of the transmission case.
3   Remove the 3rd/4th synchro hub snap-ring from the mainshaft. Do not mix up the synchro unit components which, although identical in appearance, are matched in production.
4   Remove the synchro unit, 3rd speed gear blocker ring and third speed gear from the front end of the mainshaft.
5   Depress the speedometer drivegear retaining clip and remove the gear from the mainshaft.
6   Remove the rear bearing snap-ring from its mainshaft groove.
7   Support 1st speed gear and press the mainshaft out of the rear bearing. Remove the snap-ring, the rear bearing, the wave washer, thrust washer and 1st speed gear from the rear end of the mainshaft.
8   Remove the blocker ring and 1st/2nd synchro hub snap-ring from the mainshaft and remove the synchro unit/reverse gear.
9   Remove the 2nd speed blocker ring and 2nd speed gear from the rear end of the mainshaft.
10   Carry out the operations of Steps 19 through 22 of Section 14.
11   Reassemble the transmission by first reassembling the mainshaft. Install 3rd speed gear so that the rear face of the gear butts against the flange on the mainshaft.

12   Install the blocker ring, followed by 3rd/4th synchro assembly (shift fork groove nearer mainshaft flange). Make sure that the notches of the blocker ring align with the keys of the synchro assembly.
13   Install the snap-ring that retains the synchro hub to the mainshaft.
14   To the rear end of the mainshaft, install the 2nd speed gear followed by the blocker ring.
15   Install the 1st/2nd synchro unit (shift fork groove nearer the front of the mainshaft), again making sure that the notches of the blocker ring align with the keys of the synchro unit. Install the snap-ring and blocker ring.
16   Install 1st speed gear, the steel thrust washer and the wave washer.
17   Install the mainshaft rear ball bearing with the outer snap-ring groove nearer the front of the shaft.
18   Install the rear bearing shaft snap-ring.
19   Fit the speedometer drivegear and retaining clip.
20   Carry out operations of Steps 32 through 35 of Section 14 but ignore the reference to the E-ring.
21   Insert the mainshaft pilot bearings (14 of them) into the clutch cavity and then assemble the fourth speed blocker ring onto the clutch drivegear.
22   Locate the clutch drivegear, pilot bearings and fourth speed blocker ring over the front of the mainshaft. Do not fit the drivegear bearing at this time; also make sure that the notches in the blocker ring align with the keys in the 3rd/4th synchro unit.
23   Carry out the operations of Steps 38 through 42 and Step 44 of Section 14. Note that the reference at Step 38 to second/third synchro sleeve will now be 3rd/4th synchro sleeve.

18 Muncie four-speed transmission - overhaul

1   Remove the transmission, drain the oil and remove the transmission side cover (refer to Section 10).
2   Remove the bolts and lockstrips securing the front bearing retainer. Remove the retainer and gasket.
3   Lock up the transmission by selecting two gears then use Chevrolet tool J-933 (or equivalent) to remove the drivegear retaining nut.
4   Select Neutral, then drive out the lockpin from the reverse shifter lever boss. Pull the shifter shaft out about 1/8 inch to disengage the reverse shift fork.
5   Remove the six case extension retaining bolts then tap the extension to the rear using a soft hammer. Move the extension to the left when the reverse idler is out as far as it will go. This will permit the extension to be removed.
6   Remove the reverse idler, flat thrust washer, shaft and roll pin.

7   Remove the speedometer gear and reverse gear using a suitable extractor.
8   Slide the 3rd/4th synchronizer sleeve forwards into 4th gear position, then carefully remove the rear bearing retainer and mainshaft assembly from the case by tapping the retainer with a soft hammer.
9   Remove the 17 bearing rollers from the main drivegear, and the 4th speed synchronizer blocker ring.
10   Lift the front half of the reverse idler and its thrust washer from the case.
11   Press the drivegear from the front bearing into the case.
12   Tap out the front bearing and snap-ring from inside the case.
13   Using a dummy shaft or special tool, press out the countershaft, then remove the countergear and both tanged washers.
14   Remove the 112 rollers, six 0.070-in. spacers and the roller spacer from the countergear.
15   Remove the mainshaft front snap-ring and slide the 3rd/4th speed clutch assembly, 3rd speed gear and synchronizing ring from the mainshaft.
16   Remove the rear bearing snap-ring and press the mainshaft out of the retainer.
17   The remaining steps require a press or suitable extractor. If you don't have one, the best approach may be to have the remainder of disassembly done by a transmission shop.
18   Remove the mainshaft rear snap-ring, then, while supporting on the 2nd speed gear, press on the rear of the mainshaft to remove the 1st speed gear and sleeve, first gear synchronizing ring, 1st/2nd speed synchronizing clutch assembly, 2nd speed synchronizing ring and 2nd speed gear.
19   Remove the reverse shift fork from the shifter shaft, then carefully drive the shaft in to allow the detent ball to drop out. Remove the shaft and ball detent spring.
20   Carry out the operations of Steps 19 through 21 of Section 14.
21   Place the reverse shifter shaft detent spring into its hole in the extension, then install the shifter shaft until the detent plate butts against the inside of the extension housing.
22   Commence reassembly by placing the detent ball on the spring and hold it down while moving the shifter shaft away from the case until the ball drops into the detent on the shaft detent plate.
23   Install the fork, but do not lock it at this stage.
24   To the rear of the mainshaft, assemble the 2nd speed gear with the hub toward the rear of the shaft.
25   Install the 1st/2nd speed synchronizer clutch assembly to the mainshaft (hub toward the front), together with a synchronizing ring on each side. Align the keyways with the clutch keys.
26   Press the 1st speed gear sleeve onto the mainshaft using a 1 3/4-inch inside-diameter pipe or similar tool.
27   Install the 1st speed gear (hub toward the front) and, using a 1 5/8-inch inside-

diameter pipe, press on the rear bearing.

28   Select a snap-ring to give 0 to 0.005-inch from the mainshaft groove to the rear face of the mainshaft rear bearing. New snap-rings are available in sizes of 0.087, 0.090, 0.093 and 0.096-inch.

29   Install the 3rd speed gear (hub to the front of the transmission) and the 3rd speed gear synchronizing ring (notches to the front of the transmission).

30   Install the 3rd/4th gear clutch assembly with the sleeve taper and hub towards the front. Ensure that the hub keys align with the synchronizing ring notches.

31   Install the snap-ring in the mainshaft groove in front of the 3rd/4th speed clutch assembly, with the ends seated behind the spline teeth.

32   Install the rear bearing retainer. Spread the snap-ring in the plate to allow it to drop around the rear bearing and press on the end of the mainshaft until it engages the groove in the rear bearing.

33   Install the reverse gear.

34   Install the speedometer gear, pressing it on to obtain a dimension of 4 7/8 inch from the forward side of the gear to the flat surface of the rear bearing retainer.

35   Install the tubular spacer in the counter gear.

36   Using heavy grease to retain the rollers, install one spacer, 28 rollers, one spacer, 28 rollers and one more spacer in each end of the counter gear.

37   Insert the shaft into the counter gear.

38   Lay the transmission case on its side with the cover opening towards you, the put the tanged washers in place, retaining them with grease.

39   Position the countergear, making sure that the thrust washers do not move, then position the transmission case so that it is resting on its front face.

40   Lubricate the countershaft with transmission oil and insert it in the rear of the case. Turn the countershaft so that the flat on the end is horizontal and facing the bottom of the case.

41   Align the countergear and shaft, and press in the shaft, ejecting the shaft out of the front of the case. Ensure that the thrust washers are still in place.

42   Check the overall countergear endplay using a dial indicator or similar tool. If in excess of 0.025 inch, new thrust washers must be used.

43   Install the cage and 17 rollers into the main drivegear - retaining them with heavy grease. Install the oil slinger on the main drivegear, concave side towards the gear.

44   Install the main drivegear and pilot bearing through the side cover opening and into position in the transmission front bore.

45   Position the gasket on the front face of the rear bearing retainer.

46   Install the 4th speed gear synchronizing ring on the main drivegear with the notches towards the rear of the transmission.

47   Position the reverse idler gear tanged thrust washer on the machined face of the

gear cast in the case for the reverse idler shaft, and retain with heavy grease. Position the front reverse idler gear next to the thrust washer, with the hub facing towards the rear of the case.

48   Slide the 3rd/4th synchronizing clutch sleeve forward into the fourth speed detent position, then lower the mainshaft assembly into the case. Ensure that the notches on the fourth speed synchronizing ring align with the keys in the clutch assembly.

49   Align the rear bearing retainer guide pin with the hole in the rear of the case then tap the retainer into place with a soft-faced hammer.

50   From the rear of the case, insert the rear reverse idler gear, engaging the splines with the portion of the front gear inside the case.

51   Use heavy grease to retain the gasket in position with the rear face of the bearing retainer.

52   Install the remaining flat thrust washer on the reverse idler shaft. If a new shaft is being used, drive out the old roll pin and press it into the new shaft.

53   Install the reverse idler shaft, roll pin and thrust washer into the gears and the front boss of the case, picking up the front thrust washer. The roll pin must be vertical.

54   Pull the reverse shifter shaft to the left side of the extension and rotate the shaft to bring the shift fork forwards to the reverse detent position. Move the extension onto the transmission case while slowly pushing in on the shifter shaft to engage the shift fork with the reverse gear shift collar. Now lead the reverse idler shaft into the extension housing, allowing the extension to slide onto the transmission case.

55   Install the six extension and retainer attaching bolts and tighten them to the torque listed in this Chapter's Specifications.

56   Move the reverse shifter shaft to align the shaft groove with the holes in the boss, then drive in the lock pin. Install the shifter lever.

57   With the snap-ring groove to the front, press the main drivegear bearing onto the shaft and into the case until at least three threads are exposed.

58   Lock the transmission in two gears at once, then install the main drivegear retaining nut and draw it up tight using the special spanner. With the bearing seating on the gear shoulder, tighten the nut to the torque listed in this Chapter's Specifications and lock it by staking in several places. Take care not to damage the shaft screw threads.

59   Install the bearing retainer, gasket, four attaching bolts and two lockstrips, using a suitable sealant on the screw threads. Tighten the bolts to the torque listed in this Chapter's Specifications.

60   Shift the mainshaft 3rd/4th sliding clutch sleeve into neutral and 1st/2nd sliding clutch sleeve forward into the second gear detent. Shift the side cover 3rd/4th shifter lever into the neutral detent and the first/second shifter lever into the 2nd speed gear detent.

61   Install the side cover gasket and care-

fully position the side cover to ensure proper alignment. Install the attaching bolts and tighten evenly to the torque listed in this Chapter's Specifications.

19   Warner four-speed transmission - overhaul

1   With the transmission removed from the car, clean away all external dirt.

2   Shift the transmission into second gear, remove the drain plug and drain the lubricant.

3   Unscrew and remove the side cover bolts, then withdraw the cover and gasket. Remove the shift forks.

4   From the front of the transmission, unbolt and remove the drive gear bearing retainer and gasket.

5   Remove the lock-pin from the reverse shifter lever boss, then pull the shift shaft partially out to disengage the reverse shifter fork from reverse gear.

6   Remove the rear extension housing bolts and tap the extension to the rear with a soft-face hammer, but only enough to start it moving.

7   Pull the extension until the reverse idler shaft clears the reverse idler gears. Rotate the extension to free the shift fork from the collar of reverse gear, and then withdraw the extension completely. Remove the gasket.

8   Extract the speedometer gear rear snap-ring, slide the speedometer gear from the mainshaft then extract the remaining snap-ring.

9   Slide the reverse gear from the mainshaft and then pull the reverse idler gear from the rear face of the transmission case.

10   Remove the snap-ring and spacer washer from the front bearing.

11   Using a suitable extractor, withdraw the front main drive gear bearing from the transmission case.

12   Remove the rear retainer lockbolt.

13   Move 1st/2nd and 3rd/4th synchronizer sleeves forward to provide enough clearance for removal of the mainshaft assembly.

14   Withdraw the mainshaft and rear bearing retainer from the transmission case.

15   Remove the front reverse idler gear and thrust washer from the case.

16   Using a dummy shaft or a special tool, drive the countershaft out of the transmission case, then remove the countergear and tanged thrust washers. Remove any needle bearings from the bottom of the case.

17   Unless a suitable press or extractors are available, disassembling the mainshaft should be left to a transmission shop. If suitable tools are available, proceed with the following.

18   Extract the snap-ring from the front of the 3rd/4th synchro unit. Slide the washer, synchro unit, synchro ring and 3rd speed gear from the mainshaft.

19   Expand the rear bearing retainer snap-ring and slide the retainer from the mainshaft.

20   Remove the snap-ring from the rear of

the mainshaft rear bearing.

21   Support the front face of 2nd speed gear and press the mainshaft out of the rear bearing, 1st speed gear and sleeve, 1st/2nd synchro unit and 2nd speed gear.

22   With all components removed, inspect for wear or damage, and renew as necessary.

23   The synchronizer units should be dismantled only after having marked their hub-to-sleeve relationship.

24   Replace the extension housing and drive gear bearing retainer oil seals, as a matter of routine, at major overhaul.

25   To replace the reverse shifter shaft O-ring oil seal, remove the shift fork and carefully drive the shifter shaft into the extension housing, allowing the detent ball to drop into the case. Remove the detent spring.

26   Remove the O-ring seal from the shaft.

27   When reassembling, place the detent spring into the hole and start the reverse shift shaft into its hole in the boss. Hold the ball down and push the shaft into position turning it until the ball drops into place in the detent on the shaft detent plate.

28   Fit a new O-ring and install the shift fork, but do not drive the shifter shaft lock pin into place until the extension housing has been installed.

29   Replacement of the reverse idler shaft can be accomplished if the welch plug and roll pin in the extension housing is first driven into the shaft, and the shaft then extracted.

30   Install the new idler shaft, drive in a new roll pin and finally tap in a new welch plug that has had sealant applied to it.

31   Overhaul of the transmission side cover assembly is covered in Section 11.

32   The countergear endplay should be checked as follows. Stick the thrust washers into the case using some thick grease.

33   Assemble the countergear rollers and spacers. Divide the rollers into four equal quantities, and then into each end of the countergear install rollers, spacer, rollers and spacer. Hold them in position using thick grease and insert the shaft. Install the assembly into position in the case without disturbing the thrust washers and insert the countershaft from the rear end of the case. The dummy shaft will be displaced. Make sure that the slot for the Woodruff key is correctly aligned but do not fit the key itself in case removal is required to change the thrust washers.

34   Using feeler gauges or a dial indicator, check the endplay of the countergear. If it exceeds 0.025-in. new thrust washers are required. If the endplay is correct, the countershaft and gear can remain undisturbed pending reassembly of the transmission.

35   Assemble the mainshaft by installing the 2nd speed gear to its rear end so that the boss on the gear faces the rear end of the mainshaft.

36   Install the 1st/2nd synchronizer unit with a synchro ring on both sides. Make sure that the taper is towards the rear of the mainshaft.

37   Locate the 1st speed gear sleeve on the mainshaft and press the sleeve onto the shaft until the 2nd speed gear, the synchro unit and the sleeve contact the shoulder on the mainshaft.

38   Install the first speed gear (boss towards the front).

39   Apply pressure to the inner race of the mainshaft rear bearing and press the bearing into position. Make sure that the snap-ring groove in the outer race is towards the front end of the shaft.

40   Install the spacer and the thickest snap-ring that will fit behind the rear bearing.

41   Install the 3rd speed gear (boss towards front of mainshaft) and the 3rd speed gear synchronizer ring (notches to front of mainshaft).

42   Install the 3rd/4th speed synchronizer unit (taper to front making sure that the keys in the hub correspond with the notches in the third speed ring.

43   Install the thickest possible snap-ring into the groove in front of the 3rd/4th synchronizer unit.

44   Install the rear bearing retainer over the end of the mainshaft. Expand the snap-ring to drop it round the rear bearing and into its groove.

45   Install reverse gear to the mainshaft so the shift collar is to the rear.

46   Install a snap-ring, the speedometer drive gear and the second snap-ring.

47   To reassemble the transmission, install the countergear and countershaft as described in Steps 32 and 33 (if not already done). Fit the Woodruff key.

48   Install the front reverse idler gear (teeth facing forward) and thrust washer into the transmission case.

49   Using heavy grease, install the sixteen roller bearings and washer into the main drive gear. Engage the main drive gear with the mainshaft assembly front end.

50   Push the 3rd/4th synchro sleeve forward.

51   Locate a new gasket for the rear bearing retainer on the rear of the transmission case and then carefully install the mainshaft/drive gear assembly into the transmission case.

52   Align the rear bearing retainer with the transmission case, install the locating pin and retainer lockbolt. Tighten to the torque listed in this Chapter's Specifications.

53   Locate a snap-ring around the outside of the front main bearing and then tap it into position in the front of the transmission case. Apply pressure to the inner race and make sure the snap-ring is nearer the front of the bearing.

54   Install a spacer and the thickest snap-ring from the thicknesses available to secure the bearing.

55   Install the front bearing retainer and gasket. Apply sealant to the bolt threads and tighten to the torque listed in this Chapter's Specifications.

56   Install the reverse idler gear up against the rear face of the transmission so that the splines engage with the reverse gear inside the transmission case.

57   Locate a new gasket on the rear bearing retainer.

58   Place the 1st/2nd and 3rd/4th synchro unit sleeves in Neutral. Pull the reverse shift shaft partially out of the extension housing and push the reverse shift fork as far forward as possible. Offer the extension housing to the mainshaft, at the same time pushing the shifter shaft in to engage reverse shift fork with reverse gear shift collar.

59   Place the 1st/2nd and 3rd/4th synchro unit sleeves in Neutral. Pull the reverse shift shaft partially out of the extension housing and push the reverse shift fork as far forward as possible. Offer the extension housing to the mainshaft, at the same time pushing the shifter shaft in to engage reverse shift fork with reverse gear shift collar.

60   When the fork engages, rotate the shifter shaft to move reverse gear rearward so the extension can butt against the transmission case.

61   Install the reverse shifter shaft lock pin.

62   Install the extension housing retaining bolts and the shorter rear bearing retainer bolts. It is vital that the bolt indicated in the illustration has sealer applied to its threads before installation. Tighten all bolts to the torque listed in this Chapter's Specifications.

63   Set the 1st/2nd speed synchro sleeve to the 2nd speed gear position and 3rd/4th to neutral.

64   Locate the forward shift forks in the sliding sleeves.

65   Set the 1st/2nd speed gear shifter shaft and detent plate on the transmission side cover in second gear position and install the side cover, using a new gasket to which sealer has been applied on both sides.

66   Check the gear selection. Refill the transmission with the proper lubricant (see Chapter 1) after it has been installed in the car.

Notes

Chapter 7 Part B
Automatic transmission

Contents

Specifications

Transmission fluid type and amount .... See Chapter 1

Transmission type and application

1968 through 1975	Turbo Hydra-Matic 400
1976	Turbo Hydra-Matic 350 or 400
1977	CBC350 or Turbo Hydra-Matic 400
1978 and 1979	Turbo Hydra-Matic 350
1980	
Federal	Turbo Hydra-Matic 350
California	Turbo Hydra-Matic 350 with lock-up converter
1981	Turbo Hydra-Matic 350 with lock-up converter
1982	700-R4 with lock-up converter

Torque specifications

	Ft-lbs (unless otherwise indicated)
Transmission case-to-engine bolts (all models)	40
1968 through 1977 models	
Extension housing bolts	25
Torque converter-to-driveplate bolts	32
1978 through 1980 models	
Extension housing bolts	25
Torque converter-to-driveplate bolts	35
1981	
Extension housing-to-case	35
Torque converter-to-flywheel	35
1982	
Extension housing-to-case	23
Torque converter-to-flexplate	37

1   General information

All the optional automatic transmissions installed in the 1968 through 1981 Corvettes are basically the same Turbo-Hydramatic 350 or 400 transmission. The 1980 Corvettes sold in California and all 1981 models were equipped with a Torque Converter Clutch (TCC), which provided a direct drive mechanical coupling between the engine and transmission. The torque converter clutch actually functions as a part of the C-4 system, and it is therefore recommended that diagnosis and repair be left to a dealer service department. For 1982 a completely new 4-speed automatic transmission, designated the 700-R4, was installed as standard equipment. It also was equipped with a torque converter clutch.

All information on the automatic transmission is included in this Part of Chapter 7. Information on the manual transmission can be found in Part A of this Chapter.

Due to the complexity of the automatic transmissions covered in this manual and the need for specialized equipment to perform most service operations, this Chapter contains only general diagnosis, routine maintenance, adjustment and removal and installation procedures.

If the transmission requires major repair work, it should be left to a dealer service department or an automotive or transmission repair shop. You can, however, remove and install the transmission yourself and save the expense, even if the repair work is done by a transmission shop.

2   Diagnosis - general

Note: *Automatic transmission malfunctions may be caused by five general conditions: poor engine performance, improper adjustments, hydraulic malfunctions, mechanical malfunctions or malfunctions in the computer or its signal network. Diagnosis of these problems should always begin with a check of the easily repaired items: fluid level and condition (see Chapter 1), shift linkage adjustment and throttle linkage adjustment. Next, perform a road test to determine if the problem has been corrected or if more diagnosis is necessary. If the problem persists after the preliminary tests and corrections are completed, additional diagnosis should be done by a dealer service department or transmission repair shop. Refer to the Troubleshooting Section at the front of this manual for information on symptoms of transmission problems.*

Preliminary checks

1   Drive the vehicle to warm the transmission to normal operating temperature.
2   Check the fluid level as described in Chapter 1:

a) *If the fluid level is unusually low, add enough fluid to bring the level within the designated area of the dipstick, then check for external leaks (see below).*
b) *If the fluid level is abnormally high, drain off the excess, then check the drained fluid for contamination by coolant. The presence of engine coolant in the automatic transmission fluid indicates that a failure has occurred in the internal radiator walls that separate the coolant from the transmission fluid (see Chapter 3).*
c) *If the fluid is foaming, drain it and refill the transmission, then check for coolant in the fluid or a high fluid level.*

3   Check the engine idle speed. **Note:** *If the engine is malfunctioning, do not proceed with the preliminary checks until it has been repaired and runs normally.*
4   On 1982 models, check the throttle valve cable for freedom of movement. Adjust it if necessary (see Section 7). **Note:** *The throttle cable may function properly when the engine is shut off and cold, but it may malfunction once the engine is hot. Check it cold and at normal engine operating temperature.*
5   Inspect the shift control linkage (see Section 3). Make sure that it's properly adjusted and that the linkage operates smoothly.

Fluid leak diagnosis

6   Most fluid leaks are easy to locate visually. Repair usually consists of replacing a seal or gasket. If a leak is difficult to find, the following procedure may help.
7   Identify the fluid. Make sure it's transmission fluid and not engine oil or brake fluid (automatic transmission fluid is a deep red color).
8   Try to pinpoint the source of the leak. Drive the vehicle several miles, then park it over a large sheet of cardboard. After a minute or two, you should be able to locate the leak by determining the source of the fluid dripping onto the cardboard.
9   Make a careful visual inspection of the suspected component and the area immediately around it. Pay particular attention to gasket mating surfaces. A mirror is often helpful for finding leaks in areas that are hard to see.
10   If the leak still cannot be found, clean the suspected area thoroughly with a degreaser or solvent, then dry it.
11   Drive the vehicle for several miles at normal operating temperature and varying speeds. After driving the vehicle, visually inspect the suspected component again.
12   Once the leak has been located, the cause must be determined before it can be properly repaired. If a gasket is replaced but the sealing flange is bent, the new gasket will not stop the leak. The bent flange must be straightened.
13   Before attempting to repair a leak, check to make sure that the following conditions are corrected or they may cause another leak.
Note: *Some of the following conditions cannot be fixed without highly specialized tools*

and expertise. Such problems must be referred to a transmission repair shop or a dealer service department.

Gasket leaks

14   Check the pan periodically. Make sure the bolts are tight, no bolts are missing, the gasket is in good condition and the pan is flat (dents in the pan may indicate damage to the valve body inside).
15   If the pan gasket is leaking, the fluid level or the fluid pressure may be too high, the vent may be plugged, the pan bolts may be too tight, the pan sealing flange may be warped, the sealing surface of the transmission housing may be damaged, the gasket may be damaged or the transmission casting may be cracked or porous. If sealant instead of gasket material has been used to form a seal between the pan and the transmission housing, it may be the wrong sealant.

Seal leaks

16   If a transmission seal is leaking, the fluid level or pressure may be too high, the vent may be plugged, the seal bore may be damaged, the seal itself may be damaged or improperly installed, the surface of the shaft protruding through the seal may be damaged or a loose bearing may be causing excessive shaft movement.
17   Make sure the dipstick tube seal is in good condition and the tube is properly seated. Periodically check the area around the speedometer gear or sensor for leakage. If transmission fluid is evident, check the O-ring for damage.

Case leaks

18   If the case itself appears to be leaking, the casting is porous and will have to be repaired or replaced.
19   Make sure the oil cooler hose fittings are tight and in good condition.

Fluid comes out vent pipe or fill tube

20   If this condition occurs, the transmission is overfilled, there is coolant in the fluid, the case is porous, the dipstick is incorrect, the vent is plugged or the drain back holes are plugged.

3   Shift linkage - adjustment

1968 through 1972 Turbo 400 models and 1976 and 1977 Turbo 350 models

1   Disconnect the operating cable from the transmission control lever.
2   Position the floor shift selector lever in Drive.
3   Position the control lever on the side of the transmission case in the Drive detent. This is the third detent from the fully forward position of the lever.
4   The forward end of the cable should

now be connected to the transmission lever, and the cable to support bracket securing clip inserted. If there is any tendency for the cable to deflect the transmission lever when the clip is inserted, move the cable or support bracket as necessary after releasing the bracket screws.

1973 through 1982 Turbo 400 models

5   If the floor shift cable is correctly adjusted, with the ignition key in Run, and the transmission in Reverse, the key can't be removed, but the steering wheel is unlocked.

6   With the ignition key in Lock and the transmission in Park, the key can be removed but the steering wheel is locked.

7   If adjustment is needed, loosen nut (D) so that the pin moves in the slot of the transmission lever (C).

8   Remove the floor center console cover.

9   Move the transmission lever (C) counterclockwise to L1 and then clockwise five detent positions to Park.

10   Now set the shift lever to Park and insert a 0.040-in. spacer forward of the pawl. Tighten the nut securely.

11   Turn the ignition switch to Lock.

12   Extract the backdrive cable (B) cotter pin and washer at the lever (A) on the steering column, then disconnect the cable from the lever retaining pin.

13   Working inside the car, loosen the two nuts at the steering column to dash bracket.

14   Rotate the lock tube lever counterclockwise (viewed from front of column) to remove any freeplay.

15   Reposition the bracket until the cable eye passes freely over the retaining pin on the bracket. Hold the bracket steady and have an assistant tighten the bracket retaining nuts inside the car.

16   Install the cotter pin and washer to retain the cable to the lever retaining pin.

4   Detent switch - adjustment

Note: *This procedure applies only to models equipped with the Turbo 400 transmission.*

1968 through 1971 models

Refer to illustration 4.1

1   Use a 0.092-inch diameter pin inserted to a depth of 0.10-inch to align the holes in the driver and switch **(see illustration).**

2   Depress the accelerator lever to open the throttle fully.

3   Release the switch-to-bracket screws and slide the switch toward the lever until the driver contacts the lever.

4   Tighten the switch screws and extract the pin.

1972 through 1982 models

5   The detent switch, after being installed, should have its plunger fully depressed. This will pre-set the switch, after which it is self-adjusting.

5   Neutral safety switch - adjustment

1   The switch position should be adjusted after so the car will start with the shift lever in Neutral or Park, but not in other positions.

2   A certain amount of trial and error will be required. Make sure the rear wheels are blocked and the handbrake fully applied before starting work.

3   The neutral safety switch is located on the right side of the shift lever beneath the console. Two screws secure it to the bracket. Remove the console cover for access. To adjust the switch, place the shift lever in Neutral. Loosen the switch mounting bolts. Rotate the switch slightly and turn the ignition key to the Start position - if the engine cranks over, tighten the mounting bolts and move the shift lever to the Drive position. Turn the ignition key to the Start position again - the starter should not operate. If it does, loosen the mounting bolts and turn the switch until it doesn't.

4   Recheck the adjustment of the switch in Neutral (the engine should crank over) and in Reverse (the engine should not crank over). It may take a few tries to get the adjustment right.

5   After 1973 the switch incorporates contacts for the back-up lamps and the seat belt warning buzzer.

6   Detent downshift cable - adjustment

CBC 350 transmissions (some 1977 models only)

1   The downshift cable should be adjusted by removing the snap lock and then opening the carburetor to the full throttle position.

2   Hold the carburetor at full throttle and push the snap lock into place in a downward position until its upper edge is flush with the cable.

Turbo 350 transmissions - 1978 through 1981 models

3   The detent valve is actuated by the downshift detent cable, which is connected to the carburetor linkage. When the throttle is 1/2 open, the detent valve is actuated, causing a part throttle downshift at speeds below 50 mph. When the throttle is opened completely, the detent valve is actuated, causing the transmission to downshift. The 3-1 valve is actuated, causing the transmission to downshift. The 3-1 detent downshift occurs when vehicle speed is approximately 6 to 12 mph below the maximum throttle 1-2 upshift point. The 3-2 detent downshift occurs when vehicle speed is approximately 4 to 8 mph below the maximum throttle 2-3 upshift point.

4   After the cable has been installed on the transmission, install the cable fitting into the bracket on the engine. **Note:** *The slider must not ratchet through the fitting. If it does, depress and hold the metal lock tab and move the slider back (away from the carburetor lever) until it stops against the fitting, then release the lock tab.*

5   Connect the cable terminal to the carburetor lever, then open the throttle completely. The slider will position itself automatically. **Note:** *The lock tab must not be depressed as this adjustment is performed.*

6   Release the carburetor lever and allow the throttle to close.

7   Throttle Valve (TV) cable - adjustment (1982 models only)

Refer to illustration 7.4

1   The Throttle Valve (TV) cable used on the 1982 models combines the functions of the vacuum modulator and the downshift detent cable used on previous transmissions. If the cable is broken, sticking or misadjusted, the transmission will produce delayed, early, slipping or full-throttle shifts or no detent downshifts.

2   Before attempting to adjust the cable,

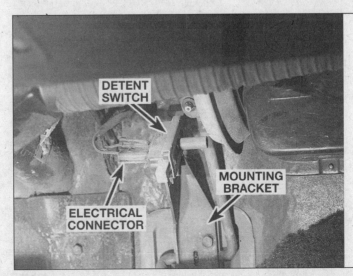

DETENT SWITCH

MOUNTING BRACKET

ELECTRICAL CONNECTOR

4.1 Typical detent switch location

check the transmission fluid level (correct as necessary) and make sure the engine and brakes are operating properly (the brakes must not be dragging). Also make sure the cable is connected at both ends. Check the cable for binding or sticking with the engine idling, the transmission in neutral and the parking brake set. Pull the cable through its full travel, then release it. It should return to the closed throttle position against the cable terminal.

3   To adjust the cable, stop the engine and depress the release tab on the cable fitting.

4   Move the slider back through the fitting (away from the throttle body) until it stops against the fitting, then release the release tab **(see illustration)**.

5   Open the throttle completely by moving the lever until it touches the stop, then release it; the cable will be adjusted automatically.

6   If a road test of the vehicle reveals that delayed or full throttle only shifts still occur, have the transmission checked by a dealer service department or a reputable transmission repair shop.

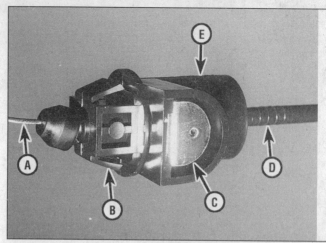

7.4 On 1982 models, adjust the TV cable by depressing the release tab, then pull the slider back until it rests on its stop - release the tab and open the throttle completely

A   TV cable
B   Locking lugs
C   Release tab
D   Cable casing
E   Slider

8   Oil seal - replacement

1   Oil leaks frequently occur due to wear of the extension housing oil seal and bushing (if equipped), and/or the speedometer drive gear oil seal and O-ring. Replacement of these seals is relatively easy, since the repairs can usually be performed without removing the transmission from the vehicle.

2   The extension housing oil seal is located at the extreme rear of the transmission, where the driveshaft is attached. If leakage at the seal is suspected, raise the vehicle and support it securely on jackstands. If the seal is leaking, transmission lubricant will be built up on the front of the driveshaft and may be dripping from the rear of the transmission.

3   Refer to Chapter 8 and remove the driveshaft.

4   Using a soft-face hammer, carefully tap the dust shield (if equipped) to the rear and remove it from the transmission. Be careful not to distort it.

5   Using a screwdriver or seal removal tool, carefully pry the oil seal and bushing (if equipped) out of the rear of the transmission. Do not damage the splines on the transmission output shaft.

6   If the oil seal and bushing cannot be removed with a screwdriver or pry bar, a special oil seal removal tool (available at auto parts stores) will be required.

7   Using a large section of pipe or a very large deep socket as a drift, install the new oil seal. Drive it into the bore squarely and make sure it's completely seated. Install a new bushing using the same method.

8   Reinstall the dust shield by carefully tapping it into place. Lubricate the splines of the transmission output shaft and the outside of

the driveshaft sleeve yoke with lightweight grease, then install the driveshaft. Be careful not to damage the lip of the new seal.

9   The speedometer cable and driven gear housing is located on the side of the extension housing. Look for transmission oil around the cable housing to determine if the seal and O-ring are leaking.

10   Disconnect the speedometer cable.

11   Using a hook, remove the seal.

12   Using a small socket as a drift, install the new seal.

13   Install a new O-ring in the driven gear housing and reinstall the driven gear housing and cable assembly on the extension housing.

9   Transmission - removal and installation

1   Disconnect the battery and then raise the car or place it over an inspection pit.

2   Remove the driveshaft (see Chapter 8).

3   Remove both exhaust systems from the car. If the car is fitted with a catalytic converter, remove it very carefully so as not to dent it.

4   On 1978 through 1981 models, disconnect the detent downshift cable from the carburetor lever and engine bracket.

5   On 1982 models only, remove the air cleaner assembly and disconnect the TV cable from the throttle lever. Remove the transmission fluid dipstick and the dipstick tube (it is held in place with one bolt).

6   Disconnect the speedometer cable from the transmission, the vacuum line at the modulator, the fluid cooler pipes and the detent downshift cable. Mark all the electrical connectors before disconnecting them from the switches on the transmission.

7   On 1982 models only, unhook the clips that attach the wiring harness to the transmission case.

8   Disconnect the shift control linkage from the transmission.

9   Support the transmission on a suitable jack, preferably one made for this purpose.

10   Disconnect the transmission rear mount from the crossmember.

11   Remove the crossmember. This will necessitate removing the two bolts from each end of the crossmember, the through bolts inside the frame and the parking brake pulley.

12   On 1982 models only, remove the splash shield and mark the driveplate and torque converter so they can be reassembled in the same relative position.

13   Remove the torque converter under pan.

14   Unscrew and remove the torque converter to driveplate bolts and/or nuts. The crankshaft will have to be turned to bring these into view through the underpan opening. Mark the relative position of the driveplate to the torque converter.

15   Lower the transmission carefully, making sure that the tachometer cable does not become damaged on the firewall. Unscrew and remove the bolts that hold the transmission to the engine. Remove the fluid filler tube.

16   Support the engine with a second jack and then withdraw the transmission to the rear and downward, at the same time turning it clockwise. Tip the front of the transmission downward and remove it from the car.

17   As the transmission is withdrawn, keep the torque converter pressed in place rearward. If it appears to be sticking to the driveplate, pry it carefully to the rear with a piece of wood before the transmission is completely removed.

18   Installation is a reversal of the removal steps, but tighten the converter-to-driveplate bolts by hand initially to prevent distortion of the converter, then to the torque listed in this Chapter's Specifications.

19   On 1982 models only, before installing the driveplate bolts, make certain the weld nuts on the converter are flush with the driveplate and the converter rotates freely in this position. Be sure to install a new seal on the dipstick tube before attaching it to the transmission.

20   Refill the transmission (see Chapter 1), then check the shift linkage and adjustment of other controls.

Chapter 8
Clutch and driveline

Contents

Specifications

Clutch
Clutch type .... Dry plate, diaphragm spring
Actuation .... Mechanical

Driveshaft type .... Open, single section, tubular steel with two universal joints and one slip joint

Rear axle
Driveaxle type .... Open, tubular steel with universal joint at inner and outer ends
Differential type
   Standard .... Hypoid rigid differential carrier driving through two open universally-jointed driveaxles
   Optional .... Eaton Positraction limited slip differential
Differential tolerances
   Ring gear to pinion backlash .... 0.005 to 0.008 in
   Pinion bearing preload (pinion shaft turning torque)
      New bearings .... 20 to 25 in-lbs
      Used bearings .... 5 to 10 in-lbs (+ new oil seal drag - see text)

Torque specifications

	Ft-lbs
Clutch pressure plate bolts	35
Flywheel housing-to-engine bolts	30
Driveshaft universal joint strap or U-bolts	15
Driveaxle universal joint strap or U-bolts	15
Driveaxle-to-wheel spindle flange	75
Driveaxle-to-differential side gear yoke	15
Camber cam bolt	
1968 through 1977	65
1978 through 1982	130
Differential carrier cover bolts	50
Filler plug	20
Transverse rear spring anchor plate bolts	70
Driveaxle-to-differential carrier	15
Driveshaft-to-pinion flange	15
Crossmember-to-differential carrier	60
Differential carrier front mount side bolts	50
Differential carrier front mount-to-crossmember bolt	65
Pinion nut (initial - see text)	100

1   General information

The information in this Chapter deals with the components from the rear of the engine to the rear wheels, except for the transmission, which is dealt with in the previous Chapter. For the purposes of this Chapter, these components are grouped into three categories: clutch, driveshaft and rear axle. Separate Sections within this Chapter offer general descriptions and checking procedures for components in each of the three groups.

Since nearly all the procedures covered in this Chapter involve working under the vehicle, make sure it's securely supported on sturdy jackstands or on a hoist where the vehicle can be easily raised and lowered.

2   Clutch - description and check

Refer to illustration 2.1

1   All vehicles with a manual transmission use a dry plate, diaphragm-spring type clutch **(see illustration)**. The standard clutch is of the single dry plate type, but in 1969 and 1970 models a dual plate clutch was optionally available on the larger capacity high performance engines. The clutch disc has a splined hub which allows it to slide along the splines of the transmission input shaft. The clutch and pressure plate are held in contact by spring pressure exerted by the diaphragm in the pressure plate.

2   The clutch release system is a mechanical type. The mechanical release system includes the clutch pedal with adjuster mechanism, the clutch linkage that actuates the clutch release lever and the release bearing.

3   When pressure is applied to the clutch pedal to release the clutch, mechanical pressure is exerted against the outer end of the clutch release lever. As the lever pivots, the shaft fingers push against the release bearing. The bearing pushes against the fingers of the diaphragm spring of the pressure plate

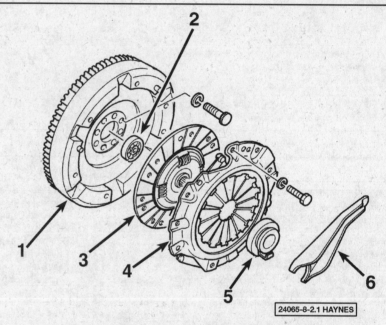

2.1 Exploded view of the clutch components

1	Flywheel	5	Clutch release bearing (throwout bearing)
2	Pilot bearing or bushing		
3	Clutch disc	6	Clutch release lever
4	Clutch cover (pressure plate)		

assembly, which in turn releases the clutch plate.

4   Terminology can be a problem when discussing the clutch components because common names are in some cases different from those used by the manufacturer. For example, the driven plate is also called the clutch plate or disc, while the clutch release bearing is sometimes called a throwout bearing.

5   Other than to replace components with obvious damage, some preliminary checks should be performed to diagnose clutch problems.

a) *To check "clutch spin down time," run the engine at normal idle speed with the transmission in Neutral (clutch pedal up - engaged). Disengage the clutch (pedal down), wait several seconds and shift the transmission into Reverse. No grinding noise should be heard. A grinding noise would most likely indicate a problem in the pressure plate or the clutch disc.*

b) *To check for complete clutch release, run the engine (with the parking brake applied to prevent movement) and hold the clutch pedal approximately 1/2-inch from the floor. Shift the transmission between 1st gear and Reverse several times. If the shift is hard or the transmission grinds, component failure is indicated.*

3.8 After removal of the transmission and bellhousing, this will be the view of the clutch components

| 1 | Pressure plate | 2 | Flywheel |

3.9a Principal clutch components

| 1 | Flywheel | 3 | Clutch cover (or pressure |
| 2 | Clutch disc | | plate) |

c) *Visually inspect the pivot bushing at the top of the clutch pedal to make sure there is no binding or excessive play.*

d) *A clutch pedal that is difficult to operate is most likely caused by faulty clutch linkage, which should be replaced.*

e) *Crawl under the vehicle and make sure the clutch release lever is solidly mounted on the ball stud.*

3 Clutch components - removal, inspection and installation

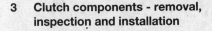

3.9b Components of the clutch driven plate

1 **Lining** - *this will wear down with use*
2 **Rivets** - *these secure the lining and will damage the flywheel or pressure plate if allowed to contact the surfaces*
3 **Markings** - *"flywheel side" or something similar*

Warning: *Dust produced by clutch wear and deposited on clutch components may contain asbestos, which is hazardous to your health. DO NOT blow it out with compressed air and DO NOT inhale it. DO NOT use gasoline or petroleum-based solvents to remove the dust. Brake system cleaner should be used to flush the dust into a drain pan. After the clutch components are wiped clean with a rag, dispose of the contaminated rags and cleaner in a covered, marked container.*

Removal

Refer to illustration 3.8

1   Access to the clutch components is normally accomplished by removing the transmission, leaving the engine in the vehicle. If the engine is being removed for major overhaul, then check the clutch for wear and replace worn components as necessary. However, the relatively low cost of the clutch components compared to the time and trouble spent gaining access to them warrants their replacement anytime the engine or transmission is removed, unless they are new or in near perfect condition. The following procedures are based on the assumption the engine will stay in place.

2   Referring to Chapter 7 Part A, remove the transmission from the vehicle. Support the engine while the transmission is out. Prefer-

ably, an engine hoist should be used to support it from above. However, if a jack is used underneath the engine, make sure a piece of wood is positioned between the jack and oil pan to spread the load. **Caution:** *The pickup for the oil pump is very close to the bottom of the oil pan. If the pan is bent or distorted in any way, engine oil starvation could occur.*

3   Disconnect the clutch fork pushrod and spring.

4   Remove the bellhousing-to-engine bolts and then detach the housing. It may have to be gently pried off the alignment dowels with a screwdriver or pry bar.

5   Remove the clutch fork and release bearing.

6   To support the clutch disc during removal, install a clutch alignment tool through the clutch disc hub.

7   Carefully inspect the flywheel and pressure plate for indexing marks. The marks are usually an X, an O or a white letter. If they cannot be found, scribe your own marks so the pressure plate and the flywheel will be in the same alignment during installation.

8   Turning each bolt only 1/4-turn at a

time, loosen the pressure plate-to-flywheel bolts. Work in a criss-cross pattern until all spring pressure is relieved. Then hold the pressure plate securely and completely remove the bolts, followed by the pressure plate and clutch disc **(see illustration)**.

Inspection

Refer to illustrations 3.9a, 3.9b and 3.14

9   Ordinarily, when a problem occurs in the clutch, it can be attributed to wear of the clutch driven plate assembly (clutch disc) **(see illustrations)**. However, all components should be inspected at this time.

10   Inspect the flywheel for cracks, heat checking, grooves and other obvious defects. If the imperfections are slight, a machine shop can machine the surface flat and smooth, which is highly recommended regardless of the surface appearance. Refer to Chapter 2 for the flywheel removal and installation procedure.

11   Inspect the pilot bearing (see Section 4).

12   Inspect the lining on the clutch disc. There should be at least 1/16 inch of lining above the rivet heads. Check for loose rivets,

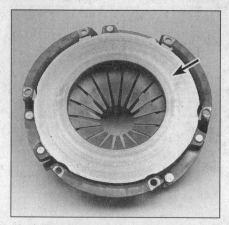

3.14 The machined face of the pressure plate must be inspected for score marks and other damage

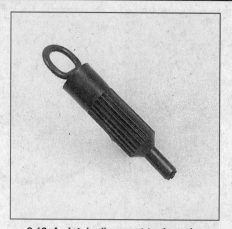

3.16 A clutch alignment tool can be purchased at most auto parts stores and eliminates the guesswork when centering the clutch disc in the pressure plate

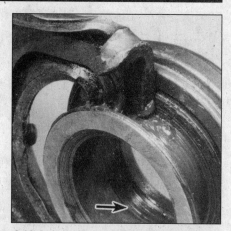

3.19 Lubricate the clutch release bearing recess (arrow) and the fork groove with high-temperature grease - note how the release fork engages the release bearing

3.20a Rear view of clutch fork and throwout bearing

3.20b Clutch fork and throwout bearing installed

distortion, cracks, broken springs and other obvious damage. As mentioned above, ordinarily the clutch disc is routinely replaced, so if you're in doubt about the condition, replace it with a new one.

13   The release bearing should also be replaced along with the clutch disc.

14   Check the machined surfaces and the diaphragm spring fingers of the pressure plate. If the surface is grooved or otherwise damaged, replace the pressure plate **(see illustration)**. Also check for obvious damage, distortion, cracking, etc. Light glazing can be removed with medium grit emery cloth. If a new pressure plate is required, new and factory-rebuilt units are available.

Installation

Refer to illustrations 3.16, 3.19, 3.20a and 3.20b

15   Before installation, clean the flywheel and pressure plate machined surfaces with lacquer thinner or acetone. It's important that no oil or grease is on these surfaces or the lining of the clutch disc. Handle the parts only with clean hands.

16   Position the clutch disc and pressure plate against the flywheel with the clutch held in place with an alignment tool **(see illustration)**. Make sure it's installed properly (most replacement clutch plates will be marked "flywheel side" or something similar - if not marked, install the clutch disc with the damper springs toward the transmission).

17   Tighten the pressure plate-to-flywheel bolts only finger tight, working around the pressure plate.

18   Center the clutch disc by ensuring the alignment tool extends through the splined hub and into the pilot bearing in the crankshaft. Wiggle the tool up, down or side-to-side as needed to bottom the tool in the pilot bearing. Tighten the pressure plate-to-flywheel bolts a little at a time, working in a criss-cross pattern to prevent distorting the cover. After all of the bolts are snug, tighten them to the torque listed in this Chapter's Specifications. Remove the alignment tool.

19   Using high-temperature grease, lubricate the inner groove of the release bearing **(see illustration)**. Also place grease on the release lever contact areas and the transmis-

sion input shaft bearing retainer. Lubricate the clutch fork fingers at the release bearing, and the ball and socket, with high melting point grease.

20   Install the clutch fork and dust boot into the clutch housing and install the release bearing **(see illustrations)**.

21   Install the bellhousing and tighten the bolts to the torque listed in this Chapter's Specifications.

22   Install the transmission, slave cylinder and all components removed previously. Tighten all fasteners to the torque listed in this Chapter's Specifications.

4   Pilot bushing - inspection and replacement

Refer to illustration 4.9

1   The clutch pilot bushing is pressed into the rear of the crankshaft. Its primary purpose is to support the front of the transmission input shaft. The pilot bushing should be inspected whenever the clutch components are removed

4.9 Pack the recess behind the pilot bearing with heavy grease and force it out hydraulically with a steel rod slightly smaller in diameter than the bore in the bearing - when the hammer strikes the rod, the bearing will be forced out

5.1 Front face of transmission showing clutch fork ball stud (arrow)

6.1a Clutch operating cross shaft (arrow)

6.1b Disconnect the clutch linkage and tension spring

from the engine. Due to its inaccessibility, if you are in doubt as to its condition, replace it with a new one. **Note:** *If the engine has been removed from the vehicle, disregard the following steps that do not apply.*

2   Remove the transmission (refer to Chapter 7 Part A).

3   Remove the clutch components (see Section 3).

4   Inspect for any excessive wear, scoring, or obvious damage. If any of these conditions are noted, the bushing should be replaced. A flashlight will be helpful to direct light into the recess.

5   Removal can be accomplished with a special puller and slide hammer, but an alternative method also works very well.

6   Find a solid steel bar that is slightly smaller in diameter than the bushing. Alternatives to a solid bar would be a wood dowel or a socket with a bolt fixed in place to make it solid.

7   Check the bar for fit - it should just slip into the bushing with very little clearance.

8   Pack the bushing and the area behind it (in the crankshaft recess) with heavy grease. Pack it tightly to eliminate as much air as possible.

9   Insert the bar into the bearing bore and strike the bar sharply with a hammer which will force the grease to the back side of the bushing and push it out **(see illustration)**. Remove the bushing and clean all grease from the crankshaft recess.

10   To install the new bushing, lightly lubricate the outside surface with oil, then drive it into the recess with a soft-face hammer (the radius in the bore in the bushing must face out). Select a socket that is slightly smaller than the outside diameter of the bushing.

11   Install the clutch components, transmission and all other components removed previously, tightening all fasteners properly.

5   Clutch fork ball stud - replacement

Refer to illustration 5.1

1   If necessary, the clutch fork ball stud can be removed from the clutch housing by unscrewing it **(see illustration)**.

2   It should be noted that the L48 and L82 engines use distinctly different ball studs. Be sure to use the correct part if replacement is necessary.

6   Clutch linkage cross-shaft - removal and installation

Refer to illustrations 6.1a, 6.1b and 6.1c

1   Disconnect the springs and rods from the levers on the cross-shaft **(see illustrations)**.

6.1c Disconnect the clutch linkage and return spring

2 Unscrew the outer ball stud nut and slide the stud out of the bracket slot.

3 Move the cross-shaft out, to clear the inner ball stud, then lift the shaft from the car.

4 Inspect and replace components as necessary.

5 Installation is a reversal of removal, but apply some graphite grease to the ball studs before reassembly.

7 Clutch start switch - replacement

1 Disconnect the negative cable at the battery.

2 At the top of the clutch pedal is a small rod that passes through the pedal. Remove the clip and washer from the end of this rod.

3 Remove the bolt that secures the clutch start switch to the clutch pedal support bracket.

4 Disconnect the electrical lead to the switch and remove the switch.

5 Install a new switch in the reverse order of removal. Check to be sure the vehicle can be started only when the clutch pedal is fully depressed.

8 Clutch pedal (1968 and 1969) - removal and installation

1 Disconnect the clutch pedal return spring.

2 Disconnect the clutch pushrod from the pedal.

3 Disconnect the brake return spring.

4 Disconnect the brake master cylinder pushrod from the brake pedal.

5 Remove the steering column (see Chapter 10).

6 Working inside the engine compartment, support the brake master cylinder and remove the four nuts from the support brace.

7 Remove the four nuts and bolts that secure the support plate to the bracket, then remove the support plate.

8 Remove the two screws that secure the bracket to the underside of the instrument panel, then lower the bracket and the pedals to the floor.

9 Remove the retainer from the right-hand side of the pedal pivot shaft and slide the clutch pedal to the left, removing it from the support brace.

10 Replace any worn components. Nylon bushings should not be cleaned in solvent, but just wiped clean with a rag.

11 Installation is the reverse of removal. Grease the bushings before installation and adjust the free movement when installation is complete.

9 Clutch pedal (1970 through 1982) - removal and installation

1 Disconnect the battery.

2 Remove the steering column (see Chapter 10).

3 Remove the instrument cluster (see Chapter 12).

4 Disconnect the clutch and brake pushrods from the pedals.

5 Working inside the engine compartment, support the brake master cylinder and then remove the four nuts from the support brace.

6 Remove the wiper cover grille so the brake bracket bolts can be unscrewed.

7 Remove the dash brace, then the brake and clutch pedal bracket. Withdraw it slightly, then disconnect the brake switch and neutral start switch.

8 Remove the retainer from the right-hand side of the pedal pivot shaft and remove the pedal from the shaft.

9 Inspect all components and replace any that are worn.

10 Installation is the reversal of removal. Adjust pedal freeplay (see Chapter 1) on completion.

10 Driveshaft and universal joints - description and check

1 The driveshaft is a tube running between the transmission and the rear end. Universal joints are located at either end of the drive-shaft and permit power to be transmitted to the rear wheels to allow for slight amounts of engine and transmission movement during normal operation modes.

2 The driveshaft features a splined yoke at the front, which slips into the extension housing of the transmission. This arrangement allows the driveshaft to slide back-and-forth within the transmission as the vehicle is in operation.

3 An oil seal is used to prevent leakage of fluid at this point and to keep dirt and contaminants from entering the transmission. If leakage is evident at the front of the drive-shaft, replace the oil seal referring to the procedures in Chapter 7A or Chapter 7B.

4 The driveshaft assembly requires very little service. The universal joints are lubricated for life and must be replaced if problems develop. The driveshaft must be removed from the vehicle for this procedure. **Note:** *Many replacement U-joints are fitted with fittings for lubrication.*

5 Since the driveshaft is a balanced unit, it's important that no undercoating, mud, etc. be allowed to stay on it. When the vehicle is raised for service it's a good idea to clean the driveshaft and inspect it for any obvious damage. Also check that the small weights used to originally balance the driveshaft are in place and securely attached. Whenever the driveshaft is removed it's important that it be reinstalled in the same relative position to preserve the balance.

6 Problems with the driveshaft are usually indicated by noise or vibration while driving the vehicle. A road test should verify if the problem is the driveshaft or another vehicle component:

a) *On an open road, free of traffic, drive the*

vehicle and note the engine speed (rpm) at which the problem is most evident.

b) *With this noted, drive the vehicle again, this time manually keeping the transmission in 1st, then 2nd, then 3rd gear ranges and running the engine up to the engine speed noted.*

c) *If the noise or vibration occurs at the same engine speed regardless of which gear the transmission is in, the driveshaft is not at fault because the speed of the driveshaft varies in each gear.*

d) *If the noise or vibration decreased or was eliminated, visually inspect the driveshaft for damage, material on the shaft that would effect balance, missing weights and damaged universal joints. Another possibility for this condition would be tires that are out-of-balance.*

7 To check for worn universal joints:

a) *On an open road, free of traffic, drive the vehicle slowly until the transmission is in High gear. Let off on the accelerator, allowing the vehicle to coast, then accelerate. A clunking or knocking noise will indicate worn universal joint(s).*

b) *Drive the vehicle at a speed of about 10 to 15 mph and then place the transmission in Neutral, allowing the vehicle to coast. Listen for abnormal driveline noises.*

c) *Raise the vehicle and support it securely on jackstands. With the transmission in Neutral, manually turn the driveshaft, watching the universal joints for excessive play.*

11 Driveshaft - removal and installation

Refer to illustration 11.4

Removal

1 Disconnect the negative cable from the battery.

2 Raise the vehicle and support it securely on jackstands. Place the transmission in Neutral with the parking brake off.

3 Using a scribe, white paint or a hammer and punch, place marks on the driveshaft and the differential flange in line with each other. This is to make sure the driveshaft is reinstalled in the same position to preserve the balance.

4 Remove the rear universal joint bolts and straps. Turn the driveshaft (or rear wheels) as necessary to bring the bolts into the most accessible position **(see illustration)**.

5 Tape the bearing caps to the spider to prevent the caps from coming off during removal.

6 Lower the rear of the driveshaft and then slide the front out of the transmission.

7 To prevent loss of fluid and protect against contamination while the driveshaft is out, wrap a plastic bag over the transmission housing and hold it in place with a rubber band.

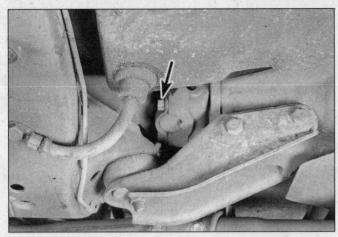

11.4 Rear universal joint straps and bolts (arrow)

12.4a To remove the U-joint from the driveshaft, use a vise as a press - the small socket will push the cross and bearing cup into the larger socket

12.4b Grip the old bearing cap with locking pliers and remove it from the yoke

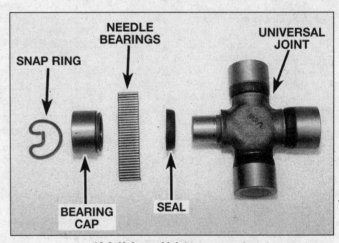

12.6 Universal joint components

Installation

8   Remove the plastic bag from the transmission and wipe the area clean. Inspect the oil seal carefully. Procedures for replacement of this seal can be found in Chapter 7A or Chapter 7B.

9   Slide the front of the driveshaft into the transmission.

10   Raise the rear of the driveshaft into position, checking to be sure the marks are in alignment. If not, turn the rear wheels to match the pinion flange and the driveshaft.

11   Remove the tape securing the bearing caps and install the straps and bolts. Tighten the bolts to the torque listed in this Chapter's Specifications.

12   Driveshaft U-joint - replacement

Refer to illustrations 12.4a, 12.4b, 12.6 and 12.8
Note: *A press or large vise will be required for this procedure. It may be a good idea to take the driveshaft to a repair or machine shop where the universal joints can be replaced for you, normally at a reasonable charge*.

1   Remove the driveshaft as outlined in the previous Section.

2   Using a small pair of pliers, remove the snap-rings from the spider.

3   Supporting the driveshaft, place it in position on either an arbor press or on a workbench equipped with a vise.

4   Place a piece of pipe or a large socket with the same inside diameter over one of the bearing caps. Position a socket which is of slightly smaller diameter than the cap on the opposite bearing cap and use the vise or press to force the cap out (inside the pipe or large socket), stopping just before it comes completely out of the yoke. Use the vise or large pliers to work the cap the rest of the way out **(see illustrations)**.

5   Transfer the sockets to the other side and press the opposite bearing cap out in the same manner.

6   Pack the new universal joint bearings with grease **(see illustration)**. Ordinarily, specific instructions for lubrication will be included with the universal joint servicing kit and should be followed carefully.

7   Position the spider in the yoke and par-

tially install one bearing cap in the yoke. If the replacement spider is equipped with a grease fitting, be sure it's offset in the proper direction (toward the driveshaft).

8   Start the spider into the bearing cap and then partially install the other cap. Align the spider and press the bearing caps into posi-

12.8 Installing bearing cups to trunnion

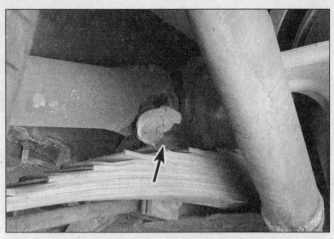

13.1 Each driveaxle is bolted to the differential (arrow), and at the rear spindle flange

15.7 Loosen the rear spring to differential cover bolts (arrows)

tion, being careful not to damage the dust seals **(see illustration)**.

9   Install the snap-rings. If difficulty is encountered in seating the snap-rings, strike the driveshaft yoke sharply with a hammer. This will spring the yoke ears slightly and allow the snap-rings to seat in the groove.

10   If so equipped, install the grease fitting (if equipped) and fill the joint with grease. Be careful not to overfill the joint, as this could blow out the grease seals.

11   Install the driveshaft. Tighten the flange bolts to the torque listed in this Chapter's Specifications.

13   Driveaxles - removal and installation

Refer to illustration 13.1

1   Disconnect the inner end of the driveaxle by unbolting it from the differential side gear yoke **(see illustration)**.

2   Bend down the four locking tabs and remove the four bolts which secure the outer shaft flange to the spindle drive flange.

3   Scribe marks on the camber adjusting cam (see Chapter 10) and the mounting bracket for subsequent alignment on reassembly.

4   Loosen the camber adjusting nut and rotate the cam so that the high point of the cam points in. This will push the control arm out to provide some clearance between the wheel spindle and the driveshaft.

5   Pry the driveaxle out of the outer drive flange, then remove the driveaxle by withdrawing the outer end first.

6   To install a driveaxle, first insert the inner U-joint into the side gear yokes and install the U-bolts.

7   Be sure that the carrier side yoke trunnion seats are at 90-degrees to each other on opposite sides of the differential.

8   Install the outer drive flange into the spindle flange pilot, install the lock plates, tighten the four bolts to the torque listed in this Chapter's Specifications and then bend

the lock plate tabs to secure the bolts.

9   Align the cam scribe marks on the cam, made before the shaft was removed, and tighten the bolts to the torque listed in this Chapter's Specifications.

14   Driveaxle U-joints - replacement

1   The operations for the dismantling, repair and reassembly of the driveaxle universal joints are very similar to those described in Section 12 of this Chapter for driveshaft U-joints.

2   Pack the bearings before reassembly with high melting point grease and make sure that the lubricant reservoir at the end of each trunnion is completely filled. Fill the reservoirs from the bottom to prevent air pockets in the grease.

3   Make sure that the new dust seals are fitted to the trunnion, with the seal cavity towards the end of the trunnion. Make sure that the seal is pressed into its recess with a piece of tubing.

15   Differential carrier - removal and installation

Refer to illustration 15.7

Note: *On 1980 through 1982 models, if problems occur in the differential,*
it is recommended that repairs be left to a dealer service department or a competent repair shop. However, the differential can be removed, delivered for repair and reinstalled by performing the following procedure.

1   Raise and support the rear of the car.

2   If necessary, the rear mufflers can be disconnected from their mountings and moved aside carefully to provide better access to the carrier.

3   Disconnect the driveaxles from the differential yokes (see Section 13).

4   Disconnect the bolt from the differential carrier front mounting bracket.

5   Remove the driveshaft (see Section 11).

6   Disconnect the strut rod bracket from the underside of the differential carrier and then lower the bracket with the strut rods attached.

7   Loosen the four bolts connecting the rear spring to the differential cover **(see illustration)**.

8   Unscrew and remove the eight carrier-to-cover bolts and let the oil drain from the carrier. If the two lower cover bolts remain trapped by the rear spring, this will not prevent removal of the carrier.

9   Set the driveshaft yokes to provide the best arrangement for removal of the carrier.

10   Pull the carrier forward partially out of its cover. Let the cover stay in the vehicle. Lower the front of the carrier to clear the crossmember and then withdraw it completely from the car.

11   To facilitate installation of the carrier, it is recommended that two suitable bolts are screwed into two of the "below center" holes in the cover mating flange. Before screwing in the bolts, cut off their heads and cut a screwdriver slot in their plain ends. The bolts, which will then act as aligning pins, can be unscrewed and removed at a later stage.

12   Make up another aligning pin and screw it into the lower face of the differential carrier to act as a guide for installing the strut rod bracket.

13   Locate a new gasket (with sealant on both sides) to the mating flange of the carrier.

14   Lift the carrier into position and install six cover-to-carrier bolts. Unscrew the two guide pin studs and screw in the remaining two bolts. Tighten to the torque listed in this Chapter's Specifications.

15   Install the strut rod bracket and remove the temporary guide pin.

16   Reconnect the front mounting bracket.

17   Tighten the four rear spring-to-cover bolts to the torque listed in this Chapter's Specifications.

18   Install the driveshaft (see Section 11).

19   Install the driveaxles (see Section 13).

20   Reconnect the rear mufflers and then lower the car to the ground.

17.4 Mark the relative positions of the pinion, nut and flange before removing the nut

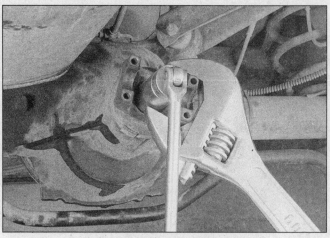

17.5 Unscrewing pinion flange nut

16   Differential cover/suspension crossmember - removal and installation

1   Raise the rear of the car and support the frame and suspension separately on jackstands.
2   On 1980 through 1982 models, remove the spare tire and cover (by removing the support hooks attached to the differential carrier cover). Remove the heat shield and the rear sections of the exhaust system.
3   Remove the transverse rear spring as described in Chapter 10.
4   On 1980 through 1982 models, mark the camber adjusting bolts, then remove the strut bracket. Remove the strut-to-carrier bolts, then lower the strut rods.
5   On 1980 through 1982 models, mark the driveshaft and differential companion flange, then disconnect the driveshaft from the differential. Support it on a jackstand or tie it up out of the way, then remove the front carrier mount bolt.
6   On 1980 through 1982 models, support the carrier on a jack or jackstand, then remove the carrier crossmember-to-frame bolts. The differential must be lowered slightly to gain access to all of the cover bolts. Loosen the cover bolts and allow the lubricant to drain into a suitable container, then remove the bolts and lift the cover/crossmember away from the differential assembly.
7   Remove the differential carrier (see Section 15).
8   Support the crossmember, unscrew and remove the crossmember insulating mount bolts from the frame.
9   Lower the crossmember complete with differential cover.
10   The cover can be unbolted from the crossmember if required.
11   The flexible mounts can be renewed if necessary by first bending back the lock tabs and then pressing out the mounts using a

piece of tubing.
12   When installing the mounts remember to bend over the lock tabs once they are fully seated.
13   Installation of the crossmember and cover is the reverse of removal. Tighten bolts to the torque listed in this Chapter's Specifications.
14   On 1980 through 1982 models, be sure to use a new cover gasket and an appropriate sealant when the cover is installed. Also the gasket surfaces must be cleaned thoroughly and the bolts tightened (in a criss-cross pattern) to the torque listed in this Chapter's Specifications.
15   Install the differential carrier (see Section 15) and install the spring (see Chapter 11).

17   Differential oil seal - replacement

Refer to illustrations 17.4, 17.5 and 17.8
1   Raise the rear of the car and remove the driveshaft (see Section 11).
2   Disconnect the driveaxles from the differential carrier (see Section 13).
3   Now measure and record the pinion turning torque. If a torque wrench is not available, wrap a length of cord around the companion flange and attach it to a spring balance. Note the force required to start the pinion flange turning.
4   Mark the relative positions of the end of the pinion shaft, the pinion nut and the companion flanges, by scribing positioning lines **(see illustration)**.
5   Unscrew and remove the pinion flange nut and washer. The nut will be very tight and the companion flange will have to be held stationary by using a suitable long wrench or by bolting a length of steel bar to two of its holes **(see illustration)**.
6   Drive off the companion flange by using a brass drift and hammer **(see illustration)**.
7   Pry the defective oil seal out of the carrier using a screwdriver.

8   Apply lithium based lubricant between the lips of the new oil seal and drive it into position (flat side of seal visible when installed) until it seats fully.
9   Lubricate the companion flange splines and tap it into position.
10   Install the washer and nut. Tighten the nut until pinion end-float is just eliminated and the scribe marks are in alignment. Do not overtighten the nut or the collapsible spacer will be over-compressed. If the nut is backed off the spacer will not be restored to it former length and the differential will have to be disassembled for a new spacer to be installed.
11   Once the scribe marks are correctly aligned, check the pinion rotating torque against the figure recorded earlier. Tighten the pinion nut by not more than 1/8 of a turn at a time until the new torque figure exceeds the original by between 1 and 5 ft-lbs and no more.
12   Install the driveshaft (see Section 11).
13   Install the driveaxles (see Section 13).
14   Lower the car to the ground and check the fluid level in the differential (see Chapter 1).

17.8 Lubricate the lips of the new pinion seal and seat it squarely in the bore, then drive it into the carrier with a seal driver, a large socket (shown) or a block of wood

Notes

Chapter 9 Brakes

Contents

Specifications

System type .... Hydraulic, four wheel disc, dual circuit with power booster. Parking brake-to-rear wheel integral drums.

Power booster type .... Bendix, Moraine or Delco according to year of production of car

Brake disc
Disc thickness (standard)	1.25 in
Minimum wear thickness*	1.215 in
Minimum refinish thickness	1.230 in
Disc runout	0.005 in maximum

*Refer to marks stamped in the disc (they supersede information printed here)

Torque specifications
	Ft-lbs
Master cylinder-to-power booster	24
Power booster-to-dash panel	24
Caliper mounting bolts	70
Caliper housing bolt	
1974 and earlier models	130
1975 on	
Front caliper	130
Rear caliper	60
Brake pedal bracket-to-dash panel	20

2.5a Remove the cotter pin from the pad-retaining pin

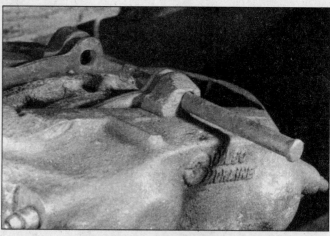

2.5b Pull the pad-retaining pin out

1   General information

The vehicles covered by this manual are equipped with hydraulically operated, power assisted four-wheel disc brakes. Both the front and rear brakes are self-adjusting. The disc brakes automatically compensate for pad wear.

Hydraulic system

The hydraulic system consists of two separate circuits. The master cylinder has separate reservoirs for the two circuits and in the event of a leak or failure in one hydraulic circuit, the other circuit will remain operative. A visual warning of circuit failure or air in the system is given by a warning light activated by displacement of the piston in the pressure differential switch portion of the combination valve from its normal "in balance" position.

Combination valve

Two basic variations of this valve have been used. On 1968 through 1974 models, the valve includes a pressure failure warning switch which illuminates a warning light if hydraulic pressure drops in either the front or rear brake circuit. On 1975 and later models, the valve also includes a proportioning function. Under heavy braking, the proportioning section reduces hydraulic pressure to the rear brakes to prevent early rear wheel lock-up. The valve is also designed to assure full pressure to one brake system should the other system fail. The design of the switch and valve are such that the switch will stay in the "warning" position once a failure has occurred. The only way to turn the light off is to repair the cause of the failure and apply very high brake pedal pressure.

Power brake booster

The power brake booster, utilizing engine manifold vacuum and atmospheric pressure to provide assistance to the hydraulically operated brakes, is mounted on the firewall in the engine compartment.

Parking brake

The parking brake operates the rear brakes only, through cable actuation. It's activated by a hand lever mounted in the center console.

Service

After completing any operation involving disassembly of any part of the brake system, always test-drive the vehicle to check for proper braking performance before resuming normal driving. When testing the brakes, perform the tests on a clean, dry flat surface. Conditions other than these can lead to inaccurate test results.

Test the brakes at various speeds with both light and heavy pedal pressure. The vehicle should stop evenly without pulling to one side or the other. Avoid locking the brakes because this slides the tires and diminishes braking efficiency and control of the vehicle.

Tires, vehicle load and front-end alignment are factors that also affect braking performance.

2   Disc brake pads - replacement

Refer to illustrations 2.5a, 2.5b and 2.6
Warning: *Disc brake pads must be replaced on both wheels at the same time - never*

2.6 Remove the inner pad, push the pistons back into the bore and install the new pad

replace the pads on only one wheel. Also, the dust created by the brake system may contain asbestos, which is harmful to your health. Never blow it out with compressed air and don't inhale any of it. An approved filtering mask should be worn when working on the brakes. Do not, under any circumstances, use petroleum-based solvents to clean brake parts. Use brake cleaner or denatured alcohol only!

Note: *The following information applies to both the front and rear brakes. When servicing the disc brakes, use only high quality, nationally-recognized name brand pads.*

1   Remove the cover from the brake fluid reservoir.

2   Loosen the wheel lug nuts, raise the vehicle and support it securely on jackstands.

3   Remove the wheels. Work on one brake assembly at a time, using the assembled brake for reference if necessary.

4   Inspect the brake disc carefully as outlined in Section 4. If machining is necessary, follow the information in that Section to remove the disc, at which time the pads can be removed from the calipers as well.

5   Remove the cotter pin from the pad-retaining pin **(see illustration)**. Pull the retaining pin out of the pads **(see illustration)**.

6   Pull the inboard pad out **(see illustration)**.

7   Carefully pry the inner pistons into their

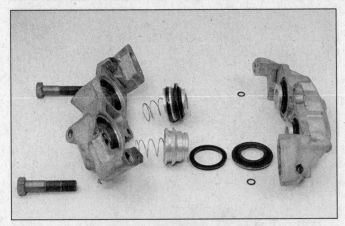

3.7 Exploded view of a brake caliper

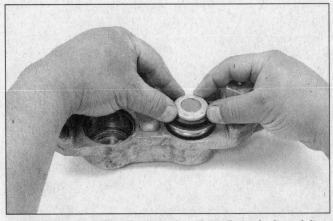

3.16 When installing the piston into the caliper, don't cock it in the bore

bores to make room for the new inner pad. Use two large screwdrivers as levers, or a flat steel bar. As the piston is depressed to the bottom of the caliper bore, the fluid in the master cylinder will rise. Make sure it doesn't overflow. If necessary, siphon off some of the fluid.

8   Replace the outer pad in the same manner as the inner pad.

9   Install the pad-retaining pin from the outer side. Push it through the outer pad, then through the inner pad. Install a new cotter pin and bend the ends over.

10   Install new pads on the opposite brake in the same manner.

11   After the job has been completed, firmly depress the brake pedal a few times to bring the pads into contact with the disc.

12   Check for fluid leakage and make sure the brakes operate normally before driving in traffic.

3   Disc brake caliper - removal, overhaul and installation

Refer to illustrations 3.7 and 3.16

Warning: *Dust created by the brake system may contain asbestos, which is harmful to your health. Never blow it out with compressed air and don't inhale any of it. An approved filtering mask should be worn when working on the brakes. Do not, under any circumstances, use petroleum-based solvents to clean brake parts. Use brake cleaner or denatured alcohol only!*

Note: *If an overhaul is indicated (usually because of fluid leakage) explore all options before beginning the job. New and factory rebuilt calipers are available on an exchange basis, which makes this job quite easy. If it's decided to rebuild the calipers, make sure a rebuild kit is available before proceeding. Always rebuild the calipers in pairs - never rebuild just one of them. If the rebuilding operation fails to cure the brake problem, consider having the piston bores of the calipers sleeved. Due to casting porosity in older Corvette calipers, an effective seal on*

the piston can't always be maintained. Several companies offer rebuilt calipers sleeved with stainless steel, on an exchange basis. Look for their advertisements in Corvette enthusiast magazines.

Removal

1   Loosen the wheel lug nuts, raise the vehicle and support it securely on jackstands. Remove the wheels.

2   If you're removing a front caliper, detach the brake hose at the frame bracket (see Section 13). Use a backup wrench to avoid twisting the metal brake line. If a rear caliper is being removed, unscrew the brake line fitting from the caliper. In either case, use a flare nut wrench, if available, to prevent rounding off the corners of the fitting. Have a rag handy to catch spilled fluid and wrap a plastic bag tightly around the end of the metal line to prevent fluid loss and contamination. **Note:** *Don't separate the hose from the metal line if you are only removing the caliper for access to other components (when removing the brake disc or suspension components, for example). If you are just removing the caliper for access to another component, secure the caliper with a piece of wire to the upper control arm.*

3   Remove the two caliper mounting bolts and pull the caliper off the disc.

Overhaul

4   With the caliper removed, clean away all external dirt.

5   Remove the brake pads from the caliper as described in Section 2.

6   Unscrew the brake hose from the caliper.

7   Separate the two halves of the caliper by removing the two large bolts **(see illustration)**.

8   Extract the two O-rings from the cavities around the fluid transfer holes in the ends of the caliper half-sections.

9   Push all the pistons into their cylinders as far as possible.

10   Pry the boot retaining rings and boots from the cylinders.

11   Extract the pistons and their springs. Store them so they can be returned to their original bores. If necessary, apply gentle air pressure to the fluid outlet port to eject the pistons. In most cases, the pistons should slide out easily.

12   At this time, examine the surfaces of the pistons and cylinder bores. If scoring or "bright" wear areas are evident, replace the complete caliper assembly with a new or rebuilt unit.

13   If these components are in good condition, discard all seals and boots and obtain a repair kit.

14   Wash all components in clean brake fluid and blow-dry them with filtered, unlubricated compressed air. Manipulate the new seals into position with your fingers only. Install the new seal into the groove closest to the flat end of the piston, with the seal lip towards the larger diameter end of the piston. **Note:** *On 1978 and later models, before installing the pistons into the caliper apply a bead of silastic sealant (RTV) to the boot grooves in the pistons (the groove closest to the concave end of the piston). The groove must be clean and dry for the sealant to adhere properly. Do not let the seal lip extend over the step in the edge of the groove.*

15   Install the springs in the piston cavities, then dip the piston seal in clean brake fluid.

16   Install the piston into the original cylinder from which it was removed **(see illustration)**. Ideally, a compressor will help to prevent the seal lips being trapped or damaged, but a thin strip of metal used to compress the lips inwards while the piston is pushed past the edge of the cylinder will usually suffice.

17   Engage the boot in the groove at the end of the piston and then install the boot-retaining ring so it fits evenly in the counterbore and will lie flush or just below the machined face of the caliper.

18   Locate new O-rings in the holes in the ends of the caliper halves and lubricate them with clean brake fluid. Dip the caliper half bolts in brake fluid, then screw them in and tighten them to the torque listed in this Chapter's Specifications.

4.4 Checking disc runout using a dial indicator

5.2 Typical master cylinder mounting

Installation

19   Install the caliper, if necessary depressing the pistons into their cylinders to provide enough clearance for the caliper to pass over the disc.
20   Install the caliper mounting bolts and tighten them to the torque listed in this Chapter's Specifications.
21   Install the pads as described in Section 2.
22   Using a new copper gasket, screw the brake hose (front) into the caliper and pass the hose through the support bracket. The hose can then be reconnected to the rigid line. If you're installing a rear caliper, connect the brake line fitting to the caliper and tighten it securely.
23   Bleed the braking system as described in Section 15.
24   Install the wheels and lower the car. Tighten the lug nuts to the torque listed in the Chapter 1 Specifications.

4   Brake disc - inspection, removal and installation

Inspection

Refer to illustration 4.4
Note: *This procedure applies to both front and rear disc brake assemblies.*
1   Loosen the wheel lug nuts, raise the vehicle and support it securely on jackstands. Remove the wheel. If you're inspecting a rear disc, reinstall three lug nuts to hold the disc to the hub.
2   Remove the brake caliper as outlined in Section 3. It's not necessary to disconnect the brake hose. After removing the caliper bolts, suspend the caliper out of the way with a piece of wire. **Warning:** *Don't let the caliper hang by the hose and don't stretch or twist the hose.*
3   Visually check the disc surface for score marks and other damage. Light scratches

and shallow grooves are normal after use and may not always be detrimental to brake operation, but deep score marks - over 0.015-inch (0.38 mm) - require disc removal and refinishing by an automotive machine shop. Be sure to check both sides of the disc. If pulsating has been noticed during application of the brakes, the disc runout may be greater than specified.
4   To check disc runout, place a dial indicator at a point about 1/2-inch from the outer edge of the disc **(see illustration)**. Set the indicator to zero and turn the disc. The indicator reading should not exceed the runout limit listed in this Chapter's Specifications. If it does, the disc should be refinished by an automotive machine shop. **Note:** *Professionals recommend resurfacing of brake discs regardless of the dial indicator reading (to produce a smooth, flat surface that will eliminate brake pedal pulsations and other undesirable symptoms related to questionable discs). At the very least, if you elect not to have the discs resurfaced, deglaze them with medium-grit emery cloth (use a swirling motion to ensure a non-directional finish).*
5   The disc must not be machined to a thickness less than the minimum refinish thickness listed in this Chapter's Specifications. The minimum wear (or discard) thickness is cast into the inside of the disc. The disc thickness can be checked with a micrometer.

Removal

6   Refer to Chapter 1, Front wheel bearing check, repack and adjustment, to remove the front disc and hub assembly. To remove the rear disc, unscrew the lug nuts that held the disc to the axle during the inspection procedure, then pull the disc off the hub.

Installation

7   Install the disc and hub assembly and adjust the wheel bearing (front discs only - see Chapter 1).
8   Install the caliper and brake pad assem-

bly over the disc and install the mounting bolts, tightening them to the torque listed in this Chapter's Specifications.
9   Install the wheel, then lower the vehicle to the ground. Tighten the lug nuts to the torque listed in the Chapter 1 Specifications. Depress the brake pedal a few times to bring the brake pads into contact with the disc. Bleeding of the system will not be necessary unless the brake line was disconnected from the caliper. Check the operation of the brakes carefully before placing the vehicle into normal service.

5   Master cylinder - removal, overhaul and installation

Refer to illustrations 5.2 and 5.6
Note: *Before deciding to overhaul the master cylinder, check on the availability and cost of a new or factory-rebuilt unit and also the availability of a rebuild kit.*

Removal

1   Disconnect the hydraulic lines from the master cylinder and cap the pipes to prevent the entry of dirt.
2   Unscrew and remove the nuts which hold the master cylinder to the brake booster and remove the master cylinder making sure that no fluid is spilled on the car's painted surfaces **(see illustration)**.
3   Clean away all external dirt, then remove the fluid reservoir cover and diaphragm. Pour out the brake fluid, then invert the cylinder. Depress the pushrod by hand to expel the remaining fluid from the cylinders.

Overhaul

4   Depress the pushrod and remove the secondary piston stop screw from the bottom of the forward fluid reservoir. The stop screw is only used on Bendix master cylinders.
5   Grip the master cylinder carefully in a

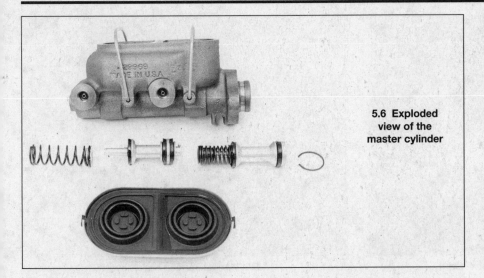

**5.6 Exploded
view of the
master cylinder**

vise and pry out the locking ring from the inside of the cylinder.

6   Remove the primary piston assembly **(see illustration)**. On some models it is necessary to first remove the piston stop screw from the bottom of the cylinder.

7   Remove the secondary piston assembly. To do this, apply air pressure to the fluid outlet port. Low air pressure, such as from a foot pump, will be enough to eject the components. An alternative to air pressure would be to tap the cylinder against a wood block.

8   Inspect the surfaces of the cylinder bore and pistons for scoring, or bright wear areas. If these are evident, replace the complete master cylinder.

9   If these main components are in good condition, then the original assembly is worth overhauling.

10   No check valves are used in fluid outlets of this type of master cylinder, but if on inspection, the tube seat inserts appear damaged, replace them in the following way.

11   Grip the master cylinder in a vise so the outlet ports are facing up.

12   Drill a 13/64 in hole through both tube seat inserts. Pry out the seats by screwing a self-tapping screw (1/4 x 20 x 3/4-inch) into them and levering against the head of the screw. Take care not to damage the master cylinder or outlet threads.

13   Remove and discard the piston seals and wash all the internal components in clean brake fluid or denatured alcohol. Do not use any other type of fluid. Mineral oil or solvent must never be allowed to come in contact with brake components.

14   Purchase a rebuild kit that contains all the necessary seals and other replaceable parts. Some repair kits will contain a complete primary piston assembly.

15   If the tube inserts were removed, install new ones into the fluid outlet holes. Remove the nut and check that no burrs are visible on the tube fitting.

16   Install three new seals into the grooves at the ends of the secondary piston using your fingers only.

17   Insert the secondary piston spring

retainer in the spring. Place the retainer and spring over the end of the secondary piston so that the retainer locates inside the lip of the cup seal.

18   Dip the secondary piston assembly into clean brake fluid and push the piston into the cylinder, so the spring will seat against the closed end of the cylinder.

19   Grip the master cylinder in a vise so the open end of the cylinder is facing up. Dip the primary piston (seals assembled) into clean brake fluid and then push the piston, spring end first, into the master cylinder. Keep the piston depressed while the piston retaining snap - ring is engaged, also the stop screw installed (where used).

Installation

20   Install the master cylinder to the brake booster, reconnect the fluid lines and refill the master cylinder reservoir.

21   Bleed the brake system as outlined in Section 15 and test the brakes carefully before driving the vehicle in traffic.

6   Power brake booster - description and maintenance

1   A power brake booster is used to reduce the effort required by the driver to operate the brakes under all braking conditions.

2   The unit operates by vacuum obtained from the intake manifold and consists basically of a booster diaphragm and check valve. The brake booster and master cylinder are connected together so the booster piston rod acts as the master cylinder pushrod. The driver's braking effort is transmitted through another pushrod to the booster piston and its built-in control system. The booster piston does not fit tightly into the cylinder, but has a strong diaphragm to keep its edges in constant contact with the cylinder wall, assuring an airtight seal between the two parts. The forward chamber is held under vacuum con-

ditions created in the intake manifold of the engine and, during periods when the brake pedal is not in use, the controls open a passage to the rear chamber to place it under vacuum conditions as well. When the brake pedal is depressed, the vacuum passage to the rear chamber is cut off and the chamber opened to atmospheric pressure. The consequent rush of air pushes the servo piston forward in the vacuum chamber and operates the main pushrod to the master cylinder.

3   The controls are designed so that assistance is given under all conditions and, when the brakes are not required, vacuum in the rear chamber is established when the brake pedal is released. All air from the atmosphere entering the rear chamber is passed through a small air filter.

4   Under normal operating conditions the booster is very reliable and does not require overhaul except at very high mileage. If a problem develops, it is recommended that a new or factory rebuilt unit is to be used.

5   Since the booster assists in reducing the braking effort required at the foot pedal and in the event of its failure, the hydraulic braking system is in no way affected except that higher pedal pressure is required.

Maintenance

6   Maintenance consists of keeping the flexible hose to the check valve tight and in good condition, also cleaning the air filter at the specified intervals.

7   To clean the air filter, disconnect the pushrod from the brake pedal and remove it from the booster.

8   Remove the flexible dust boot and the silencer, then remove the air filter.

9   The filter element should be washed clean in soap and water, then thoroughly dried before installing by reversing the removal process.

7   Power brake booster - removal and installation

1   Disconnect the flexible hose from the booster check valve.

2   Remove the nuts that hold the master cylinder to the front of the booster.

3   Pull the master cylinder forward very carefully without straining the brake lines until the cylinder clears the mounting studs. Support the master cylinder to one side **(see illustration 5.2)**.

4   Unscrew the nuts that hold the power booster to the dash panel.

5   Disconnect the pushrod from the brake pedal and then withdraw the booster from the car.

6   Replace the gasket that is located between the power booster and the dash panel and then install by reversing the removal operations. Tighten all nuts and bolts to the torque listed in this Chapter's Specifications.

8.2 Parking brake equalizer and spring

8.6 Typical parking brake lever

8.7 Parking brake primary cable pulley

8.8 Parking brake rear cable retaining clip and bracket

8 Parking brake lever and cables - removal and installation

Refer to illustrations 8.2, 8.6, 8.7 and 8.8

1   Release the parking brake lever fully.
2   Raise the car on ramps or place it over an inspection pit. Disconnect the return spring at the equalizer **(see illustration)**.
3   Remove the rear nut from the cable end fitting at the equalizer and allow the front cable to hang down.
4   Working inside the car, remove the screws which hold the cover to the underbody. The seat cushion will have to be pushed down to gain access to the lower mounting screw on each side of the cover.
5   Remove the screw and washer that secure the warning switch to the side of the parking brake assembly.
6   Unbolt the parking brake lever, remove it and the front mounting bracket **(see illustration)**.
7   The front cable and the brake lever can now be removed from the car. If necessary,

to remove the cable, the pulley wheel pivot bolt can be removed and the pulley disconnected **(see illustration)**.
8   To remove the rear cable, disconnect the cable clip retainers at the rear support brackets **(see illustration)**.
9   Disconnect the cables from the equalizer and also from the rear wheel brake operating levers on the backplate.
10   Installation of the parking brake lever and cables is a reversal of removal. Adjust the parking brake assembly as described in Section 9.

9 Parking brake - adjustment

Refer to illustration 9.5

1   Whenever the parking brake lever has to be pulled over an excessive number of clicks of the ratchet, then adjustment is necessary. Such adjustment will almost certainly be due to cable stretch, as the linings will not normally wear, unless the parking brake has been applied when the car is in motion as a

routine practice.
2   To adjust the parking brake, raise the rear of the car and remove the rear wheels.
3   Loosen the brake cables at the equalizer until the parking brake levers are fully off, with a little slack in the cables.
4   Rotate the brake disc until the adjuster screw can be seen through the hole in the drum section of the disc assembly.
5   Insert a screwdriver and turn the adjuster screw until the brake is locked and then back it off between 6 and 8 notches **(see illustration)**.
6   Adjust the nuts at the equalizer to remove any slack from the cable, but not so much that the levers at the backplates are moved from their fully off position.
7   Check that the parking brake lever, when fully applied over fourteen clicks, will lock the rear wheels. When released, the rear wheels should be able to be turned by hand without any evidence of brake drag.
8   Install the rear wheels and lower the car to the ground. Tighten the lug nuts to the torque listed in the Chapter 1 Specifications.

9.5 With the disc turned to this position, the access hole will be directly over the star wheel inside - a standard screwdriver is then used to move the star wheel and adjust the brake

10.8a A screwdriver is used to pry the shoe back so the adjuster assembly can be lifted out

10.8b Needle-nose pliers are used to disconnect the adjuster return spring from each of the shoes

10.9 Pull the parking brake shoes apart

10 Parking brake shoes - replacement

Refer to illustrations 10.8a, 10.8b and 10.9

1 Due to the fact that the parking brake is usually applied after the car has stopped, wear to the brake linings does not normally occur. However, if due to abuse or grease contamination they must be replaced, proceed with the following.

2 Raise the rear of the car and remove the rear wheels and the calipers (see Section 3). It is not necessary to disconnect the hydraulic line from the caliper - simply remove the pipe clip at the suspension control arm and then tie the caliper up out of the way with a piece of wire.

3 Drill out the rivet heads which attach the disc/drum. On some cars, screws are used instead of rivets.

4 Using a screwdriver, turn the adjuster screw several turns to expand the brake shoes.

5 Push the shoes inwards so that the front shoe hold-down spring retainer is visible from the side. Now turn the axle flange plate until the access hole in the plate is in alignment with the head of the shoe hold-down spring pin.

6 Insert a pair of needle-nosed pliers through the hole in the plate, grip the pin and turn it 90-degrees, after first having depressed the spring retaining cup. Remove the spring and cup.

7 Repeat Steps 5 and 6 for the remaining shoe.

8 Turn the adjuster screw until the shoes are fully retracted, pry the shoes apart at the adjuster, and then remove the adjuster and spring **(see illustrations)**.

9 Pry the shoes apart at the anchor pin. Lift them up and remove them, allowing the straight section of the shoe return spring to pass between the outer end of the anchor pin and the axle flange plate **(see illustration)**.

10 Before installing the new shoes, apply a light coat of brake lubricant to the shoe slid-ing surfaces on the brake backplate, also to the anchor pin and adjuster screw threads.

11 Attach the shoe return spring to the new shoes and locate the shoes onto the anchor pin. Make sure that the shoe actuator is engaged in the shoe cutouts.

12 Install the adjuster spring and the adjuster. Then expand the shoes by means of the adjuster screw and install the hold down springs, cups and pins, by reversing the removal operations.

13 Retract the shoes using the adjuster screw.

14 Install the disc/drum assembly making sure that the adjuster screw access holes are in alignment with each other on the axle flange plate and drum.

15 Re-riveting is not necessary as this is only done during production to facilitate assembly. If screws are used, reinstall them.

16 Install the caliper as described in Section 3.

17 Adjust the parking brake as described in Section 9.

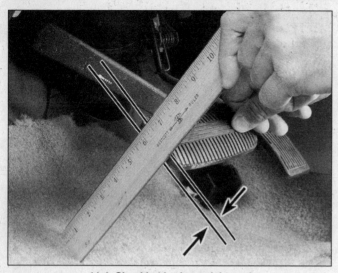

11.4 Checking brake pedal travel

13.3 It's a good idea to mark the position of the brake hose to the frame bracket (arrow) so the hose isn't twisted when it's reinstalled

18   Install the rear wheels and lower the car to the ground.

11   Brake pedal - removal, installation and travel check

Removal and installation

1   The brake pedal operates on a common cross shaft with the clutch pedal. Refer to Chapter 8, Section 8 or 9 for a full description of removal and installation instructions.

Brake pedal travel check (1978 and later models only)

Refer to illustration 11.4

2   At frequent intervals, the brakes should be checked for correct pedal travel (the distance the pedal moves toward the floor from a fully released position). This check should be made with the brake pedal firmly depressed (with approximately an 80 lb. load) while the brakes are cold.
3   Pump the pedal a minimum of 3 times with the engine off before making the pedal travel check. This will exhaust all vacuum from the power booster and ensure an accurate result.
4   Pedal travel should not exceed 1.80 inches (see illustration).

12   Brake light switch - removal, installation and adjustment

Removal

1   Disconnect the electrical connector at the brake light switch.
2   Remove the retaining nut, if so equipped, and unscrew the switch from the bracket.

Installation and adjustment (1968 through 1977 models)

3   Install the switch and the retaining nut, if so equipped.
4   Check that the brake pedal is in its fully released position. The switch should actuate the stop lamps when the pedal has been depressed between 1/4 and 5/8 inch.
5   Adjust the switch setting by turning it in its bracket.
6   Connect the wiring at the switch.

Installation and adjustment (1978 and later models)

7   Install the switch and the retaining nut, if so equipped.
8   The design of the switch and mount provides for automatic adjustment when the brake pedal is manually returned to it stop as follows:
9   With the brake pedal depressed, insert the switch and/or valve assembly into the tubular clip until the switch body and/or the valve assembly seats on the tube clip. Note that subtle clicks can be heard as the threaded portion of the switch and/or valve is pushed through the clip toward the pedal.
10   Pull the brake pedal back as far as possible (against the pedal stop) until the clicks can no longer be heard. The switch and/or valve assembly will be moved in the tubular clip, providing proper adjustment.
11   Release the brake pedal and repeat Step 10 to ensure that no clicks can be heard.

13   Brake hoses and lines - inspection and replacement

Inspection

1   About every six months, with the vehicle raised and supported securely on jackstands, the rubber hoses which connect the steel brake lines with the front and rear brake assemblies should be inspected for cracks, chafing of the outer cover, leaks, blisters and other damage. These are important and vulnerable parts of the brake system and inspection should be complete. A light and mirror will be helpful for a thorough check. If a hose exhibits any of the above conditions, replace it with a new one immediately.

Replacement

Front brake hose

Refer to illustrations 13.3 and 13.11

2   Using a back-up wrench, disconnect the brake line from the hose fitting, being careful not to bend the frame bracket or brake line.
3   Use a pair of pliers to remove the U-clip from the female fitting at the bracket, then detach the hose from the bracket (see illustration).
4   Unscrew the brake hose from the caliper.
5   To install the hose, first thread it into the caliper, tightening it securely.
6   Without twisting the hose, install the female fitting in the hose bracket. It will fit the bracket in only one position.
7   Install the U-clip retaining the female fitting to the frame bracket.
8   Using a back-up wrench, attach the brake line to the hose fitting.
9   When the brake hose installation is complete, there should be no kinks in the hose. Make sure the hose doesn't contact any part of the suspension. Check this by turning the wheels to the extreme left and right positions. If the hose makes contact, remove it and correct the installation as necessary. After installation, check the master cylinder fluid level and add fluid as necessary. Bleed the brake system as outlined in Section 15 and test the brakes carefully before driving the vehicle in traffic.

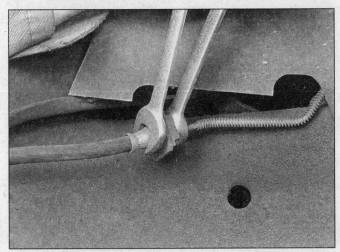

13.11 Place a wrench on the hose fitting to prevent it from turning and disconnect the line with a flare-nut wrench

14.1 The proportioning valve is mounted to the front frame rail

Rear brake hose

10   Using a back-up wrench, disconnect the hose at the frame bracket, being careful not to bend the bracket or steel lines.

11   Remove the U-clip with a pair of pliers and separate the female fitting from the bracket **(see illustration)**.

12   Disconnect the two hydraulic lines at the junction block, then unbolt and remove the hose.

13   Bolt the junction block to the axle housing and connect the lines, tightening them securely. Without twisting the hose, install the female end of the hose in the frame bracket.

14   Install the U-clips retaining the female end to the bracket.

15   Using a back-up wrench, attach the steel line fittings to the female fittings. Again, be careful not to bend the bracket or steel line.

16   Make sure the hose installation did not loosen the frame bracket. Tighten the bracket if necessary.

17   After installation, check the master cylinder fluid level and add fluid as necessary. Bleed the brake system as outlined in Section 15 and test the brakes carefully before driving the vehicle in traffic.

Metal brake lines

18   When replacing brake lines, be sure to use the correct parts.
Don't use copper tubing for any brake system components. Purchase steel brake lines from a dealer or auto parts store.

19   Prefabricated brake lines, with the tube ends already flared and fittings installed, are available at auto parts stores and dealers. These lines are also bent to the proper shapes.

20   When installing the new line make sure it's securely supported in the brackets and has plenty of clearance between moving or hot components.

21   After installation, check the master cylinder fluid level and add fluid as necessary. Bleed the brake system as outlined in Section 15 and test the brakes carefully before driving the vehicle in traffic.

14   Combination valve - check

Refer to illustration 14.1

1   This is a combination switch and valve which also serves as the front hydraulic line junction block **(see illustration)**.

2   The failure switch is actuated if pressure in either of the two hydraulic circuits drops. The switch is essentially a piston which is maintained "in balance" by equal circuit pressures but can be displaced if pressure in one circuit falls, thereby making electrical contact to illuminate a warning lamp.

3   The regulating valve, used on 1975 and later models, is essentially a pressure proportioning valve which improves front to rear wheel braking characteristics during heavy braking, when weight is transferred from the rear to the front wheels.

4   Once the pressure failure switch piston has been displaced and then the system repaired and bled, the piston can only be returned to its "in balance" state by a very hard application of the brake pedal.

15   Brake system bleeding

Refer to illustration 15.9

Warning: *Wear eye protection when bleeding the brake system. If the fluid comes in contact with your eyes, immediately rinse them with water and seek medical attention.*

Note: *Bleeding the hydraulic system is necessary to remove any air that manages to find its way into the system when it's been opened during removal and installation of a hose, line, caliper or master cylinder.*

1   It will probably be necessary to bleed the system at all four brakes if air has entered the system due to low fluid level, or if the brake lines have been disconnected at the master cylinder.

2   If a brake line was disconnected only at a wheel, then only that caliper or wheel cylinder must be bled.

3   If a brake line is disconnected at a fitting located between the master cylinder and any of the brakes, that part of the system served by the disconnected line must be bled.

4   Remove any residual vacuum from the brake power booster by applying the brake several times with the engine off.

5   Remove the master cylinder reservoir cover and fill the reservoir with brake fluid. Reinstall the cover. **Note:** *Check the fluid level often during the bleeding operation and add fluid as necessary to prevent the fluid level from falling low enough to allow air bubbles into the master cylinder.*

6   Have an assistant on hand, as well as a supply of new brake fluid, a clear container partially filled with clean brake fluid, a length of 3/16-inch plastic, rubber or vinyl tubing to fit over the bleeder valve and a wrench to open and close the bleeder valve.

7   The full bleeding sequence is as follows:

1968 through 1977 models:
Left rear
Right rear
Left front
Right front

1978 through 1982 models:
Left rear (inner)
Left rear (outer)
Right rear (inner)
Right rear (outer)
Left front
Right front

8   Beginning at the indicated wheel location, loosen the bleeder valve slightly, then tighten it to a point where it is snug but can still be loosened quickly and easily.

9   Place one end of the tubing over the bleeder valve and submerge the other end in

brake fluid in the container **(see illustration)**.

10   Have the assistant pump the brakes slowly a few times to get pressure in the system, then hold the pedal firmly depressed.

11   While the pedal is held depressed, open the bleeder valve just enough to allow a flow of fluid to leave the valve. Watch for air bubbles to exit the submerged end of the tube. When the fluid flow slows after a couple of seconds, close the valve and have your assistant release the pedal.

12   Repeat Steps 8 and 9 until no more air is seen leaving the tube, then tighten the bleeder valve and proceed to the next indicated wheel location and perform the same procedure. Be sure to check the fluid level in the master cylinder reservoir frequently.

13   Never use old brake fluid. It contains moisture that will deteriorate the brake system components.

14   Refill the master cylinder with fluid at the end of the operation.

15.9 Bleeding a front caliper

15   Check the operation of the brakes. The pedal should feel solid when depressed, with no sponginess. If necessary, repeat the entire process. **Warning:** *Do not operate the vehicle if you are in doubt about the effectiveness of the brake system.*

Chapter 10
Suspension and steering systems

Contents

Specifications

General

Front suspension type	Independent, upper and lower control arms with coil springs, telescopic shock absorbers and stabilizer bar.
Rear suspension type	Independent with torque control arms, transverse leaf spring and telescopic shock absorbers. Optional stabilizer bar.

Steering gear
Type	Worm and sector, recirculating ball with collapsible column. Linkage, outer tie-rods with center relay and idler
Lubricant	Steering Gear Lubricant
Worm bearing preload	5 to 8 in-lbs
Sector lash adjustment	9 to 16 in-lbs turning torque
Over-center preload	6 to 9 in-lbs

Torque specifications

Front suspension

	Ft-lbs
Upper balljoint stud nut	50
Lower balljoint stud nut	90
Balljoint attaching bolt (repair kit)	25
Steering arm-to-knuckle	70
Upper control arm pivot-to-frame bolts/nuts	55
Upper control arm shaft bolts	60
Lower control arm shaft-to-crossmember	
Front bolt	70
Rear bolt	95

Torque specifications

Rear suspension

	Ft-lbs
Control arm front pivot bolt	50
Leaf spring center plate	70
Camber cam bolt	65
Spindle flange nut	100
Strut rod-to-spindle support	75
Strut rod bracket-to-carrier	35
Strut rod bracket-to-control arm	15

Manual steering gear

Steering gear mounting bolts	30
Pitman shaft nut	140
Pitman arm-to-relay rod	45
Idler arm-to-relay rod	35
Idler arm-to-frame	35
Tie-rod end ball stud nuts	36
Tie-rod clamp bolts	18
Flexible coupling flange nuts	20
Flexible coupling pinch bolt	30
Steering wheel nut	30
Worm adjuster locknut	85
Lash adjuster screw locknut	19
Steering column support bolts	15

Power steering gear

Same as manual steering gear except for:

Pitman shaft nut	185
Steering pump mounting bolts	25
Power cylinder-to-relay rod ball stud nut	45
Power cylinder-to-bracket nut	23
Power cylinder bracket-to-frame nuts	17
Control valve-to-relay rod clamp pinch bolt	25
Control valve ball stud-to-Pitman arm nut	45
Wheel lug nuts	See Chapter 1

1   General information

The front suspension is an independent type with upper and lower control arms, coil springs and telescopic shock absorbers. A stabilizer bar is also installed.

The rear suspension is also an independent type with a frame-mounted differential carrier transmitting power through open driveshafts to the wheels. The suspension strut rods, driveshafts and torque control arms form the links together with a transversely-mounted leaf spring. Telescopic type shock absorbers are used and a stabilizer bar is optionally available.

The steering gear is of the recirculating ball type with worm and sector gear. All cars have an energy-absorbing type steering column with optional tilt and telescopic versions. Power steering is optionally available and comprises a ball-driven pump and a power piston operating through the relay rod of the steering linkage, controlled by a valve assembly.

Frequently, when working on the suspension or steering system components, you may come across fasteners which seem impossible to loosen. These fasteners on the underside of the vehicle are continually subjected to water, road grime, mud, etc., and can become rusted or "frozen," making them extremely difficult to remove. In order to unscrew these stubborn fasteners without damaging them (or other components), be sure to use lots of penetrating oil and allow it to soak in for a while. Using a wire brush to clean exposed threads will also ease removal of the nut or bolt and prevent damage to the threads. Sometimes a sharp blow with a hammer and punch will break the bond between a nut and bolt threads, but care must be taken to prevent the punch from slipping off the fastener and ruining the threads. Heating the stuck fastener and surrounding area with a torch sometimes helps too, but isn't recommended because of the obvious dangers associated with fire. Long breaker bars and extension, or "cheater," pipes will increase leverage, but never use an extension pipe on a ratchet - the ratcheting mechanism could be damaged. Sometimes tightening the nut or bolt first will help to break it loose. Fasteners that require drastic measures to remove should always be replaced with new ones.

Since most of the procedures dealt with in this Chapter involve jacking up the vehicle and working underneath it, a good pair of jackstands will be needed. A hydraulic floor jack is the preferred type of jack to lift the vehicle, and it can also be used to support certain components during various operations. **Warning:** *Never, under any circumstances, rely on a jack to support the vehicle while working on it. Whenever any of the suspension or steering fasteners are loosened or removed they must be inspected and, if necessary, replaced with new ones of the same part number or of original equipment quality and design. Torque specifications must be followed for proper reassembly and component retention. Never attempt to heat or straighten any suspension or steering components. Instead, replace any bent or damaged part with a new one.*

2   Front shock absorbers - removal and installation

Refer to illustration 2.2

1   Any sign of oil on the outside of shock absorber bodies will indicate that the seals have started to leak and the complete units must be replaced. Where the shock absorber has failed internally, this is more difficult to detect although wheel hop or a wallowing sensation, particularly on uneven road surfaces, may provide a clue. When a shock absorber is suspected to have failed, remove it from the vehicle and, holding it in a vertical position, operate it for the full length of its stroke a few times. Any lack of resistance in either direction will indicate the need for a

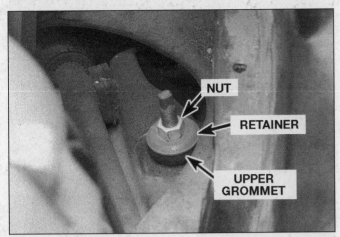

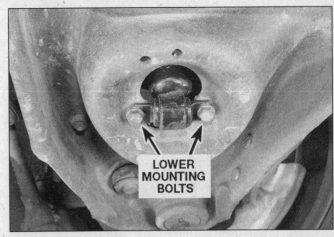

2.2 Typical front shock absorber mounting details

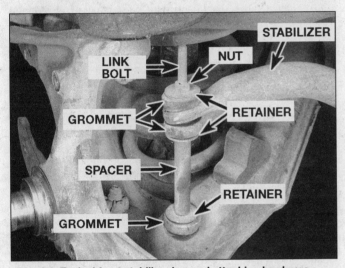

3.1 Typical front stabilizer bar and attaching hardware

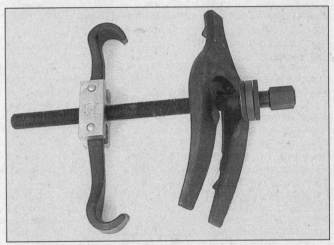

4.4 A typical aftermarket internal-type spring compressor - the hooked arms grip the upper coils of the spring, the plate is inserted between the lower coils, and when the nut on the threaded rod is turned, the spring is compressed

new shock absorber.

2   Raise the front end of the vehicle and place it securely on jackstands. Use an open-end wrench to prevent the upper (squared) end from turning, then remove the upper stem retaining nut, retainer and rubber grommet **(see illustration)**.

3   Remove the two shock absorber lower mounting bolts.

4   Pull the assembly out from the bottom.

5   When installing, slip the lower retainer and rubber grommet in place over the stem.

6   Install the shock absorber in the fully extended position up through the lower control arm and spring.

7   Install the upper rubber grommet, retainer and attaching nut after the shock absorber upper stem has passed through the frame bracket.

8   Using an open-end wrench, hold the upper stem and tighten the retaining nut securely.

9   Install the bolts at the shock absorber lower mount and tighten them securely.

10   Remove the jackstands and lower the vehicle.

3   Front stabilizer bar - removal and installation

Refer to illustration 3.1

1   Raise the front end of the vehicle and place it securely on jackstands. Disconnect the stabilizer bar from the lower control arm **(see illustration)**.

2   Remove the stabilizer bar brackets from the frame, then lift away the stabilizer bar.

3   Remove the link bolts, spacers and rubber grommets from the lower control arms or stabilizer bar.

4   Inspect all the parts for damage, wear and deterioration. Install new parts as necessary.

5   If new frame bushings are required, slide them into position along the stabilizer bar.

6   Install the brackets over the bushings and connect them (loosely) to the frame. Install the link bolts with the nuts pointing up.

7   Ensure the stabilizer bar is centered, then tighten all the bolts securely.

8   Remove the jackstands and lower the vehicle to the ground.

4   Front coil spring - removal and installation

Refer to illustrations 4.4 and 4.7

1   Remove the shock absorber as described in Section 2.

2   Support the front of the vehicle securely on jackstands placed under the frame rails.

3   Disconnect the stabilizer bar from the lower control arm.

4   Jack up the lower control arm to relieve the tension on the control arm pivot bolts.

Warning: *The coil spring is under great tension. It must be secured so it can't fly out and cause injury. Wrap a chain around the spring and through the control arm, and bolt the ends of the chain together. The coil spring must be held compressed at this stage. To do this, use spring compressors designed for an automotive coil spring. These can be rented inexpensively from tool rental outlets and some auto parts stores* **(see illustration)**.

5   Remove the pivot cross shaft nut and bolts from the inner end of the control arm.

6   Lower the jack slowly until the com-

4.7 When installing new front springs, the bottom of the spring must be positioned as described in the text before releasing the spring compressor

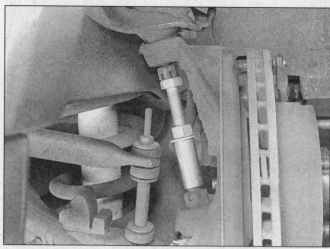

5.15 A special tool is used to push the balljoint out of the steering knuckle, but an alternative tool can be fabricated from a large bolt, nut, washer and socket - in this view, it is being used for the upper ball-joint stud, when reversed it can be used on the lower stud

pressed spring can be removed. **Warning:** *Handle the compressed spring carefully.*

7   Installation is the reverse of the removal steps. Compress the spring either before installing, or after locating it on the control arm, depending upon the type of compressor being used. The closer spring coils should be at the top on all but the very latest models. On these vehicles, tape is located on one of the lower coils. The tape should be at its lowest position compatible with the end of the bottom coil, covering all or part of one inspection hole in the lower control arm. The other hole must be partly or completely uncovered **(see illustration)**.

8   Tighten all nuts and bolts to the torque listed in this Chapter's Specifications.

5   Balljoints - check and replacement

Refer to illustration 5.15

Lower balljoints

1   For precise determination of wear in the control arm lower balljoints, perform the following operations.

2   With the weight of the vehicle on its wheels, use an outside micrometer or calipers to measure the distance from the top of the lubrication fitting to the bottom of the ball stud. Measure both sides and record the dimensions.

3   Now raise the car under the lower control arms so the wheels hang free. Measure the previously taken dimensions again.

4   If the comparative measurements for each side vary by more than 1/16-inch between the first and second dimensions then the joints are worn and must be replaced.

5   A further check should be made to confirm wear in the joint by cleaning out the lubri-

cator hole and inspecting it to see if the joint liner is partially blocking the hole. If it is, replace both lower balljoints. Where excessive pressure is needed to lubricate a balljoint, this is an indication of wear in the joint.

6   To replace a balljoint, support the outer end of the lower control arm on a jack.

7   Remove the brake caliper and tie it up out of the way as described in Chapter 9.

8   Disconnect the upper and lower balljoint studs from the steering knuckle. A heavy duty puller will be needed for this. Support the steering knuckle in the upright position and install the puller as shown **(see illustration 5.15)**. Loosen the balljoint nut one turn, extend the puller to free the balljoint stud from the knuckle, then remove the balljoint nut.

9   Drill out or grind off the rivets that hold the balljoint, taking care not to enlarge the rivet holes.

10   The new balljoint is supplied with the necessary retaining bolts to replace the original rivets. The special thick-headed bolt supplied must be installed on the forward side of the control arm.

11   Tighten the nuts to the torque listed in this Chapter's Specifications and then lubricate the balljoint. Install the grease fitting.

12   Reinstall the caliper.

Upper balljoints

13   For precise determination of wear in the upper control arm balljoint, jack up the front of the vehicle under the outer ends of the lower control arm so that the wheels hang free. Support the vehicle securely on jackstands.

14   Remove the wheel.

15   Disconnect the upper balljoint from the steering knuckle. A heavy duty balljoint separator will be needed for this **(see illustration)**. Loosen the balljoint nut one turn, extend the

puller to free the balljoint stud from the knuckle, then remove the balljoint nut.

16   The turning torque of the ball stud should now be measured. Either screw a nut onto the ball stud and use a torque wrench, or wind a cord around the stud and attach it to a spring balance. The correct turning torque for a ball stud is 3 to 10 ft-lbs. If it is outside these limits, replace the balljoint as it is either seized or worn.

17   To replace a joint, cut off the heads of the original rivets.

18   Enlarge the rivet holes to 21/64-in diameter to accept the 5/16-inch bolts supplied with the new balljoint. Install the new assembly and tighten the nuts to the torque listed in this Chapter's Specifications.

19   Reconnect the ball stud to the steering knuckle, install the wheel and lower the car.

20   Lubricate the joint. Remove the original grease fitting and screw it into the new balljoint. The fitting has a self-tapping thread.

6   Front lower control arm - removal and installation

1   Remove the coil spring (see Section 4).

2   Disconnect the lower balljoint stud from the steering knuckle.

3   The control arm bushings are pressed in and it is recommended that new bushings be installed by a dealer service department or other repair shop.

4   If a press is available, press the cross shaft first from one end and then from the other to force out the bushings. When reassembling, make sure that the end of the cross shaft that has the two bolt holes is on the leading edge of the control arm.

5   Installation is the reverse of the removal steps. Tighten all nuts and bolts to the torques listed in this Chapter's Specifications.

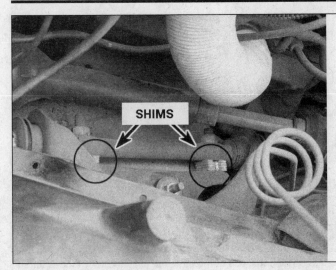

SHIMS

7.4 Note the original positions of the alignment shims and reinstall them just as they were

7 Front upper control arm - removal and installation

Refer to illustration 7.4

1   Raise the front of the car by placing a jack under the outer end of the lower control arm. The jack must remain in this location during the entire procedure.
2   Remove the wheel.
3   Disconnect the upper balljoint from the steering knuckle. A heavy duty balljoint separator will be needed for this **(see illustration 5.15)**.
4   Inspect and record the number and position of shims used at the cross shaft retaining bolts **(see illustration)**. These control caster and camber angles and must be reinstalled to their original locations. Remove the two nuts that hold the cross shaft to the crossmember, remove the shims and withdraw the control arm.
5   Cross shaft bushing replacement should be left to a dealer service department or other repair shop unless a suitable press is available. In this case, apply pressure to each end of the cross shaft in turn, to drive out the bushings.
6   Installation is the reverse of the removal steps. Tighten the nuts and bolts to the torques listed in this Chapter's Specifications.

8 Steering knuckle - removal and installation

1   Raise the front of the car and support it securely on jackstands. Support the lower control arm on a jack. The jack must remain in this location during the entire procedure.
2   Remove the wheel.
3   Remove the brake caliper and tie it up out of the way (see Chapter 9).
4   Remove the hub/disc assembly (see Chapter 1, Front wheel bearing check, repack and adjustment).
5   Remove the splash shield.

6   Support the lower control arm with a floor jack. **Warning:** *The jack must remain in this position throughout the entire procedure. Disconnect the upper and lower balljoints from the steering knuckle* **(see illustration 5.15)**.
7   Installation is the reverse of the removal steps. Tighten all nuts and bolts to the torques listed in this Chapter's Specifications.

9 Rear wheel bearings - adjustment

1   At the specified intervals, inspect and adjust the rear wheel bearings as follows:
2   Raise the rear of the vehicle until the wheel is free. Support the vehicle securely on jackstands.
3   Remove the bolts and disconnect the outer end of the driveaxle from the wheel spindle flange.
4   Mark the camber cam in relation to the bracket. Loosen and turn the camber bolt until the strut rod forces the torque control arm outward.
5   Position the loose end of the driveaxle to one side for access to the wheel spindle.
6   Remove the wheel and mount a dial indicator on the torque control arm so that the pointer rests on the flange or end of the spindle.
7   Grip the spindle flange and try to move it in-and-out. Observe the movement of the dial indicator. If the reading is between 0.001 and 0.008-inch adjustment is not required. If it is outside these limits, record the readings and then adjust as follows:
8   Fully apply the parking brake to prevent the spindle from turning. Remove the cotter pin and nut from the spindle.
9   Release the parking brake and pull the drive spindle flange from the splined end of the wheel spindle.
10   Remove the brake caliper and the drum/disc assembly as described in Chapter 9.
11   Use a bolt-on, plate type puller to press

out the spindle from the spindle support. Remove the shim and bearing spacer from the spindle support.
12   Measure the thickness of the original shim using a micrometer. If the maximum reading on the dial indicator was in excess of 0.008-inch then select a shim from the available thicknesses (0.097 to 0.148-inch in increments of 0.003-inch) that's thinner by the necessary amount to bring the endplay within the specified limits. If the endplay was less than 0.001-inch select a thicker shim to bring the endplay within that specified.
13   Install the spacer and newly selected shim on the spindle.
14   Locate the spindle in the spindle support. Make sure the larger end of the spacer is facing the outer bearing with the shim located between the spacer and the inner bearing.
15   Draw the spindle/bearing assembly into the support using the washer and nut without the drive flange. Then remove the nut and washer and ensure that the flange can be installed leaving sufficient thread exposed for the nut and washer to be screwed on, and the drive spindle drawn fully into position. Use a new nut for final assembly.
16   Tighten the nut to the torque listed in this Chapter's Specifications and insert a new cotter pin. If necessary, tighten the nut further to align the cotter pin hole; do not back it off to achieve alignment.
17   Install the spindle support outer seal.
18   Install the brake disc and caliper.
19   Connect the driveaxle and install the wheel.
20   Set the camber cam to the original alignment mark and tighten all nuts and bolts to the torques listed in this Chapter's Specifications.

10 Rear wheel bearings - replacement

1   Press out the drive spindle as described in the preceding Section.
2   The bearings may be removed and installed without removing the control arm, as long as support is provided when the bearing cups are tapped out.
3   If preferred, the spindle support can first be removed as follows:
4   Disconnect the parking brake cable from the actuating lever on the brake backplate.
5   Remove the four nuts that hold the support to the control arm. Withdraw the brake backplate and tie it out of the way.
6   Disconnect the shock absorber lower end from the strut rod. Take care that the shock absorber is not under load before disconnecting it. If necessary, jack up the outer end of the rear spring.
7   Remove the deflector, the inner oil seal and inner bearing race and drive out the bearing cups.
8   The outer bearing should be pressed

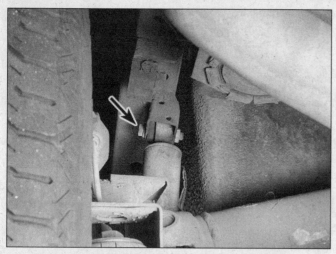

11.2 Rear shock absorber upper mounting bolt (arrow)

12.3a The outer end of the strut rod is secured by a castellated nut and a cotter pin (arrow)

from the spindle, or a suitable bearing puller used.

9   Reassembly is the reverse of disassembly. Pack the bearings with high melting point grease and install new inner and outer oil seals.

10   Adjust the bearings as described in the preceding Section.

11 Rear shock absorber - removal and installation

Refer to illustration 11.2

1   Make sure the shock absorber is not fully extended (wheels hanging free) before unbolting it. If it is, support the outer end of the transverse rear spring and jack it up.

2   Remove the shock absorber upper mounting bolt, then remove the lower mounting nut with its lockwasher **(see illustration)**.

3   Slide the upper end of the shock absorber out of the frame bracket and then pull the lower mounting eye from the strut rod.

4   Inspect the shock absorbers as described in Section 2.

5   Installation is the reverse of the removal.

12 Strut rod and bracket - removal and installation

Refer to illustrations 12.3a and 12.3b

1   Raise the rear of the car and support it securely on jackstands.

2   Remove the shock absorber lower mounting bolt (see Section 11).

3   Remove the cotter pin and nut from the strut rod shaft and withdraw the shaft **(see illustrations). Note:** *The shaft may be very tight. If necessary, use a tie-rod separator to force it out. Don't hammer on the threaded end or the threads will be damaged.*

4   Mark the relative position of the camber adjusting cam and bracket so that the com-

ponents may be installed in their original positions.

5   Loosen the camber bolt and nut and then remove the four bolts that hold the strut rod bracket to the differential carrier. Lower the bracket.

6   Remove the cam and bolt assembly, pull the strut down out of the bracket and remove the bushing caps.

7   Remove the bushings and replace them if worn. A press is needed to remove them and it is preferable to have this done by a dealer or machine shop.

8   Place the bushing caps over the inner bushing and slide the strut rod into the bracket.

9   Install the cam and bolt assembly and adjust the cam to align the positioning marks. Tighten the cam bolt nut just enough to hold the rod.

10   Bolt the strut rod bracket to the underside of the differential carrier.

11   Raise the outer end of the strut rod into the spindle support fork and insert the strut rod shaft into the fork so that the flat on the shaft lines up with the corresponding flat in the spindle fork. Install the retaining nut but do not tighten.

12   Connect and fully tighten the shock absorber lower mounting bolt.

13   Lower the car to the ground and tighten the cam bolt nut and strut rod shaft nut to the torques listed in this Chapter's Specifications. Install a new cotter pin to the strut rod shaft nut.

14   The rear wheel camber should be checked, especially if new components have been installed.

13 Rear spring - removal and installation

1   Raise the rear of the car and support it securely on jackstands under the frame just forward of the rear suspension control arm pivot points.

12.3b Mark the position of the camber adjusting cam (arrow) on the inner strut rod end before disassembling it from the bracket

2   Remove the wheels.

3   Position a jack under the end of the spring just below the link bolt. Raise the spring with the jack until it appears nearly flat.

4   At this stage, fit a C-clamp to the spring to prevent the jack from sliding along the spring when it is lowered. Secure it very tightly and use a block of wood between the threads of the clamp and the jack as a thread protector.

5   Disconnect the link bolt. Do not score the shank of the bolt during removal. If you do, replace it.

6   Carefully lower the jack until all spring tension is removed.

7   Repeat the spring disconnection operations on the other end of the spring.

8   Unbolt the spring center plate and slide the spring out sideways.

9   With the spring removed, examine the leaves carefully for cracks. The spring can be disassembled to replace a leaf by first clamping it in a vise and then unscrewing the center bolt. The cushion retainers can be removed

by cutting off their flared portions. Peen the new ones on installation. Worn or damaged liners should be replaced where necessary.

10 Installation is the reverse of removal; partially tighten the center plate first and then raise each end of the spring in turn and connect the link bolts.

11 Fully tighten the center plate bolts after the weight of the car is on the wheels. Refer to this Chapter's Specifications for torque settings.

14 Rear suspension torque (control) arm - removal and installation

1 Disconnect the rear spring on the side from which the control arm is to be removed. Refer to Steps 1 through 6 of the preceding Section.

2 If the car is equipped with a stabilizer bar, disconnect it (refer to Section 16).

3 Disconnect the shock absorber lower mounting bolt.

4 Disconnect the strut rod and swing it down.

5 Remove the four bolts that hold the outer end of the driveaxle to the spindle flange. Lower the driveaxle.

6 Disconnect the brake line from the caliper and from the control arm. Plug the line to prevent loss of fluid.

7 Disconnect the parking brake cable.

8 Remove the control arm pivot bolt and remove the shims that control the rear wheel toe-in. Tape these shims together and note their location.

9 New bushings can be installed to the control arms but retaining flares will have to be drilled out before the old ones can be removed. After installing new bushings, the retainers will have to be flared with a special tool. In view of this, it is recommended that new bushings be installed by a dealer or machine shop.

10 Insert the control arm into the frame opening.

11 Install the pivot bolt and toe-in shims in their original locations on both sides of the control arm. Insert a new cotter pin (so its loop is as shown in illustration 14.8) to retain the shims.

12 Do not tighten the pivot bolt at this time.

13 Reconnect the driveaxle.

14 Raise the strut rod and insert the strut rod shaft so that its flat lines up with the one on the spindle support fork. Install the nut and tighten to the torque listed in this Chapter's Specifications.

15 Reconnect the shock absorber lower mounting bolt.

16 Reconnect the end of the rear spring.

17 Reconnect the stabilizer bar (if equipped).

18 Reconnect the brake line and bleed the hydraulic circuit (see Chapter 9)

19 Install the wheel and lower the car to the ground.

20 With the weight of the car on the wheels,

tighten the control arm pivot bolt to the torque listed in this Chapter's Specifications, then insert the cotter pin.

15 Rear suspension crossmember - removal and installation

Refer to Chapter 8 for details of this in conjunction with the differential carrier.

16 Rear stabilizer bar - removal and installation

1 To remove this optional piece of equipment, raise the rear of the car and support it on the frame side rails.

2 Disconnect the end of the stabilizer bar from both suspension control arms.

3 Unbolt the brackets from the frame and remove the stabilizer bar.

4 Installation is the reverse of removal.

17 Steering linkage - removal and installation

Tie-rod

Refer to illustrations 17.2 and 17.9

1 Clean away external dirt and record the number of exposed threads on each side of the center sleeve.

2 Remove the cotter pin from the slotted nut on the ball stud of the tie-rod which is to be removed. Unscrew and remove the nut **(see illustration)**.

3 Disconnect the tie-rod ball stud from the eye of the steering arm. This can be done in one of several different ways. Either strike both sides of the eye simultaneously using two hammers, or use a two-jaw puller or a picklefork-type balljoint separator.

4 Loosen the clamp bolt on the end of the sleeve from which the tie-rod is to be unscrewed.

5 Unscrew and remove the tie-rod from

the sleeve.

6 Install the new tie-rod, screwing it into the sleeve so that the same number of threads are exposed as was originally recorded.

7 Position the clamp but do not tighten the bolt at this stage.

8 Reconnect the tie-rod to the steering arm, tighten the nut to the torque listed in this Chapter's Specifications and insert a new cotter pin.

9 Tighten the sleeve clamps **(see illustration)**. The clamps must be between and clear of the small dimples on the sleeve ends. The sleeves must be between 0.060-inch and 0.50-inch from the end of each tie-rod. The slots in the adjuster tube must not be between the jaws of the clamps or within 0.10-inch of them.

10 Have the front wheel alignment checked as soon as possible.

Relay rod

11 Disconnect the inner ends of the tie-rods from the relay rod (refer to Step 3).

12 Disconnect the relay rod from the idler arm again using one of the methods described in Step 3.

13 On vehicles without power steering, disconnect the relay rod from the Pitman arm.

14 On vehicles with power steering, disconnect the relay rod from the power cylinder. Remove the control valve clamp bolt and lockwasher, then disconnect the relay rod from the control valve by backing out the threaded end of the rod.

15 Installation of the relay rod is simply the reverse of removal on vehicles with manual steering. On vehicles with power steering, install the relay rod as follows:

a) *Thread the relay rod onto the control valve, leaving 0.06 to 0.12-inch clearance.*

b) *Fit the control valve clamp bolt and lock washer. Tighten to the torque listed in this Chapter's Specifications.*

c) *Install the power cylinder to the relay rod and tighten the securing nut to the specified torque. If the cotter pin holes are*

17.2 After the castellated nut is loosened, a small puller can be used to detach the tie-rod end from the steering knuckle. Don't use a picklefork unless you plan to replace the tie-rod end - it will tear the boot

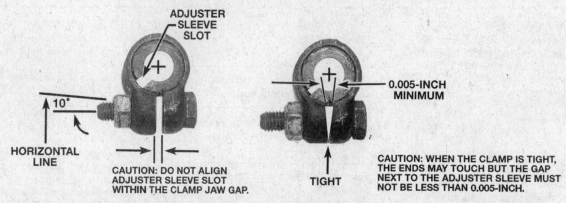

ADJUSTER SLEEVE SLOT

10°

HORIZONTAL LINE

CAUTION: DO NOT ALIGN ADJUSTER SLEEVE SLOT WITHIN THE CLAMP JAW GAP.

0.005-INCH MINIMUM

TIGHT

CAUTION: WHEN THE CLAMP IS TIGHT, THE ENDS MAY TOUCH BUT THE GAP NEXT TO THE ADJUSTER SLEEVE MUST NOT BE LESS THAN 0.005-INCH.

17.9 Tie-rod clamp setting diagram

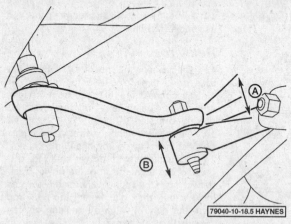

79040-10-18.5 HAYNES

17.19 Check for excessive idler arm play by pushing up and down (B) on the idler arm - if the total movement at A exceeds 1/4-inch, replace the idler arm

not in alignment, tighten the nut further; do not back it off.

16   Reconnect the tie-rods to the relay rod and then the relay rod to the idler arm.
17   Have the front wheel alignment checked as soon as possible.

Idler arm

Refer to illustration 17.19

18   To remove the idler arm, first raise the front of the vehicle so the wheels hang free and then set them in the straight ahead position. Support the vehicle securely on jackstands.
19   If the reason for removal is suspected wear, first check this by attaching a spring balance to the idler arm as near as possible to the relay rod. Exert a pull of 25-lb, first upward and then downward **(see illustration)**. The total movement of the end of the idler arm should not exceed 1/4-inch; if it does, replace the idler arm as an assembly.
20   To remove the idler arm, unbolt it from the frame (no washer is used under the nut).
21   Disconnect the idler arm from the relay rod and remove the arm.
22   Installation is the reverse of the removal steps.

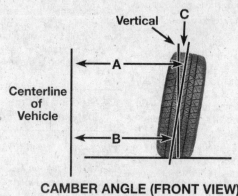

Vertical   **C**

A

Centerline of Vehicle

B

CAMBER ANGLE (FRONT VIEW)

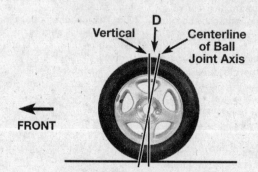

D

Vertical   **Centerline of Ball Joint Axis**

FRONT

CASTER ANGLE (SIDE VIEW)

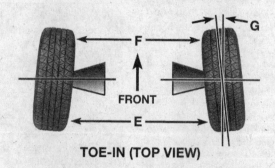

G

F

FRONT

E

TOE-IN (TOP VIEW)

18.1 Typical front end alignment details

A minus B = C (degrees camber)
D = degrees caster

E minus F = toe-in (measured in inches)
G = toe-in (expressed in degrees)

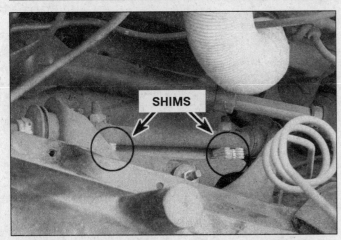

18.4 Front caster and camber are adjusted with shims at the upper control arm mounting points

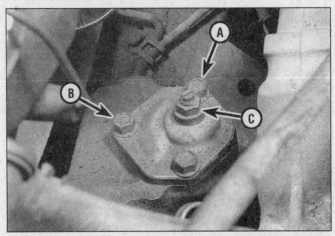

19.2 Remove bolt A to add lubricant to the steering box - remove bolt B to check the level - C is the lash adjuster screw and jam-nut

18 Wheel alignment - general information

Front wheels

Refer to illustrations 18.1 and 18.4

A front end alignment refers to the adjustments made to the front wheels so they are in proper angular relationship to the suspension and the ground. Front wheels that are out of proper alignment not only affect steering control, but also increase tire wear. The front end adjustments normally required are camber, caster and toe-in **(see illustration)**.

Getting the proper front wheel alignment is a very exacting process, one in which complicated and expensive machines are necessary to perform the job properly. Because of this, you should have a technician with the proper equipment perform these tasks. We will, however, use this space to give you a basic idea of what is involved with front end alignment so you can better understand the process and deal intelligently with the shop that does the work.

Toe-in is the turning in of the front wheels. The purpose of a toe specification is to ensure parallel rolling of the front wheels. In a vehicle with zero toe-in, the distance between the front edges of the wheels will be the same as the distance between the rear edges of the wheels. The actual amount of toe-in is normally only a fraction of an inch. Toe-in adjustment is controlled by the tie-rod end position on the inner end of each tie-rod. Incorrect toe-in will cause the tires to wear improperly by making them scrub against the road surface.

Camber is the tilting of the front wheels from the vertical when viewed from the front of the vehicle. When the wheels tilt out at the top, the camber is said to be positive (+). When the wheels tilt in at the top the camber is negative (-). The amount of tilt is measured in degrees from the vertical and this measurement is called the camber angle. This angle affects the amount of tire tread which contacts the road and compensates for changes in the suspension geometry when the vehicle is cornering or traveling over an undulating surface. Camber is adjusted by adding or subtracting shims at the upper control arm pivot mounting points **(see illustration)**.

Caster is the tilting of the top of the front steering axis from the vertical. A tilt toward the rear is positive caster and a tilt toward the front is negative caster. It's adjusted by moving shims from one end of the upper control arm mount to the other.

Rear wheels

On the rear, the only adjustments possible are camber and toe-in. These angles are set during production and do not normally require alteration. If the rear suspension is to be dismantled, always mark the setting of the cam adjuster bolt and the location of the toe-in shims.

Special equipment will again be required to measure the camber and toe-in for the rear wheels, and it is recommended that this work is left to an alignment shop, but the method of adjustment should be understood.

Camber is adjusted by loosening the nut on the cam bolt and turning the cam bolt until the specified angle is obtained.

Toe-in is adjusted by inserting or removing shims at the frame side member on both sides of the torque control arm pivot bushing. Shim removal and installation procedure is described in conjunction with removal of the control arm in Section 14.

19 Steering gear - lubrication and adjustment

Early models

Refer to illustration 19.2

1 The manual steering gear is filled during production with a water-resistant grease and normally requires no further attention. However as a precaution against a worn seal or crack permitting loss of lubricant, check the lubricant at the mileages specified in Chapter 1.

2 Unscrew and remove the two lower screws from the cover on the steering gear **(see illustration)**.

3 Install a lubricator in the indicated hole and inject lubricant of the correct type until it appears level with the other screw hole. Remove the lubricator and screw in the cover screws.

4 After a considerable mileage the following two adjustments may become necessary as the internal components of the steering gear wear.

Worm bearing pre-load adjustment

5 Unscrew and remove the Pitman arm retaining nut.

6 Mark the relative position of the Pitman arm to the shaft. Remove the Pitman arm using a heavy duty puller.

7 Loosen the Pitman shaft lash adjuster screw jam nut, and unscrew the screw a few turns **(see illustration 19.2)**.

8 With the front wheels raised off the ground, turn the steering wheel gently to full lock and then return it one turn of the steering wheel. Do not turn the steering hard against its stops or the steering gear ball guides may be damaged.

9 On vehicles without a tilt - telescopic steering column, remove the steering wheel horn button or contact ring and apply a 3/4-inch socket to the steering wheel retaining nut.

10 On vehicles with a tilt/telescopic column, disconnect the steering flexible coupling as an additional operation. Also as a means of turning the steering wheel, a Phillips adapter socket must be applied to the wheel center screw.

11 Using a torque wrench (the beam type is preferred), check the turning torque of the steering column.

12 On cars with tilt/telescopic steering columns, the turning torque must be estab-

lished first on the column (previously disconnected at the flexible coupling) and then on the gear. Subtract the first reading from the second.

13   If the turning torque is not within that given in this Chapter's Specifications, adjust the steering gear as follows:

14   The worm bearing adjuster is the large lock-nut and hex located at the bottom of he steering box. Loosen the worm bearing adjuster locknut and turn the adjuster until any endplay is just eliminated from the worm. Re-check the turning torque and then tighten the locknut.

Pitman shaft lash adjustment

15   Once worm bearing pre-load is adjusted, adjust the shaft lash. Turn the steering wheel gently from one stop to the other and count the exact number of turns. Now turn the steering wheel back exactly half way to center the steering gear.

16   Gently turn the lash adjuster screw until all lash is removed from the gear teeth. This can be established if the Pitman shaft is gripped and pushed and pulled as the screw is turned. When correctly adjusted, a force of between 9 and 16 in-lbs should be in the steering wheel through the center position. Use a beam-type torque wrench to check this.

17   Install the Pitman arm (marks in alignment), lower the car and install the horn button components.

Later models

18   The steering gear is filled at the factory with the proper lubricant. Change of lubricant is not necessary and the housing should not be drained. No additional lubrication is required for the life of the steering gear.

19   At the specified intervals (refer to Chapter 1), the steering gear should be inspected for seal leakage (actual solid grease, not just an oily film). If a seal is replaced or the gear is overhauled, the housing should be refilled with steering gear lubricant. **Note:** *Do not use EP chassis lube and do not overfill the gear housing.*

20   Before any adjustments are made to the steering gear in an attempt to correct such conditions as shimmy, loose or hard steering, etc., a careful check should be made of front end alignment, the shock absorbers, wheel balance and tire pressure (which may also cause steering related problems).

21   Correct adjustment of the steering gear is very important. Begin by disconnecting the battery ground cable.

22   Raise the vehicle and support it securely on jackstands. Remove the Pitman arm nut. Mark the relationship of the Pitman arm to the shaft, then remove the Pitman arm. This requires a special Pitman arm puller, which can be rented, or a heavy duty two-jaw puller.

23   Loosen the adjuster plug locknut and back the adjuster off 1/4 turn.

24   Remove the horn button cap or shroud.

25   Turn the steering wheel gently in one direction until it contacts the stop, then turn it back 1/2-turn. **Note:** *Do not turn the steering*

wheel hard against the stops when the steering linkage is disconnected from the gear, as damage to the ball guides could result.

26   Measure and record "bearing drag" by applying a torque wrench with an appropriate size socket to the steering wheel nut and rotating it through a 90-degree arc. **Note:** *Do not use a torque wrench with a maximum torque reading greater than 50 in-lbs.*

27   Adjust the thrust bearing preload by tightening the adjuster plug until the proper preload is obtained (see this Chapter's Specifications). When the proper preload has been obtained, tighten the adjuster plug locknut to the torque listed in this Chapter's Specifications and recheck the preload. If the steering gear feels "lumpy" after adjustment, damage to the bearings has probably occurred (due to severe impact or improper adjustment). The steering gear must be disassembled for replacement of damaged parts (refer to Section 25).

28   Adjust the over-center preload as follows:

a) *Turn the steering wheel gently from one stop to the other and carefully count the total number of turns required. Turn the wheel back half way, to the center position.*

b) *Turn the over-center adjuster screw clockwise to take out all lash between the ball nut and Pitman shaft sector teeth, then tighten the locknut.*

c) *Check the torque at the steering wheel, taking the highest reading as the wheel is through the center position (see this Chapter's Specifications for proper over-center preload).*

d) *If necessary, loosen the locknut and readjust the over-center adjusting screw to obtain the proper torque. Tighten the locknut to the torque listed in this Chapter's Specifications and again check the torque reading through the center of travel. **Note:** If the maximum torque value is exceeded, turn the over-center adjusting screw counterclockwise, then come up on the adjustment by turning the adjuster locknut in a clockwise direction.*

29   Connect the Pitman arm to the shaft by lining up the marks made during disassembly, then install the nut and tighten it to the torque listed in this Chapter's Specifications.

---

20   Manual steering - ratio changes

1   To suit individual preference, the steering ratio may be altered by moving both tie-rod ends to engage in one of the two holes in the steering arms.

2   Engagement in the forward hole will give a steering ratio of 17.6:1, while the rear hole gives a ratio of 20.2:1 which is the standard ratio.

3   After changing the positions of the tie-rod ends on the steering arms, have the front end alignment checked and, if necessary, adjusted.

---

21   Steering wheel - removal and installation

1968 through 1972 models (standard steering wheel)

Refer to illustration 21.6

1   Disconnect the battery negative cable from the battery.

2   Disconnect the electrical connector at the side of the steering column.

3   Remove the horn button cap or center ornament from the steering wheel.

4   Remove the three screws from the cup now exposed, followed by the belleville spring, bushing and pivot ring.

5   Unscrew the steering wheel nut and washer.

6   Use a suitable puller with anchor bolts screwed into the threaded holes in the hub of the wheel and remove the steering wheel **(see illustration)**.

7   Installation is the reverse of the removal steps but make sure that the turn signal control assembly is in its neutral position before installing the wheel, or the canceling cam may be damaged. Tighten the steering wheel

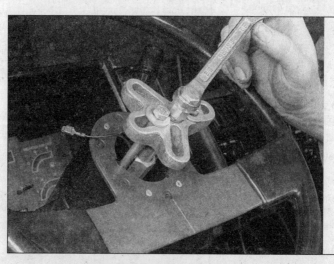

21.6 Remove the steering wheel with a puller - DO NOT pound on the wheel or use an impact-type puller

nut to the torque listed in this Chapter's Specifications.

1968 through 1982 models (deluxe steering wheel)

8 Disconnect the battery negative cable from the battery.
9 Disconnect the electrical connector at the side of the steering column.
10 Remove the three screws from the underside of the steering wheel. Remove the horn button securing screws and the steering wheel shroud.
11 Remove the steering wheel as described in Steps 5 and 6.
12 Installation is the reverse of the removal steps. Tighten the steering wheel nut to the torque listed in this Chapter's Specifications.

1968 through 1972 models (tilt/telescopic steering wheel)

13 With this type of steering wheel, the upper bearing preload spring is located below the canceling cam. Otherwise the removal operations are similar to those previously described.
14 Disconnect the battery ground cable.
15 Disconnect the electrical connector at the side of the steering column.
16 Pry off the horn button cap.
17 Remove the three screws that secure the horn contact to the spacer and hub.
18 Remove the two screws which hold the lock screw to the locking knob. Remove the screw, knob and spacer.
19 The steering wheel can be removed independently from the hub at this stage by unscrewing the securing screws. If the complete wheel/hub assembly is to be removed, proceed with the following operations.
20 Remove the shaft nut and washer and draw off the steering wheel using a puller. Remove the canceling cam and spring.
21 Installation is the reverse of the removal steps. Tighten nuts and bolts to the torque listed in this Chapter's Specifications.

1973 and later models (regular steering wheel)

22 Disconnect the battery ground cable.
23 Pry off the horn button cap.
24 Remove the snap-ring and then unscrew the steering wheel retaining nut.
25 Use a steering wheel puller bolted into the threaded holes in the steering wheel hub to pull the steering wheel off the shaft.
26 Installation is the reverse of the removal steps. Make sure that the direction indicator is in the neutral position. Tighten the steering wheel nut to the torque listed in this Chapter's Specifications and install the snap-ring.

1973 and later models (tilt/telescopic steering wheel)

27 Disconnect the battery ground cable, then pry off the horn button and remove the horn contact.

28 Remove the shim (if used), followed by the star screw and lever.
29 Remove the snap-ring and unscrew the steering wheel retaining nut. Remove the steering wheel with a puller.
30 The steering wheel can be disassembled by removing the three wheel-to-hub screws and the four screws that hold the extension to the steering wheel.
31 Installation is the reverse of the removal procedure.

22 Steering flexible coupling - removal and installation

1968 through 1977 models

Refer to illustration 22.2
1 Disconnect the cable from the negative terminal of the battery.
2 Remove the bolts that attach the flange of the intermediate steering shaft to the flexible coupling **(see illustration)**.
3 Unscrew and remove the bolts that hold the steering gear to the frame and lower the gear until the intermediate shaft can be pushed to the rear and turned aside out of the way.
4 Unscrew the pinch bolt from the coupling clamp and remove the flexible coupling. The pinch bolt will require a 12-point socket or box-end wrench to unscrew it.
5 Installation is the reverse of the removal steps. Make sure the flat on the coupling aligns with the matching scribed line or flat on the wormshaft.

1978 and later models

6 Disconnect the battery negative cable from the battery.
7 Remove the two nuts that connect the steering shaft flange to the flexible coupling bolts.
8 Detach the steering column from the firewall and the lower trim plate (below the steering column).
9 Remove the two bolts holding the steering column to the support, then slide the column to the rear until the steering shaft is disengaged from the flexible coupling. Let the column assembly rest on the seat.
10 Remove the through bolt from the coupling on the steering gear shaft, then remove the coupling.
11 Installation is the reverse of the removal steps.

23 Pitman shaft seal - replacement

1 A leaking grease seal can be replaced without removing the steering gear from the car.

Early models

2 Remove the Pitman arm from the steering gear. This is the arm that connects the steering gear to the linkage. Removal requires a special Pitman arm puller, which can be rented, or a heavy duty two-jaw puller.
3 Loosen the lash adjuster locknut and unscrew the lash adjuster screw several turns.
4 Remove the three side cover screws from the steering gear, then pull the side cover complete with Pitman shaft from the steering gear housing. Do not separate the components.
5 Pry the defective seal from the housing. Apply grease to the lips of a new one and install it. Use a socket or piece of tubing to drive it into position.
6 Tape the splines on the Pitman shaft to prevent them cutting the lips of the seal and install the cover/shaft assembly. Before installing the two lower cover bolts, fill the housing with grease as described in Section 19.
7 Adjust the steering gear also as described in Section 19. Install the Pitman arm and tighten the securing bolt to the torque listed in this Chapter's Specifications.

Later models

8 Remove the Pitman arm (refer to Step 2).
9 Rotate the steering wheel from stop to stop, counting the total number of turns, then turn it back exactly half way, placing the gear

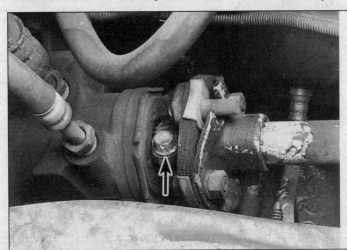

22.2 Remove the coupling clamp pinch bolt (arrow) - some models may require a 12-point socket

on center (the wormshaft flat should be at the 12 o'clock position).

10   Remove the three self-locking bolts attaching the side cover to the housing and lift the Pitman shaft/side cover assembly out of the housing.

11   Using a screwdriver, pry the Pitman shaft seal out of the housing (be careful not to damage the housing bore). **Note:** *Inspect the lubricant in the gear for contamination. If the lubricant is contaminated in any way, the gear must be removed from the vehicle and completely overhauled (refer to Section 25).*

12   Coat the new Pitman shaft seal with steering gear lubricant. Position the seal in the shaft bore and tap it into position with a large socket and hammer.

13   Remove the lash adjuster locknut, then disconnect the side cover from the Pitman shaft by turning the lash adjuster screw clockwise.

14   Place the Pitman shaft in the steering gear so the center tooth of the Pitman shaft sector enters the center tooth space of the ball nut.

15   Fill the housing with steering gear lubricant, then install a new side cover gasket onto the gear housing.

16   Install the side cover onto the lash adjuster screw by reaching through the threaded hole in the side cover with a small screwdriver and turning in the lash adjuster screw until it bottoms, then turn it back in 1/4-turn.

17   Install the side cover bolts and tighten them securely.

18   Install the lash adjuster screw locknut, then perform the steering gear adjustments. Install the Pitman arm.

24   Steering gear - removal and installation

1   Remove the flange nuts and pinch bolt from the steering coupling.

2   Unscrew and remove the nut and washer that secure the Pitman arm to the steering shaft.

3   Mark the relative position of the arm to the shaft and then pull off the Pitman arm. This requires a special Pitman arm puller, which can be rented, or a heavy-duty two-jaw puller.

4   Unscrew and remove the steering gear securing bolts and remove it from the vehicle.

5   Installation is the reverse of the removal steps. Make sure that the coupling pinch bolt passes through the undercut in the wormshaft and tighten all bolts and nuts to the torques listed in this Chapter's Specifications.

25   Steering gear - overhaul

1   Remove the steering gear as described in the preceding Section and clean away external dirt.

2   Mount the steering gear in a vise so it is clamped by means of one of its mounting tabs. Position the wormshaft in a horizontal attitude.

3   Rotate the wormshaft from stop-to-stop and count the total number of turns. Now turn it back exactly half way (confirmed by the wormshaft flat being at the 12 o'clock position).

4   Loosen the wormshaft adjuster screw locknut.

5   Remove the housing side cover (three bolts).

6   Tap the end of the Pitman shaft lightly with a plastic hammer and withdraw the shaft with side cover.

7   Remove the wormshaft adjuster plug and locknut assembly which incorporates the upper bearing race for the wormshaft. Do not allow the ball nut to run down to the ends of the worm under its own weight or the ball guides may be damaged.

8   Remove the wormshaft lower bearing from inside the gear housing.

9   Remove the locknut from the lash adjuster screw in the side cover, then screw the adjuster out of the side cover by turning it in a clockwise direction. Slide the adjuster screw and shim out of the slot in the end of the Pitman shaft.

10   Pry out and discard the Pitman shaft and wormshaft seals.

11   With the steering gear disassembled, inspect all components for wear.

12   Replace the oil seals as a matter of routine.

13   Replacement of the Pitman shaft bushings should be left to a dealer service department or other repair shop, as a press is required. New bushings require no reaming as they are supplied bored to size.

14   If the side cover bushing is worn, the complete side cover must be replaced.

15   The wormshaft adjuster plug bearing race can be replaced by driving it out with a punch and pressing in the new one.

16   The wormshaft housing races can be removed by inserting a punch into the housing from the adjuster plug end and then driving the expansion plug out of the lower end of the housing. Drive out the bearing race.

17   Press in the new bearing and install a new expansion plug. Depress the center of the plug to deform it sufficiently to make a tight seal.

18   Binding or tightness of the ball nut on the worm is unusual, but if such conditions are evident, disassemble it as follows:

19   Remove the screws and the clamp that hold the ball guides in the nut. Draw the guides out of the nut.

20   Turn the nut upside down and rotate the wormshaft back and forth until all the balls have dropped out of the nut. Be sure to catch the balls as they fall out. Now pull the nut from the worm.

21   Using a magnifier, examine the balls, grooves and worm for wear, scoring or damage. Replace parts as necessary.

22   Reassemble the ball nut in the following way. Place the wormshaft flat on a bench and slide the nut onto the worm so that the ball guide holes are uppermost and the shallow end of the rack teeth are to the left with respect to the steering wheel (as if the steering gear was in the vehicle).

23   Align the worm and nut grooves by looking through the ball guide holes.

24   Place 27 balls into a container and then insert balls, one at a time into the guide holes, at the same time turning the worm gradually away from the hole.

25   Lay one half of the ball guide (groove up) on the bench and install the remainder of the 27 balls in it.

26   Cover this half of the ball guide with the other half guide and plug each open end of the guide with petroleum jelly to prevent the balls from dropping out.

27   Insert the guide into the guide holes in the nut. One circuit of the balls is now completely installed. Repeat the operations with the remaining 27 balls and the second circuit.

28   Assemble the ball guide clamp to the ball nut and tighten the screws to the torque listed in this Chapter's Specifications.

29   Before reassembling, smear the internal components with the specified steering gear lubricant.

30   Place a wormshaft bearing in the housing race. Slide the other bearing and the adjuster plug assembly over the upper end of the wormshaft.

31   Insert the wormshaft, nut and adjuster into the housing, guiding the lower end of the wormshaft into the housing bearing.

32   Thread the adjuster into the housing until nearly all endplay is eliminated from the wormshaft.

33   Engage the lash adjuster screw together with its shim in the groove at the end of the Pitman shaft. Now check the end clearance of the adjuster groove. This should not be more than 0.002-inch. If it is, change the shim for one of an alternative thickness, which is supplied as a selection of four in a repair pack.

34   Keep packing the steering gear lubricant into the components and housing as reassembly progresses.

35   Rotate the wormshaft until the ballnut is at the center of its travel. Install the Pitman shaft with the adjuster screw so the center tooth of the shaft sector enters the center space on the ballnut.

36   Install a near side cover gasket to the housing.

37   Install the side cover to the Pitman shaft by inserting a screwdriver through the lash adjuster hole in the side cover and turning the screw counterclockwise until the screw bottoms. Now back off the screw 1/2-turn. Loosely fit a locknut to the adjuster screw.

38   Screw in and tighten the side cover bolts.

39   Adjust the worm bearing preload and the Pitman shaft lash as described in Section 19 and also fill the housing with lubricant as instructed in the same Section.

26 Steering lock cylinder - removal and installation

1 The lock cylinder is located on the upper right-hand side of the column. The lock cylinder should only be removed in the Run position, or damage to the buzzer switch will occur.

1968 through 1977 models

2 Remove the steering wheel (see Section 21) and turn signal switch (see Chapter 12). The turn signal switch need not be fully removed provided that it is pushed rearward far enough for it to be slipped over the end of the shaft. Do not pull the harness out of the column.

3 Insert a thin blade or driver into the slot in the turn signal switch housing. Break the housing flash loose and at the same time depress the spring latch at the lower end of the lock cylinder. Hold the latch down and withdraw the lock cylinder from the housing.

4 The lock cylinder can't be disassembled; a new one (coded to accept the original key) must be installed in the original cylinder sleeve after the assembly has been dismantled by releasing the cylinder-to-sleeve staking.

5 To assemble the new lock cylinder to the sleeve, insert the ignition key part way into the lock and then place the wave washer and anti-theft ring onto the lower end of the lock cylinder.

6 Now align the lock bolt in the cylinder and the tab of the anti-theft washer with the slot in the sleeve. Push the sleeve fully onto the sleeve and then insert the ignition key fully and rotate the cylinder clockwise.

7 Rotate the lock counterclockwise to the Lock position.

8 Secure the lock assembly in the jaws of a vise suitably protected with wood or cloth. Install the adapter ring onto the lower end of the cylinder so that the finger of the adapter is located at the step in the sleeve and the serrated edge of the adapter can be seen after assembly to the cylinder. The key must also be free to rotate at least 120-degrees.

9 Tap the adapter onto the cylinder until it is at the bottom of the cylinder flats and the cylinder projects about 1/16-inch above the adapter.

10 Using a small punch, stake the lock cylinder over the adapter ring in four positions just outside of the four dimples.

11 To install the lock cylinder/sleeve assembly, hold the sleeve and rotate the knob clockwise against the stop.

12 Insert the cylinder/sleeve assembly into the housing so that the key on the cylinder sleeve is aligned with the housing key way.

13 Push the cylinder into the abutment of the lock cylinder and sector, then rotate the cylinder counter-clockwise, maintaining pressure on the cylinder until the snap-ring engages in the grooves and secures the cylinder in the housing. Check the lock action.

14 Install the turn signal switch and the steering wheel.

1978 and later models

15 Remove the steering wheel (see Section 21) and turn signal switch (see Chapter 12).

16 With the lock in the Run position, remove the lock plate and key buzzer (see Chapter 12).

17 Remove the screw and take out the cylinder. **Note:** *Do not drop the screw into the steering column. Complete disassembly of the column would be required to retrieve it. Use a magnetic screwdriver.*

18 To install the cylinder, rotate the key clockwise to the stop, align the key on the cylinder with the keyway in the housing and push the lock in as far as possible.

19 Install the screw and tighten it securely.

27 Steering column - removal and installation

1968 through 1977 models

1 The vehicle may be equipped with a standard column or tilt/telescopic column. Both types are removed and installed in the same way.

2 Disconnect the cable from the negative terminal of the battery.

3 Remove the steering wheel (see Section 21).

4 Remove the pinch bolt from the intermediate steering shaft coupling and separate the coupling from the lower end of the steering shaft.

5 Disconnect the backdrive linkage from the base of the steering column.

6 Disconnect the steering column harness at the electrical connector.

7 Disconnect the neutral start switch and back-up lamp switch connectors, if so equipped.

8 Remove the floorpan trim cover screws and remove the cover.

9 Remove the two nuts that secure the floorpan bracket to the mounting studs.

10 Remove the instrument panel trim cover.

11 Move the front seat as far back as it will go and then remove the two nuts that hold the column bracket to the instrument panel.

12 With the help of an assistant, withdraw the steering column assembly.

13 To install the steering column, first loosely assemble the support to the bracket using the shoulder bolts and nuts.

14 Assemble the upper end of the rag joint to the steering gear, tightening to the specified torque.

15 Pass the column assembly into the car, sliding the splined end of the steering shaft into the upper end of the rag joint. Connect all the electrical wiring.

16 Start the two support attaching screws.

17 Fit the transmission control cable bracket using the bolt.

18 Maintain a gap of 0.030-inch (± 0.05-inch) between the mast jacket and the inside (semi-circular) surface of the instrument panel. Screw on the nuts and tighten to the specified torque.

19 Pull the support to the rear in order to accommodate the height differential of the instrument panel and the bracket. Tighten the screws followed by the nuts to the specified torque.

20 Loosen the nuts and check that one of the following gaps exists (according to coupling type) between the flexible coupling rivets and the steering shaft flange. The steering must be in the straight-ahead position and no turning torque applied to the steering wheel.

> *Four-ply coupling - 0.04-inch*
> *Seven-ply flexible coupling - 0.07-inch*
> *If the gap is less than specified, realign the column.*

21 To complete the installation, reverse the operations described in Steps 2 through 10.

1978 and later models

22 To remove the steering column, perform Steps 1 through 12 of this Section.

23 To install the steering column, position the steering column in the vehicle with the splined end of the shaft inserted into the flange.

24 Loosely attach the column to the bracket with screws and washers.

25 Locate the steering column lower bracket assembly with screw and washers. Hold the bracket in place.

26 While maintaining a 0.030 ± 0.030-inch gap between the mast jacket of the column and the inside semi-circular surface of the instrument panel, position the steering column seal and plate on the inside of the dash panel. Install the nuts and tighten them securely.

27 Pull the support to the rear to accommodate the height difference between the instrument panel and the bracket. Tighten screws and nuts to the torque listed in this Chapter's Specifications. **Note:** *Do not tighten the column to the instrument panel until the vehicle is placed on its wheels/suspension.*

28 Loosen nuts and tighten flange bolt to the torque listed in this Chapter's Specifications while maintaining the flexible coupling dimension.

29 Remove the plastic spacer from the flexible coupling safety pins, then secure the steering column lower seal and plate to the dash panel by tightening the nuts to the specified torque.

30 Maximum misalignment of the steering shaft (in relation to the steering gear) must not exceed 0.152-inch. Also, the rivets in the flexible coupling must not ground out on the steering shaft flange when the shaft is rotated 360-degrees.

28.4a Remove the turn signal switch lever. On some models this is accomplished by pulling straight out; on other models it's attached to the switch with a screw. Remove the turn signal switch (see Chapter 12)

28.4b Remove the three screws (arrows) which retain the switch cover assembly

28.4c Remove the switch cover assembly and set it on the floor; be careful not to damage the cruise control wire

28.4d Remove the high-beam/turn signal switch actuator (if equipped)

28.4e To release the tilt mechanism retainer, push it in and turn it counterclockwise - be careful, since it's under spring pressure

28 Tilt/telescopic steering column - repair

Refer to illustrations 28.4a through 28.4p

1   Disconnect the negative battery cable.

2   Remove the steering wheel (see Section 21).

3   Remove the turn signal switch and the key lock cylinder (see Chapter 12).

4   Follow the accompanying photo sequence on a typical GM column **(see illustrations)**. Stay in order and read each caption carefully.

5   Installation is the reverse of removal.

28.4f The tilt pivot pins (arrow) are located on each side of the housing

28.4g A small slide hammer and an 8-32 machine screw . . .

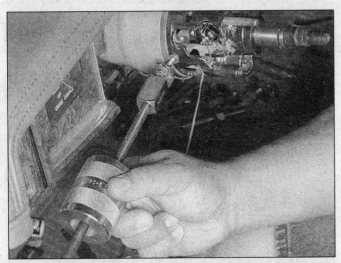

28.4h . . . is the best way to remove the pivot pins

28.4i If you don't have a small slide hammer, screw an 8-32 machine screw into each pin, clamp a pair of locking pliers onto the screw and use a large screwdriver to pry out the pins as shown

28.4j Before you remove the housing, pay very close attention to the relationship between the rack (A) and the sector (B); when the housing is installed again, this is how these two parts must fit together

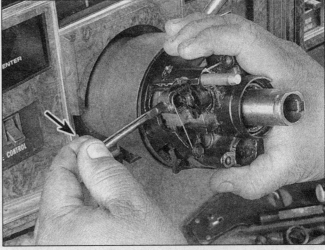

28.4k Temporarily screw the tilt lever back in and pull toward you to release the tilt shoes from the shaft . . .

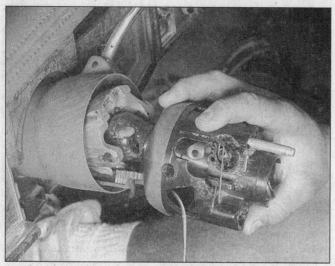

28.4l . . . and remove the housing (you will need to use this same procedure to install the housing)

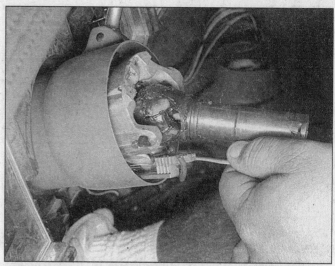

28.4m After disconnecting the cruise control lead down at the base of the column, carefully fish it out of the column and set the housing on the floor

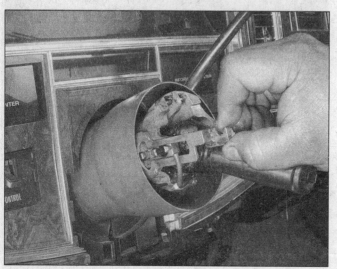

28.4n Remove the rack; note how the rack is oriented - it must go back in exactly this way

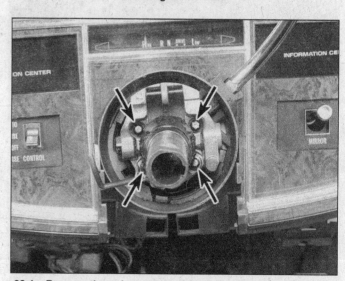

28.4o Remove these four screws (arrows), apply some Loctite to the threads, install the screws and tighten them securely; this will eliminate the "sloppiness" in the steering column

28.4p Install the rack and housing and pass the cruise control harness through the column (remember to pull back on the tilt lever when installing the housing). To install the pivot pins, carefully tap them into place with a hammer. The remainder of installation is the reverse of removal

29 Power steering cylinder - removal, overhaul and installation

Refer to illustration 29.3

1   Raise the front of the vehicle and support it securely on jackstands.

2   Disconnect the two flexible hoses from the power cylinder. Let the fluid drain into a container, then discard it.

3   Remove the cotter pin and unscrew the nut that holds the piston rod to the chassis frame (see illustration).

4   Remove the cotter pin and nut, then disconnect the power cylinder from the steering linkage relay rod. A balljoint separator will be required to disconnect the ball stud. A two-jaw puller may work also.

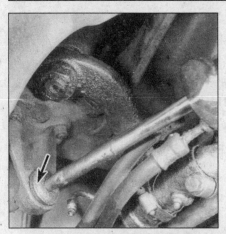

29.3 Power steering cylinder rod attachment to frame bracket (arrow)

30.2 Power steering control valve

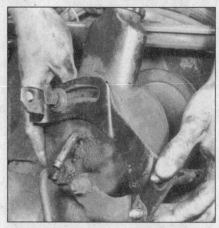

31.3 Removing the power steering pump

5   Remove the power cylinder and clean away all external dirt.

6   To disassemble the power cylinder, remove the snap-ring from the end of the cylinder and pull out the rod.

7   Remove the internal components from the rod.

8   Remove the ball stud seal and then remove the snap-ring that retains the end plug and lubrication fitting. Push on the ball stud to eject the ball stud components. Remove the O-ring seal.

9   If the ball stud seat is to be replaced, it will require the use of a press; or a bolt, nut and suitable spacers may be used as an alternative.

10   Replace all worn components, especially the seals.

11   Reassembly is the reverse of disassembly, but dip the internal components in clean power steering fluid as work progresses.

12   Installation is the reverse of the removal steps.

13   Bleed the hydraulic system as described in Section 33.

30 Power steering control valve - removal, overhaul and installation

Refer to illustration 30.2

1   Raise the front of the vehicle and place it securely on jackstands.

2   Remove the clamp pinch bolt from the point of attachment of the control valve and the relay rod **(see illustration)**.

3   Disconnect the two flexible hoses from the control valve and allow the fluid to drain, then discard it. Disconnect the two remaining hoses.

4   Disconnect the control valve from the Pitman arm. A balljoint separator will be required for this. A two-jaw puller might also work.

5   Push the Pitman arm to the right to clear the control valve and unscrew the control valve from the relay rod. Remove the control valve.

6   Clean away all external dirt and then grip the valve in a vise.

7   Pry off the dust cover and unscrew the adjuster nut.

8   Remove the bolts that hold the valve to the adapter, then withdraw the valve housing and spool.

9   Remove the spool from the housing.

10   Remove the spring, the reaction spool, the washer reaction spring, the spring retainer and the seal. Pry off the O-ring from the reaction spool.

11   Remove the annulus spacer valve shaft washer and the key that retains the plug to the sleeve.

12   Remove the clamp by unscrewing the nut, bolt and spacer. On some models, a crimped type of clamp is used. With this, straighten the clamp end and pull the clamp and the seal from the end of the stud.

13   Carefully turn the adjuster plug out of the sleeve.

14   Remove the valve from the vise and invert it to allow the spring and one of the two ball seats to fall free.

15   By removing the ball stud, the remaining ball seat and sleeve will fall free.

16   Clean and inspect all components and replace any that are worn or damaged.

17   Reassembly is the reverse of disassembly. Observe the following points:

  a) *Screw in the adjuster plug until it is tight and then back it off until the slot aligns with the notches in the sleeve.*

  b) *Install the reaction seal with its lip up, and the washer with its chamfer up.*

  c) *Always use a new nut on the shaft, turning it on about four turns. The valve assembly must now be adjusted (see Steps 18 to 21). This adjustment may also be required if the power steering system shows a need for more effort in one direction than in the other).*

18   Install the control valve to the car by reversing the removal operations. Disconnect the power cylinder piston rod from the frame bracket. Connect the flexible hoses and fill the pump reservoir with fluid.

19   Start the engine and observe the piston

rod. If the rod remains retracted, turn the adjusting nut clockwise until the rod begins to move out, then mark the position of the nut. Now turn the nut counterclockwise until the rod just begins to move in. Again mark the position of the nut. Finally turn the nut to the halfway position between the two marks.

20   If the rod extends as soon as the engine is started, turn the nut counterclockwise until the rod begins to move in. Mark the position of the nut. Now turn the nut clockwise until the rod just begins to move out. Again mark the position of the nut. Finally turn the nut to the halfway position between the two marks.

21   If the valve is correctly balanced, it should be possible to move the rod in and out using hand pressure alone.

22   Turn off the engine and connect the piston rod to the frame bracket.

23   Restart the engine, bleed the system (see Section 33) and then check the operation of the steering by turning the steering wheel in both directions.

24   Lubricate the end of the valve and install the dust cap.

25 . Lower the car to the ground.

31 Power steering pump - removal and installation

Refer to illustrations 31.3 and 31.6

1   Disconnect the flexible hoses that run between the pump and the control valve. Plug or cap the ends of the hoses.

2   Release the pump pivot bolt and brace bolt, push the pump in towards the engine and remove the drivebelt. On vehicles with a 454 cubic inch engine, loosen the alternator mounting bolts and adjuster to remove the drivebelt.

3   Unbolt and remove the pump, drain the fluid and clean off external dirt **(see illustration)**.

4   Unscrew the pump pulley nut and withdraw the pulley with a suitable puller. These can be rented.

5   To install the pulley on a new pump, draw the pulley onto the hub using a bolt, nut

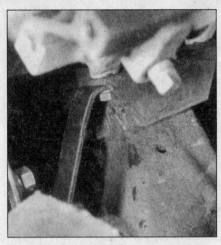

31.6 Power steering pump rear support strut

and washer. Do not hammer it into position.
6   Install the pump by reversing the removal steps. Position the strut that supports the rear of the pump**(see illustration)**. Tension the drivebelt and fill the reservoir with fluid of specified type. Bleed the system (Section 33).

32   Power steering system - bleeding

1   This is not a routine operation and is normally required only when the system has been disassembled and reassembled. Air in the power steering system is often indicated by a noisy pump, but a low fluid level can also cause this.
2   Fill the reservoir to its correct level with fluid of the recommended type (see Chapter 1), and allow it to remain undisturbed for at least two minutes.
3   . Start the engine and run it for two or three seconds only. Check the reservoir fluid level and top up if necessary.
4   Repeat the operations described in Step 3 until the fluid level remains constant.
5   Raise the front of the vehicle until the tires clear the ground. Support it securely on jackstands.
6   Start the engine and increase its speed to about 1500 rpm. Turn the steering wheel gently from stop to stop. Check the fluid level in the reservoir and top up if necessary.
7   Remove the jackstands and lower the vehicle to the ground. With the engine running, drive forward enough that the steering wheel can be turned to full right lock and full

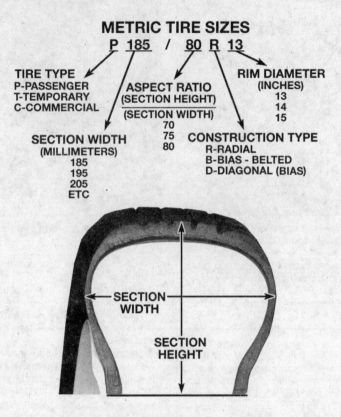

33.1 Metric tire size code

left lock. Recheck the fluid level. If the fluid is extremely foamy, let the vehicle stand for a few minutes with the engine off, then repeat the preceding steps.

33   Wheels and tires - general information

Refer to illustration 33.1
        The standard wheels are of the pressed steel type. Construction of original equipment tires varies to the production date of the vehicle. Early cars were equipped with crossply tires, while later models were fitted with bias belted or radial tires. Alloy wheels are optionally available on certain models. Today, only metric-sized, radial-ply tires are available **(see illustration)**.
        Tires affect the ride and handling of the vehicle. Don't mix different types of tires, such as radials and bias belted, on the same vehicle as handling may be seriously

affected. It's recommended that tires be replaced in pairs on the same axle, but if only one tire is being replaced, make sure it's the same size, structure and tread design as the other.
        Because tire pressure has a substantial effect on handling and wear, the pressure on all tires should be checked at least once a month or before any extended trips (see Chapter 1).
        Wheels must be replaced if they are bent, dented, leak air, have elongated holes, are heavily rusted, out of vertical symmetry or if the lug nuts won't stay tight. Wheel repairs that use welding or peening are not recommended.
        Tire and wheel balance is important to the overall handling, braking and performance of the vehicle. Unbalanced wheels can adversely affect handling and ride characteristics as well as tire life. Whenever a tire is installed on a wheel, the tire and wheel should be balanced by a shop with the proper equipment.

Chapter 11   Body

Contents

1   General information

The body utilizes a structural steel framework combined with fiberglass reinforced plastic body panels. This arrangement provides exceptional torsional rigidity and beaming strength. On later models, the steel underbody section is welded to the pillar support panel, which in turn is bonded to a fiberglass rear section.

A full-frame, rigid-perimeter, ladder-type chassis is used with five crossmembers and the body shell is bolted to it.

Two body styles are available - a convertible with a folding top or removable hardtop, and a coupe with removable roof panels.

The body styling has changed very little during the production run, although there are some differences with the front and rear end panels.

2   Body - maintenance

1   The condition of your vehicle's body is very important, because the resale value depends a great deal on it. It's much more difficult to repair a neglected or damaged body than it is to repair mechanical components. The hidden areas of the body, such as the wheel wells, the frame and the engine compartment, are equally important, although they don't require as frequent attention as the rest of the body.

2   Once a year, or every 12,000 miles, it's a good idea to have the underside of the body steam cleaned. All traces of dirt and oil will be removed and the area can then be inspected carefully for rust, damaged brake lines, frayed electrical wires, damaged cables and other problems. Body drain holes should be cleared of obstructions. The front suspension components should be greased after completion of this job.

3   At the same time, clean the engine and the engine compartment with a steam cleaner or water-soluble degreaser.

4   The wheel wells should be given close attention, since undercoating can peel away and stones and dirt thrown up by the tires can cause the paint to chip and flake.

5   The body should be washed about once a week. Wet the vehicle thoroughly to soften the dirt, then wash it down with a soft sponge and plenty of clean soapy water. If the surplus dirt is not washed off very carefully, it can wear down the paint.

6   Spots of tar or asphalt thrown up from the road should be removed with a cloth soaked in solvent.

7   Once every six months, wax the body and chrome trim. If a chrome cleaner is used to remove rust from any of the vehicle's

plated parts, remember that the cleaner also removes part of the chrome, so use it sparingly.

3   Upholstery and carpets - maintenance

1   Remove the carpets or mats, and thoroughly vacuum the interior of the car every three months or more frequently if necessary.
2   Beat the carpets and vacuum them if they're very dirty. If the upholstery is soiled, apply an upholstery cleaner with a damp sponge and wipe off with a clean, dry cloth.

4   Vinyl and folding tops - maintenance

1   Every three months, or more frequently if necessary, wash with a solution of lukewarm water and a neutral soap using a soft bristle brush, then rinse with plenty of clean water.
2   If additional cleaning is needed, a mild foaming cleaner can be used together with a little lukewarm water and a soft bristle brush. Remove the foam with a sponge or cloth, then repeat the operation if necessary. Rinse with plenty of clean water afterwards.
3   Never keep the top folded when wet, either from cleaning or wet-weather usage. Allow it to dry out in the raised position.

5   Body repair - minor damage

Repair of minor scratches in bodywork

1   Where a scratched panel involves no more than a paint refinishing job, it will be necessary to remove the existing paint down to the fiberglass laminate using a lacquer removing solvent.
2   Obtain a feather-edge on the remaining paint around the repair area using No. 220 wet-or-dry abrasive paper, then use a suitable plastic or wood block and No. 320 wet-or-dry paper to finally prepare the whole area to be repainted. Take care not to rub down too deeply or you'll cut into the fiberglass mat, which will mean filling the area as described later.
3   Carefully clean the repair area and an inch or two of the surrounding area with solvent, finishing off with a tack rag.
4   The repair area is now ready for spraying as described later in this Section.
5   If the damaged area requires any build-up to bring it up to the original contour, but where there is no structural damage to the fiberglass, remove the paint as described earlier.
6   Grind or file around the edge of the damaged area to form a V-groove to allow

the repair material to obtain a satisfactory bond. **Warning:** *Don't inhale the fiberglass dust, as it can be harmful to the lungs.*
7   Scuff the surrounding area with a sander or file to obtain a suitable surface for the repair to get a good bond.
8   Using a fiberglass repair kit, mix the epoxy solder or resin and hardener by carefully following the manufacturer's instructions.
9   Apply the filling material using a putty knife or rubber squeegee so that the filler is slightly higher than the surrounding body contour.
10   If possible, heat the area using a fan-type heater (a hair dryer will do if you can support it) or radiated heat from an electric light bulb. Don't overheat the repair, but just heat it gently to speed up the curing process. If you don't have a heat source, allow the repair to cure at room temperature. When curing by heat, about one hour is sufficient, but eight to ten hours will be required at 70 to 75-degrees and proportionately longer at lower temperatures.
11   Finish the repair by sanding down as described earlier. If you find that you've still got some low spots, a further local repair will be needed.
12   The repair area is now ready for spraying as described later in this Section.

Repair of cracks and holes where rear of panel is accessible

13   First, apply hand pressure all around the damaged area to see if there's any concealed damage which will also require attention.
14   Remove the existing paint from the damaged area using a lacquer removing solvent.
15   Grind or file a V-groove around the edge of the damaged area, making sure that the side of the V has a shallow pitch for a maximum bonding surface. Remove all the damaged material from the center of the repair area. **Warning:** *Don't inhale the fiberglass dust, as it can be harmful to the lungs.*
16   Scuff-sand around the edges of the repair area, and carefully clean and scuff the rear of the panel to provide a good bonding surface for the backing patch.
17   Carefully clean the repair area on both sides of the panel with a very fine cutting paste or car body polish remover.
18   If necessary, align the panel sections around the repair area using weights or clamps to re-establish the original panel profile.
19   Cut a piece of fiberglass cloth that will overlap the repair area by about two-inches, then mix up fiberglass resin and hardener according to the manufacturer's instructions. Don't mix too much - only enough for your immediate use.
20   Saturate the fiberglass cloth with the liquid resin mixture, and lay it over the repair area, smoothing out any wrinkles to maintain the general contour.

21   Repeat this procedure to build up a total thickness of three-to-five layers.
22   If possible, heat the repair area as described in Step 10; if you can't heat the area, allow it to cure at room temperature (70 to 75-degrees F) for about ten hours.
23   Finish the repair by sanding down, using progressively finer grades of wet-or-dry paper to obtain a good surface for painting. If necessary, further local filling may be done as described earlier.
24   The repair area is now ready for spraying as described later in this Section.

Repair of cracks and holes where rear of panel is inaccessible

25   First, apply hand pressure all around the damaged area to see if there's any concealed damage which will also require attention.
26   Remove the existing paint from the damaged area using a lacquer-removing solvent.
27   Using a file or hacksaw blade, remove all the damaged material from the repair area to form a hole through which a backing patch can be inserted.
28   Cut a piece of polyethylene film (food wrap) about three-inches larger all around than the repair area, and tape it in place so that the repair area is approximately in the middle. The repair area will serve as a form to give the backing patch the correct shape; the polyethylene will keep the patch from sticking to the vehicle.
29   Mix up resin and hardener, and build up to three-to-five layers of fiberglass cloth on top of the polyethylene as described for normal panel repair in Steps 19 through 22.
30   After curing, take off the patch and peel the polyethylene from the patch or vehicle body. Trim the patch to provide about two-inches overlap all round, so that it can be used as a backing on which to build up the repair.
31   Sand the mating surface of the backing patch and the rear of the hole to provide a rough bonding surface, then grind or file a V-groove around the edge of the damaged area, making sure that the side of the V has a shallow pitch for a maximum bonding surface.
32   Drill two holes about 3/4-inch apart in the backing patch and thread through a piece of wire (if the wire surface is waxed or very lightly greased, it will help with removal later). The wire is used for holding the patch in place while the rest of the repair is carried out.
33   Mix up more resin and hardener and apply it to the mating surface of the patch and the rear of the panel.
34   Slip the patch through the hole and pull hard on the wire until the filler squeezes out. Twist the wire around a strip of wood to support the backing patch in this position.
35   Allow the fiberglass resin to cure as described earlier to obtain a suitable surface for paint spraying.

Paint spraying

36 Initially make sure that the area to be sprayed is clean and dry. If not already done as part of the preparation process, clean the whole of the area to be sprayed with a very fine cutting paste or a car body polish remover, then wash down and carefully dry.

37 The repair area is now ready for spraying. Paint spraying must be carried out in a warm, dry, windless and dust-free atmosphere. This condition can be created artificially if you have access to a large indoor working area, but if you're forced to work in the open, you'll have to pick your day carefully. If you're working indoors, dousing the floor in the work area with water will settle the dust that would otherwise be in the atmosphere. If the repair area is confined to one body panel, mask off the surrounding panels; this will help to minimize the effects of a slight mismatch in paint colors. Bodywork fittings such as chrome strips and door handles will also need to be masked off. Use non-staining masking tape and several thicknesses of newspaper for the masking operation.

38 Spray the whole repair area with a light coat of grey primer; this will show up any imperfections on the surface. Repair these imperfections with fresh filler or glazing putty, and once more smooth the surface with sandpaper. If glazing putty is used it can be mixed with cellulose thinners to form a really thin paste which is ideal for filling small holes. Repeat this spray and repair procedure until you're satisfied that the surface of the filler, and the feathered edge of the paint are perfect. Clean the repair area with clean water and allow to dry fully.

39 Before spraying, agitate the aerosol can thoroughly, then spray a test area until the technique is mastered. Cover the repair area with a thick coat of primer; the thickness should be built up using several thin layers of paint rather than one thick one. Using 400 grade wet-or-dry paper, rub down the surface of the primer until it is really smooth. While doing this, the work area should be thoroughly doused with water, and the wet-or-dry paper periodically rinsed in water. Allow to dry before spraying on more paint.

40 Spray on the top coat, again building up the thickness by using several thin layers of paint. Start spraying in the center of the repair area, then use a circular motion, working outward until the whole repair area and about two-inches of the surrounding original paint is covered. Remove all masking material 10 to 15 minutes before spraying on the final coat of paint.

41 Allow the new paint at least two weeks to harden fully; then, using a very fine polishing compound, blend the edges of the new paint into the existing paint. Finally, apply wax polish.

6 Body repair - major damage

Repair of major damage cannot be readily carried out by the home mechanic. Whether it is a complete body panel, or a major part of one where the original contour has been lost, it is a job either for your Corvette dealer or a body repair shop.

7 Front bumper - removal and installation

1968 through 1972 models

Refer to illustration 7.3

1 Raise the front of the vehicle for access beneath the front bumper. Support the vehicle securely on jackstands.

2 Remove the decorative radiator grilles (see Section 9).

3 Remove the face bar attaching bolts, and the bolts attaching the lower edge of the bumper guards to the crossmember **(see illustration)**.

4 Lift off the bumper assembly, and remove the guards from the face bar. Note the shim locations when dismantling, for ease of assembly.

5 Installation is the reverse of the removal procedure, but do not finally tighten the various bolts until the alignment has been checked at the appropriate assembly stage.

1973 and 1974 models

6 Raise the headlight assemblies, then remove the retainers and take off the urethane bumper cover.

7 Remove the slider bracket bolt and shims.

8 Remove the bolt, and detach the impact bar from the side brackets.

9 Remove the nuts, and detach the energy absorbing bolts.

10 Remove the side bolt, and detach the slider bracket from the frame.

11 Remove the bolt and detach the side bracket from the brace assembly on the fender reinforcement.

12 Remove the bolts and nuts, and detach the brace assembly and support rods from the frame.

13 Installation is the reverse of the removal procedure, but do not finally tighten any bolts until everything is correctly aligned.

1975 through 1979 models

14 Raise the headlights, then remove the lower cover plate.

15 Remove the license plate and bracket from the front cover.

16 Remove the 14 nuts from the studs and take off the bumper cover.

17 Remove the parking light bulbs.

18 Remove the three center bolts and one at each end, and detach the bumper bar and honeycomb cushion assembly.

19 If necessary, remove the two long upper bolts (from the rear), and the three lower bolts (from the front), and detach the reinforcement. Remove the bolts and screws to separate the honeycomb cushion from the bumper bar.

20 Installation is the reverse of the removal process, but make check as you proceed that the bumper bar is mounted correctly before any final tightening of fasteners is done.

1980 through 1982 models

21 Raise both headlights to gain working clearance, then remove the splash shield and lower cover plate.

22 Remove the license plate and bracket from the front cover and remove the bulbs from the parking lamps.

23 Remove the grilles and lenses.

24 Remove the corner reinforcements from each side of the vehicle.

25 Remove the nuts from the studs holding the bumper cover to the body, then remove the cover.

26 Remove the bolts from both outboard ends of the bumper bar and the bolts from the lower guard reinforcement, then remove the center bolts from the frame extension brace.

27 Lift the bumper and cushion assembly away from the vehicle.

28 To disassemble the bumper, remove the 2 bolts holding the reinforcement to the bumper bar (at the front).

29 Remove the reinforcement from the

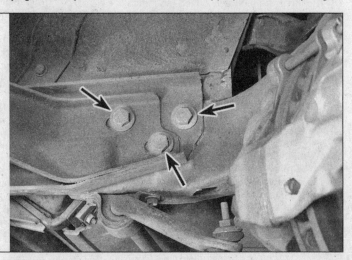

7.3 The front bumper brackets are attached to the frame by these bolts (arrows) - 1975 vehicle shown

8.15 The rear bumper cover is retained to the bumper bar by eighteen fasteners (arrows)

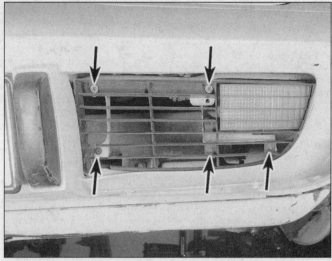

9.1a The 1975 and later grille can be lifted out after removing the fasteners (arrows)

bumper bar, then separate the cushion from the bar by drilling out the pop rivets.
30   Installation is the reverse of removal.

9.1b The lower extension panel on 1975 and later vehicles can be removed after raising the vehicle and supporting it securely on jackstands

8   Rear bumper - removal and installation

1968 through 1973 models

1   Raise the rear of the vehicle and place it securely on jackstands.
2   From beneath the vehicle, starting at the outboard ends, remove the bolts, washers and nuts securing the bumper assembly to the braces and rods.
3   Detach the braces and rods from the frame assembly.
4   Installation is the reverse of the removal steps, but do not tighten any of the bolts until alignment has been checked.

1974 models

5   Raise the rear of the vehicle and place it securely on jackstands.
6   Disconnect the license plate lights.
7   Remove the license plate and two license plate housing brace bolts.
8   Disconnect the two rubber straps.
9   Remove the two Phillips screws from the taillight housing cover.
10   Remove the sixteen stud nuts to release the bumper cover; the nuts over the inboard taillight should be removed last, after disconnecting the inboard taillights.
11   Remove the bumper cover.
12   To remove the bumper bracket and reinforcement, remove the rivets and bolts.
13   Reassembly and installation are basically the reverse of the removal steps, but it must be understood that the procedure is time-consuming. Time may be gained by sawing off the studs over the inboard taillights, and replacing the stud assembly with a new one during installation.

1975 through 1979 models

Refer to illustration 8.15

14   Remove the license plate and disconnect the lamps from the bumper cover.
15   Remove the eighteen cover retaining nuts **(see illustration)**.
16   Remove the license plate carrier bolts.
17   Remove the four lenses and housings, disconnecting the electrical wires.
18   Remove the three screws from each housing well, and disconnect the rear cover.
19   Disconnect the four bolts from each side, and detach the bumper bar from the enersorbers.
20   If necessary, enersorber brackets, lamp housing supports, center reinforcement, cover reinforcement and the two end brackets can be removed.
21   Reassembly and installation are basically the reverse of the removal steps, but correct alignment is very important. With the rear cover removed, tape a string exactly at the rear edge of the peak line across both sides.

Align the bumpers to maintain the dimensions shown, using shims where necessary.

1980 and later models

22   The rear bumper components for 1980 and later models are similar to those on 1975 through 1979 vehicles.

9   Radiator grille - removal and installation

Refer to illustrations 9.1a and 9.1b

1   Removal of the grille is straightforward, after removing the attaching screws **(see illustrations)**. On pre-1972 models it is necessary to remove the parking lights, and on some models it may also be necessary to remove the license plate bracket.
2   On 1975 and later models, the grille panel extension and grille lower support panel can be taken off after retaining bolts have been removed.

10.2 Scribe carefully around all hinge brackets prior to removing the hood bolts (arrows) so that it can installed in the same position - an assistant is required to support and help lift the hood

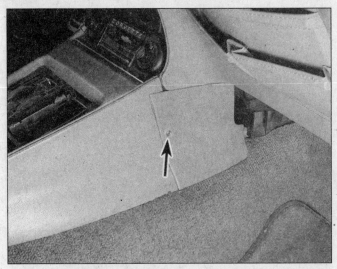

11.16 The console side covers are secured with screws (arrow)

10 Hood - removal, installation and adjustment

Refer to illustration 10.2

1 If the same hood is to be reinstalled, scribe around the hinges as a guide to installation.

2 With an assistant to support the hood, remove the hinge bolts and lift the hood off **(see illustration)**. Collect any shims that may have been used for adjustment.

3 Installation is straightforward, but make sure that the hinges and scribe marks are aligned.

4 If adjustment is required, shims may be added or removed from the hinges, or the hinges may be repositioned fore-and-aft. For adjustment at the forward end of the hood, reposition the two catch bolt mounting screws as necessary.

5 Synchronization of the catch release can be made by adjustment of the cable retainer located at the left-hand catch bolt assembly.

11 Console - removal and installation

1968 models

1 Using a sheet of heavy cardboard or a similar item to compress the seat cushion, remove one screw on each side of the rear console assembly.

2 Remove the rear storage compartment box, then remove the bolt and washer located at the center of the underbody panel.

3 Carefully lift up the rear console assembly housing clear of the parking brake lever.

4 With the left and right side trim panels removed, remove the two side flange screws on the front console assembly.

5 Remove the heater and side vent controls, the shift knob assembly, boot assembly and trim-plate, then lift the front console assembly rearward and upward.

6 Installation is the reverse of the removal steps, but make sure that the parking brake lever seal is properly positioned.

1969 through 1974 models

7 Disconnect the battery ground cable.

8 With the storage compartment, glovebox and battery lids opened, remove the storage compartment interior, the lid hinge screws (three per lid) and the eight compartment lid trim plate screws. Lift off the trim-plate, lids and glove compartment as an assembly.

9 Remove the bolt at the rear of the console, and the two bolts on each side of the rear portion of the console.

10 Lift up the console and disconnect the electric window switch connectors, then move it rearward to allow the parking brake handle seal to slide out of the slot. Remove the rear portion completely.

11 Remove the heater and side vent controls, the shift knob assembly, boot assembly and trim-plate, then lift the front console assembly rearward and upward.

12 Installation is the reverse of the removal procedure, but make sure that the parking brake lever seal is properly positioned.

1975 and later models

Refer to illustration 11.16

13 Disconnect the battery ground cable.

14 Remove the shifter knob assembly.

15 Remove the screws and take off the trim-plate; remove the cigarette lighter assembly.

16 Remove the front side panels of the console **(see illustration)**; where applicable, disconnect the rear window defogger wiring switch.

17 Remove the two attaching screws on each side of the rear console.

18 Remove the storage compartment tray, then remove the console rear attaching screw.

19 Slide the rear console rearward to remove the housing and the parking brake seal.

20 Remove one screw from each side of the front console, then working through the left panel opening, loosen the console-to-instrument panel securing nut.

21 Working through the console center opening, loosen the right-hand console-to-instrument panel securing nut.

22 Lift the console and slide it rearward, pushing down on the heater control for additional clearance.

23 Installation is the reverse of the removal procedure, but make sure that the parking brake seal is properly positioned.

12 Instrument panel pad - removal and installation

1968 through 1971 models (right-hand pad)

1 Remove the two screws on the outboard flange and the two screws at the inner flange of the center cluster.

2 Pull the pad outward to release the retaining clips along the top of the trim side panel.

3 Remove the pad.

4 Installation is the reverse of the removal procedure.

1972 through 1977 models (right-hand pad)

Refer to illustration 12.5

5 Remove the two screws on the out-

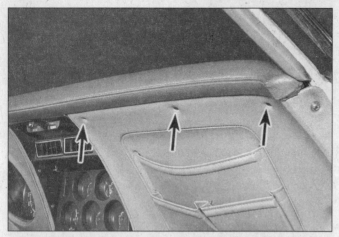

12.5 The right instrument panel pad on 1975 through 1978 vehicles can be taken off after removing seven retaining screws (arrows indicate four upper screws)

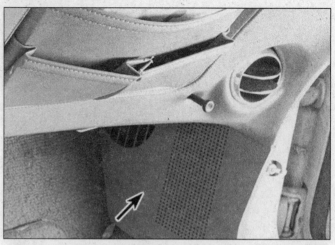

13.3 The fronts of the door sill covers must be raised in order to allow the kick panels (arrow) to be unclipped

board flange, the two screws at the inner flange of the center cluster panel, and the three screws at the top of the pad **(see illustration).**

6   Pull the trim pad outward, disconnecting the clips and wiring harness, as applicable.

7   Installation is the reverse of the removal procedure.

1978 and later models (one-piece pad)

8   Disconnect the negative battery cable from the battery.

9   Remove the six glove compartment attaching screws and lift out the glove compartment.

10   Remove the four screws attaching the instrument panel to the hinge pillars.

11   Remove the lower air distribution ducts and the console side panels.

12   Remove the two center console-to-instrument panel attaching screws from the front edge of the console.

13   Remove the radio, then release the two clips from the instrument panel brackets by pulling down on them.

14   Pull the center instrument cluster out slightly, disconnect the electrical connector from the rear of the cluster, then remove the cluster from the panel.

15   Remove the instrument panel steering column cover and the two nuts attaching the steering column to the dash brace and lower column.

16   To remove the left instrument cluster, proceed as follows:

a)   *Remove the lens-to-bezel attaching screws and lift off the lens.*

b)   *Remove the cluster-to-instrument panel attaching screws.*

c)   *Pull the cluster slightly forward to obtain clearance for removal of the speedometer cable housing and illuminating lamps.*

d)   *Remove the instrument cluster.*

17   Disconnect the windshield wiper switch connector, the headlamp switch connector and the speaker connectors.

18   The instrument panel assembly is now free and can be removed from the vehicle.

19   Installation is the reverse of removal.

13   Cowl ventilator cover and kick panel - removal and installation

1968 through 1978 models

Refer to illustration 13.3

1   Loosen four of the sill plate screws sufficiently to release the force of the kick panel.

2   Remove one screw at the center of the kick panel, then pull the panel out in the rearward direction.

3   The side trim panels can now be lifted out by pulling them forward and upward to release the two spring clips at the front console assembly **(see illustration).**

4   Installation is the reverse of the removal procedure.

1979 and later models

5   Remove the courtesy light from the right-hand kick panel.

6   Remove the screw from the rear of the panel, then pull to the rear to remove the panel. Repeat the procedure for the remaining panel.

7   Installation is the reverse of the removal steps.

14   Cowl ventilator - removal, installation and adjustment

Removal and installation

1   Remove the cowl kick panel.

2   Detach the control cable from the bracket, then remove the knob assembly retaining screw.

3   With the console trim plate lifted out, remove the nut retaining guide.

4   Remove the cable retaining screw at the inside front of the console assembly.

5   Disassemble the control mechanism, then remove the cable assembly by disconnecting it at the adjusting link and pulling it through.

6   Installation is the reverse of the removal procedure; if necessary adjust as described in Step 1.

Adjustment

7   Turn the plastic adjustment link in the middle of the central cable beneath the dash panel as necessary. When the knob is in the forward position the ventilator valve should be completely closed.

15   Windshield and rear window glass - replacement

This job, which involves the use of special tools and self-curing adhesives, is considered beyond the scope of the home mechanic. Where a replacement item is required, the job should be carried out by a windshield replacement specialist.

16   Doors - adjustment

Door lock striker

Refer to illustration 16.3

1   To check whether adjustment is required, make sure that the door is properly aligned (Steps 15 through 20).

2   Stick some modeling clay around the lock bolt opening, then gently close the door as far as necessary for the striker bolt to form an impression.

3   Check the striker impression. It should be centered fore and aft as well as up and down. If adjustment is necessary, mark the position of the striker on the body pillar before removing it **(see illustration).**

4   Using either a hexagonal wrench (early models) or a six-point socket wrench (later models), remove the striker.

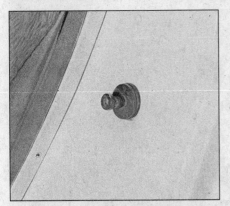

16.3 The door striker can be moved slightly up or down and in and out, or shimmed to bring it closer or further away from the latch

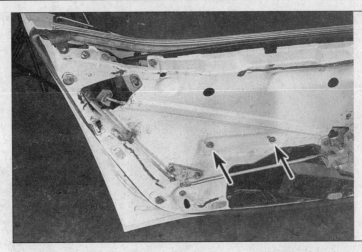

16.10 Adjusting the glass at the front and rear (arrows) bolts can change the tilt of the glass

5   Using a combination of spacers to make up the adjustment, install and tighten the bolt. Spacers are available in 5/64-inch, 5/32-inch, 1/4-inch and 5/16-inch sizes.

Door wedge pin (convertible)

6   The wedge pin in the door is not adjustable, and is not interchangeable from side-to-side of the vehicle.
7   Adjustments are made by moving the housing bracket. Vertical adjustment is made by loosening the six mounting screws. Side-to-side and in-and-out adjustments are made by loosening the three mounting bolts. Shims must not be used for adjustment.
8   To adjust, loosen the screws and bolts and move the bracket as needed. Tighten the screws or bolts just snug (no tighter) and close the door gently. Tighten all 9 screws and bolts, then open the door.
9   Tighten the screws and bolts to 70 in-lbs, then close the door and check the fit.

Door window

Refer to illustrations 16.10 and 16.11
10   Window tilted: Loosen the two channel adjustment bolts **(see illustration)**, then

move the glass until a constant distance is achieved between the front edge of the glass and the windshield pillar. Retighten the bolts.
11   Window rolls up too far: Loosen the front and rear stop screws **(see illustration)**, then roll the glass up until it seats properly in the roof weather strip. Move the front and rear stops until they contact the window rollers then retighten the screws.
12   Incorrect gap between window forward edge and windshield pillar: Loosen the through bolts and move the glass until it seats properly in the stripping. Retighten the bolts.
13   Glass too far inboard or outboard: Loosen the bolts that hold the top of the front glass channel, then back off the adjusting screws. Move the top of the glass inboard until it seats properly against the roof rail weatherstrip, then tighten the bolts. Move the felt weatherstrip until it is even against the window, then tighten the bolts. Turn the adjusting screws until the nylon pads are just contacting the wedges.
14   Window rolls down too far: Loosen the screw at the bottom of the window channel and roll the glass down until the top edge is flush with the outer panel. Move the stop to contact the window roller, then tighten the screw.

Door hinges

15   Remove the door trim panel (Section 17).
16   Remove the lock striker bolt (Steps 3 and 4).
17   For up-and-down adjustment, remove the hinge cover (two screws) for access to the upper hinge retaining screws.
18   For in-and-out, and fore-and-aft adjustment it is necessary to first remove the instrument panel (for the left door only), right dash pad (for the right door only), the cowl kick panel and inlet air duct, for access to the hinge retaining screws.
19   During any door adjustment, do not allow the door to hang on one hinge only.
20   After adjustment, recheck the lock striker adjustment (Steps 1 through 5).

17 Trim panel and inside handles - removal and installation

1968 through 1977 models
Refer to illustrations 17.1a, 17.1b, 17.1c and 17.3
1   Using a suitable tool **(see illustration)**

16.11 There are adjustment points at the rear (arrow) and front of each door

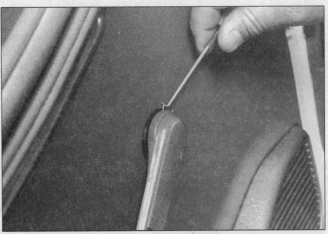

17.1a Auto parts stores carry special tools for door handle/window crank clip removal - you can also use a small hooked tool like this

17.1b The clip inside the window and door lock handle fits into a groove in the shaft

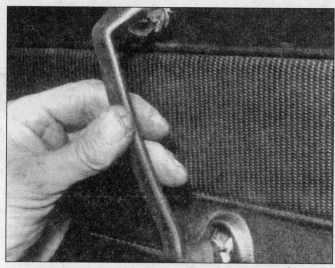

17.1c The door grab handle is secured by two screws

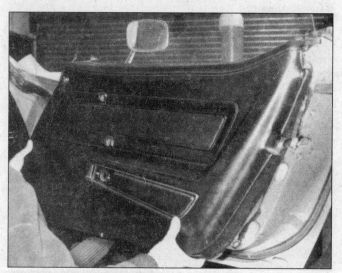

17.3 Once the clips and fasteners have been released, lift the trim panel up and away from the door

18.2 The door latch control rod uses this bellcrank - the lock control rod runs on the inside of the door

remove the spring clips retaining the window handle and lock control **(see illustration)**. Remove two screws and take off the grab handle **(see illustration)**.

2   Remove the four trim panel securing screws, one at each inside corner of the door inner panel.

3   Carefully pry alongside the plastic retaining clips to release the trim panel. Lift the panel off **(see illustration)**.

4   Remove the retaining screw and slide the handle forward to remove it.

5   Remove the formed plastic cover by peeling along the edge at the adhesive bead.

6   Installation is the reverse of the removal procedure.

1978 and later models

7   Using a suitable tool, remove the window crank retaining clip (if so equipped) **(see**

illustration 17.1a)**.

8   Unscrew the inside door handle cover-plate attaching screw and remove the cover.

9   Remove the door lock knob and unscrew the three arm rest-to-inner door panel attaching screws.

10   If equipped with a remotely adjustable mirror, remove the screws retaining the mirror trim. Loosen the set screw to disengage the end of the mirror control cable from the trim.

11   If equipped with power door locks, remove the switch and disconnect the wire harness at the switch.

12   Remove the three trim panel attaching screws and carefully pry out the plastic fastener clips located around the perimeter of the panel.

13   Remove the plastic liner by carefully peeling along its edge at the adhesive bead.

14   Installation is the reverse of the removal steps.

18   Door latch and remote controls - removal and installation

Refer to illustrations 18.2, 18.3 and 18.4

1   With the window fully raised, remove the trim panel (Section 17).

2   Disengage the upper control rod by removing the plastic guide clip (early models only) **(see illustration)**, and releasing the retaining clips at both ends; remove the rod through the access hole.

3   Disengage the control rods by releasing the clips at both ends and lifting outward **(see illustration)**.

4   Remove the four screws on the inner door panel to release the remote control assembly **(see illustration)**.

5   Remove the two screws and take off the crank link.

18.3 Door latch control rod and clip

18.4 Door latch remote control assembly

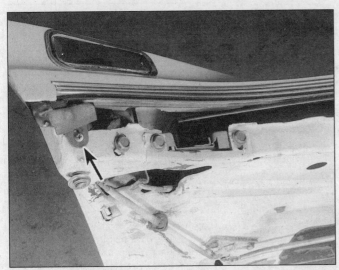

19.1 The door weatherstrip seal is held in place by adhesive,
except at the front and rear (shown), where a screw must
be removed

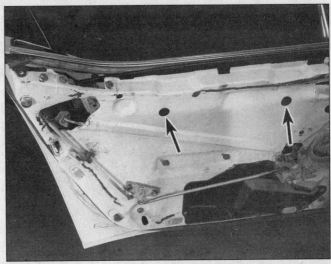

20.2 The sash screws are accessed through these holes (arrows)

6   Remove the three screws and withdraw the door lock through the access hole.
7   Installation is the reverse of the removal procedure.

19 Door window seals, anti-rattle strips and weatherstrips - removal and installation

Refer to illustration 19.1
1   Removal of the weatherstrip is straightforward. Pull off the old one **(see illustration)**, make sure that the area is clean and then install the replacement using a suitable adhesive.
2   Replacement of window seals and anti-rattle strips is straightforward after the door panels have been removed.

20 Window glass - removal and installation

Refer to illustration 20.2
1   Remove the door trim panel (Section 17) and the window outer seal assembly.
2   Raise the window fully to line up the two sash screws through the access holes **(see illustration)**.
3   Hold the nuts so they can't turn and remove the two screws.
4   Remove the crosshead screw at the top of the channel assembly to disengage the stop.
5   Adjust the front and rear channels fully outward to provide maximum clearance, then carefully pull the window upward. Make sure that the window clears the roller assemblies through the opening in the inner door panel.

6   Installation is basically the reverse of the removal procedure. If a new glass is being used, remove the pads, fasteners and frame assembly, and attach them to the new glass before installation. Adjust the glass position as necessary (refer to Section 16).

21 Window regulator - removal and installation

All 1968 through 1977 models; 1978 and later manual regulators

Refer to illustration 21.9
1   Remove the trim panel (refer to Section 17).
2   With the window fully up, remove the sash bolts.

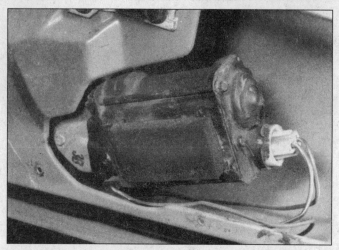

21.9 Power window motor - 1968 through 1977 models

21.10 Remove the screws (arrows) and the inner cover over the window motor/regulator

3   Remove the nuts retaining the glass.
4   Remove the window crank housing (three screws).
5   Remove the crankshaft, pin and spring washer.
6   Remove two retaining screws adjacent to the spring.
7   Remove the front glass channel lower securing bolt.
8   Remove the adjusting stud securing nut, and position the front channel outward for maximum clearance.
9   Collapse the linkage to the elongated position, then press the front channel outward and slide the regulator back and forth to draw it out of the access hole **(see illustration)**.

1978 and later power window regulators

Refer to illustration 21.10
10   Remove the door armrest, the trim panel and the plastic liner, then unfasten the inner door panel access cover **(see illustration)**.
11   With the window in the fully raised position, fasten it to the door frame with cloth-backed tape.
12   Disconnect the wire harness from the motor.
13   Remove the inner panel cam.
14   Punch out the window regulator rivet center pins with a hammer and suitable size pin punch, then drill out the rivets with a 1/4-inch drill bit.
15   Disengage the regulator rollers from the sash channel cam and remove the regulator from the door.
16   To install the regulator, reverse the removal procedure. Attach the regulator to the inner panel with 1/4-20 x 1/2-inch screws. Tighten the screws to 72 in-lbs.

22   Power window motor - replacement

Warning: *Do not attempt to detach the motor*

until the arm is locked as described in Steps 1 and 2.
1   Remove the regulator assembly (refer to Section 21).
2   With the regulator assembly secured in a vise, use jumper leads from a 12-volt battery to run the motor until the semi-circular hole in the sector gear centers over one of the two weld nuts on the mounting plate.
3   Screw a 1/4-20 x 1-inch bolt into the weld so that the end passes through the hole in the sector gear. (If necessary, enlarge the hole slightly.) Secure the bolt with a nut to prevent it from moving.
4   Detach the motor from the regulator unit.
5   Reassembly is the reverse of the removal procedure. Don't forget to remove the nut and bolt on completion.

23   Outside handle and lock cylinder - removal and installation

1   Remove the trim pad (Section 17).
2   Where applicable, remove the lock water shield.
3   Disconnect the link rod, remove the retaining clip (working through the opening in the door, and take off the handle lock (except 1968 models).
4   Remove the two nuts on the handle studs, and lift the handle after prying loose the pivot link clip (except 1968 models).
5   Remove the handle assembly by removing the three nuts securing the handle studs (1968 models only).
6   Remove the lock cylinder by removing the two clips on the rear (except 1968 models).
7   Remove the lock cylinder by removing the two screws at the top of the assembly (1968 models only).
8   Installation is the reverse of the removal procedure. The use of a new lock cylinder seal is recommended.

24   Door hinges - removal and installation

Caution: *During the removal and installation procedure, do not allow the door to hang on one hinge or permanent damage may occur.*
1   Remove the trim panel (Section 17).
2   Remove the access panel from the door inner panel.
3   For access to the lower hinge, remove the door sill plate and the cowl kick panel.
4   For access to the upper hinge, remove the lower mast jacket cover and instrument panel pad (left side) or the dash panel pad (right side), and the air inlet ducts.
5   On power window models, if the door is to be removed completely, disconnect the wiring between the hinge pillar and door.
6   If a hinge is to be used again in the same position, scribe around the inner strap on the door panel, and record the number of shims between the hinge strap and the door panel.
7   Remove the hinge-to-door and hinge-to-body retaining bolts.
8   Installation is the reversal of the removal procedure, but on completion adjust the door position and lock striker as necessary (Section 16).

25   Underbody storage compartment - removal and installation

1   Remove the right-hand box by opening the lid and lifting the box upward.
2   Remove the eight screws along the inner flange of the frame and the lower door hinges. This releases the storage compartment assembly so that it can be lifted out.
3   To remove the doors, remove three screws (outer doors) and two screws (inner doors) at the upper hinge strap.
4   The center storage compartment box can be removed by taking out the seven

screws from around the top inside edge of the box.

5   Installation is the reverse of the removal procedure.

26 Folding top compartment lid - adjustment

Hinges

1   The compartment lid is correctly adjusted when there is 1/16 to 3/16-inch clearance at the sides and 3/16 to 1/4-inch clearance at the rear; the surface should also be flush with the surrounding body panels.

2   To adjust the hinge position, scribe around the hinge following the contour of the hinge strap.

3   Remove the hinge bolts, and add or remove shims as necessary to raise or lower the top surface of the lid.

Latch

4   The latch striker can be adjusted in or out to the extent of the slotted mounting holes.

5   The latch release is adjusted by loosening the latch assembly retaining bolts and utilizing the fore-and-aft adjustment slots.

Closing

6   Adjust the screw and bumper to the fully down position.

7   Close the lid, allowing the pin to engage in the bushing and locate the housing. Tighten the nuts.

8   Tighten the screw until the bumper is firmly seated against the lower surface of the lid assembly.

27 Folding top compartment lid hinges - removal and installation

1   This operation requires the use of a special tool to restrain the spring, and it should therefore be carried out by a Chevrolet dealer service department or other repair shop.

28 Folding top compartment lock - removal and installation

1   For the locks on either side, remove the screw to allow the rod mounting clamps to be removed.

2   Remove the two nut-and-washer assemblies.

3   With the lock removed, carefully remove the cover and gasket from the compartment lid.

4   Installation is the reverse of the removal procedure.

29 Folding top compartment latch - removal and installation

1   Remove the rod mounting clamps. Remove the retainer from the control rod assembly and disengage the rod from the control.

2   Scribe a mark around the contour of the latch assembly.

3   Remove the three retaining screws, and detach the latch from the compartment lid.

4   Installation is the reverse of the removal procedure; adjust the latch, if necessary, on completion (refer to Section 26).

30 Folding top compartment control - removal and installation

1   Remove the inner mounting clamps from both cables, then disengage the rod from the control by removing the retainers.

2   Remove the four screws and detach the control from the compartment lid.

3   Installation is the reverse of the removal procedure; adjust if necessary for satisfactory operation.

31 Seats and seat belts

1   Two different seat styles have been used on Corvette models, but removal and installation is straightforward. If the car has a seat belt warning system, do not forget to unplug the sensor leads.

2   Lap belt and shoulder harness type seat belts are installed in 1972 and later models.

32 Interior quarter trim panel (Sport Coupe) - removal and installation

1   Remove the rear window assembly.

2   Gently pry off the back window lower garnish molding by pulling the lower edge forward, unhooking the nylon fasteners, and lifting up.

3   Remove the left or right rear roof trim panel latch cover.

4   Remove the left or right rear roof trim panel.

5   Remove the left or right quarter trim panel screws, and lift the panel out. Note that four of the screws are removed from inside the door joints.

6   Installation is the reverse of the removal procedure.

33 Astro-ventilation components

Side outlets and ducts

1   Disconnect the battery ground cable.

2   Remove the duct-to-cowl wingnut, and remove the duct.

3   Remove the adapter-to-instrument panel screws and detach the ball outlet assemblies.

4   Installation is the reverse of the removal procedure.

Rear exhaust doors

5   Disconnect the battery ground cable.

6   Remove the vacuum valve attaching screws.

7   Disconnect the vacuum valve at the door actuating rod, detach the hose and remove the valve assembly.

8   With the doors closed, remove the screws and detach the door assemblies from the rear plenum.

9   Installation is the reverse of the removal procedure.

Chapter 12
Chassis electrical system

Contents

1 General information

Warning: *To prevent electrical shorts, fires and injury, always disconnect the cable from the negative terminal of the battery before checking, repairing or replacing electrical components.*

The chassis electrical system of this vehicle is a 12-volt, negative ground type. Power for the lights and all electrical accessories is supplied by a lead/acid-type battery, which is charged by the alternator.

This Chapter covers repair and service procedures for various chassis (non-engine related) electrical components. For information regarding the engine electrical system components (battery, alternator, distributor and starter motor), see Chapter 5.

2 Electrical troubleshooting - general information

Refer to illustration 1.16

A typical electrical circuit consists of an electrical component, any switches, relays, motors, fuses, fusible links or circuit breakers, etc. related to that component and the wiring and connectors that link the components to both the battery and the chassis. To help you pinpoint an electrical circuit problem, wiring diagrams are included at the end of this book.

Before tackling any troublesome electrical circuit, first study the appropriate wiring diagrams to get a complete understanding of what makes up that individual circuit. Trouble spots, for instance, can often be narrowed down by noting if other components related to the circuit are operating properly. If several components or circuits fail at one time, chances are the problem is a fuse or ground connection, because several circuits are often routed through the same fuse and ground connections.

Electrical problems usually stem from simple causes such as loose or corroded connectors, a blown fuse, a melted fusible link or a bad relay. Visually inspect the condition of all fuses, wires and connectors in a problem circuit before troubleshooting it.

If testing instruments are going to be utilized, use the diagrams to plan ahead of time where you will make the necessary connections in order to accurately pinpoint the trouble spot.

The basic tools needed for electrical

troubleshooting include a circuit tester, a high impedance (10 K-ohm) digital voltmeter, a continuity tester and a jumper wire with an inline circuit breaker for bypassing electrical components. Before attempting to locate or define a problem with electrical test instruments, use the wiring diagrams to decide where to make the necessary connections.

Voltage checks

Voltage checks should be performed if a circuit is not functioning properly. Connect one lead of a circuit tester to either the negative battery terminal or a known good ground. Connect the other lead to a connector in the circuit being tested, preferably nearest to the battery or fuse. If the bulb of the tester lights up, voltage is present, which means that the part of the circuit between the connector and the battery is problem free. Continue checking the rest of the circuit in the same fashion.

When you reach a point at which no voltage is present, the problem lies between that point and the last test point with voltage. Most of the time the problem can be traced to a loose connection. **Note:** *Keep in mind that some circuits receive voltage only when the ignition key is in the Accessory or Run position.*

Finding a short circuit

One method of finding shorts in a circuit is to remove the fuse and connect a test light or voltmeter in its place. There should be no voltage present in the circuit. Move the wiring harness from side-to-side while watching the test light. If the bulb goes on, there is a short to ground somewhere in that area, probably where the insulation has been rubbed through. The same test can be performed on each component in a circuit, even a switch.

Ground check

Perform a ground test to check whether a component is properly grounded. Disconnect the battery and connect one lead of a self-powered test light, known as a continuity tester, to a known good ground. Connect the other lead to the wire or ground connection being tested. If the bulb goes on, the ground is good.

If the bulb does not go on, the ground is not good.

Continuity check

A continuity check determines if there are any breaks in a circuit - if it is conducting electricity properly. With the circuit off (no power in the circuit), a self-powered continuity tester can be used to check the circuit. Connect the test leads to both ends of the circuit (or to the "power" end and a good ground), and if the test light comes on the circuit is passing current properly. If the light doesn't come on, there is a break somewhere in the circuit. The same procedure can be used to test a switch, by connecting the continuity tester to the power in and power out

1.16 To backprobe a connector, insert a straight pin into the back of the connector alongside the desired wire until it contacts the metal terminal inside; connect your meter leads to the probes - this allows you to test a functioning circuit

sides of the switch. With the switch turned on, the test light should come on.

Finding an open circuit

When diagnosing for possible open circuits it is often difficult to locate them by sight because oxidation or terminal misalignment are hidden by the connectors. Merely wiggling a connector on a sensor or in the wiring harness may correct the open circuit condition. Remember this if an open circuit is indicated when troubleshooting a circuit. Intermittent problems may also be caused by oxidized or loose connections.

Electrical troubleshooting is simple if you keep in mind that all electrical circuits are basically electricity running from the battery, through the wires, switches, relays, fuses and fusible links to each electrical component (light bulb, motor, etc.) and then to ground, from which it is passed back to the battery. Any electrical problem is an interruption in the flow of electricity to and from the battery.

Connectors

Most electrical connections on these vehicles are made with multiwire plastic connectors. The mating halves of many connectors are secured with locking clips molded into the plastic connector shells. The mating halves of large connectors, such as some of those under the instrument panel, are held together by a bolt through the center of the connector.

To separate a connector with locking clips, use a small screwdriver to pry the clips apart carefully, then separate the connector halves. Pull only on the shell, never pull on the wiring harness as you may damage the individual wires and terminals inside the connectors. Look at the connector closely before trying to separate the halves. Often the locking clips are engaged in a way that is not immediately clear. Additionally, many connectors have more than one set of clips.

Each pair of connector terminals has a male half and a female half. When you look at the end view of a connector in a diagram, be sure to understand whether the view shows the harness side or the component side of the connector. Connector halves are mirror

images of each other, and a terminal shown on the right side end view of one half will be on the left side end view of the other half.

It is often necessary to take circuit voltage measurements with a connector connected. Whenever possible, carefully insert the test probes of your meter into the rear of the connector shell to contact the terminal inside. This kind of connection is called "backprobing" **(see illustration)**. When inserting a test probe into a male terminal, be careful not to distort the terminal opening. Doing so can lead to a poor connection and corrosion at that terminal later.

3   Fuses - general information

Refer to illustrations 3.2 and 3.4

The electrical circuits are protected by a combination of fuses, fusible links and circuit breakers. The fuse panel is located under the instrument panel.

Each of the fuses is designed to protect a specific circuit, and the various circuits are identified on the fuse panel itself **(see illustration)**.

Glass fuses are used on early models. Miniaturized fuses are used on later models. These compact fuses, with blade terminal design, allow fingertip removal and replacement.

If an electrical component fails, always check the fuse first. A blown fuse, which is nothing more than a broken element, is easily identified through the clear glass or plastic body. Visually inspect the element for evidence of damage **(see illustration)**. If you aren't sure about a fuse's condition, you can check it with an ohmmeter - connect it to the metal ends of a glass fuse or to the terminals in the plastic body of a miniaturized fuse. A good fuse will indicate continuity on the ohmmeter - a blown fuse will indicate infinite resistance.

Remove and insert the fuse straight in and out without twisting. Twisting could force the terminal open too far, resulting in a bad connection.

Be sure to replace blown fuses with the correct type and amp rating. Fuses of differ-

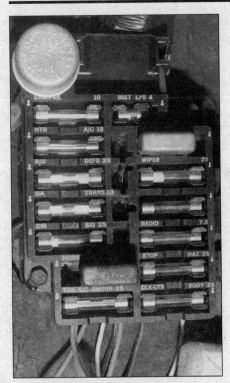

3.2 Fuse panel - typical

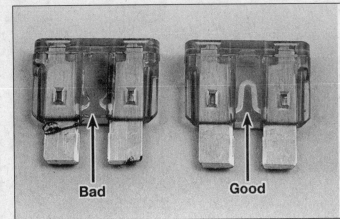

3.4 Late model miniaturized fuses. The one on the right is good - the left one is blown

ent ratings are physically interchangeable, but replacing a fuse with one of a higher or lower value than specified is not recommended. A fuse with too low a value will blow too easily; a fuse with too high a value could cause an electrical fire. Each electrical circuit needs a specific amount of protection. The amperage value of glass fuses is inscribed in one of the metal ends. The amperage value of miniaturized fuses is usually molded into the fuse body. **Caution:** *Always turn off all electrical components and the ignition switch before replacing a fuse. Never bypass a fuse with pieces of metal or foil. Serious damage to the electrical system could result.*

If the replacement fuse immediately fails, do not replace it again until the cause of the problem is isolated and corrected. In most cases, this will be a short circuit in the wiring caused by a broken or deteriorated wire.

4   Fusible links - general information

Some circuits are protected by fusible links. These links are used in circuits that are not ordinarily fused, such as the ignition circuit. If a circuit protected by a fusible link becomes inoperative, inspect for a blown fusible link. A blown fusible link appears as a short length of heavy wire that has had the insulation completely melted.

Although fusible links appear to be of heavier gauge that the wire they are protecting, their appearance is due to thicker insula-

tion. All fusible links are several wire gauges smaller than the wire they are designed to protect. The location of the fusible links on your particular vehicle can be determined by referring to the wiring diagrams at the end of this book.

Fusible links cannot be repaired. If you must replace one, make sure that the new fusible link is a duplicate of the one removed with respect to gauge, length and insulation. Original and replacement fusible links have insulation that is flame proof. Do not fabricate a fusible link from ordinary wire - the insulation may not be flame proof. Replace fusible links as follows:

a) *Disconnect the negative cable from the battery.*
b) *Disconnect the fusible link from the wiring harness.*
c) *Cut the damaged fusible link out of the wiring just behind the connector.*
d) *Strip the insulation back approximately 1/2-inch.*
e) *Position the connector on the new fusible link and crimp it into place.*
f) *Use rosin core solder at each end of the new link to obtain a good solder joint.*
g) *Use plenty of electrical tape around the soldered joint.*
h) *Connect the battery negative cable. Test the circuit for proper operation.*

5   Circuit breakers - general information

Circuit breakers protect components such as power windows, power door locks and headlights. Some circuit breakers are located in the fuse panel. Some later models have circuit breakers that are integral with the headlight and wiper switches.

On some models the circuit breaker resets itself automatically, so an electrical overload in a circuit breaker protected system will cause the circuit to fail momentarily, then come back on. If the circuit does not come back on, check it immediately. Once the condition is corrected, the breaker will resume its normal function. Some circuit breakers must be reset manually.

6   Switches - removal and installation

1   Before removing any switch, disconnect the battery ground cable.

Ignition switch
Early models

2   Insert the ignition key in the lock.
3   Remove the screws that secure the Corvette cover plate to the top center of the instrument cluster.
4   Remove the ashtray and radio (refer to Section 24).
5   Turn the ignition key to Acc and then insert a piece of wire or a thin rod into the hole in the face of the lock cylinder. Depress the wire to actuate the plunger, at the same time turning the key counterclockwise until the lock cylinder can be withdrawn.
6   Unscrew the ignition switch bezel nut and remove the switch.
7   Using a screwdriver, release the anti-theft locking tangs and unplug the connector.
8   Snap the connector into the new ignition switch and install by reversing the removal operations.

Later models
Refer to illustration 6.15
9   The ignition switch is mounted on top of the steering column jacket near the front of the dash. The switch is located inside the channel section of the brake pedal support and is actuated by a rod and rack assembly that is operated when the steering column lock is turned.
10   To remove the switch, first lower the steering column by releasing its upper and lower mounting bolts as described in Chapter 10. The steering wheel need not be removed.
11   Turn the switch to the Off-Unlock position.
12   Remove the switch retaining screw and withdraw the switch.
13   To install the switch, turn the lock cylinder to the Off-Unlock position.
14   Place the gearshift lever in Neutral.
15   Locate the ignition switch as shown in

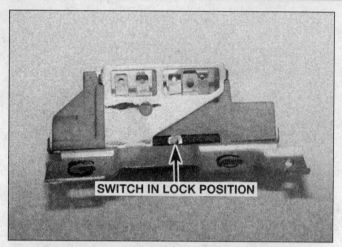

6.15 The ignition switch used on later models is secured to the steering column and is actuated by a rod - it must be installed when the slider is in the Lock position

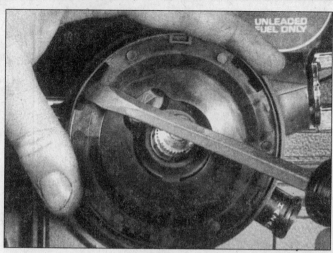

6.43 Pry out the turn signal lockplate with a screwdriver as shown

the accompanying illustration, then move the slider two positions to the right from Accessory to Off-Unlock.

16   Insert the actuator rod into the slider hole and attach it to the steering column with the two screws. Take care not to move the switch out of its detent. Do not overtighten the lower screw.

17   Raise the steering column and secure it.

Ignition key warning buzzer switch

18   Remove the steering wheel and release the directional signal switch. Push the switch to the rear far enough for it to be slipped over the end of the steering shaft. Do not pull the harness out of the column. Set the steering column lock to On.

19   Using a hooked piece of wire, pull the switch-retaining clip so that the switch/clip assembly can be removed. Be very careful not to drop the clip into the steering column.

20   To install the switch, set the steering column lock to Run and then fit the buzzer switch so that the contacts are toward the upper end of the steering column and with the formed end of the spring clip around the lower end of the switch.

21   Install the directional signal switch and the steering wheel.

Headlight switch

1968 through 1970 models

22   Pull the headlamp control switch knob to On.

23   Remove the screws at the top and left-hand side of the instrument panel and pull the panel forward to gain access to the switch.

24   Depress the switch shaft retainer and then remove the knob and shaft assembly.

25   Remove the switch retaining nut and the switch itself from the instrument panel.

26   Mark the headlight vacuum hoses so they can be reconnected in their original positions, then disconnect them.

27   Disconnect the electrical connector

from the headlight switch and install it to a new switch if one is being used.

28   The installation steps are the reverse of those for removal.

1971 through 1977 models

29   Access to the switch is obtained by first removing the mast jacket trim covers in order to reach the instrument panel mounting bracket.

30   Unclip and remove the left-hand side console forward trim panel.

31   Lower the steering column.

32   Remove the screws that secure the left-hand instrument panel.

33   Pull the instrument cluster downward and then tip it forward to obtain access to the lighting switch.

34   Removal and installation operations for the switch itself are described in Steps 10 through 16 of this Section.

1978 and later models

35   Remove the left air distribution duct.

36   Remove the instrument cluster-to-instrument panel screws and carefully pull the cluster to the rear.

37   Disconnect the speedometer cable and the cluster electrical connector, then remove the cluster.

38   Remove the 2 instrument panel-to-left door pillar attaching screws, then pull the left side of the instrument panel slightly to the rear for access to the switch.

39   Depress the switch shaft retainer and pull the knob and shaft assembly out. Remove the switch retaining bezel.

40   Label the vacuum hoses for correct installation, then unplug the hoses and the electrical connector and take the switch out.

41   Installation is the reverse of the removal steps. Check switch operation.

Turn signal switch

Except tilt/telescopic

Refer to illustration 6.43

42   Remove the steering wheel (refer to

Chapter 10).

43   Remove the column-to-instrument panel trim cover, the three cover screws and the cover. (The cover screws have plastic retainers and need not be fully removed). On later models, the lockplate cover must be removed by prying it out with a screwdriver **(see illustration).**

44   The lockplate will now have to be depressed using a U-shaped tool and utilizing the steering wheel retaining nut, so that the snap-ring can be removed from the shaft groove. Remove the lockplate.

45   From the steering shaft, slide the directional signal canceling cam, the preload spring and the thrust washer.

46   Unscrew the turn signal lever screw and remove the lever.

47   Depress the hazard-warning knob and then unscrew it.

48   All columns: Pull out the switch connector from the bracket on the jacket and tape the wire ends to prevent snagging on removal.

49   Remove the wire protector by pulling downward on the tab.

50   Tilt columns: Position the directional signal and shifter housing to the low position, then remove the harness cover. Be careful not to damage the wires.

51   Unscrew the three switch mounting screws and pull the turn signal switch straight up, guiding the wiring harness carefully through the opening in the steering column housing.

52   Installation is the reverse of the removal steps. Make sure that the switch is in Neutral and the hazard-warning knob is pulled fully out. Always use a new snap-ring in the steering shaft groove.

Tilt/telescopic

53   Remove the steering wheel (refer to Chapter 10).

54   Remove the trim panel that is located between the steering column and the instrument panel.

6.91 Remove the screws securing the center vent panel -
wiper/washer switch is above the vents

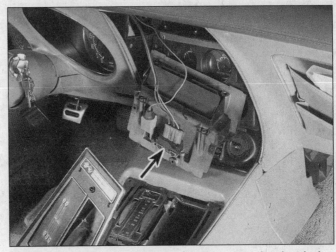

6.92 With the panel pulled forward, disconnect the electrical
connector (arrow), then unbolt the switch

55   From the upper end of the steering column remove the rubber bumper and the C-ring plastic retainer.

56   A compressor will now be required to compress the lockplate sufficiently to be able to remove the C-ring.

57   Lift the lockplate, the horn contact carrier and the upper bearing preload spring from the end of the shaft.

58   Pull the switch connector out of the bracket on the steering column jacket. Remove the harness cover and wrap the upper part of the connector in adhesive tape to prevent the wires snagging as the switch is withdrawn.

59   Push the hazard warning knob in, then remove the knob.

60   Remove the turn signal lever and then the switch actuator arm and screw.

61   Place the directional signal and shifter housing in the low position. Remove the three directional switch screws and pull the switch straight up. Guide the wiring out of the housing.

62   Installation is the reverse of the removal steps.

Headlamp dimmer switch

Floor mounted type

63   Fold back the corner of the floor mat and disconnect the electrical connector from the switch.

64   Remove the two screws that hold the switch to the toe board.

65   Installation is the reverse of the removal steps.

Steering column mounted type

66   The dimmer switch is mounted on the steering column jacket next to the ignition switch.

67   To gain access to the switch, first lower the steering column by releasing its upper and lower mounting bolts (refer to Chapter 10).

68   Remove the flat head screw from the

ignition switch bracket, but leave the hex head screw that passes through both the dimmer switch bracket and the ignition switch bracket in place.

69   Install and tighten the stud and nut (supplied with the new dimmer switch) in the hole that the flat head screw was removed from, then remove the hex head screw and lift off the old dimmer switch.

70   Position the new dimmer switch, then install the hex head screw and the remaining nut (do not tighten them completely at this time). Note that the new switch bracket attaches to the column at 2 points.

71   Connect the actuating rod to the new switch, then depress the switch and slip a 3/32-inch drill bit shank into the hole in the side of the switch.

72   Push the switch up against the actuating rod until all clearance is eliminated, then tighten the hex head screw and the nut to 35 in-lbs.

73   Remove the drill bit, return the column to its normal position, reconnect the battery cable and check the switch function.

Windshield wiper/washer switch

1968 through 1970 models

74   Remove the screws from the upper part of the center console that carries the Corvette emblem.

75   Disconnect the electrical connector from the switch.

76   Remove the switch and plate from the center console.

77   Pull the knob from the switch, carefully using a pair of pliers.

78   Remove the switch screws and remove the switch.

79   Installation is the reverse of the removal steps.

1971 through 1977 models

80   The washer/wiper switch is located on the left side of the steering column under the

turn signal switch.

81   Remove the steering wheel, the turn signal switch and the lock cylinder as described earlier in this Chapter and in Chapter 10.

82   Remove the tilt release lever followed by the three housing screws. Then withdraw the housing, at the same time guiding the switch connector up through the shroud. Turn the housing over and remove the 7/16-inch bolt.

83   Withdraw the switch.

84   Installation is the reverse of the removal steps.

1978 and later models

Refer to illustrations 6.91 and 6.92

85   Remove the left air distribution duct.

86   Remove the instrument cluster-to-instrument panel screws and carefully pull the cluster to the rear.

87   Disconnect the speedometer cable and the cluster electrical connector, then remove the cluster.

88   Remove the two instrument panel-to-left door pillar attaching screws, then pull the left side of the instrument panel slightly to the rear for access to the switch.

89   Remove the switch mounting screws and unplug the electrical connector.

90   Installation is the reverse of the removal steps. Check switch operation.

91   On some models, the switch is located in the center vent panel, above the center gauge cluster **(see illustration)**.

92   Remove the screws and pull the vent panel forward enough to access the electrical connectors on the rear of the switch **(see illustration)**.

93   Installation is the reverse of the removal steps. Check switch operation.

Glove compartment switch

94   Reach into the glove compartment, depress the bulb in the end of the switch and remove the bulb by turning it counterclockwise.

95   Remove the switch from its socket and disconnect the wire.

9.3a Remove the springs (arrow) from the retaining rings . . .

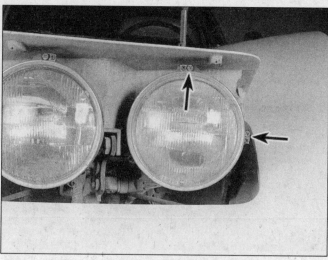

9.3b . . . then remove the screws securing the rings and remove the headlight bulb

96   Install by reversing the removal operation.

Air door switch

97   The switch that controls the actuation of the hood air door solenoid is mounted on a bracket above the accelerator pedal (refer also to Chapter 4).
98   To replace the switch, simply unscrew it and screw in a new one.
99   When a new switch is installed, depress the plunger as far as it will go. This pre-sets the switch, which will automatically adjust itself at the first full opening of the accelerator pedal.

7   Alarm system

1   This system is fitted to later vehicles. If the doors or hood are tampered with, a horn, mounted within the wheelhouse above the left rear tire, is activated.
2   The system is armed by inserting a key into a lock cylinder mounted on the left-hand front fender.
3   The location of the anti-theft relay and flasher within the center console should be noted.

8   Seat belt warning system - general information

1972 through 1975

1   The lap belts are linked to a buzzer and lamp.
2   On vehicles with automatic transmission, the buzzer and light will come on, under the following conditions:

a) *The ignition switch in the On position*
b) *The speed selector lever in a forward speed position*

c) *Either of the front seat belts not fastened*

3   On vehicles with manual transmission, the visual and audible warnings will come on when the gearshift lever is in any gear position, except when the parking brake is still applied.
4   The front passenger seat incorporates a weight-sensitive switch so that the warning system will not operate if the seat belt is left unfastened when a passenger is not being carried.

1976 on

5   The system on these vehicles is designed to remind the driver to fasten the seat belt in the following way.
6   When the ignition key is turned to On or Start, a warning light comes on for a period of between four and eight seconds and a buzzer sounds for the same period.

All models

7   Any malfunction in either system should first be checked out by inspecting all the wiring and terminal connections, together with the circuit fuse and bulb.
8   If these components are in order, have the timer and buzzer tested by your dealer.

9   Headlight bulbs - replacement

Refer to illustrations 9.3a and 9.3b
1   Open the headlight doors by using the manual control knob, or by turning on the headlights to open the doors, then removing the headlight fuse to keep the doors open.
2   Remove the headlight bezel retaining screws and remove the bezel.
3   Disengage the spring from the retaining ring and remove the two securing screws **(see illustrations)**.
4   Remove the retaining ring, disconnect the sealed beam unit wiring connector and then withdraw the unit.

5   Plug the connector into the back of the new sealed beam unit and install the unit, making sure that the numbers molded into the lens are at the top.
6   Install the retaining ring and screws, reconnect the spring and install the bezel.
7   Provided the adjuster screws have not been disturbed, the headlight beam alignment should not have been altered.

10   Headlight door - description, adjustment, removal and installation

Description

1   The retractable headlights are vacuum-operated. The vacuum circuit incorporates a vacuum tank to provide a reserve for several actuations of the headlights, even without the engine running.
2   If the light control knob is pulled, the headlights will be raised and switched on.
3   If the manual control knob is pulled then the headlights will be raised, but without being switched on.
4   In the event of a fault or during overhauls, the headlights can be raised manually in the following way.
5   Open the hood and disconnect the vacuum hoses from the actuators at the rear of the headlight.
6   Reach under the grille and push upward on the light housing. Pull the headlight door to its fully open position. Never close the headlight doors by hand.

Adjustment

Refer to illustration 10.7
7   To adjust the headlight door **(see illustration)**, turn the screws to provide:

1) *In-and-out movement (the main bracket)*
2) *Up-and-down movement (the rod attached to the servo)*

10.7 Headlight door adjustment points (shown through valance hole from below)

1 In and out adjusting bolts
2 Up and down adjustment
3 Opening rod adjustment (bolt head is on opposite side of this view)

3) Opening rod adjustment (the small lower adjustment screw)

8   When correctly adjusted, the micro-switch on the door opening linkage must shut off the warning light when the lights are fully extended.

Headlight door - removal and installation

Refer to illustration 10.14
9   Open the doors fully.
10   Remove the radiator grille.
11   Remove the headlight bezel and apply protective tape to the headlight door aperture edge.
12   Remove the headlight sealed beam units (see Section 9).
13   Remove the front screw and bushing, which attach the headlight housing to the support assembly link.
14   Remove the J bar from the side of the headlight housing **(see illustration)**.
15   Reach in through the grille opening and remove the three cap screws which retain the bearing and headlight housing to the support.

16   Lift the headlight door assembly forward and out of the opening.
17   Installation is the reverse of the removal steps. Adjust as described in Steps 7 and 8.

Actuator - removal and installation

Refer to illustration 10.20
18   Remove the radiator grille.
19   Partially raise the headlights and remove the long spring on either side of the pivot link pin.
20   Disconnect the two vacuum hoses attached to the actuator **(see illustration)**.
21   Remove the cotter pin and slide out the pivot pin to free the actuator rod.
22   Remove the four nuts from the actuator studs and slide the actuator down and out of the grille opening.
23   Installation is the reverse of the removal steps.

Vacuum relay valve - removal and installation

24   Raise the hood.

25   Carefully disconnect the four hoses from the relay. These hoses are normally color-coded with corresponding letters molded into the relay valve connectors. If there is any doubt, mark the hose locations before removal.
26   Remove the two screws that secure the relay and remove it from the engine compartment.
27   Installation is the reverse of the removal steps.

Vacuum reserve tank - removal and installation

28   Remove the power brake booster and the brake master cylinder.
29   Note the fitting of the hoses (mark them if necessary) and then disconnect them from the vacuum tank.
30   Reach under the left-hand fender and remove the screws from the vacuum tank mountings.
31   Withdraw the tank from the engine compartment.
32   Installation is the reverse of the removal steps.

11   Headlights - adjustment

Refer to illustrations 11.1 and 11.3
Note: *The headlights must be aimed correctly. If adjusted incorrectly they could blind the driver of an oncoming vehicle and cause a serious accident or seriously reduce your ability to see the road. The headlights should be checked for proper aim every 12 months and any time a new headlight is installed or front bodywork performed. It should be emphasized that the following procedure is only an interim step, which will provide temporary adjustment until the headlights can be adjusted by a properly equipped shop.*
1   Headlights have two spring loaded adjusting screws, one on the top controlling up-and-down movement and one on the side

10.14 Remove the two J-bar bolts (arrows) at the sides of the headlight door assembly - there is another bolt at the inner end of the bar

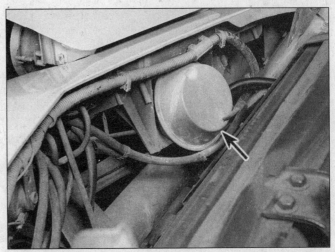

10.20 Remove the vacuum hoses from the actuator (arrow)

11.1 The upper screw (A) adjusts the vertical aiming, while the side screw (B) adjusts the left-and-right aiming

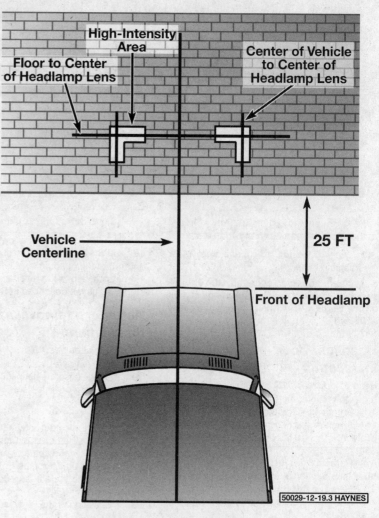

11.3 Headlight adjustment details

controlling left-and-right movement **(see illustration)**.

2   There are several methods of adjusting the headlights. The simplest method requires a blank wall 25 feet in front of the vehicle and a level floor.

3   Position masking tape vertically on the wall in reference to the vehicle centerline and the centerlines of both headlights **(see illustration)**.

4   Position a horizontal tapeline in reference to the centerline of all the headlights. **Note:** *It may be easier to position the tape on the wall with the vehicle parked only a few inches away.*

5   Adjustment should be made with the vehicle sitting level, the gas tank half-full and no unusually heavy load in the vehicle.

6   Starting with the low beam adjustment, position the high intensity zone so it is two inches below the horizontal line and two inches to the right of the headlight vertical line. Adjustment is made by turning the top adjusting screw clockwise to raise the beam and counterclockwise to lower the beam. The adjusting screw on the side should be used in the same manner to move the beam left or right.

7   With the high beams on, the high intensity zone should be vertically centered with the exact center just below the horizontal line. **Note:** *It may not be possible to position the headlight aim exactly for both high and low beams. If a compromise must be made, keep in mind that the low beams are the most used and have the greatest effect on driver safety.*

8   Have the headlights adjusted by a dealer service department or service station at the earliest opportunity.

---

12 Headlight reminder buzzer

---

1   This device is fitted to later vehicles to provide an audible warning that the main lighting switch is on when the ignition switch is turned to the Off or Lock positions, and the vehicle is about to be left unattended.

2   Where the lights are required to be left on although the ignition key is in the Off position, the buzzer can be shut off by turning the lighting switch knob until the instrument cluster lights go out.

3   The headlight-warning buzzer is mounted in the fuse panel.

---

13 Bulbs and light assemblies - removal and installation

Front parking and direction indicator light

Refer to illustrations 13.1 and 13.2

1   Access to the bulb is obtained by removing the lens. Depending on the design, this may be held in position by two front-mounted screws or by two nuts at the rear of the light body **(see illustration)**.

2   To remove the bulb **(see illustration)** push it in, turn counterclockwise and pull it out.

Marker light

Refer to illustration 13.5

3   Access to the bulb is obtained after removal of the light housing.

13.1 To replace a front parking light bulb, remove the lens

13.2 Then push the bulb into its socket, turn counterclockwise and pull it out

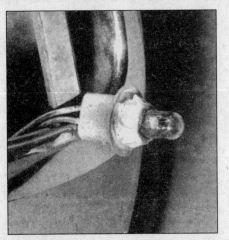

13.5 Side marker light bulbs are accessible by removing the light socket

13.8a To replace a rear lamp bulb, remove the lens screws . . .

13.8b . . . take off the lens . . .

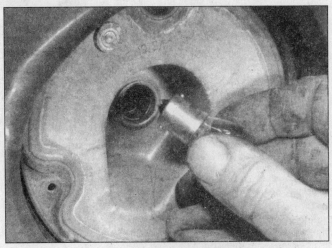

13.8c . . . and remove the bulb

4   Remove the light retaining nuts or screws from inside the fender and pull the light from the fender.

5   Disconnect the light socket and remove the bulb **(see illustration)**.

6   Installation is the reverse of the removal steps.

Rear light

Refer to illustrations 13.8a, 13.8b and 13.8c

7   The bulbs for the tail, stop, directional and back-up lights can be replaced after removing the light lenses.

8   The light housing securing screws are accessible once the lenses have been removed **(see illustrations)**.

Rear license plate light

9   Remove the two securing screws and lower the light from the trim panel. Replace the bulb and install the light.

Quadrant light (automatic transmission)

10   Remove the quadrant trim plate from the console.

11   Snap the socket out of the retainer, replace the bulb, then reinstall the socket and quadrant trim plate.

Interior lights

Refer to illustration 13.12

12   Access to the bulbs in interior lights is obtained by removing the lens **(see illustration)**.

13   Instrument panel lights can be reached after removing the instrument cluster and trim panel as described in the next Section.

Fiber optics

14   These are used to transmit light to various locations in the vehicle, and as a means of indicating that the lights are working.

---

14   Instruments - removal and installation

---

1   This Section describes instrument removal and installation for 1968 through

13.12 To gain access to an interior light, remove the lens (luggage lamp shown)

1977 models. The procedure for 1978 and later models is described as part of instrument panel pad removal in Chapter 11.

1968 through 1972 models

2   Before removing any instrument cluster, disconnect the battery ground cable.

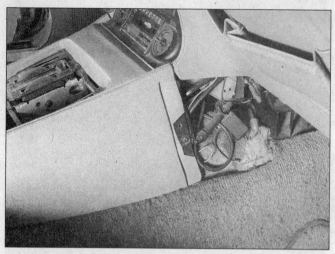

15.1 Access to electrical components in the console is achieved by removing the front side panel (one screw) of the console

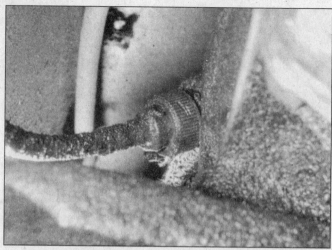

17.4 Speedometer drive cable connection to transmission

3   To remove the left-hand cluster, first lower the steering column (see Chapter 10).
4   Remove all the left-hand instrument panel securing screws.
5   Unclip and remove the floor console forward trim panel.
6   Pull the instrument cluster slightly forward until the speedometer cable nut and the nut for the tachometer cable can be reached. Disconnect the electrical connectors.
7   To remove the center cluster, remove the screws from the right-hand dash panel.
8   Remove the radio (see Section 24).
9   Remove the upper center cluster trim plate screws, tip the trim plate forward so that the windshield wiper switch connector can be reached and disconnected, and withdraw the trim plate. Do not bend the trim plate excessively as it is designed to collapse under impact.
10   Remove the screws from the left-hand side of the center cluster and the nuts from the underside of the cluster studs.
11   Tilt the center cluster forward and disconnect all attachments from the rear.
12   Lift the cluster up and remove it.
13   Individual instruments can now be removed from the cluster assemblies as necessary.
14   Installation is the reverse of the removal steps.

1973 through 1976 models

15   The procedure is similar to that for 1968 through 1972 models, but the radio need not be removed all the way. Remove the knobs and bezel retaining nuts, and the mounting bolt from the rear of the cluster. Push the radio toward the engine firewall while the cluster is pulled forward.
16   Note the difference in some of the left-hand cluster fixing components.

1977 and later models

17   Remove the left-hand instrument cluster as described in Steps 2 through 5.

18   To remove the center instrument cluster, first detach the console tunnel side panels.
19   Pull off the radio control knobs.
20   Remove the two screws that secure the console trim plate to the instrument cluster.
21   Remove the rear window defogger switch.
22   Remove the five screws from around the upper edge of the instrument cluster.
23   Withdraw the instrument cluster slightly so that the electrical connector at the rear can be disconnected.
24   Individual instruments, light bulbs or printed circuit boards can be removed as necessary.
25   Installation is the reverse of the removal steps.

15   Console controls and trim plate - removal and installation

Refer to illustration 15.1
1   All console-mounted controls can be removed without removing the trim plate. Access is obtained by taking off the tunnel side panels **(see illustration)**.
2   The power window relay and the anti-theft warning system installed in later models are accessible in this way.
3   If the trim plate must be removed, refer to Chapter 11.

16   Cigarette lighter - removal and installation

1   Disconnect the battery ground cable.
2   Remove the vent control set screws on vehicles not equipped with air conditioning.
3   Remove the retaining screws, then remove the gearshift trim plate.
4   Compress the clip that holds the lighter lamp and unplug the connector from beneath the lighter housing.

5   Unscrew the retainer from the rear of the lighter housing and disengage the assembly from the trim plate.
6   Installation is the reverse of the removal steps.

17   Speedometer cable - replacement

Refer to illustration 17.4
1   Pull the instrument cluster forward as described in Section 14.
2   Release the drive cable from the back of the speedometer or tachometer as necessary.
3   Grip the exposed end of the inner cable with a pair of pliers and remove it.
4   If the inner cable has broken, then the lower end of the cable assembly will have to be disconnected from the transmission **(see illustration)** and the lower end of the inner cable pulled out.
5   Apply a small amount of multi-purpose grease to the lower two-thirds of the new inner cable, then insert it from the top end of the outer casing. Make sure that the cable is pushed fully into engagement with the drive pinion at the transmission end of the outer casing.
6   Connect the upper end of the cable to the speedometer and install the instrument cluster.

18   Horns - description and maintenance

1   Dual horns are fitted and the circuit incorporates a relay.
2   Periodically check the security of the wiring and connections.
3   If the horns don't work, first check the wiring and the fuse. If these are in order, the relay may be at fault. This can be checked

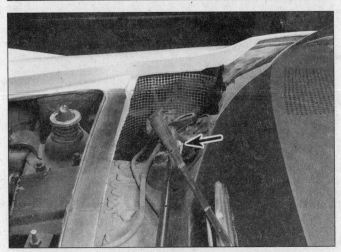

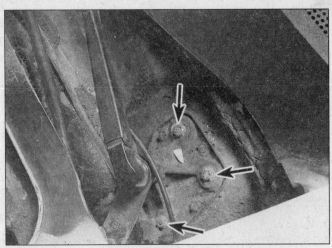

19.4 Remove or flip up the wiper arm, then remove the nut (arrow) where the linkage rod attaches at each wiper

19.5 Remove the bolts (arrows) and pull the wiper linkage from the cowl

out by temporarily disconnecting the wires from the horns and bypassing the relay by connecting two leads direct to the battery. If the horns now operate, replace the relay.

19 Windshield wiper linkage - removal and installation

Refer to illustrations 19.4 and 19.5

1   Make sure that the wiper motor is in the parked position and open the hood. Disconnect the battery ground cable.
2   On 1968 through 1975 models, remove the rubber plug from the front of the wiper door actuator, then insert a screwdriver and push the internal piston to the rear to open the wiper door.
3   Pull the wiper arm/blades from the driving spindle.
4   Loosen the nuts that retain the drive rod ball stud to the crankarm and detach the drive

rod from the crankarm (see illustration).
5   Remove the linkage retaining screws and withdraw the linkage from its cavity (see illustration).
6   Installation is the reverse of the removal steps, but make sure that the wiper arms are installed in their original parked positions (± 3/8 inch from reveal molding stop).

20 Windshield wiper motor - removal and installation

Refer to illustration 20.4

1   The motor is of two-speed type and incorporates a relay control, located in the gearbox section, which controls starting and stopping of the wiper mechanism through a latching mechanism.
2   Also mounted in the gearbox section is a washer pump which is driven by the wiper unit gear assembly.

3   To remove the motor, make sure that it is in the parked position, then disconnect all washer hoses and electrical connections from it.
4   Remove the plenum chamber grille and then unscrew the nut that retains the crankarm to the motor assembly (see illustration).
5   Remove the ignition shield and distributor cap to gain access to the motor mounting screws and nuts.
6   Remove the screws and nuts and lift away the motor.
7   Installation is the reverse of the removal steps.

21 Windshield washer pump - removal and installation

Refer to illustration 21.1

1   The washer pump can be removed from

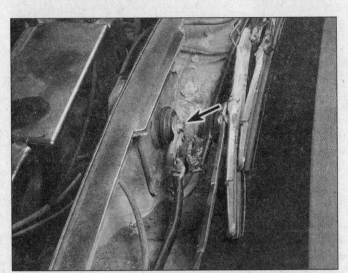

20.4 Remove the nut (arrow) at the cowl side of the motor, then remove the wiper motor mounting bolts on the firewall side

21.1 The washer pump (arrow) can be removed from the wiper motor without removing the entire motor assembly from the vehicle

the wiper motor without having to withdraw the complete motor/pump unit **(see illustration)**.

2   Once removed, individual components of the pump or valve assembly can be replaced as necessary.

---

22   Wiper cover panels

General information

1   This system, installed on vehicles built up until 1972, is an automatically controlled wiper mechanism cover panel which is actuated by vacuum when the wipers are switched on.

2   The same vacuum source is used to open the headlight doors.

3   A limit switch is incorporated in the circuit to prevent the wiper motor operating until the cover panel is fully open. Also, an interlock valve prevents the panel closing until the wiper arms are safely parked.

4   Maintenance consists of regularly inspecting the electrical and vacuum connections and replacing the cover panel bumpers when they have become compressed below 3/16-inch thick.

Removal and installation

5   Disconnect the battery ground cable.

6   Raise the hood.

7   Remove the eight screws from the vent grille and then move the grille forward and up to remove it.

8   If vacuum is still present in the system, open the cover panels by pulling the panel switch downward. If the panel does not open, pry out the plug from the front of the vacuum actuator and insert a screwdriver. Depress the actuator piston until the cover panels are raised to the fully open position. Install the plug.

9   Remove the four bolts and bushings that hold the cover panel to the actuating arms and lift the panel from the vehicle.

10   Installation is the reverse of the removal steps. With the actuator in the closed position, align the vent grille to the mounting brackets and install the screws to the brackets.

11   Reconnect the battery ground cable.

12   Actuate the system and check both panels for alignment with the adjacent bodywork. Where adjustment is required, use the adjusting screws to control the panel-to-windshield adjustment. Release the jam nuts and turn the screws so that the underside of the panel (at the reveal molding clip) has a gap of 0.060-inch at the windshield center. The adjustment stop screws seat against plastic pads mounted on top of the plenum.

13   Nuts control up-and-down alignment of the entire assembly at the engine compartment firewall and the grille panel itself has elongated screw holes to permit fore-and-aft adjustment.

---

23   Cruise Master

General information

1   This system is designed to let the driver maintain a constant highway speed without having to continuously apply foot pressure to the accelerator pedal.

2   Speed variations are easily made and override features allow the vehicle to be slowed, accelerated or stopped without delay.

3   To engage the Cruise Master, accelerate to the desired speed and then depress the switch button on the end of the steering tilt lever. The road speed will then be maintained (within the power limitations of the engine) irrespective of gradients.

4   Operation of the engagement switch button should be understood. The button has three positions.

   a) *The released or normal position.*
   b) *Partially depressed at speeds above 30 mph - the system is engaged.*
   c) *Fully depressed and held there (trim-down position) - the system is disengaged. The road speed can be allowed to decrease or increase to a new required level and the switch button then very gradually released, which will cause the system to re-engage.*

5   An override facility is built in. Whenever the accelerator pedal is depressed, the system is overridden, but when the pedal is released, the control system will re-engage at its previous cruising speed.

6   The main components of the Cruise Master system are:

   a) *The regulator, which is mounted in the speedometer cable line. It is a controlled speed sensing device and control unit.*
   b) *The servo unit, which is mounted on the left front inner fender and connected by cable to the throttle linkage. The servo unit is controlled by the regulator.*
   c) *The cruise brake release switch, which is mounted on the brake pedal bracket. It disengages the system electrically when the brake pedal is depressed.*
   d) *The cruise brake release valve, which is mounted on the brake pedal bracket. It disengages the system pneumatically when the brake pedal is depressed.*

Maintenance and adjustment

7   Maintenance consists of periodically checking the wires and hoses of the system for secure connections.

8   The following adjustments should be maintained at all times.

Engagement cruising speed

9   If engagement of the Cruise Master causes a cruising speed to be maintained slightly above or below that selected, first check the adjustment of the servo cable. To do this, set the fast idle cam (manually) on its lowest step with the ignition switch off.

Adjust the tension of the cable so that virtually all slack is eliminated.

10   Once the servo cable is set, check the system by engaging the Cruise Master at 55 mph. If the vehicle then settles down to a cruising speed below this level, screw the orifice tube outward after releasing the locknut on the regulator. If the vehicle cruises at a level higher than the engagement speed level, screw the orifice tube inward.

11   Each 1/4-turn of the orifice tube will change the cruise speed by one mph. Tighten the locknut on completion. Never unscrew the orifice tube completely from the regulator; it cannot be refitted.

12   The brake release switch contacts should be open when the brake pedal is depressed between 0.38 and 0.64-inch measured at the brake pedal.

13   The vacuum valve plunger in the brake release valve must clear the pedal arm when the arm is moved through 5/16-inch measured at the switch.

14   Any faulty components must be replaced.

---

24   Radio - removal and installation

Radio receiver

1   Disconnect the battery ground cable.

2   Pull the radio control knobs from their shafts.

3   Remove the instrument cluster (see Section 14).

4   Remove the screw that secures the radio receiver-mounting bracket to the reinforcement on the floor pan.

5   Pull the receiver forward and disconnect the electrical connector and antenna lead from the rear.

Left-hand speaker

6   Disconnect the battery ground cable.

7   Loosen the windshield upper trim molding and remove the windshield side trim moldings.

8   Remove one screw from the instrument panel reinforcement and one screw from the center console.

9   Lift up the instrument panel top pad and disconnect the speaker plug.

10   Remove the instrument panel and then unscrew the nuts that secure the speaker to the underside of the instrument panel top pad. Remove the speaker.

Right-hand speaker

11   Disconnect the battery ground cable.

12   Remove the right-hand dash pad including the knob from the air valve.

13   Disconnect the speaker lead.

14   Remove the speaker retaining nuts from the underside of the instrument panel top pad and then remove the speaker.

Antenna

15   Unscrew the nut that secures the

antenna mast to the socket. Withdraw the mast from its mounting plate and then pull the antenna lead and plug through the grommets and clips.

16   Installing all components is the reverse of removal, but make sure that the speakers are connected before applying power to the radio receiver.

25   Radio antenna - trimming

1   Trimming is normally only carried out if a new antenna or receiver is installed.

2   Switch on the radio and turn to maximum volume with the receiver turned to a weak station (near 1400 KHz) on the AM scale.

3   Remove the control knob from the tuner

and withdraw the bezel.

4   Use a small screwdriver to turn the trimmer screw until maximum volume is obtained.

5   Install the knob, bezel and switch.

26   Tape player - maintenance

1   The only maintenance operation required is periodic cleaning of the tape player head using a head cleaning tape or a proprietary cleaning kit.

2   Never bring magnetized tools near the tape head. If the head becomes magnetized every cartridge played will become degraded.

3   Do not leave cartridges in direct sunlight or fully inserted in the tape player for long periods.

27   Wiring diagrams - general information

Since it isn't possible to include all wiring diagrams for every year covered by this manual, the following diagrams are those that are typical and most commonly needed.

Prior to troubleshooting any circuits, check the fuse and circuit breakers (if equipped) to make sure they're in good condition. Make sure the battery is properly charged and check the cable connections (Chapter 1).

When checking a circuit, make sure that all connectors are clean, with no broken or loose terminals. When unplugging a connector, do not pull on the wires. Pull only on the connector housings themselves.

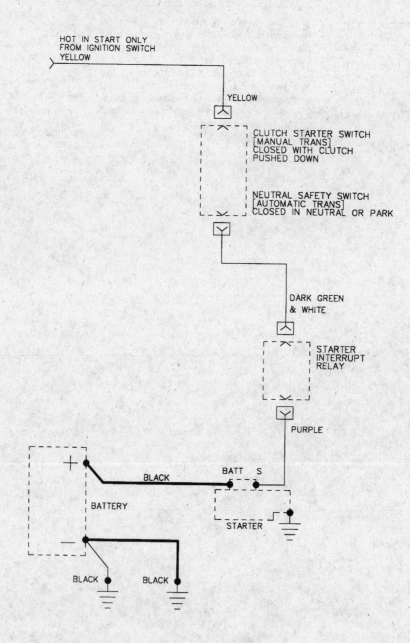

HOT IN START ONLY
FROM IGNITION SWITCH
YELLOW

YELLOW

CLUTCH STARTER SWITCH
[MANUAL TRANS]
CLOSED WITH CLUTCH
PUSHED DOWN

NEUTRAL SAFETY SWITCH
[AUTOMATIC TRANS]
CLOSED IN NEUTRAL OR PARK

DARK GREEN
& WHITE

STARTER
INTERRUPT
RELAY

PURPLE

BLACK   BATT   S

BATTERY

STARTER

BLACK   BLACK

Starting system - typical

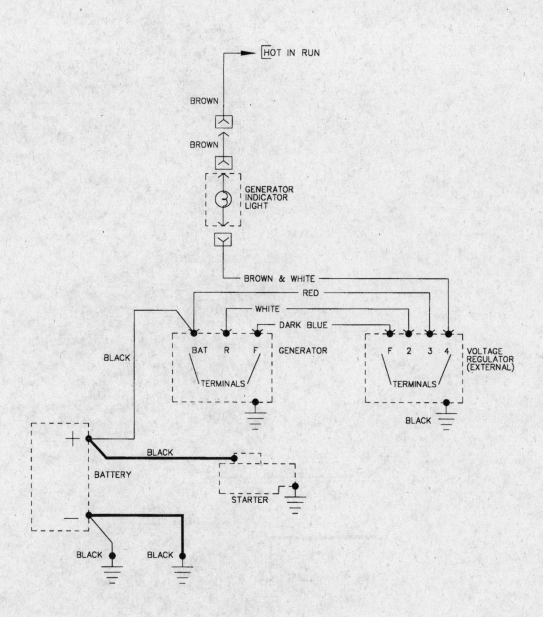

Charging system - typical early models

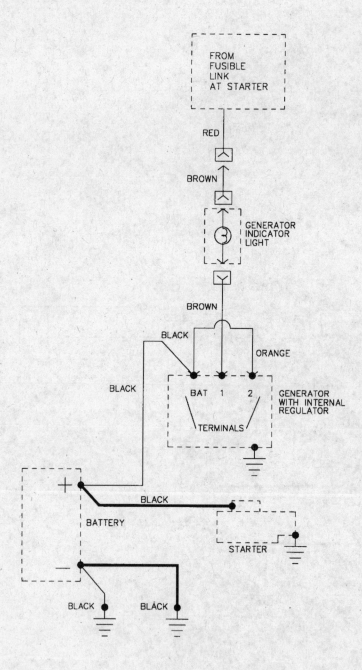

Charging system - typical later models

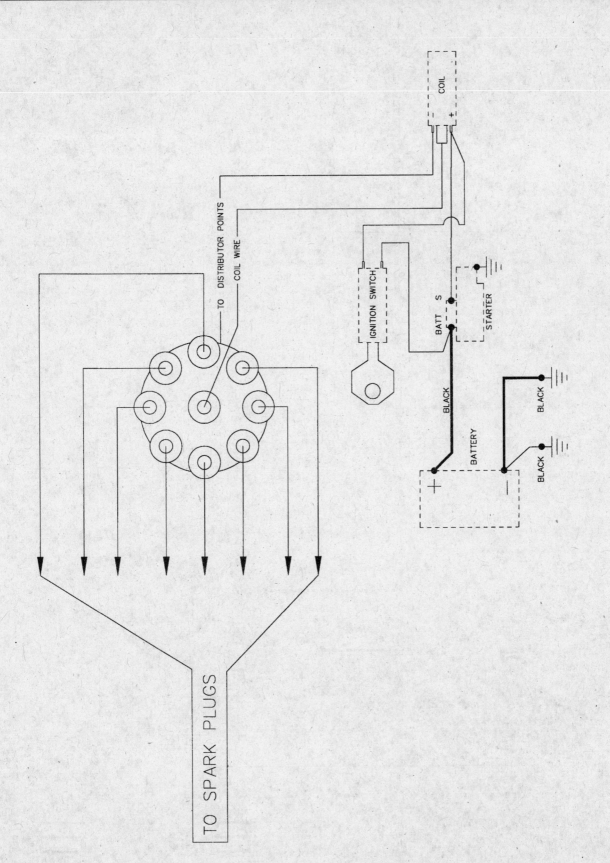

Ignition system - typical early models with breaker points

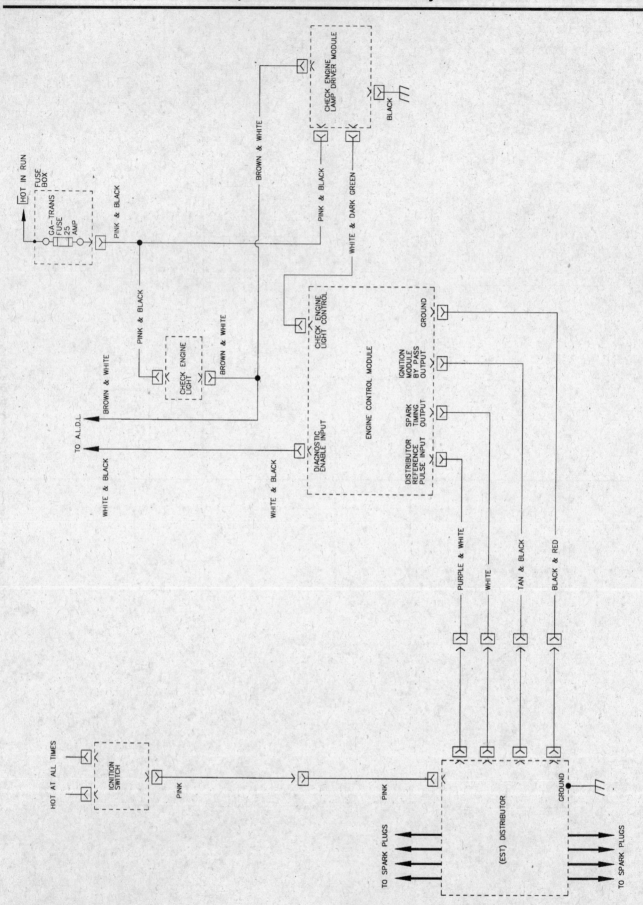

Engine control system - typical later models

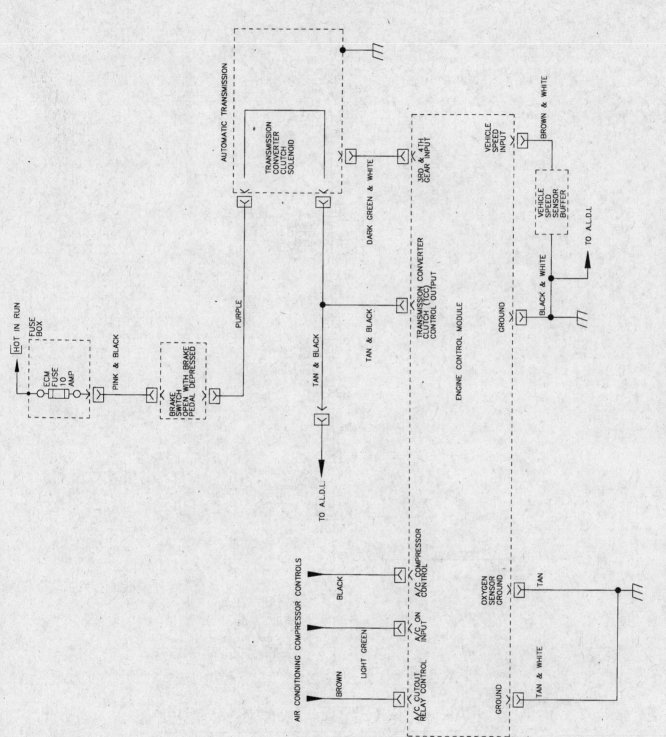

Vehicle sensors and transmission converter clutch system - typical later models

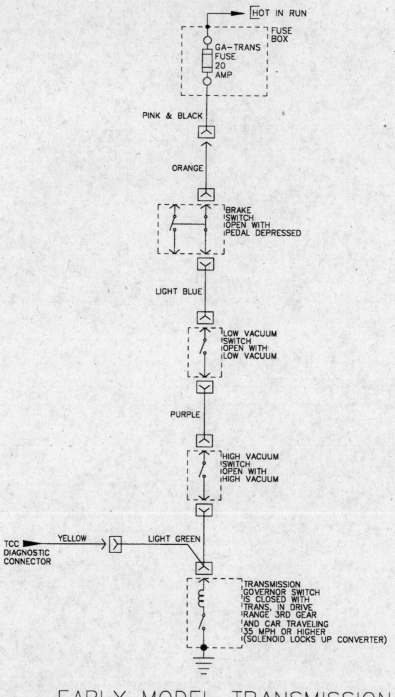

HOT IN RUN

FUSE
BOX

GA-TRANS
FUSE
20
AMP

PINK & BLACK

ORANGE

BRAKE
SWITCH
OPEN WITH
PEDAL DEPRESSED

LIGHT BLUE

LOW VACUUM
SWITCH
OPEN WITH
LOW VACUUM

PURPLE

HIGH VACUUM
SWITCH
OPEN WITH
HIGH VACUUM

TCC
DIAGNOSTIC
CONNECTOR
YELLOW
LIGHT GREEN

TRANSMISSION
GOVERNOR SWITCH
IS CLOSED WITH
TRANS. IN DRIVE
RANGE 3RD GEAR
AND CAR TRAVELING
35 MPH OR HIGHER
(SOLENOID LOCKS UP CONVERTER)

EARLY MODEL TRANSMISSION

Transmission controls system - typical early models

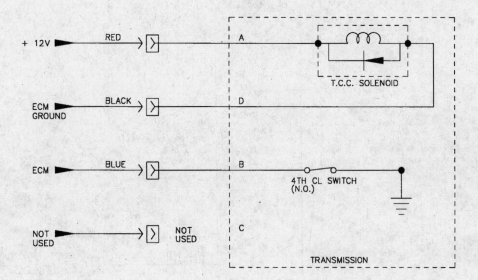

LATE MODEL TRANSMISSION

Transmission controls system - typical later models

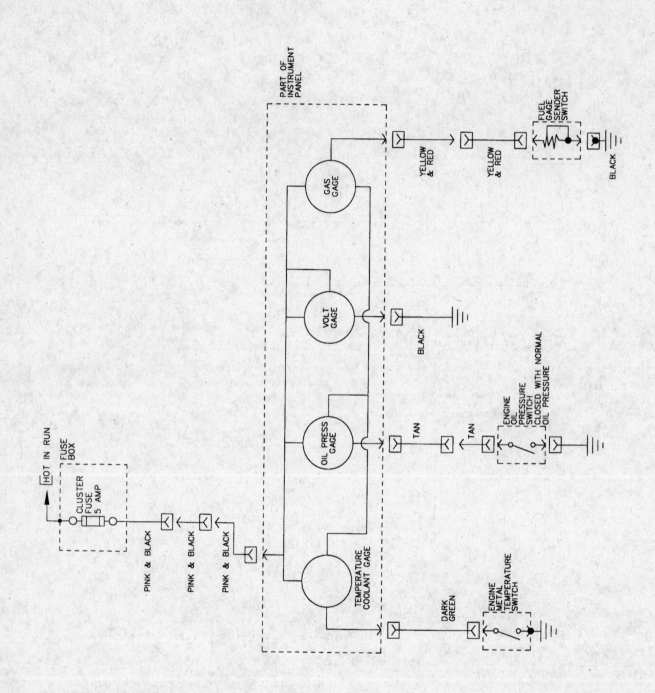

Engine warning systems - typical

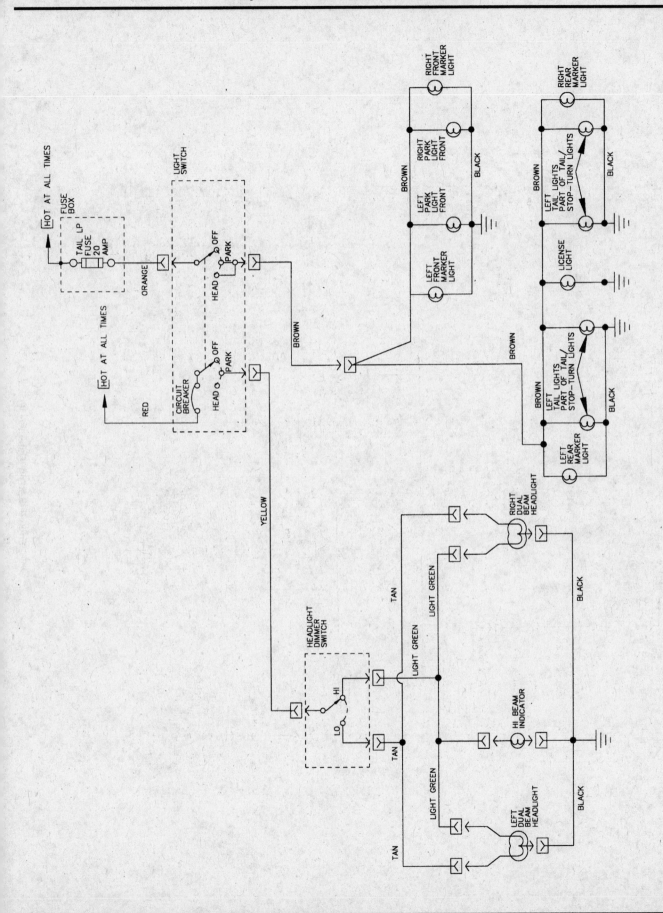

Exterior lighting system - typical (part 1 of 2)

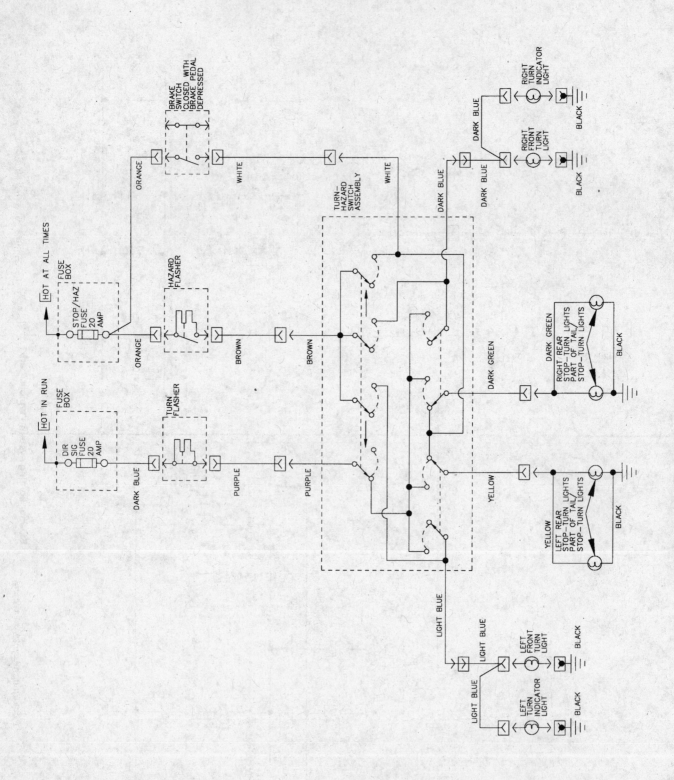

Exterior lighting system - typical (part 2 of 2)

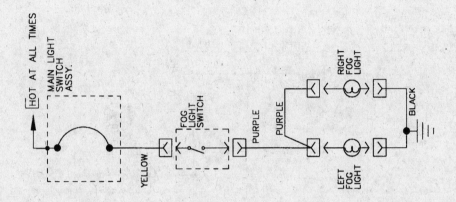

Fog light system - typical

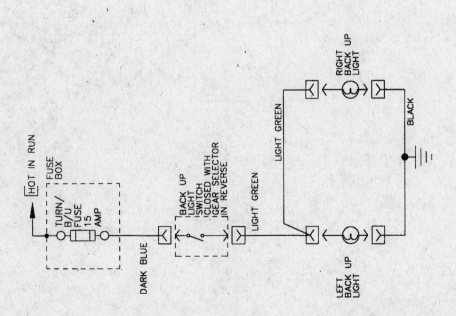

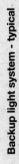

Backup light system - typical

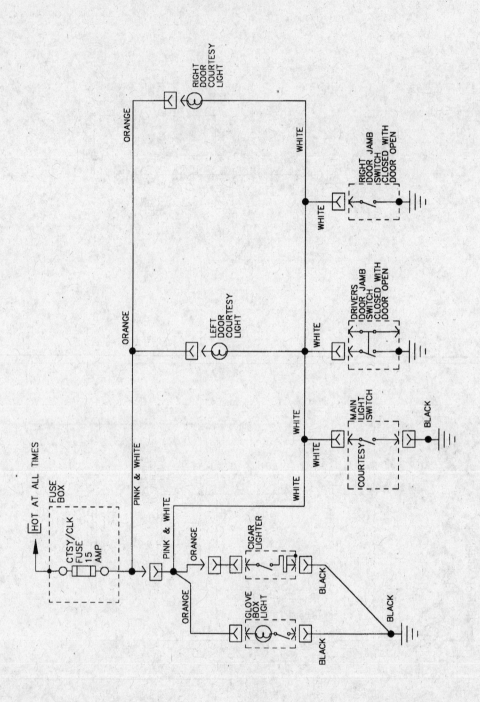

Interior lighting system - typical (part 1 of 2)

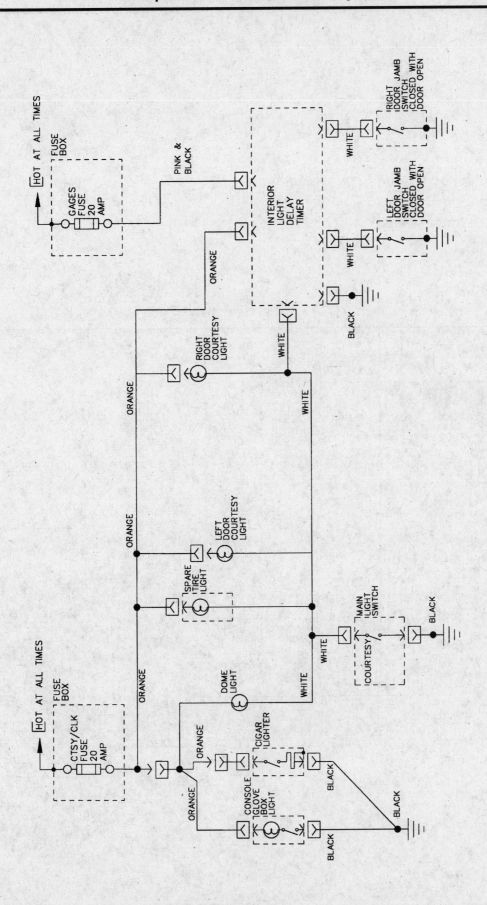

Interior lighting system - typical (part 2 of 2)

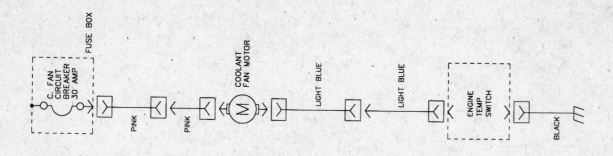

Auxiliary cooling fan system - typical later models

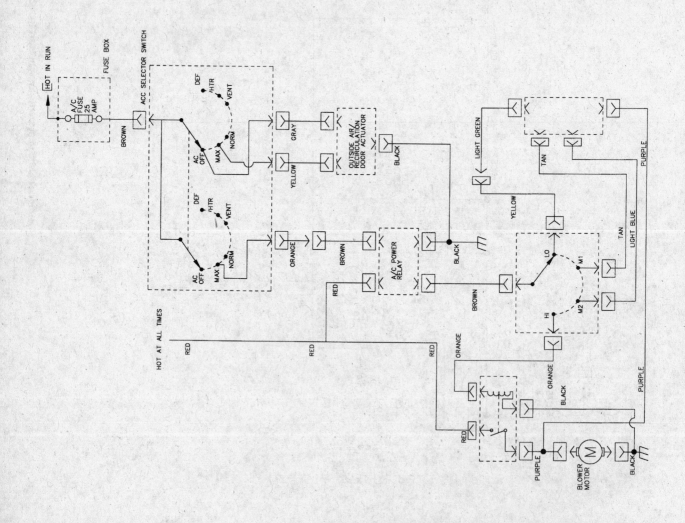

Heating and air-conditioning system - typical

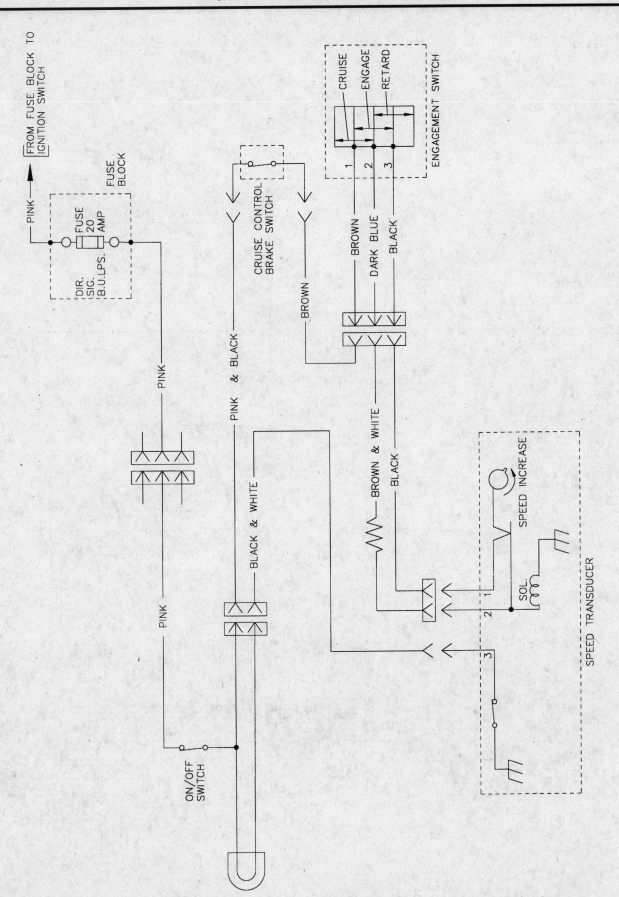

Cruise control system - typical early models

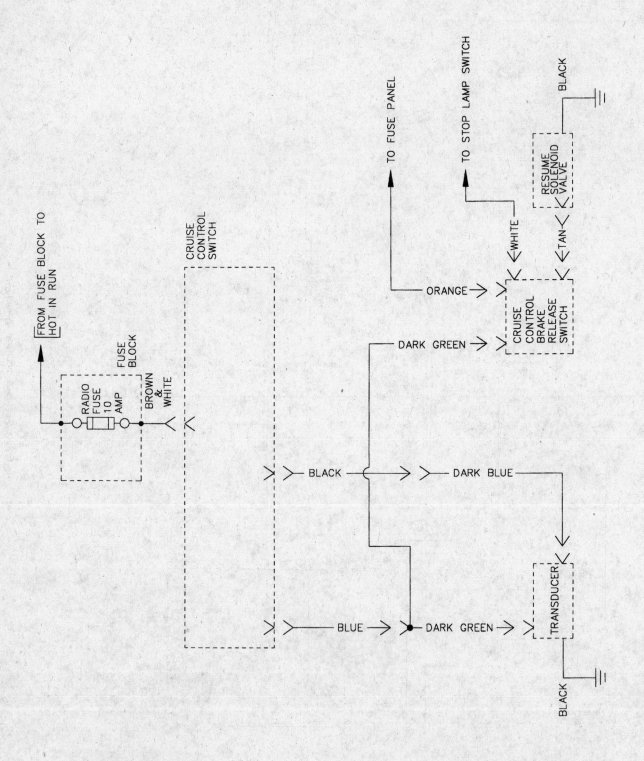

Cruise control system - typical later models

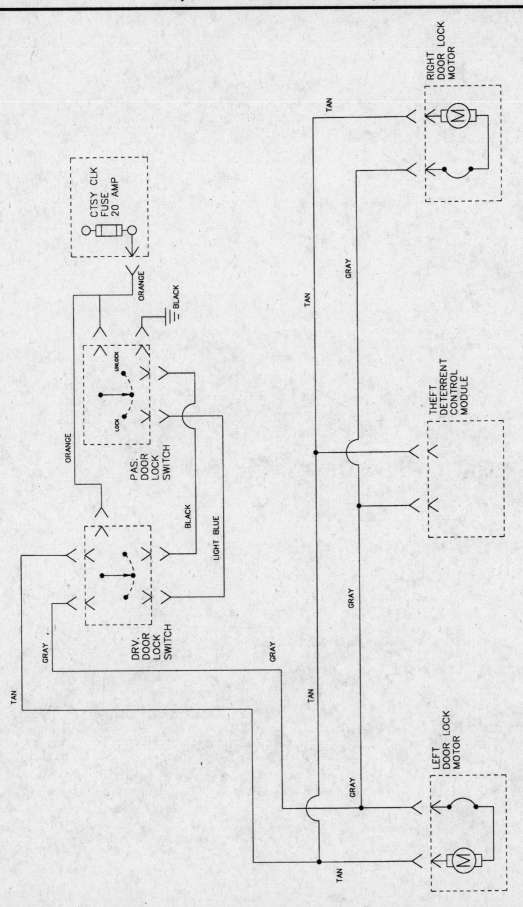

Power door lock system - typical

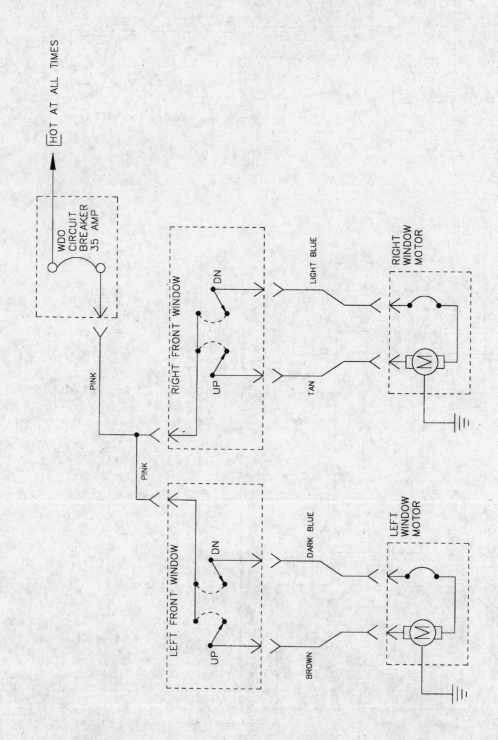

Power window system - typical

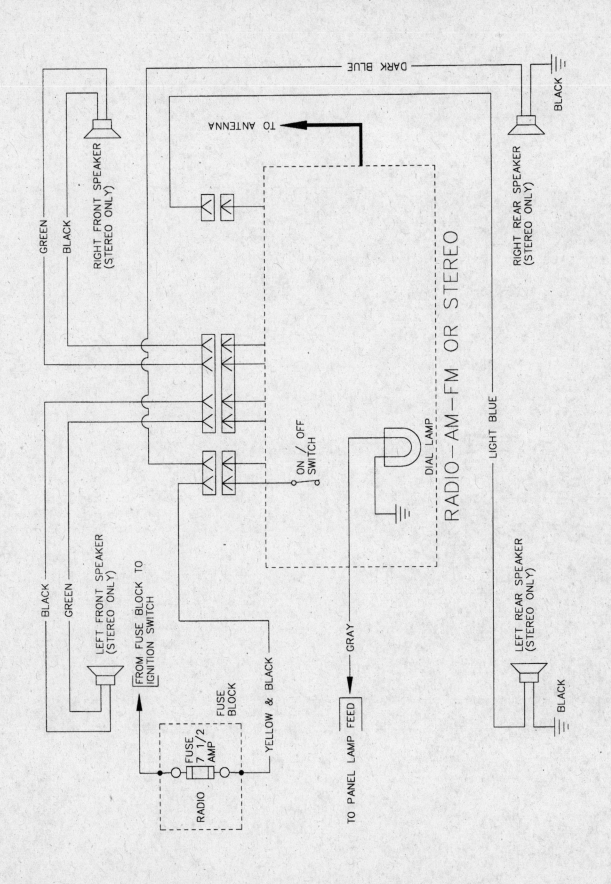

Audio system (base model) - typical early models

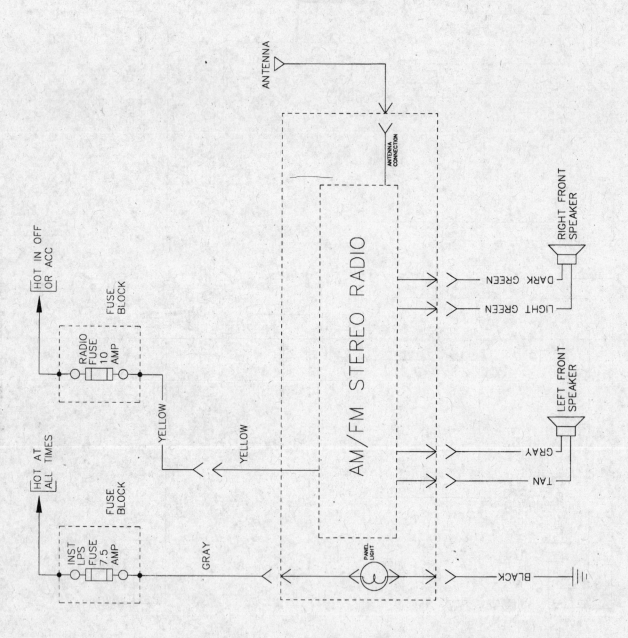

Audio system (base model) – typical later models

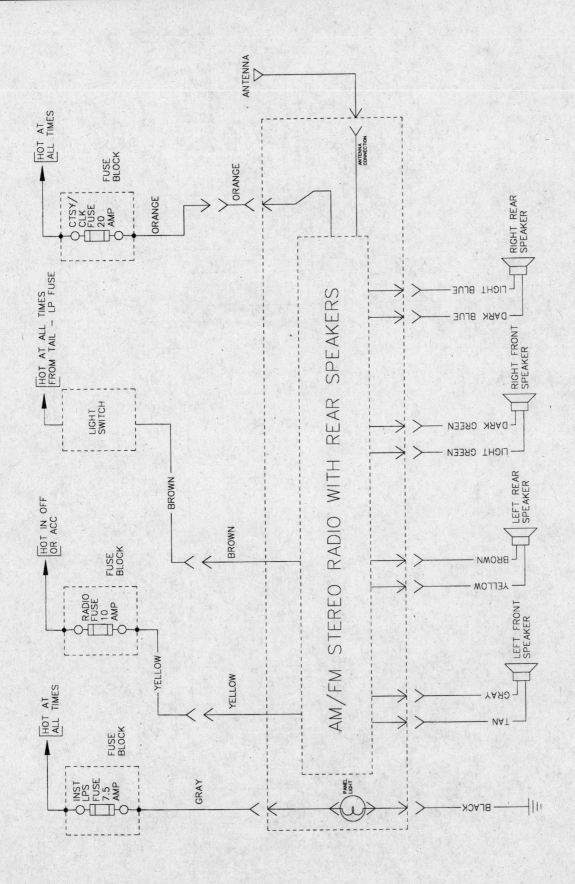

Audio system with rear speakers - typical later models

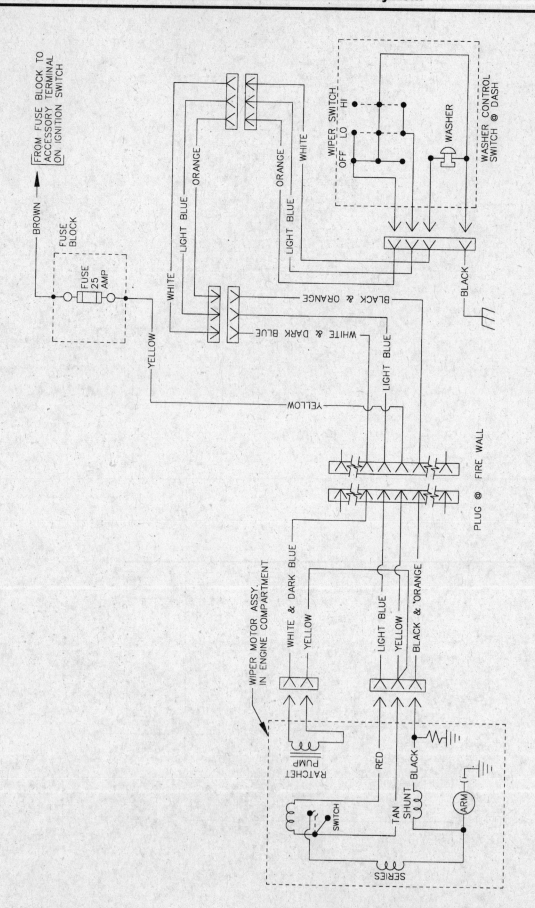

Windshield wiper/washer system - typical early models

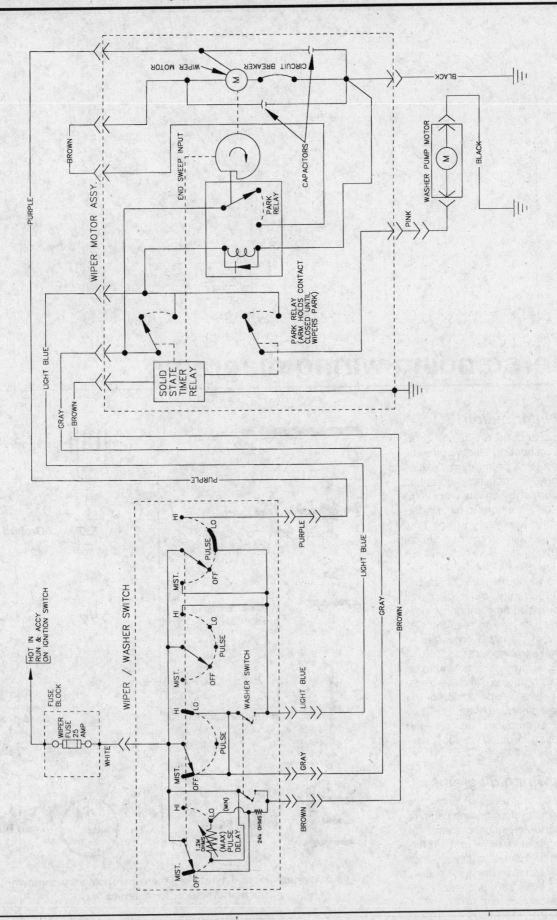

Windshield wiper/washer system - typical later models

Understanding wiring diagrams

General information

Wiring diagrams are useful tools when troubleshooting electric circuits. Electrical systems on modern vehicles have become increasingly complex, making a correct diagnosis more difficult. If you take the time to fully understand wiring diagrams, you can take much of the guesswork out of electrical troubleshooting.

If you have an older vehicle, you may find the wiring diagrams difficult to decipher. Frequently, older diagrams give no information on component location, operation or how to read the diagram. Many of them are organized in ways that make tracing wires difficult.

Today's wiring diagrams tend to be more carefully organized, and the cross-references between each portion of the diagram are clearly explained. They often have component locators and some are even in color (to show wire colors).

Reading wiring diagrams

Wiring diagrams either show the entire electrical system on one page, or they split up the electrical system onto multiple pages and have cross-references which tie them all together. When a diagram is split up, there are usually charts with the diagram that explain the cross-referencing system.

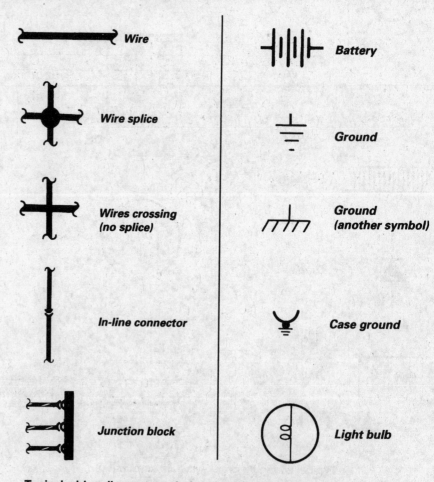

Typical wiring diagram symbols – these symbols vary somewhat from manufacturer to manufacturer

Most diagrams show the power source at the top of the page and the grounds at the bottom.

Components of a wiring diagram

Wiring diagrams can be broken down into three main components: symbols, color codes and wire gage numbers.

Symbols

On wiring diagrams, symbols are used to represent the components of the electrical system. The most obvious symbol is a line to represent a wire. Some other symbols are not so obvious, since they do not necessarily look like the components they're representing. That's because most wiring diagram symbols, which are sometimes called *schematic* symbols, show the way the component functions electrically rather than how it appears physically.

Color codes

Since wiring diagrams are usually in black-and-white, color codes are used to indicate the color of each wire. These codes are normally one or two-character abbreviations. These codes vary somewhat from manufacturer to manufacturer; however, most diagrams include a color code chart so its easy to check the meaning of each code.

Occasionally, manufacturing difficulties cause a manufacturer to deviate slightly from the wiring colors shown on the diagram. If the wire colors at a connector do not match the diagram, and you're sure you're looking at the correct diagram, you can usually identify the incorrect color by comparing all the colors at the connector with the diagram.

Wires are not always solid colors. Often they have markings on them such as a stripe, dots or hash marks. When a diagram shows two colors for a wire, the first color is the basic color of the wire. The second color is the marking.

Wire gage numbers

The wire gage number represents the wire thickness. In a wiring diagram, the gage number for each wire is usually listed either before or after the color code.

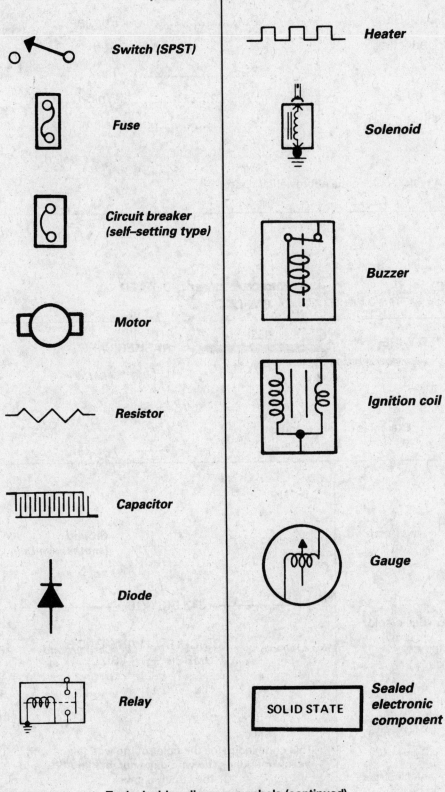

Typical wiring diagram symbols (continued)

BK	Black	**O**	Orange
BR	Brown	**PK**	Pink
DB	Dark Blue	**P**	Purple
DG	Dark Green	**R**	Red
GY	Gray	**T**	Tan
LB	Light Blue	**W**	White
LG	Light Green	**Y**	Yellow
N	Natural		

A typical color code abbreviation chart

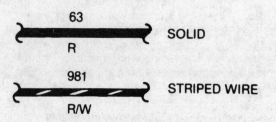

63
R
SOLID

981
R/W
STRIPED WIRE

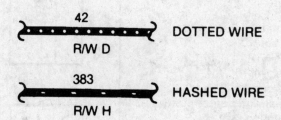

42
R/W D
DOTTED WIRE

383
R/W H
HASHED WIRE

Examples of wire markings

Example: 1.25F - GB

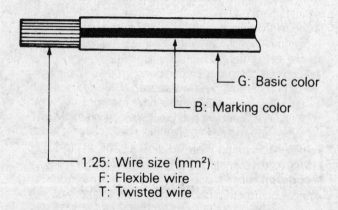

G: Basic color
B: Marking color

1.25: Wire size (mm²)
F: Flexible wire
T: Twisted wire

This example code is for a green wire with a black stripe – the 1.25 is the metric wire gage number

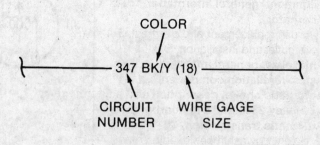

COLOR

347 BK/Y (18)

CIRCUIT
NUMBER

WIRE GAGE
SIZE

This code indicates the color of the wire (black with a yellow marking), the wire gage number (in AWG) and the circuit number

Index

Haynes Automotive Manuals

NOTE: If you do not see a listing for your vehicle, consult your local Haynes dealer for the latest product information.

HAYNES XTREME CUSTOMIZING
- **11101 Sport Compact Customizing**
- **11102 Sport Compact Performance**
- **11110 In-car Entertainment**
- **11150 Sport Utility Vehicle Customizing**
- **11213 Acura**
- **11255 GM Full-size Pick-ups**
- **11314 Ford Focus**
- **11315 Full-size Ford Pick-ups**
- **11373 Honda Civic**

ACURA
- **12020 Integra '86 thru '89 & Legend '86 thru '90**
- **12021 Integra '90 thru '93 & Legend '91 thru '95**

AMC
- Jeep CJ - *see JEEP (50020)*
- **14020 Mid-size models '70 thru '83**
- **14025 (Renault) Alliance & Encore '83 thru '87**

AUDI
- **15020 4000 all models '80 thru '87**
- **15025 5000 all models '77 thru '83**
- **15026 5000 all models '84 thru '88**

AUSTIN-HEALEY
- Sprite - *see MG Midget (66015)*

BMW
- **18020 3/5 Series** not including diesel or all-wheel drive models '82 thru '92
- **18021 3-Series** incl. Z3 models '92 thru '98
- **18022 3-Series, E46 chassis '99 thru '05, Z4 models '03 thru '05**
- **18025 320i** all 4 cyl models '75 thru '83
- **18050 1500 thru 2002** except Turbo '59 thru '77

BUICK
- **19010 Buick Century '97 thru '05**
  Century (front-wheel drive) - *see GM (38005)*
- **19020 Buick, Oldsmobile & Pontiac Full-size (Front-wheel drive) '85 thru '05**
  Buick Electra, LeSabre and Park Avenue; Oldsmobile Delta 88 Royale, Ninety Eight and Regency; Pontiac Bonneville
- **19025 Buick Oldsmobile & Pontiac Full-size (Rear wheel drive)**
  Buick Estate '70 thru '90, Electra '70 thru '84, LeSabre '70 thru '85, Limited '74 thru '79 Oldsmobile Custom Cruiser '70 thru '90, Delta 88 '70 thru '85, Ninety-eight '70 thru '84 Pontiac Bonneville '70 thru '81, Catalina '70 thru '81, Grandville '70 thru '75, Parisienne '83 thru '86
- **19030 Mid-size Regal & Century** all rear-drive models with V6, V8 and Turbo '74 thru '87
  Regal - *see GENERAL MOTORS (38010)*
  Riviera - *see GENERAL MOTORS (38030)*
  Roadmaster - *see CHEVROLET (24046)*
  Skyhawk - *see GENERAL MOTORS (38015)*
  Skylark - *see GM (38020, 38025)*
  Somerset - *see GENERAL MOTORS (38025)*

CADILLAC
- **21030 Cadillac Rear Wheel Drive** all gasoline models '70 thru '93
  Cimarron - *see GENERAL MOTORS (38015)*
  DeVille - *see GM (38031 & 38032)*
  Eldorado - *see GM (38030 & 38031)*
  Fleetwood - *see GM (38031)*
  Seville - *see GM (38030, 38031 & 38032)*

CHEVROLET
- **24010 Astro & GMC Safari Mini-vans '85 thru '03**
- **24015 Camaro V8** all models '70 thru '81
- **24016 Camaro** all models '82 thru '92
- **24017 Camaro & Firebird '93 thru '02**
  Cavalier - *see GENERAL MOTORS (38016)*
  Celebrity - *see GENERAL MOTORS (38005)*
- **24020 Chevelle, Malibu & El Camino '69 thru '87**
- **24024 Chevette & Pontiac T1000 '76 thru '87**
  Citation - *see GENERAL MOTORS (38020)*
- **24027 Colorado & GMC Canyon '04 thru '06**
- **24032 Corsica/Beretta** all models '87 thru '96
- **24040 Corvette** all V8 models '68 thru '82
- **24041 Corvette** all models '84 thru '96
- **10305 Chevrolet Engine Overhaul Manual**
- **24045 Full-size Sedans** Caprice, Impala, Biscayne, Bel Air & Wagons '69 thru '90
- **24046 Impala SS & Caprice and Buick Roadmaster '91 thru '96**
  Impala - *see LUMINA (24048)*
  Lumina '90 thru '94 - *see GM (38010)*
- **24048 Lumina & Monte Carlo '95 thru '05**
  Lumina APV - *see GM (38035)*

- **24050 Luv Pick-up** all 2WD & 4WD '72 thru '82
  Malibu '97 thru '00 - *see GM (38026)*
- **24055 Monte Carlo** all models '70 thru '88
  Monte Carlo '95 thru '01 - *see LUMINA (24048)*
- **24059 Nova** all V8 models '69 thru '79
- **24060 Nova and Geo Prizm '85 thru '92**
- **24064 Pick-ups '67 thru '87** - Chevrolet & GMC, all V8 & in-line 6 cyl, 2WD & 4WD '67 thru '87; Suburbans, Blazers & Jimmys '67 thru '91
- **24065 Pick-ups '88 thru '98** - Chevrolet & GMC, full-size pick-ups '88 thru '98, C/K Classic '99 & '00, Blazer & Jimmy '92 thru '94; Suburban '92 thru '99; Tahoe & Yukon '95 thru '99
- **24066 Pick-ups '99 thru '06** - Chevrolet Silverado & GMC Sierra '99 thru '06, Suburban/Tahoe/Yukon/Yukon XL/Avalanche '00 thru '06
- **24070 S-10 & S-15 Pick-ups '82 thru '93, Blazer & Jimmy '83 thru '94,**
- **24071 S-10 & Sonoma Pick-ups '94 thru '04, Blazer & Jimmy '95 thru '04, Hombre '96 thru '01**
- **24072 Chevrolet TrailBlazer & TrailBlazer EXT, GMC Envoy & Envoy XL, Oldsmobile Bravada '02 thru '06**
- **24075 Sprint '85 thru '88 & Geo Metro '89 thru '01**
- **24080 Vans - Chevrolet & GMC '68 thru '96**
- **24081 Chevrolet Express & GMC Savana Full-size Vans '96 thru '05**

CHRYSLER
- **25015 Chrysler Cirrus, Dodge Stratus, Plymouth Breeze '95 thru '00**
- **10310 Chrysler Engine Overhaul Manual**
- **25020 Full-size Front-Wheel Drive '88 thru '93**
  K-Cars - *see DODGE Aries (30008)*
  Laser - *see DODGE Daytona (30030)*
- **25025 Chrysler LHS, Concorde, New Yorker, Dodge Intrepid, Eagle Vision, '93 thru '97**
- **25026 Chrysler LHS, Concorde, 300M, Dodge Intrepid, '98 thru '03**
- **25027 Chrysler 300, Dodge Charger & Magnum '05 thru '07**
- **25030 Chrysler & Plymouth Mid-size** front wheel drive '82 thru '95
  Rear-wheel Drive - *see Dodge (30050)*
- **25035 PT Cruiser** all models '01 thru '03
- **25040 Chrysler Sebring, Dodge Avenger '95 thru '05, Dodge Stratus '01 thru 05**

DATSUN
- **28005 200SX** all models '80 thru '83
- **28007 B-210** all models '73 thru '78
- **28009 210** all models '79 thru '82
- **28012 240Z, 260Z & 280Z Coupe '70 thru '78**
- **28014 280ZX Coupe & 2+2 '79 thru '83**
  300ZX - *see NISSAN (72010)*
- **28018 510 & PL521 Pick-up '68 thru '73**
- **28020 510** all models '78 thru '81
- **28022 620 Series Pick-up** all models '73 thru '79
  720 Series Pick-up - *see NISSAN (72030)*
- **28025 810/Maxima** all gasoline models, '77 thru '84

DODGE
- 400 & 600 - *see CHRYSLER (25030)*
- **30008 Aries & Plymouth Reliant '81 thru '89**
- **30010 Caravan & Plymouth Voyager '84 thru '95**
- **30011 Caravan & Plymouth Voyager '96 thru '02**
- **30012 Challenger/Plymouth Saporro '78 thru '83**
- **30013 Caravan, Chrysler Voyager, Town & Country '03 thru '06**
- **30016 Colt & Plymouth Champ '78 thru '87**
- **30020 Dakota Pick-ups** all models '87 thru '96
- **30021 Durango '98 & '99, Dakota '97 thru '99**
- **30022 Dodge Durango** models '00 thru '03
  Dodge Dakota models '00 thru '04
- **30023 Dodge Durango '04 thru '06, Dakota '05 and '06**
- **30025 Dart, Demon, Plymouth Barracuda, Duster & Valiant** 6 cyl models '67 thru '76
- **30030 Daytona & Chrysler Laser '84 thru '89**
  Intrepid - *see CHRYSLER (25025, 25026)*
- **30034 Neon** all models '95 thru '99
- **30035 Omni & Plymouth Horizon '78 thru '90**
- **30036 Dodge and Plymouth Neon '00 thru '05**
- **30040 Pick-ups** all full-size models '74 thru '93
- **30041 Pick-ups** all full-size models '94 thru '01
- **30042 Dodge Full-size Pick-ups '02 thru '05**
- **30045 Ram 50/D50 Pick-ups & Raider and Plymouth Arrow Pick-ups '79 thru '93**
- **30050 Dodge/Plymouth/Chrysler RWD '71 thru '89**
- **30055 Shadow & Plymouth Sundance '87 thru '94**
- **30060 Spirit & Plymouth Acclaim '89 thru '95**
- **30065 Vans - Dodge & Plymouth '71 thru '03**

EAGLE
- Talon - *see MITSUBISHI (68030, 68031)*
- Vision - *see CHRYSLER (25025)*

FIAT
- **34010 124 Sport Coupe & Spider '68 thru '78**
- **34025 X1/9** all models '74 thru '80

FORD
- **10355 Ford Automatic Transmission Overhaul**
- **36004 Aerostar Mini-vans** all models '86 thru '97
- **36006 Contour & Mercury Mystique '95 thru '00**
- **36008 Courier Pick-up** all models '72 thru '82
- **36012 Crown Victoria & Mercury Grand Marquis '88 thru '06**
- **10320 Ford Engine Overhaul Manual**
- **36016 Escort/Mercury Lynx** all models '81 thru '90
- **36020 Escort/Mercury Tracer '91 thru '00**
- **36022 Ford Escape & Mazda Tribute '01 thru '03**
- **36024 Explorer & Mazda Navajo '91 thru '01**
- **36025 Ford Explorer & Mercury Mountaineer '02 thru '06**
- **36028 Fairmont & Mercury Zephyr '78 thru '83**
- **36030 Festiva & Aspire '88 thru '97**
- **36032 Fiesta** all models '77 thru '80
- **36034 Focus** all models '00 thru '05
- **36036 Ford & Mercury Full-size '75 thru '87**
- **36044 Ford & Mercury Mid-size '75 thru '86**
- **36048 Mustang V8** all models '64-1/2 thru '73
- **36049 Mustang II** 4 cyl, V6 & V8 models '74 thru '78
- **36050 Mustang & Mercury Capri** all models Mustang, '79 thru '93; Capri, '79 thru '86
- **36051 Mustang** all models '94 thru '04
- **36052 Mustang '05 thru '07**
- **36054 Pick-ups & Bronco '73 thru '79**
- **36058 Pick-ups & Bronco '80 thru '96**
- **36059 F-150 & Expedition '97 thru '03, F-250 '97 thru '99 & Lincoln Navigator '98 thru '02**
- **36060 Super Duty Pick-ups, Excursion '99 thru '06**
- **36061 F-150 full-size '04 thru '06**
- **36062 Pinto & Mercury Bobcat '75 thru '80**
- **36066 Probe** all models '89 thru '92
- **36070 Ranger/Bronco II** gasoline models '83 thru '92
- **36071 Ranger '93 thru '05 & Mazda Pick-ups '94 thru '05**
- **36074 Taurus & Mercury Sable '86 thru '95**
- **36075 Taurus & Mercury Sable '96 thru '05**
- **36078 Tempo & Mercury Topaz '84 thru '94**
- **36082 Thunderbird/Mercury Cougar '83 thru '88**
- **36086 Thunderbird/Mercury Cougar '89 and '97**
- **36090 Vans** all V8 Econoline models '69 thru '91
- **36094 Vans** full size '92 thru '05
- **36097 Windstar Mini-van '95 thru '03**

GENERAL MOTORS
- **10360 GM Automatic Transmission Overhaul**
- **38005 Buick Century, Chevrolet Celebrity, Oldsmobile Cutlass Ciera & Pontiac 6000** all models '82 thru '96
- **38010 Buick Regal, Chevrolet Lumina, Oldsmobile Cutlass Supreme & Pontiac Grand Prix (FWD) '88 thru '05**
- **38015 Buick Skyhawk, Cadillac Cimarron, Chevrolet Cavalier, Oldsmobile Firenza & Pontiac J-2000 & Sunbird '82 thru '94**
- **38016 Chevrolet Cavalier & Pontiac Sunfire '95 thru '04**
- **38017 Chevrolet Cobalt & Pontiac G5 '05 thru '07**
- **38020 Buick Skylark, Chevrolet Citation, Olds Omega, Pontiac Phoenix '80 thru '85**
- **38025 Buick Skylark & Somerset, Oldsmobile Achieva & Calais and Pontiac Grand Am** all models '85 thru '98
- **38026 Chevrolet Malibu, Olds Alero & Cutlass, Pontiac Grand Am '97 thru '03**
- **38027 Chevrolet Malibu '04 thru '07**
- **38030 Cadillac Eldorado '71 thru '85, Seville '80 thru '85, Oldsmobile Toronado '71 thru '85, Buick Riviera '79 thru '85**
- **38031 Cadillac Eldorado & Seville '86 thru '91, DeVille '86 thru '93, Fleetwood & Olds Toronado '86 thru '92, Buick Riviera '86 thru '93**
- **38032 Cadillac DeVille '94 thru '05 & Seville '92 thru '04**
- **38035 Chevrolet Lumina APV, Olds Silhouette & Pontiac Trans Sport** all models '90 thru '96
- **38036 Chevrolet Venture, Olds Silhouette, Pontiac Trans Sport & Montana '97 thru '05**
  General Motors Full-size Rear-wheel Drive - *see BUICK (19025)*

GEO
- Metro - *see CHEVROLET Sprint (24075)*
- Prizm - '85 thru '92 *see CHEVY (24060)*, '93 thru '02 *see TOYOTA Corolla (92036)*

(Continued on other side)

Haynes North America, Inc., 861 Lawrence Drive, Newbury Park, CA 91320-1514 • (805) 498-6703

Haynes Automotive Manuals (continued)

NOTE: If you do not see a listing for your vehicle, consult your local Haynes dealer for the latest product information.

40030 Storm all models '90 thru '93
Tracker - see SUZUKI Samurai (90010)

GMC
Vans & Pick-ups - see CHEVROLET

HONDA
42010 Accord CVCC all models '76 thru '83
42011 Accord all models '84 thru '89
42012 Accord all models '90 thru '93
42013 Accord all models '94 thru '97
42014 Accord all models '98 thru '02
42015 Honda Accord models '03 thru '05
42020 Civic 1200 all models '73 thru '79
42021 Civic 1300 & 1500 CVCC '80 thru '83
42022 Civic 1500 CVCC all models '75 thru '79
42023 Civic all models '84 thru '91
42024 Civic & del Sol '92 thru '95
42025 Civic '96 thru '00, CR-V '97 thru '01, Acura Integra '94 thru '00
42026 Civic '01 thru '04, CR-V '02 thru '04
42035 Honda Odyssey all models '99 thru '04
42037 Honda Pilot '03 thru '07, Acura MDX '01 thru '07
42040 Prelude CVCC all models '79 thru '89

HYUNDAI
43010 Elantra all models '96 thru '01
43015 Excel & Accent all models '86 thru '98

ISUZU
Hombre - see CHEVROLET S-10 (24071)
47017 Rodeo '91 thru '02; Amigo '89 thru '94 and '98 thru '02; Honda Passport '95 thru '02
47020 Trooper & Pick-up '81 thru '93

JAGUAR
49010 XJ6 all 6 cyl models '68 thru '86
49011 XJ6 all models '88 thru '94
49015 XJ12 & XJS all 12 cyl models '72 thru '85

JEEP
50010 Cherokee, Comanche & Wagoneer Limited all models '84 thru '01
50020 CJ all models '49 thru '86
50025 Grand Cherokee all models '93 thru '04
50029 Grand Wagoneer & Pick-up '72 thru '91 Grand Wagoneer '84 thru '91, Cherokee & Wagoneer '72 thru '83, Pick-up '72 thru '88
50030 Wrangler all models '87 thru '03
50035 Liberty '02 thru '04

KIA
54070 Sephia '94 thru '01, Spectra '00 thru '04

LEXUS
ES 300 - see TOYOTA Camry (92007)

LINCOLN
Navigator - see FORD Pick-up (36059)
59010 Rear-Wheel Drive all models '70 thru '05

MAZDA
61010 GLC Hatchback (rear-wheel drive) '77 thru '83
61011 GLC (front-wheel drive) '81 thru '85
61015 323 & Protegé '90 thru '00
61016 MX-5 Miata '90 thru '97
61020 MPV all models '89 thru '94
Navajo - see Ford Explorer (36024)
61030 Pick-ups '72 thru '93
Pick-ups '94 thru '00 - see Ford Ranger (36071)
61035 RX-7 all models '79 thru '85
61036 RX-7 all models '86 thru '91
61040 626 (rear-wheel drive) all models '79 thru '82
61041 626/MX-6 (front-wheel drive) '83 thru '92
61042 626 '93 thru '01, MX-6/Ford Probe '93 thru '01

MERCEDES-BENZ
63012 123 Series Diesel '76 thru '85
63015 190 Series four-cyl models, '84 thru '88
63020 230/250/280 6 cyl sohc models '68 thru '72
63025 280 123 Series gasoline models '77 thru '81
63030 350 & 450 all models '71 thru '80

MERCURY
64200 Villager & Nissan Quest '93 thru '01
All other titles, see FORD Listing.

MG
66010 MGB Roadster & GT Coupe '62 thru '80
66015 MG Midget, Austin Healey Sprite '58 thru '80

MITSUBISHI
68020 Cordia, Tredia, Galant, Precis & Mirage '83 thru '93

68030 Eclipse, Eagle Talon & Ply. Laser '90 thru '94
68031 Eclipse '95 thru '01, Eagle Talon '95 thru '98
68035 Mitsubishi Galant '94 thru '03
68040 Pick-up '83 thru '96 & Montero '83 thru '93

NISSAN
72010 300ZX all models including Turbo '84 thru '89
72015 Altima all models '93 thru '04
72020 Maxima all models '85 thru '92
72021 Maxima all models '93 thru '04
72030 Pick-ups '80 thru '97 Pathfinder '87 thru '95
72031 Frontier Pick-up '98 thru '04, Xterra '00 thru '04, Pathfinder '96 thru '04
72040 Pulsar all models '83 thru '86
Quest - see MERCURY Villager (64200)
72050 Sentra all models '82 thru '94
72051 Sentra & 200SX all models '95 thru '04
72060 Stanza all models '82 thru '90

OLDSMOBILE
73015 Cutlass V6 & V8 gas models '74 thru '88
For other OLDSMOBILE titles, see BUICK, CHEVROLET or GENERAL MOTORS listing.

PLYMOUTH
For PLYMOUTH titles, see DODGE listing.

PONTIAC
79008 Fiero all models '84 thru '88
79018 Firebird V8 models except Turbo '70 thru '81
79019 Firebird all models '82 thru '92
79040 Mid-size Rear-wheel Drive '70 thru '87
For other PONTIAC titles, see BUICK, CHEVROLET or GENERAL MOTORS listing.

PORSCHE
80020 911 except Turbo & Carrera 4 '65 thru '89
80025 914 all 4 cyl models '69 thru '76
80030 924 all models including Turbo '76 thru '82
80035 944 all models including Turbo '83 thru '89

RENAULT
Alliance & Encore - see AMC (14020)

SAAB
84010 900 all models including Turbo '79 thru '88

SATURN
87010 Saturn all models '91 thru '02
87011 Saturn Ion '03 thru '07
87020 Saturn all L-series models '00 thru '04

SUBARU
89002 1100, 1300, 1400 & 1600 '71 thru '79
89003 1600 & 1800 2WD & 4WD '80 thru '94
89100 Legacy all models '90 thru '99
89101 Legacy & Forester '00 thru '06

SUZUKI
90010 Samurai/Sidekick & Geo Tracker '86 thru '01

TOYOTA
92005 Camry all models '83 thru '91
92006 Camry all models '92 thru '96
92007 Camry, Avalon, Solara, Lexus ES 300 '97 thru '01
92008 Toyota Camry, Avalon and Solara and Lexus ES 300/330 all models '02 thru '05
92015 Celica Rear Wheel Drive '71 thru '85
92020 Celica Front Wheel Drive '86 thru '99
92025 Celica Supra all models '79 thru '92
92030 Corolla all models '75 thru '79
92032 Corolla all rear wheel drive models '80 thru '87
92035 Corolla all front wheel drive models '84 thru '92
92036 Corolla & Geo Prizm '93 thru '02
92037 Corolla models '03 thru '05
92040 Corolla Tercel all models '80 thru '82
92045 Corona all models '74 thru '82
92050 Cressida all models '78 thru '82
92055 Land Cruiser FJ40, 43, 45, 55 '68 thru '82
92056 Land Cruiser FJ60, 62, 80, FZJ80 '80 thru '96
92065 MR2 all models '85 thru '87
92070 Pick-up all models '69 thru '78
92075 Pick-up all models '79 thru '95
92076 Tacoma '95 thru '04, 4Runner '96 thru '02, & T100 '93 thru '98
92078 Tundra '00 thru '05 & Sequoia '01 thru '05
92080 Previa all models '91 thru '95
92081 Prius all models '01 thru '08
92082 RAV4 all models '96 thru '05
92085 Tercel all models '87 thru '94
92090 Toyota Sienna all models '98 thru '02
92095 Highlander & Lexus RX-330 '99 thru '06

TRIUMPH
94007 Spitfire all models '62 thru '81
94010 TR7 all models '75 thru '81

VW
96008 Beetle & Karmann Ghia '54 thru '79
96009 New Beetle '98 thru '05
96016 Rabbit, Jetta, Scirocco & Pick-up gas models '75 thru '92 & Convertible '80 thru '92
96017 Golf, GTI & Jetta '93 thru '98 & Cabrio '95 thru '98
96018 Golf, GTI, Jetta & Cabrio '99 thru '02
96020 Rabbit, Jetta & Pick-up diesel '77 thru '84
96023 Passat '98 thru '01, Audi A4 '96 thru '01
96030 Transporter 1600 all models '68 thru '79
96035 Transporter 1700, 1800 & 2000 '72 thru '79
96040 Type 3 1500 & 1600 all models '63 thru '73
96045 Vanagon all air-cooled models '80 thru '83

VOLVO
97010 120, 130 Series & 1800 Sports '61 thru '73
97015 140 Series all models '66 thru '74
97020 240 Series all models '76 thru '93
97040 740 & 760 Series all models '82 thru '88
97050 850 Series all models '93 thru '97

TECHBOOK MANUALS
10205 Automotive Computer Codes
10206 OBD-II & Electronic Engine Management Systems
10210 Automotive Emissions Control Manual
10215 Fuel Injection Manual, 1978 thru 1985
10220 Fuel Injection Manual, 1986 thru 1999
10225 Holley Carburetor Manual
10230 Rochester Carburetor Manual
10240 Weber/Zenith/Stromberg/SU Carburetors
10305 Chevrolet Engine Overhaul Manual
10310 Chrysler Engine Overhaul Manual
10320 Ford Engine Overhaul Manual
10330 GM and Ford Diesel Engine Repair Manual
10333 Building Engine Power Manual
10340 Small Engine Repair Manual, 5 HP & Less
10341 Small Engine Repair Manual, 5.5 - 20 HP
10345 Suspension, Steering & Driveline Manual
10355 Ford Automatic Transmission Overhaul
10360 GM Automatic Transmission Overhaul
10405 Automotive Body Repair & Painting
10410 Automotive Brake Manual
10411 Automotive Anti-lock Brake (ABS) Systems
10415 Automotive Detailing Manual
10420 Automotive Electrical Manual
10425 Automotive Heating & Air Conditioning
10430 Automotive Reference Manual & Dictionary
10435 Automotive Tools Manual
10440 Used Car Buying Guide
10445 Welding Manual
10450 ATV Basics
10452 Scooters, Automatic Transmission 50cc to 250cc

SPANISH MANUALS
98903 Reparación de Carrocería & Pintura
98904 Carburadores para los modelos Holley & Rochester
98905 Códigos Automotrices de la Computadora
98910 Frenos Automotriz
98913 Electricidad Automotriz
98915 Inyección de Combustible 1986 al 1999
99040 Chevrolet & GMC Camionetas '67 al '87 Incluye Suburban, Blazer & Jimmy '67 al '91
99041 Chevrolet & GMC Camionetas '88 al '98 Incluye Suburban '92 al '98, Blazer & Jimmy '92 al '94, Tahoe y Yukon '95 al '98
99042 Chevrolet & GMC Camionetas Cerradas '68 al '95
99055 Dodge Caravan & Plymouth Voyager '84 al '95
99075 Ford Camionetas y Bronco '80 al '94
99077 Ford Camionetas Cerradas '69 al '91
99088 Ford Modelos de Tamaño Mediano '75 al '86
99091 Ford Taurus & Mercury Sable '86 al '95
99095 GM Modelos de Tamaño Grande '70 al '90
99100 GM Modelos de Tamaño Mediano '70 al '88
99106 Jeep Cherokee, Wagoneer & Comanche '84 al '00
99110 Nissan Camioneta '80 al '96, Pathfinder '87 al '95
99118 Nissan Sentra '82 al '94
99125 Toyota Camionetas y 4Runner '79 al '95

Over 100 Haynes motorcycle manuals also available

10-07

Haynes North America, Inc., 861 Lawrence Drive, Newbury Park, CA 91320-1514 • (805) 498-6703